Blackstone's Sta

Evidence

Blackstone's Statutes
Evidence

· ·

2004/2005

Eighth Edition

Edited by

Phil Huxley

LLB, LLM

Principal Lecturer in Law, The Nottingham Trent University

and

Michael O'Connell

BL, M Phil

(King's Inns, Dublin), Barrister, of the Midland Circuit

OXFORD
UNIVERSITY PRESS

OXFORD
UNIVERSITY PRESS

Great Clarendon Street, Oxford OX2 6DP

Oxford University Press is a department of the University of Oxford.
It furthers the University's objective of excellence in research, scholarship,
and education by publishing worldwide in

Oxford New York

Auckland Bangkok Buenos Aires Cape Town Chennai
Dar es Salaam Delhi Hong Kong Istanbul Karachi Kolkata
Kuala Lumpur Madrid Melbourne Mexico City Mumbai Nairobi
São Paulo Shanghai Taipei Tokyo Toronto

Oxford is a registered trade mark of Oxford University Press
in the UK and in certain other countries

Published in the United States
by Oxford University Press Inc., New York
First published by Blackstone Press

© Phil Huxley and Michael O'Connell 2004

The moral rights of the authors have been asserted

Database right Oxford University Press (maker)

First edition 1991	Fifth edition 1999
Second edition 1993	Sixth edition 2001
Reprinted 1995	Fifth edition 1999
Third edition 1995	Seventh edition 2003
Fourth edition 1997	Eighth edition 2004

British Library Cataloguing in Publication Data
Data available

Library of Congress Cataloging in Publication Data
Data applied for

Crown Copyright material is reproduced with the permission of the
Controller of HMSO and the Queen's Printer for Scotland

ISBN 0–19–927644–7

1 3 5 7 9 10 8 6 4 2

Typeset in Stone Serif and Stone Sans
by RefineCatch Limited, Bungay, Suffolk
Printed in Great Britain by
Ashford Colour Press Ltd, Gosport, Hampshire

CONTENTS

PART B   Rules and Guidelines   397

ALPHABETICAL CONTENTS

CHRONOLOGICAL CONTENTS

EDITORS' PREFACE

The appearance of the 8th edition of *Blackstone's Statutes on Evidence* within a year of the previous edition is easily explained in three words—the Criminal Justice Act. The Act received Royal Assent on 20 November 2003 and is said to be controversial, far reaching and the most significant overhaul of the criminal justice system in a generation. In the view of the Home Office the Act has some aims including an 'inclusionary approach to evidence to make trials a search for the truth' which may come as something of a surprise to those practicing criminal lawyers who for years laboured under the impression that unless there is truth there cannot be justice, and 'trusting juries and magistrates to make a decision based on as wide a range of evidence as possible, while protecting the rights of defendants'. No doubt it was for this laudable purpose that the rules relating to disclosure are overhauled, the rule against oral and documentary hearsay is very substantially changed, the common law rules governing the admissibility of evidence of bad character in criminal proceedings are abolished and there is a new definition of bad character. There is even a definition of 'criminal proceedings' in section 112 of the Act—these are 'criminal proceedings in relation to which the strict rules of evidence apply'. A 'defendant' is also defined in the same section and means, in relation to criminal proceedings, a person charged with an offence in those proceedings'. Not exactly rocket science on any view. All this is apparently calculated to improve the criminal justice system, where if anything goes wrong under the new arrangements and the accused is acquitted, the double jeopardy rule is abolished and there can be a retrial with fresh evidence in a substantial number of serious cases.

The fairly extensive evidential provisions of the Sexual Offences Act 2003 are also included in this book. This Statute, too, is likely to provoke controversy.

We have included evidential material that may not yet have the force of law at the date of writing—July 2004—and we wish to thank those many colleagues and friends who have helped us in compiling the material for this edition. Most especially we would like to thank Rebecca Huxley-Binns for her enthusiasm and support.

Phil Huxley
Michael O'Connell

PART A

Criminal Statutes

Criminal Procedure Act 1865
(1865, c. 18)

3   How far witnesses may be discredited by the party producing
A party producing a witness shall not be allowed to impeach his credit by general evidence of bad character; but he may, in case the witness shall in the opinion of the judge prove adverse, contradict him by other evidence, or, by leave of the judge, prove that he has made at other times a statement inconsistent with his present testimony; but before such last-mentioned proof can be given the circumstances of the supposed statement, sufficient to designate the particular occasion, must be mentioned to the witness, and he must be asked whether or not he has made such statement.

4   As to proof of contradictory statements of adverse witness
If a witness, upon cross-examination as to a former statement made by him relative to the subject matter of the indictment or proceeding, and inconsistent with his present testimony, does not distinctly admit that he has made such statement, proof may be given that he did in fact make it; but before such proof can be given the circumstances of the supposed statement, sufficient to designate the particular occasion, must be mentioned to the witness, and he must be asked whether or not he has made such statement.

5   Cross-examinations as to previous statements in writing
A witness may be cross-examined as to previous statements made by him in writing, or reduced into writing, relative to the subject matter of the indictment or proceeding, without such writing being shown to him; but if it is intended to contradict such witness by the writing, his attention must, before such contradictory proof can be given, be called to those parts of the writing which are to be used for the purpose of so contradicting him: Provided always, that it shall be competent for the judge, at any time during the trial, to require the production of the writing for his inspection, and he may thereupon make such use of it for the purposes of the trial as he may think fit.

Banker's Books Evidence Act 1879
(1879, c. 11)

3   Mode of proof of entries in bankers' books
Subject to the provisions of this Act, a copy of any entry in a banker's book shall in all legal proceedings be received as prima facie evidence of such entry, and of the matters, transactions, and accounts therein recorded.

4   Proof that book is a banker's book
A copy of an entry in a banker's book shall not be received in evidence under this Act unless it be first proved that the book was at the time of the making of the entry one of the ordinary

books of the bank, and that the entry was made in the usual and ordinary course of business, and that the book is in the custody or control of the bank.

Such proof may be given by a partner or officer of the bank, and may be given orally or by an affidavit sworn before any commissioner or person authorised to take affidavits.

5 Verification of copy
A copy of an entry in a banker's book shall not be received in evidence under this Act unless it be further proved that the copy has been examined with the original entry and is correct.

Such proof shall be given by some person who has examined the copy with the original entry, and may be given either orally or by an affidavit sworn before any commissioner or person authorised to take affidavits.

6 Case in which banker, etc., not compellable to produce book, etc.
A banker or officer of a bank shall not, in any legal proceeding to which the bank is not a party, be compellable to produce any banker's book the contents of which can be proved under this Act, or to appear as a witness to prove the matters, transactions, and accounts therein recorded, unless by order of a judge made for special cause.

7 Court or judge may order inspection, etc.
On the application of any party to a legal proceeding a court or judge may order that such party be at liberty to inspect and take copies of any entries in a banker's book for any of the purposes of such proceedings. An order under this section may be made either with or without summoning the bank or any other party, and shall be served on the bank three clear days before the same is to be obeyed, unless the court or judge otherwise directs.

9 Interpretation of 'bank', 'banker', and 'bankers' books'
[(1) In this Act the expressions 'bank' and 'banker' mean—
   (a) an institution recognised under the Banking Act 1987 or a municipal bank within the meaning of that Act;
   (aa) a building society within the meaning of the Building Societies Act 1986;
   (b) *a trustee savings bank within the meaning [the Trustee Savings Banks Act 1981]*;
   (c) the National Savings Bank; and
   (d) the Post Office, in the exercise of its powers to provide banking services.

(2) Expressions in this Act relating to 'bankers' books' include ledgers, day books, cash books, account books and other records used in the ordinary business of the bank, whether those records are in written form or are kept on microfilm, magnetic tape or any other form of mechanical or electronic data retrieval mechanism.]

11 Computation of time
Sunday, Christmas Day, Good Friday, and any bank holiday shall be excluded from the computation of time under this Act.

Criminal Evidence Act 1898
(1898, c. 36)

1 Competency of witnesses in criminal cases
(1) A person charged in criminal proceedings shall not be called as a witness in the proceedings except upon his own application.

(2) Subject to section 101 of the Criminal Justice Act 2003 (admissibility of evidence of defendant's bad character), a person charged in criminal proceedings who is called as a witness in the proceedings may be asked any question in cross-examination notwithstanding that it would tend to criminate him as to any offence with which he is charged in the proceedings.

(3) . . .

(4) Every person charged in criminal proceedings who is called as a witness in the proceedings shall, unless otherwise ordered by the court, give his evidence from the witness box or other place from which the other witnesses give their evidence.

2 Evidence of person charged

Where the only witness to the facts of the case called by the defence is the person charged, he shall be called as a witness immediately after the close of the evidence for the prosecution.

3 Right of reply

The fact that the person charged has been called as a witness shall not of itself confer on the prosecution the right of reply.

Perjury Act 1911
(1911, c. 6)

13 Corroboration

A person shall not be liable to be convicted of any offence against this Act, or of any offence declared by any other Act to be perjury or subornation of perjury, or to be punishable as perjury or subornation of perjury, solely upon the evidence of one witness as to the falsity of any statement alleged to be false.

14 Proof of certain proceedings on which perjury is assigned

On a prosecution—

      (a) for perjury alleged to have been committed on the trial of an indictment . . .; or

      (b) for procuring or suborning the commission of perjury on any such trial,

the fact of the former trial shall be sufficiently proved by the production of a certificate containing the substance and effect (omitting the formal parts) of the indictment and trial purporting to be signed by the clerk of the court, or other person having the custody of the records of the court where the indictment was tried, or by the deputy of that clerk or other person, without proof of the signature or official character of the clerk or person appearing to have signed the certificate.

Indictments Act 1915
(1915, c. 90)

5 Orders for amendment of indictment, separate trial, and postponement of trial

(1) Where, before trial, or at any stage of a trial, it appears to the court that the indictment is defective, the court shall make such order for the amendment of the indictment as the court thinks necessary to meet the circumstances of the case, unless, having regard to the merits of the case, the required amendments cannot be made without injustice, . . .

(2) Where an indictment is so amended, a note of the order for amendment shall be endorsed on the indictment, and the indictment shall be treated for the purposes of the trial and for the purposes of all proceedings in connection therewith as having been found by the grand jury in the amended form.

(3) Where, before trial, or at any stage of a trial, the court is of opinion that a person accused may be prejudiced or embarrassed in his defence by reason of being charged with more than one offence in the same indictment, or that for any other reason it is desirable to direct that the person should be tried separately for any one or more offences charged in an indictment, the court may order a separate trial of any count or counts of such indictment.

(4) Where, before trial, or at any stage of a trial, the court is of opinion that the postponement of the trial of a person accused is expedient as a consequence of the exercise of any power of the court under this Act to amend an indictment or to order a separate trial of a count, the court shall make such order as to the postponement of the trial as appears necessary.

(5) Where an order of the court is made under this section for a separate trial or for the postponement of a trial—

    (a) if such an order is made during a trial the court may order that the jury are to be discharged from giving a verdict on the count or counts the trial of which is postponed or on the indictment, as the case may be; and

    (b) the procedure on the separate trial of a count shall be the same in all respects as if the count had been found in a separate indictment, and the procedure on the postponed trial shall be the same in all respects (if the jury has been discharged) as if the trial had not commenced; and

    (c) the court may make such order . . . as to [granting the accused person bail] and as to the enlargement of recognizances and otherwise as the court thinks fit.

(6) Any power of the court under this section shall be in addition to and not in derogation of any other power of the court for the same or similar purposes.

Prevention of Corruption Act 1916
(1916, c. 64)

2   Presumption of corruption in certain cases

Where in any proceedings against a person for an offence under the Prevention of Corruption Act 1906, or the Public Bodies Corrupt Practices Act 1889, it is proved that any money, gift, or other consideration has been paid or given to or received by a person in the employment of Her Majesty or any Government Department or a public body by or from a person, or agent of a person, holding or seeking to obtain a contract from His Majesty or any Government Department or public body, the money, gift, or consideration shall be deemed to have been paid or given and received corruptly as such inducement or reward as is mentioned in such Act unless the contrary is proved.

Children and Young Persons Act 1933
(1933, c. 12)

42   Extension of power to take deposition of child or young person

(1) Where a justice of the peace is satisfied by the evidence of a duly qualified medical practitioner that the attendance before the court of any child or young person in respect of whom any of the offences mentioned in the First Schedule to this Act is alleged to have been committed would involve serious danger to his life or health, the justice may take in writing the deposition of the child or young person on oath, and shall thereupon subscribe the deposition and add thereto a statement of his reason for taking it and of the day when and place where it was taken, and of the names of the person (if any) present at the taking thereof.

(2) The justice taking any such deposition shall transmit it with his statement—

    (a) if the deposition relates to an offence for which any accused person is already sent for trial, to the proper officer of the court for trial at which the accused person has been sent; and

    (b) in any other case, to the proper officer of the court before which proceedings are pending in respect of the offence.

43   Admission of deposition of child or young person in evidence
Where, in any proceedings in respect of any of the offences mentioned in the First Schedule to this Act, the court is satisfied by the evidence of a duly qualified medical practitioner that the attendance before the court of any child or young person in respect of whom the offence is alleged to have been committed would involve serious danger to his life or health, any deposition of the child or young person taken under the Indictable Offences Act 1848, or this Part of this Act, shall be admissible in evidence either for or against the accused person without further proof thereof if it purports to be signed by the justice by or before whom it purports to be taken:

   Provided that the deposition shall not be admissible in evidence against the accused person unless it is proved that reasonable notice of the intention to take the deposition has been served upon him and that he or his counsel or solicitor had, or might have had if he had chosen to be present, an opportunity of cross-examining the child or young person making the deposition.

50   Age of criminal responsibility
It shall be conclusively presumed that no child under the age of [ten] years can be guilty of any offence.

Prevention of Crime Act 1953
(1953, c. 14)

1   Prohibition of the carrying of offensive weapons without lawful authority or reasonable excuse
   (1) Any person who without lawful authority or reasonable excuse, the proof whereof shall lie on him, has with him in any public place any offensive weapon shall be guilty of an offence, and shall be liable—
   (a)   on summary conviction, to imprisonment for a term not exceeding [six months] or a fine not exceeding the prescribed sum or both;
   (b)   on conviction on indictment, to imprisonment for a term not exceeding [four] years or a fine . . . or both.
   (2) Where any person is convicted of an offence under subsection (1) of this section the court may make an order for the forfeiture or disposal of any weapon in respect of which the offence was committed.
   (3) . . .
   (4) In this section 'public place' includes any highway and any other premises or place to which at the material time the public have or are permitted to have access, whether on payment or otherwise; and 'offensive weapon' means any article made or adapted for use for causing injury to the person, or intended by the person having it with him for such use by him or by some other person.

Homicide Act 1957
(1957, c. 11)

2   Persons suffering from diminished responsibility
   (1) Where a person kills or is a party to the killing of another, he shall not be convicted of murder if he was suffering from such abnormality of mind (whether arising from a condition of arrested or retarded development of mind or any inherent causes or induced by disease or injury) as substantially impaired his mental responsibility for his acts and omissions in doing or being a party to the killing.

(2) On a charge of murder, it shall be for the defence to prove that the person charged is by virtue of this section not liable to be convicted of murder.

(3) A person who but for this section would be liable, whether as principal or as accessory, to be convicted of murder shall be liable instead to be convicted of manslaughter.

(4) The fact that one party to a killing is by virtue of this section not liable to be convicted of murder shall not affect the question whether the killing amounted to murder in the case of any other party to it.

3 Provocation

Where on a charge of murder there is evidence on which the jury can find that the person charged was provoked (whether by things done or by things said or by both together) to lose his self-control, the question whether the provocation was enough to make a reasonable man do as he did shall be left to be determined by the jury; and in determining that question the jury shall take into account everything both done and said according to the effect which, in their opinion, it would have on a reasonable man.

Criminal Procedure (Right of Reply) Act 1964
(1964, c. 34)

1   Right of reply at trials on indictment
(1) Upon the trial of any person on indictment—
- (a) the prosecution shall not be entitled to the right of reply on the ground only that the Attorney General or the Solicitor General appears for the Crown at the trial; and
- (b) the time at which the prosecution is entitled to exercise that right shall, notwithstanding anything in section 2 of the Criminal Procedure Act, 1865, be after the close of the evidence for the defence and before the closing speech (if any) by or on behalf of the accused.

Criminal Justice Act 1967
(1967, c. 80)

9   Proof by written statement
(1) In any criminal proceedings, a written statement by any person shall, if such of the conditions mentioned in the next following subsection as are applicable are satisfied, be admissible as evidence to the like extent as oral evidence to the like effect by that person.

(2) The said conditions are—
- (a) the statement purports to be signed by the person who made it;
- (b) the statement contains a declaration by the person to the effect that it is true to the best of his knowledge and belief and that he made the statement knowing that, if it were tendered in evidence, he would be liable to prosecution if he wilfully stated in it anything which he knew to be false or did not believe to be true;
- (c) before the hearing at which the statement is tendered in evidence, a copy of the statement is served, by or on behalf of the party proposing to tender it, on each of the other parties to the proceedings; and
- (d) none of the other parties or their solicitors, within seven days from the service of the copy of the statement, serves a notice on the party so proposing objecting to the statement being tendered in evidence under this section:

Provided that the conditions mentioned in paragraphs (c) and (d) of this subsection shall not apply if the parties agree before or during the hearing that the statement shall be so tendered.

(3) The following provisions shall also have effect in relation to any written statement tendered in evidence under this section, that is to say—

    (a) if the statement is made by a person under the age of eighteen, it shall give his age;

    (b) if it is made by a person who cannot read it, it shall be read to him before he signs it and shall be accompanied by a declaration by the person who so read the statement to the effect that it was so read; and

    (c) if it refers to any other document as an exhibit, the copy served on any other party to the proceedings under paragraph (c) of the last foregoing subsection shall be accompanied by a copy of that document or by such information as may be necessary in order to enable the party on whom it is served to inspect that document or a copy thereof.

(3A) In the case of a statement which indicates in pursuance of subsection (3)(a) of this section that the person making it has not attained the age of 14, subsection (2)(b) of this section shall have effect as if for the words from 'made' onwards there were substituted the words 'understands the importance of telling the truth in it'.

(4) Notwithstanding that a written statement made by any person may be admissible as evidence by virtue of this section—

    (a) the party by whom or on whose behalf a copy of the statement was served may call that person to give evidence; and

    (b) the court may, of its own motion or on the application of any party to the proceedings, require that person to attend before the court and give evidence.

(5) An application under paragraph (b) of the last foregoing subsection to a court other than a magistrates' court may be made before the hearing and on any such application the powers of the court shall be exercisable [by a puisne judge of the High Court, a Circuit judge or Recorder sitting alone].

(6) So much of any statement as is admitted in evidence by virtue of this section shall, unless the court otherwise directs, be read aloud at the hearing and where the court so directs an account shall be given orally of so much of any statement as is not read aloud.

(7) Any document or object referred to as an exhibit and identified in a written statement tendered in evidence under this section shall be treated as if it had been produced as an exhibit and identified in court by the maker of the statement.

(8) A document required by this section to be served on any person may be served—

    (a) by delivering it to him or to his solicitor; or

    (b) by addressing it to him and leaving it at his usual or last known place of abode or place of business or by addressing it to his solicitor and leaving it at his office; or

    (c) by sending it in a registered letter or by the recorded delivery service addressed to him at his usual or last known place of abode or place of business or addressed to his solicitor at his office; or

    (d) in the case of a body corporate, by delivering it to the secretary or clerk of the body at its registered or principal office or sending it in a registered letter or by the recorded delivery service addressed to the secretary or clerk of that body at that office.

10   Proof by formal admission

(1) Subject to the provisions of this section, any fact of which oral evidence may be given in any criminal proceedings may be admitted for the purpose of those proceedings by or on behalf of the prosecutor or defendant, and the admission by any party of any such fact under this section shall as against that party be conclusive evidence in those proceedings of the fact admitted.

(2) An admission under this section—

    (a) may be made before or at the proceedings;

    (b) if made otherwise than in court, shall be in writing;

    (c) if made in writing by an individual, shall purport to be signed by the person making it and, if so made by a body corporate, shall purport to be signed by a director or manager, or the secretary or clerk, or some other similar officer of the body corporate;

    (d) if made on behalf of a defendant who is an individual, shall be made by his counsel or solicitor;

    (e) if made at any stage before the trial by a defendant who is an individual, must be approved by his counsel or solicitor (whether at the time it was made or subsequently) before or at the proceedings in question.

(3) An admission under this section for the purpose of proceedings relating to any matter shall be treated as an admission for the purpose of any subsequent criminal proceedings relating to that matter (including any appeal or retrial).

(4) An admission under this section may with the leave of the court be withdrawn in the proceedings for the purpose of which it is made or any subsequent criminal proceedings relating to the same matter.

Criminal Appeal Act 1968
(1968, c. 19)

PART I   APPEAL TO COURT OF APPEAL IN CRIMINAL CASES

Appeal against conviction on indictment

1   Right of appeal

(1) [Subject to subsection (3) below] a person convicted of an offence on indictment may appeal to the Court of Appeal against his conviction.

    [(2) An appeal under this section lies only—

    (a) with the leave of the Court of Appeal; or

    (b) if the judge of the court of trial grants a certificate that the case is fit for appeal.]

    [(3) Where a person is convicted before the Crown Court of a scheduled offence it shall not be open to him to appeal to the Court of Appeal against the conviction on the ground that the decision of the court which sent him to the Crown Court for trial as to the value involved was mistaken.

(4) In subsection (3) above 'scheduled offence' and 'the value involved' have the same meanings as they have in section 22 of the Magistrates' Courts Act 1980 (certain offences against property to be tried summarily if value of property or damage is small).]

2   Grounds for allowing an appeal under s. 1

    [(1) Subject to the provisions of this act, the Court of Appeal—

    (a) shall allow an appeal against conviction if they think the conviction is unsafe; and

    (b) shall dismiss such an appeal in any other case.]

(2) In the case of an appeal against conviction the Court shall, if they allow the appeal, quash the conviction.

(3) An order of the Court of Appeal quashing a conviction shall, except when under section 7 below the appellant is ordered to be retired, operate as a direction to the court of trial to enter, instead of the record of conviction, a judgment and verdict of acquittal.

3   Power to substitute conviction of alternative offence

(1) This section applies on an appeal against conviction, where the appellant has been convicted of an offence and the jury could on the indictment have found him guilty of some other offence, and on the finding of the jury it appears to the Court of Appeal that the jury must have been satisfied of facts which proved him guilty of the other offence.

(2) The Court may, instead of allowing or dismissing the appeal, substitute for the verdict found by the jury a verdict of guilty of the other offence, and pass such sentence in substitution for the sentence passed at the trial as may be authorised by law for the other offence, not being a sentence of greater severity.

4   Sentence when appeal allowed on part of an indictment

(1) This section applies where, on an appeal against conviction on an indictment containing two or more counts, the Court of Appeal allow the appeal in respect of part of the indictment.

(2) Except as provided by subsection (3) below the Court may in respect of any count on which the appellant remains convicted pass such sentence, in substitution for any sentence passed thereon at the trial, as they think proper and is authorised by law for the offence of which he remains convicted on the count.

(3) The Court shall not under this section pass any sentence such that the appellant's sentence on the indictment as a whole will, in consequence of the appeal, be of greater severity than the sentence (taken as a whole) which was passed at the trial for all offences of which he was convicted on the indictment.

5   Disposal of appeal against conviction on special verdict

(1) This section applies on an appeal against conviction [in a case where] the jury have found a special verdict.

(2) If the Court of Appeal consider that a wrong conclusion has been arrived at by the court of trial on the effect of the jury's verdict they may, instead of allowing the appeal, order such conclusion to be recorded as appears to them to be in law required by the verdict, and pass such sentence in substitution for the sentence passed at the trial as may be authorised by law.

[6   Substitution of finding of insanity or findings of unfitness to plead etc.

(1) This section applies where, on an appeal against conviction, the Court of Appeal, on the written or oral evidence of two or more registered medical practitioners at least one of whom is duly approved, are of opinion—

(a) that the proper verdict would have been one of not guilty by reason of insanity;

or

(b) that the case is not one where there should have been a verdict of acquittal, but that there should have been findings that the accused was under a disability and that he did the act or made the omission charged against him.

(2) Subject to subsection (3) below, the Court of Appeal shall either—

(a) make an order that the appellant be admitted, in accordance with the provisions of Schedule 1 to the Criminal Procedure (Insanity and Unfitness to Plead) Act 1991, to such hospital as may be specified by the Secretary of State; or

(b) where they have the power to do so by virtue of section 5 of that Act, make in respect of the appellant such one of the following orders as they think most suitable in all the circumstances of the case, namely—

(i) a guardianship order within the meaning of the Mental Health Act 1983;

(ii) a supervision and treatment order within the meaning of Schedule 2 to the said Act of 1991; and

(iii) an order for his absolute discharge.

(3) Paragraph (b) of subsection (2) above shall not apply where the offence to which the appeal relates is an offence the sentence for which is fixed by law.]

7 Power to order retrial

(1) Where the Court of Appeal allow an appeal against conviction . . . and it appears to the Court that the interests of justice so require, they may order the appellant to be retried.

(2) A person shall not under this section be ordered to be retired for any offence other than—

> (a) the offence of which he was convicted at the original trial and in respect of which his appeal is allowed as mentioned in subsection (1) above;
>
> (b) an offence of which he could have been convicted at the original trial on an indictment for the first-mentioned offence; or
>
> (c) an offence charged in an alternative count of the indictment in respect of which no verdict was given in consequence of his being convicted of the first-mentioned offence.

8 Supplementary provisions as to retrial

(1) A person who is to be retried for an offence in pursuance of an order under section 7 of this Act shall be tried on a fresh indictment preferred by direction of the Court of Appeal, . . . [but after the end of two months from the date of the order for his retrial he may not be arraigned on an indictment preferred in pursuance of such a direction unless the Court of Appeal give leave.]

[(1A) Where a person has been ordered to be retired but may not be arraigned without leave, he may apply to the Court of Appeal to set aside the order for retrial and to direct the court of trial to enter a judgment and verdict of acquittal of the offence for which he was ordered to be retired.

(1B) On an application under subsection (1) or (1A) above the Court of Appeal shall have power—

> (a) to grant leave to arraign; or
>
> (b) to set aside the order for retrial and direct the entry of a judgment and verdict of acquittal, but shall not give leave to arraign unless they are satisfied—
>> (i) that the prosecution has acted with all due expedition; and
>> (ii) that there is a good and sufficient cause for a retrial in spite of the lapse of time since the order under section 7 of the Act was made.]

(2) The Court of Appeal may, on ordering a retrial, make such orders as appear to them to be necessary or expedient—

> (a) for the custody or subject to section 25 of Criminal Justice and Public Order Act 1994 release on bail of the person ordered to be retried pending his retrial; or
>
> (b) for the retention pending the retrial of any property or money forfeited, restored or paid by virtue of the original conviction or any order made on that conviction.

(3) If the person ordered to be retried was, immediately before the determination of his appeal, liable to be detained in pursuance of an order or direction under Part V of the Mental Health Act 1959 [or under Part III of the Mental Health Act 1983 (other than under section 35, 36 or 38 of that Act)],—

> (a) that order or direction shall continue in force pending the retrial as if the appeal had not been allowed; and
>
> (b) any order made by the Court of Appeal under this section for his custody or release on bail shall have effect subject to the said order or direction.

[(3A) If the person ordered to be retried was, immediately before the determination of his appeal, liable to be detained in pursuance of a remand under section 36 of the Mental Health Act 1983 or an interim hospital order under section 38 of that Act, the Court of Appeal may, if they think fit, order that he shall continue to be detained in a hospital or mental nursing home, and in that event Part III of that Act shall apply as if he had been ordered under this section to be kept in custody pending his retrial and was detained in pursuance of a transfer direction together with a restriction direction.]

(4) Schedule 2 to this Act has effect with respect to the procedure in the case of a person ordered to be retried, the sentence which may be passed if the retrial results in his conviction and the order for costs which may be made if he is acquitted.

9 Appeal against sentence following conviction on indictment

[(1)] A person who has been convicted of an offence on indictment may appeal to the Court of Appeal against any sentence (not being a sentence fixed by law) passed on him for the offence, whether passed on his conviction or in subsequent proceedings.

[(2) A person who on conviction on indictment has also been convicted of a summary offence under paragraph 6 of Schedule 3 to the Crime & Disorder Act 1998 (power of Crown Court to deal with summary offences where person sent for trial for indictable-only offence) may appeal to the Court of Appeal against any sentence passed on him for the summary offence (whether on his conviction or in subsequent proceedings) under subsection (7) of that section or sub-paragraph (4) of that paragraph.]

10 Appeal against sentence in other cases dealt with at the Crown Court

(1) This section has effect for providing rights of appeal against sentence when a person is dealt with by the Crown Court (otherwise than on appeal from a magistrates' court) for an offence of which he was not convicted on indictment.

(2) The proceedings from which an appeal against sentence lies under this section are those where an offender convicted of an offence by a magistrates' court—

(a) is committed by the court to be dealt with for his offence at the Crown Court, or

[(b) having been made the subject of an order for conditional discharge, or a community order within the meaning of the Powers of Criminal Courts (Sentencing) Act 2000 or given a suspended sentence, appears or is brought before the Crown Court to be further dealt with for his offence.]

(3) An offender dealt with for an offence at the Crown Court in a proceeding to which subsection (2) of this section applies may appeal to the Court of Appeal against sentence in any of the following cases:—

(a) where either for that offence alone or for that offence and other offences for which sentence is passed in the same proceeding, he is sentenced to imprisonment [or to [detention in a young offender institution]] for a term of six months or more; or

(b) where the sentence is one which the court convicting him had not power to pass; or

(c) where the court in dealing with him for the offence makes in respect of him—
(i) a recommendation for deportation; or
(ii) an order disqualifying him from holding or obtaining a licence to drive a motor vehicle under Part II of the Road Traffic Offenders Act 1988; or
(iii) an order under section 119 of the Powers of Criminal Courts (Sentencing) Act 2000 (orders as to existing suspended sentence when person subject to the sentence is again convicted);
(iv) a banning order under section 14A of the Football Spectators Act 1989;] [or
(v) a declaration of relevance under the Football Spectators Act 1989;] [or

(cc) where the court makes such an order with regard to him as is mentioned in section 116(2) or (4) of the Powers of Criminal Courts (Sentencing) Act 2000.

(d) ...

11 Supplementary provisions as to appeal against sentence

(1) [Subject to subsection (1A) below, an] appeal against sentence, whether under section 9 or under section 10 of this Act, lies only with the leave of the Court of Appeal.

[(1A) If the judge who passed the sentence grants a certificate that the case is fit for appeal under section 9 or 10 of this Act, an appeal lies under this section without the leave of the Court of Appeal.]

(2) Where [the Crown Court], in dealing with an offender either on his conviction on indictment or in a proceeding to which section 10(2) of this Act applies, has passed on him two or more sentences in the same proceeding, being sentences against which an appeal lies under section 9[(1)] or section 10, an appeal or application for leave to appeal against any one of those sentences shall be treated as an appeal or application in respect of both or all of them.

[(2A) Where following conviction on indictment a person has been convicted under section 41 of the Criminal Justice Act 1988 of a summary offence an appeal or application for leave to appeal against any sentence for the offence triable either way shall be treated also as an appeal or application in respect of any sentence for the summary offence and an appeal or application for leave to appeal against any sentence for the summary offence shall be treated also as an appeal or application in respect of the offence triable either way.

(2B) If the appellant or applicant was convicted on indictment of two or more offences triable either way, the references to the offence triable either way in subsection (2A) above are to be construed, in relation to any summary offence of which he was convicted under section 41 of the Criminal Justice Act 1988 following the conviction on indictment, as references to the offence triable either way specified in the notice relating to that summary offence which was given under subsection (2) of that section.]

(3) On an appeal against sentence the Court of Appeal, if they consider that the appellant should be sentenced differently for an offence for which he was dealt with by the court below may—

(a) quash any sentence or order which is the subject of the appeal; and
(b) in place of it pass such sentence or make such order as they think appropriate for the case and as the court below had power to pass or make when dealing with him for the offence;

but the Court shall so exercise their powers under this subsection that, taking the case as a whole, the appellant is not more severely dealt with on appeal than he was dealt with by the court below.

(4) The power of the Court of Appeal under subsection (3) of this section to pass a sentence which the court below had power to pass for an offence shall, notwithstanding that the court below made no order under section 23(1) of the Powers of Criminal Courts Act 1973 or section 119 of the Powers of Criminal Courts (Sentencing) Act 2000 in respect of a suspended sentence previously passed on the appellant for another offence include power to deal with him in respect of that sentence where the court below made no order in respect of it.]

[(5) The fact that an appeal is pending against an interim hospital order under [the Mental Health Act 1983] shall not affect the power of the court below to renew or terminate the order or to deal with the appellant on its termination; and where the Court of Appeal quash such an order but do not pass any sentence or make any other order in its place the Court may subject to section 25 of the Criminal Justice and Public Order Act 1994 direct the appellant to be kept in custody or released on bail pending his being dealt with by the court below.

(6) Where the Court of Appeal make an interim hospital order by virtue of subsection (3) of this section—

(a) the power of renewing or terminating it and of dealing with the appellant on its termination shall be exercisable by the court below and not by the Court of Appeal; and
(b) the court below shall be treated for the purposes of [section 38(7) of the said Act of 1983] (absconding offenders) as the court that made the order.]

12   Appeal against verdict of not guilty by reason of insanity
A person in whose case there is returned a verdict of not guilty by reason of insanity may appeal to the Court of Appeal against the verdict—
  (a) with the leave of the Court of Appeal; or
  (b) if the judge of the court of trial grants a certificate that the case is fit for appeal.

13   Disposal of appeal under s. 12
  (1) Subject to the provisions of this section, the Court of Appeal—
    (a) shall allow an appeal under section 12 of this Act if they think that the conviction is unsafe; and
    (b) shall dismiss such an appeal in any other case.
  (2) . . .
  (3) Where apart from this subsection—
    (a) an appeal under section 12 of this Act would fall to be allowed; and
    (b) none of the grounds for allowing it relates to the question of the insanity of the accused,
the Court of Appeal may dismiss the appeal if they are of opinion that, but for the insanity of the accused, the proper verdict would have been that he was guilty of an offence other than the offence charged.
  (4) Where an appeal under section 12 of this Act is allowed, the following provisions apply:—
    (a) If the ground, or one of the grounds, for allowing the appeal is that the finding of the jury as to the insanity of the accused ought not to stand and the Court of Appeal are of opinion that the proper verdict would have been that he was guilty of an offence (whether the offence charged or any other offence of which the jury could have found him guilty), the Court—
      (i)   shall substitute for the verdict of not guilty by reason of insanity a verdict of guilty of that offence; and
      (ii) shall, subject to subsection (5) below, have the like powers of punishing or otherwise dealing with the appellant, and other powers, as the court of trial would have had if the jury had come to the substituted verdict; and
    (b) in any other case, the Court of Appeal shall substitute for the verdict of the jury a verdict of acquittal.
  (5) The Court of Appeal shall not by virtue of subsection (4)(a) above sentence any person to death; but where under that paragraph they substitute a verdict of guilty of an offence for which apart from this subsection they would be required to sentence the appellant to death, their sentence shall (whatever the circumstances) be one of imprisonment for life.
  (6) An order of the Court of Appeal allowing an appeal in accordance with this section shall operate as a direction to the court of trial to amend the record to conform with the order.

[14   Substitution of findings of unfitness to plead etc.
  (1) This section applies where, on an appeal under section 12 of this Act, the Court of Appeal, on the written or oral evidence of two or more registered medical practitioners at least one of whom is duly approved, are of opinion that—
    (a) the case is not one where there should have been a verdict of acquittal; but
    (b) there should have been findings that the accused was under a disability and that he did the act or made the omission charged against him.
  (2) Subject to subsection (3) below, the Court of Appeal shall either—
    (a) make an order that the appellant be admitted, in accordance with the provisions of Schedule 1 to the Criminal Procedure (Insanity and Unfitness to Plead) Act 1991, to such hospital as may be specified by the Secretary of State; or

(b) where they have the power to do so by virtue of section 5 of that Act, make in respect of the appellant such one of the following orders as they think most suitable in all the circumstances of the case, namely—
    (i)   a guardianship order within the meaning of the Mental Health Act 1983;
    (ii) a supervision and treatment order within the meaning of Schedule 2 to the said Act of 1991; and
    (iii) an order for his absolute discharge.
(3) Paragraph (b) of subsection (2) above shall not apply where the offence to which the appeal relates is an offence the sentence for which is fixed by law.

14A   Substitution of verdict of acquittal

(1) This section applies where, in accordance with section 13(4)(b) of this Act, the Court of Appeal substitute a verdict of acquittal and the Court, on the written or oral evidence of two or more registered medical practitioners at least one of whom is duly approved, are of opinion—
    (a) that the appellant is suffering from mental disorder of a nature or degree which warrants his detention in a hospital for assessment (or for assessment followed by medical treatment) for at least a limited period; and
    (b) that he ought to be so detained in the interests of his own health or safety or with a view to the protection of other persons.
(2) The Court of Appeal shall make an order that the appellant be admitted for assessment, in accordance with the provisions of Schedule 1 to the Criminal Procedure (Insanity and Unfitness to Plead) Act 1991, to such hospital as may be specified by the Secretary of State.]

15   Right of appeal against finding of disability

(1) Where there has been a determination under section 4 of the Criminal Procedure (Insanity) Act 1964 of the question of a person's fitness to be tried, and the jury has returned [findings that he is under a disability and that he did the act or made the omission charged against him, the person may appeal to the Court of Appeal against either or both of those findings].
[(2) An appeal under this section lies only—
    (a) with the leave of the Court of Appeal; or
    (b) if the judge of the court of trial grants a certificate that the case is fit for appeal.]

16   Disposal of appeal under s. 15

(1) The Court of Appeal—
    (a) shall allow an appeal under section 15 of this Act against a finding if they think that the finding is unsafe; and
    (b) shall dismiss such an appeal in any other case.
(2) . . .
[(3) Where the Court of Appeal allow an appeal under section 15 of this Act against a finding that the appellant is under a disability—
    (a) the appellant may be tried accordingly for the offence with which he was charged; and
    (b) the Court may make such orders as appear to them necessary or expedient pending any such trial for his custody, release on bail or continued detention under the Mental Health Act 1983;
and Schedule 3 to this Act has effect for applying provisions in Part III of that Act to persons in whose case an order is made by the Court under this subsection.
(4) Where, otherwise than in a case falling within subsection (3) above, the Court of Appeal allow an appeal under section 15 of this Act against a finding that the appellant did the act or made the omission charged against him, the Court shall, in addition to quashing the

verdict, direct a verdict of acquittal to be recorded (but not a verdict of not guilty by reason of insanity).]

17 Repealed

18 Initiating procedure
    (1) A person who wishes to appeal under this Part of this Act to the Court of Appeal, or to obtain the leave of that court to appeal, shall give notice of appeal or, as the case may be, notice of application for leave to appeal, in such manner as may be directed by rules of court.
    (2) Notice of appeal, or of application for leave to appeal, shall be given within twenty-eight days from the date of the conviction, verdict or finding appealed against, or in the case of appeal against sentence, from the date on which sentence was passed or, in the case of an order made or treated as made on conviction, from the date of the making of the order.
    (3) The time for giving notice under this section may be extended, either before or after it expires, by the Court of Appeal.

18A Appeals in cases of contempt of court
    (1) A person who wishes to appeal under section 13 of the Administration of Justice Act 1960 from any order or decision of the Crown Court in the exercise of jurisdiction to punish for contempt of court shall give notice of appeal in such manner as may be directed by rules of court.
    (2) Notice of appeal shall be given within twenty-eight days from the date of the order or decision appealed against.
    (3) The time for giving notice under this section may be extended, either before or after its expiry, by the Court of Appeal.

19 Bail
    (1) The Court of Appeal may, subject to section 25 of the Criminal Justice and Public Order Act 1994 if they think fit,—
        (a) grant an appellant bail pending the determination of his appeal; or
        (b) revoke bail granted to an appellant by the Crown Court under paragraph (f) of section 81 (1) of the Supreme Court Act 1981 [or paragraph (a) above]; or
        (c) vary the conditions of bail granted to an appellant in the exercise of the power conferred by [either of those paragraphs].
    (2) The powers conferred by subsection (1) above may be exercised—
        (a) on the application of an appellant; or
        (b) if it appears to the registrar of criminal appeals of the Court of Appeal (hereafter referred to as 'the registrar') that any of them ought to be exercised, on a reference to the court by him.

20 Disposal of groundless appeal or application for leave to appeal
If it appears to the registrar that a notice of appeal or application for leave to appeal does not show any substantial ground of appeal, he may refer the appeal or application for leave to the Court for summary determination; and where the case is so referred the Court may, if they consider that the appeal or application for leave is frivolous or vexatious, and can be determined without adjourning it for a full hearing, dismiss the appeal or application for leave summarily, without calling on anyone to attend the hearing or to appear for the Crown thereon.

21 Preparation of case for hearing
    (1) The registrar shall—
        (a) take all necessary steps for obtaining a hearing of any appeal or application of which notice is given to him and which is not referred and dismissed summarily under the foregoing section; and

(b) obtain and lay before the Court of Appeal in proper form all documents, exhibits and other things which appear necessary for the proper determination of the appeal or application.

(2) Rules of court may enable an appellant to obtain from the registrar any documents or things, including copies or reproductions of documents, required for his appeal and may authorise the registrar to make charges for them in accordance with scales and rates fixed from time to time by the Treasury.

22   Right of appellant to be present

(1) Except as provided by this section, an appellant shall be entitled to be present, if he wishes it, on the hearing of his appeal, although he may be in custody.

(2) A person in custody shall not be entitled to be present—

(a) where his appeal is on some ground involving a question of law alone; or
(b) on an application by him for leave to appeal; or
(c) on any proceedings preliminary or incidental to an appeal; or
(d) where he is in custody in consequence of a verdict of not guilty by reason of insanity or of a finding of disability,

unless the Court of Appeal give him leave to be present.

(3) The power of the Court of Appeal to pass sentence on a person may be exercised although he is for any reason not present.

23   Evidence

(1) For the purposes of an appeal under this Part of this Act the Court of Appeal may, if they think it necessary or expedient in the interests of justice—

(a)   order the production of any document, exhibit or other thing connected with the proceedings, the production of which appears to them necessary for the determination of the case;
(b)   order any witness who would have been a compellable witness in the proceedings from which the appeal lies to attend for examination and be examined before the Court, whether or not he was called in those proceedings; and
[(c)   receive any evidence which was not adduced in the proceedings from which the appeal lies.]

[(2) The Court of Appeal shall, in considering whether to receive any evidence, have regard in particular to—

(a)   whether the evidence appears to the Court to be capable of belief;
(b)   whether it appears to the Court that the evidence may afford any ground for allowing the appeal;
(c)   whether the evidence would have been admissible in the proceedings from which the appeal lies on an issue which is the subject of the appeal; and
(d)   whether there is a reasonable explanation for the failure to adduce the evidence in those proceedings.]

(3) Subsection (1)(c) above applies to [evidence of a] witness (including the appellant) who is competent but not compellable.

(4) For [the purposes of an appeal under] this Part of this Act, the Court of Appeal may, if they think it necessary or expedient in the interests of justice, order the examination of any witness whose attendance might be required under subsection (1)(b) above to be conducted, in manner provided by rules of court, before any judge or officer of the Court or other person appointed by the Court for the purpose, and allow the admission of any depositions so taken as evidence before the Court.

23A   Power to order investigations

(1) On an appeal against conviction the Court of Appeal may direct the Criminal Cases Review Commission to investigate and report to the Court on any matter if it appears to the Court that—

(a) the matter is relevant to the determination of the case and ought, if possible, to be resolved before the case is determined;

(b) an investigation of the matter by the Commission is likely to result in the Court being able to resolve it; and

(c) the matter cannot be resolved by the Court without an investigation by the Commission.

(2) A direction by the Court of Appeal under subsection (1) above shall be given in writing and shall specify the matter to be investigated.

(3) Copies of such a direction shall be made available to the appellant and the respondent.

(4) Where the Commission have reported to the Court of Appeal on any matter which they have been directed under subsection (1) above to investigate, the Court—

(a) shall notify the appellant and the respondent that the Commission have reported; and

(b) may make available to the appellant and the respondent the report of the Commission and any statements, opinions and reports which accompanied it.

24–28   Repealed

29   Effect of appeal on sentence

(1) The time during which an appellant is in custody pending the determination of his appeal shall, subject to any direction which the Court of Appeal may give to the contrary, be reckoned as part of the term of any sentence to which he is for the time being subject.

(2) Where the Court of Appeal give a contrary direction under subsection (1) above, they shall state their reasons for doing so; and they shall not give any such direction where—

(a) leave to appeal has been granted; or

(b) a certificate has been given by the judge of the court of trial under—

(i)   section 1 or 11 (1A) of this Act; or

(ii) section 81(1B) of the Supreme Court Act 1981; or

(c) the case has been referred to them [under section 9 of the Criminal Appeal Act 1995.]

(3) When an appellant is [granted] bail under section 19 of this Act, the time during which he is [released on bail] shall be disregarded in computing the term of any sentence to which he is for the time being subject.

(4) The term of any sentence passed by the Court of Appeal under section 3, 4, 5, 11 or 13(4) of this Act shall, unless the Court otherwise direct, begin to run from the time when it would have begun to run if passed in the proceedings from which the appeal lies.

30   Restitution of property

(1) The operation of an order for the restitution of property to a person made by the Crown Court shall, unless the Court direct to the contrary in any case in which, in their opinion, the title to the property is not in dispute, be suspended until (disregarding any power of a court to grant leave to appeal out of time) there is no further possibility of an appeal on which the order could be varied or set aside, and provision may be made by rules of court for the custody of any property in the meantime.

(2) The Court of Appeal may by order annul or vary any order made by the court of trial for the restitution of property to any person, although the conviction is not quashed; and the order, if annulled, shall not take effect and, if varied, shall take effect as so varied.

(3) Where the House of Lords restores a conviction, it may make any order for the restitution of property which the court of trial could have made.

31   Powers of Court under Part I which are exercisable by single judge

(1) There may be exercised by a single judge in the same manner as by the Court of Appeal and subject to the same provisions—

(a) the powers of the Court of Appeal under this Part of this Act specified in sub-section (2) below;

(b) the power to give directions under section 3(4) of the Sexual Offences (Amendment) Act 1992; and

(c) the powers to make orders for the payment of costs under sections 16 to 18 of the Prosecution of Offences Act 1985 in proceedings under this Part of this Act.

(2) The powers mentioned in subsection (1)(a) above are the following:—

(a) to give leave to appeal;

(b) to extend the time within which notice of appeal or of application for leave to appeal may be given;

(c) to allow an appellant to be present at any proceedings;

(d) to order a witness to attend for examination;

(e) to exercise the powers conferred by section 19 of this Act;

(f) to make orders under section 8(2) of this Act and discharge or vary such orders;

(g) ...

(h) to give directions under section 29(I) of this Act.

(2A) The power of the Court of Appeal to suspend a person's disqualification under [section 40(2) of the Road Traffic Offenders Act 1988] may be exercised by a single judge in the same manner as it may be exercised by the Court.

(2B) The power of the Court of Appeal to grant leave to appeal under section 159 of the Criminal Justice Act 1988 may be exercised by a single judge in the same manner as it may be exercised by the Court.

(3) If the single judge refuses an application on the part of an appellant to exercise in his favour any of the powers above specified, the appellant shall be entitled to have the application determined by the Court of Appeal.

31A   Powers of Court under Part I which are exercisable by registrar

(1) The powers of the Court of Appeal under this Part of this Act which are specified in subsection (2) below may be exercised by the registrar.

(2) The powers mentioned in subsection (1) above are the following—

(a) to extend the time within which notice of appeal or of application for leave to appeal may be given;

(b) to order a witness to attend for examination; and

(c) to vary the conditions of bail granted to an appellant by the Court of Appeal or the Crown Court.

(3) No variation of the conditions of bail granted to an appellant may be made by the registrar unless he is satisfied that the respondent does not object to the variation; but, subject to that, the powers specified in that subsection are to be exercised by the registrar in the same manner as by the Court of Appeal and subject to the same provisions.

(4) If the registrar refuses an application on the part of an appellant to exercise in his favour any of the powers specified in subsection (2) above, the appellant shall be entitled to have the application determined by a single judge.

32   Transcripts

(1) Rules of court may provide—

(a) for the making of a record (whether by means of shorthand notes, by mechanical means or otherwise) of any proceedings in respect of which an appeal lies (with or without leave) to the Court of Appeal; and

(b) for the making and verification of a transcript of any such record and for supplying the transcript (on payment of such charge, if any, as may be fixed for the time being by the Treasury) to the registrar for the use of the Court of Appeal or any judge exercising the powers of a judge of the Court, and to such other person and in such circumstances as may be prescribed by the rules.

(2) Without prejudice to subsection (1) above, the Secretary of State may, if he thinks fit, in any case direct that a transcript shall be made of any such record made in pursuance of the rules and be supplied to him.

(3) The cost—

(a) of making any such record in pursuance of the rules; and

(b) of making and supplying in pursuance of this section any transcript ordered to be supplied to the registrar or the Secretary of State,

shall be defrayed, in accordance with scales of payment fixed for the time being by the Treasury, out of moneys provided by Parliament; and the cost of providing and installing at a court any equipment required for the purpose of making such a record or transcript shall also be defrayed out of moneys so provided.

PART II   APPEAL TO HOUSE OF LORDS FROM COURT OF APPEAL (CRIMINAL DIVISION)

33   Right of appeal to House of Lords

(1) An appeal lies to the House of Lords, at the instance of the defendant or the prosecutor, from any decision of the Court of Appeal on an appeal to that court under Part I of this Act or Part 9 of the Criminal Justice Act 2003 [or section 9 (preparatory hearings) of the Criminal Justice Act 1987] or section 35 of the Criminal Procedure and Investigations Act 1996.

(1A) In subsection (1) above the reference to the prosecutor includes a reference to the Director of Assets Recovery Agency in a case where (and to the extent that) he is a party to the appeal to the Court of Appeal.

(2) The appeal lies only with the leave of the Court of Appeal or the House of Lords; and leave shall not be granted unless it is certified by the Court of Appeal that a point of law of general public importance is involved in the decision and it appears to the Court of Appeal or the House of Lords (as the case may be) that the point is one which ought to be considered by the House.

[(3) Except as provided by this Part of this Act and section 13 of the Administration of Justice Act 1960 (appeal in cases of contempt of court), no appeal shall lie from any decision of the criminal division of the Court of Appeal.]

34   Application for leave to appeal

(1) An application to the Court of Appeal for leave to appeal to the House of Lords shall be made within the period of fourteen days beginning with the date of the decision of the Court; and an application to the House of Lords for leave shall be made within the period of fourteen days beginning with the date on which the application for leave is refused by the Court of Appeal.

(2) The House of Lords or the Court of Appeal may, upon application made at any time by the defendant, extend the time within which an application may be made by him to that House or the Court under subsection (1) above.

(3) An appeal to the House of Lords shall be treated as pending until any application for leave to appeal is disposed of and, if leave to appeal is granted, until the appeal is disposed of; and for purposes of this Part of this Act an application for leave to appeal shall be treated as disposed of at the expiration of the time within which it may be made, if it is not made within that time.

35   Hearing and disposal of appeal

(1) An appeal under this Part of this Act shall not be heard and determined by the House of Lords unless there are present at least three of the persons designated Lords of Appeal by section 5 of the Appellate Jurisdiction Act 1876.

(2) Any order of the House of Lords which provides for the hearing of applications for leave to appeal by a committee constituted in accordance with section 5 of the said Act

of 1876 may direct that the decision of that committee shall be taken on behalf of the House.

(3) For the purpose of disposing of an appeal, the House of Lords may exercise any powers of the Court of Appeal or may remit the case to the Court.

36   Bail on appeal by defendant

The Court of Appeal may, subject to section 25 of the Criminal Justice and Public Order Act 1994, if it seems fit, on the application of a person appealing or applying for leave to appeal to the House of Lords, [other than a person appealing or applying for leave to appeal from a decision on an appeal under Part 9 of the Criminal Justice Act 2003 or section 9(11) of the Criminal Justice Act 1987 or section 35 of the Criminal Procedure and Investigations Act 1996 (appeals against orders and rulings at preparatory hearings) grant him bail pending the determination of his appeal.

37   Detention of defendant on appeal by the Crown

(1) The following provisions apply where, immediately after a decision of the Court of Appeal from which an appeal lies to the House of Lords, the prosecutor is granted or gives notice that he intends to apply for, leave to appeal.

(2) If, but for the decision of the Court of Appeal, the defendant would be liable to be detained, the Court of Appeal may make an order providing for his detention, or directing that he shall not be released except on bail (which may be granted by the Court as under section 36 above), so long as an appeal to the House of Lords is pending.

(3) An order under this section shall (unless the appeal has previously been disposed of) cease to have effect at the expiration of the period for which the defendant would have been liable to be detained but for the decision of the Court of Appeal.

(4) Where an order is made under this section in the case of a defendant who, but for the decision of the Court of Appeal, would be liable to be detained in pursuance of—

    (a) an order or direction under [Part III of the Mental Health Act 1983 (otherwise than under section 35, 36 or 38 of that Act)] (admission to hospital of persons convicted by criminal courts); or

    (b) an order under section 5(1) of the Criminal Procedure (Insanity) Act 1964 (admission to hospital following verdict of insanity or unfitness to stand trial), the order under this section shall be one authorising his continued detention in pursuance of the order or direction referred to in paragraph (a) or (b) of this subsection; and the provisions of [the Mental Health Act 1983] with respect to persons liable to be detained as mentioned in this subsection (including provisions as to the renewal of authority for detention and the removal or discharge of patients) shall apply accordingly.

[(4A) Where an order is made under this section in the case of a defendant who, but for the decision of the Court of Appeal, would be liable to be detained in pursuance of a remand under [section 36 of the Mental Health Act 1983] or an interim hospital order under [section 38] of that Act, the order may, if the Court of Appeal thinks fit, be one authorising his continued detention in a hospital or mental nursing home and in that event—

    (a) subsection (3) of this section shall not apply to the order;

    (b) [Part III of the said Act of 1983] shall apply to him as if he had been ordered under this section to be detained in custody so long as an appeal to the House of Lords is pending and were detained in pursuance of a transfer direction together with a restriction direction; and

    (c) if the defendant, having been subject to an interim hospital order, is detained by virtue of this subsection and the appeal by the prosecutor succeeds, subsection (2) of the said [section 38] (power of court to make hospital order in the absence of an offender who is subject to an interim hospital order) shall apply as if the defendant were still subject to an interim hospital order.]

(5) Where the Court of Appeal have power to make an order under this section, and either no such order is made or the defendant is released or discharged, by virtue of [subsection (3), (4) or (4A)] of this section, before the appeal is disposed of, the defendant shall not be liable to be again detained as the result of the decision of the House of Lords on the appeal.

38 Presence of defendant at hearing

A defendant who has been convicted of an offence and who is detained pending an appeal to the House of Lords shall not be entitled to be present on the hearing of the appeal or of any proceedings preliminary or incidental thereto, except where an order of the House of Lords authorises him to be present, or where the House or the Court of Appeal, as the case may be, give him leave to be present.

39–42 Repealed

43 Effect of appeal on sentence

(1) Where a person subject to a sentence is [granted] bail under section 36 or 37 of this Act, the time during which he is [released on bail] shall be disregarded in computing the term of his sentence.

(2) Subject to the foregoing subsection, any sentence passed on an appeal to the House of Lords in substitution for another sentence shall, unless that House or the Court of Appeal otherwise direct, begin to run from the time when the other sentence would have begun to run.

44 Powers of Court of Appeal under Part II which are exercisable by single judge

[(1)] [There may be exercised by a single judge—

    (a) the powers of the Court of Appeal under this Part of this Act—
        (i) to extend the time for making an application for leave to appeal;
        (ii) to make an order for or in relation to bail; and
        (iii) to give leave for a person to be present at the hearing of any proceedings preliminary or incidental to an appeal; and
    (b) their powers to make orders for the payment of costs under sections 16 and 17 of the Prosecution of Offences Act 1985 in proceedings under this Part of this Act], but where the judge refuses an application to exercise any of the said powers the applicant shall be entitled to have the application determined by the Court of Appeal.

(2) The power of the Court of Appeal to suspend a person's disqualification under section 40(3) of the Road Traffic Offenders Act 1988 may be exercised by a single judge, but where the judge refuses an application to exercise that power the applicant shall be entitled to have the application determined by the Court of Appeal.

PART III   MISCELLANEOUS AND GENERAL

44A Appeals in cases of death

(1) Where a person has died—
    (a) any relevant appeal which might have been begun by him had he remained alive may be begun by a person approved by the Court of Appeal; and
    (b) where any relevant appeal was begun by him while he was alive or is begun in relation to his case by virtue of paragraph (a) above or by a reference by the Criminal Cases Review Commission, any further step which might have been taken by him in connection with the appeal if he were alive may be taken by a person so approved.

(2) In this section 'relevant appeal' means—
    (a) an appeal under section 1, 9, 12 or 15 of this Act; or

(b) an appeal under section 33 of this Act from any decision of the Court of Appeal on an appeal under any of those sections.

(3) Approval for the purposes of this section may only be given to—

(a) the widow or widower of the dead person;

(b) a person who is the personal representative (within the meaning of section 55(1)(xi) of the Administration of Estates Act 1925) of the dead person; or

(c) any other person appearing to the Court of Appeal to have, by reason of a family or similar relationship with the dead person, a substantial financial or other interest in the determination of a relevant appeal relating to him.

(4) Except in the case of an appeal begun by a reference by the Criminal Cases Review Commission, an application for such approval may not be made after the end of the period of one year beginning with the date of death.

(5) Where this section applies, any reference in this Act to the appellant shall, where appropriate, be construed as being or including a reference to the person approved under this section.

(6) The power of the Court of Appeal to approve a person under this section may be exercised by a single judge in the same manner as by the Court of Appeal and subject to the same provisions; but if the single judge refuses the application, the applicant shall be entitled to have the application determined by the Court of Appeal.

45   Construction of references in Parts I and II to Court of Appeal and a single judge

[(1) References in Parts I and II [and section 44A] of this Act to the Court of Appeal shall be construed as references to the criminal division of the Court.]

(2) The references in section 31[, 31A, 44 and 44A] of this Act to a single judge are to any judge of the Court of Appeal or . . . of the High Court.

49   Saving for prerogative of mercy

Nothing in this Act is to be taken as affecting Her Majesty's prerogative of mercy.

50   Meaning of 'sentence'

[(1) In this Act 'sentence', in relation to an offence, includes any order made by a court when dealing with an offender including, in particular—

(a) a hospital order under Part III of the Mental Health Act 1983, with or without a restriction order;

(b) an interim hospital order under that Part;

(c) a recommendation for deportation;

'(ca) a confiscation order under Part 2 of the Proceeds of Crime Act 2002;

(cb) an order which varies a confiscation order made under Part 2 of the Proceeds of Crime Act 2002 if the varying order is made under section 21, 22 or 29 of that Act (but not otherwise);'

(d) a confiscation order under the Drug Trafficking Offences Act 1986 other than one made by the High Court;

(e) a confiscation order under Part VI of the Criminal Justice Act 1988;

(f) an order varying a confiscation order of a kind which is included by virtue of paragraph (d) or (e) above;

(g) an order made by the Crown Court varying a confiscation order which was made by the High Court by virtue of section 4A of the Act of 1986; and

(h) a declaration of relevance under the Football Spectators Act 1989.]

[(1A) Section 14 of the Powers of Criminal Courts (Sentencing) Act 2000 (under which a conviction of an offence for which . . . an order for conditional or absolute discharge is made is deemed not to be a conviction except for certain purposes) shall not prevent an appeal under this Act, whether against conviction or otherwise.]

(2) Any power of the criminal division of the Court of Appeal to pass a sentence includes a power to make a recommendation for deportation in cases where the court from which the appeal lies had power to make such a recommendation.

(3) An order under section 17 of the Access to Justice Act 1999 is not a sentence for the purposes of this Act.

51 Interpretation

(1) In this Act, except where the context otherwise requires—

'appeal', where used in Part I or II of this Act, means appeal under that Part, and 'appellant' has a corresponding meaning and in Part I includes a person who has given notice of application for leave to appeal;

'the court of trial', in relation to an appeal, means the court from which the appeal lies;

'duly approved', in relation to a registered medical practitioner, means approved for the purposes of section 12 of the Mental Health Act 1983 by the Secretary of State as having special experience in the diagnosis or treatment of mental disorder; 'the judge of the court of trial' means, where the Crown Court comprises justices of the peace, the judge presiding;

['registered medical practitioner' means a fully registered person within the meaning of the Medical Act 1983;]

'under disability' has the meaning assigned to it by section 4 of the Criminal Procedure (Insanity) Act 1964 (unfitness to plead); and

. . .

(2) Any expression used in this Act which is defined in [section 145(1) and (1AA) of the Mental Health Act 1983] has the same meaning in this Act as in that Act.

[(2A) Subsections (2) and (3) of section 54 of the Mental Health Act 1983 shall have effect with respect to proof of the appellant's medical condition for the purposes of section 6, 14 or 14A of this Act as they have effect with respect to proof of an offender's mental condition for the purposes of section 37(2)(a) of that Act.]

(3) . . .

Courts-Martial (Appeals) Act 1968
(1968, c. 20)

28 Evidence

(1) The Appeal Court may—

    (a) order the production of any document, exhibit or other thing connected with the proceedings the production of which appears to them necessary for the determination of the case;

    (b) order any witness who would have been a compellable witness at the trial to attend for examination and be examined before the Court, whether or not he was called at the trial; and

    (c) receive [any evidence which was not adduced at the trial].

[(2) The Appeal Court shall, in considering whether to receive any evidence, have regard in particular to—

    (a) whether the evidence appears to the Court to be capable of belief;

    (b) whether it appears to the Court that the evidence may afford any ground for allowing the appeal;

    (c) whether the evidence would have been admissible at the trial on an issue which is the subject of the appeal; and

    (d) whether there is a reasonable explanation for the failure to adduce the evidence at the trial.]

(3) Subsection (1)(c) above applies to [evidence of a] witness (including the appellant) who is competent but not compellable . . .

(4) The Appeal Court may order the examination of any witness whose attendance may be required under subsection (1)(b) of this section to be conducted in the prescribed manner before any judge of the Court or before any other person appointed by the Court for that purpose, and allow the admission of any depositions so taken as evidence before the Court.

Theft Act 1968
(1968, c. 60)

22   Handling stolen goods

(1) A person handles stolen goods if (otherwise than in the course of the stealing) knowing or believing them to be stolen goods he dishonestly receives the goods, or dishonestly undertakes or assists in their retention, removal, disposal or realisation by or for the benefit of another person, or if he arranges to do so.

(2) A person guilty of handling stolen goods shall on conviction on indictment be liable to imprisonment for a term not exceeding fourteen years.

25   Going equipped for stealing, etc.

(1) A person shall be guilty of an offence if, when not at his place of abode, he has with him any article for use in the course of or in connection with any burglary, theft or cheat.

(2) A person guilty of an offence under this section shall on conviction on indictment be liable to imprisonment for a term not exceeding three years.

(3) Where a person is charged with an offence under this section, proof that he had with him any article made or adapted for use in committing a burglary, theft or cheat shall be evidence that he had it with him for such use.

(4) Any person may arrest without warrant anyone who is, or whom he, with reasonable cause, suspects to be, committing an offence under this section.

(5) For purposes of this section an offence under section 12(1) of this Act of taking a conveyance shall be treated as theft, and 'cheat' means an offence under section 15 of this Act.

27   Evidence and procedure on charge of theft or handling stolen goods

(1) Any number of persons may be charged in one indictment, with reference to the same theft, with having at different times or at the same time handled all or any of the stolen goods, and the persons so charged may be tried together.

(2) On the trial of two or more persons indicted for jointly handling any stolen goods the jury may find any of the accused guilty if the jury are satisfied that he handled all or any of the stolen goods, whether or not he did so jointly with the other accused or any of them.

(3) Where a person is being proceeded against for handling stolen goods (but not for any offence other than handling stolen goods), then at any stage of the proceedings, if evidence has been given of his having or arranging to have in his possession the goods the subject of the charge, or of his undertaking or assisting in, or arranging to undertake or assist in, their retention, removal, disposal or realisation, the following evidence shall be admissible for the purpose of proving that he knew or believed the goods to be stolen goods:—

(a) evidence that he has had in his possession, or has undertaken or assisted in the retention, removal, disposal or realisation of, stolen goods from any theft taking place not earlier than twelve months before the offence charged; and

(b) (provided that seven days' notice in writing has been given to him of the intention to prove the conviction) evidence that he has within the five years preceding the date of the offence charged been convicted of theft or of handling stolen goods.

(4) In any proceedings for the theft of anything in the course of transmission (whether by post or otherwise), or for handling stolen goods from such a theft, a statutory declaration made by any person that he despatched or received or failed to receive any goods or postal packet, or that any goods or postal packet when despatched or received by him were in a particular state or condition, shall be admissible as evidence of the facts stated in the declaration, subject to the following conditions:—

(a) a statutory declaration shall only be admissible where and to the extent to which oral evidence to the like effect would have been admissible in the proceedings; and

(b) a statutory declaration shall only be admissible if at least seven days before the hearing or trial a copy of it has been given to the person charged, and he has not, at least three days before the hearing or trial or within such further time as the court may in special circumstances allow, given the prosecutor written notice requiring the attendance at the hearing or trial of the person making the declaration.

(5) This section is to be construed in accordance with section 24 of this Act; and in subsection (3)(b) above the reference to handling stolen goods shall include any corresponding offence committed before the commencement of this Act.

30 Husband and wife

(1) This Act shall apply in relation to the parties to a marriage, and to property belonging to the wife or husband whether or not by reason of an interest derived from the marriage, as it would apply if they were not married and any such interest subsisted independently of the marriage.

(2) Subject to subsection (4) below, a person shall have the same right to bring proceedings against that person's wife or husband for any offence (whether under this Act or otherwise), as if they were not married.

[(3) *Repealed by the Police and Criminal Evidence Act 1984, s. 18, Sched. 7.*]

(4) Proceedings shall not be instituted against a person for any offence of stealing or doing unlawful damage to property which at the time of the offence belongs to that person's wife or husband, or for any attempt, incitement or conspiracy to commit such an offence, unless the proceedings are instituted by or with the consent of the Director of Public Prosecutions:

Provided that—

(a) this subsection shall not apply to proceedings against a person for an offence—

(i) if that person is charged with committing the offence jointly with the wife or husband; or

(ii) if by virtue of any judicial decree or order (wherever made) that person and the wife or husband are at the time of the offence under no obligation to cohabit [*and*

(b) *Repealed by the Criminal Jurisdiction Act 1975, s. 14(5), Sched. 6.*]

(5) Notwithstanding [section 6 of the Prosecution of Offences Act 1979] subsection (4) of this section shall apply—

(a) to an arrest (if without warrant) made by the wife or husband, and

(b) to a warrant of arrest issued on an information laid by the wife or husband.

31 Effect on civil proceedings and rights

(1) A person shall not be excused, by reason that to do so may incriminate that person or the wife or husband of that person of an offence under this Act—

(a) from answering any question put to that person in proceedings for the recovery or administration of any property, for the execution of any trust or for an account of any property or dealings with property; or

(b) from complying with any order made in any such proceedings;

but no statement or admission made by a person in answering a question put or complying with an order made as aforesaid shall, in proceedings for an offence under this Act, be admissible in evidence against that person or (unless they married after the making of the statement of admission) against the wife or husband of that person.

(2) Notwithstanding any enactment to the contrary, where property has been stolen or obtained by fraud or other wrongful means, the title to that or any other property shall not be affected by reason only of the conviction of the offender.

Criminal Damage Act 1971
(1971, c. 48)

9   Evidence in connection with offences under this Act

A person shall not be excused, by reason that to do so may incriminate that person or the wife or husband of that person of an offence under this Act—

(a) from answering any question put to that person in proceedings for the recovery or administration of any property, for the execution of any trust or for an account of any property or dealings with property; or

(b) from complying with any order made in any such proceedings; but no statement or admission made by a person in answering a question put or complying with an order made as aforesaid shall, in proceedings for an offence under the Act, be admissible in evidence against that person or (unless they married after the making of the statement or admission) against the wife or husband of that person.

Misuse of Drugs Act 1971
(1971, c. 38)

5   Restriction of possession of controlled drugs

(1) Subject to any regulations under section 7 of this Act for the time being in force, it shall not be lawful for a person to have a controlled drug in his possession.

(2) Subject to section 28 of this Act and to subsection (4) below, it is an offence for a person to have a controlled drug in his possession in contravention of subsection (1) above.

(3) Subject to section 28 of this Act, it is an offence for a person to have a controlled drug in his possession, whether lawfully or not, with intent to supply it to another in contravention of section 4(1) of this Act.

(4) In any proceedings for an offence under subsection (2) above in which it is proved that the accused had a controlled drug in his possession, it shall be a defence for him to prove—

(a) that, knowing or suspecting it to be a controlled drug, he took possession of it for the purpose of preventing another from committing or continuing to commit an offence in connection with that drug and that as soon as possible after taking possession of it he took all such steps as were reasonably open to him to destroy the drug or to deliver it into the custody of a person lawfully entitled to take custody of it; or

(b) that, knowing or suspecting it to be a controlled drug, he took possession of it for the purpose of delivering it into the custody of a person lawfully entitled to take custody of it and that as soon as possible after taking possession of it he took all such steps as were reasonably open to him to deliver it into the custody of such a person.

(5) ...

(6) Nothing in subsection (4) . . . above shall prejudice any defence which it is open to a person charged with an offence under this section to raise apart from that subsection.

Rehabilitation of Offenders Act 1974

(1974, c. 53)

4   Effect of rehabilitation

(1) Subject to sections 7 and 8 below, a person who has become a rehabilitated person for the purposes of this Act in respect of a conviction shall be treated for all purposes in law as a person who has not committed or been charged with or prosecuted for or convicted of or sentenced for the offence or offences which were the subject of that conviction; and, notwithstanding the provisions of any other enactment or rule of law to the contrary, but subject as aforesaid—

    (a) no evidence shall be admissible in any proceedings before a judicial authority exercising its jurisdiction or functions in Great Britain to prove that any such person has committed or been charged with or prosecuted for or convicted of or sentenced for any offence which was the subject of a spent conviction; and

    (b) a person shall not, in any such proceedings, be asked, and, if asked, shall not be required to answer, any question relating to his past which cannot be answered without acknowledging or referring to a spent conviction or spent convictions or any circumstances ancillary thereto.

(2) Subject to the provisions of any order made under subsection (4) below, where a question seeking information with respect to a person's previous convictions, offences, conduct or circumstances is put to him or to any other person otherwise than in proceedings before a judicial authority—

    (a) the question shall be treated as not relating to spent convictions or to any circumstances ancillary to spent convictions, and the answer thereto may be framed accordingly; and

    (b) the person questioned shall not be subjected to any liability or otherwise prejudiced in law by reason of any failure to acknowledge or disclose a spent conviction or any circumstances ancillary to a spent conviction in his answer to the question.

(3) Subject to the provisions of any order made under subsection (4) below,—

    (a) any obligation imposed on any person by any rule of law or by the provisions of any agreement or arrangement to disclose any matters to any other person shall not extend to requiring him to disclose a spent conviction or any circumstances ancillary to a spent conviction (whether the conviction is his own or another's); and

    (b) a conviction which has become spent or any circumstances ancillary thereto, or any failure to disclose a spent conviction or any such circumstances, shall not be a proper ground for dismissing or excluding a person from any office, profession, occupation or employment, or for prejudicing him in any way in any occupation or employment.

(4) The Secretary of State may by order—

    (a) make such provisions as seems to him appropriate for excluding or modifying the application of either or both of paragraphs (a) and (b) of subsection (2) above in relation to questions put in such circumstances as may be specified in the order;

    (b) provide for such exceptions from the provisions of subsection (3) above as seem to him appropriate, in such cases or classes of case, and in relation to convictions of such a description, as may be specified in the order.

(5) For the purposes of this section and section 7 below any of the following are circumstances ancillary to a conviction, that is to say—

    (a) the offence or offences which were the subject of that conviction;

    (b) the conduct constituting that offence or those offences; and

    (c) any process or proceedings preliminary to the conviction, any sentence imposed in respect of that conviction, any proceedings (whether by way of appeal or otherwise) for reviewing that conviction or any such sentence, and anything done in pursuance of or undergone in compliance with any such sentence.

(6) For the purposes of this section and section 7 below 'proceedings before a judicial authority' includes, in addition to proceedings before any of the ordinary courts of law, proceedings before any tribunal, body or person having power—

    (a) by virtue of any enactment, law, custom or practice;

    (b) under the rules governing any association, institution, profession, occupation or employment; or

    (c) under any provision of an agreement providing for arbitration with respect to questions arising thereunder;

to determine any question affecting the rights, privileges, obligations or liabilities of any person, or to receive evidence affecting the determination of any such question.

5   Rehabilitation periods for particular sentences

(1) The sentences excluded from rehabilitation under this Act are—

    (a) a sentence of imprisonment for life;

    (b) a sentence of imprisonment [youth custody] [detention in a young offender institution] or corrective training for a term exceeding thirty months;

    (c) a sentence of preventive detention; . . .

    (d) a sentence of detention during Her Majesty's pleasure or for life under section 90 or 91 of the Powers of Criminal Court (Sentencing) Act 2000 [or under section 205(2) or (3) of the Criminal Procedure (Scotland) Act 1975,] or a sentence of detention for a term exceeding thirty months passed under section 91 of the said Act of 2000 [(young offenders convicted of grave crimes) or under section 206 of the said Act of 1975 (detention of children convicted on indictment)] [or a corresponding court-martial punishment]; [and

    (e) a sentence of custody for life] and any other sentence is a sentence subject to rehabilitation under this Act.

[(1A) In subsection (1)(d) above 'corresponding court-martial punishment' means a punishment awarded under section 71A(3) or (4) of the Army Act 1955, section 71A(3) or (4) of the Air Force Act 1955 or section 43A(3) or (4) of the Naval Discipline Act 1957.]

(2) For the purposes of this Act—

    (a) the rehabilitation period applicable to a sentence specified in the first column of Table A below is the period specified in the second column of that Table in relation to that sentence, or, where the sentence was imposed on a person who was under seventeen years of age at the date of his conviction, half that period; and

    (b) the rehabilitation period applicable to a sentence specified in the first column of Table B below is the period specified in the second column of that Table in relation to that sentence;

reckoned in either case from the date of the conviction in respect of which the sentence was imposed.

(3) The rehabilitation period applicable—

    (a) to an order discharging a person absolutely for an offence; and

    (b) to the discharge by a children's hearing under section 43(2) of the Social Work (Scotland) Act 1968 of the referral of a child's case;

shall be six months from the date of conviction.

Table A   Rehabilitation periods subject to reduction by half for persons under 17

Sentence	Rehabilitation period
A sentence of imprisonment [detention in a young offender institution] [or youth custody] or corrective training for a term exceeding six months but not exceeding thirty months.	Ten years.
A sentence of cashiering, discharge with ignominy or dismissal with disgrace from Her Majesty's service.	Ten years.
A sentence of imprisonment [detention in a young offender institution] [or youth custody] for a term not exceeding six months.	Seven years.
A sentence of dismissal from Her Majesty's service.	Seven years.
Any sentence of detention in respect of a conviction in service disciplinary proceedings.	Five years.
A fine or any other sentence subject to rehabilitation under this Act, not being a sentence to which Table B below or any of subsections (3) or (8) below applies.	Five years.

Table B   Rehabilitation periods for certain sentences confined to young offenders

Sentence	Rehabilitation period
A sentence of Borstal training.	Seven years.
[A custodial order under Schedule 5A to the Army Act 1955 or the Air Force Act 1955, or under Schedule 4A to the Naval Discipline Act 1957, where the maximum period of detention specified in the order is more than six months.	Seven years.]
[A custodial order under section 71AA of the Army Act 1955 or the Air Force Act 1955, or under section 43AA of the Naval Discipline Act 1957, where the maximum period of detention specified in the order is more than six months.	Seven years.]
A sentence of detention for a term exceeding six months but not exceeding thirty months passed under section 91 of the Power of Criminal Courts (Sentencing) Act 2000 or under section [206 of the Criminal Procedure (Scotland) Act 1975].	Five years.
A sentence of detention for a term not exceeding six months passed under either of those provisions.	Three years.
An order for detention in a detention centre made under [section 4 of the Criminal Justice Act 1982,] section 4 of the Criminal Justice Act 1961 . . .	Three years.
[A custodial order under any of the Schedules to the said Acts of 1955 and 1957 mentioned above, where the maximum period of detention specified in the order is six months or less.	Three years.]
[A custodial order under section 71AA of the said Acts of 1955, or section 43AA of the said Act of 1957, where the maximum period of detention specified in the order is six months or less.	Three years.]

(4) Where in respect of a conviction a person was conditionally discharged, bound over to keep the peace or be of good behaviour, the rehabilitation period applicable to the sentence shall be one year from the date of conviction or a period beginning with that date and ending when the order for conditional discharge or (as the case may be) the recognisance or bond of

caution to keep the peace or be of good behaviour ceases to have effect, whichever is the longer.

(4A) Where in respect of a conviction a probation order was made, the rehabilitation period applicable to the sentence shall be—

    (a) in the case of a person aged eighteen years or over at the date of his conviction, five years from the date of conviction;

    (b) in the case of a person aged under the age of eighteen years at the date of his conviction, two and a half years from the date of conviction or a period beginning with the date of conviction and ending when the order in question ceases or ceased to have effect, whichever is the longer.

(4B) Where in respect of a conviction a referral order (within the meaning of the Powers of Criminal Courts (Sentencing) Act 2000) is made in respect of the person convicted, the rehabilitation period applicable to the sentence shall be—

    (a) if a youth offender contract takes effect under section 23 of that Act between him and a youth offender panel, the period beginning with the date of conviction and ending on the date when (in accordance with section 24 of that Act) the contract ceases to have effect;

    (b) if no such contract so takes effect, the period beginning with the date of conviction and having the same length as the period for which such a contract would (ignoring any order under paragraph 11 or 12 of Schedule 1 to that Act) have had effect had one so taken effect.

(4C) Where in respect of a conviction an order is made in respect of the person convicted under paragraph 11 or 12 of Schedule 1 to the Powers of Criminal Courts (Sentencing) Act 2000 (extension of period for which youth offender contract has effect), the rehabilitation period applicable to the sentence shall be—

    (a) if a youth offender contract takes effect under section 23 of that Act between the offender and a youth offender panel, the period beginning with the date of conviction and ending on the date when (in accordance with section 24 of that Act) the contract ceases to have effect;

    (b) if no such contract so takes effect, the period beginning with the date accordance with the order such a contract would have had effect had one so taken effect.

(5) Where in respect of a conviction any of the following sentences was imposed, that is to say—

    (a) an order under section 57 of the Children and Young Persons Act 1933 or section 61 of the Children and Young Persons (Scotland) Act 1937 committing the person convicted to the care of a fit person;

    (b) a supervision order under any provision of either of those Acts or of the Children and Young Persons Act 1963;

    [(c) an order under section 413 of the Criminal Procedure (Scotland) Act 1975 committing a child for the purpose of his undergoing residential training;]

    (d) an approved school order under section 61 of the said Act of 1937;

    (e) a care order or a supervision order under section 63(1) of the Powers of Criminal Courts (Sentencing) Act 2000; or

    (f) a supervision requirement under any provision of the Social Work (Scotland) Act 1968;

    [(g) a community supervision order under Schedule 5A to the Army Act 1955 or the Air Force Act 1955, or under Schedule 4A to the Naval Discipline Act 1957;

    (h) a reception order under any of those Schedules;]

the rehabilitation period applicable to the sentence shall be one year from the date of conviction or a period beginning with that date and ending when the order or requirement ceases or ceased to have effect, whichever is the longer.

(6) Where in respect of a conviction any of the following orders was made, that is to say—

(a) an order under section 54 of the said Act of 1933 committing the person convicted to custody in a remand home;

(b) an approved school order under section 57 of the said Act of 1933; or

(c) an attendance centre order under section 60 of the Powers of Criminal Courts (Sentencing) Act 2000;

the rehabilitation period applicable to the sentence shall be a period beginning with the date of conviction and ending one year after the date on which the order ceases or ceased to have effect; or

(d) a secure training order under section 1 of the Criminal Justice and Public Order Act 1994.

(6A) Where in respect of a conviction a detention and training order was made under section 100 of the Powers of Criminal Courts (Sentencing) Act 2000, the rehabilitation period applicable to the sentence shall be—

(a) in the case of a person aged fifteen years or over at the date of his conviction, five years if the order was, and three and a half years if the order was not, for a term exceeding six months;

(b) in the case of a person aged under fifteen years at the date of his conviction, a period beginning with that date and ending one year after the date on which the order ceases to have effect.

(7) Where in respect of a conviction a hospital order under [Part III of the Mental Health Act 1983] or under [Part VI of the Mental Health (Scotland) Act 1984] (with or without [a restriction order]) was made, the rehabilitation period applicable to the sentence shall be the period of five years from the date of conviction or a period beginning with that date and ending two years after the date on which the hospital order ceases or ceased to have effect, whichever is the longer.

(8) Where in respect of a conviction an order was made imposing on the person convicted any disqualification, disability, prohibition or other penalty, the rehabilitation period applicable to the sentence shall be a period beginning with the date of conviction and ending on the date on which the disqualification, disability, prohibition or penalty (as the case may be) ceases or ceased to have effect.

(9) For the purposes of this section—

(a) 'sentence of imprisonment' includes a sentence of detention [under section 207 or 415 of the Criminal Procedure (Scotland) Act 1975] and a sentence of penal servitude, and 'term of imprisonment' shall be construed accordingly;

(b) consecutive terms of imprisonment or of detention under section 91 of the Powers of Criminal Courts (Sentencing) Act 2000 or (section 206 of the said Act 1975)], and terms which are wholly or partly concurrent (being terms of imprisonment or detention imposed in respect of offences of which a person was convicted in the same proceedings) shall be treated as a single term;

(c) no account shall be taken of any subsequent variation, made by a court in dealing with a person in respect of a suspended sentence of imprisonment, or the term originally imposed; and

(d) a sentence imposed by a court outside Great Britain shall be treated as a sentence of that one of the descriptions mentioned in this section which most nearly corresponds to the sentence imposed.

(10) References in this section to the period during which a probation order, or a care order or supervision order under the Powers of Criminal Courts (Sentencing) Act 2000, or a supervision requirement under the Social Work (Scotland) Act 1968, is or was in force include references to any period during which any order or requirement to which this subsection applies, being an order or requirement made or imposed directly or indirectly in substitution for the first-mentioned order or requirement, is or was in force.

This subsection applies—

(a) to any such order or requirement as is mentioned above in this subsection;

(b) to any order having effect under section 25(2) of the Children and Young Persons Act 1969 as if it were a training school order in Northern Ireland; and

(c) to any supervision order made under section 72(2) of the said Act of 1968 and having effect as a supervision order under the Children and Young Persons Act (Northern Ireland) 1950.

[(10A) The reference in subsection (5) above to the period during which a reception order has effect includes a reference to any subsequent period during which by virtue of the order having been made the Social Work (Scotland) Act 1968 or the Children and Young Persons Act (Northern Ireland) 1968 has effect in relation to the person in respect of whom the order was made and subsection (10) above shall accordingly have effect in relation to any such subsequent period.]

(11) The Secretary of State may by order—

(a) substitute different periods or terms for any of the periods or terms mentioned in subsections (1) to (8) above; and

(b) substitute a different age for the age mentioned in subsection (2)(a) above.

7 Limitations on rehabilitation under this Act, etc.

(1) Nothing in section 4(1) above shall affect—

(a) any right of Her Majesty, by virtue of Her Royal prerogative or otherwise, to grant a free pardon, to quash any conviction or sentence, or to commute any sentence;

(b) the enforcement by any process or proceedings of any fine or other sum adjudged to be paid by or imposed on a spent conviction;

(c) the issue of any process for the purpose of proceedings in respect of any breach of a condition or requirement applicable to a sentence imposed in respect of a spent conviction; or

(d) the operation of any enactment by virtue of which, in consequence of any conviction, a person is subject, otherwise than by way of sentence, to any disqualification, disability, prohibition or other penalty the period of which extends beyond the rehabilitation period applicable in accordance with section 6 above to the conviction.

(2) Nothing in section 4(1) above shall affect the determination of any issue, or prevent the admission or requirement of any evidence, relating to a person's previous convictions or to circumstances ancillary thereto—

(a) in any criminal proceedings before a court in Great Britain (including any appeal or reference in a criminal matter);

(b) in any service disciplinary proceedings or in any proceedings on appeal from any service disciplinary proceedings;

(bb) in any proceedings under Part 2 of the Sexual Offences Act 2003 or on an appeal from any such proceedings;

(c) in any proceedings relating to adoption or to the guardianship, wardship, marriage, custody, care or control of, or access to, any minor, or to the provision by any person of accommodation, care or schooling for minors;

(d) in any care proceedings under section 1 of the Powers of Criminal Courts (Sentencing) Act 2000 or on appeal from any such proceedings, or in any proceedings relating to the variation or discharge of a care order or supervision order under that Act;

(e) in any proceedings before a children's hearing under the Social Work (Scotland) Act 1968 or on appeal from any such hearing; or

(f) in any proceedings in which he is a party or a witness, provided that, on the occasion when the issue or the admission or requirement of the evidence falls to be determined, he consents to the determination of the issue or, as the case may be, the admission or requirement of the evidence notwithstanding the provisions of section 4(1); [or,

(g)   ...]

In the application of this subsection to Scotland, 'minor' means a child under the age of eighteen, including a pupil child.

(3) If at any stage in any proceedings before a judicial authority in Great Britain (not being proceedings to which, by virtue of any of paragraphs (a) to (e) of subsection (2) above or of any order for the time being in force under subsection (4) below, section 4(1) above has no application, or proceedings to which section 8 below applies) the authority is satisfied, in the light of any considerations which appear to it to be relevant (including any evidence which has been or may thereafter be put before it), that justice cannot be done in the case except by admitting or requiring evidence relating to a person's spent convictions or to circumstances ancillary thereto, that authority may admit or, as the case may be, require the evidence in question notwithstanding the provisions of subsection (1) of section 4 above, and may determine any issue to which the evidence relates in disregard, so far as necessary, of those provisions.

(4) The Secretary of State may by order exclude the application of section 4(1) above in relation to any proceedings specified in the order (other than proceedings to which section 8 below applies) to such extent and for such purposes as may be so specified.

(5) No order made by a court with respect to any person otherwise than on a conviction shall be included in any list or statement of that person's previous convictions given or made to any court which is considering how to deal with him in respect of any offence.

Protection of Children Act 1978

(1978, c. 37)

1   Indecent photographs of children

(1) It is an offence for a person—

(a) to take, or permit to be taken, or to make any indecent photograph or pseudo-photograph of a child; or

(b) to distribute or show such indecent photographs or pseudo-photographs; or

(c) to have in his possession such indecent photographs or pseudo-photographs, with a view to their being distributed or shown by himself or others; or

(d) to publish or cause to be published any advertisement likely to be understood as conveying that the advertiser distributes or shows such indecent photographs or pseudo-photographs, or intends to do so.

(2) For purposes of this Act, a person is to be regarded as distributing an indecent photograph or pseudo-photograph if he parts with possession of it to, or exposes or offers it for acquisition by another person.

(3) Proceedings for an offence under this Act shall not be instituted except by or with the consent of the Director of Public Prosecutions.

(4) Where a person is charged with an offence under subsection (1)(b) or (c), it shall be a defence for him to prove—

(a) that he had a legitimate reason for distributing or showing the photographs or pseudo-photographs or (as the case may be) having them in his possession; or

(b) that he had not himself seen the photographs or pseudo-photographs and did not know, nor had any cause to suspect, them to be indecent.

(5) References in the Children and Young Persons Act 1933 (except in sections 15 and 99) to the offences mentioned in Schedule 1 to that Act shall include an offence under subsection (1)(a) above.

2   Evidence

(1), (2) . . .

(3) In proceedings under this Act relating to indecent photographs of children a person is to be taken as having been a child at any material time if it appears, from the evidence as a whole, that he was then under the age of 16.

Magistrates' Courts Act 1980
(1980, c. 43)

98   Evidence on oath

Subject to the provisions of any enactment or rule of law authorising the reception of unsworn evidence, evidence given before a magistrates' court shall be given on oath.

101   Onus of proving exceptions, etc.

Where the defendant to an information or complaint relies for his defence on any exception, exemption, proviso, excuse or qualification, whether or not it accompanies the description of the offence or matter of complaint in the enactment creating the offence or on which the complaint is founded, the burden of proving the exception, exemption, proviso, excuse or qualification shall be on him; and this notwithstanding that the information or complaint contains an allegation negativing the exception, exemption, proviso, excuse or qualification.

104   Proof of previous convictions

Where a person is convicted of a summary offence by a magistrates' court, other than a juvenile court, and—

(a) it is proved to the satisfaction of the court, on oath or in such other manner as may be prescribed, that not less than 7 days previously a notice was served on the accused in the prescribed form and manner specifying any alleged previous conviction of the accused of a summary offence proposed to be brought to the notice of the court in the event of his conviction of the offence charged; and

(b) the accused is not present in person before the court, the court may take account of any such previous conviction so specified as if the accused had appeared and admitted it.

107   False statements in declaration proving service, etc.

If, in any solemn declaration, certificate or other writing made or given for the purpose of its being used in pursuance of the rules as evidence of the service of any document or the handwriting or seal of any person, a person makes a statement that he knows to be false in a material particular, or recklessly makes any statement that is false in a material particular, he shall be liable on summary conviction to imprisonment for a term not exceeding 6 months or a fine not exceeding [level 3 on the standard scale] or both.

Criminal Attempts Act 1981
(1981, c. 47)

1   Attempting to commit an offence

(1) If, with intent to commit an offence to which this section applies, a person does an act which is more than merely preparatory to the commission of the offence, he is guilty of attempting to commit the offence.

(1A) Subject to section 8 of the Computer Misuse Act 1990 (relevance of external law) if this subsection applies to an act, what the person doing it had in view shall be treated as an offence to which this section applies.

(1B) Subsection (1A) above applies to an act if—
  (a) it is done in England and Wales; and
  (b) it would fall within subsection (1) above as more than merely preparatory to the commission of an offence under section 3 of the Computer Misuse Act 1990 but for the fact that the offence, if completed, would not be an offence triable in England and Wales.

(2) A person may be guilty of attempting to commit an offence to which this section applies even though the facts are such that the commission of the offence is impossible.

(3) In any case where—
  (a) apart from this subsection a person's intention would not be regarded as having amounted to an intent to commit an offence; but
  (b) if the facts of the case had been as he believed them to be, his intention would be so regarded, then, for the purposes of subsection (1) above, he shall be regarded as having had an intent to commit that offence.

(4) This section applies to any offence which, if it were completed, would be triable in England and Wales as an indictable offence, other than—
  (a) conspiracy (at common law or under section 1 of the Criminal Law Act 1977 or any other enactment);
  (b) aiding, abetting, counselling, procuring or suborning the commission of an offence;
  (c) offences under section 4(1) (assisting offenders) or 5(1) (accepting or agreeing to accept consideration for not disclosing information about an arrestable offence) of the Criminal Law Act 1967.

1A   Extended jurisdiction in relation to certain attempts

(1) If this section applies to an act, what the person doing the act had in view shall be treated as an offence to which section 1(1) above applies.

(2) This section applies to an act if—
  (a) it is done in England and Wales, and
  (b) it would fall within section 1(1) above as more than merely preparatory to the commission of a Group A offence but for the fact that that offence, if completed, would not be an offence triable in England and Wales.

(3) In this section 'Group A offence' has the same meaning as in Part I of the Criminal Justice Act 1993.

(4) Subsection (1) above is subject to the provisions of section 6 of the Act of 1993 (relevance of external law).

(5) Where a person does an act to which this section applies, the offence which he commits shall for all purposes be treated as the offence of attempting to commit the relevant Group A offence.

2   Application of procedural and other provisions to offences under s.1

(1) Any provision to which this section applies shall have effect with respect to an offence under section 1 above of attempting to commit an offence as it has effect with respect to the offence attempted.

(2) This section applies to provisions of any of the following descriptions made by or under any enactment (whenever passed)—
  (a) provisions whereby proceedings may not be instituted or carried on otherwise than by, or on behalf or with the consent of, any person (including any provisions which also make other exceptions to the prohibition);
  (b) provisions conferring power to institute proceedings;

    (c) provisions as to the venue of proceedings;

    (d) provisions whereby proceedings may not be instituted after the expiration of a time limit;

    (e) provisions conferring a power of arrest or search;

    (f) provisions conferring a power of seizure and detention of property;

    (g) provisions whereby a person may not be convicted on the uncorroborated evidence of one witness (including any provision requiring the evidence of not less than two credible witnesses);

    (h) provisions conferring a power of forfeiture, including any power to deal with anything liable to be forfeited;

    (i) provisions whereby, if an offence committed by a body corporate is proved to have been committed with the consent or connivance of another person, that person also is guilty of the offence.

3 Offences of attempt under other enactments

(1) Subsections (2) to (5) below shall have effect, subject to subsection (6) below and to any inconsistent provision in any other enactment, for the purpose of determining whether a person is guilty of an attempt under a special statutory provision.

(2) For the purposes of this Act an attempt under a special statutory provision is an offence which—

    (a) is created by an enactment other than section 1 above, including an enactment passed after this Act; and

    (b) is expressed as an offence of attempting to commit another offence (in this section referred to as 'the relevant full offence').

(3) A person is guilty of an attempt under a special statutory provision if, with intent to commit the relevant full offence, he does an act which is more than merely preparatory to the commission of that offence.

(4) A person may be guilty of an attempt under a special statutory provision even though the facts are such that the commission of the relevant full offence is impossible.

(5) In any case where—

    (a) apart from this subsection a person's intention would not be regarded as having amounted to an intent to commit the relevant full offence; but

    (b) if the facts of the case had been as he believed them to be, his intention would be so regarded, then, for the purposes of subsection (3) above, he shall be regarded as having had an intent to commit that offence.

(6) Subsections (2) to (5) above shall not have effect in relation to an act done before the commencement of this Act.

4 Trial and penalties

(1) A person guilty by virtue of section 1 above of attempting to commit an offence shall—

    (a) if the offence attempted is murder or any other offence the sentence for which is fixed by law, be liable on conviction on indictment to imprisonment for life; and

    (b) if the offence attempted is indictable but does not fall within paragraph (a) above, be liable on conviction on indictment to any penalty to which he would have been liable on conviction on indictment of that offence; and

    (c) if the offence attempted is triable either way, be liable on summary conviction to any penalty to which he would have been liable on summary conviction of that offence.

(2) In any case in which a court may proceed to summary trial of an information charging a person with an offence and an information charging him with an offence under section 1

above of attempting to commit it or an attempt under a special statutory provision, the court may, without his consent, try the informations together.

(3) Where, in proceedings against a person for an offence under section 1 above, there is evidence sufficient in law to support a finding that he did an act falling within subsection (1) of that section, the question whether or not his act fell within that subsection is a question of fact.

(4) Where, in proceedings against a person for an attempt under a special statutory provision, there is evidence sufficient in law to support a finding that he did an act falling within subsection (3) of section 3 above, the question whether or not his act fell within that subsection is a question of fact.

(5) Subsection (1) above shall have effect—
    (b) notwithstanding anything—
        (i) in section 32(1) (no limit to fine on conviction on indictment) of the Criminal Law Act 1977; or
        (ii) in section 78(1) and (2) (maximum of six months' imprisonment on summary conviction unless express provision made to the contrary) of the Powers of Criminal Courts (Sentencing) Act 2000.

Contempt of Court Act 1981

(1981, c. 49)

10   Sources of information

No court may require a person to disclose, nor is any person guilty of contempt of court for refusing to disclose, the source of information contained in a publication for which he is responsible, unless it be established to the satisfaction of the court that disclosure is necessary in the interests of justice or national security or for the prevention of disorder or crime.

Criminal Justice Act 1982

(1982, c. 48)

Unsworn statements

72   Abolition of right of accused to make unsworn statement

(1) Subject to subsections (2) and (3) below, in any criminal proceedings the accused shall not be entitled to make a statement without being sworn, and accordingly, if he gives evidence, he shall do so (subject to sections 55 and 56 of the Youth Justice and Criminal Evidence Act 1999) on oath and be liable to cross-examination; but this section shall not affect the right of the accused, if not represented by counsel or a solicitor, to address the court of jury otherwise than on oath on any matter on which, if he were so represented, counsel or a solicitor could address the court or jury on his behalf.

(2) Nothing in subsection (1) above shall prevent the accused making a statement without being sworn—
    (a) if it is one which he is required by law to make personally; or
    (b) if he makes it by way of mitigation before the court passes sentence upon him.

(3) Nothing in this section applies—
    (a) to a trial; or
    (b) to proceedings before a magistrates' court acting as examining justices, which began before the commencement of this section.

Police and Criminal Evidence Act 1984
(1984, c. 60)

PART I   POWERS TO STOP AND SEARCH

1   Power of constable to stop and search persons, vehicles etc.

(1) A constable may exercise any power conferred by this section—

(a) in any place to which at the time when he proposes to exercise the power the public or any section of the public has access, on payment or otherwise, as of right or by virtue of express or implied permission; or

(b) in any other place to which people have ready access at the time when he proposes to exercise the power but which is not a dwelling.

(2) Subject to subsection (3) to (5) below, a constable—

(a) may search—

(i) any person or vehicle;

(ii) anything which is in or on a vehicle, for stolen or prohibited articles or any article to which subsection (8A) below applies; and

(b) may detain a person or vehicle for the purpose of such a search.

(3) This section does not give a constable power to search a person or vehicle or anything in or on a vehicle unless he has reasonable grounds for suspecting that he will find stolen or prohibited articles or any article to which subsection (8A) below applies.

(4) If a person is in a garden or yard occupied with and used for the purposes of a dwelling or on other land so occupied and used, a constable may not search him in the exercise of the power conferred by this section unless the constable has reasonable grounds for believing—

(a) that he does not reside in the dwelling; and

(b) that he is not in the place in question with the express or implied permission of a person who resides in the dwelling.

(5) If a vehicle is in a garden or yard occupied with and used for the purposes of a dwelling or on other land so occupied and used, a constable may not search the vehicle or anything in or on it in the exercise of the power conferred by this section unless he has reasonable grounds for believing—

(a) that the person in charge of the vehicle does not reside in the dwelling; and

(b) that the vehicle is not in the place in question with the express or implied permission of a person who resides in the dwelling.

(6) If in the course of such a search a constable discovers an article which he has reasonable grounds for suspecting to be a stolen or prohibited article or any article to which subsection (8A) below applies, he may seize it.

(7) An article is prohibited for the purposes of this Part of this Act if it is—

(a) an offensive weapon; or

(b) an article—

(i) made or adapted for use in the course of or in connection with an offence to which this sub-paragraph applies; or

(ii) intended by the person having it with him for such use by him or by some other person.

(8) The offences to which subsection (7)(b)(i) above applies are—

(a) burglary;

(b) theft;

(c) offences under section 12 of the Theft Act 1968 (taking motor vehicle or other conveyance without authority); and

(d) offences under section 15 of that Act (obtaining property by deception); and

(e) offences under section 1 of the Criminal Damage Act 1971 (damaging or destroying property).

(8A) This subsection applies to any article in relation to which a person has committed, or is committing or is going to commit an offence under section 139 of the Criminal Justice Act 1988.

(9) In this Part of this Act 'offensive weapon' means any article—

(a) made or adapted for use for causing injury to persons; or

(b) intended by the person having it with him for such use by him or by some other person.

2 Provisions relating to search under section 1 and other powers

(1) A constable who detains a person or vehicle in the exercise—

(a) of the power conferred by section 1 above; or

(b) of any other power—

(i) to search a person without first arresting him; or

(ii) to search a vehicle without making an arrest,

need not conduct a search if it appears to him subsequently—

(i) that no search is required; or

(ii) that a search is impracticable.

(2) If a constable contemplates a search, other than a search of an unattended vehicle, in the exercise—

(a) of the power conferred by section 1 above; or

(b) of any other power, except the power conferred by section 6 below and the power conferred by section 27(2) of the Aviation Security Act 1982—

(i) to search a person without first arresting him; or

(ii) to search a vehicle without making an arrest,

it shall be his duty, subject to subsection (4) below, to take reasonable steps before he commences the search to bring to the attention of the appropriate person—

(i) if the constable is not in uniform, documentary evidence that he is a constable; and

(ii) whether he is in uniform or not, the matter specified in subsection (3) below;

and the constable shall not commence the search until he has performed that duty.

(3) The matters referred to in subsection (2)(ii) above are—

(a) the constable's name and the name of the police station to which he is attached;

(b) the object of the proposed search;

(c) the constable's grounds for proposing to make it; and

(d) the effect of section 3(7) or (8) below, as may be appropriate.

(4) A constable need not bring the effect of section 3(7) or (8) below to the attention of the appropriate person if it appears to the constable that it will not be practicable to make the record in section 3(1) below.

(5) In this section 'the appropriate person' means—

(a) if the constable proposes to search a person, that person; and

(b) if he proposes to search a vehicle, or anything in or on a vehicle, the person in charge of the vehicle.

(6) On completing a search of an unattended vehicle or anything in or on such a vehicle in the exercise of any such power as is mentioned in subsection (2) above a constable shall leave a notice—

(a) stating that he has searched it;

(b) giving the name of the police station to which he is attached;

(c) stating that an application for compensation for any damage caused by the search may be made to that police station; and

(d) stating the effect of section 3(8) below.

(7) The constable shall leave the notice inside the vehicle unless it is not reasonably practicable to do so without damaging the vehicle.

(8) The time for which a person or vehicle may be detained for the purposes of such a search is such time as is reasonably required to permit a search to be carried out either at the place where the person or vehicle was first detained or nearby.

(9) Neither the power conferred by section 1 above nor any other power to detain and search a person without first arresting him or to detain and search a vehicle without making an arrest is to be construed—

(a) as authorising a constable to require a person to remove any of his clothing in public other than an outer coat, jacket or gloves; or

(b) as authorising a constable not in uniform to stop a vehicle.

(10) This section and section 1 above apply to vessels, aircraft and hovercraft as they apply to vehicles.

3   Duty to make records concerning searches

(1) Where a constable has carried out a search in the exercise of any such power as is mentioned in section 2(1) above, other than a search—

(a) under section 6 below; or

(b) under section 27(2) of the Aviation Security Act 1982, he shall make a record of it in writing unless it is not practicable to do so.

(2) If—

(a) a constable is required by subsection (1) above to make a record of a search; but

(b) it is not practicable to make the record on the spot,

he shall make it as soon as practicable after the completion of the search.

(3) The record of a search of a person shall include a note of his name, if the constable knows it, but a constable may not detain a person to find out his name.

(4) If a constable does not know the name of a person whom he has searched, the record of the search shall include a note otherwise describing that person.

(5) The record of a search of a vehicle shall include a note describing the vehicle.

(6) The record of a search of a person or a vehicle—

(a) shall state—

(i)   the object of the search;

(ii) the grounds for making it;

(iii) the date and time when it was made;

(iv) the place where it was made;

(v)   whether anything, and if so what, was found;

(vi) whether any, and if so what, injury to a person or damage to property appears to the constable to have resulted from the search; and

(b) shall identify the constable making it.

(7) If a constable who conducted a search of a person made a record of it, the person who was searched shall be entitled to a copy of the record if he asks for one before the end of the period specified in subsection (9) below.

(8) If—

(a) the owner of a vehicle which has been searched or the person who was in charge of the vehicle at the time when it was searched asks for a copy of the record of the search before the end of the period specified in subsection (9) below; and

(b) the constable who conducted the search made a record of it, the person who made the request shall be entitled to a copy.

(9) The period mentioned in subsections (7) and (8) above is the period of 12 months beginning with the date on which the search was made.

(10) The requirements imposed by this section with regard to records of searches of vehicles shall apply also to records of searches of vessels, aircraft and hovercraft.

4   Road checks

(1) This section shall have effect in relation to the conducting of road checks by police officers for the purpose of ascertaining whether a vehicle is carrying—

(a) a person who has committed an offence other than a road traffic offence or a vehicle excise offence;

(b) a person who is a witness to such an offence;

(c) a person intending to commit such an offence; or

(d) a person who is unlawfully at large.

(2) For the purposes of this section a road check consists of the exercise in a locality of the power conferred by section 163 of the Road Traffic Act 1988 in such a way as to stop during the period for which its exercise in that way in that locality continues all vehicles or vehicles selected by any criterion.

(3) Subject to subsection (5) below, there may only be such a road check if a police officer of the rank of superintendent or above authorises it in writing.

(4) An officer may only authorise a road check under subsection (3) above—

(a) for the purpose specified in subsection (1)(a) above, if he has reasonable grounds—

   (i)   for believing that the offence is a serious arrestable offence; and

   (ii) for suspecting that the person is, or is about to be, in the locality in which vehicles would be stopped if the road check were authorised;

(b) for the purpose specified in subsection (1)(b) above, if he has reasonable grounds for believing that the offence is a serious arrestable offence;

(c) for the purpose specified in subsection (1)(c) above, if he has reasonable grounds—

   (i)   for believing that the offence would be a serious arrestable offence; and

   (ii) for suspecting that the person is, or is about to be, in the locality in which vehicles would be stopped if the road check were authorised;

(d) for the purpose specified in subsection (1)(d) above, if he has reasonable grounds for suspecting that the person is, or is about to be, in that locality.

(5) An officer below the rank of superintendent may authorise such a road check if it appears to him that it is required as a matter of urgency for one of the purposes specified in subsection (1) above.

(6) If an authorisation is given under subsection (5) above, it shall be the duty of the officer who gives it—

(a) to make a written record of the time at which he gives it; and

(b) to cause an officer of the rank of superintendent or above to be informed that it has been given.

(7) The duties imposed by subsection (6) above shall be performed as soon as it is practicable to do so.

(8) An officer to whom a report is made under subsection (6) above may, in writing, authorise the road check to continue.

(9) If such an officer considers that the road checks should not continue, he shall record in writing—

(a) the fact that it took place; and

(b) the purpose for which it took place.

(10) An officer giving an authorisation under this section shall specify the locality in which vehicles are to be stopped.

(11) An officer giving an authorisation under this section, other than an authorisation under subsection (5) above—

(a) shall specify a period, not exceeding seven days, during which the road check may continue; and

(b) may direct that the road check—
  (i) shall be continuous; or
  (ii) shall be conducted at specified times, during that period.

(12) If it appears to an officer of the rank of superintendent or above that a road check ought to continue beyond the period for which it has been authorised he may, from time to time, in writing specify a further period, not exceeding seven days, during which it may continue.

(13) Every written authorisation shall specify—
  (a) the name of the officer giving it;
  (b) the purpose of the road check; and
  (c) the locality in which vehicles are to be stopped.

(14) The duties to specify the purposes of a road check imposed by subsections (9) and (13) above include duties to specify any relevant serious arrestable offence.

(15) Where a vehicle is stopped in a road check, the person in charge of the vehicle at the time when it is stopped shall be entitled to obtain a written statement of the purpose of the road check if he applies for such a statement not later than the end of the period of twelve months from the day on which the vehicle was stopped.

(16) Nothing in this section affects the exercise by police officers of any power to stop vehicles for purposes other than those specified in subsection (1) above.

5   Reports of recorded searches and of road checks

(1) Every annual report—
  (a) under [section 22 of the Police Act 1996]; or
  (b) made by the Commissioner of Police of the Metropolis, shall contain information—
    (i) about searches recorded under section 3 above which have been carried out in the area to which the report relates during the period to which it relates; and
    (ii) about road checks authorised in that area during that period under section 4 above.

[(1A) Every annual report under section 57 of the Police Act 1997 (reports by Director General of the National Crime Squad) shall contain information—
  (a) about searches recorded under section 3 above which have been carried out by members of the National Crime Squad during the period to which the report relates, and
  (b) about road checks authorised by members of the National Crime Squad during that period under section 4 above.]

(2) The information about searches shall not include information about specific searches but shall include—
  (a) the total number of searches in each month during the period to which the report relates—
    (i)   for stolen articles;
    (ii) for offensive weapons or articles to which section 1(8A) above applies; and
    (iii) for other prohibited articles;
  (b) the total number of persons arrested in each such month in consequence of searches of each of the descriptions specified in paragraph (a)(i) to (iii) above.

(3) The information about road checks shall include information—
  (a) about the reason for authorising each road check; and
  (b) about the result of each of them.

6   Statutory undertakers etc.

(1) A constable employed by statutory undertakers may stop, detain and search any vehicle before it leaves a goods area included in the premises of the statutory undertakers.

(1A) Without prejudice to any powers under subsection (1) above, a constable employed by the Strategic Rail Authority may stop, detain and search any vehicle before it leaves a goods area which is included in the premises of any successor of the British Railways Board and is used wholly or mainly for the purpose of a relevant undertaking.

(2) In this section 'goods area' means any area used wholly or mainly for the storage or handling of goods.

(3) For the purposes of section 6 of the Public Stores Act 1875, any person appointed under the Special Constables Act 1923 to be a special constable within any premises which are in the possession or under the control of British Nuclear Fuels Limited shall be deemed to be a constable deputed by a public department and any goods and chattels belonging to or in the possession of British Nuclear Fuels Limited shall be deemed to be Her Majesty's Stores.

(4) In the application of subsection (3) above to Northern Ireland, for the reference to the Special Constables Act 1923 there shall be substituted a reference to paragraph 1(2) of Schedule 2 to the Emergency Laws (Miscellaneous Provisions) Act 1947.

7   Part I—supplementary

(1) The following enactments shall cease to have effect—
(a) section 8 of the Vagrancy Act 1824;
(b) section 66 of the Metropolitan Police Act 1839;
(c) section 11 of the Canals (Offences) Act 1840;
(d) section 19 of the Pedlars Act 1871;
(e) section 33 of the County of Merseyside Act 1980; and
(f) section 42 of the West Midlands County Council Act 1980.

(2) There shall also cease to have effect—
(a) so much of any enactment contained in an Act passed before 1974, other than—
   (i)   an enactment contained in a public general Act; or
   (ii) an enactment relating to statutory undertakers, as confers power on a constable to search for stolen or unlawfully obtained goods; and
(b) so much of any enactment relating to statutory undertakers as provides that such a power shall not be exercisable after the end of a specified period.

(3) In this Part of this Act 'statutory undertakers' means persons authorised by any enactment to carry on any railway, light railway, road transport, water transport, canal, inland navigation, dock or harbour undertaking.

PART II   POWERS OF ENTRY, SEARCH AND SEIZURE

Search warrants

8   Power of justice of the peace to authorise entry and search of premises

(1) If on an application made by a constable a justice of the peace is satisfied that there are reasonable grounds for believing—
(a) that a serious arrestable offence has been committed; and
(b) that there is material on premises specified in the application which is likely to be of substantial value (whether by itself or together with other material) to the investigation of the offence; and
(c) that the material is likely to be relevant evidence; and
(d) that it does not consist of or include items subject to legal privilege, excluded material or special procedure material; and
(e) that any of the conditions specified in subsection (3) below applies, he may issue a warrant authorising a constable to enter and search the premises.

(2) A constable may seize and retain anything for which a search has been authorised under subsection (1) above.

(3) The conditions mentioned in subsection (1)(e) above are—

    (a) that it is not practicable to communicate with any person entitled to grant entry to the premises;

    (b) that it is practicable to communicate with a person entitled to grant entry to the premises but it is not practicable to communicate with any person entitled to grant access to the evidence;

    (c) that entry to the premises will not be granted unless a warrant is produced;

    (d) that the purpose of a search may be frustrated or seriously prejudiced unless a constable arriving at the premises can secure immediate entry to them.

(4) In this Act 'relevant evidence', in relation to an offence, means anything that would be admissible in evidence at a trial for the offence.

(5) The power to issue a warrant conferred by this section is in addition to any such power otherwise conferred.

(6) This section applies in relation to a relevant offence (as defined in section 28D of the Immigration Act 1971) as it applies to a serious arrestable offence.

9   Special provisions as to access

(1) A constable may obtain access to excluded material or special procedure material for the purposes of a criminal investigation by making an application under Schedule 1 below and in accordance with that Schedule.

(2) Any Act (including a local Act) passed before this Act under which a search of premises for the purposes of a criminal investigation could be authorised by the issue of a warrant to a constable shall cease to have effect so far as it relates to the authorisation of searches—

    (a) for items subject to legal privilege; or

    (b) for excluded material; or

    (c) for special procedure material consisting of documents or records other than documents.

(2A) Section 4 of the Summary Jurisdiction (Process) Act 1881 (c. 24) (which includes provision for the execution of process of English courts in Scotland) and section 29 of the Petty Sessions (Ireland) Act 1851 (c. 93) (which makes equivalent provision for execution in Northern Ireland) shall each apply to any process issued by a circuit judge under Schedule 1 to this Act as it applies to process issued by a magistrates' court under the Magistrates' Courts Act 1980 (c. 43).

10   Meaning of 'items subject to legal privilege'

(1) Subject to subsection (2) below, in this Act 'items subject to legal privilege' means—

    [(a) communications between a professional legal adviser and his client or any person representing his client made in connection with the giving of legal advice to the client;]

    [(b)] communications between a professional legal adviser and his client or any person representing his client or between such an adviser or his client or any such representative and any other person made in connection with or in contemplation of legal proceedings and for the purpose of such proceedings; and

    (c) items enclosed with or referred to in such communications and made—

        (i) in connection with the giving of legal advice; or

        (ii) in connection with or in contemplation of legal proceedings and for the purposes of such proceedings,

when they are in the possession of a person who is entitled to possession of them.

(2) Items held with the intention of furthering a criminal purpose are not items subject to legal privilege.

11   Meaning of 'excluded material'

(1) Subject to the following provisions of this section, in this Act 'excluded material' means—

(a) personal records which a person has acquired or created in the course of any trade, business, profession or other occupation or for the purposes of any paid or unpaid office and which he holds in confidence;

(b) human tissue or tissue fluid which has been taken for the purposes of diagnosis or medical treatment and which a person holds in confidence;

(c) journalistic material which a person holds in confidence and which consists—

(i) of documents; or

(ii) of records other than documents.

(2) A person holds material other than journalistic material in confidence for the purposes of this section if he holds it subject—

(a) to an express or implied undertaking to hold it in confidence; or

(b) to a restriction on disclosure or an obligation of secrecy contained in any enactment, including an enactment contained in an Act passed after this Act.

(3) A person holds journalistic material in confidence for the purposes of this section if—

(a) he holds it subject to such an undertaking, restriction or obligation; and

(b) it has been continuously held (by one or more persons) subject to such an undertaking, restriction or obligation since it was first acquired or created for the purposes of journalism.

12 Meaning of 'personal records'

In this Part of this Act 'personal records' means documentary and other records concerning an individual (whether living or dead) who can be identified from them and relating—

(a) to his physical or mental health;

(b) to spiritual counselling or assistance given or to be given to him; or

(c) to counselling or assistance given or to be given to him, for the purposes of his personal welfare, by any voluntary organisation or by any individual who—

(i) by reason of his office or occupation has responsibilities for his personal welfare; or

(ii) by reason of an order of a court has responsibilities for his supervision.

13 Meaning of 'journalistic material'

(1) Subject to subsection (2) below, in this Act 'journalistic material' means material acquired or created for the purposes of journalism.

(2) Material is only journalistic material for the purposes of this Act if it is in the possession of a person who acquired or created it for the purposes of journalism.

(3) A person who receives material from someone who intends that the recipient shall use it for the purposes of journalism is to be taken to have acquired it for those purposes.

14 Meaning of 'special procedure material'

(1) In this Act 'special procedure material' means—

(a) material to which subsection (2) below applies; and

(b) journalistic material, other than excluded material.

(2) Subject to the following provisions of this section, this subsection applies to material, other than items subject to legal privilege and excluded material, in the possession of a person who—

(a) acquired or created it in the course of any trade, business, profession or other occupation or for the purpose of any paid or unpaid office; and

(b) holds it subject—

(i) to an express or implied undertaking to hold it in confidence; or

(ii) to a restriction or obligation such as is mentioned in section 11(2)(b) above.

(3) Where material is acquired—

    (a) by an employee from his employer and in the course of his employment; or

    (b) by a company from an associated company,

it is only special procedure material if it was special procedure material immediately before the acquisition.

    (4) Where material is created by an employee in the course of his employment, it is only special procedure material if it would have been special procedure material had his employer created it.

    (5) Where material is created by a company on behalf of an associated company, it is only special procedure material if it would have been special procedure material had the associated company created it.

    (6) A company is to be treated as another's associated company for the purposes of this section if it would be so treated under section 302 of the Income and Corporation Taxes Act 1970.

15   Search warrants—safeguards

    (1) This section and section 16 below have effect in relation to the issue to constables under any enactment, including an enactment contained in an Act passed after this Act, of warrants to enter and search premises; and an entry on or search of premises under a warrant is unlawful unless it complies with this section 16 below.

    (2) Where a constable applies for any such warrant, it shall be his duty—

        (a) to state—

            (i) the ground on which he makes the application; and

            (ii) the enactment under which the warrant would be issued;

        (b) to specify the premises which it is desired to enter and search; and

        (c) to identify, so far as is practicable, the articles or persons to be sought.

    (3) An application for such a warrant shall be made ex parte and supported by an information in writing.

    (4) The constable shall answer on oath any question that the justice of the peace or judge hearing the application asks him.

    (5) A warrant shall authorise an entry on one occasion only.

    (6) A warrant—

        (a) shall specify—

            (i)   the name of the person who applies for it;

            (ii) the date on which it is issued;

            (iii) the enactment under which it is issued; and

            (iv) the premises to be searched; and

        (b) shall identify, so far as is practicable, the articles or persons to be sought.

    (7) Two copies shall be made of a warrant.

    (8) The copies shall be clearly certified as copies.

16   Execution of warrants

    (1) A warrant to enter and search premises may be executed by any constable.

    (2) Such a warrant may authorise persons to accompany any constable who is executing it.

    (2A) A person so authorised has the same powers as the constable whom he accompanies in respect of—

        (a) the execution of the warrant, and

        (b) the seizure of anything to which the warrant relates.

    (2B) But he may exercise those powers only in the company, and under the supervision, of a constable.

    (3) Entry and search under a warrant must be within one month from the date of its issue.

    (4) Entry and search under a warrant must be at a reasonable hour unless it appears to the constable executing it that the purpose of a search may be frustrated on an entry at a reasonable hour.

(5) Where the occupier of premises which are to be entered and searched is present at the time when a constable seeks to execute a warrant to enter and search them, the constable—

    (a) shall identify himself to the occupier and, if not in uniform, shall produce to him documentary evidence that he is a constable;

    (b) shall produce a warrant to him; and

    (c) shall supply him with a copy of it.

(6) Where—

    (a) the occupier of such premises is not present at the time when a constable seeks to execute such a warrant; but

    (b) some other person who appears to the constable to be in charge of the premises is present,

subsection (5) above shall have effect as if any reference to the occupier were a reference to that other person.

(7) If there is no person present who appears to the constable to be in charge of the premises, he shall leave a copy of the warrant in a prominent place on the premises.

(8) A search under a warrant may only be a search to the extent required for the purpose for which the warrant was issued.

(9) A constable executing a warrant shall make an endorsement on it stating—

    (a) whether the articles or persons sought were found; and

    (b) whether any articles were seized, other than articles which were sought.

(10) A warrant which—

    (a) has been executed; or

    (b) has not been executed within the time authorised for its execution, shall be returned—

        (i) if it was issued by a justice of the peace, to the designated officer for the local justice area in which the justice was acting when he issued the warrant; and

        (ii) if it was issued by a judge, to the appropriate officer of the court from which he issued it.

(11) A warrant which is returned under subsection (10) above shall be retained for 12 months from its return—

    (a) by the designated officer for the local justice area, if it was returned under paragraph (i) of that subsection; and

    (b) by the appropriate officer, if it was returned under paragraph (ii).

(12) If during the period for which a warrant is to be retained the occupier of the premises to which it relates asks to inspect it, he shall be allowed to do so.

Entry and search without search warrant

17 Entry for purpose of arrest etc.

(1) Subject to the following provisions of this section, and without prejudice to any other enactment, a constable may enter and search any premises for the purpose—

    (a) of executing—

        (i) a warrant of arrest issued in connection with or arising out of criminal proceedings; or

        (ii) a warrant of commitment issued under section 76 of the Magistrates' Courts Act 1980;

    (b) of arresting a person for an arrestable offence;

    (c) of arresting a person for an offence under—

        (i) section 1 (prohibition of uniforms in connection with political objects), of the Public Order Act 1936;

        (ii) any enactment contained in sections 6 to 8 or 10 of the Criminal Law Act 1977 (offences relating to entering and remaining on property);

    (iii)   section 4 of the Public Order Act 1986 (fear or provocation of violence);

    (iiia) section 163 of the Road Traffic Act 1988 (failure to stop when required to do so by a police officer in uniform);

    (iv)   section 76 of the Criminal Justice and Public Order Act 1994 (failure to comply with interim possession order);

(ca) of arresting, in pursuance of section 32(1A) of the Children and Young Persons Act 1969, any child or young person who has been remanded or committed to local authority accommodation under section 23(1) of that Act;

(cb) of recapturing any person who is, or is deemed for any purpose to be, unlawfully at large while liable to be detained—

    (i)   in a prison, remand centre, young offender institution or secure housing centre, or

    (ii) in pursuance of section 92 of the Powers of Criminal Courts (Sentencing) Act 2000 (dealing with children and young persons guilty of grave crimes), in any other place.

(d) of recapturing any person whatsoever who is unlawfully at large and whom he is pursuing; or

(e) of saving life or limb or preventing serious damage to property.

(2) Except for the purpose specified in paragraph (e) of subsection (1) above, the powers of entry and search conferred by this section—

(a) are only exercisable if the constable has reasonable grounds for believing that the person whom he is seeking is on the premises; and

(b) are limited, in relation to premises consisting of two or more separate dwellings, to powers to enter and search—

    (i)   any parts of the premises which the occupiers of any dwelling comprised in the premises use in common with the occupiers of any other such dwelling; and

    (ii) any such dwelling in which the constable has reasonable grounds for believing that the person whom he is seeking may be.

(3) The powers of entry and search conferred by this section are only exercisable for the purposes specified in subsection (1)(c)(ii) or (iv) above by a constable in uniform.

(4) The power of search conferred by this section is only a power to search to the extent that is reasonably required for the purpose for which the power of entry is exercised.

(5) Subject to subsection (6) below, all the rules of common law under which a constable has power to enter premises without a warrant are hereby abolished.

(6) Nothing in subsection (5) above affects any power of entry to deal with or prevent a breach of the peace.

18   Entry and search after arrest

(1) Subject to the following provisions of this section, a constable may enter and search any premises occupied or controlled by a person who is under arrest for an arrestable offence, if he has reasonable grounds for suspecting that there is on the premises evidence, other than items subject to legal privilege, that relates—

(a) to that offence; or

(b) to some other arrestable offence which is connected with or similar to that offence.

(2) A constable may seize and retain anything for which he may search under subsection (1) above.

(3) The power to search conferred by subsection (1) above is only a power to search to the extent that is reasonably required for the purpose of discovering such evidence.

(4) Subject to subsection (5) below, the powers conferred by this section may not be exercised unless an officer of the rank of inspector or above has authorised them in writing.

(5) A constable may conduct a search under subsection (1)—

    (a) before the person is taken to a police station or released on bail under section 30A, and

    (b) without obtaining an authorisation under subsection (4),

if the condition in subsection (5A) is satisfied.

(5A) The condition is that the presence of the person at a place (other than a police station) is necessary for the effective investigation of the offence.

(6) If a constable conducts a search by virtue of subsection (5) above, he shall inform an officer of the rank of inspector or above that he has made the search as soon as practicable after he has made it.

(7) An officer who—

    (a) authorises a search; or

    (b) is informed of a search under subsection (6) above,

shall make a record in writing—

        (i) of the grounds for the search; and

       (ii) of the nature of the evidence that was sought.

(8) If the person who was in occupation or control of the premises at the time of the search is in police detention at the time the record is to be made, the officer shall make the record as part of his custody record.

Seizure etc.

19   General power of seizure etc.

(1) The powers conferred by subsections (2), (3) and (4) below are exercisable by a constable who is lawfully on any premises.

(2) The constable may seize anything which is on the premises if he has reasonable grounds for believing—

    (a) that it has been obtained in consequence of the commission of an offence; and

    (b) that it is necessary to seize it in order to prevent it being concealed, lost, damaged, altered or destroyed.

(3) The constable may seize anything which is on the premises if he has reasonable grounds for believing—

    (a) that it is evidence in relation to an offence which he is investigating or any other offence; and

    (b) that it is necessary to seize it in order to prevent it being concealed, lost, altered or destroyed.

(4) The constable may require any information which is stored in any electronic form and is accessible from the premises to be produced in a form in which it can be taken away and in which it is visible and legible [or from which it can readily be produced in a visible and legible form] if he has reasonable grounds for believing—

    (a) that—

        (i) it is evidence in relation to an offence which he is investigating or any other offence; or

       (ii) it has been obtained in consequence of the commission of an offence; and

    (b) that it is necessary to do so in order to prevent it being concealed, lost, tampered with or destroyed.

(5) The powers conferred by this section are in addition to any power otherwise conferred.

(6) No power of seizure conferred on a constable under any enactment (including an enactment contained in an Act passed after this Act) is to be taken to authorise the seizure of an item which the constable exercising the power has reasonable grounds for believing to be subject to legal privilege.

20   Extension of powers of seizure to computerised information

(1) Every power of seizure which is conferred by an enactment to which this section applies on a constable who has entered premises in the exercise of a power conferred by an enactment shall be construed as including a power to require any information stored in any electronic form and accessible from the premises to be produced in a form in which it can be taken away and in which it is visible and legible [or from which it can readily be produced in a visible and legible form].

(2) This section applies—

(a) to any enactment contained in an Act passed before this Act;

(b) to sections 8 and 18 above;

(c) to paragraph 13 of Schedule 1 to this Act; and

(d) to any enactment contained in an Act passed after this Act.

21   Access and copying

(1) A constable who seizes anything in the exercise of a power conferred by any enactment, including an enactment contained in an Act passed after this Act, shall, if so requested by a person showing himself—

(a) to be the occupier of premises on which it was seized; or

(b) to have had custody or control of it immediately before the seizure,

provide that person with a record of what he seized.

(2) The officer shall provide the record within a reasonable time from the making of the request for it.

(3) Subject to subsection (8) below, if a request for permission to be granted access to anything which—

(a) has been seized by a constable; and

(b) is retained by the police for the purpose of investigating an offence,

is made to the officer in charge of the investigation by a person who had custody or control of the thing immediately before it was so seized or by someone acting on behalf of such a person, the officer shall allow the person who made the request access to it under the supervision of a constable.

(4) Subject to subsection (8) below, if a request for a photograph or copy of any such thing is made to the officer in charge of the investigation by a person who had custody or control of the thing immediately before it was so seized, or by someone acting on behalf of such a person, the officer shall—

(a) allow the person who made the request access to it under the supervision of a constable for the purpose of photographing or copying it; or

(b) photograph or copy it, or cause it to be photographed or copied.

(5) A constable may also photograph or copy, or have photographed or copied, anything which he has power to seize, without a request being made under subsection (4) above.

(6) Where anything is photographed or copied under subsection (4)(b) above, the photograph or copy shall be supplied to the person who made the request.

(7) The photograph or copy shall be so supplied within a reasonable time from the making of the request.

(8) There is no duty under this section to grant access to, or to supply a photograph or copy of, anything if the officer in charge of the investigation for the purposes of which it was seized has reasonable grounds for believing that to do so would prejudice—

(a) that investigation;

(b) the investigation of an offence other than the offence for the purposes of investigating which the thing was seized; or

(c) any criminal proceedings which may be brought as a result of—

(i) the investigation of which he is in charge; or

(ii) any such investigation as is mentioned in paragraph (b) above.

(9) The references to a constable in subsections (1), (2), (3)(a) and (5) include a person authorised under section 16(2) to accompany a constable executing a warrant.

22   Retention

(1) Subject to subsection (4) below, anything which has been seized by a constable or taken away by a constable following a requirement made by virtue of section 19 or 20 above may be retained so long as is necessary in all the circumstances.

(2) Without prejudice to the generality of subsection (1) above—

    (a) anything seized for the purposes of a criminal investigation may be retained, except as provided by subsection (4) below,—

        (i)   for use as evidence at a trial for an offence; or

        (ii) for forensic examination or for investigation in connection with an offence; and

    (b) anything may be retained in order to establish its lawful owner, where there are reasonable grounds for believing that it has been obtained in consequence of the commission of an offence.

(3) Nothing seized on the ground that it may be used—

    (a) to cause physical injury to any person;

    (b) to damage property;

    (c) to interfere with evidence; or

    (d) to assist in escape from police detention or lawful custody,

may be retained when the person from whom it was seized is no longer in police detention or the custody of a court or is in the custody of a court but has been released on bail.

(4) Nothing may be retained for either of the purposes mentioned in subsection (2)(a) above if a photograph or copy would be sufficient for that purpose.

(5) Nothing in this section affects any power of a court to make an order under section 1 of the Police (Property) Act 1897.

(6) This section also applies to anything retained by the police under section 28H(5) of the Immigration Act 1971.

(7) The reference in subsection (1) to anything seized by a constable includes anything seized by a person authorised under section 16(2) to accompany a constable executing a warrant.

Supplementary

23   Meaning of 'premises' etc.

In this Act—

    'premises' includes any place and, in particular, includes—

    (a) any vehicle, vessel, aircraft or hovercraft;

    (b) any offshore installation; and

    (c) any tent or movable structure; and

    'offshore installation' has the meaning given to it by section 1 of the Mineral Workings (Offshore Installations) Act 1971.

PART III   ARREST

24   Arrest without warrant for arrestable offences

(1) The powers of summary arrest conferred by the following subsections shall apply—

    (a) to offences for which the sentence is fixed by law;

    (b) to offences for which a person of 18 years of age or over (not previously convicted) may be sentenced to imprisonment for a term of five years (or might be so sentenced but for the restrictions imposed by section 33 of the Magistrates' Courts Act 1980); and

(c) to the offences listed in Schedule 1A, and in this Act 'arrestable offence' means any such offence.

(2) Schedule 1A (which lists the offences referred to in subsection (1)(c)) shall have effect.

(a) offences for which a person may be arrested under the customs and excise Acts, as defined in section 1(1) of the Customs and Excise Management Act 1979;

(b) offences under the Official Secrets Act 1920 that are not arrestable offences by virtue of the term of imprisonment for which a person may be sentenced in respect of them;

(bb) offences under any provision of the Official Secrets Act 1989 except section 8(1), (4) or (5);

(c) offences under section 22 (causing prostitution of women) or 23 (procuration of girl under 21) of the Sexual Offences Act 1956;

(ca) an offence under section 46 of the Criminal Justice and Police Act 2001;

(d) offences under section 12(1) (taking motor vehicle or other conveyance without authority etc.) or 25(1) (going equipped for stealing, etc.) of the Theft Act 1968;

(e) any offence under the Football (Offences) Act 1991.

(f) an offence under section 2 of the Obscene Publications Act 1959 (publication of obscene matter);

(g) an offence under section 1 of the Protection of Children Act 1978 (indecent photographs and pseudo-photographs of children);

(ga) an offence under section 1 of the Sexual Offences Act 1985 (kerb-crawling);

(gb) an offence under subsection (4) of section 170 of the Road Traffic Act 1988 (failure to stop and report an accident) in respect of an accident to which that section applies by virtue of subsection (1)(a) of that section (accidents causing personal injury);

(h) an offence under section 166 of the Criminal Justice and Public Order Act 1994 (sale of tickets by unauthorised persons);

(i) an offence under section 19 of the Public Order Act 1986 (publishing etc. material intended or likely to stir up racial hatred);

(j) an offence under section 167 of the Criminal Justice and Public Order Act 1994 (touting for car hire services);

[(k) an offence under section 1(1) of the Prevention of Crime Act 1953 (prohibition of the carrying of offensive weapons without lawful authority or reasonable excuse);

(l) an offence under section 139(1) of the Criminal Justice Act 1988 (offence of having article with blade or point in public place);

(m) an offence under section 139A(1) or (2) of the Criminal Justice Act 1988 (offence of having article with blade or point (or offensive weapon) on school premises).]

(n) an offence under section 2 of the Protection from Harassment Act (harassment).

(o) an offence under section 60(AA)(7) of the Criminal Justice and Public Order Act 1994 (failing to comply with requirements to remove mask etc.);

(p) an offence falling within section 32(1)(a) of the Crime and Disorder Act 1998 (racially aggravated harassment);

(q) an offence under section 14J or 21C of the Football Spectators Act 1989 (failure to comply with requirements imposed by or under a banning order or a notice under section 21B).

(qa) an offence under section 12(4) of the Criminal Justice and Police Act 2001;

(r)   (repealed)

(s)   an offence under section 1(1) or (2) or 6 of the Wildlife and Countryside Act 1981 (taking, possessing, selling etc. of wild birds) in respect of a bird included in Schedule 1 to that Act or any part of, or anything derived from, such a bird;

(t)   an offence under any of the following provisions of the Wildlife and Countryside Act 1981—

    (i)   section 1(5) (disturbance of wild birds);

    (ii)   section 9 or 13(1)(a) or (2) (taking, possessing, selling etc. of wild animals or plants);

    (iii) section 14 (introduction of new species etc.);

(u)   an offence under section 21C(1) or 21D(1) of the Aviation Security Act 1982 (c. 36) (unauthorised presence in restricted zone or on aircraft);

(v)   an offence under section 39(1) of the Civil Aviation Act 1982 (c. 16) (trespass on an aerodrome).

(3) Without prejudice to section 2 of the Criminal Attempts Act 1981, the powers of summary arrest conferred by the following subsections shall also apply to the offences of—

(a)   conspiring to commit any of the offences listed in Schedule 1A;

(b)   attempting to commit any such offence [other than one which is a summary offence];

(c)   inciting, aiding, abetting, counselling or procuring any such offence; and such offences are also arrestable offences for the purposes of this Act.

(4) Any person may arrest without a warrant—

(a)   anyone who is in the act of committing an arrestable offence;

(b)   anyone whom he has reasonable grounds for suspecting to be committing such an offence.

(5) Where an arrestable offence has been committed, any person may arrest without a warrant—

(a)   anyone who is guilty of the offence;

(b)   anyone whom he has reasonable grounds for suspecting to be guilty of it.

(6) Where a constable has reasonable grounds for suspecting that an arrestable offence has been committed, he may arrest without a warrant anyone whom he has reasonable grounds for suspecting to be guilty of the offence.

(7) A constable may arrest without a warrant—

(a)   anyone who is about to commit an arrestable offence;

(b)   anyone whom he has reasonable grounds for suspecting to be about to commit an arrestable offence.

25   General arrest conditions

(1) Where a constable has reasonable grounds for suspecting that any offence which is not an arrestable offence has been committed or attempted, or is being committed or attempted, he may arrest the relevant person if it appears to him that service of a summons is impracticable or inappropriate because any of the general arrest conditions is satisfied.

(2) In this section 'the relevant person' means any person whom the constable has reasonable grounds to suspect of having committed or having attempted to commit the offence or of being in the course of committing or attempting to commit it.

(3) The general arrest conditions are—

(a)   that the name of the relevant person is unknown to, and cannot be readily ascertained by, the constable;

(b)   that the constable has reasonable grounds for doubting whether a name furnished by the relevant person as his name is his real name;

(c)   that—

(i)   the relevant person has failed to furnish a satisfactory address for service; or

(ii) the constable has reasonable grounds for doubting whether an address furnished by the relevant person is a satisfactory address for service;

(d) that the constable has reasonable grounds for believing that arrest is necessary to prevent the relevant person—

(i)   causing physical injury to himself or any other person;

(ii)   suffering physical injury;

(iii) causing loss of or damage to property;

(iv)   committing an offence against public decency; or

(v)   causing an unlawful obstruction of the highway;

(e) that the constable has reasonable grounds for believing that arrest is necessary to protect a child or other vulnerable person from the relevant person.

(4) For the purposes of subsection (3) above an address is a satisfactory address for service if it appears to the constable—

(a) that the relevant person will be at it for a sufficiently long period for it to be possible to serve him with a summons; or

(b) that some other person specified by the relevant person will accept service of a summons for the relevant person at it.

(5) Nothing in subsection (3)(d) above authorises the arrest of a person under sub-paragraph (iv) of that paragraph except where members of the public going about their normal business cannot reasonably be expected to avoid the person to be arrested.

(6) This section shall not prejudice any power of arrest conferred apart from this section.

26   Repeal of statutory powers of arrest without warrant or order

(1) Subject to subsection (2) below, so much of any Act (including a local Act) passed before this Act as enables a constable—

(a) to arrest a person for an offence without a warrant; or

(b) to arrest a person otherwise than for an offence without a warrant or an order of a court,

shall cease to have effect.

(2) Nothing in subsection (1) above affects the enactments specified in Schedule 2 to this Act.

27   Fingerprinting of certain offenders

(1) If a person—

(a) has been convicted of a recordable offence;

(b) has not at any time been in police detention for the offence; and

(c) has not had his fingerprints taken—

(i)   in the course of the investigation of the offence by the police; or

(ii) since the conviction,

any constable may at any time not later than one month after the date of the conviction require him to attend a police station in order that his fingerprints may be taken.

(1A) Where a person convicted of a recordable offence has already had his fingerprints taken as mentioned in paragraph (c) of subsection (1) above, that fact (together with any time when he has been in police detention for the offence) shall be disregarded for the purposes of that subsection if—

(a) the fingerprints taken on the previous occasion do not constitute a complete set of his fingerprints; or

(b) some or all of the fingerprints taken on the previous occasion are not of sufficient quality to allow satisfactory analysis, comparison or matching.

(1B) Subsections (1) and (1A) above apply—

(a) where a person has been given a caution in respect of a recordable offence which, at the time of the caution, he has admitted, or

(b) where a person has been warned or reprimanded under section 65 of the Crime and Disorder Act 1998 (c. 37) for a recordable offence,

as they apply where a person has been convicted of an offence, and references in this section to a conviction shall be construed accordingly.

(2) A requirement under subsection (1) above—

(a) shall give the person a period of at least 7 days within which he must so attend; and

(b) may direct him to so attend at a specified time of day or between specified times of a day.

(3) Any constable may arrest without warrant a person who has failed to comply with a requirement under subsection (1) above.

(4) The Secretary of State may by regulations make provision for recording in national police records convictions for such offences as are specified in the regulations.

(5) Regulations under this section shall be made by statutory instrument and shall be subject to annulment in pursuance of a resolution of either House of Parliament.

28   Information to be given on arrest

(1) Subject to subsection (5) below, where a person is arrested, otherwise than by being informed that he is under arrest, the arrest is not lawful unless the person arrested is informed that he is under arrest as soon as is practicable after his arrest.

(2) Where a person is arrested by a constable, subsection (1) above applies regardless of whether the fact of the arrest is obvious.

(3) Subject to subsection (5) below, no arrest is lawful unless the person arrested is informed of the ground for the arrest at the time of, or as soon as is practicable after, the arrest.

(4) Where a person is arrested by a constable, subsection (3) above applies regardless of whether the ground for the arrest is obvious.

(5) Nothing in this section is to be taken to require a person to be informed—

(a) that he is under arrest; or

(b) of the ground for the arrest,

if it was not reasonably practicable for him to be so informed by reason of his having escaped from arrest before the information could be given.

29   Voluntary attendance at police station etc.

Where for the purpose of assisting with an investigation a person attends voluntarily at a police station or at any other place where a constable is present or accompanies a constable to a police station or any such other place without having been arrested—

(a) he shall be entitled to leave at will unless he is placed under arrest;

(b) he shall be informed at once that he is under arrest if a decision is taken by a constable to prevent him from leaving at will.

30   Arrest elsewhere than at police station

(1) Subsection (1A) applies where a person is, at any place other than a police station—

(a) arrested by a constable for an offence, or

(b) taken into custody by a constable after being arrested for an offence by a person other than a constable.

(1A) The person must be taken by a constable to a police station as soon as practicable after the arrest.

(1B) Subsection (1A) has effect subject to section 30A (release on bail) and subsection (7) (release without bail).

(2) Subject to subsections (3) and (5) below, the police station to which an arrested person is taken under subsection (1A) above shall be a designated police station.

(3) A constable to whom this subsection applies may take an arrested person to any police station unless it appears to the constable that it may be necessary to keep the arrested person in police detention for more than six hours.

(4) Subsection (3) above applies—

    (a) to a constable who is working in a locality covered by a police station which is not a designated police station; and

    (b) to a constable belonging to a body of constables maintained by an authority other than a police authority.

(5) Any constable may take an arrested person to any police station if—

    (a) either of the following conditions is satisfied—

        (i) the constable has arrested him without the assistance of any other constable and no other constable is available to assist him;

        (ii) the constable has taken him into custody from a person other than a constable without the assistance of any other constable and no other constable is available to assist him; and

    (b) it appears to the constable that he will be unable to take the arrested person to a designated police station without the arrested person injuring himself, the constable or some other person.

(6) If the first police station to which an arrested person is taken after his arrest is not a designated police station, he shall be taken to a designated police station not more than six hours after his arrival at the first police station unless he is released previously.

(7) A person arrested by a constable at any place other than a police station must be released without bail if the condition in subsection (7A) is satisfied.

(7A) The condition is that, at any time before the person arrested reaches a police station, a constable is satisfied that there are no grounds for keeping him under arrest or releasing him on bail under section 30A.

(8) A constable who releases a person under subsection (7) above shall record the fact that he has done so.

(9) The constable shall make the record as soon as is practicable after the release.

(10) Nothing in subsection (1A) or in section 30A prevents a constable delaying taking a person to a police station or releasing him on bail if the condition in subsection (10A) is satisfied.

(10A) The condition is that the presence of the person at a place (other than a police station) is necessary in order to carry out such investigations as it is reasonable to carry out immediately.

(11) Where there is any such delay the reasons for the delay must be recorded when the person first arrives at the police station or (as the case may be) is released on bail.

(12) Nothing in subsection (1A) or section 30A above shall be taken to affect—

    (a) paragraphs 16(3) or 18(1) of Schedule 2 to the Immigration Act 1971;

    (b) section 34(1) of the Criminal Justice Act 1972; or

    (c) any provision of the Terrorism Act 2000.

(13) Nothing in subsection (10) above shall be taken to affect paragraph 18(3) of Schedule 2 to the Immigration Act 1971.

30A   Bail elsewhere than at police station

(1) A constable may release on bail a person who is arrested or taken into custody in the circumstances mentioned in section 30(1).

(2) A person may be released on bail under subsection (1) at any time before he arrives at a police station.

(3) A person released on bail under subsection (1) must be required to attend a police station.

(4) No other requirement may be imposed on the person as a condition of bail.

(5) The police station which the person is required to attend may be any police station.

30B   Bail under section 30A: notices

(1) Where a constable grants bail to a person under section 30A, he must give that person a notice in writing before he is released.

(2) The notice must state—

    (a) the offence for which he was arrested, and

    (b) the ground on which he was arrested.

(3) The notice must inform him that he is required to attend a police station.

(4) It may also specify the police station which he is required to attend and the time when he is required to attend.

(5) If the notice does not include the information mentioned in subsection (4), the person must subsequently be given a further notice in writing which contains that information.

(6) The person may be required to attend a different police station from that specified in the notice under subsection (1) or (5) or to attend at a different time.

(7) He must be given notice in writing of any such change as is mentioned in subsection (6) but more than one such notice may be given to him.

30C   Bail under section 30A: supplemental

(1) A person who has been required to attend a police station is not required to do so if he is given notice in writing that his attendance is no longer required.

(2) If a person is required to attend a police station which is not a designated police station he must be—

    (a) released, or

    (b) taken to a designated police station,

not more than six hours after his arrival.

(3) Nothing in the Bail Act 1976 applies in relation to bail under section 30A.

(4) Nothing in section 30A or 30B or in this section prevents the re-arrest without a warrant of a person released on bail under section 30A if new evidence justifying a further arrest has come to light since his release.

30D   Failure to answer to bail under section 30A

(1) A constable may arrest without a warrant a person who—

    (a) has been released on bail under section 30A subject to a requirement to attend a specified police station, but

    (b) fails to attend the police station at the specified time.

(2) A person arrested under subsection (1) must be taken to a police station (which may be the specified police station or any other police station) as soon as practicable after the arrest.

(3) In subsection (1), "specified" means specified in a notice under subsection (1) or (5) of section 30B or, if notice of change has been given under subsection (7) of that section, in that notice.

(4) For the purposes of—

    (a) section 30 (subject to the obligation in subsection (2)), and

    (b) section 31,

an arrest under this section is to be treated as an arrest for an offence.

31   Arrest for further offence

Where—

    (a) a person—

    (i) has been arrested for an offence; and

    (ii) is at a police station in consequence of that arrest; and

(b) it appears to a constable that, if he were released from that arrest, he would be liable to arrest for some other offence,

he shall be arrested for that other offence.

32 Search upon arrest

(1) A constable may search an arrested person, in any case where the person to be searched has been arrested at a place other than a police station, if the constable has reasonable grounds for believing that the arrested person may present a danger to himself or others.

(2) Subject to subsections (3) to (5) below, a constable shall also have power in any such case—

(a) to search the arrested person for anything—

    (i) which he might use to assist him to escape from lawful custody; or

    (ii) which might be evidence relating to an offence; and

(b) to enter and search any premises in which he was when arrested or immediately before he was arrested for evidence relating to the offence for which he has been arrested.

(3) The power to search conferred by subsection (2) above is only a power to search to the extent that is reasonably required for the purpose of discovering any such thing or any such evidence.

(4) The powers conferred by this section to search a person are not to be construed as authorising a constable to require a person to remove any of his clothing in public other than an outer coat, jacket or gloves but they do authorise a search of a person's mouth.

(5) A constable may not search a person in the exercise of the power conferred by subsection (2)(a) above unless he has reasonable grounds for believing that the person to be searched may have concealed on him anything for which a search is permitted under that paragraph.

(6) A constable may not search premises in the exercise of the power conferred by subsection (2) (b) above unless he has reasonable grounds for believing that there is evidence for which a search is permitted under that paragraph on the premises.

(7) In so far as the power of search conferred by subsection (2)(b) above relates to premises consisting of two or more separate dwellings, it is limited to a power to search—

(a) any dwelling in which the arrest took place or in which the person arrested was immediately before his arrest; and

(b) any parts of the premises which the occupier of any such dwelling uses in common with the occupiers of any other dwellings comprised in the premises.

(8) A constable searching a person in the exercise of the power conferred by subsection (1) above may seize and retain anything he finds, if he has reasonable grounds for believing that the person searched might use it to cause physical injury to himself or to any other person.

(9) A constable searching a person in the exercise of the power conferred by subsection (2)(a) above may seize and retain anything he finds, other than an item subject to legal privilege, if he has reasonable grounds for believing—

(a) that he might use it to assist him to escape from lawful custody; or

(b) that it is evidence of an offence or has been obtained in consequence of the commission of an offence.

(10) Nothing in this section shall be taken to affect the power conferred by section 43 of the Terrorism Act 2000.

. . .

PART IV   DETENTION

Detention—conditions and duration

34   Limitations on police detention

(1) A person arrested for an offence shall not be kept in police detention except in accordance with the provisions of this Part of this Act.

(2) Subject to subsection (3) below, if at any time a custody officer—

    (a) becomes aware, in relation to any person in police detention, that the grounds for the detention of that person have ceased to apply and

    (b) is not aware of any other grounds on which the continued detention of that person could be justified under the provisions of this Part of this Act,

it shall be the duty of the custody officer, subject to subsection (4) below, to order his immediate release from custody.

(3) No person in police detention shall be released except on the authority of a custody officer at the police station where his detention was authorised, or if it was authorised at more than one station, a custody officer at the station where it was last authorised.

(4) A person who appears to the custody officer to have been unlawfully at large when he was arrested is not to be released under subsection (2) above.

(5) A person whose release is ordered under subsection (2) above shall be released without bail unless it appears to the custody officer—

    (a) that there is need for further investigation of any matter in connection with which he was detained at any time during the period of his detention; or

    (b) that proceedings may be taken against him in respect of any such matter, and if it so appears, he shall be released on bail.

(6) For the purposes of this Part of this Act a person arrested under section 6(5) of the Road Traffic Act 1988 or section 30(2) of the Transport and Works Act 1992 is arrested for an offence.

(7) For the purposes of this Part a person who—

    (a) attends a police station to answer to bail granted under section 30A,

    (b) returns to a police station to answer to bail granted under this Part, or

    (c) is arrested under section 30D or 46A,

is to be treated as arrested for an offence and that offence is the offence in connection with which he was granted bail.

35   Designated police stations

(1) The chief officer of police for each police area shall designate the police stations in his area which, subject to sections 30(3) and (5), 30A(5) and 30D(2) above, are to be the stations in that area to be used for the purpose of detaining arrested persons.

(2) A chief officer's duty under subsection (1) above is to designate police stations appearing to him to provide enough accommodation for that purpose.

(2A) The Chief Constable of the British Transport Police Force may designate police stations which (in addition to those designated under subsection (1) above) may be used for the purpose of detaining arrested persons.

(3) Without prejudice to section 12 of the Interpretation Act 1978 (continuity of duties) a chief officer—

    (a) may designate a station which was not previously designated; and

    (b) may direct that a designation of a station previously made shall cease to operate.

(4) In this Act 'designated police station' means a police station designated under this section.

36   Custody officers at police stations

(1) One or more custody officers shall be appointed for each designated police station.

(2) A custody officer for a police station designated under section 35(1) above shall be appointed—

    (a) by the chief officer of police for the area in which the designated police station is situated; or

    (b) by such other police officer as the chief officer of police for that area may direct.

(2A) A custody officer for a police station designated under section 35(2A) above shall be appointed—

    (a) by the Chief Constable of the British Transport Police Force; or

    (b) by such other member of that Force as that Chief Constable may direct.

(3) No officer may be appointed a custody officer unless he is of at least the rank of sergeant.

(4) An officer of any rank may perform the functions of a custody officer at a designated police station if a custody officer is not readily available to perform them.

(5) Subject to the following provisions of this section and to section 39(2) below, none of the functions of a custody officer in relation to a person shall be performed by an officer who at the time when the function fails to be performed is involved in the investigation of an offence for which that person is in police detention at that time.

(6) Nothing in subsection (5) above is to be taken to prevent a custody officer—

    (a) performing any function assigned to custody officers—

        (i) by this Act; or

        (ii) by a code of practice issued under this Act;

    (b) carrying out the duty imposed on custody officers by section 39 below;

    (c) doing anything in connection with the identification of a suspect; or

    (d) doing anything under sections 7 and 8 of the Road Traffic Act 1988.

(7) Where an arrested person is taken to a police station which is not a designated police station, the functions in relation to him which at a designated police station would be the functions of a custody officer shall be performed—

    (a) by an officer who is not involved in the investigation of an offence for which he is in police detention, if such an officer is readily available; and

    (b) if no such officer is readily available, by the officer who took him to the station or any other officer.

(7A) Subject to subsection (7B), subsection (7) applies where a person attends a police station which is not a designated station to answer to bail granted under section 30A as it applies where a person is taken to such a station.

(7B) Where subsection (7) applies because of subsection (7A), the reference in subsection (7)(b) to the officer who took him to the station is to be read as a reference to the officer who granted him bail.

(8) References to a custody officer in the following provisions of this Act include references to an officer other than a custody officer who is performing the functions of a custody officer by virtue of subsection (4) or (7) above.

(9) Where by virtue of subsection (7) above an officer of a force maintained by a police authority who took an arrested person to a police station is to perform the functions of a custody officer in relation to him, the officer shall inform an officer who—

    (a) is attached to a designated police station; and

    (b) is of at least the rank of inspector,

that he is to do so.

(10) The duty imposed by subsection (9) above shall be performed as soon as it is practicable to perform it.

37 Duties of custody officer before charge

(1) Where—

    (a) a person is arrested for an offence—

      (i) without a warrant; or

      (ii) under a warrant not endorsed for bail,

the custody officer at each police station where he is detained after his arrest shall determine whether he has before him sufficient evidence to charge that person with the offence for which he was arrested and may detain him at the police station for such period as is necessary to enable him to do so.

    (2) If the custody officer determines that he does not have such evidence before him, the person arrested shall be released either on bail or without bail, unless the custody officer has reasonable grounds for believing that his detention without being charged is necessary to secure or preserve evidence relating to an offence for which he is under arrest or to obtain such evidence by questioning him.

    (3) If the custody officer has reasonable grounds for so believing, he may authorise the person arrested to be kept in police detention.

    (4) Where a custody officer authorises a person who has not been charged to be kept in police detention, he shall, as soon as is practicable, make a written record of the grounds for the detention.

    (5) Subject to subsection (6) below, the written record shall be made in the presence of the person arrested who shall at that time be informed by the custody officer of the grounds for his detention.

    (6) Subsection (5) above shall not apply where the person arrested is, at the time when the written record is made—

      (a) incapable of understanding what is said to him;

      (b) violent or likely to become violent; or

      (c) in urgent need of medical attention.

    (7) Subject to section 41(7) below, if the custody officer determines that he has before him sufficient evidence to charge the person arrested with the offence for which he was arrested, the person arrested—

      (a) shall be released without charge and on bail for the purpose of enabling the Director of Public Prosecutions to make a decision under section 37B below,

      (b) shall be released without charge and on bail but not for that purpose,

      (c) shall be released without charge and without bail, or

      (d) shall be charged.

    (7A) The decision as to how a person is to be dealt with under subsection (7) above shall be that of the custody officer.

    (7B) Where a person is released under subsection (7)(a) above, it shall be the duty of the custody officer to inform him that he is being released to enable the Director of Public Prosecutions to make a decision under section 37B below.

    (8) Where—

      (a) a person is released under subsection (7)(b) above; and

      (b) at the time of his release a decision whether he should be prosecuted for the offence for which he was arrested has not been taken,

it shall be the duty of the custody officer so to inform him.

    (9) If the person arrested is not in a fit state to be dealt with under subsection (7) above, he may be kept in police detention until he is.

    (10) The duty imposed on the custody officer under subsection (1) above shall be carried out by him as soon as practicable after the person arrested arrives at the police station or, in the case of a person arrested at the police station, as soon as practicable after the arrest.

    (15) In this Part of this Act—

'arrested juvenile' means a person arrested with or without a warrant who appears to be under the age of 17;

'endorsed for bail' means endorsed with a direction for bail in accordance with section 117(2) of the Magistrates' Courts Act 1980.

37A   Guidance

(1) The Director of Public Prosecutions may issue guidance—

 (a) for the purpose of enabling custody officers to decide how persons should be dealt with under section 37(7) above or 37C(2) below, and

 (b) as to the information to be sent to the Director of Public Prosecutions under section 37B(1) below.

(2) The Director of Public Prosecutions may from time to time revise guidance issued under this section.

(3) Custody officers are to have regard to guidance under this section in deciding how persons should be dealt with under section 37(7) above or 37C(2) below.

(4) A report under section 9 of the Prosecution of Offences Act 1985 (report by DPP to Attorney General) must set out the provisions of any guidance issued, and any revisions to guidance made, in the year to which the report relates.

(5) The Director of Public Prosecutions must publish in such manner as he thinks fit—

 (a) any guidance issued under this section, and

 (b) any revisions made to such guidance.

(6) Guidance under this section may make different provision for different cases, circumstances or areas.

37B   Consultation with the Director of Public Prosecutions

(1) Where a person is released on bail under section 37(7)(a) above, an officer involved in the investigation of the offence shall, as soon as is practicable, send to the Director of Public Prosecutions such information as may be specified in guidance under section 37A above.

(2) The Director of Public Prosecutions shall decide whether there is sufficient evidence to charge the person with an offence.

(3) If he decides that there is sufficient evidence to charge the person with an offence, he shall decide—

 (a) whether or not the person should be charged and, if so, the offence with which he should be charged, and

 (b) whether or not the person should be given a caution and, if so, the offence in respect of which he should be given a caution.

(4) The Director of Public Prosecutions shall give written notice of his decision to an officer involved in the investigation of the offence.

(5) If his decision is—

 (a) that there is not sufficient evidence to charge the person with an offence, or

 (b) that there is sufficient evidence to charge the person with an offence but that the person should not be charged with an offence or given a caution in respect of an offence,

a custody officer shall give the person notice in writing that he is not to be prosecuted.

(6) If the decision of the Director of Public Prosecutions is that the person should be charged with an offence, or given a caution in respect of an offence, the person shall be charged or cautioned accordingly.

(7) But if his decision is that the person should be given a caution in respect of the offence and it proves not to be possible to give the person such a caution, he shall instead be charged with the offence.

(8) For the purposes of this section, a person is to be charged with an offence either—

 (a) when he is in police detention after returning to a police station to answer bail or is otherwise in police detention at a police station, or

 (b) in accordance with section 29 of the Criminal Justice Act 2003.

(9) In this section 'caution' includes—

(a) a conditional caution within the meaning of Part 3 of the Criminal Justice Act 2003, and

(b) a warning or reprimand under section 65 of the Crime and Disorder Act 1998.

37C   Breach of bail following release under section 37(7)(a)

(1) This section applies where—

    (a) a person released on bail under section 37(7)(a) above or subsection (2)(b) below is arrested under section 46A below in respect of that bail, and

    (b) at the time of his detention following that arrest at the police station mentioned in section 46A(2) below, notice under section 37B(4) above has not been given.

(2) The person arrested—

    (a) shall be charged, or

    (b) shall be released without charge, either on bail or without bail.

(3) The decision as to how a person is to be dealt with under subsection (2) above shall be that of a custody officer.

(4) A person released on bail under subsection (2)(b) above shall be released on bail subject to the same conditions (if any) which applied immediately before his arrest.

37D   Release under section 37(7)(a): further provision

(1) Where a person is released on bail under section 37(7)(a) or section 37C(2)(b) above, a custody officer may subsequently appoint a different time, or an additional time, at which the person is to attend at the police station to answer bail.

(2) The custody officer shall give the person notice in writing of the exercise of the power under subsection (1).

(3) The exercise of the power under subsection (1) shall not affect the conditions (if any) to which bail is subject.

(4) Where a person released on bail under section 37(7)(a) or 37C(2)(b) above returns to a police station to answer bail or is otherwise in police detention at a police station, he may be kept in police detention to enable him to be dealt with in accordance with section 37B or 37C above or to enable the power under subsection (1) above to be exercised.

(5) If the person is not in a fit state to enable him to be so dealt with or to enable that power to be exercised, he may be kept in police detention until he is.

(6) Where a person is kept in police detention by virtue of subsection (4) or (5) above, section 37(1) to (3) and (7) above (and section 40(8) below so far as it relates to section 37(1) to (3)) shall not apply to the offence in connection with which he was released on bail under section 37(7)(a) or 37C(2)(b) above.

38   Duties of custody officer after charge

(1) Where a person arrested for an offence otherwise than under a warrant endorsed for bail is charged with an offence, the custody officer shall, subject to section 25 of the Criminal Justice and Public Order Act 1994, order his release from police detention, either on bail or without bail, unless—

    (a) if the person arrested is not an arrested juvenile—

        (i) his name or address cannot be ascertained or the custody officer has reasonable grounds for doubting whether a name or address furnished by him as his name or address is his real name or address;

        (ii) the custody officer has reasonable grounds for believing that the person arrested will fail to appear in court to answer to bail;

        (iii) in the case of a person arrested for an imprisonable offence, the custody officer has reasonable grounds for believing that the detention of the person arrested is necessary to prevent him from committing an offence;

        (iiia) except in a case where (by virtue of subsection (9) of section 63B below) that section does not apply, the custody officer has reasonable grounds for believing that the detention of the person is necessary to enable a sample to be taken from him under that section;

(iv) in the case of a person arrested for an offence which is not an imprisonable offence, the custody officer has reasonable grounds for believing that the detention of the person arrested is necessary to prevent him from causing physical injury to any other person or from causing loss of or damage to property;

(v) the custody officer has reasonable grounds for believing that the detention of the person arrested is necessary to prevent him from interfering with the administration of justice or with the investigation of offences or of a particular offence; or

(vi) the custody officer has reasonable grounds for believing that the detention of the person arrested is necessary for his own protection;

(b) if he is an arrested juvenile—

(i) any of the requirements of paragraph (a) above is satisfied (but, in the case of paragraph (a)(iiia) above, only if the arrested juvenile has attained the minimum age); or

(ii) the custody officer has reasonable grounds for believing that he ought to be detained in his own interests.

(2) If the release of a person arrested is not required by subsection (1) above, the custody officer may authorise him to be kept in police detention but may not authorise a person to be kept in police detention by virtue of subsection (1)(a)(iiia) after the end of the period of six hours beginning with when he was charged with the offence.

(2A) The custody officer, in taking the decisions required by subsection (1)(a) and (b) above (except (a)(i) and (vi) and (b)(ii), shall have regard to the same considerations as those which a court is required to have regard to in taking the corresponding decisions under paragraph 2 of Part I of Schedule 1 to the Bail Act 1976.

(3) Where a custody officer authorises a person who has been charged to be kept in police detention, he shall, as soon as practicable, make a written record of the grounds for the detention.

(4) Subject to subsection (5) below, the written record shall be made in the presence of the person charged who shall at that time be informed by the custody officer of the grounds for his detention.

(5) Subsection (4) above shall not apply where the person charged is, at the time when the written record is made—

(a) incapable of understanding what is said to him;

(b) violent or likely to become violent; or

(c) in urgent need of medical attention.

(6) Where a custody officer authorises an arrested juvenile to be kept in police detention under subsection (1) above, the custody officer shall, unless he certifies—

(a) that, by reason of such circumstances as are specified in the certificate, it is impracticable for him to do so; or

(b) in the case of an arrested juvenile who has attained the age of 12 years, that no secure accommodation is available and that keeping him in other local authority accommodation would not be adequate to protect the public from serious harm from him,

secure that the arrested juvenile is moved to local authority accommodation.

(6A) In this section, 'local authority accommodation' means accommodation provided 'minimum age' means the age specified in section 63B(3) below;

'secure accommodation' means accommodation provided for the purpose of restricting liberty;

'sexual offence' and 'violent offence' have the same meanings as in the Powers of Criminal Courts (Sentencing) Act 2000; and any reference, in relation to an arrested juvenile charged with a violent or sexual offence, to protecting the public from serious harm from him shall be construed as a reference to protecting members of the public from death or serious injury, whether physical or psychological, occasioned by further such offences committed by him.

(6B) Where an arrested juvenile is moved to local authority accommodation under subsection (6) above, it shall be lawful for any person acting on behalf of the authority to detain him.

(7) A certificate made under subsection (6) above in respect of an arrested juvenile shall be produced to the court before which he is first brought thereafter.

(7A) In this section 'imprisonable offence' has the same meaning as in Schedule 1 to the Bail Act 1976.

(8) In this Part of this Act 'local authority' has the same meaning as in the Children Act 1989.

39 Responsibilities in relation to persons detained

(1) Subject to subsections (2) and (4) below, it shall be the duty of the custody officer at a police station to ensure—

    (a) that all persons in police detention at that station are treated in accordance with this Act and any code of practice issued under it and relating to the treatment of persons in police detention; and

    (b) that all matters relating to such persons which are required by this Act or by such codes of practice to be recorded are recorded in the custody records relating to such persons.

(2) If this custody officer, in accordance with any code of practice issued under this Act, transfers or permits the transfer of a person in police detention—

    (a) to the custody of a police officer investigating an offence for which that person is in police detention; or

    (b) to the custody of an officer who has charge of that person outside the police station,

the custody officer shall cease in relation to that person to be subject to the duty imposed on him by subsection (1)(a) above; and it shall be the duty of the officer to whom the transfer is made to ensure that he is treated in accordance with the provisions of this Act and of any such codes of practice as are mentioned in subsection (1) above.

(3) If the person detained is subsequently returned to the custody of the custody officer, it shall be the duty of the officer investigating the offence to report to the custody officer as to the manner in which this section and the codes of practice have been complied with while that person was in his custody.

(4) If an arrested juvenile is moved to local authority accommodation under section 38(6) above, the custody officer shall cease in relation to that person to be subject to the duty imposed on him by subsection (1) above.

(6) Where—

    (a) an officer of higher rank than the custody officer gives directions relating to a person in police detention; and

    (b) the directions are at variance—

        (i) with any decision made or action taken by the custody officer in the performance of a duty imposed on him under this Part of this Act; or

        (ii) with any decision or action which would but for the directions have been made or taken by him in the performance of such a duty,

the custody officer shall refer the matter at once to an officer of the rank of superintendent or above who is responsible for the police station for which the custody officer is acting as custody officer.

40   Review of police detention

(1) Reviews of the detention of each person in police detention in connection with the investigation of an offence shall be carried out periodically in accordance with the following provisions of this section—

(a) in the case of a person who has been arrested and charged, by the custody officer; and

(b) in the case of a person who has been arrested but not charged, by an officer of at least the rank of inspector who has not been directly involved in the investigation.

(2) The officer to whom it falls to carry out a review is referred to in this section as a 'review officer'.

(3) Subject to subsection (4) below—

(a) the first review shall be not later than six hours after the detention was first authorised;

(b) the second review shall be not later than nine hours after the first;

(c) subsequent reviews shall be at intervals of not more than nine hours.

(4) A review may be postponed—

(a) if, having regard to all the circumstances prevailing at the latest time for it specified in subsection (3) above, it is not practicable to carry out the review at that time;

(b) without prejudice to the generality of paragraph (a) above—

(i) if at that time the person in detention is being questioned by a police officer and the review officer is satisfied that an interruption of the questioning for the purpose of carrying out the review would prejudice the investigation in connection with which he is being questioned; or

(ii) if at that time no review officer is readily available.

(5) If a review is postponed under subsection (4) above it shall be carried out as soon as practicable after the latest time specified for it in subsection (3) above.

(6) If a review is carried out after postponement under subsection (4) above, the fact that it was so carried out shall not affect any requirement of this section as to the time at which any subsequent review is to be carried out.

(7) The review officer shall record the reasons for any postponement of a review in the custody record.

(8) Subject to subsection (9) and (10A) below, where the person whose detention is under review has not been charged before the time of the review, section 37(1) to (6) above shall have effect in relation to him, but with the modifications specified in subsection (8A).

'(8A) The modifications are—

(a) the substitution of references to the person whose detention is under review for references to the person arrested;

(b) the substitution of references to the review officer for references to the custody officer; and

(c) in subsection (6), the insertion of the following paragraph after paragraph (a)— "(aa) asleep;".'

(9) Where a person has been kept in police detention by virtue of section 37(9) and (10A) or 37D(5) above, section 37(1) to (6) shall not have effect in relation to him but it shall be the duty of the review officer to determine whether he is yet in a fit state.

(10) Where the person whose detention is under review has been charged before the time of the review, section 38(1) to (6B) above shall have effect in relation to him, but with the modifications specified in subsection (10A).

'(10A) The modifications are—

(a) the substitution of a reference to the person whose detention is under review for any reference to the person arrested or to the person charged; and

(b) in subsection (5), the insertion of the following paragraph after paragraph (a)— "(aa) asleep;".'

(11) Where—
  (a) an officer of higher rank than the review officer gives directions relating to a person in police detention; and
  (b) the directions are at variance—
     (i) with any decision made or action taken by the review officer in the performance of a duty imposed on him under this Part of this Act; or
     (ii) with any decision or action which would but for the directions have been made or taken by him in the performance of such a duty,
the review officer shall refer the matter at once to an officer of the rank of superintendent or above who is responsible for the police station for which the review officer is acting as review officer in connection with the detention.

(12) Before determining whether to authorise a person's continued detention the review officer shall give—
  (a) that person (unless he is asleep); or
  (b) any solicitor representing him who is available at the time of the review,
an opportunity to make representations to him about the detention.

(13) Subject to subsection (14) below, the person whose detention is under review or his solicitor may make representations under subsection (12) above either orally or in writing.

(14) The review officer may refuse to hear oral representations from the person whose detention is under review if he considers that he is unfit to make such representations by reason of his condition or behaviour.

40A   Use of telephone for review under s. 40

(1) A review under section 40(1)(b) may be carried out by means of a discussion, conducted by telephone, with one or more persons at the police station where the arrested person is held.

(2) But subsection (1) does not apply if—
  (a) the review is of a kind authorised by regulations under section 45A to be carried out using video-conferencing facilities; and
  (b) it is reasonably practicable to carry it out in accordance with those regulations.

(3) Where any review is carried out under this section by an officer who is not present at the station where the arrested person is held—
  (a) any obligation of that officer to make a record in connection with the carrying out of the review shall have effect as an obligation to cause another officer to make the record;
  (b) any requirement for the record to be made in the presence of the arrested person shall apply to the making of that record by that other officer; and
  (c) the requirements under section 40(12) and (13) above for—
     (i) the arrested person, or
     (ii) solicitor representing him,
to be given any opportunity to make representations (whether in writing or orally to that officer shall have effect as a requirement for that person, or such a solicitor, to be given an opportunity to make representations in a manner authorised by subsection (4) below.

(4) Representations are made in a manner authorised by this subsection—
  (a) in a case where facilities exist for the immediate transmission of written representations to the officer carrying out the review, if they are made either—
     (i) orally by telephone to that officer; or
     (ii) in writing to that officer by means of those facilities;
     and
  (b) in any other case, if they are made orally by telephone to that officer.

(5) In this section 'video-conferencing facilities' has the same meaning as in section 45A below.

41   Limits on period of detention without charge

(1) Subject to the following provisions of this section and to sections 42 and 43 below, a person shall not be kept in police detention for more than 24 hours without being charged.

(2) The time from which the period of detention of a person is to be calculated (in this Act referred to as 'the relevant time')—

(a)   in the case of a person to whom this paragraph applies, shall be—

(i)   the time at which that person arrives at the relevant police station; or

(ii)   the time 24 hours after the time of that person's arrest,

whichever is the earlier;

(b)   in the case of a person arrested outside England and Wales, shall be—

(i)   the time at which that person arrives at the first police station to which he is taken in the police area in England or Wales in which the offence for which he was arrested is being investigated; or

(ii)   the time 24 hours after the time of that person's entry into England and Wales,

whichever is the earlier;

(c)   in the case of a person who—

(i)   attends voluntarily at a police station; or

(ii)   accompanies a constable to a police station without having been arrested, and is arrested at the police station, the time of his arrest;

(ca)   in the case of a person who attends a police station to answer to bail granted under section 30A, the time when he arrives at the police station;'.

(d)   in any other case, except where subsection (5) below applies, shall be the time at which the person arrested arrives at the first police station to which he is taken after his arrest.

(3) Subsection (2)(a) above applies to a person if—

(a)   his arrest is sought in one police area in England and Wales;

(b)   he is arrested in another police area; and

(c)   he is not questioned in the area in which he is arrested in order to obtain evidence in relation to an offence for which he is arrested;

and in sub-paragraph (i) of that paragraph 'the relevant police station' means the first police station to which he is taken in the police area in which his arrest was sought.

(4) Subsection (2) above shall have effect in relation to a person arrested under section 31 above as if every reference in it to his arrest or his being arrested were a reference to his arrest or his being arrested for the offence for which he was originally arrested.

(5) If—

(a)   a person is in police detention in a police area in England and Wales ('the first area'); and

(b)   his arrest for an offence is sought in some other police area in England and Wales ('the second area'); and

(c)   he is taken to the second area for the purposes of investigating that offence, without being questioned in the first area in order to obtain evidence in relation to it, the relevant time shall be—

(i)   the time 24 hours after he leaves the place where he is detained in the first area; or

(ii)   the time at which he arrives at the first police station to which he is taken in the second area,

whichever is the earlier.

(6) When a person who is in police detention at a police station is removed to hospital because he is in need of medical treatment, any time during which he is being questioned in hospital or on the way there or back by a police officer for the purpose of obtaining evidence

relating to an offence shall be included in any period which falls to be calculated for the purposes of this Part of this Act, but any other time while he is in hospital or on his way there or back shall not be so included.

(7) Subject to subsection (8) below, a person who at the expiry of 24 hours after the relevant time is in police detention and has not been charged shall be released at that time either on bail or without bail.

(8) Subsection (7) above does not apply to a person whose detention for more than 24 hours after the relevant time has been authorised or is otherwise permitted in accordance with section 42 or 43 below.

(9) A person released under subsection (7) above shall not be re-arrested without a warrant for the offence for which he was previously arrested unless new evidence justifying a further arrest has come to light since his release; but this subsection does not prevent an arrest under section 46A below.

42   Authorisation of continued detention

(1) Where a police officer of the rank of superintendent or above who has not been directly involved in the investigation has reasonable grounds for believing that—

    (a) the detention of that person without charge is necessary to secure or preserve evidence relating to an offence for which he is under arrest or to obtain such evidence by questioning him;

    (b) an offence for which he is under arrest is an arrestable offence; and

    (c) the investigation is being conducted diligently and expeditiously,

he may authorise the keeping of that person in police detention for a period expiring at or before 36 hours after the relevant time.

(2) Where an officer such as is mentioned in subsection (1) above has authorised the keeping of a person in police detention for a period expiring less than 36 hours after the relevant time, such an officer may authorise the keeping of that person in police detention for a further period expiring not more than 36 hours after that time if the conditions specified in subsection (1) above are still satisfied when he gives the authorisation.

(3) If it is proposed to transfer a person in police detention to another police area, the officer determining whether or not to authorise keeping him in detention under subsection (1) above shall have regard to the distance and the time the journey would take.

(4) No authorisation under subsection (1) above shall be given in respect of any person—

    (a) more than 24 hours after the relevant time; or

    (b) before the second review of his detention under section 40 above has been carried out.

(5) Where an officer authorises the keeping of a person in police detention under subsection (1) above, it shall be his duty—

    (a) to inform that person of the grounds for his continued detention; and

    (b) to record the grounds in that person's custody record.

(6) Before determining whether to authorise the keeping of a person in detention under subsection (1) or (2) above, an officer shall give—

    (a) that person; or

    (b) any solicitor representing him who is available at the time when it falls to the officer to determine whether to give the authorisation,

an opportunity to make representations to him about the detention.

(7) Subject to subsection (8) below, the person in detention or his solicitor may make representations under subsection (6) above either orally or in writing.

(8) The officer to whom it falls to determine whether to give the authorisation may refuse to hear oral representations from the person in detention if he considers that he is unfit to make such representations by reason of his condition or behaviour.

(9) Where—

(a) an officer authorises the keeping of a person in detention under subsection (1) above; and

(b) at the time of the authorisation he has not yet exercised a right conferred on him by section 56 or 58 below,

the officer—

    (i)   shall inform him of that right;

    (ii) shall decide whether he should be permitted to exercise it;

    (iii) shall record the decision in his custody record; and

    (iv) if the decision is to refuse to permit the exercise of the right, shall also record the grounds for the decision in that record.

(10) Where an officer has authorised the keeping of a person who has not been charged in detention under subsection (1) or (2) above, he shall be released from detention, either on bail or without bail, not later than 36 hours after the relevant time, unless—

(a) he has been charged with an offence; or

(b) his continued detention is authorised or otherwise permitted in accordance with section 43 below.

(11) A person released under subsection (10) above shall not be re-arrested without a warrant for the offence for which he was previously arrested unless new evidence justifying a further arrest has come to light since his release; but this subsection does not prevent an arrest under section 46A below.

43 Warrants of further detention

(1) Where, on an application on oath made by a constable and supported by an information, a magistrates' court is satisfied that there are reasonable grounds for believing that the further detention of the person to whom the application relates is justified, it may issue a warrant of further detention authorising the keeping of that person in police detention.

(2) A court may not hear an application for a warrant of further detention unless the person to whom the application relates—

(a) has been furnished with a copy of the information; and

(b) has been brought before the court for the hearing.

(3) The person to whom the application relates shall be entitled to be legally represented at the hearing and, if he is not so represented but wishes to be so represented—

(a) the court shall adjourn the hearing to enable him to obtain representation; and

(b) he may be kept in police detention during the adjournment.

(4) A person's further detention is only justified for the purposes of this section or section 44 below if—

(a) his detention without charge is necessary to secure or preserve evidence relating to an offence for which he is under arrest or to obtain such evidence by questioning him;

(b) an offence for which he is under arrest is a serious arrestable offence; and

(c) the investigation is being conducted diligently and expeditiously.

(5) Subject to subsection (7) below, an application for a warrant of further detention may be made—

(a) at any time before the expiry of 36 hours after the relevant time; or

(b) in a case where—

    (i)   it is not practicable for the magistrates' court to which the application will be made to sit at the expiry of 36 hours after the relevant time; but

    (ii) the court will sit during the 6 hours following the end of that period, at any time before the expiry of the said 6 hours.

(6) In a case to which subsection (5)(b) above applies—

(a) the person to whom the application relates may be kept in police detention until the application is heard; and

    (b) the custody officer shall make a note in that person's custody record—
        (i) of the fact that he was kept in police detention for more than 36 hours after the relevant time; and
        (ii) of the reason why he was so kept.

(7) If—
    (a) an application for a warrant of further detention is made after the expiry of 36 hours after the relevant time; and
    (b) it appears to the magistrates' court that it would have been reasonable for the police to make it before the expiry of that period,

the court shall dismiss the application.

(8) Where on an application such as is mentioned in subsection (1) above a magistrates' court is not satisfied that there are reasonable grounds for believing that the further detention of the person to whom the application relates is justified, it shall be its duty—
    (a) to refuse the application; or
    (b) to adjourn the hearing of it until a time not later than 36 hours after the relevant time.

(9) The person to whom the application relates may be kept in police detention during the adjournment.

(10) A warrant of further detention shall—
    (a) state the time at which it is issued;
    (b) authorise the keeping in police detention of the person to whom it relates for the period stated in it.

(11) Subject to subsection (12) below, the period stated in a warrant of further detention shall be such period as the magistrates' court thinks fit, having regard to the evidence before it.

(12) The period shall not be longer than 36 hours.

(13) If it is proposed to transfer a person in police detention to a police area other than that in which he is detained when the application for a warrant of further detention is made, the court hearing the application shall have regard to the distance and the time the journey would take.

(14) Any information submitted in support of an application under this section shall state—
    (a) the nature of the offence for which the person to whom the application relates has been arrested;
    (b) the general nature of the evidence on which that person was arrested;
    (c) what inquiries relating to the offence have been made by the police and what further inquiries are proposed by them;
    (d) the reasons for believing the continued detention of that person to be necessary for the purposes of such further inquiries.

(15) Where an application under this section is refused, the person to whom the application relates shall forthwith be charged or, subject to subsection (16) below, released, either on bail or without bail.

(16) A person need not be released under subsection (15) above—
    (a) before the expiry of 24 hours after the relevant time; or
    (b) before the expiry of any longer period for which his continued detention is or has been authorised under section 42 above.

(17) Where an application under this section is refused, no further application shall be made under this section in respect of the person to whom the refusal relates, unless supported by evidence which has come to light since the refusal.

(18) Where a warrant of further detention is issued, the person to whom it relates shall be released from police detention, either on bail or without bail, upon or before the expiry of the warrant unless he is charged.

(19) A person released under subsection (18) above shall not be re-arrested without a warrant for the offence for which he was previously arrested unless new evidence justifying a further arrest has come to light since his release; but this subsection does not prevent an arrest under section 46A below.

44   Extension of warrants of further detention

(1) On an application made by a constable and supported by an information a magistrates' court may extend a warrant of further detention issued under section 43 above if it is satisfied that there are reasonable grounds for believing that the further detention of the person to whom the application relates is justified.

(2) Subject to subsection (3) below, the period for which a warrant of further detention may be extended shall be such period as the court thinks fit, having regard to the evidence before it.

(3) The period shall not—

    (a) be longer than 36 hours; or

    (b) end later than 96 hours after the relevant time.

(4) Where a warrant of further detention has been extended under subsection (1) above, or further extended under this subsection, for a period ending before 96 hours after the relevant time, on an application such as is mentioned in that subsection a magistrates' court may further extend the warrant if it is satisfied as there mentioned; and subsections (2) and (3) above apply to such further extensions as they apply to extensions under subsection (1) above.

(5) A warrant of further detention shall, if extended under this section, be endorsed with a note of the period of the extension.

(6) Subsections (2), (3), (14) and (15) of section 43 above shall apply to an application made under this section as they apply to an application made under that section.

(7) Where an application under this section is refused, the person to whom the application relates shall forthwith be charged or, subject to subsection (8) below, released, either on bail or without bail.

(8) A person need not be released under subsection (7) above before the expiry of any period for which a warrant of further detention issued in relation to him has been extended or further extended on an earlier application made under this section.

45   Detention before charge—supplementary

(1) In sections 43 and 44 of this Act 'magistrates' court' means a court consisting of two or more justices of the peace sitting otherwise than in open court.

(2) Any reference in this Part of this Act to a period of time or a time of day is to be treated as approximate only.

45A   Use of video-conferencing facilities for decisions about detention

(1) Subject to the following provisions of this section, the Secretary of State may by regulations provide that, in the case of an arrested person who is held in a police station, some or all of the functions mentioned in subsection (2) may be performed (notwithstanding anything in the preceding provisions of this Part) by an officer who—

    (a) is not present in that police station; but

    (b) has access to the use of video-conferencing facilities that enable him to communicate with persons in that station.

(2) Those functions are—

    (a) the functions in relation to an arrested person taken to or answering to bail at a police station that is not a designated police station which, in the case of an arrested person taken to a station that is a designated police station, are functions of a custody officer under section 37, 38 or 40 above; and

    (b) the function of carrying out a review under section 40(1)(b) above (review, by an officer of at least the rank of inspector, of the detention of person arrested but not charged).

(3) Regulations under this section shall specify the use to be made in the performance of the functions mentioned in subsection (2) above of the facilities mentioned in subsection (1) above.

(4) Regulations under this section shall not authorise the performance of any of the functions mentioned in subsection (2)(a) above by such an officer as is mentioned in subsection (1) above unless he is a custody officer for a designated police station.

(5) Where any functions mentioned in subsection (2) above are performed in a manner authorised by regulations under this section—

(a) any obligation of the officer performing those functions to make a record in connection with the performance of those functions shall have effect as an obligation to cause another officer to make the record; and

(b) any requirement for the record to be made in the presence of the arrested person shall apply to the making of that record by that other officer.

(6) Where the functions mentioned in subsection (2)(b) are performed in a manner authorised by regulations under this section, the requirements under section 40(12) and (13) above for—

(a) the arrested person, or

(b) a solicitor representing him,

to be given any opportunity to make representations (whether in writing or orally) to the person performing those functions shall have effect as a requirement for that person, or such a solicitor, to be given an opportunity to make representations in a manner authorised by subsection (7) below.

(7) Representations are made in a manner authorised by this subsection—

(a) in a case where facilities exist for the immediate transmission of written representations to the officer performing the functions, if they are made either—

(i) orally to that officer by means of the video-conferencing facilities used by him for performing those functions; or

(ii) in writing to that officer by means of the facilities available for the immediate transmission of the representations;

and

(b) in any other case if they are made orally to that officer by means of the video-conferencing facilities used by him for performing the functions.

(8) Regulations under this section may make different provision for different cases and may be made so as to have effect in relation only to the police stations specified or described in the regulations.

(9) Regulations under this section shall be made by statutory instrument and shall be subject to annulment in pursuance of a resolution of either House of Parliament.

(10) Any reference in this section to video-conferencing facilities, in relation to any functions, is a reference to any facilities (whether a live television link or other facilities) by means of which the functions may be performed with the officer performing them, the person in relation to whom they are performed and any legal representative of that person all able to both see and to hear each other.

Detention—miscellaneous

46   Detention after charge

(1) Where a person—

(a) is charged with an offence; and

(b) after being charged—

(i) is kept in police detention; or

(ii) is detained by a local authority in pursuance of arrangements made under section 38(6) above, he shall be brought before a magistrates' court in accordance with the provisions of this section.

(1A) A person who has been released on bail under section 37(7)(a) or 37C(2)(b) above may be arrested without warrant by a constable if the constable has reasonable grounds for suspecting that the person has broken any of the conditions of bail.

(2) If he is to be brought before a magistrates' court in the local justice area in which the police station at which he was charged is situated, he shall be brought before such a court as soon as is practicable and in any event not later than the first sitting after he is charged with the offence.

(3) If no magistrates' court in that area is due to sit either on the day on which he is charged or on the next day, the custody officer for the police station at which he was charged shall inform the designated officer for the area that there is a person in the area to whom subsection (2) above applies.

(4) If the person charged is to be brought before a magistrates' court in a local justice area other than that in which the police station at which he was charged is situated, he shall be removed to that area as soon as is practicable and brought before such a court as soon as is practicable after his arrival in the area and in any event not later than the first sitting of a magistrates' court in that area after his arrival in the area.

(5) If no magistrates' court in that area is due to sit either on the day on which he arrives in the area or on the next day—

(a) he shall be taken to a police station in the area; and
(b) the custody officer at that station shall inform the designated officer for the area that there is a person in the area to whom subsection (4) applies.

(6) Subject to subsection (8) below, where the designated officer for a local justice area has been informed—

(a) under subsection (3) above that there is a person in the area to whom subsection (2) above applies; or
(b) under subsection (5) above that there is a person in the area to whom subsection (4) above applies,

the designated officer shall arrange for a magistrates' court to sit not later than the day next following the relevant day.

(7) In this section 'the relevant day'—

(a) in relation to a person who is to be brought before a magistrates' court in the local justice area in which the police station at which he was charged is situated, means the day on which he was charged; and
(b) in relation to a person who is to be brought before a magistrates' court in any other local justice area, means the day on which he arrives in the area.

(8) Where the day next following the relevant day is Christmas Day, Good Friday or a Sunday, the duty of the designated officer under subsection (6) above is a duty to arrange for a magistrates' court to sit not later than the first day after the relevant day which is not one of those days.

(9) Nothing in this section requires a person who is in hospital to be brought before a court if he is not well enough.

46A   Power of arrest for failure to answer to police bail

(1) A constable may arrest without a warrant any person who, having been released on bail under this Part of this Act subject to a duty to attend at a police station, fails to attend at that police station at the time appointed for him to do so.

(2) A person who is arrested under this section shall be taken to the police station appointed as the place at which he is to surrender to custody as soon as practicable after the arrest.

(3) For the purposes of—

(a) section 30 above (subject to the obligation in subsection (2) above), and

(b) section 31 above,

an arrest under this section shall be treated as an arrest for an offence.

47   Bail after arrest

(1) Subject to the following provisions of this section, a release on bail of a person under this Part of this Act shall be a release on bail granted in accordance with sections 3, 3A, 5 and 5A of the Bail Act 1976 as they apply to bail granted by a constable.

(1A) The normal powers to impose conditions of bail shall be available to him where a custody officer releases a person on bail under section 37(7)(a) above or 38(1) above (including that subsection as applied by section 40(10) above) but not in any other cases.

In this subsection, 'the normal powers to impose conditions of bail' has the meaning given in section 3(b) of the Bail Act 1976.

(1B) No application may be made under section 5B of the Bail Act 1976 if a person is released on bail under section 37(7)(a) or 37C(2)(b) above.

(1C) Subsections (1D) to (1F) below apply where a person released on bail under section 37(7)(a) or 37C(2)(b) above is on bail subject to conditions.

(1D) The person shall not be entitled to make an application under section 43B of the Magistrates' Courts Act 1980.

(1E) A magistrates' court may, on an application by or on behalf of the person, vary the conditions of bail; and in this subsection "vary" has the same meaning as in the Bail Act 1976.

(1F) Where a magistrates' court varies the conditions of bail under subsection (1E) above, that bail shall not lapse but shall continue subject to the conditions as so varied.

(2) Nothing in the Bail Act 1976 shall prevent the re-arrest without warrant of a person released on bail subject to a duty to attend at a police station if new evidence justifying a further arrest has come to light since his release.

(3) Subject to subsections (3A) and (4) below, in this Part of this Act references to 'bail' are references to bail subject to a duty—

(a) to appear before a magistrates' court at such time and such place; or

(b) to attend at such police station at such time,

as the custody officer may appoint.

(3A) Where a custody officer grants bail to a person subject to a duty to appear before a magistrates' court, he shall appoint for the appearance—

(a) a date which is not later than the first sitting of the court after the person is charged with the offence; or

(b) where he is informed by the designated officer for the relevant local justice area that the appearance cannot be accommodated until a later date, that later date.

(4) Where a custody officer has granted bail to a person subject to a duty to appear at a police station, the custody officer may give notice in writing to that person that his attendance at the police station is not required.

(6) Where a person who has been granted bail under this Part and has either attended at the police station in accordance with the grant of bail or has been arrested under section 46A above is detained at a police station, any time during which he was in police detention prior to being granted bail shall be included as part of any period which falls to be calculated under this Part of this Act.

(7) Where a person who was released on bail under this Part subject to a duty to attend at a police station is re-arrested, the provisions of this Part of this Act shall apply to him as they apply to a person arrested for the first time but this subsection does not apply to a person who is arrested under section 46A above or has attended a police station in accordance with the grant of bail (and who accordingly is deemed by section 34(7) above to have been arrested for an offence).

(8) In the Magistrates' Courts Act 1980—

(a) the following section shall be substituted for section 43—

'**43**   Bail on arrest

(1) Where a person has been granted bail under the Police and Criminal Evidence Act 1984 subject to a duty to appear before a magistrates' court, the court before which he is to appear may appoint a later time as the time at which he is to appear and may enlarge the recognizances of any sureties for him at that time.

(2) The recognizance of any surety for any person granted bail subject to a duty to attend at a police station may be enforced as if it were conditioned for his appearance before a magistrates' court for the petty sessions area in which the police station named in the recognizance is situated.'; and

(b) the following subsection shall be substituted for section 117(3)—

'(3) Where a warrant has been endorsed for bail under subsection (1) above—

(a) where the person arrested is to be released on bail on his entering into a recognizance without sureties, it shall not be necessary to take him to a police station, but if he is so taken, he shall be released from custody on his entering into the recognizance; and

(b) where he is to be released on his entering into a recognizance with sureties, he shall be taken to a police station on his arrest, and the custody officer there shall (subject to his approving any surety tendered in compliance with the endorsement) release him from custody as directed in the endorsement.'.

47A   Early administrative hearings conducted by justices' clerk

Where a person has been charged with an offence at a police station, any requirement imposed under this Part for the person to appear or be brought before a magistrates' court shall be taken to be satisfied if the person appears or is brought before a justices' clerk in order for the clerk to conduct a hearing under section 50 of the Crime and Disorder Act 1998 (early administrative hearings).

48   Remands to police detention

In section 128 of the Magistrates' Courts Act 1980—

(a) in subsection (7) for the words 'the custody of a constable' there shall be substituted the words 'detention at a police station';

(b) after subsection (7) there shall be inserted the following subsection—

'(8) Where a person is committed to detention at a police station under subsection (7) above—

(a) he shall not be kept in such detention unless there is a need for him to be so detained for the purposes of inquiries into other offences;

(b) if kept in such detention, he shall be brought back from the magistrates' court which committed him as soon as that need ceases;

(c) he shall be treated as a person in police detention to whom the duties under section 39 of the Police and Criminal Evidence Act 1984 (responsibilities in relation to persons detained) relate;

(d) his detention shall be subject to periodic review at the times set out in section 40 of that Act (review of police detention).'.

49   Police detention to count towards custodial sentence

(1) In subsection (1) of section 67 of the Criminal Justice Act 1967 (computation of custodial sentences) for the words from 'period', in the first place where it occurs, to 'the offender' there shall be substituted the words 'relevant period, but where he'.

(2) The following subsection shall be inserted after that subsection—

'(1A) In subsection (1) above "relevant period" means—

(a) any period during which the offender was in police detention in connection with the offence for which the sentence was passed; or

(b) any period during which he was in custody—

(i) by reason only of having been committed to custody by an order of a court made in connection with any proceedings relating to that sentence or the offence for which it was passed or any proceedings from which those proceedings arose; or

(ii) by reason of his having been so committed and having been concurrently detained otherwise than by order of a court.'.

(3) The following subsections shall be added after subsection (6) of that section—

'(7) A person is in police detention for the purposes of this section—

(a) at any time when he is in police detention for the purposes of the Police and Criminal Evidence Act 1984; and

(b) at any time when he is detained under section 41 of the Terrorism Act 2000.

(8) No period of police detention shall be taken into account under this section unless it falls after the coming into force of section 49 of the Police and Criminal Evidence Act 1984.'.

50　Records of detention

(1) Each police force shall keep written records showing on an annual basis—

(a) the number of persons kept in police detention for more than 24 hours and subsequently released without charge;

(b) the number of applications for warrants of further detention and the results of the applications; and

(c) in relation to each warrant of further detention—

(i) the period of further detention authorised by it;

(ii) the period which the person named in it spent in police detention on its authority; and

(iii) whether he was charged or released without charge.

(2) Every annual report—

(a) under [section 22 of the Police Act 1996]; or

(b) made by the Commissioner of Police of the Metropolis,

shall contain information about the matters mentioned in subsection (1) above in respect of the period to which the report relates.

51　Savings

Nothing in this Part of this Act shall affect—

(a) the powers conferred on immigration officers by section 4 of and Schedule 2 to the Immigration Act 1971 (administrative provisions as to control on entry etc.);

(b) the powers conferred by or by virtue of section 41 of, or Schedule 7 to, the Terrorism Act 2000 (Powers of Arrest and Detention);

(c) any duty of a police officer under—

(i) section 129, 190 or 202 of the Army Act 1955 (duties of governors of prisons and others to receive prisoners, deserters, absentees and persons under escort);

(ii) section 129, 190 or 202 of the Air Force Act 1955 (duties of governors of prisons and others to receive prisoners, deserters, absentees and persons under escort);

(iii) section 107 of the Naval Discipline Act 1957 (duties of governors of civil prisons etc.); or

    (iv) paragraph 5 of Schedule 5 to the Reserve Forces Act 1980 (duties of governors of civil prisons); or
  (d) any right of a person in police detention to apply for a writ of habeas corpus or other prerogative remedy.

PART V   QUESTIONING AND TREATMENT OF PERSONS BY POLICE

53   Abolition of certain powers of constables to search persons

(1) Subject to subsection (2) below, there shall cease to have effect any Act (including a local Act) passed before this Act in so far as it authorises—
  (a) any search by a constable of a person in police detention at a police station; or
  (b) an intimate search of a person by a constable;
and any rule of common law which authorises a search such as is mentioned in paragraph (a) or (b) above is abolished.

54   Searches of detained persons

(1) The custody officer at a police station shall ascertain everything which a person has with him when he is—
  (a) brought to the station after being arrested elsewhere or after being committed to custody by an order or sentence of a court; or
  (b) arrested at the station or detained there, as a person falling within section 34(7), under section 37 above.

(2) The custody officer may record or cause to be recorded all or any of the things which he ascertains under subsection (1).

(2A) In the case of an arrested person, any such record may be made as part of his custody record.

(3) Subject to subsection (4) below, a custody officer may seize and retain any such thing or cause any such thing to be seized and retained.

(4) Clothes and personal effects may only be seized if the custody officer—
  (a) believes that the person from whom they are seized may use them—
    (i)   to cause physical injury to himself or any other person;
    (ii)   to damage property;
    (iii) to interfere with evidence; or
    (iv)   to assist him to escape; or
  (b) has reasonable grounds for believing that they may be evidence relating to an offence.

(5) Where anything is seized, the person from whom it is seized shall be told the reason for the seizure unless he is—
  (a) violent or likely to become violent; or
  (b) incapable of understanding what is said to him.

(6) Subject to subsection (7) below, a person may be searched if the custody officer considers it necessary to enable him to carry out his duty under subsection (1) above and to the extent that the custody officer considers necessary for that purpose.

(6A) A person who is in custody at a police station or is in police detention otherwise than at a police station may at any time be searched in order to ascertain whether he has with him anything which he could use for any of the purposes specified in subsection 4(a) above.

(6B) Subject to subsection (6C) below, a constable may seize and detain, or cause to be seized and detained, anything found in such a search.

(6C) A constable may only seize clothes and personal effects in the circumstances specified in subsection (4) above.

(7) An intimate search may not be conducted under this section.

(8) A search under this section shall be carried out by a constable.

(9) The constable carrying out a search shall be of the same sex as the person searched.

'54A   Searches and examination to ascertain identity

(1) If an officer of at least the rank of inspector authorises it, a person who is detained in a police station may be searched or examined, or both—

    (a) for the purpose of ascertaining whether he has any mark that would tend to identify him as a person involved in the commission of an offence; or

    (b) for the purpose of facilitating the ascertainment of his identity.

(2) An officer may only give an authorisation under subsection (1) for the purpose mentioned in paragraph (a) of that subsection if—

    (a) the appropriate consent to a search or examination that would reveal whether the mark in question exists has been withheld; or

    (b) it is not practicable to obtain such consent.

(3) An officer may only give an authorisation under subsection (1) in a case in which subsection (2) does not apply if—

    (a) the person in question has refused to identify himself; or

    (b) the officer has reasonable grounds for suspecting that that person is not who he claims to be.

(4) An officer may give an authorisation under subsection (1) orally or in writing but, if he gives it orally, he shall confirm it in writing as soon as is practicable.

(5) Any identifying mark found on a search or examination under this section may be photographed—

    (a) with the appropriate consent; or

    (b) if the appropriate consent is withheld or it is not practicable to obtain it, without it.

(6) Where a search or examination may be carried out under this section, or a photograph may be taken under this section, the only persons entitled to carry out the search or examination, or to take the photograph, are constables.

(7) A person may not under this section carry out a search or examination of a person of the opposite sex or take a photograph of any part of the body of a person of the opposite sex.

(8) An intimate search may not be carried out under this section.

(9) A photograph taken under this section—

    (a) may be used by, or disclosed to, any person for any purpose related to the prevention or detection of crime, the investigation of an offence or the conduct of a prosecution; and

    (b) after being so used or disclosed, may be retained but may not be used or disclosed except for a purpose so related.

(10) In subsection—

    (a) the reference to crime includes a reference to any conduct which—

        (i) constitutes one or more criminal offences (whether under the law of a part of the United Kingdom or of a country or territory outside the United Kingdom); or

        (ii) is, or corresponds to, any conduct which, if it all took place in any one part of the United Kingdom, would constitute one or more criminal offences; and

    (b) the references to an investigation and to a prosecution include references, respectively, to any investigation outside the United Kingdom of any crime or suspected crime and to a prosecution brought in respect of any crime in a country or territory outside the United Kingdom.

(11) In this section—
  (a) references to ascertaining a person's identity include references to showing that he is not a particular person; and
  (b) references to taking a photograph include references to using any process by means of which a visual image may be produced, and references to photographing a person shall be construed accordingly.

(12) In this section "mark" includes features and injuries; and a mark is an identifying mark for the purposes of this section if its existence in any person's case facilitates the ascertainment of his identity or his identification as a person involved in the commission of an offence.'

55 Intimate searches

(1) Subject to the following provisions of this section, if an officer of at least the rank of inspector has reasonable grounds for believing—
  (a) that a person who has been arrested and is in police detention may have concealed on him anything which—
    (i) he could use to cause physical injury to himself or others; and
    (ii) he might so use while he is in police detention or in the custody of a court;
    or
  (b) that such a person—
    (i) may have a Class A drug concealed on him; and
    (ii) was in possession of it with the appropriate criminal intent before his arrest,
he may authorise an intimate search of that person.

(2) An officer may not authorise an intimate search of a person for anything unless he has reasonable grounds for believing that it cannot be found without his being intimately searched.

(3) An officer may give an authorisation under subsection (1) above orally or in writing but, if he gives it orally, he shall confirm it in writing as soon as is practicable.

(4) An intimate search which is only a drug offence search shall be by way of examination by a suitably qualified person.

(5) Except as provided by subsection (4) above, an intimate search shall be by way of examination by a suitably qualified person unless an officer of at least the rank of inspector considers that this is not practicable.

(6) An intimate search which is not carried out as mentioned in subsection (5) above shall be carried out by a constable.

(7) A constable may not carry out an intimate search of a person of the opposite sex.

(8) No intimate search may be carried out except—
  (a) at a police station;
  (b) at a hospital;
  (c) at a registered medical practitioner's surgery; or
  (d) at some other place used for medical purposes.

(9) An intimate search which is only a drug offence search may not be carried out at a police station.

(10) If an intimate search of a person is carried out, the custody record relating to him shall state—
  (a) which parts of his body were searched; and
  (b) why they were searched.

(11) The information required to be recorded by subsection (10) above shall be recorded as soon as practicable after the completion of the search.

(12) The custody officer at a police station may seize and retain anything which is found on an intimate search of a person, or cause any such thing to be seized and retained—
  (a) if he believes that the person from whom it is seized may use it—

(i)   to cause physical injury to himself or any other person;

(ii)   to damage property;

(iii) to interfere with evidence; or

(iv) to assist him to escape; or

(b) if he has reasonable grounds for believing that it may be evidence relating to an offence.

(13) Where anything is seized under this section, the person from whom it is seized shall be told the reason for the seizure unless he is—

(a) violent or likely to become violent; or

(b) incapable of understanding what is said to him.

(14)–(16) [Information to be contained in annual reports.]

(17) In this section—

'the appropriate criminal intent' means an intent to commit an offence under—

(a) section 5(3) of the Misuse of Drugs Act 1971 (possession of controlled drug with intent to supply to another); or

(b) section 68(2) of the Customs and Excise Management Act 1979 (exportation etc, with intent to evade a prohibition or restriction);

'Class A drug' has the meaning assigned to it by section 2(1)(b) of the Misuse of Drugs Act 1971;

'drug offence search' means an intimate search for a Class A drug which an officer has authorised by virtue of subsection (1)(b) above; and

'suitably qualified person' means—

(a) a registered medical practitioner; or

(b) a registered nurse.

56   Right to have someone informed when arrested

(1) Where a person has been arrested and is being held in custody in a police station or other premises, he shall be entitled, if he so requests, to have one friend or relative or other person who is known to him or who is likely to take an interest in his welfare told, as soon as is practicable except to the extent that delay is permitted by this section, that he has been arrested and is being detained there.

(2) Delay is only permitted—

(a) in the case of a person who is in police detention for a serious arrestable offence; and

(b) if an officer of at least the rank of inspector authorises it.

(3) In any case the person in custody must be permitted to exercise the right conferred by subsection (1) above within 36 hours from the relevant time, as defined in section 41(2) above.

(4) An officer may give an authorisation under subsection (2) above orally or in writing but, if he gives it orally, he shall confirm it in writing as soon as is practicable.

(5) Subject to subsection (5A) below an officer may only authorise delay where he has reasonable grounds for believing that telling the named person of the arrest—

(a) will lead to interference with or harm to evidence connected with a serious arrestable offence or interference with or physical injury to other persons; or

(b) will lead to the alerting of other persons suspected of having committed such an offence but not yet arrested for it; or

(c) will hinder the recovery of any property obtained as a result of such an offence.

'(5A) An officer may also authorise delay where he has reasonable grounds for believing that—

(a) the person detained for the serious arrestable offence has benefited from his criminal conduct, and

(b) the recovery of the value of the property constituting the benefit will be hindered by telling the named person of the arrest.

(5B) For the purposes of subsection (5A) above the question whether a person has benefited from his criminal conduct is to be decided in accordance with Part 2 of the Proceeds of Crime Act 2002.'

(6) If a delay is authorised—

(a) the detained person shall be told the reason for it, and

(b) the reason shall be noted on his custody record.

(7) The duties imposed by subsection (6) above shall be performed as soon as is practicable.

(8) The rights conferred by this section on a person detained at a police station or other premises are exercisable whenever he is transferred from one place to another; and this section applies to each subsequent occasion on which they are exercisable as it applies to the first such occasion.

(9) There may be no further delay in permitting the exercise of the right conferred by subsection (1) above once the reason for authorising delay ceases to subsist.

(10) Nothing in this section applies to a person arrested or detained under the terrorism provisions.

57   Additional rights of children and young persons

The following subsections shall be substituted for section 34(2) of the Children and Young Persons Act 1933—

'(2) Where a child or young person is in police detention, such steps as are practicable shall be taken to ascertain the identity of a person responsible for his welfare.

(3) If it is practicable to ascertain the identity of a person responsible for the welfare of the child or young person, that person shall be informed, unless it is not practicable to do so—

(a) that the child or young person has been arrested;

(b) why he has been arrested; and

(c) where he is being detained.

(4) Where information falls to be given under subsection (3) above, it shall be given as soon as it is practicable to do so.

(5) For the purposes of this section the persons who may be responsible for the welfare of a child or young person are—

(a) his parent or guardian; or

(b) any other person who has for the time being assumed responsibility for his welfare.

(6) If it is practicable to give a person responsible for the welfare of the child or young person the information required by subsection (3) above, that person shall be given it as soon as it is practicable to do so.

(7) If it appears that at the time of his arrest a supervision order, as defined in section 163 of the Powers of Criminal Courts (Sentencing) Act 2000 or Part IV of the Children Act 1989, is in force in respect of him, the person responsible for his supervision shall also be informed as described in subsection (3) above as soon as it is reasonably practicable to do so.

(8) The reference to a parent or guardian in subsection (5) above is—

(a) in the case of a child or young person in the care of a local authority, a reference to that authority; and

(b) in the case of a child or young person in the care of a voluntary organisation in which parental rights and duties with respect to him are vested by virtue of a resolution under section 64(1) of the Child Care Act 1980, a reference to that organisation.

(9) The rights conferred on a child or young person by subsections (2) to (8) above are in addition to his rights under section 56 of the Police and Criminal Evidence Act 1984.

(10) The reference in subsection (2) above to a child or young person who is in police detention includes a reference to a child or young person who has been detained under the terrorism provisions; and in subsection (3) above "arrest" includes such detention.

(11) In subsection (10) above "the terrorism provisions" has the meaning assigned to it by section 65 of the Police and Criminal Evidence Act 1984.'.

58   Access to legal advice

(1) A person arrested and held in custody in a police station or other premises shall be entitled, if he so requests, to consult a solicitor privately at any time.

(2) Subject to subsection (3) below, a request under subsection (1) above and the time at which it was made shall be recorded in the custody record.

(3) Such a request need not be recorded in the custody record of a person who makes it at a time while he is at a court after being charged with an offence.

(4) If a person makes such a request, he must be permitted to consult a solicitor as soon as is practicable except to the extent that delay is permitted by this section.

(5) In any case he must be permitted to consult a solicitor within 36 hours from the relevant time, as defined in section 41(2) above.

(6) Delay in compliance with a request is only permitted—
   (a) in the case of a person who is in police detention for a serious arrestable offence; and
   (b) if an officer of at least the rank of superintendent authorises it.

(7) An officer may give an authorisation under subsection (6) above orally or in writing but, if he gives it orally, he shall confirm it in writing as soon as is practicable.

(8) Subject to subsection (8A) below an officer may only authorise delay where he has reasonable grounds for believing that the exercise of the right conferred by subsection (1) above at the time when the person detained desires to exercise it—
   (a) will lead to interference with or harm to evidence connected with a serious arrestable offence or interference with or physical injury to other persons; or
   (b) will lead to the alerting of other persons suspected of having committed such an offence but not yet arrested for it; or
   (c) will hinder the recovery of any property obtained as a result of such an offence.

'(8A) An officer may also authorise delay where he has reasonable grounds for believing that—
   (a) the person detained for the serious arrestable offence has benefited from his criminal conduct, and
   (b) the recovery of the value of the property constituting the benefit will be hindered by the exercise of the right conferred by subsection (1) above.

(8B) For the purposes of subsection (8A) above the question whether a person has benefited from his criminal conduct is to be decided in accordance with Part 2 of the Proceeds of Crime Act 2002.'

(9) If delay is authorised—
   (a) the detained person shall be told the reason for it; and
   (b) the reason shall be noted on his custody record.

(10) The duties imposed by subsection (9) above shall be performed as soon as is practicable.

(11) There may be no further delay in permitting the exercise of the right conferred by subsection (1) above once the reason for authorising delay ceases to subsist.

(12) Nothing in this section applies to a person arrested or detained under the terrorism provisions.

60   Tape-recording of interviews

(1) It shall be the duty of the Secretary of State—
   (a) to issue a code of practice in connection with the tape-recording of interviews of persons suspected of the commission of criminal offences which are held by police officers at police stations; and

(b) to make an order requiring the tape-recording of interviews of persons suspected of the commission of criminal offences, or of such descriptions of criminal offences as may be specified in the order, which are so held, in accordance with the code as it has effect for the time being.

(2) An order under subsection (1) above shall be made by statutory instrument and shall be subject to annulment in pursuance of a resolution of either House of Parliament.

60A   Visual recording of interviews

(1) The Secretary of State shall have power—
  (a) to issue a code of practice for the visual recording of interviews held by police officers at police stations; and
  (b) to make an order requiring the visual recording of interviews so held, and requiring the visual recording to be in accordance with the code for the time being in force under this section.

(2) A requirement imposed by an order under this section may be imposed in relation to such cases or police stations in such areas, or both, as may be specified or described in the order.

(3) An order under subsection (1) above shall be made by statutory instrument and shall be subject to annulment in pursuance of a resolution of either House of Parliament.

(4) In this section—
  (a) references to any interview are references to an interview of a person suspected of a criminal offence; and
  (b) references to a visual recording include references to a visual recording in which an audio recording is comprised.

61   Fingerprinting

(1) Except as provided by this section no person's fingerprints may be taken without the appropriate consent.

(2) Consent to the taking of a person's fingerprints must be in writing if it is given at a time when he is at a police station.

(3) The fingerprints of a person detained at a police station may be taken without the appropriate consent if—
  (a) he is detained in consequence of his arrest for a recordable offence; and
  (b) he has not had his fingerprints taken in the course of the investigation of the offence by the police.

(3A) Where a person mentioned in paragraph (a) of subsection (3) or (4) has already had his fingerprints taken in the course of the investigation of the offence by the police that fact shall be disregarded for the purposes of that subsection if—
  (a) the fingerprints taken on the previous occasion do not constitute a complete set of his fingerprints; or
  (b) some or all of the fingerprints taken on the previous occasion are not of sufficient quality to allow satisfactory analysis, comparison or matching (whether in the case in question or generally).

(4) The fingerprints of a person detained at a police station may be taken without the appropriate consent if—
  (a) he has been charged with a recordable offence or informed that he will be reported for such an offence; and
  (b) he has not had his fingerprints taken in the course of the investigation of the offence by the police.'

(4A) The fingerprints of a person who has answered to bail at a court or police station may be taken without the appropriate consent at the court or station if—
  (a) the court, or

(b) an officer of at least the rank of inspector,

authorises them to be taken.

(4B) A court or officer may only give an authorisation under subsection (4A) if—

(a) the person who has answered to bail has answered to it for a person whose finger-prints were taken on a previous occasion and there are reasonable grounds for believing that he is not the same person; or

(b) the person who has answered to bail claims to be a different person from a person whose fingerprints were taken on a previous occasion.

(5) An officer may give an authorisation under subsection (4A) above orally or in writing but, if he gives it orally, he shall confirm it in writing as soon as is practicable.

(6) Any person's fingerprints may be taken without the appropriate consent if—

(a) he has been convicted of a recordable offence;

(b) he has been given a caution in respect of a recordable offence which, at the time of the caution, he has admitted; or

(c) he has been warned or reprimanded under section 65 of the Crime and Disorder Act 1998 (c. 37) for a recordable offence.

(7) In a case where by virtue of subsection (3), (4) or (6) above a person's fingerprints are taken without the appropriate consent—

(a) he shall be told the reason before his fingerprints are taken; and

(b) the reason shall be recorded as soon as is practicable after the fingerprints are taken.

(7A) If a person's fingerprints are taken at a police station, whether with or without the appropriate consent—

(a) before the fingerprints are taken, an officer shall inform him that they may be the subject of a speculative search; and

(b) the fact that the person has been informed of this possibility shall be recorded as soon as is practicable after the fingerprints have been taken; and

(8) If he is detained at a police station when the fingerprints are taken, the reason for taking them and in the case falling within subsection (7A) above, the fact referred to in paragraph (b) of that subsection shall be recorded on his custody record.

(8A) Where a person's fingerprints are taken electronically, they must be taken only in such manner, and using such devices, as the Secretary of State has approved for the purposes of electronic fingerprinting.

(8B) The power to take the fingerprints of a person detained at a police station without the appropriate consent shall be exercisable by any constable.

(9) Nothing in this section—

(a) affects any power conferred by paragraph 18(2) of Schedule 2 to the Immigration Act 1971; or

(b) applies to a person arrested or detained under the terrorism provisions.

62   Intimate samples

(1) Subject to section 63B below an intimate sample may be taken from a person in police detention only—

(a) if a police officer of at least the rank of inspector authorises it to be taken; and

(b) if the appropriate consent is given.

(1A) An intimate sample may be taken from a person who is not in police detention but from whom, in the course of the investigation of an offence, two or more non-intimate samples suitable for the same means of analysis have been taken which have proved insufficient—

(a) if a police officer of at least the rank of inspector authorises it to be taken; and

(b) if the appropriate consent is given.

(2) An officer may only give an authorisation under subsection (1) or (1A) above if he has reasonable grounds—

(a) for suspecting the involvement of the person from whom the sample is to be taken in a recordable offence; and

(b) for believing that the sample will tend to confirm or disprove his involvement.

(3) An officer may give an authorisation under subsection (1) or (1A) above orally or in writing but, if he gives it orally, he shall confirm it in writing as soon as is practicable.

(4) The appropriate consent must be given in writing.

(5) Where—

(a) an authorisation has been given; and

(b) it is proposed that an intimate sample shall be taken in pursuance of the authorisation,

an officer shall inform the person from whom the sample is to be taken—

(i)   of the giving of the authorisation; and

(ii) of the grounds for giving it.

(6) The duty imposed by subsection (5)(ii) above includes a duty to state the nature of the offence in which it is suspected that the person from whom the sample is taken has been involved.

(7) If an intimate sample is taken from a person—

(a) the authorisation by virtue of which it was taken;

(b) the grounds for giving the authorisation; and

(c) the fact that the appropriate consent was given,

shall be recorded as soon as is practicable after the sample is taken.

(7A) If an intimate sample is taken from a person at a police station—

(a) before the sample is taken, an officer shall inform him that it may be the subject of a speculative search; and

(b) the fact that the person has been informed of this possibility shall be recorded as soon as practicable after the sample has been taken; and

(8) If an intimate sample is taken from a person detained at a police station, the matters required to be recorded by subsection (7) or (7A) above shall be recorded in his custody record.

'(9) In the case of an intimate sample which is a dental impression, the sample may be taken from a person only by a registered dentist.

(9A) In the case of any other form of intimate sample, except in the case of a sample of urine, the sample may be taken from a person only by—

(a) a registered medical practitioner; or

(b) a registered health care professional.'

(10) Where the appropriate consent to the taking of an intimate sample from a person was refused without good cause, in any proceedings against that person for an offence—

(a) the court, in determining—

(i)   ...

(ii) whether there is a case to answer; and

(aa) a judge, in deciding whether to grant an application made by the accused under—

(i)   paragraph 2 of Schedule 3 to the Crime and Disorder Act 1998 (applications for dismissal); and

(b) the court or jury, in determining whether that person is guilty of the offence charged,

may draw such inferences from the refusal as appear proper.

(11) Nothing in this section applies to the taking of a specimen for the purposes of any of the provisions of sections 4 to 11 of the Road Traffic Act 1988 or of sections 26 to 38 of the Transport and Works Act 1992.

(12) Nothing in this section applies to a person arrested or detained under the terrorism

provisions; and subsection (1A) shall not apply where the non-intimate samples mentioned in that subsection were taken under paragraph 10 of Schedule 8 to the Terrorism Act 2000.

63   Other samples

(1) Except as provided by this section, a non-intimate sample may not be taken from a person without the appropriate consent.

(2) Consent to the taking of a non-intimate sample must be given in writing.

(2A) A non-intimate sample may be taken from a person without the appropriate consent if two conditions are satisfied.

(2B) The first is that the person is in police detention in consequence of his arrest for a recordable offence.

(2C) The second is that—

(a) he has not had a non-intimate sample of the same type and from the same part of the body taken in the course of the investigation of the offence by the police, or

(b) he has had such a sample taken but it proved insufficient.

(3) A non-intimate sample may be taken from a person without the appropriate consent if—

(a) he is being held in custody by the police on the authority of a court; and

(b) an officer of at least the rank of inspector authorises it to be taken without the appropriate consent.

(3A) A non-intimate sample may be taken from a person (whether or not he is in police detention or held in custody by the police on the authority of a court) without the appropriate consent if—

(a) he has been charged with a recordable offence or informed that he will be reported for such an offence; and

(b) either he has not had a non-intimate sample taken from him in the course of the investigation of the offence by the police or he has had a non-intimate sample taken from him but either it was not suitable for the same means of analysis or, though so suitable, the sample proved insufficient.

(3B) A non-intimate sample may be taken from a person without the appropriate consent if he has been convicted of a recordable offence.

(3C) A non-intimate sample may also be taken from a person without the appropriate consent if he is a person to whom section 2 of the Criminal Evidence (Amendment) Act 1997 applies (persons detained following acquittal on grounds of insanity or finding of unfitness to plead).

(4) An officer may only give an authorisation under subsection (3) above if he has reasonable grounds—

(a) for suspecting the involvement of the person from whom the sample is to be taken in a recordable offence; and

(b) for believing that the sample will tend to confirm or disprove his involvement.

(5) An officer may give an authorisation under subsection (3) above orally or in writing but, if he gives it orally, he shall confirm it in writing as soon as is practicable.

(5A) An officer shall not give an authorisation under subsection (3) above for the taking from any person of a non-intimate sample consisting of a skin impression if—

(a) a skin impression of the same part of the body has already been taken from that person in the course of the investigation of the offence; and

(b) the impression previously taken is not one that has proved insufficient.

(6) Where—

(a) an authorisation has been given; and

(b) it is proposed that a non-intimate sample shall be taken in pursuance of the authorisation, an officer shall inform the person from whom the sample is to be taken—

    (i) of the giving of the authorisation; and

    (ii) of the grounds for giving it.

(7) The duty imposed by subsection (6)(ii) above, includes a duty to state the nature of the offence in which it is suspected that the person from whom the sample is to be taken has been involved.

(8) If a non-intimate sample is taken from a person by virtue of subsection (3) above—

    (a) the authorisation by virtue of which it was taken; and

    (b) the grounds for giving the authorisation,

shall be recorded as soon as is practicable after the sample is taken.

(8A) In a case whereby by virtue of subsection (2A), (3A), (3B) or (3C) above a sample is taken from a person without the appropriate consent—

    (a) he shall be told the reason before the sample is taken; and

    (b) the reason shall be recorded as soon as practicable after the sample is taken.

(8B) If a non-intimate sample is taken from a person at a police station, whether with or without the appropriate consent—

    (a) before the sample is taken, an officer shall inform him that it may be the subject of a speculative search; and

    (b) the fact that the person has been informed of this possibility shall be recorded as soon as practicable after the sample has been taken.

(9) If a non-intimate sample is taken from a person detained at a police station, the matters required to be recorded by subsection (8) or (8A) or (8B) above shall be recorded in his custody record.

[(9ZA) The power to take a non-intimate sample from a person without the appropriate consent shall be exercisable by any constable.]

(9A) Subsection (3B) above shall not apply to any person convicted before 10 April 1995 unless he is a person to whom section 1 of the Criminal Evidence (Amendment) Act 1997 applies (persons imprisoned or detained by virtue of pre-existing conviction for sexual offence etc.).

[(9A) Where a non-intimate sample consisting of a skin impression is taken electronically from a person, it must be taken only in such manner, and using such devices, as the Secretary of State has approved for the purpose of the electronic taking of such an impression.]

[(10) Nothing in this section applies to a person arrested or detained under the terrorism provisions.]

63A   Fingerprints and samples: supplementary provisions

(1) Where a person has been arrested on suspicion of being involved in a recordable offence or has been charged with such an offence or has been informed that he will be reported for such an offence, fingerprints or samples or the information derived from samples taken under any power conferred by this Part of this Act from the person may be checked against—

    (a) other fingerprints or samples to which the person seeking to check has access and which are held by or on behalf of any one or more relevant law enforcement authorities or which are held in connection with or as a result of an investigation of an offence;

    (b) information derived from other samples if the information is contained in records to which the person seeking to check has access and which are held as mentioned in paragraph (a) above.

(1A) In subsection (1) above 'relevant law-enforcement authority' means—

    (a) a police force;

    (b) the National Criminal Intelligence Service;

    (c) the National Crime Squad;

(d) a public authority (not falling within paragraphs (a) to (c)) with functions in any part of the British Islands which consist of or include the investigation of crimes or the charging of offenders;

(e) any person with functions in any country or territory outside the United Kingdom which—
  (i) correspond to those of a police force; or
  (ii) otherwise consist of or include the investigation of conduct contrary to the law of that country or territory, or the apprehension of persons guilty of such conduct;

(f) any person with functions under any international agreement which consist of or include the investigation of conduct which is—
  (i) unlawful under the law of one or more places,
  (ii) prohibited by such an agreement, or
  (iii) contrary to international law, or the apprehension of persons guilty of such conduct.

(1B) The reference in subsection (1A) above to a police force is a reference to any of the following—

(a) any police force maintained under section 2 of the Police Act 1996 (c. 16) (police forces in England and Wales outside London);
(b) the metropolitan police force;
(c) the City of London police force;
(d) any police force maintained under or by virtue of section 1 of the Police (Scotland) Act 1967 (c. 77);
(e) the Police Service of Northern Ireland;
(f) the Police Service of Northern Ireland Reserve;
(g) the Ministry of Defence Police;
(h) the Royal Navy Regulating Branch;
(i) the Royal Military Police;
(j) the Royal Air Force Police;
(k) the Royal Marines Police;
(l) the British Transport Police;
(m) the States of Jersey Police Force;
(n) the salaried police force of the Island of Guernsey;
(o) the Isle of Man Constabulary.

(1C) Where—
(a) fingerprints or samples have been taken from any person in connection with the investigation of an offence but otherwise than in circumstances to which subsection (1) above applies, and
(b) that person has given his consent in writing to the use in a speculative search of the fingerprints or of the samples and of information derived from them, the fingerprints or, as the, case may be, those samples and that information may be checked against any of the fingerprints, samples or information mentioned in paragraph (a) or (b) of that subsection.

(1D) A consent given for the purposes of subsection (1C) above shall not be capable of being withdrawn.

(2) Where a sample of hair other than public hair is to be taken the sample may be taken either by cutting hairs or by plucking hairs with their roots so long as no more are plucked than the person taking the sample reasonably considers to be necessary for a sufficient sample.

(3) Where any power to take a sample is exercisable in relation to a person the sample may be taken in a prison or other institution to which the Prison Act 1952 applies.

(3A) Where—

(a) the power to take a non-intimate sample under section 63(3B) above is exercisable in relation to any person who is detained under Part III of the Mental Health Act 1983 in pursuance of—

    (i) a hospital order or interim hospital order made following his conviction for the recordable offence in question, or

    (ii) a transfer direction given at a time when he was detained in pursuance of any sentence or order imposed following that conviction, or

(b) the power to take a non-intimate sample under section 63(3C) above is exercisable in relation to any person,

the sample may be taken in the hospital in which he is detained under that Part of that Act. Expressions used in this subsection and in the Mental Health Act 1983 have the same meaning as in that Act.

(3B) Where the power to take a non-intimate sample under section 63(3B) above is exercisable in relation to a person detained in pursuance of directions of the Secretary of State under section 92 of the Powers of Criminal Courts (Sentencing) Act 2000 the sample may be taken at the place where he is so detained.

(4) Any constable may, within the allowed period, require a person who is neither in police detention nor held in custody by the police on the authority of a court to attend a police station in order to have a sample taken where—

(a) the person has been charged with a recordable offence or informed that he will be reported for such an offence and either he has not had a sample taken from him in the course of the investigation of the offence by the police or he has had a sample so taken from him but either it was not suitable for the same means of analysis or, though so suitable, the sample proved insufficient; or

(b) the person has been convicted of a recordable offence and either he has not had a sample taken from him since the conviction or he has had a sample taken from him (before or after his conviction) but either it was not suitable for the same means of analysis or, though so suitable, the sample proved insufficient.

(5) The period allowed for requiring a person to attend a police station for the purpose specified in subsection (4) above is—

(a) in the case of a person falling within paragraph (a), one month beginning with the date of the charge or of his being informed as mentioned in that paragraph or one month beginning with the date on which the appropriate officer is informed of the fact that the sample is not suitable for the same means of analysis or has proved insufficient, as the case may be;

(b) in the case of a person falling within paragraph (b), one month beginning with the date of the conviction or one month beginning with the date on which the appropriate officer is informed of the fact that the sample is not suitable for the same means of analysis or has proved insufficient, as the case may be.

(6) A requirement under subsection (4) above—

(a) shall give the person at least 7 days within which he must so attend; and

(b) may dirct him to attend at a specified time of day or between specified times of day.

(7) Any constable may arrest without a warrant a person who has failed to comply with a requirement under subsection (4) above.

(8) In this section 'the appropriate officer' is—

(a) in the case of a person falling within subsection (4)(a), the officer investigating the offence with which that person has been charged or as to which he was informed that he would be reported;

(b) in the case of a person falling within subsection (4)(b), the officer in charge of the police station from which the investigation of the offence of which he was convicted was conducted.

63B   Testing for presence of Class A drugs

(1) A sample of urine or a non-intimate sample may be taken from a person in police detention for the purpose of ascertaining whether he has any specified Class A drug in his body if the following conditions are met.

(2) The first condition is—

  (a) that the person concerned has been charged with a trigger offence; or

  (b) that the person concerned has been charged with an offence and a police officer of at least the rank of inspector, who has reasonable grounds for suspecting that the misuse by that person of any specified Class A drug caused or contributed to the offence, has authorised the sample to be taken.

(3) The second condition is that the person concerned has attained the age of 18.

(4) The third condition is that a police officer has requested the person concerned to give the sample.

(5) Before requesting the person concerned to give a sample, an officer must—

  (a) warn him that if, when so requested, he fails without good cause to do so he may be liable to prosecution, and

  (b) in a case within subsection (2)(b) above, inform him of the giving of the authorisation and of the grounds in question.

(5A) In the case of a person who has not attained the age of 17—

  (a) the making of the request under subsection (4) above;

  (b) the giving of the warning and (where applicable) the information under subsection (5) above; and

  (c) the taking of the sample,

may not take place except in the presence of an appropriate adult.

(6) A sample may be taken under this section only by a person prescribed by regulations made by the Secretary of State by statutory instrument. No regulations shall be made under this subsection unless a draft has been laid before, and approved by resolution of, each House of Parliament.

(6A) The Secretary of State may by order made by statutory instrument amend subsection (3) above by substituting for the age for the time being specified a different age specified in the order.

(6B) A statutory instrument containing an order under subsection (6A) above shall not be made unless a draft of the instrument has been laid before, and approved by a resolution of, each House of Parliament.

(7) Information obtained from a sample taken under this section may be disclosed—

  (a) for the purpose of informing any decision about granting bail in criminal proceedings (within the meaning of the Bail Act 1976) to the person concerned;

  (b) where the person concerned is in police detention or is remanded in or committed to custody by an order of a court or has been granted such bail, for the purpose of informing any decision about his supervision;

  (c) where the person concerned is convicted of an offence, for the purpose of informing any decision about the appropriate sentence to be passed by a court and any decision about his supervision or release;

  (d) for the purpose of ensuring that appropriate advice and treatment is made available to the person concerned.

(8) A person who fails without good cause to give any sample which may be taken from him under this section shall be guilty of an offence.

(9) In relation to a person who has not attained the age of 18, this section applies only where—

  (a) the relevant chief officer has been notified by the Secretary of State that arrangements for the taking of samples under this section from persons who have not

attained the age of 18 have been made for the police area as a whole, or for the particular police station, in which the person is in police detention; and
(b) the notice has not been withdrawn.
(10) In this section—
"appropriate adult", in relation to a person who has not attained the age of 17, means—
(a) his parent or guardian or, if he is in the care of a local authority or voluntary organisation, a person representing that authority or organisation; or
(b) a social worker of a local authority social services department; or
(c) if no person falling within paragraph (a) or (b) is available, any responsible person aged 18 or over who is not a police officer or a person employed by the police;
"relevant chief officer" means—
(a) in relation to a police area, the chief officer of police of the police force for that police area; or
(b) in relation to a police station, the chief officer of police of the police force for the police area in which the police station is situated."

63C Testing for presence of Class A drugs: supplementary

(1) A person guilty of an offence under section 63B above shall be liable on summary conviction to imprisonment for a term not exceeding three months, or to a fine not exceeding level 4 on the standard scale, or to both.

(2) A police officer may give an authorisation under section 63B above orally or in writing but, if he gives it orally, he shall confirm it in writing as soon as is practicable.

(3) If a sample is taken under section 63B above by virtue of an authorisation, the authorisation and the grounds for the suspicion shall be recorded as soon as is practicable after the sample is taken.

(4) If the sample is taken from a person detained at a police station, the matters required to be recorded by subsection (3) above shall be recorded in his custody record.

(5) Subsections (11) and (12) of section 62 above apply for the purposes of section 63B above as they do for the purposes of that section; and section 63B above does not prejudice the generality of sections 62 and 63 above.

(6) In section 63B above—
'Class A drug' and 'misuse' have the same meanings as in the Misuse of Drugs Act 1971;
'specified' (in relation to a Class A drug) and 'trigger offence' have the same meanings as in Part III of the Criminal Justice and Court Services Act 2000.

As to the definitions in subsection (6), see section 70 of, and Schedule 6 to, the 2000 Act.

64 Destruction of fingerprints and samples

(1A) Where—
(a) fingerprints or samples are taken from a person in connection with the investigation of an offence, and
(b) subsection (3) below does not require them to be destroyed,
the fingerprints or samples may be retained after they have fulfilled the purposes for which they were taken but shall not be used by any person except for purposes related to the prevention or detection of crime, the investigation of an offence or the conduct of a prosecution.

(1B) In subsection (1A) above—
(a) the reference to using a fingerprint includes a reference to allowing any check to be made against it under section 63A(1) or (1C) above and to disclosing it to any person;
(b) the reference to using a sample includes a reference to allowing any check to be made under section 63A(1) or (1C) above against it or against information derived from it and to disclosing it or any such information to any person;

  (c) the reference to crime includes a reference to any conduct which—
    (i) constitutes one or more criminal offences (whether under the law of a part of the United Kingdom or of a country or territory outside the United Kingdom); or
    (ii) is, or corresponds to, any conduct which, if it all took place in any one part of the United Kingdom, would constitute one or more criminal offences; and
  (d) the references to an investigation and to a prosecution include references, respectively, to any investigation outside the United Kingdom of any crime or suspected crime and to a prosecution brought in respect of any crime in a country or territory outside the United Kingdom.

(3) If—
  (a) fingerprints or samples are taken from a person in connection with the investigation of an offence; and
  (b) that person is not suspected of having committed the offence, they must, except as provided by the following provisions of this section, be destroyed as soon as they have fulfilled the purpose for which they were taken.

(3AA) Samples and fingerprints are not required to be destroyed under subsection (3) above if—
  (a) they were taken for the purposes of the investigation of an offence of which a person has been convicted; and
  (b) a sample or, as the case may be, fingerprint was also taken from the convicted person for the purposes of that investigation.

(3AB) Subject to subsection (3AC) below, where a person is entitled under subsection (3) above to the destruction of any fingerprint or sample taken from him (or would be but for subsection (3AA) above), neither the fingerprint nor the sample, nor any information derived from the sample, shall be used—
  (a) in evidence against the person who is or would be entitled to the destruction of that fingerprint or sample; or
  (b) for the purposes of the investigation of any offence;
and subsection (1B) above applies for the purposes of this subsection as it applies for the purposes of subsection (1A) above.

(3AC) Where a person from whom a fingerprint or sample has been taken consents in writing to its retention—
  (a) that sample need not be destroyed under subsection (3) above;
  (b) subsection (3AB) above shall not restrict the use that may be made of the fingerprint or sample or, in the case of a sample, of any information derived from it; and
  (c) that consent shall be treated as comprising a consent for the purposes of section 63A(1C) above;
and a consent given for the purpose of this subsection shall not be capable of being withdrawn.

(3AD) For the purposes of subsection (3AC) above it shall be immaterial whether the consent is given at, before or after the time when the entitlement to the destruction of the fingerprint or sample arises.

(5) If fingerprints are destroyed—
  (a) any copies of the fingerprints shall also be destroyed; and
  (b) any chief officer of police controlling access to computer data relating to the fingerprints shall make access to the data impossible, as soon as it is practicable to do so.

(6) A person who asks to be allowed to witness the destruction of his fingerprints or copies of them shall have a right to witness it.

(6A) If—

    (a) subsection (5)(b) above falls to be complied with; and

    (b) the person to whose fingerprints the data relate asks for a certificate that it has been complied with,

such a certificate shall be issued to him, not later than the end of the period of three months beginning with the day on which he asks for it, by the responsible chief officer of police or a person authorised by him or on his behalf for the purposes of this section.

(6B) In this section—

'the responsible chief officer of police' means the chief officer of police in whose police area the computer data were put on to the computer.

(7) Nothing in this section—

    (a) affects any power conferred by paragraph 18(2) of Schedule 2 to the Immigration Act 1971 or section 20 of the Immigration and Asylum Act 1999 (disclosure of police information to the Secretary of State for use for immigration purposes); or

    (b) applies to a person arrested or detained under the terrorism provisions.

'64A   Photographing of suspects etc.

(1) A person who is detained at a police station may be photographed—

    (a) with the appropriate consent; or

    (b) if the appropriate consent is withheld or it is not practicable to obtain it, without it.

(2) A person proposing to take a photograph of any person under this section—

    (a) may, for the purpose of doing so, require the removal of any item or substance worn on or over the whole or any part of the head or face of the person to be photographed; and

    (b) if the requirement is not complied with, may remove the item or substance himself.

(3) Where a photograph may be taken under this section, the only persons entitled to take the photograph are constables.

(4) A photograph taken under this section—

    (a) may be used by, or disclosed to, any person for any purpose related to the prevention or detection of crime, the investigation of an offence or the conduct of a prosecution; and

    (b) after being so used or disclosed, may be retained but may not be used or disclosed except for a purpose so related.

(5) In subsection (4)—

    (a) the reference to crime includes a reference to any conduct which—

        (i) constitutes one or more criminal offences (whether under the law of a part of the United Kingdom or of a country or territory outside the United Kingdom); or

        (ii) is, or corresponds to, any conduct which, if it all took place in any one part of the United Kingdom, would constitute one or more criminal offences;

    and

    (b) the references to an investigation and to a prosecution include references, respectively, to any investigation outside the United Kingdom of any crime or suspected crime and to a prosecution brought in respect of any crime in a country or territory outside the United Kingdom.

(6) References in this section to taking a photograph include references to using any process by means of which a visual image may be produced; and references to photographing a person shall be construed accordingly.'

65   Part V—supplementary

(1) In this Part of this Act—

'analysis', in relation to a skin impression, includes comparison and matching;

'appropriate consent' means—
  (a) in relation to a person who has attained the age of 17 years, the consent of that person;
  (b) in relation to a person who has not attained that age but has attained the age of 14 years, the consent of that person and his parent or guardian; and
  (c) in relation to a person who has not attained the age of 14 years, the consent of his parent or guardian;
'fingerprints', in relation to any person, means a record (in any form and produced by any method) of the skin pattern and other physical characteristics or features of—
  (a) any of that person's fingers; or
  (b) either of his palms;
'intimate sample' means
  (a) a sample of blood, semen or any other tissue fluid, urine or pubic hair;
  (b) a dental impression;
  (c) a swab taken from a person's body orifice other than the mouth.
'intimate search' means a search which consists of the physical examination of a person's body orifices other than the mouth;
'non-intimate sample' means—
  (a) a sample of hair other than public hair;
  (b) a sample taken from a nail or from under a nail;
  (c) a swab taken from any part of a person's body including the mouth but not any other body orifice;
  (d) saliva;
  (e) a skin impression;
'registered dentist' has the same meaning as in the Dentists Act 1984;
'registered health care professional' means a person (other than a medical practitioner) who is—
  (a) a registered nurse; or
  (b) a registered member of a health care profession which is designated for the purposes of this paragraph by an order made by the Secretary of State;
'skin impression', in relation to any person, means any record (other than a fingerprint) which is a record (in any form and produced by any method) of the skin pattern and other physical characteristics or features of the whole or any part of his foot or of any other part of his body;
'speculative search', in relation to a person's fingerprints or samples, means such a check against other fingerprints or samples or against information derived from other samples as is referred to in section 63A(1) above;
'sufficient' and 'insufficient', in relation to a sample, (subject to subsection (2) below) means sufficient or insufficient (in point of quantity or quality) for the purpose of enabling information to be produced by the means of analysis used or to be used in relation to the sample.
['the terrorism provisions' means—
  (a) section 41 of the Terrorism Act 2000 and any provision of Schedule 7 to that Act conferring a power of arrest or detention]; and
'terrorism' has the meaning given in section 1 of that Act;
  (2) References in this Part of this Act to a sample's proving insufficient include references to where, as a consequence of—
  (a) the loss, destruction or contamination of the whole or any part of the sample,
  (b) any damage to the whole or a part of the sample, or
  (c) the use of the whole or a part of the sample for an analysis which produced no results or which produced results some or all of which must be regarded, in the circumstances, as unreliable,

the sample has become unavailable or insufficient for the purpose of enabling information, or information of a particular description, to be obtained by means of analysis of the sample.

'(1A) A health care profession is any profession mentioned in section 60(2) of the Health Act 1999 (c. 8) other than the profession of practising medicine and the profession of nursing.

(1B) An order under subsection (1) shall be made by statutory instrument and shall be subject to annulment in pursuance of a resolution of either House of Parliament.'

PART VI   CODES OF PRACTICE—GENERAL

66   Codes of practice
The Secretary of State shall issue codes of practice in connection with—
- (a) the exercise by police officers of statutory powers—
  - (i) to search a person without first arresting him; or
  - (ii) to search a vehicle without making an arrest;
- (b) the detention, treatment, questioning and identification of persons by police officers;
- (c) searches of premises by police officers; and
- (d) the seizure of property found by police officers on persons or premises.

(2) Codes shall (in particular) include provision in connection with the exercise by police officers of powers under section 63B above.

67   Codes of practice—supplementary
(1) In this section, "code" means a code of practice under section 60, 60A or 66.

(2) The Secretary of State may at any time revise the whole or any part of a code.

(3) A code may be made, or revised, so as to—
- (a) apply only in relation to one or more specified areas,
- (b) have effect only for a specified period,
- (c) apply only in relation to specified offences or descriptions of offender.

(4) Before issuing a code, or any revision of a code, the Secretary of State must consult—
- (a) persons whom he considers to represent the interests of police authorities,
- (b) persons whom he considers to represent the interests of chief officers of police,
- (c) the General Council of the Bar,
- (d) the Law Society of England and Wales,
- (e) the Institute of Legal Executives, and
- (f) such other persons as he thinks fit.

(5) A code, or a revision of a code, does not come into operation until the Secretary of State by order so provides.

(6) The power conferred by subsection (5) is exercisable by statutory instrument.

(7) An order bringing a code into operation may not be made unless a draft of the order has been laid before Parliament and approved by a resolution of each House.

(7A) An order bringing a revision of a code into operation must be laid before Parliament if the order has been made without a draft having been so laid and approved by a resolution of each House.

(7B) When an order or draft of an order is laid, the code or revision of a code to which it relates must also be laid.

(7C) No order or draft of an order may be laid until the consultation required by subsection (4) has taken place.

(7D) An order bringing a code, or a revision of a code, into operation may include transitional or saving provisions.

(9) Persons other than police officers who are charged with the duty of investigating offences or charging offenders shall in the discharge of that duty have regard to any relevant provision of a code.

(9A) Persons on whom powers are conferred by—

(a) any designation under section 38 or 39 of the Police Reform Act 2002 (c. 30) (police powers for police authority employees), or

(b) any accreditation under section 41 of that Act (accreditation under community safety accreditation schemes),

shall have regard to any relevant provision of a code in the exercise or performance of the powers and duties conferred or imposed on them by that designation or accreditation.

(10) A failure on the part—

(a) of a police officer to comply with any provision of a code;

(b) of any person other than a police officer who is charged with the duty of investigating offences or charging offenders to have regard to any relevant provision of a code in the discharge of that duty; or

(c) of a person designated under section 38 or 39 or accredited under section 41 of the Police Reform Act 2002 to have regard to any relevant provision of a code in the exercise or performance of the powers and duties conferred or imposed on him by that designation or accreditation,

shall not of itself render him liable to any criminal or civil proceedings.

(11) In all criminal and civil proceedings any code shall be admissible in evidence; and if any provision of a code appears to the court or tribunal conducting the proceedings to be relevant to any question arising in the proceedings it shall be taken into account in determining that question.

(12) In this section 'criminal proceedings' includes—

(a) proceedings in the United Kingdom or elsewhere before a court-martial constituted under the Army Act 1955, the Air Force Act 1955 or the Naval Discipline Act 1957 or a disciplinary court constituted under section [52G] of the said Act of 1957;

(b) proceedings before the Courts-Martial Appeal Court; and

(c) proceedings before a Standing Civilian Court.

PART VII DOCUMENTARY EVIDENCE IN CRIMINAL PROCEEDINGS

71 Microfilm copies

In any proceedings the contents of a document may (whether or not the document is still in existence) be proved by the production of an enlargement of a microfilm copy of that document or of the material part of it, authenticated in such manner as the court may approve.

72 Part VII—supplementary

(1) In this Part of this Act—

'copy' in relation to a document means anything onto which information recorded in the document has been copied, by whatever means and whether directly or indirectly, and 'statement' means any representation of fact however made; and

'proceedings' means criminal proceedings, including—

(b) proceedings in the United Kingdom or elsewhere before the courts-martial constituted under the Army Act 1955 or the Air Force Act 1955 or the Naval Discipline Act 1957;

(b) proceedings in the United Kingdom or elsewhere before the Courts-Martial Appeal Court—

(i) on an appeal from a court-martial so constituted; or

(ii) on a reference under section 34 of the Courts-Martial (Appeals) Act 1968; and

(c) proceedings before a Standing Civilian Court.

(2) Nothing in this Part of this Act shall prejudice any power of a court to exclude evidence (whether by preventing questions from being put or otherwise) at its discretion.

PART VIII   EVIDENCE IN CRIMINAL PROCEEDINGS—GENERAL

Convictions and acquittals

73 Proof of convictions and acquittals

(1) Where in any proceedings the fact that a person has in the United Kingdom been convicted or acquitted of an offence otherwise than by a Service court is admissible in evidence, it may be proved by producing a certificate of conviction or, as the case may be, of acquittal relating to that offence, and proving that the person named in the certificate as having been convicted or acquitted of the offence is the person whose conviction or acquittal of the offence is to be proved.

(2) For the purposes of this section a certificate of conviction or of acquittal—

(a) shall, as regards a conviction or acquittal on indictment, consist of a certificate, signed by the proper officer where the conviction or acquittal took place, giving the substance and effect (omitting the formal parts) of the indictment and of the conviction or acquittal; and

(b) shall, as regards a conviction or acquittal on a summary trial, consist of a copy of the conviction or of the dismissal of the information, signed by the clerk of the court where the conviction or acquittal took place or by the clerk of the court, if any, to which a memorandum of the conviction or acquittal was sent;

and a document purporting to be a duly signed certificate of conviction or acquittal under this section shall be taken to be such a certificate unless the contrary is proved.

(3) In subsection (2) above 'proper officer' means:

(a) in relation to a magistrates' court in England and Wales, the designated officer for the court; and

(b) in relation to any other court, the clerk of a court, his deputy and to any other person having the custody of the court record.

(4) The method of proving a conviction or acquittal authorised by this section shall be in addition to and not to the exclusion of any other authorised manner of proving a conviction or acquittal.

74 Conviction as evidence of commission of offence

(1) In any proceedings the fact that a person other than the accused has been convicted of an offence by or before any court in the United Kingdom or by a Service court outside the United Kingdom shall be admissible in evidence for the purpose of proving, where to do so is relevant to any issue in those proceedings, that that person committed that offence, whether or not any other evidence of his having committed that offence is given.

(2) In any proceedings in which by virtue of this section a person other than the accused is proved to have been convicted of an offence by or before any court in the United Kingdom or by a Service court outside the United Kingdom, he shall be taken to have committed that offence unless the contrary is proved.

(3) In any proceedings where evidence is admissible of that fact that the accused has committed an offence, if the accused is proved to have been convicted of the offence—

(a) by or before any court in the United Kingdom; or

(b) by a Service court outside the United Kingdom,

he shall be taken to have committed that offence unless the contrary is proved.

(4) Nothing in this section shall prejudice—

    (a) the admissibility in evidence of any conviction which would be admissible apart from this section; or

    (b) the operation of any enactment whereby a conviction or a finding of fact in any proceedings is for the purposes of any other proceedings made conclusive evidence of any fact.

75 Provisions supplementary to section 74

(1) Where evidence that a person has been convicted of an offence is admissible by virtue of section 74 above, then without prejudice to the reception of any other admissible evidence for the purpose of identifying the facts on which the conviction was based—

    (a) the contents of any document which is admissible as evidence of the conviction; and

    (b) the contents of the information, complaint, indictment or charge-sheet on which the person in question was convicted,

shall be admissible in evidence for that purpose.

(2) Where in any proceedings the contents of any document are admissible in evidence by virtue of subsection (1) above, a copy of that document, or of the material part of it, purporting to be certified or otherwise authenticated by or on behalf of the court or authority having custody of that document shall be admissible in evidence and shall be taken to be a true copy of that document or part unless the contrary is shown.

(3) Nothing in any of the following—

    (a) section 14 of the Powers of Criminal Courts (Sentencing) Act 2000 (under which a conviction leading to probation or discharge is to be disregarded except as mentioned in that section);

    (b) section 247 of the Criminal Procedure (Scotland) Act 1995 (which makes similar provision in respect of convictions on indictment in Scotland); and

    (c) section 8 of the Probation Act (Northern Ireland) 1950 (which corresponds to section 13 of the Powers of Criminal Courts Act 1973) or any legislation which is in force in Northern Ireland for the time being and corresponds to that section,

shall affect the operation of section 74 above; and for the purposes of that section any order made by a court of summary jurisdiction in Scotland under section 228 or section 246(3) of the said Act of 1995 shall be treated as a conviction.

(4) Nothing in section 74 above shall be construed as rendering admissible in any proceedings evidence of any conviction other than a subsisting one.

Confessions

76 Confessions

(1) In any proceedings a confession made by an accused person may be given in evidence against him in so far as it is relevant to any matter in issue in the proceedings and is not excluded by the court in pursuance of this section.

(2) If, in any proceedings where the prosecution proposes to give in evidence a confession made by an accused person, it is represented to the court that the confession was or may have been obtained—

    (a) by oppression of the person who made it; or

    (b) in consequence of anything said or done which was likely, in the circumstances existing at the time, to render unreliable any confession which might be made by him in consequence thereof,

the court shall not allow the confession to be given in evidence against him except in so far as the prosecution proves to the court beyond reasonable doubt that the confession (notwithstanding that it may be true) was not obtained as aforesaid.

(3) In any proceedings where the prosecution proposes to give in evidence a confession made by an accused person, the court may of its own motion require the prosecution, as a condition of allowing it to do so, to prove that the confession was not obtained as mentioned in subsection (2) above.

(4) The fact that a confession is wholly or partly excluded in pursuance of this section shall not affect the admissibility in evidence—

(a) of any facts discovered as a result of the confession; or

(b) where the confession is relevant as showing that the accused speaks, writes or expresses himself in a particular way, of so much of the confession as is necessary to show that he does so.

(5) Evidence that a fact to which this subsection applies was discovered as a result of a statement made by an accused person shall not be admissible unless evidence of how it was discovered is given by him or on his behalf.

(6) Subsection (5) above applies—

(a) to any fact discovered as a result of a confession which is wholly excluded in pursuance of this section; and

(b) to any fact discovered as a result of a confession which is partly so excluded, if the fact is discovered as a result of the excluded part of the confession.

(7) Nothing in Part VII of this Act shall prejudice the admissibility of a confession made by an accused person.

(8) In this section 'oppression' includes torture, inhuman or degrading treatment, and the use or threat of violence (whether or not amounting to torture).

'76A Confessions may be given in evidence for co-accused

(1) In any proceedings a confession made by an accused person may be given in evidence for another person charged in the same proceedings (a co-accused) in so far as it is relevant to any matter in issue in the proceedings and is not excluded by the court in pursuance of this section.

(2) If, in any proceedings where a co-accused proposes to give in evidence a confession made by an accused person, it is represented to the court that the confession was or may have been obtained—

(a) by oppression of the person who made it; or

(b) in consequence of anything said or done which was likely, in the circumstances existing at the time, to render unreliable any confession which might be made by him in consequence thereof,

the court shall not allow the confession to be given in evidence for the co-accused except in so far as it is proved to the court on the balance of probabilities that the confession (notwithstanding that it may be true) was not so obtained.

(3) Before allowing a confession made by an accused person to be given in evidence for a co-accused in any proceedings, the court may of its own motion require the fact that the confession was not obtained as mentioned in subsection (2) above to be proved in the proceedings on the balance of probabilities.

(4) The fact that a confession is wholly or partly excluded in pursuance of this section shall not affect the admissibility in evidence—

(a) of any facts discovered as a result of the confession; or

(b) where the confession is relevant as showing that the accused speaks, writes or expresses himself in a particular way, of so much of the confession as is necessary to show that he does so.

(5) Evidence that a fact to which this subsection applies was discovered as a result of a statement made by an accused person shall not be admissible unless evidence of how it was discovered is given by him or on his behalf.

(6) Subsection (5) above applies—

(a) to any fact discovered as a result of a confession which is wholly excluded in pursuance of this section; and

(b) to any fact discovered as a result of a confession which is partly so excluded, if the fact is discovered as a result of the excluded part of the confession.

(7) In this section 'oppression' includes torture, inhuman or degrading treatment, and the use or threat of violence (whether or not amounting to torture)."

77 Confessions by mentally handicapped persons

(1) Without prejudice to the general duty of the court at a trial on indictment with a jury to direct the jury on any matter on which it appears to the court appropriate to do so, where at such a trial—

(a) the case against the accused depends wholly or substantially on a confession by him; and

(b) the court is satisfied—

(i) that he is mentally handicapped; and

(ii) that the confession was not made in the presence of an independent person, the court shall warn the jury that there is special need for caution before convicting the accused in reliance on the confession, and shall explain that the need arises because of the circumstances mentioned in paragraphs (a) and (b) above.

(2) In any case where at the summary trial of a person for an offence it appears to the court that a warning under subsection (1) above would be required if the trial were on indictment with a jury, the court shall treat the case as one in which there is a special need for caution before convicting the accused on his confession.

(2A) In any case where at the trial on indictment without a jury of a person for an offence it appears to the court that a warning under subsection (1) above would be required if the trial were with a jury, the court shall treat the case as one in which there is a special need for caution before convicting the accused on his confession.

(3) In this section—

'independent person' does not include a police officer or a person employed for, or engaged on, police purposes;

'mentally handicapped', in relation to a person, means that he is in a state of arrested or incomplete development of mind which includes significant impairment of intelligence and social functioning; and

'police purposes' has the meaning assigned to it by section 101(2) of the Police Act 1996.

78 Exclusion of unfair evidence

(1) In any proceedings the court may refuse to allow evidence on which the prosecution proposes to rely to be given if it appears to the court that, having regard to all the circumstances, including the circumstances in which the evidence was obtained, the admission of the evidence would have such an adverse effect on the fairness of the proceedings that the court ought not to admit it.

(2) Nothing in this section shall prejudice any rule of law requiring a court to exclude evidence.

79 Time for taking accused's evidence

If at the trial of any person for an offence—

(a) the defence intends to call two or more witnesses to the facts of the case; and

(b) those witnesses include the accused,

the accused shall be called before the other witness or witnesses unless the court in its discretion otherwise directs.

80 Competence and compellability of accused's spouse

(2) In any proceedings the wife or husband of a person charged in the proceedings shall, subject to subsection (4) below, be compellable to give evidence on behalf of that person.

(2A) In any proceedings the wife or husband of a person charged in the proceedings shall, subject to subsection (4) below, be compellable—

(a) to give evidence on behalf of any other person charged in the proceedings but only in respect of any specified offence with which that other person is charged; or

(b) to give evidence for the prosecution but only in respect of any specified offence with which any person is charged in the proceedings.

(3) In relation to the wife or husband of a person charged in any proceedings, an offence is a specified offence for the purposes of subsection (2A) above if—

(a) it involves an assault on, or injury or a threat of injury to, the wife or husband or a person who was at the material time under the age of 16;

(b) it is a sexual offence alleged to have been committed in respect of a person who was at the material time under that age; or

(c) it consists of attempting or conspiring to commit, or of aiding, abetting, counselling, procuring or inciting the commission of, an offence falling within paragraph (a) or (b) above.

(4) No person who is charged in any proceedings shall be compellable by virtue of subsection (2) or (2A) above to give evidence in the proceedings.

(4A) References in this section to a person charged in any proceedings do not include a person who is not, or is no longer, liable to be convicted of any offence in the proceedings (whether as a result of pleading guilty or for any other reason).

(5) In any proceedings a person who has been but is no longer married to the accused shall be compellable to give evidence as if that person and the accused had never been married.

(6) Where in any proceedings the age of any person at any time is material for the purposes of subsection (3) above, his age at the material time shall for the purposes of that provision be deemed to be or to have been that which appears to the court to be or to have been his age at that time.

(7) In subsection (3)(b) above 'sexual offence' means an offence under the Protection of Children Act 1978 or Part I of the Sexual Offences Act 2003.

(9) Section 1(d) of the Criminal Evidence Act 1898 (communications between husband and wife) and section 43(1) of the Matrimonial Causes Act 1965 (evidence as to marital intercourse) shall cease to have effect.

80A The failure of the wife or husband of a person charged in any proceedings to give evidence shall not be made the subject of any comment by the prosecution.

81 Advance notice of expert evidence in crown court

(1) Criminal Procedure Rules may make provision for—

(a) requiring any party to proceedings before the Court to disclose to the other party or parties any expert evidence which he proposes to adduce in the proceedings; and

(b) prohibiting a party who fails to comply in respect of any evidence with any requirement imposed by virtue of paragraph (a) above from adducing that evidence without the leave of the court.

(2) Criminal Procedure Rules made by virtue of this section may specify the kinds of expert evidence to which they apply and may exempt facts or matters of any description specified in the rules.

PART VIII   SUPPLEMENTARY

82 Part VIII—interpretation

(1) In this Part of this Act—

'confession' includes any statement wholly or partly adverse to the person who made it, whether made to a person in authority or not and whether made in words or otherwise;

'court-martial' means a court-martial constituted under the Army Act 1955, the Air Force Act 1955 or the Naval Discipline Act 1957;

'proceedings' means criminal proceedings, including—

    (a) proceedings in the United Kingdom or elsewhere before a court-martial;

    (b) proceedings in the United Kingdom or elsewhere before the Courts-Martial (Appeals) Court—

        (i) on an appeal from a court-martial; or

        (ii) on a reference under section 34 of the Courts-Martial (Appeals) Act 1968; and

    (c) proceedings before a Standing Civilian Court; and

'Service court' means a court-martial or a Standing Civilian Court.

(2) In this Part of this Act references to conviction before a Service court are references—

    (a) as regards a court-martial constituted under the Army Act 1955 or the Air Force Act 1955, to a finding of guilty which is, or falls to be treated as, a finding of the court duly confirmed;

    (b) as regards—

        (i) a court-martial; or

        (ii) a disciplinary court;

constituted under the Naval Discipline Act 1957, to a finding of guilty which is, or falls to be treated as, the finding of the court;

and 'convicted' shall be construed accordingly.

(3) Nothing in this Part of this Act shall prejudice any power of a court to exclude evidence (whether by preventing questions from being put or otherwise) at its discretion.

PART X   POLICE—GENERAL

107   Police officers performing duties of higher rank

(1) For the purpose of any provision of this Act or any other Act under which a power in respect of the investigation of offences or the treatment of persons in police custody is exercisable only by or with the authority of a police officer of at least the rank of superintendent, an officer of the rank of chief inspector shall be treated as holding the rank of superintendent if—

    (a) he has been authorised by an officer holding a rank above the rank of superintendent to exercise the power or, as the case may be, to give his authority for its exercise, or

    (b) he is acting during the absence of an officer holding the rank of superintendent who has authorised him, for the duration of that absence, to exercise the power, or as the case may be, to give his authority for its exercise.

(2) For the purpose of any provision of this Act or any other Act under which such a power is exercisable only by or with the authority of an officer of at least the rank of inspector, an officer of the rank of sergeant shall be treated as holding the rank of inspector if he has been authorised by an officer of at least the rank of superintendent to exercise the power or, as the case may be, to give this authority for its exercise.

108   Deputy chief constables

(6) In section 23(2) of the Police (Scotland) Act 1967 (under which a chief constable affected by an amalgamation holds the rank of assistant chief constable) for the word 'assistant' there shall be substituted the word 'deputy'.

110   Functions of special constables in Scotland

Subsection (6) of section 17 of the Police (Scotland) Act 1967 (restriction on functions of special constables) is hereby repealed.

111   Regulations for Police Forces and Police Cadets—Scotland

(1) In section 26 to the Police (Scotland) Act 1967 (regulations as to government and administration of police forces)—

    (a) after subsection (1) there shall be inserted the following subsection—

        '(1A) Regulations under this section may authorise the Secretary of State, the police authority or the chief constable to make provision for any purpose specified in the regulations.'; and

    (b) at the end there shall be inserted the following subsection—

        '(10) Any statutory instrument made under this section shall be subject to annulment in pursuance of a resolution of either House of Parliament'.

(2) In section 27 of the said Act of 1967 (regulations for police cadets) in subsection (3) for the word '(9)' there shall be substituted the words '(1A), (9) and (10)'.

PART XI   MISCELLANEOUS AND SUPPLEMENTARY

113   Application of Act to Armed Forces

(1) The Secretary of State may by order direct that any provision of Part II of this Act (or Part II of this Act so far as relating to that Part) which relates to the investigations of offences conducted by police officers or to persons detained by the police shall apply, subject to such modifications as he may specify, to investigations of offences conducted under the Army Act 1955, the Air Force Act 1955 or the Naval Discipline Act 1957 or to persons under arrest under any of those Acts.

(2) Section 67(9) above shall not have effect in relation to investigations of offences conducted under the Army Act 1955, the Air Force Act 1955 or the Naval Discipline Act 1957.

(3) The Secretary of State shall issue a code of practice or a number of such codes, for persons other than police officers who are concerned with—

    (a) the exercise of powers conferred by Part 2 of the Armed Force Act 2001, or

    (b) enquiries into offences under the Army Act 1955, the Air Force Act 1955 or the Naval Discipline Act 1957.

(3A) In subsections (4) to (10), "code" means a code of practice under subsection (3).

(4) Without prejudice to the generality of subsection (3) above, a code may contain provisions, in connection with the power mentioned in subsection (3)(a) above or the enquiries mentioned in subsection (3)(b) above, as to the following matters—

    (a) the tape-recording of interviews;

    (b) searches of persons and premises; and

    (c) the seizure of things found on searches.

(5) The Secretary of State may at any time revise the whole or any part of a code.

(6) A code may be made, or revised, so as to—

    (a) apply only in relation to one or more specified areas,

    (b) have effect only for a specified period,

    (c) apply only in relation to specified offences or descriptions of offender.

(7) The Secretary of State must lay a code, or any revision of a code, before Parliament.

(8) A failure on the part of any person to comply with any provision of a code shall not of itself render him liable to any criminal or civil proceedings except those to which this subsection applies.

(9) Subsection (8) above applies—

    (a) to proceedings under any provision of the Army Act 1955 or the Air Force Act 1955 other than section 70; and

    (b) to proceedings under any provision of the Naval Discipline Act 1957 other than section 42.

(10) In all criminal and civil proceedings any code shall be admissible in evidence and

if any provision of a code appears to the court or tribunal conducting the proceedings to be relevant to any question arising in the proceedings it shall be taken into account in determining that question.

(11) In subsection (10) above 'criminal proceedings' includes—

(a) proceedings in the United Kingdom or elsewhere before a court-martial constituted under the Army Act 1955, the Air Force Act 1955 or the Naval Discipline Act 1957;

(b) proceedings before the Courts-Martial Appeal Court; and

(c) proceedings before a Standing Civilian Court.

(12) Parts VII and VIII of this Act have effect for the purposes of proceedings—

(a) before a court-martial constituted under the Army Act 1955 or the Air Force Act 1955;

(b) before a Courts-Martial Appeal Court; and

(c) before a Standing Civilian Court,

subject to any modifications which the Secretary of State may by order specify.

(13) An order under this section shall be made by statutory instrument and shall be subject to annulment in pursuance of a resolution of either House of Parliament.

114 Application of Act to Customs and Excise

(1) 'Arrested', 'arresting', 'arrest' and 'to arrest' shall respectively be substituted for 'detained', 'detaining', 'detention' and 'to detain' wherever in the customs and excise Acts, as defined in section 1(1) of the Customs and Excise Management Act 1979, those words are used in relation to persons.

(2) The Treasury may by order direct—

(a) that any provision of this Act which relates to investigations of offences conducted by police officers or to persons detained by the police shall apply, subject to such modifications as the order may specify, to investigations conducted by officers of Customs and Excise of offences which relate to assigned matters, as defined in section 1 of the Customs and Excise Management Act 1979, or to persons detained by officers of Customs and Excise; and

(b) that, in relation to investigations of offences conducted by officers of Customs and Excise—

(i) this Act shall have effect as if the following section were inserted after section 14—

'**14A Exception for Customs and Excise**

Material in the possession of a person who acquired or created it in the course of any trade, business, profession or other occupation or for the purpose of any paid or unpaid office and which relates to an assigned matter, as defined in section 1 of the Customs and Excise Management Act 1979, is neither excluded material nor special procedure material for the purposes of any enactment such as is mentioned in section 9(2) above.'; and

(ii) section 55 above shall have effect as if it related only to things such as are mentioned in subsection (1)(a) of that section; and

(c) that in relation to customs detention (as defined in any order made under this subsection) the Bail Act 1976 shall have effect as if references in it to a constable were references to an officer of Customs and Excise of such grade as may be specified in the order.

(3) Nothing in any order under subsection (2) above shall be taken to limit any powers exercisable under section 164 of the Customs and Excise Management Act 1979.

(4) In this section 'officers of Customs and Excise' means officers commissioned by the Commissioners of Customs and Excise under section 6(3) of the Customs and Excise Management Act 1979.

(5) An order under this section shall be made by statutory instrument and shall be subject to annulment in pursuance of a resolution of either House of Parliament.

114A   Power to apply Act to officers of the Secretary of State etc.
(1) The Secretary of State may by order direct that—
  (a) the provisions of Schedule 1 to this Act so far as they relate to special procedure material, and
  (b) the other provisions of this Act so far as they relate to the provisions falling within paragraph (a) above,
shall apply, with such modifications as may be specified in the order, for the purposes of investigations falling within subsection (2) as they apply for the purposes of investigations of offences conducted by police officers.
(2) An investigation falls within this subsection if—
  (a) it is conducted by an officer of the department of the Secretary of State for Trade and Industry or by another person acting on that Secretary of State's behalf;
  (b) it is conducted by that officer or other person in the discharge of a duty to investigate offences; and
  (c) the investigations relates to a serious arrestable offence or to anything which there are reasonable grounds for suspecting has involved the commission of a serious arrestable offence.
(3) The investigations for the purposes of which provisions of this Act may be applied with modifications by an order under this section include investigations of offences committed, or suspected of having been committed, before the coming into force of the order or of this section.
(4) An order under this section shall be made by statutory instrument and shall be subject to annulment in pursuance of a resolution of either House of Parliament.

115   Expenses
Any expenses of a Minister of the Crown incurred in consequence of the provisions of this Act, including any increase attributable to those provisions in sums payable under any other Act, shall be defrayed out of money provided by Parliament.

116   Meaning of 'serious arrestable offence'
(1) This section has effect for determining whether an offence is a serious arrestable offence for the purposes of this Act.
(2) The following arrestable offences are always serious—
  (a) an offence (whether at common law or under any enactment) specified in Part I of Schedule 5 to this Act; and
  (b) an offence under an enactment specified in Part II of that Schedule;
  '(c) any offence which is specified in paragraph 1 of Schedule 2 to the Proceeds of Crime Act 2002 (drug trafficking offences);
  (d) any offence under section 327, 328 or 329 of that Act (certain money laundering offences).'
(3) Subject to subsection (4) below, any other arrestable offence is serious only if its commission—
  (a) has led to any of the consequences specified in subsection (6) below; or
  (b) is intended or is likely to lead to any of those consequences.
(4) An arrestable offence which consists of making a threat is serious if carrying out the threat would be likely to lead to any of the consequences specified in subsection (6) below.
(6) The consequences mentioned in subsections (3) and (4) above are
  (a) serious harm to the security of the State or to public order;
  (b) serious interference with the administration of justice or with the investigation of offences or of a particular offence;

    (c) the death of any person;

    (d) serious injury to any person;

    (e) substantial financial gain to any person; and

    (f) serious financial loss to any person.

(7) Loss is serious for the purposes of this section, if having regard to all the circumstances, it is serious for the person who suffers it.

(8) In this section 'injury' includes any disease and any impairment of a person's physical or mental condition.

117 Power of constable to use reasonable force

Where any provision of this Act—

    (a) confers a power on a constable; and

    (b) does not provide that the power may only be exercised with the consent of some person, other than a police officer,

the officer may use reasonable force, if necessary, in the exercise of the power.

118 General interpretation

(1) In this Act—

'arrestable offence' has the meaning assigned to it by section 24 above;

'British Transport Police' means the constables appointed under section 53 of the British Transport Commission Act 1949;

'designated police station' has the meaning assigned to it by section 35 above;

'document' means anything in which information of any description is recorded;

'item subject to legal privilege' has the meaning assigned to it by section 10 above;

'parent or guardian' means—

    (a) in the case of a child or young person in the care of a local authority, that authority;

'premises' has the meaning assigned to it by section 23 above;

'recordable offence' means any offence to which regulations under section 23 above apply;

'vessel' includes any ship, boat, raft or other apparatus constructed or adapted for floating on water.

(2) Subject to subsection (2A) a person is in police detention for the purposes of this Act if—

    (a) he has been taken to a police station after being arrested for an offence or after being arrested under section 41 of the Terrorism Act 2000;

    (b) he is arrested at a police station after attending voluntarily at the station or accompanying a constable to it,

and is detained there or is detained elsewhere in the charge of a constable, except that a person who is at a court after being charged is not in police detention for those purposes.

'(2A) Where a person is in another's lawful custody by virtue of paragraph 22, 34(1) or 35(3) of Schedule 4 to the Police Reform Act 2002, he shall be treated as in police detention.'

119 Amendments and repeals

(1) The enactments mentioned in Schedule 6 to this Act shall have effect with the amendments there specified.

(2) The enactments mentioned in Schedule 7 to this Act (which include enactments already obsolete or unnecessary) are repealed to the extent specified in the third column of that Schedule.

(3) The repeals in Parts II and IV of Schedule 7 to this Act have effect only in relation to criminal proceedings.

120 Extent

(1) Subject to the following provisions of this section, this Act extends to England and Wales only.

(2) The following extend to Scotland only—

section 108(4) and (5);

section 110;

section 111;

section 112(1); and

section 119(2), so far as it relates to the provisions of the Pedlars Act 1871 repealed by Part VI of Schedule 7.

(3) The following extend to Northern Ireland only—

section 6(4), and

section 112(2).

(4) The following extend to England and Wales and Scotland—

section 6(1) and (2);

section 7;

section 83(2), so far as it relates to paragraph 8 of Schedule 4;

section 108(1) and (6);

section 109; and

section 119(2), so far as it relates to section 19 of the Pedlars Act 1871.

(5) The following extend to England and Wales, Scotland and Northern Ireland—

section 6(3);

section 9(2A);

section 83(2), so far as it relates to paragraph 7(1) of Schedule 4; and

section 114(1).

(6) So far as they relate to proceedings before courts-martial and Standing Civilian Courts, the relevant provisions extend to any place at which such proceedings may be held.

(7) So far as they relate to proceedings before the Courts-Martial Appeal Court, the relevant provisions extend to any place at which such proceedings may be held.

(8) In this section 'the relevant provisions' means—

    (a) subsection (11) of section 67 above;

    (b) subsection (12) of that section as far as it relates to subsection (11);

    (c) Parts VII and VIII of this Act, except paragraph 10 of Schedule 3;

    (d) subsections (2) and (8) to (12) of section 113 above; and

    (e) subsection (13) of that section, so far as it relates to an order under subsection (12).

(9) Except as provided by the foregoing provisions of this section, section 113 above extends to any place to which the Army Act 1955, the Air Force Act 1955 or the Naval Discipline Act 1957 extends.

(9A) Section 119(1), so far as it relates to any provision amended by Part II of Schedule 6, extends to any place to which that provision extends.

(11) Section 119(2), so far as it relates—

    (a) to any provision contained in—

the Army Act 1955;

the Air Force Act 1955;

the Armed Forces Act 1981; or

the Value Added Tax Act 1983;

    (b) to any provision mentioned in Part VI of Schedule 7, other than section 18 of the Pedlars Act 1871,

extends to any place to which that provision extends.

(12) So far as any of the following—

section 115;

in section 118, the definition of 'document';

this section;

section 121; and

section 122,

has effect in relation to any other provision of this Act, it extends to any place to which that provision extends.

121 Commencement

(1) This Act, except section 120 above, this section and section 122 below, shall come into operation on such day as the Secretary of State may by order made by statutory instrument appoint, and different days may be so appointed for different provisions and for different purposes.

(2) Different days may be appointed under this section for the coming force of section 60 above in different areas.

(3) When an order under this section provides by virtue of subsection (2) above that section 60 above shall come into force in an area specified in the order, the duty imposed on the Secretary of State by that section shall be construed as a duty to make an order under it in relation to interviews in that area.

(4) An order under this section may make such transitional provision as appears to the Secretary of State to be necessary or expedient in connection with the provisions thereby brought into operation.

122 Short title

This Act may be cited as the Police and Criminal Evidence Act 1984.

SCHEDULES

(Section 9)   SCHEDULE 1   SPECIAL PROCEDURE

Making of orders by circuit judge

1. If on an application made by a constable a circuit judge is satisfied that one or other of the sets of access conditions is fulfilled, he may make an order under paragraph 4 below.

2. The first set of access conditions is fulfilled if—
  - (a) there are reasonable grounds for believing—
    - (i)   that a serious arrestable offence has been committed;
    - (ii) that there is material which consists of special procedure material or includes special procedure material and does not also include excluded material on premises specified in the application;
    - (iii) that the material is likely to be of substantial value (whether by itself or together with other material) to the investigation in connection with which the application is made; and
    - (iv) that the material is likely to be relevant evidence;
  - (b) other methods of obtaining the material—
    - (i)   have been tried without success; or
    - (ii) have not been tried because it appeared that they were bound to fail; and
  - (c) it is in the public interest, having regard—
    - (i)   to the benefit likely to accrue to the investigation if the material is obtained; and
    - (ii) to the circumstances under which the person in possession of the material holds it.

that the material should be produced or that access to it should be given.

3. The second set of access conditions is fulfilled if—
  - (a) there are reasonable grounds for believing that there is material which consists of or includes excluded material or special procedure material on premises specified in the application;

(b) but for section 9(2) above a search of the premises for that material could have been authorised by the issue of a warrant to a constable under an enactment other than this Schedule; and

(c) the issue of such a warrant would have been appropriate.

4.   An order under this paragraph is an order that the person who appears to the circuit judge to be in possession of the material to which the application relates shall—

(a) produce it to a constable for him to take away; or

(b) give a constable access to it,

not later than the end of the period of seven days from the date of the order or the end of such longer period as the order may specify.

5.   Where the material consists of information stored in any electronic form

(a) an order under paragraph 4(a) above shall have effect as an order to produce the material in a form in which it can be taken away and in which it is visible and legible or from which it can readily be produced in a visible and legible form, and

(b) an order under paragraph 4(b) above shall have effect as an order to give a constable access to the material in a form in which it is visible and legible.

6.   For the purposes of sections 21 and 22 above material produced in pursuance of an order under paragraph 4(a) above shall be treated as if it were material seized by a constable.

Notices of applications for orders

7.   An application for an order under paragraph 4 above shall be made inter partes.

8.   Notice of an application for such an order may be served on a person either by delivering it to him or by leaving it at his proper address or by sending it by post to him in a registered letter or by the recorded delivery service.

9.   Such a notice may be served—

(a) on a body corporate, by serving it on the body's secretary or clerk or other similar officer; and

(b) on a partnership, by serving it on one of the partners.

10.   For the purposes of this Schedule, and of section 7 of the Interpretation Act 1978 in its application to this Schedule, the proper address of a person, in the case of secretary or clerk or other similar officer of a body corporate, shall be that of the registered or principal office of that body, in the case of a partner of a firm shall be that of the principal office of the firm, and in any other case shall be the last known address of the person to be served.

11.   Where notice of an application for an order under paragraph 4 above has been served on a person, he shall not conceal, destroy, alter or dispose of the material to which the application relates except—

(a) with the leave of a judge; or

(b) with the written permission of a constable,

until—

(i) the application is dismissed or abandoned; or

(ii) he has complied with an order under paragraph 4 above made on the application.

Issue of warrants by circuit judge

12.   If on an application made by a constable a circuit judge—

(a) is satisfied—

(i) that either set of access conditions is fulfilled; and

(ii) that any of the further conditions set out in paragraph 14 below is also fulfilled; or

(b) is satisfied—
    (i) that the second set of access conditions is fulfilled; and
    (ii) that an order under paragraph 4 above relating to the material has not been complied with,

he may issue a warrant authorising a constable to enter and search the premises.

13. A constable may seize and retain anything for which a search has been authorised under paragraph 12 above.

14. The further conditions mentioned in paragraph 12(a)(ii) above are—
(a) that it is not practicable to communicate with any person entitled to grant entry to the premises to which the application relates;
(b) that it is practicable to communicate with a person entitled to grant entry to the premises but it is not practicable to communicate with any person entitled to grant access to the material;
(c) that the material contains information which—
    (i) is subject to a restriction or obligation such as is mentioned in section 11(2)(b) above; and
    (ii) is likely to be disclosed in breach of it if a warrant is not issued;
(d) that service of notice of an application for an order under paragraph 4 above may seriously prejudice the investigation.

15.—(1) If a person fails to comply with an order under paragraph 4 above, a circuit judge may deal with him as if he had committed a contempt of the Crown Court.

(2) Any enactment relating to contempt of the Crown Court shall have effect in relation to such a failure as if it were such a contempt.

Costs

16. The costs of any application under this Schedule and of anything done or to be done in pursuance of an order made under it shall be in the discretion of the judge.

(Section 26) **'SCHEDULE 1A   SPECIFIC OFFENCES WHICH ARE ARRESTABLE OFFENCES**

Customs and Excise Acts
1. An offence for which a person may be arrested under the customs and excise Acts (within the meaning of the Customs and Excise Management Act 1979 (c. 2)).

Official Secrets Act 1920
2. An offence under the Official Secrets Act 1920 (c. 75) which is not an arrestable offence by virtue of the term of imprisonment for which a person may be sentenced in respect of them.

Criminal Justice Act 1925
2ZA. An offence under section 36 of the Criminal Justice Act 1925 (untrue statement for procuring a passport)

Prevention of Crime Act 1953
3. An offence under section 1(1) of the Prevention of Crime Act 1953 (c. 14) (prohibition of carrying offensive weapons without lawful authority or excuse).

Obscene Publications Act 1959
5. An offence under section 2 of the Obscene Publications Act 1959 (c. 66) (publication of obscene matter).

Theft Act 1968
>   6.   An offence under—
>>   (a) section 12(1) of the Theft Act 1968 (c. 60) (taking motor vehicle or other conveyance without authority etc.); or
>>   (b) section 25(1) of that Act (going equipped for stealing etc.)

Misuse of Drugs Act 1971
>   6A.   An offence under section 5(2) of the Misuse of Drugs Act 1971 (having possession of a controlled drug) in respect of cannabis or cannabis resin (within the meaning of that Act).

Theft Act 1978
>   7.   An offence under section 3 of the Theft Act 1978 (c. 31) (making off without payment).

Protection of Children Act 1978
>   8.   An offence under section 1 of the Protection of Children Act 1978 (c. 37) (indecent photographs and pseudo-photographs of children).

Wildlife and Countryside Act 1981
>   9.   An offence under section 1(1) or (2) or 6 of the Wildlife and Countryside Act 1981 (c. 69) (taking, possessing, selling etc. of wild birds) in respect of a bird included in Schedule 1 to that Act or any part of, or anything derived from, such a bird.
>   10.   An offence under—
>>   (a) section 1(5) of the Wildlife and Countryside Act 1981 (disturbance of wild birds);
>>   (b) section 9 or 13(1)(a) or (2) of that Act (taking, possessing, selling etc. of wild animals or plants); or
>>   (c) section 14 of that Act (introduction of new species etc.).

Civil Aviation Act 1982
>   11.   An offence under section 39(1) of the Civil Aviation Act 1982 (c. 16) (trespass on aerodrome).
>   11A.   An offence of contravening a provision of an Order in Council under section 60 of that Act (air navigation order) where the offence relates to:
>>   (a) a provision which prohibits specified behaviour by a person in an aircraft towards or in relation to a member of the crew, or
>>   (b) a provision which prohibits a person from being drunk in an aircraft, in so far as it applies to passengers.'

Aviation Security Act 1982
>   12.   An offence under section 21C(1) or 21D(1) of the Aviation Security Act 1982 (c. 36) (unauthorised presence in a restricted zone or on an aircraft).

Sexual Offences Act 1985
>   13.   An offence under section 1 of the Sexual Offences Act 1985 (c. 44) (kerb-crawling).

Public Order Act 1986
>   14.   An offence under section 19 of the Public Order Act 1986 (c. 64) (publishing etc. material likely to stir up racial or religious hatred).

Criminal Justice Act 1988
>   15.   An offence under—

(a) section 139(1) of the Criminal Justice Act 1988 (c. 33) (offence of having article with a blade or point in public place); or

(b) section 139A(1) or (2) of that Act (offence of having article with a blade or point or offensive weapon on school premises).

Road Traffic Act 1988

16.   An offence under section 103(1)(b) of the Road Traffic Act 1988 (c. 52) (driving while disqualified).

17.   An offence under subsection (4) of section 170 of the Road Traffic Act 1988 (failure to stop and report an accident) in respect of an accident to which that section applies by virtue of subsection (1)(a) of that section (accidents causing personal injury).

17A.   An offence under section 174 of the Road Traffic Act 1988 (false statements and withholding material information).

Official Secrets Act 1989

18.   An offence under any provision of the Official Secrets Act 1989 (c. 6) other than subsection (1), (4) or (5) of section 8 of that Act.

Football Spectators Act 1989

19.   An offence under section 14J or 21C of the Football Spectators Act 1989 (c. 37) (failing to comply with requirements imposed by or under a banning order or a notice under section 21B).

Football (Offences) Act 1991

20.   An offence under any provision of the Football (Offences) Act 1991 (c. 19).

Criminal Justice and Public Order Act 1994

21.   An offence under—

(a) section 60AA(7) of the Criminal Justice and Public Order Act 1994 (c. 33) (failing to comply with requirement to remove disguise);

(b) section 166 of that Act (sale of tickets by unauthorised persons); or

(c) section 167 of that Act (touting for car hire services).

Police Act 1996

22.   An offence under section 89(1) of the Police Act 1996 (c. 16) (assaulting a police officer in the execution of his duty or a person assisting such an officer).

Protection from Harassment Act 1997

23.   An offence under section 2 of the Protection from Harassment Act 1997 (c. 40) (harassment).

Crime and Disorder Act 1998

24.   An offence falling within section 32(1)(a) of the Crime and Disorder Act 1998 (c. 37) (racially or religiously aggravated harassment).

Criminal Justice and Police Act 2001

25.   An offence under—

(a) section 12(4) of the Criminal Justice and Police Act 2001 (c. 16) (failure to comply with requirements imposed by constable in relation to consumption of alcohol in public place); or

(b) section 46 of that Act (placing of advertisements in relation to prostitution).'

(Section 26) SCHEDULE 2   PRESERVED POWERS OF ARREST

1892 c.43.	Section 17(2) of the Military Lands Act 1892.
1911 c.27.	Section 12(1) of the Protection of Animals Act 1911.
1920 c.55.	Section 2 of the Emergency Powers Act 1920.
1936 c.6.	Section 7(3) of the Public Order Act 1936.
1952 c.52	Section 49 of the Prison Act 1952.
1952 c.67.	Section 13 of the Visiting Forces Act 1952.
1955 c.18.	Sections 186 and 190B of the Army Act 1955.
1955 c.19.	Sections 186 and 190B of the Air Force Act 1955.
1957 c.53.	Section 104 and 105 of the Naval Discipline Act 1957.
1959 c.37.	Section 1(3) of the Street Offences Act 1959.
1969 c.54.	Section 32 of the Children and Young Persons Act 1969.
1971 c.77.	Section 24(2) of the Immigration Act 1971 and paragraphs 17, 24 and 33 of Schedule 2 and paragraph 7 of Schedule 3 of that Act.
1976 c.63.	Section 7 of the Bail Act 1976.
1977 c.45.	Sections 6(6), 7(11), 8(4), 9(7) and 10(5) of the Criminal Law Act 1977.
1981 c.22.	Sections 60(5) and 61(1) of the Animal Health Act 1981.
1983 c.2.	Rule 36 in Schedule 1 to the Representation of the People Act 1983.
1983 c.20.	Sections 18, 35(10), 36(8), 38(7), 136(1) and 138 of the Mental Health Act 1983.
1984 c.47.	Section 5(5) of the Repatriation of Prisoners Act 1984.

Sexual Offences Act 2003
   27.   An offence under—
      (a)   section 66 of the Sexual Offences Act 2003 (exposure);
      (b)   section 67 of that Act (voyeurism);
      (c)   section 69 of that Act (intercourse with an animal);
      (d)   section 70 of that Act (sexual penetration of a corpse); or
      (e)   section 71 of that Act (sexual activity in public lavatory).

(Section 116)   SCHEDULE 5   SERIOUS ARRESTABLE OFFENCES

PART I   OFFENCES MENTIONED IN SECTION 116(2)(a)

   1.   Treason.
   2.   Murder.
   3.   Manslaughter.
   5.   Kidnapping.
   9.   An offence under section 170 of the Customs and Excise Management Act 1979 of being knowingly concerned, in relation to any goods, in the fraudulent evasion or attempt at evasion of a prohibition in force with respect to the goods under section 42 of the Customer Consolidation Act 1876 (prohibition on importing indecent or obscene articles).

PART II   OFFENCES MENTIONED IN SECTION 116(2)(b)

Explosive Substances Act 1883 (c. 3)
   1.   Section 2 (causing explosion likely to endanger life or property).

Firearms Act 1968 (c. 27)
 3.   Section 16 (possession of firearms with intent to injure).
 4.   Section 17(1) (use of firearms and imitation firearms to resist arrest).
 5.   Section 18 (carrying firearms with criminal intent).

Taking of Hostages Act 1982 (c. 28)
 7.   Section 1 (hostage-taking).

Aviation Security Act 1982 (c. 36)
 8.   Section 1 (hi-jacking).

[*Criminal Justice Act 1988 (c. 33)*
 9.   Section 134 (torture).]

[*Road Traffic Act 1988 (c. 52)*
 [10.]   Section 1 (causing death by [dangerous] driving).
          Section 3A (causing death by careless driving when under the influence of drink or drugs).]

[*Aviation and Maritime Security Act 1990 (c. 31)*
 11.   Section 1 (endangering safety at aerodromes).
 12.   Section 9 (hi-jacking of ships).
 13.   Section 10 (seizing or exercising control of fixed platforms).

[*Channel Tunnel (Security) Order 1994 No. 570*
 14.   Article 4 (hi-jacking of Channel Tunnel trains).
 15.   Article 5 (seizing or exercising control of the tunnel system).]

Protection of Children Act 1978 (c.37)
 16.   Section 1 (indecent photographs and pseudo-photographs of children).

Obscene Publications Act 1959 (c. 66)
 17.   Section 2 (publication of obscene matter).

Sexual Offences Act 2003
 18.   Section 1 (rape).
 19.   Section 2 (assault by penetration).
 20.   Section 4 (causing a person to engage in sexual activity without consent), where the activity caused involved penetration within subsection (4)(a) to (d) of that section.
 21.   Section 5 (rape of a child under 13).
 22.   Section 6 (assault of a child under 13 by penetration).
 23.   Section 8 (causing or inciting a child under 13 to engage in sexual activity), where an activity involving penetration within subsection (3)(a) to (d) of that section was caused.
 24.   Section 30 (sexual activity with a person with a mental disorder impeding choice), where the touching involved penetration within subsection (3)(a) to (d) of that section.
 25.   Section 31 (causing or inciting a person, with a mental disorder impeding choice, to engage in sexual activity), where an activity involving penetration within subsection (3)(a) to (d) of that section was caused.

(Section 119)   SCHEDULE 6   MINOR AND
                        CONSEQUENTAL AMENDMENTS

                    PART I   ENGLAND AND WALES

Game Act 1831 (c. 32)
 1.   The following section shall be inserted after section 31 of the Game Act 1831—

'31A Powers of constables in relation to trespassers

The powers conferred by section 31 above to require a person found on land as mentioned in that section to quit the land and to tell his christian name, surname, and place of abode shall also be exercisable by a police constable.'.

Metropolitan Police Act 1839 (c. 47)

2. In section 39 of the Metropolitan Police Act 1839 (fairs within the metropolitan police district) after the word 'amusement' there shall be inserted the words 'shall be guilty of an offence'.

Railway Regulation Act 1840 (c. 97)

3. In section 16 of the Railway Regulation Act 1840 (persons obstructing officers of railway company or trespassing upon railway) for the words from 'and' in the third place where it occurs to 'justice,' in the third place where it occurs there shall be substituted the words ',upon conviction by a magistrates' court, at the discretion of the court,'.

London Hackney carriages Act 1843 (c. 86)

4. In section 27 of the London Hackney Carriages Act 1843 (no person to act as driver of carriage without consent of proprietor) for the words after 'constable' there shall be substituted the words 'if necessary, to take charge of the carriage and every horse in charge of any person unlawfully acting as a driver or as a conductor and to deposit the same in some place of safe custody until the same can be applied for by the proprietor.'.

Town Gardens Protection Act 1863 (c. 13)

5. In section 5 of the Town Gardens Protection Act 1863 (penalty for injuring garden) for the words from the beginning to 'district' there shall be substituted the words 'Any person who throws any rubbish into any such garden, or trespasses therein, or gets over the railings or fence, or steals or damages the flowers or plants, or commits any nuisance therein, shall be guilty of an offence and'.

Parks Regulation Act 1872 (c. 15)

6. The following section shall be substituted for section 5 of the Parks Regulation Act 1872 (apprehension of offender whose name or residence is not known)—

'5. Any person who—
  (a) within the view of a park constable acts in contravention of any of the said regulations in the park where the park constable has jurisdiction; and
  (b) when required by any park constable or by any police constable to give his name and address gives a false name or false address.

shall be liable on summary conviction to a penalty of an amount not exceeding level I on the standard scale, as defined in section 75 of the Criminal Justice Act 1982.'.

Dogs (Protection of Livestock) Act 1953 (c. 28)

7. In the Dogs (Protection of Livestock) Act 1953 the following section shall be inserted after section 2—

'2A Power of justice of the peace to authorise entry and search

If on an application made by a constable a justice of the peace is satisfied that there are reasonable grounds for believing—
  (a) that an offence under this Act has been committed; and
  (b) that the dog in respect of which the offence has been committed is on premises specified in the application.

he may issue a warrant authorising a constable to enter and search the premises in order to identify the dog.

Army Act 1955 (c. 18)

Air Force Act 1955 (c. 19)

8.   The following subsection shall be substituted for section 195(3) of the Army Act 1955 and section 195(3) of the Air Force Act 1955—

'(3) A constable may seize any property which he has reasonable grounds for suspecting of having been the subject of an offence against this section.'.

Games Laws (Amendment) Act 1960 (c. 36)

10.   In subsection (1) of section 2 of the Game Laws (Amendment) Act 1960 (power of police to enter on land) for the words 'purpose of exercising any power conferred on him by the foregoing section' there shall be substituted the words

'purpose—
(a) of exercising in relation to him the powers under section 31 of the Game Act 1831 which section 31A of the Act confers on police constables; or
(b) of arresting him in accordance with section 25 of the Police and Criminal Evidence Act 1984.'.

11.   In subsection (1) of section 4 of that Act (enforcement powers) for the words from 'under', in the first place where it occurs, to 'thirty-one' there shall be substituted the words ', in accordance with section 25 of the Police and Criminal Evidence Act 1984, for an offence under section one or section nine of the Night Poaching Act 1828, or under section thirty'.

Betting, gaming and lotteries Act 1963 (c.2)

12.   The following subsection shall be substituted for subsection (2) of section 8 of the Betting, Gaming and Lotteries Act 1963 (prohibition of betting in streets and public places)—

'(2) Where a person is found committing an offence under this section, any constable may seize and detain any article liable to be forfeited under this section.'.

Criminal Law Act 1967 (c. 58)

17.   The following subsection shall be inserted after section 4(1) of the Criminal Law Act 1967—

'(1A) In this section and section 5 below "arrestable offence" has the meaning assigned to it by section 24 of the Police and Criminal Evidence Act 1984.'.

Theatres Act 1968 (c. 54)

18.   In section 15(1) of the Theatres Act 1968 (powers of entry and inspection); for the words 'fourteen days' there shall be substituted the words 'one month'.

Children and Young Persons Act 1969 (c. 54)

19.   In the Children and Young Persons Act 1969—
(b) the following section shall be substituted for section 29—

'29.   Recognisance on release of arrested child or young person

A child or young person arrested in pursuance of a warrant shall not be released unless he or his parent or guardian (with or without sureties) enters into a recognisance for such amount as the custody officer at the police station where he is detained considers will secure his attendance at the hearing of the charge; and the recognisance entered into in pursuance of this section may, if the custody officer thinks fit, be conditioned for the attendance of the parent or guardian at the hearing in addition to the child or young person.'.

Immigration Act 1971 (c. 77)

20.   In section 25(3) of the Immigration Act 1971 for the words 'A constable or' there shall be substituted the word 'An'.

Criminal Justice Act 1972 (c. 71)

21.   In subsection (1) of section 34 of the Criminal Justice Act 1972 (powers of constable to take drunken offender to treatment centre) for the words from the beginning to

'section the' there shall be substituted the words 'On arresting an offender for an offence under—

    (a) section 12 of the Licensing Act 1872; or

    (b) section 91(1) of the Criminal Justice Act 1967, a'.

Animal Health Act 1981 (c. 22)

    24. In subsection (5) of section 60 of the Animal Health Act 1981 (enforcement powers) for the words 'a constable or other officer' there shall be substituted the words 'an officer other than a constable'.

Wildlife and Countryside Act 1981 (c. 69)

    25. In subsection (2) of section 19 of the Wildlife and Countryside Act 1981 (enforcement powers) after the words 'subsection (1)' there shall be inserted the words 'or arresting a person, in accordance with section 25 of the Police and Criminal Evidence Act 1984, for such an offence'.

Mental Health Act 1983 (c. 20)

    26. In section 135(4) of the Mental Health Act 1983 for the words 'the constable to whom it is addressed', in both places where they occur, there shall be substituted the words 'a constable'.

PART II   OTHER AMENDMENTS

Army Act 1955 (c. 18)

    28.—(1) The Army Act 1955 shall be amended as follows.

    (2) In section 99—

    (a) in subsection (1), after the word 'below' there shall be inserted the words 'and to service modifications'; and

    (b) the following subsections shall be inserted after that subsection—

'(1A) In this section 'service modifications' means such modifications as the Secretary of State may by regulations made by statutory instrument prescribe, being modifications which appear to him to be necessary or proper for the purpose of proceedings before a court-martial; and it is hereby declared that in this section—

'rules' includes rules contained in or made by virtue of an enactment; and

'enactment' includes an enactment contained in an Act passed after this Act.

(1B) Regulations under subsection (1A) above may not modify section 99A below.

(1C) Regulations under subsection (1A) above shall be subject to annulment in pursuance of a resolution of either House of Parliament.'.

    (3) In section 99A(1) for the word 'Section' there shall be substituted the words 'Without prejudice to section 99 above, section'.

Air Force Act 1955 (c. 19)

    29.—(1) The Air Force Act 1955 shall be amended as follows.

    (2) In section 99—

    (a) in subsection (1), after the word 'below' there shall be inserted the words 'and to service modifications'; and

    (b) the following subsections shall be inserted after that subsection—

'(1A) In this section 'service modifications' means such modifications as the Secretary of State may by regulations made by statutory instrument prescribe, being modifications which appear to him to be necessary or proper for the purpose of proceedings before a court-martial; and it is hereby declared that in this section—

'rules' include rules contained in or made by virtue of an enactment; and 'enactment' includes an enactment contained in an Act passed after this Act.

(1B) Regulations under subsection (1A) above may not modify section 99A below.

(1C) Regulations under subsection (1A) above shall be subject to annulment in pursuance of a resolution of either House of Parliament.'.

(3) In section 99A(1) for the word 'Section' there shall be substituted the words 'Without prejudice to section 99 above, section'.

Police (Scotland) Act 1967 (c. 77)

30.   In section 6(2) of the Police (Scotland) Act 1967 (constables below rank of assistant chief constable) for the words 'an assistant chief constable or a constable holding the office of deputy chief constable' there shall be substituted the words 'a deputy chief constable or an assistant chief constable'.

31.   In section 7(1) of that Act (ranks) after the words 'chief constable,' there shall be inserted the words 'deputy chief constable,'.

32.   In section 26(7) of that Act (disciplinary authority) immediately before the words 'deputy chief constable' there shall be inserted the word 'any'.

33.   In section 31(2) of that Act (compulsory retirement of chief constable etc.) for the words 'the deputy or an assistant chief constable' there shall be substituted the words 'a deputy or assistant chief constable'.

Northern Ireland Assembly Disqualification Act 1975 (c. 25)

35.   In Part II of Schedule 1 to the House of Commons Disqualification Act 1975 and Part II of Schedule 1 to the Northern Ireland Assembly Disqualification Act 1975 (bodies of which all members are disqualified under those Acts) there shall be inserted at the appropriate place in alphabetical order—

'The Police Complaints Authority'.

Customs and Excise Management Act 1979 (c. 2)

37.   The following subsection shall be substituted for section 138(4) of the Customs and Excise Management Act 1979—

'(4) Where any person has been arrested by a person who is not an officer—
(a) by virtue of this section; or
(b) by virtue of section 24 of the Police and Criminal Evidence Act 1984 in its application to offences under the customs and excise Acts,

the person arresting him shall give notice of the arrest to an officer at the nearest convenient office of customs and excise.'.

38.   In section 161 of that Act—
(a) in subsection (3), for the words from 'that officer' to the end of the subsection there shall be substituted the words 'any officer and any person accompanying an officer to enter and search the building or place named in the warrant within one month from that day'; and
(b) in subsection (4), for the words 'person named in a warrant under subsection (3) above' there shall be substituted the words 'other person so authorised'.

Betting and Gaming Duties Act 1981 (c. 63)

39.   In the following provisions of the Betting and Gaming Duties Act 1981, namely—
(b) paragraph 16(1) of Schedule 1;
(c) paragraph 17(1) of Schedule 3; and
(d) paragraph 17(1) of Schedule 4,

for the words 'fourteen days' there shall be substituted the words 'one month'.

Car Tax Act 1983 (c. 53)
    40.   In paragraph 7(3) of Schedule 1 to the Car Tax Act 1983 for the words 'fourteen days' there shall be substituted the words 'one month'.

Police and Criminal Evidence Act 1984
Revised Codes of Practice A–F
(Effective 1 April 2003)

Code of Practice for the Exercise by Police Officers of Statutory Powers of Stop and Search (Code A)

General
This code of practice must be readily available at all police stations for consultation by police officers, detained persons and members of the public.

The notes for guidance included are not provisions of this code, but are guidance to police officers and others about its application and interpretation. Provisions in the annexes to the code are provisions of this code.

This code governs the exercise by police officers of statutory powers to search a person or a vehicle without first making an arrest. The main stop and search powers to which this code applies are set out in Annex A, but that list should not be regarded as definitive. [See Note 1]

This code does not apply to;
  (a) the powers of stop and search under;
      (i)   Aviation Security Act 1982, section 27(2);
      (ii) Police and Criminal Evidence Act 1984, section 6(1) (which relates specifically to powers of constables employed by statutory undertakers on the premises of the statutory undertakers).
  (b) searches carried out for the purposes of examination under Schedule 7 to the Terrorism Act 2000 and to which the Code of Practice issued under paragraph 6 of Schedule 14 to the Terrorism Act 2000 applies.

1   Principles governing stop and search
1.1   Powers to stop and search must be used fairly, responsibly, with respect for people being searched and without unlawful discrimination. The Race Relations (Amendment) Act 2000 makes it unlawful for police officers to discriminate on the grounds of race, colour, ethnic origin, nationality or national origins when using their powers.

1.2   The intrusion on the liberty of the person stopped or searched must be brief and detention for the purposes of a search must take place at or near the location of the stop.

1.3   If these fundamental principles are not observed the use of powers to stop and search may be drawn into question. Failure to use the powers in the proper manner reduces their effectiveness. Stop and search can play an important role in the detection and prevention of crime, and using the powers fairly makes them more effective.

1.4   The primary purpose of stop and search powers is to enable officers to allay or confirm suspicions about individuals without exercising their power of arrest. Officers may be required to justify the use or authorisation of such powers, in relation both to individual searches and the overall pattern of their activity in this regard, to their supervisory officers or in court. Any misuse of the powers is likely to be harmful to policing and lead to mistrust of the police. Officers must also be able to explain their actions to the member of the public searched. The misuse of these powers can lead to disciplinary action.

1.5   An officer must not search a person, even with his or her consent, where no power to search is applicable. Even where a person is prepared to submit to a search voluntarily, the person must not be searched unless the necessary legal power exists, and the search must be in accordance with the relevant power and the provisions of this Code. The only exception, where an officer does not require a specific power, applies to searches of persons entering sports grounds or other premises carried out with their consent given as a condition of entry.

2   Explanation of powers to stop and search

2.1   This code applies to powers of stop and search as follows:

   (a)   powers which require reasonable grounds for suspicion, before they may be exercised; that articles unlawfully obtained or possessed are being carried, or under Section 43 of the Terrorism Act 2000 that a person is a terrorist;
   (b)   authorised under section 60 of the Criminal Justice and Public Order Act 1994, based upon a reasonable belief that incidents involving serious violence may take place or that people are carrying dangerous instruments or offensive weapons within any locality in the police area;
   (c)   authorised under section 44(1) and (2) of the Terrorism Act 2000 based upon a consideration that the exercise of one or both powers is expedient for the prevention of acts of terrorism;
   (d)   powers to search a person who has not been arrested in the exercise of a power to search premises (see Code B paragraph 1.3a).

Searches requiring reasonable grounds for suspicion

2.2   Reasonable grounds for suspicion depend on the circumstances in each case. There must be an objective basis for that suspicion based on facts, information, and/or intelligence which are relevant to the likelihood of finding an article of a certain kind or, in the case of searches under section 43 of the Terrorism Act 2000, to the likelihood that the person is a terrorist. Reasonable suspicion can never be supported on the basis of personal factors alone without reliable supporting intelligence or information or some specific behaviour by the person concerned. For example, a person's race, age, appearance, or the fact that the person is known to have a previous conviction, cannot be used alone or in combination with each other as the reason for searching that person. Reasonable suspicion cannot be based on generalisations or stereotypical images of certain groups or categories of people as more likely to be involved in criminal activity.

2.3   Reasonable suspicion can sometimes exist without specific information or intelligence and on the basis of some level of generalisation stemming from the behaviour of a person. For example, if an officer encounters someone on the street at night who is obviously trying to hide something, the officer may (depending on the other surrounding circumstances) base such suspicion on the fact that this kind of behaviour is often linked to stolen or prohibited articles being carried. Similarly, for the purposes of section 43 of the Terrorism Act 2000, suspicion that a person is a terrorist may arise from the person's behaviour at or near a location which has been identified as a potential target for terrorists.

2.4   However, reasonable suspicion should normally be linked to accurate and current intelligence or information, such as information describing an article being carried, a suspected offender, or a person who has been seen carrying a type of article known to have been stolen recently from premises in the area. Searches based on accurate and current intelligence or information are more likely to be effective. Targeting searches in a particular area at specified crime problems increases their effectiveness and minimises inconvenience to law-abiding members of the public. It also helps in justifying the use of searches both to those who are searched and to the general public. This does not however prevent stop and search powers being exercised in other locations where such powers may be exercised and reasonable suspicion exists.

2.5   Searches are more likely to be effective, legitimate, and secure public confidence when reasonable suspicion is based on a range of factors. The overall use of these powers is more likely to be effective when up to date and accurate intelligence or information is communicated to officers and they are well-informed about local crime patterns.

2.6   Where there is reliable information or intelligence that members of a group or gang habitually carry knives unlawfully or weapons or controlled drugs, and wear a distinctive item of clothing or other means of identification to indicate their membership of the group or gang, that distinctive item of clothing or other means of identification may provide reasonable grounds to stop and search a person. [See Note 9]

2.7   A police officer may have reasonable grounds to suspect that a person is in innocent possession of a stolen or prohibited article or other item for which he or she is empowered to search. In that case the officer may stop and search the person even though there would be no power of arrest.

2.8   Under section 43(1) of the Terrorism Act 2000 a constable may stop and search a person whom the officer reasonably suspects to be a terrorist to discover whether the person is in possession of anything which may constitute evidence that the person is a terrorist. These searches may only be carried out by an officer of the same sex as the person searched.

2.9   An officer who has reasonable grounds for suspicion may detain the person concerned in order to carry out a search. Before carrying out a search the officer may ask questions about the person's behaviour or presence in circumstances which gave rise to the suspicion. As a result of questioning the detained person, the reasonable grounds for suspicion necessary to detain that person may be confirmed or, because of a satisfactory explanation, be eliminated. [See Notes 2 and 3] Questioning may also reveal reasonable grounds to suspect the possession of a different kind of unlawful article from that originally suspected. Reasonable grounds for suspicion however cannot be provided retrospectively by such questioning during a person's detention or by refusal to answer any questions put.

2.10   If, as a result of questioning before a search, or other circumstances which come to the attention of the officer, there cease to be reasonable grounds for suspecting that an article is being carried of a kind for which there is a power to stop and search, no search may take place. [See Note 3] In the absence of any other lawful power to detain, the person is free to leave at will and must be so informed.

2.11   There is no power to stop or detain a person in order to find grounds for a search. Police officers have many encounters with members of the public which do not involve detaining people against their will. If reasonable grounds for suspicion emerge during such an encounter, the officer may search the person, even though no grounds existed when the encounter began. If an officer is detaining someone for the purpose of a search, he or she should inform the person as soon as detention begins.

Searches authorised under section 60 of the Criminal Justice and Public Order Act 1994

2.12   Authority for a constable in uniform to stop and search under section 60 of the Criminal Justice and Public Order Act 1994 may be given if the authorising officer reasonably believes;

(a) that incidents involving serious violence may take place in any locality in the officer's police area, and it is expedient to use these powers to prevent their occurrence, or

(b) that persons are carrying dangerous instruments or offensive weapons without good reason in any locality in the officer's police area.

2.13   An authorisation under section 60 may only be given by an officer of the rank of inspector or above, in writing, specifying the grounds on which it was given, the locality in which the powers may be exercised and the period of time for which they are in force. The period authorised shall be no longer than appears reasonably necessary to prevent, or seek to prevent incidents of serious violence, or to deal with the problem of carrying dangerous instruments or offensive weapons. It may not exceed 24 hours. [See Notes 10–13]

2.14   If an inspector gives an authorisation, he or she must, as soon as practicable, inform an officer of or above the rank of superintendent. This officer may direct that the authorisation shall be extended for a further 24 hours, if violence or the carrying of dangerous instruments or offensive weapons has occurred, or is suspected to have occurred, and the continued use of the powers is considered necessary to prevent or deal with further such activity. That direction must also be given in writing at the time or as soon as practicable afterwards. [See Note 12]

Powers to require removal of face coverings

2.15   Section 60AA of the Criminal Justice and Public Order Act 1994 also provides a power to demand the removal of disguises. The officer exercising the power must reasonably believe that someone is wearing an item wholly or mainly for the purpose of concealing identity. There is also a power to seize such items where the officer believes that a person intends to wear them for this purpose. There is no power to stop and search for disguises. An officer may seize any such item which is discovered when exercising a power of search for something else, or which is being carried, and which the officer reasonably believes is intended to be used for concealing anyone's identity. This power can only be used if an authorisation under section 60 or an authorisation under section 60AA is in force.

2.16   Authority for a constable in uniform to require the removal of disguises and to seize them under section 60AA may be given if the authorising officer reasonably believes that activities may take place in any locality in the officer's police area that are likely to involve the commission of offences and it is expedient to use these powers to prevent or control these activities.

2.17   An authorisation under section 60AA may only be given by an officer of the rank of inspector or above, in writing, specifying the grounds on which it was given, the locality in which the powers may be exercised and the period of time for which they are in force. The period authorised shall be no longer than appears reasonably necessary to prevent, or seek to prevent the commission of offences. It may not exceed 24 hours. [See Notes 10–13]

2.18   If an inspector gives an authorisation, he or she must, as soon as practicable, inform an officer of or above the rank of superintendent. This officer may direct that the authorisation shall be extended for a further 24 hours, if crimes have been committed, or is suspected to have been committed, and the continued use of the powers is considered necessary to prevent or deal with further such activity. This direction must also be given in writing at the time or as soon as practicable afterwards. [See Note 12]

Searches authorised under section 44 of the Terrorism Act 2000

2.19   An officer of the rank of assistant chief constable (or equivalent) or above, may give authority for the following powers of stop and search under section 44 of the Terrorism Act 2000 to be exercised in the whole or part of his or her police area if the officer considers it is expedient for the prevention of acts of terrorism;

   (a) under section 44(1) of the Terrorism Act 2000, to give a constable in uniform power to stop and search any vehicle, its driver, any passenger in the vehicle and anything in or on the vehicle or carried by the driver or any passenger; and
   (b) under section 44(2) of the Terrorism Act 2000, to give a constable in uniform power to stop and search any pedestrian and anything carried by the pedestrian.

An authorisation under section 44(1) may be combined with one under section 44(2).

2.20   If an authorisation is given orally at first, it must be confirmed in writing by the officer who gave it as soon as reasonably practicable.

2.21   When giving an authorisation, the officer must specify the geographical area in which the power may be used, and the time and date that the authorisation ends (up to a maximum of 28 days from the time the authorisation was given). [See Notes 12 and 13]

2.22   The officer giving an authorisation under section 44(1) or (2) must cause the Secretary of State to be informed, as soon as reasonably practicable, that such an authorisation has been given. An authorisation which is not confirmed by the Secretary of State within 48 hours of its having been given, shall have effect up until the end of that 48 hour period or the end of the period specified in the authorisation (whichever is the earlier). [See Note 14]

2.23   Following notification of the authorisation, the Secretary of State may:
  (i)   cancel the authorisation with immediate effect or with effect from such other time as he or she may direct;
  (ii) confirm it but for a shorter period than that specified in the authorisation; or
  (iii) confirm the authorisation as given.

2.24   When an authorisation under section 44 is given, a constable in uniform may exercise the powers;
  (a)   only for the purpose of searching for articles of a kind which could be used in connection with terrorism (see paragraph 2.25);
  (b)   whether or not there are any grounds for suspecting the presence of such articles.

2.25   The selection of persons stopped under section 44 of Terrorism Act 2000 should reflect an objective assessment of the threat posed by the various terrorist groups active in Great Britain. The powers must not be used to stop and search for reasons unconnected with terrorism. Officers must take particular care not to discriminate against members of minority ethnic groups in the exercise of these powers. There may be circumstances, however, where it is appropriate for officers to take account of a person's ethnic origin in selecting persons to be stopped in response to a specific terrorist threat (for example, some international terrorist groups are associated with particular ethnic identities). [See Notes 12 and 13]

2.26   The powers under sections 43 and 44 of the Terrorism Act 2000 allow a constable to search only for articles which could be used for terrorist purposes. However, this would not prevent a search being carried out under other powers if, in the course of exercising these powers, the officer formed reasonable grounds for suspicion.

Powers to search in the exercise of a power to search premises

2.27   The following powers to search premises also authorise the search of a person, not under arrest, who is found on the premises during the course of the search:
  (a)   section 139B of the Criminal Justice Act 1988 under which a constable may enter school premises and search the premises and any person on those premises for any bladed or pointed article or offensive weapon; and
  (b)   under a warrant issued under section s.23(3) of the Misuse of Drugs Act 1971 to search premises for drugs or documents but only if the warrant specifically authorises the search of persons found on the premises.

2.28   Before the power under section 139B of the Criminal Justice Act 1988 may be exercised, the constable must have reasonable grounds to believe that an offence under section 139A of the Criminal Justice Act 1988 (having a bladed or pointed article or offensive weapon on school premises) has been or is being committed. A warrant to search premises and persons found therein may be issued under section s.23(3) of the Misuse of Drugs Act 1971 if there are reasonable grounds to suspect that controlled drugs or certain documents are in the possession of a person on the premises.

2.29   The powers in paragraph 2.27(a) or (b) do not require prior specific grounds to suspect that the person to be searched is in possession of an item for which there is an existing power to search. However, it is still necessary to ensure that the selection and treatment of those searched under these powers is based upon objective factors connected with the search of the premises, and not upon personal prejudice.

3   Conduct of searches

3.1   All stops and searches must be carried out with courtesy, consideration and respect for the person concerned. This has a significant impact on public confidence in the police. Every reasonable effort must be made to minimise the embarrassment that a person being searched may experience. [See Note 4]

3.2   The co-operation of the person to be searched must be sought in every case, even if the person initially objects to the search. A forcible search may be made only if it has been established that the person is unwilling to co-operate or resists. Reasonable force may be used as a last resort if necessary to conduct a search or to detain a person or vehicle for the purposes of a search.

3.3   The length of time for which a person or vehicle may be detained must be reasonable and kept to a minimum. Where the exercise of the power requires reasonable suspicion, the thoroughness and extent of a search must depend on what is suspected of being carried, and by whom. If the suspicion relates to a particular article which is seen to be slipped into a person's pocket, then, in the absence of other grounds for suspicion or an opportunity for the article to be moved elsewhere, the search must be confined to that pocket. In the case of a small article which can readily be concealed, such as a drug, and which might be concealed anywhere on the person, a more extensive search may be necessary. In the case of searches mentioned in paragraph 2.1(b), (c), and (d), which do not require reasonable grounds for suspicion, officers may make any reasonable search to look for items for which they are empowered to search. [See Note 5]

3.4   The search must be carried out at or near the place where the person or vehicle was first detained. [See Note 6]

3.5   There is no power to require a person to remove any clothing in public other than an outer coat, jacket or gloves except under section 45(3) of the Terrorism Act 2000 (which empowers a constable conducting a search under section 44(1) or 44(2) of that Act to require a person to remove headgear and footwear in public) and under section 60AA of the Criminal Justice and Public Order Act 1994 (which empowers a constable to require a person to remove any item worn to conceal identity). [See Notes 4 and 6] A search in public of a person's clothing which has not been removed must be restricted to superficial examination of outer garments. This does not, however, prevent an officer from placing his or her hand inside the pockets of the outer clothing, or feeling round the inside of collars, socks and shoes if this is reasonably necessary in the circumstances to look for the object of the search or to remove and examine any item reasonably suspected to be the object of the search. For the same reasons, subject to the restrictions on the removal of headgear, a person's hair may also be searched in public (see paragraphs 3.1 and 3.3).

3.6   Where on reasonable grounds it is considered necessary to conduct a more thorough search (e.g. by requiring a person to take off a T-shirt), this must be done out of public view, for example, in a police van unless paragraph 3.7 applies, or police station if there is one nearby. [See *Note* 6] Any search involving the removal of more than an outer coat, jacket, gloves, headgear or footwear, or any other item concealing identity, may only be made by an officer of the same sex as the person searched and may not be made in the presence of anyone of the opposite sex unless the person being searched specifically requests it. [See Notes 4, 7 and 8]

3.7   Searches involving exposure of intimate parts of the body must not be conducted as a routine extension of a less thorough search, simply because nothing is found in the course of the initial search. Searches involving exposure of intimate parts of the body may be carried out only at a nearby police station or other nearby location which is out of public view (but not a police vehicle). These searches must be conducted in accordance with paragraph 11 of Annex A to Code C except that an intimate search mentioned in paragraph 11(f) of Annex A to Code C may not be authorised or carried out under any stop and search powers. The other provisions of Code C do not apply to the conduct and recording of searches of persons detained at police stations in the exercise of stop and search powers. [See Note 7]

Steps to be taken prior to a search

3.8   Before any search of a detained person or attended vehicle takes place the officer must take reasonable steps to give the person to be searched or in charge of the vehicle the following information:

(a)   that they are being detained for the purposes of a search;

(b)   the officer's name (except in the case of enquiries linked to the investigation of terrorism, or otherwise where the officer reasonably believes that giving his or her name might put him or her in danger, in which case a warrant or other identification number shall be given) and the name of the police station to which the officer is attached;

(c)   the legal search power which is being exercised; and

(d)   a clear explanation of;

    (i)   the purpose of the search in terms of the article or articles for which there is a power to search; and

    (ii)   in the case of powers requiring reasonable suspicion (see paragraph 2.1(a)), the grounds for that suspicion; or

    (iii) in the case of powers which do not require reasonable suspicion (see paragraph 2.1(b), and (c)), the nature of the power and of any necessary authorisation and the fact that it has been given.

3.9   Officers not in uniform must show their warrant cards. Stops and searches under the powers mentioned in paragraphs 2.1(b), and (c) may be undertaken only by a constable in uniform.

3.10   Before the search takes place the officer must inform the person (or the owner or person in charge of the vehicle that is to be searched) of his or her entitlement to a copy of the record of the search, including his entitlement to a record of the search if an application is made within 12 months, if it is wholly impracticable to make a record at the time. If a record is not made at the time the person should also be told how a copy can be obtained (see section 4). The person should also be given information about police powers to stop and search and the individual's rights in these circumstances.

3.11   If the person to be searched, or in charge of a vehicle to be searched, does not appear to understand what is being said, or there is any doubt about the person's ability to understand English, the officer must take reasonable steps to bring information regarding the person's rights and any relevant provisions of this Code to his or her attention. If the person is deaf or cannot understand English and is accompanied by someone, then the officer must try to establish whether that person can interpret or otherwise help the officer to give the required information.

4   Recording requirements

4.1   An officer who has carried out a search in the exercise of any power to which this Code applies, must make a record of it at the time, unless there are exceptional circumstances which would make this wholly impracticable (e.g. in situations involving public disorder or when the officer's presence is urgently required elsewhere). If a record is not made at the time, the officer must do so as soon as practicable afterwards. There may be situations in which it is not practicable to obtain the information necessary to complete a record, but the officer should make every reasonable effort to do so.

4.2   A copy of a record made at the time must be given immediately to the person who has been searched. The officer must ask for the name, address and date of birth of the person searched, but there is no obligation on a person to provide these details and no power of detention if the person is unwilling to do so.

4.3   The following information must always be included in the record of a search even if the person does not wish to provide any personal details:

(i) the name of the person searched, or (if it is withheld) a description;
(ii) a note of the person's self-defined ethnic background; [See Note 18]
(iii) when a vehicle is searched, its registration number; [See Note 17]
(iv) the date, time, and place that the person or vehicle was first detained;
(v) the date, time and place the person or vehicle was searched (if different from (iv));
(vi) the purpose of the search;
(vii) the grounds for making it, or in the case of those searches mentioned in paragraph 2.1(b) and (c), the nature of the power and of any necessary authorisation and the fact that it has been given; [See Note 17]
(viii) its outcome (e.g. arrest or no further action);
(ix) a note of any injury or damage to property resulting from it;
(x) subject to paragraph 3.8(a), the identity of the officer making the search. [See Note 15]

4.4   Nothing in paragraph 4.3 (x) requires the names of police officers to be shown on the search record or any other record required to be made under this code in the case of enquiries linked to the investigation of terrorism or otherwise where an officer reasonably believes that recording names might endanger the officers. In such cases the record must show the officers' warrant or other identification number and duty station.

4.5   A record is required for each person and each vehicle searched. However, if a person is in a vehicle and both are searched, and the object and grounds of the search are the same, only one record need be completed. If more than one person in a vehicle is searched, separate records for each search of a person must be made. If only a vehicle is searched, the name of the driver and his or her self-defined ethnic background must be recorded, unless the vehicle is unattended.

4.6   The record of the grounds for making a search must, briefly but informatively, explain the reason for suspecting the person concerned, by reference to the person's behaviour and/or other circumstances.

4.7   Where officers detain an individual with a view to performing a search, but the search is not carried out due to the grounds for suspicion being eliminated as a result of questioning the person detained, a record must still be made in accordance with the procedure outlined above.

4.8   After searching an unattended vehicle, or anything in or on it, an officer must leave a notice in it (or on it, if things on it have been searched without opening it) recording the fact that it has been searched.

4.9   The notice must include the name of the police station to which the officer concerned is attached and state where a copy of the record of the search may be obtained and where any application for compensation should be directed.

4.10   The vehicle must if practicable be left secure.

5   Monitoring and supervising the use of stop and search powers

5.1   Supervising officers must monitor the use of stop and search powers and should consider in particular whether there is any evidence that they are being exercised on the basis of stereotyped images or inappropriate generalisations. Supervising officers should satisfy themselves that the practice of officers under their supervision in stopping, searching and recording is fully in accordance with this Code. Supervisors must also examine whether the records reveal any trends or patterns which give cause for concern, and if so take appropriate action to address this

5.2   Senior officers with area or force-wide responsibilities must also monitor the broader use of stop and search powers and, where necessary, take action at the relevant level.

5.3   Supervision and monitoring must be supported by the compilation of comprehensive statistical records of stops and searches at force, area and local level. Any apparently disproportionate use of the powers by particular officers or groups of officers or in relation to specific sections of the community should be identified and investigated.

5.4   In order to promote public confidence in the use of the powers, forces in consultation with police authorities must make arrangements for the records to be scrutinised by representatives of the community, and to explain the use of the powers at a local level. [See Note 19].

Notes for Guidance

Officers exercising stop and search powers

1   This code does not affect the ability of an officer to speak to or question a person in the ordinary course of the officer's duties without detaining the person or exercising any element of compulsion. It is not the purpose of the code to prohibit such encounters between the police and the community with the co-operation of the person concerned and neither does it affect the principle that all citizens have a duty to help police officers to prevent crime and discover offenders. This is a civic rather than a legal duty; but when a police officer is trying to discover whether, or by whom, an offence has been committed he or she may question any person from whom useful information might be obtained, subject to the restrictions imposed by Code C. A person's unwillingness to reply does not alter this entitlement, but in the absence of a power to arrest, or to detain in order to search, the person is free to leave at will and cannot be compelled to remain with the officer.

2   In some circumstances preparatory questioning may be unnecessary, but in general a brief conversation or exchange will be desirable not only as a means of avoiding unsuccessful searches, but to explain the grounds for the stop/search, to gain cooperation and reduce any tension there might be surrounding the stop/search.

3   Where a person is lawfully detained for the purpose of a search, but no search in the event takes place, the detention will not thereby have been rendered unlawful.

4   Many people customarily cover their heads or faces for religious reasons – for example, Muslim women, Sikh men, Sikh or Hindu women, or Rastarfarian men or women. A police officer cannot order the removal of a head or face covering except where there is reason to believe that the item is being worn by the individual wholly or mainly for the purpose of disguising identity, not simply because it disguises identity. Where there may be religious sensitivities about ordering the removal of such an item, the officer should permit the item to be removed out of public view. Where practicable, the item should be removed in the presence of an officer of the same sex as the person and out of sight of anyone of the opposite sex.

5   A search of a person in public should be completed as soon as possible.

6   A person may be detained under a stop and search power at a place other than where the person was first detained, only if that place, be it a police station or elsewhere, is nearby. Such a place should be located within a reasonable travelling distance using whatever mode of travel (on foot or by car) is appropriate. This applies to all searches under stop and search powers, whether or not they involve the removal of clothing or exposure of intimate parts of the body (see paragraphs 3.6 and 3.7) or take place in or out of public view. It means, for example, that a search under the stop and search power in section 23 of the Misuse of Drugs Act 1971 which involves the compulsory removal of more than a person's outer coat, jacket or gloves cannot be carried out unless a place which is both nearby the place they were first detained and out of public view, is available. If a search involves exposure of intimate parts of the body and a police station is not nearby, particular care must be taken to ensure that the location is suitable in that it enables the search to be conducted in accordance with the requirements of paragraph 11 of Annex A to Code C.

7   A search in the street itself should be regarded as being in public for the purposes of paragraphs 3.6 and 3.7 above, even though it may be empty at the time a search begins. Although there is no power to require a person to do so, there is nothing to prevent an officer

from asking a person voluntarily to remove more than an outer coat, jacket or gloves (and headgear or footwear under section 45(3) of the Terrorism Act 2000) in public.

8   Where there may be religious sensitivities about asking someone to remove headgear using a power under section 45(3) of the Terrorism Act 2000, the police officer should offer to carry out the search out of public view (for example, in a police van or police station if there is one nearby).

9   Other means of identification might include jewellery, insignias, tattoos or other features which are known to identify members of the particular gang or group.

Authorising officers

10   The powers under section 60 are separate from and additional to the normal stop and search powers which require reasonable grounds to suspect an individual of carrying an offensive weapon (or other article). Their overall purpose is to prevent serious violence and the widespread carrying of weapons which might lead to persons being seriously injured by disarming potential offenders in circumstances where other powers would not be sufficient. They should not therefore be used to replace or circumvent the normal powers for dealing with routine crime problems. The purpose of the powers under section 60AA is to prevent those involved in intimidatory or violent protests using face coverings to disguise identity.

11   Authorisations under section 60 require a reasonable belief on the part of the authorising officer. This must have an objective basis, for example: intelligence or relevant information such as a history of antagonism and violence between particular groups; previous incidents of violence at, or connected with, particular events or locations; a significant increase in knife-point robberies in a limited area; reports that individuals are regularly carrying weapons in a particular locality; or in the case of section 60AA previous incidents of crimes being committed while wearing face coverings to conceal identity.

12   It is for the authorising officer to determine the period of time during which the powers mentioned in paragraph 2.1 (b) and (c) may be exercised. The officer should set the minimum period he or she considers necessary to deal with the risk of violence, the carrying of knives or offensive weapons, or terrorism. A direction to extend the period authorised under the powers mentioned in paragraph 2.1(b) may be given only once. Thereafter further use of the powers requires a new authorisation. There is no provision to extend an authorisation of the powers mentioned in paragraph 2.1(c); further use of the powers requires a new authorisation.

13   It is for the authorising officer to determine the geographical area in which the use of the powers is to be authorised. In doing so the officer may wish to take into account factors such as the nature and venue of the anticipated incident, the number of people who may be in the immediate area of any possible incident, their access to surrounding areas and the anticipated level of violence. The officer should not set a geographical area which is wider than that he or she believes necessary for the purpose of preventing anticipated violence, the carrying of knives or offensive weapons, acts of terrorism, or, in the case of section 60AA, the prevention of commission of offences. It is particularly important to ensure that constables exercising such powers are fully aware of where they may be used. If the area specified is smaller than the whole force area, the officer giving the authorisation should specify either the streets which form the boundary of the area or a divisional boundary within the force area. If the power is to be used in response to a threat or incident that straddles police force areas, an officer from each of the forces concerned will need to give an authorisation.

14   An officer who has authorised the use of powers under section 44 of the Terrorism Act 2000 must take immediate steps to send a copy of the authorisation to the National Joint Unit, Metropolitan Police Special Branch, who will forward it to the Secretary of State. The Secretary of State should be informed of the reasons for the authorisation. The National Joint Unit will inform the force concerned, within 48 hours of the authorisation being made, whether the Secretary of State has confirmed or cancelled or altered the authorisation.

Recording

15   Where a stop and search is conducted by more than one officer the identity of all the officers engaged in the search must be recorded on the record. Nothing prevents an officer who is present but not directly involved in searching from completing the record during the course of the encounter.

16   Where a vehicle has not been allocated a registration number (e.g. a rally car or a trials motorbike) that part of the requirement under 4.3(iii) does not apply.

17   It is important for monitoring purposes to specify whether the authority for exercising a stop and search power was given under section 60 of the Criminal Justice and Public Order Act 1994, or under section 44(1) or 44(2) of the Terrorism Act 2000.

18   Officers should record the self-defined ethnicity of every person stopped according to the categories used in the 2001 census question listed in Annex B. Respondents should be asked to select one of the five main categories representing broad ethnic groups and then a more specific cultural background from within this group. The ethnic classification should be coded for recording purposes using the coding system in Annex B. An additional 'Not stated' box is available but should not be offered to respondents explicitly. Officers should be aware and explain to members of the public, especially where concerns are raised, that this information is required to obtain a true picture of stop and search activity and to help improve ethnic monitoring, tackle discriminatory practice, and promote effective use of the powers. If the person gives what appears to the officer to be an 'incorrect' answer (e.g. a person who appears to be white states that they are black), the officer should record the response that has been given. Officers should also record their own perception of the ethnic background of every person stopped and this must be done by using the PNC/Phoenix classification system. If the 'Not stated' category is used the reason for this must be recorded on the form.

19   Arrangements for public scrutiny of records should take account of the right to confidentiality of those stopped and searched. Anonymised forms and/or statistics generated from records should be the focus of the examinations by members of the public.

ANNEX A   SUMMARY OF MAIN STOP AND SEARCH POWERS

POWER	OBJECT OF SEARCH	EXTENT OF SEARCH	WHERE EXERCISABLE
Unlawful articles general			
1. Public Stores Act 1875, s. 6	HM Stores stolen or unlawfully obtained	Persons, vehicles and vessels	Anywhere where the constabulary powers are exercisable
2. Firearms Act 1968, s. 47	Firearms	Persons and vehicles	A public place, or anywhere in the case of reasonable suspicion of offences of carrying firearms with criminal intent or trespassing with firearms
3. Misuse of Drugs Act 1971, s. 23	Controlled drugs	Persons and vehicles	Anywhere
4. Customs and Excise Management Act 1979, s. 163	Goods: (a) on which duty has not been paid; (b) being unlawfully removed, imported or exported; (c) otherwise liable to forfeiture to HM Customs and Excise	Vehicles and vessels only	Anywhere
5. Aviation Security Act 1982, s. 27(1)	Stolen or unlawfully obtained goods	Airport employees and vehicles carrying airport employees or aircraft or any vehicle in a cargo area whether or not carrying an employee	Any designated airport
6. Police and Criminal Evidence Act 1984, s. 1	Stolen goods; articles for use in certain Theft Act offences; offensive weapons, including bladed or sharply-pointed articles (except folding pocket knives with a bladed cutting edge not exceeding 3 inches)	Persons and vehicles	Where there is public access
Police and Criminal Evidence Act 1984, s. 6(3) (by a constable of the United Kingdom Atomic Energy Authority Constabulary in respect of property owned or controlled by British Nuclear Fuels plc	HM Stores (in the form of goods and chattels belonging to British Nuclear Fuels plc)	Persons, vehicles and vessels	Anywhere where the constabulary powers are exercisable

ANNEX A SUMMARY OF MAIN STOP AND SEARCH POWERS—*(continued)*

POWER	OBJECT OF SEARCH	EXTENT OF SEARCH	WHERE EXERCISABLE
7. Sporting events (Control of Alcohol etc.) Act 1985, s. 7	Intoxicating liquor	Persons, coaches and trains	Designated sports grounds or coaches and trains travelling to or from a designated sporting event
8. Crossbows Act 1987, s. 4	Crossbows or parts of crossbows (except crossbows with a draw weight of less than 1.4 kilograms)	Persons and vehicles	Anywhere except dwellings
9. Criminal Justice Act 1988 s. 139B	Offensive weapons, bladed or sharply pointed article	Persons	School premises
Evidence of game and wildlife offences			
10. Poaching Prevention Act 1862, s. 2	Game or poaching equipment	Persons and vehicles	A public place
11. Deer Act 1991, s. 12	Evidence of offences under the Act	Persons and vehicles	Anywhere except dwellings
12. Conversation of Seals Act 1970, s. 4	Seals or hunting equipment	Vehicles only	Anywhere
13. Badgers Act 1992, s. 11	Evidence of offences under the Act	Persons and vehicles	Anywhere
14. Wildlife and Countryside Act 1981, s. 19	Evidence of wildlife offences	Persons and vehicles	Anywhere except dwellings
Other			
15. Terrorism Act 2000, s. 43	*Evidence of liability to arrest under section 14 of the Act*	Persons	Anywhere
16. Terrorism Act 2000, s. 44(1)	Articles which could be used for a purpose connected with the commission, preparation or instigation of acts of terrorism	*Vehicles, driver and passengers*	Anywhere within the area or locality authorised under subsection (1)

17. Terrorism Act 2000, s. 44(2)	Articles which could be used for a purpose connected with the commission, preparation or instigation of acts of terrorism	*Pedestrians*	Anywhere within the area of locality authorised
18. Paragraphs 7 and 8 of Schedule 7 to the Terrorism Act 2000	Anything relevant to determining if a person being examined falls within paragraph 2(1)(a) to (c) of Schedule 5	Persons, vehicles, vessels etc.	*Ports and airports*
19. Section 60 Criminal Justice and Public Order Act 1994, *as amended by s. 8 of the Knives Act 1997*	Offensive weapons or dangerous instruments to prevent incidents of serious violence or to deal with the carrying of such items	Persons and vehicles	Anywhere within a locality authorised under subsection (1)

ANNEX B   SELF-DEFINED ETHNIC CLASSIFICATION CATEGORIES

White	*W*
A. White – British	W1
B. White – Irish	W2
C. Any other White background	W9
Mixed	*M*
D. White and Black Caribbean	M1
E. White and Black African	M2
F. White and Asian	M3
G. Any other Mixed Background	M9
Asian/Asian – British	*A*
H. Asian – Indian	A1
I. Asian – Pakistani	A2
J. Asian – Bangladeshi	A3
K. Any other Asian background	A9
Black/Black – British	*B*
L. Black – Caribbean	B1
M. Black African	B2
N. Any other Black background	B9
Other	*O*
O. Chinese	O1
P. Any other	O9
Not Stated	**NS**

Code of Practice for Searches of Premises by Police Officers and the Seizure of Property Found by Police Officers on Persons or Premises (Code B)

1   Introduction

1.1   This Code of Practice deals with police powers to:
- search premises
- seize and retain property found on premises and persons

1.1A   These powers may be used to find:
- property and material relating to a crime
- wanted persons
- children who abscond from local authority accommodation where they have been remanded or committed by a court

1.2   A justice of the peace may issue a search warrant granting powers of entry, search and seizure, e.g. warrants to search for stolen property, drugs, firearms and evidence of serious offences. Police also have powers without a search warrant. The main ones provided by the Police and Criminal Evidence Act 1984 (PACE) include powers to search premises:
- to make an arrest
- after an arrest

1.3   The right to privacy and respect for personal property are key principles of the Human Rights Act 1998. Powers of entry, search and seizure should be fully and clearly justified before use because they may significantly interfere with the occupier's privacy. Officers should consider if the necessary objectives can be met by less intrusive means.

1.4   In all cases, police should:
- exercise their powers courteously and with respect for persons and property
- only use reasonable force when this is considered necessary and proportionate to the circumstances

1.5   If the provisions of PACE and this Code are not observed, evidence obtained from a search may be open to question.

2   General

2.1   This Code must be readily available at all police stations for consultation by:
- police officers;
- detained persons;
- members of the public.

2.2   The *Notes for Guidance* included are not provisions of this Code.

2.3   This Code applies to searches of premises:
(a) by police for the purposes of an investigation into an alleged offence, with the occupier's consent, other than:
  - routine scene of crime searches;
  - calls to a fire or burglary made by or on behalf of an occupier or searches following the activation of fire or burglar alarms or discovery of insecure premises;
  - searches when paragraph 5.4 applies;
  - bomb threat calls;
(b) under powers conferred on police officers by PACE, sections 17, 18 and 32;
(c) undertaken in pursuance of search warrants issued to and executed by constables in accordance with PACE, sections 15 and 16. See Note 2A;
(d) subject to paragraph 2.6, under any other power given to police to enter premises with or without a search warrant for any purpose connected with the investigation into an alleged or suspected offence. See Note 2B.

For the purposes of this Code, 'premises' as defined in PACE, section 23, includes any place, vehicle, vessel, aircraft, hovercraft, tent or movable structure and any offshore installation as defined in the Mineral Workings (Offshore Installations) Act 1971, section 1. See Note 2D

2.4   A person who has not been arrested but is searched during a search of premises should be searched in accordance with Code A. See Note 2C

2.5   This Code does not apply to the exercise of a statutory power to enter premises or to inspect goods, equipment or procedures if the exercise of that power is not dependent on the existence of grounds for suspecting that an offence may have been committed and the person exercising the power has no reasonable grounds for such suspicion.

2.6   This Code does not affect any directions of a search warrant or order, lawfully executed in England or Wales that any item or evidence seized under that warrant or order be handed over to a police force, court, tribunal, or other authority outside England or Wales. For example, warrants and orders issued in Scotland or Northern Ireland, see Note 2B(f) and search warrants issued under the Criminal Justice (International Co-operation) Act 1990, section 7.

2.7   When this Code requires the prior authority or agreement of an officer of at least inspector or superintendent rank, that authority may be given by a sergeant or chief inspector authorised to perform the functions of the higher rank under PACE, section 107.

2.8   Written records required under this Code not made in the search record shall, unless otherwise specified, be made:

- in the recording officer's pocket book ('pocket book' includes any official report book issued to police officers) or
- on forms provided for the purpose

2.9   Nothing in this Code requires the identity of officers (or anyone accompanying them during a search of premises) to be recorded or disclosed:

   (a) in the case of enquiries linked to the investigation of terrorism; or
   (b) if officers reasonably believe recording or disclosing their names might put them in danger.

In these cases officers should use warrant or other identification numbers and the name of their police station. See Note 2E

2.10   The 'officer in charge of the search' means the officer assigned specific duties and responsibilities under this Code. Whenever there is a search of premises to which this Code applies one officer must act as the officer in charge of the search. See Note 2F

2.11   In this Code:

   (a) 'designated person' means a person other than a police officer, designated under the Police Reform Act 2002, Part 4 who has specified powers and duties of police officers conferred or imposed on them;
   (b) any reference to a police officer includes a designated person acting in the exercise or performance of the powers and duties conferred or imposed on them by their designation.

2.12   If a power conferred on a designated person:

   (a) allows reasonable force to be used when exercised by a police officer, a designated person exercising that power has the same entitlement to use force;
   (b) includes power to use force to enter any premises, that power is not exercisable by that designated person except:
      (i) in the company and under the supervision of a police officer; or
      (ii) for the purpose of:
         - saving life or limb; or
         - preventing serious damage to property.

2.13   Designated persons must have regard to any relevant provisions of the Codes of Practice.

Notes for Guidance

2A   PACE sections 15 and 16 apply to all search warrants issued to and executed by constables under any enactment, e.g. search warrants issued by a:

   (a) justice of the peace under the:
      - Theft Act 1968, section 26 – stolen property;
      - Misuse of Drugs Act 1971, section 23 – controlled drugs;
      - PACE, section 8 – evidence of serious arrestable offence;
      - Terrorism Act 2000, Schedule 5, paragraph 1;
   (b) circuit judge under the:
      - PACE, Schedule 1;
      - Terrorism Act 2000, Schedule 5, paragraph 11.

2B   Examples of the other powers in paragraph 2.3(d) include:

   (a) Road Traffic Act 1988 giving police power to enter premises:
      (i) under section 4(7) to:
         - arrest a person for driving or being in charge of a vehicle when unfit;
      (ii) under section 6(6) to:
         - require a person to provide a specimen of breath; or
         - arrest a person following:
            ~ a positive breath test;
            ~ failure to provide a specimen of breath;

  (b) Transport and Works Act 1992, sections 30(3) and 30(4) giving police powers to enter premises mirroring the powers in (a) in relation to specified persons working on transport systems to which the Act applies;
  (c) Criminal Justice Act 1988, section 139B giving police power to enter and search school premises for offensive weapons, bladed or pointed articles;
  (d) Terrorism Act 2000, Schedule 5, paragraphs 3 and 15 empowering a superintendent in urgent cases to give written authority for police to enter and search premises for the purposes of a terrorist investigation;
  (e) Explosives Act 1875, section 73(b) empowering a superintendent to give written authority for police to enter premises, examine and search them for explosives;
  (f) search warrants and production orders or the equivalent issued in Scotland or Northern Ireland endorsed under the Summary Jurisdiction (Process) Act 1881 or the Petty Sessions (Ireland) Act 1851 respectively for execution in England and Wales.

2C   The Criminal Justice Act 1988, section 139B provides that a constable who has reasonable grounds to believe an offence under the Criminal Justice Act 1988, section 139A has or is being committed may enter school premises and search the premises and any persons on the premises for any bladed or pointed article or offensive weapon. Persons may be searched under a warrant issued under the Misuse of Drugs Act 1971, section 23(3) to search premises for drugs or documents only if the warrant specifically authorises the search of persons on the premises.

2D   The Immigration Act 1971, Part III and Schedule 2 gives immigration officers powers to enter and search premises, seize and retain property, with and without a search warrant. These are similar to the powers available to police under search warrants issued by a justice of the peace and without a warrant under PACE, sections 17, 18, 19 and 32 except they only apply to specified offences under the Immigration Act 1971 and immigration control powers. For certain types of investigations and enquiries these powers avoid the need for the Immigration Service to rely on police officers becoming directly involved. When exercising these powers, immigration officers are required by the Immigration and Asylum Act 1999, section 145 to have regard to this Code's corresponding provisions. When immigration officers are dealing with persons or property at police stations, police officers should give appropriate assistance to help them discharge their specific duties and responsibilities.

2E   The purpose of paragraph 2.9(b) is to protect those involved in serious organised crime investigations or arrests of particularly violent suspects when there is reliable information that those arrested or their associates may threaten or cause harm to the officers. In cases of doubt, an officer of inspector rank or above should be consulted.

2F   For the purposes of paragraph 2.10, the officer in charge of the search should normally be the most senior officer present. Some exceptions are:
  (a) a supervising officer who attends or assists at the scene of a premises search may appoint an officer of lower rank as officer in charge of the search if that officer is:
    • more conversant with the facts;
    • a more appropriate officer to be in charge of the search;
  (b) when all officers in a premises search are the same rank. The supervising officer if available must make sure one of them is appointed officer in charge of the search, otherwise the officers themselves must nominate one of their number as the officer in charge;
  (c) a senior officer assisting in a specialist role. This officer need not be regarded as having a general supervisory role over the conduct of the search or be appointed or expected to act as the officer in charge of the search.

Except in (c), nothing in this Note diminishes the role and responsibilities of a supervisory officer who is present at the search or knows of a search taking place.

3 Search warrants and production orders

(a) Before making an application

3.1   When information appears to justify an application, the officer must take reasonable steps to check the information is accurate, recent and not provided maliciously or irresponsibly. An application may not be made on the basis of information from an anonymous source if corroboration has not been sought. See Note 3A

3.2   The officer shall ascertain as specifically as possible the nature of the articles concerned and their location.

3.3   The officer shall make reasonable enquiries to:
- (i) establish if:
  - anything is known about the likely occupier of the premises and the nature of the premises themselves;
  - the premises have been searched previously and how recently;
- (ii) obtain any other relevant information.

3.4   An application:
- (a) to a justice of the peace for a search warrant or to a circuit judge for a search warrant or production order under PACE, Schedule 1

  must be supported by a signed written authority from an officer of inspector rank or above:

  Note: If the case is an urgent application to a justice of the peace and an inspector or above is not readily available, the next most senior officer on duty can give the written authority.
- (b) to a circuit judge under the Terrorism Act 2000, Schedule 5 for
  - a production order;
  - search warrant; or
  - an order requiring an explanation of material seized or produced under such a warrant or production order

  must be supported by a signed written authority from an officer of superintendent rank or above.

3.5   Except in a case of urgency, if there is reason to believe a search might have an adverse effect on relations between the police and the community, the officer in charge shall consult the local police/community liaison officer:
- before the search; or
- in urgent cases, as soon as practicable after the search

(b) Making an application

3.6   A search warrant application must be supported in writing, specifying:
- (a) the enactment under which the application is made, see Note 2A;
- (b) the premises to be searched;
- (c) the object of the search, see Note 3B;
- (d) the grounds for the application, including, when the purpose of the proposed search is to find evidence of an alleged offence, an indication of how the evidence relates to the investigation;
- (e) there are no reasonable grounds to believe the material to be sought, when making application to a:
  - (i) justice of the peace or a circuit judge, consists of or includes items subject to legal privilege;
  - (ii) justice of the peace, consists of or includes excluded material or special procedure material;

  Note: this does not affect the additional powers of seizure in the Criminal Justice and Police Act 2001, Part 2 covered in paragraph 7.7, see Note 3B;

(f) if applicable, a request for the warrant to authorise a person or persons to accompany the officer who executes the warrant, see Note 3C.

3.7 A search warrant application under PACE, Schedule 1, paragraph 12(a), shall if appropriate indicate why it is believed service of notice of an application for a production order may seriously prejudice the investigation. Applications for search warrants under the Terrorism Act 2000, Schedule 5, paragraph 11 must indicate why a production order would not be appropriate.

3.8 If a search warrant application is refused, a further application may not be made for those premises unless supported by additional grounds.

Notes for Guidance

3A The identity of an informant need not be disclosed when making an application, but the officer should be prepared to answer any questions the magistrate or judge may have about:

- the accuracy of previous information from that source
- any other related matters

3B The information supporting a search warrant application should be as specific as possible, particularly in relation to the articles or persons being sought and where in the premises it is suspected they may be found. The meaning of 'items subject to legal privilege', 'special procedure material' and 'excluded material' are defined by PACE, sections 10, 11 and 14 respectively.

3C Under PACE, section 16(2), a search warrant may authorise persons other than police officers to accompany the constable who executes the warrant. This includes, e.g. any suitably qualified or skilled person or an expert in a particular field whose presence is needed to help accurately identify the material sought or to advise where certain evidence is most likely to be found and how it should be dealt with. It does not give them any right to force entry, to search for or seize property but it gives them the right to be on the premises during the search without the occupier's permission.

4 Entry without warrant – particular powers

(a) Making an arrest etc

4.1 The conditions under which an officer may enter and search premises without a warrant are set out in PACE, section 17. It should be noted that this section does not create or confer any powers of arrest. See other powers in Note 2B(a).

(b) Search of premises where arrest takes place or the arrested person was immediately before arrest

4.2 The powers of an officer to search premises where that officer arrested a person or where the person was immediately before being arrested are set out in PACE, section 32.

(c) Search of premises occupied or controlled by the arrested person

4.3 The specific powers to search premises occupied or controlled by an arrested person are set out in PACE, section 18. They may not be exercised, except if section 18 (5) applies, unless an officer of inspector rank or above has given written authority. That authority should only be given when the authorising officer is satisfied the necessary grounds exist. If possible the authorising officer should record the authority on the Notice of Powers and Rights and, subject to paragraph 2.9, sign the Notice. The record of the grounds for the search and the nature of the evidence sought as required by section 18(7) of the Act should be made in:

- the custody record if there is one, otherwise
- the officer's pocket book, or
- the search record.

5 Search with consent

5.1 Subject to paragraph 5.4, if it is proposed to search premises with the consent of a person entitled to grant entry the consent must, if practicable, be given in writing on the

Notice of Powers and Rights before the search. The officer must make any necessary enquiries to be satisfied the person is in a position to give such consent. See Notes 5A and 5B

5.2   Before seeking consent the officer in charge of the search shall state the purpose of the proposed search and its extent. This information must be as specific as possible, particularly regarding the articles or persons being sought and the parts of the premises to be searched. The person concerned must be clearly informed they are not obliged to consent and anything seized may be produced in evidence. If at the time the person is not suspected of an offence, the officer shall say this when stating the purpose of the search.

5.3   An officer cannot enter and search or continue to search premises under *paragraph 5.1* if consent is given under duress or withdrawn before the search is completed.

5.4   It is unnecessary to seek consent under paragraphs 5.1 and 5.2 if this would cause disproportionate inconvenience to the person concerned. See Note 5C

Notes for Guidance

5A   In a lodging house or similar accommodation, every reasonable effort should be made to obtain the consent of the tenant, lodger or occupier. A search should not be made solely on the basis of the landlord's consent unless the tenant, lodger or occupier is unavailable and the matter is urgent.

5B   If the intention is to search premises under the authority of a warrant or a power of entry and search without warrant, and the occupier of the premises co-operates in accordance with paragraph 6.4, there is no need to obtain written consent.

5C   Paragraph 5.4 is intended to apply when it is reasonable to assume innocent occupiers would agree to, and expect, police to take the proposed action, e.g. if:

- a suspect has fled the scene of a crime or to evade arrest and it is necessary quickly to check surrounding gardens and readily accessible places to see if the suspect is hiding
- police have arrested someone in the night after a pursuit and it is necessary to make a brief check of gardens along the pursuit route to see if stolen or incriminating articles have been discarded

6   Searching premises – general considerations

(a) Time of searches

6.1   Searches made under warrant must be made within one calendar month of the date of the warrant's issue.

6.2   Searches must be made at a reasonable hour unless this might frustrate the purpose of the search.

6.3   A warrant authorises an entry on one occasion only. When the extent or complexity of a search mean it is likely to take a long time, the officer in charge of the search may consider using the seize and sift powers referred to in section 7.

(b) Entry other than with consent

6.4   The officer in charge of the search shall first try to communicate with the occupier, or any other person entitled to grant access to the premises, explain the authority under which entry is sought and ask the occupier to allow entry, unless:

(i)   the search premises are unoccupied;

(ii) the occupier and any other person entitled to grant access are absent;

(iii) there are reasonable grounds for believing that alerting the occupier or any other person entitled to grant access would frustrate the object of the search or endanger officers or other people.

6.5   Unless sub-paragraph 6.4(iii) applies, if the premises are occupied the officer, subject to paragraph 2.9, shall, before the search begins:

(i)   identify him or herself, show their warrant card (if not in uniform) and state the purpose of and grounds for the search;

    (ii) identify and introduce any person accompanying the officer on the search (such persons should carry identification for production on request) and briefly describe that person's role in the process.

6.6   Reasonable and proportionate force may be used if necessary to enter premises if the officer in charge of the search is satisfied the premises are those specified in any warrant, or in exercise of the powers described in paragraphs 4.1 to 4.3, and if:

    (i)   the occupier or any other person entitled to grant access has refused entry;

    (ii) it is impossible to communicate with the occupier or any other person entitled to grant access; or

    (iii) any of the provisions of paragraphs 6.4 apply.

(c) Notice of powers and rights

6.7   If an officer conducts a search to which this Code applies the officer shall, unless it is impracticable to do so, provide the occupier with a copy of a Notice in a standard format:

    (i)   specifying if the search is made under warrant, with consent, or in the exercise of the powers described in paragraphs 4.1 to 4.3. Note: the notice format shall provide for authority or consent to be indicated, see paragraphs 4.3 and 5.1;

    (ii) summarising the extent of the powers of search and seizure conferred by PACE;

    (iii) explaining the rights of the occupier, and the owner of the property seized;

    (iv) explaining compensation may be payable in appropriate cases for damages caused entering and searching premises, and giving the address to send a compensation application, see Note 6A;

    (v)   stating this Code is available at any police station.

6.8   If the occupier is:

- present, copies of the Notice and warrant shall, if practicable, be given to them before the search begins, unless the officer in charge of the search reasonably believes this would frustrate the object of the search or endanger officers or other people;

- not present, copies of the Notice and warrant shall be left in a prominent place on the premises or appropriate part of the premises and endorsed, subject to paragraph 2.9 with the name of the officer in charge of the search, the date and time of the search.

The warrant shall be endorsed to show this has been done.

(d) Conduct of searches

6.9   Premises may be searched only to the extent necessary to achieve the object of the search, having regard to the size and nature of whatever is sought.

6.9A   A search may not continue under:

- a warrant's authority once all the things specified in that warrant have been found;

- any other power once the object of that search has been achieved.

6.9B   No search may continue once the officer in charge of the search is satisfied whatever is being sought is not on the premises. See Note 6B. This does not prevent a further search of the same premises if additional grounds come to light supporting a further application for a search warrant or exercise or further exercise of another power. For example, when, as a result of new information, it is believed articles previously not found or additional articles are on the premises.

6.10   Searches must be conducted with due consideration for the property and privacy of the occupier and with no more disturbance than necessary. Reasonable force may be used only when necessary and proportionate because the co-operation of the occupier cannot be obtained or is insufficient for the purpose. See Note 6C

6.11   A friend, neighbour or other person must be allowed to witness the search if the occupier wishes unless the officer in charge of the search has reasonable grounds for believing the presence of the person asked for would seriously hinder the investigation or endanger officers or other people. A search need not be unreasonably delayed for this purpose. A record of the action taken should be made on the premises search record including the grounds for refusing the occupier's request.

6.12   A person is not required to be cautioned prior to being asked questions that are solely necessary for the purpose of furthering the proper and effective conduct of a search, see Code C, paragraph 10.1(c). For example, questions to discover the occupier of specified premises, to find a key to open a locked drawer or cupboard or to otherwise seek co-operation during the search or to determine if a particular item is liable to be seized.

6.12A   If questioning goes beyond what is necessary for the purpose of the exemption in Code C, the exchange is likely to constitute an interview as defined by Code C, paragraph 11.1A and would require the associated safeguards included in Code C, section 10.

(e) Leaving premises

6.13   *If premises have been entered by force, before leaving the officer in charge of the search must make sure they are secure by:*
- arranging for the occupier or their agent to be present;
- any other appropriate means.

(f) Searches under PACE Schedule 1 or the Terrorism Act 2000, Schedule 5

6.14   An officer of inspector rank or above shall be the officer in charge of the search, see paragraph 2.10, in respect of any search made under a warrant issued under PACE Act 1984, Schedule 1 or the Terrorism Act 2000, Schedule 5. They are responsible for making sure the search is conducted with discretion and in a manner that causes the least possible disruption to any business or other activities carried out on the premises.

6.15   Once the officer in charge of the search is satisfied material may not be taken from the premises without their knowledge, they shall ask for the documents or other records concerned. The officer in charge of the search may also ask to see the index to files held on the premises, and the officers conducting the search may inspect any files which, according to the index, appear to contain the material sought. A more extensive search of the premises may be made only if:
- the person responsible for them refuses to:
  - ~ produce the material sought, or
  - ~ allow access to the index
- it appears the index is:
  - ~ inaccurate, or
  - ~ incomplete
- for any other reason the officer in charge of the search has reasonable grounds for believing such a search is necessary in order to find the material sought.

Notes for Guidance

6A   Whether compensation is appropriate depends on the circumstances in each case. Compensation for damage caused when effecting entry is unlikely to be appropriate if the search was lawful, and the force used can be shown to be reasonable, proportionate and necessary to effect entry. If the wrong premises are searched by mistake everything possible should be done at the earliest opportunity to allay any sense of grievance and there should normally be a strong presumption in favour of paying compensation.

6B   It is important that, when possible, all those involved in a search are fully briefed about any powers to be exercised and the extent and limits within which it should be conducted.

6C   In all cases the number of officers and other persons involved in executing the warrant should be determined by what is reasonable and necessary according to the particular circumstances.

7   Seizure and retention of property

(a) Seizure

7.1   Subject to paragraph 7.2, an officer who is searching any person or premises under any statutory power or with the consent of the occupier may seize anything:

(a)   covered by a warrant;

(b)   the officer has reasonable grounds for believing is evidence of an offence or has been obtained in consequence of the commission of an offence but only if seizure is necessary to prevent the items being concealed, lost, disposed of, altered, damaged, destroyed or tampered with;

(c)   covered by the powers in the Criminal Justice and Police Act 2001, Part 2 allowing an officer to seize property from persons or premises and retain it for sifting or examination elsewhere.

See Note 7B

7.2   No item may be seized which an officer has reasonable grounds for believing to be subject to legal privilege, as defined in PACE, section 10, other than under the Criminal Justice and Police Act 2001, Part 2.

7.3   Officers must be aware of the provisions in the Criminal Justice and Police Act 2001, section 59, allowing for applications to a judicial authority for the return of property seized and the subsequent duty to secure in section 60, see paragraph 7.12(iii).

7.4   An officer may decide it is not appropriate to seize property because of an explanation from the person holding it but may nevertheless have reasonable grounds for believing it was obtained in consequence of an offence by some person. In these circumstances, the officer should identify the property to the holder, inform the holder of their suspicions and explain the holder may be liable to civil or criminal proceedings if they dispose of, alter or destroy the property.

7.5   An officer may arrange to photograph, image or copy, any document or other article they have the power to seize in accordance with paragraph 7.1. This is subject to specific restrictions on the examination, imaging or copying of certain property seized under the Criminal Justice and Police Act 2001, Part 2. An officer must have regard to their statutory obligation to retain an original document or other article only when a photograph or copy is not sufficient.

7.6   If an officer considers information stored in any electronic form and accessible from the premises could be used in evidence, they may require the information to be produced in a form:

•   which can be taken away and in which it is visible and legible; or

•   from which it can readily be produced in a visible and legible form.

(b) Criminal Justice and Police Act 2001: Specific procedures for seize and sift powers

7.7   The Criminal Justice and Police Act 2001, Part 2 gives officers limited powers to seize property from premises or persons so they can sift or examine it elsewhere. Officers must be careful they only exercise these powers when it is essential and they do not remove any more material than necessary. The removal of large volumes of material, much of which may not ultimately be retainable, may have serious implications for the owners, particularly when they are involved in business or activities such as journalism or the provision of medical services. Officers must carefully consider if removing copies or images of relevant material or data would be a satisfactory alternative to removing originals. When originals are taken, officers must be prepared to facilitate the provision of copies or images for the owners when reasonably practicable. See Note 7C

7.8   Property seized under the Criminal Justice and Police Act 2001, sections 50 or 51 must be kept securely and separately from any material seized under other powers. An examination under section 53 to determine which elements may be retained must be carried out at the earliest practicable time, having due regard to the desirability of allowing the person from whom the property was seized, or a person with an interest in the property, an opportunity of being present or represented at the examination.

7.8A   All reasonable steps should be taken to accommodate an interested person's request to be present, provided the request is reasonable and subject to the need to prevent harm to, interference with, or unreasonable delay to the investigatory process. If an examination proceeds in the absence of an interested person who asked to attend or their representative, the officer who exercised the relevant seizure power must give that person a written notice of why the examination was carried out in those circumstances. If it is necessary for security reasons or to maintain confidentiality officers may exclude interested persons from decryption or other processes which facilitate the examination but do not form part of it. See Note 7D

7.9   It is the responsibility of the officer in charge of the investigation to make sure property is returned in accordance with sections 53 to 55. Material which there is no power to retain must be:

- separated from the rest of the seized property
- returned as soon as reasonably practicable after examination of all the seized property

7.9A   Delay is only warranted if very clear and compelling reasons exist, e.g. the:

- unavailability of the person to whom the material is to be returned
- need to agree a convenient time to return a large volume of material

7.9B   Legally privileged, excluded or special procedure material which cannot be retained must be returned:

- as soon as reasonably practicable
- without waiting for the whole examination

7.9C   As set out in section 58, material must be returned to the person from whom it was seized, except when it is clear some other person has a better right to it. See Note 7E

7.10   When an officer involved in the investigation has reasonable grounds to believe a person with a relevant interest in property seized under section 50 or 51 intends to make an application under section 59 for the return of any legally privileged, special procedure or excluded material, the officer in charge of the investigation should be informed as soon as practicable and the material seized should be kept secure in accordance with section 61. See Note 7C

7.11   The officer in charge of the investigation is responsible for making sure property is properly secured. Securing involves making sure the property is not examined, copied, imaged or put to any other use except at the request, or with the consent, of the applicant or in accordance with the directions of the appropriate judicial authority. Any request, consent or directions must be recorded in writing and signed by both the initiator and the officer in charge of the investigation. See Notes 7F and 7G

7.12   When an officer exercises a power of seizure conferred by sections 50 or 51 they shall provide the occupier of the premises or the person from whom the property is being seized with a written notice:

(i)   specifying what has been seized under the powers conferred by that section;

(ii)   specifying the grounds for those powers;

(iii)   setting out the effect of sections 59 to 61 covering the grounds for a person with a relevant interest in seized property to apply to a judicial authority for its return and the duty of officers to secure property in certain circumstances when an application is made;

(iv)   specifying the name and address of the person to whom:

- notice of an application to the appropriate judicial authority in respect of any of the seized property must be given;
- an application may be made to allow attendance at the initial examination of the property.

7.13   If the occupier is not present but there is someone in charge of the premises, the notice shall be given to them. If no suitable person is available, so the notice will easily be found it should either be:
  - left in a prominent place on the premises;
  - attached to the exterior of the premises.

(c) Retention

7.14   Subject to paragraph 7.15, anything seized in accordance with the above provisions may be retained only for as long as is necessary. It may be retained, among other purposes:
  (i)   for use as evidence at a trial for an offence;
  (ii)   to facilitate the use in any investigation or proceedings of anything to which it is inextricably linked, see Note 7H;
  (iii) for forensic examination or other investigation in connection with an offence;
  (iv)   in order to establish its lawful owner when there are reasonable grounds for believing it has been stolen or obtained by the commission of an offence.

7.15   Property shall not be retained under paragraph 7.14(i), (ii) or (iii) if a copy or image would be sufficient.

(d) Rights of owners etc.

7.16   If property is retained, the person who had custody or control of it immediately before seizure must, on request, be provided with a list or description of the property within a reasonable time.

7.17   That person or their representative must be allowed supervised access to the property to examine it or have it photographed or copied, or must be provided with a photo-graph or copy, in either case within a reasonable time of any request and at their own expense, unless the officer in charge of an investigation has reasonable grounds for believing this would:
  (i)   prejudice the investigation of any offence or criminal proceedings; or
  (ii)   lead to the commission of an offence by providing access to unlawful material such as pornography;
A record of the grounds shall be made when access is denied.

Notes for Guidance

7A   Any person claiming property seized by the police may apply to a magistrates' court under the Police (Property) Act 1897 for its possession and should, if appropriate, be advised of this procedure.

7B   The powers of seizure conferred by PACE, sections 18(2) and 19(3) extend to the seizure of the whole premises when it is physically possible to seize and retain the premises in their totality and practical considerations make seizure desirable. For example, police may remove premises such as tents, vehicles or caravans to a police station for the purpose of preserving evidence.

7C   Officers should consider reaching agreement with owners and/or other interested parties on the procedures for examining a specific set of property, rather than awaiting the judicial authority's determination. Agreement can sometimes give a quicker and more satis-factory route for all concerned and minimise costs and legal complexities.

7D   What constitutes a relevant interest in specific material may depend on the nature of that material and the circumstances in which it is seized. Anyone with a reasonable claim to ownership of the material and anyone entrusted with its safe keeping by the owner should be considered.

7E   Requirements to secure and return property apply equally to all copies, images or other material created because of seizure of the original property.

7F   The mechanics of securing property vary according to the circumstances; 'bagging up', i.e. placing material in sealed bags or containers and strict subsequent control of access is the appropriate procedure in many cases.

7G   When material is seized under the powers of seizure conferred by PACE, the duty to retain it under the Code of Practice issued under the Criminal Procedure and Investigations Act 1996 is subject to the provisions on retention of seized material in PACE, section 22.

7H   Paragraph 7.14 (ii) applies if inextricably linked material is seized under the Criminal Justice and Police Act 2001, sections 50 or 51. Inextricably linked material is material it is not reasonably practicable to separate from other linked material without prejudicing the use of that other material in any investigation or proceedings. For example, it may not be possible to separate items of data held on computer disk without damaging their evidential integrity. Inextricably linked material must not be examined, imaged, copied or used for any purpose other than for proving the source and/or integrity of the linked material.

8   Action after searches

8.1   If premises are searched in circumstances where this Code applies, unless the exceptions in paragraph 2.3(a) apply, on arrival at a police station the officer in charge of the search shall make or have made a record of the search, to include:
- (i)   the address of the searched premises;
- (ii)   the date, time and duration of the search;
- (iii)   the authority used for the search:
  - if the search was made in exercise of a statutory power to search premises without warrant, the power which was used for the search:
  - if the search was made under a warrant or with written consent;
    - ~ a copy of the warrant and the written authority to apply for it, see paragraph 3.4; or
    - ~ the written consent;

    shall be appended to the record or the record shall show the location of the copy warrant or consent.
- (iv)   subject to paragraph 2.9, the names of:
  - the officer(s) in charge of the search;
  - all other officers who conducted the search;
- (v)   the names of any people on the premises if they are known;
- (vi)   any grounds for refusing the occupier's request to have someone present during the search, see paragraph 6.11;
- (vii)   a list of any articles seized or the location of a list and, if not covered by a warrant, the grounds for their seizure;
- (viii) whether force was used, and the reason;
- (ix)   details of any damage caused during the search, and the circumstances;
- (x)   if applicable, the reason it was not practicable:
  - (a) to give the occupier a copy of the Notice of Powers and Rights, see paragraph 6.7;
  - (b) before the search to give the occupier a copy of the Notice, see paragraph 6.8;
- (xi)   when the occupier was not present, the place where copies of the Notice of Powers and Rights and search warrant were left on the premises, see paragraph 6.8.

8.2   When premises are searched under warrant, the warrant shall be endorsed to show:
- (i)   if any articles specified in the warrant were found;
- (ii)   if any other articles were seized;
- (iii)   the date and time it was executed;
- (iv)   subject to paragraph 2.9, the names of the officers who executed it;
- (v)   if a copy, together with a copy of the Notice of Powers and Rights was:
  - handed to the occupier; or
  - endorsed as required by paragraph 6.8; and left on the premises and where.

8.3   Any warrant shall be returned within one calendar month of its issue, if it was issued by a:

- justice of the peace, to the clerk to the justices for the petty sessions area concerned;
- judge, to the appropriate officer of the court concerned.

9   Search registers

9.1   A search register will be maintained at each sub-divisional or equivalent police station. All search records required under paragraph 8.1 shall be made, copied, or referred to in the register. See Note 9A

Note for Guidance

9A   Paragraph 9.1 also applies to search records made by immigration officers. In these cases, a search register must also be maintained at an immigration office. See also Note 2D

Code of Practice for the Detention, Treatment and Questioning of Persons by Police Officers (Code C)

1   General

1.1   All persons in custody must be dealt with expeditiously, and released as soon as the need for detention no longer applies.

1.1A   A custody officer must perform the functions in this Code as soon as practicable. A custody officer will not be in breach of this Code if delay is justifiable and reasonable steps are taken to prevent unnecessary delay. The custody record shall show when a delay has occurred and the reason. See Note 1H

1.2   This Code of Practice must be readily available at all police stations for consultation by:

- police officers;
- detained persons;
- members of the public.

1.3   The provisions of this Code:

- include the *Annexes*;
- do not include the *Notes for Guidance*.

1.4   If an officer has any suspicion, or is told in good faith, that a person of any age may be mentally disordered or otherwise mentally vulnerable, in the absence of clear evidence to dispel that suspicion, the person shall be treated as such for the purposes of this Code. See Note 1G.

1.5   If anyone appears to be under 17, they shall be treated as a juvenile for the purposes of this Code in the absence of clear evidence that they are older.

1.6   If a person appears to be blind, seriously visually impaired, deaf, unable to read or speak or has difficulty orally because of a speech impediment, they shall be treated as such for the purposes of this Code in the absence of clear evidence to the contrary.

1.7   'The appropriate adult' means, in the case of a:

- (a) juvenile:
    - (i) the parent, guardian or, if the juvenile is in local authority or voluntary organisation care, or is otherwise being looked after under the Children Act 1989, a person representing that authority or organisation;
    - (ii) a social worker of a local authority social services department;
    - (iii) failing these, some other responsible adult aged 18 or over who is not a police officer or employed by the police.
- (b) person who is mentally disordered or mentally vulnerable: See Note 1D

(i)   a relative, guardian or other person responsible for their care or custody;
(ii) someone experienced in dealing with mentally disordered or mentally vulnerable people but who is not a police officer or employed by the police;
(iii) failing these, some other responsible adult aged 18 or over who is not a police officer or employed by the police.

1.8   If this Code requires a person be given certain information, they do not have to be given it if at the time they are incapable of understanding what is said, are violent or may become violent or in urgent need of medical attention, but they must be given it as soon as practicable.

1.9   References to a custody officer include those performing the functions of a custody officer.

1.9A   When this Code requires the prior authority or agreement of an officer of at least inspector or superintendent rank, that authority may be given by a sergeant or chief inspector authorised to perform the functions of the higher rank under the Police and Criminal Evidence Act 1984 (PACE), section 107.

1.10   Subject to paragraph 1.12, this Code applies to people in custody at police stations in England and Wales, whether or not they have been arrested, and to those removed to a police station as a place of safety under the Mental Health Act 1983, sections 135 and 136. Section 15 applies solely to people in police detention, e.g. those brought to a police station under arrest or arrested at a police station for an offence after going there voluntarily.

1.11   People in police custody include anyone detained under the Terrorism Act 2000, Schedule 8 and section 41, having been taken to a police station after being arrested under the Terrorism Act 2000, section 41. In these cases, reference to an offence in this Code includes the commission, preparation and instigation of acts of terrorism.

1.12   This Code's provisions do not apply to people in custody:
(i)   arrested on warrants issued in Scotland by officers under the Criminal Justice and Public Order Act 1994, section 136(2), or arrested or detained without warrant by officers from a police force in Scotland under section 137(2). In these cases, police powers and duties and the person's rights and entitlements whilst at a police station in England or Wales are the same as those in Scotland;
(ii) arrested under the Immigration and Asylum Act 1999, section 142(3) in order to have their fingerprints taken;
(iii) whose detention is authorised by an immigration officer under the Immigration Act 1971;
(iv) who are convicted or remanded prisoners held in police cells on behalf of the Prison Service under the Imprisonment (Temporary Provisions) Act 1980;
(v)   detained for examination under the Terrorism Act 2000, Schedule 7 and to whom the Code of Practice issued under that Act, Schedule 14, paragraph 6 applies;
(vi) detained for searches under stop and search powers except as required by Code A.
The provisions on conditions of detention and treatment in sections 8 and 9 must be considered as the minimum standards of treatment for such detainees.

1.13   In this Code:
(a) 'designated person' means a person other than a police officer, designated under the Police Reform Act 2002, Part 4 who has specified powers and duties of police officers conferred or imposed on them;
(b) reference to a police officer includes a designated person acting in the exercise or performance of the powers and duties conferred or imposed on them by their designation.

1.14   If a power conferred on a designated person:
(a) allows reasonable force to be used when exercised by a police officer, a person exercising that power has the same entitlement to use force;

(b) includes power to use force to enter any premises, that power is not exercisable by that designated person except:

  (i) in the company, and under the supervision, of a police officer;

  (ii) for the purpose of:
  - saving life or limb; or
  - preventing serious damage to property.

1.15   Nothing in this Code prevents the custody officer, or other officer given custody of the detainee, from allowing civilian support staff who are not designated persons to carry out individual procedures or tasks at the police station if the law allows. However, the officer remains responsible for making sure the procedures and tasks are carried out correctly in accordance with the Codes of Practice. Any such civilian must be:

  (a) a person employed by a police authority maintaining a police force and under the control and direction of the Chief Officer of that force;

  (b) employed by a person with whom a police authority has a contract for the provision of services relating to persons arrested or otherwise in custody.

1.16   Designated persons and other civilian support staff must have regard to any relevant provisions of the Codes of Practice.

1.17   References to pocket books include any official report book issued to police officers or civilian support staff.

Notes for Guidance

1A   Although certain sections of this Code apply specifically to people in custody at police stations, those there voluntarily to assist with an investigation should be treated with no less consideration, e.g. offered refreshments at appropriate times, and enjoy an absolute right to obtain legal advice or communicate with anyone outside the police station.

1B   A person, including a parent or guardian, should not be an appropriate adult if they:
- are
  - ~ suspected of involvement in the offence;
  - ~ the victim;
  - ~ a witness;
  - ~ involved in the investigatio;
- received admissions prior to attending to act as the appropriate adult.

Note: If a juvenile's parent is estranged from the juvenile, they should not be asked to act as the appropriate adult if the juvenile expressly and specifically objects to their presence.

1C   If a juvenile admits an offence to, or in the presence of, a social worker or member of a youth offending team other than during the time that person is acting as the juvenile's appropriate adult, another appropriate adult should be appointed in the interest of fairness.

1D   In the case of people who are mentally disordered or otherwise mentally vulnerable, it may be more satisfactory if the appropriate adult is someone experienced or trained in their care rather than a relative lacking such qualifications. But if the detainee prefers a relative to a better qualified stranger or objects to a particular person their wishes should, if practicable, be respected.

1E   A detainee should always be given an opportunity, when an appropriate adult is called to the police station, to consult privately with a solicitor in the appropriate adult's absence if they want.

1F   A solicitor or independent custody visitor (formerly a lay visitor) present at the police station in that capacity may not be the appropriate adult.

1G   'Mentally vulnerable' applies to any detainee who, because of their mental state or capacity, may not understand the significance of what is said, of questions or of their replies. 'Mental disorder' is defined in the Mental Health Act 1983, section 1(2) as 'mental illness, arrested or incomplete development of mind, psychopathic disorder and any other disorder or disability of mind'. When the custody officer has any doubt about the mental state or capacity of a detainee, that detainee should be treated as mentally vulnerable and an appropriate adult called.

1H   Paragraph 1.1A is intended to cover delays which may occur in processing detainees e.g. if:

- a large number of suspects are brought into the station simultaneously to be placed in custody;
- interview rooms are all being used;
- there are difficulties contacting an appropriate adult, solicitor or interpreter.

1I   The custody officer must remind the appropriate adult and detainee about the right to legal advice and record any reasons for waiving it in accordance with section 6.

2   Custody records

2.1   A separate custody record must be opened as soon as practicable for each person brought to a police station under arrest or arrested at the station having gone there voluntarily. All information recorded under this Code must be recorded as soon as practicable in the custody record unless otherwise specified. Any audio or video recording made in the custody area is not part of the custody record.

2.2   If any action requires the authority of an officer of a specified rank, subject to paragraph 2.6A, their name and rank must be noted in the custody record.

2.3   The custody officer is responsible for the custody record's accuracy and completeness and for making sure the record or copy of the record accompanies a detainee if they are transferred to another police station. The record shall show the:

- time and reason for transfer;
- time a person is released from detention.

2.4   A solicitor or appropriate adult must be permitted to consult a detainee's custody record as soon as practicable after their arrival at the station and at any other time whilst the person is detained. Arrangements for this access must be agreed with the custody officer and may not unreasonably interfere with the custody officer's duties.

2.4A   When a detainee leaves police detention or is taken before a court they, their legal representative or appropriate adult shall be given, on request, a copy of the custody record as soon as practicable. This entitlement lasts for 12 months after release.

2.5   The detainee, appropriate adult or legal representative shall be permitted to inspect the original custody record after the detainee has left police detention provided they give reasonable notice of their request. Any such inspection shall be noted in the custody record.

2.6   Subject to paragraph 2.6A, all entries in custody records must be timed and signed by the maker. Records entered on computer shall be timed and contain the operator's identification.

2.6A   Nothing in this Code requires the identity of officers or civilian support staff to be recorded or disclosed:

- (a) in the case of enquiries linked to the investigation of terrorism; or
- (b) if the officer or civilian support staff reasonably believe recording or disclosing their name might put them in danger.

In these cases, they shall use their warrant or other identification numbers and the name of their police station. See Note 2A

2.7   The fact and time of any detainee's refusal to sign a custody record, when asked in accordance with this Code, must be recorded.

Note for Guidance

2A   The purpose of paragraph 2.6A(b) is to protect those involved in serious organised crime investigations or arrests of particularly violent suspects when there is reliable information that those arrested or their associates may threaten or cause harm to those involved. In cases of doubt, an officer of inspector rank or above should be consulted.

3   Initial action

(a) Detained persons – normal procedure

3.1   When a person is brought to a police station under arrest or arrested at the station having gone there voluntarily, the custody officer must make sure the person is told clearly about the following continuing rights which may be exercised at any stage during the period in custody:

   (i)   the right to have someone informed of their arrest as in section 5;

   (ii)   the right to consult privately with a solicitor and that free independent legal advice is available;

   (iii)   the right to consult these Codes of Practice. See Note 3D

3.2   The detainee must also be given:

- a written notice setting out:
  - ~ the above three rights;
  - ~ the arrangements for obtaining legal advice;
  - ~ the right to a copy of the custody record as in paragraph 2.4A;
  - ~ the caution in the terms prescribed in section 10.
- an additional written notice briefly setting out their entitlements while in custody, see Notes 3A and 3B.

Note: The detainee shall be asked to sign the custody record to acknowledge receipt of these notices. Any refusal must be recorded on the custody record.

3.3   A citizen of an independent Commonwealth country or a national of a foreign country, including the Republic of Ireland, must be informed as soon as practicable about their rights of communication with their High Commission, Embassy or Consulate. See section 7

3.4   The custody officer shall:

- note on the custody record any comment the detainee makes in relation to the arresting officer's account but shall not invite comment. If the custody officer authorises a person's detention the detainee must be informed of the grounds as soon as practicable and before they are questioned about any offence;
- note any comment the detainee makes in respect of the decision to detain them but shall not invite comment;
- not put specific questions to the detainee regarding their involvement in any offence, nor in respect of any comments they may make in response to the arresting officer's account or the decision to place them in detention. Such an exchange is likely to constitute an interview as in paragraph 11.1A and require the associated safeguards in section 11.

See paragraph 11.13 in respect of unsolicited comments.

3.5   The custody officer shall:

   (a)   ask the detainee, whether at this time, they:

     (i)   would like legal advice, see paragraph 6.5;

     (ii)   want someone informed of their detention, see section 5;

   (b)   ask the detainee to sign the custody record to confirm their decisions in respect of (a);

   (c)   determine whether the detainee:

     (i)   is, or might be, in need of medical treatment or attention, see section 9;

     (ii)   requires:

- an appropriate adult;
- help to check documentation;
- an interpreter;

   (d)   record the decision in respect of (c).

3.6   When determining these needs the custody officer is responsible for initiating an assessment to consider whether the detainee is likely to present specific risks to custody staff or themselves. Such assessments should always include a check on the Police National Computer, to be carried out as soon as practicable, to identify any risks highlighted in relation to the detainee. Although such assessments are primarily the custody officer's responsibility, it may be necessary for them to consult and involve others, e.g. the arresting officer or an appropriate health care professional, see paragraph 9.13. Reasons for delaying the initiation or completion of the assessment must be recorded.

3.7   Chief Officers should ensure that arrangements for proper and effective risk assessments required by paragraph 3.6 are implemented in respect of all detainees at police stations in their area.

3.8   Risk assessments must follow a structured process which clearly defines the categories of risk to be considered and the results must be incorporated in the detainee's custody record. The custody officer is responsible for making sure those responsible for the detainee's custody are appropriately briefed about the risks. If no specific risks are identified by the assessment, that should be noted in the custody record. See Note 3E and paragraph 9.14

3.9   The custody officer is responsible for implementing the response to any specific risk assessment, e.g.:
- reducing opportunities for self harm;
- calling a health care professional;
- increasing levels of monitoring or observation.

3.10   Risk assessment is an ongoing process and assessments must always be subject to review if circumstances change.

3.11   If video cameras are installed in the custody area, notices shall be prominently displayed showing cameras are in use. Any request to have video cameras switched off shall be refused.

(b) Detained persons – special groups

3.12   If the detainee appears deaf or there is doubt about their hearing or speaking ability or ability to understand English, and the custody officer cannot establish effective communication, the custody officer must, as soon as practicable, call an interpreter for assistance in the action under paragraphs 3.1–3.5. See section 13

3.13   If the detainee is a juvenile, the custody officer must, if it is practicable, ascertain the identity of a person responsible for their welfare. That person:
- may be:
  - ~ the parent or guardian;
  - ~ if the juvenile is in local authority or voluntary organisation care, or is otherwise being looked after under the Children Act 1989, a person appointed by that authority or organisation to have responsibility for the juvenile's welfare;
  - ~ any other person who has, for the time being, assumed responsibility for the juvenile's welfare.
- must be informed as soon as practicable that the juvenile has been arrested, why they have been arrested and where they are detained. This right is in addition to the juvenile's right in section 5 not to be held incommunicado. See Note 3C

3.14   If a juvenile known to be subject to a court order under which a person or organisation is given any degree of statutory responsibility to supervise or otherwise monitor them, reasonable steps must also be taken to notify that person or organisation (the 'responsible officer'). The responsible officer will normally be a member of a Youth Offending Team, except for a curfew order which involves electronic monitoring when the contractor providing the monitoring will normally be the responsible officer.

3.15   If the detainee is a juvenile, mentally disordered or otherwise mentally vulnerable, the custody officer must, as soon as practicable:

- inform the appropriate adult, who in the case of a juvenile may or may not be a person responsible for their welfare, as in paragraph 3.13, of:
  - ~ the grounds for their detention;
  - ~ their whereabouts.
- ask the adult to come to the police station to see the detainee.

3.16   It is imperative a mentally disordered or otherwise mentally vulnerable person, detained under the Mental Health Act 1983, section 136, be assessed as soon as possible. If that assessment is to take place at the police station, an approved social worker and a registered medical practitioner shall be called to the station as soon as possible in order to interview and examine the detainee. Once the detainee has been interviewed, examined and suitable arrangements made for their treatment or care, they can no longer be detained under section 136. A detainee must be immediately discharged from detention under section 136 if a registered medical practitioner, having examined them, concludes they are not mentally disordered within the meaning of the Act.

3.17   If the appropriate adult is:
- already at the police station, the provisions of paragraphs 3.1 to 3.5 must be complied with in the appropriate adult's presence;
- not at the station when these provisions are complied with, they must be complied with again in the presence of the appropriate adult when they arrive.

3.18   The detainee shall be advised that:
- the duties of the appropriate adult include giving advice and assistance;
- they can consult privately with the appropriate adult at any time.

3.19   If the detainee, or appropriate adult on the detainee's behalf, asks for a solicitor to be called to give legal advice, the provisions of section 6 apply.

3.20   If the detainee is blind, seriously visually impaired or unable to read, the custody officer shall make sure their solicitor, relative, appropriate adult or some other person likely to take an interest in them and not involved in the investigation is available to help check any documentation. When this Code requires written consent or signing the person assisting may be asked to sign instead, if the detainee prefers. This paragraph does not require an appropriate adult to be called solely to assist in checking and signing documentation for a person who is not a juvenile, or mentally disordered or otherwise mentally vulnerable (see paragraph 3.15).

(c) Persons attending a police station voluntarily

3.21   Anybody attending a police station voluntarily to assist with an investigation may leave at will unless arrested. If it is decided they shall not be allowed to leave, they must be informed at once that they are under arrest and brought before the custody officer, who is responsible for making sure they are notified of their rights in the same way as other detainees. If they are not arrested but are cautioned as in section 10, the person who gives the caution must, at the same time, inform them they are not under arrest, they are not obliged to remain at the station but if they remain at the station they may obtain free and independent legal advice if they want. They shall be told the right to legal advice includes the right to speak with a solicitor on the telephone and be asked if they want to do so.

3.22   If a person attending the police station voluntarily asks about their entitlement to legal advice, they shall be given a copy of the notice explaining the arrangements for obtaining legal advice. See paragraph 3.2

(d) Documentation

3.23   The grounds for a person's detention shall be recorded, in the person's presence if practicable.

3.24   Action taken under paragraphs 3.12 to 3.20 shall be recorded.

Notes for Guidance

3A   The notice of entitlements should:

- list the entitlements in this Code, including:
  - ~ visits and contact with outside parties, including special provisions for Commonwealth citizens and foreign nationals;
  - ~ reasonable standards of physical comfort;
  - ~ adequate food and drink;
  - ~ access to toilets and washing facilities, clothing, medical attention, and exercise when practicable.
- *mention the:*
  - ~ provisions relating to the conduct of interviews;
  - ~ circumstances in which an appropriate adult should be available to assist the detainee and them statutory rights to make representation whenever the period of them detention is reviewed.

3B   In addition to notices in English, translations should be available in Welsh, the main minority ethnic languages and the principal European languages, whenever they are likely to be helpful.

3C   If the juvenile is in local authority or voluntary organisation care but living with their parents or other adults responsible for their welfare, although there is no legal obligation to inform them, they should normally be contacted, as well as the authority or organisation unless suspected of involvement in the offence concerned. Even if the juvenile is not living with their parents, consideration should be given to informing them.

3D   The right to consult the Codes of Practice does not entitle the person concerned to delay unreasonably any necessary investigative or administrative action whilst they do so. Examples of action which need not be delayed unreasonably include:

- procedures requiring the provision of breath, blood or urine specimens under the Road Traffic Act 1988 or the Transport and Works Act 1992;
- searching detainees at the police station;
- taking fingerprints or non-intimate samples without consent for evidential purposes.

3E   Home Office Circular 32/2000 provides more detailed guidance on risk assessments and identifies key risk areas which should always be considered.

4   Detainee's property

(a) Action

4.1   The custody officer is responsible for:
  (a) ascertaining what property a detainee:
    (i) has with them when they come to the police station, whether on:
      - arrest or re-detention on answering to bail;
      - commitment to prison custody on the order or sentence of a court;
      - lodgement at the police station with a view to their production in court from prison custody;
      - transfer from detention at another station or hospital;
      - detention under the Mental Health Act 1983, section 135 or 136;
    (ii) might have acquired for an unlawful or harmful purpose while in custody;
  (b) the safekeeping of any property taken from a detainee which remains at the police station.

The custody officer may search the detainee or authorise their being searched to the extent they consider necessary, provided a search of intimate parts of the body or involving the removal of more than outer clothing is only made as in Annex A. A search may only be carried out by an officer of the same sex as the detainee. See Note 4A

4.2   Detainees may retain clothing and personal effects at their own risk unless the custody officer considers they may use them to cause harm to themselves or others, interfere with evidence, damage property, effect an escape or they are needed as evidence. In this event the custody officer may withhold such articles as they consider necessary and must tell the detainee why.

4.3   Personal effects are those items a detainee may lawfully need, use or refer to while in detention but do not include cash and other items of value.

(b) Documentation

4.4   The custody officer is responsible for recording all property brought to the police station which a detainee had with them, or had taken from them on arrest. The detainee shall be allowed to check and sign the record of property as correct. Any refusal to sign shall be recorded.

4.5   If a detainee is not allowed to keep any article of clothing or personal effects, the reason must be recorded.

Notes for Guidance

4A   PACE, section 54(1) and paragraph 4.1 require a detainee to be searched when it is clear the custody offices will have continuing duties in relation to that detainee or when that detainee's behaviour or offence makes an inventory appropriate. They do not require every detainee to be searched, e.g. if it is clear a person will only be detained for a short period and is not to be placed in a cell, the custody officer may decide not to search them. In such a case the custody record will be endorsed 'not searched', paragraph 4.4 will not apply, and the detainee will be invited to sign the entry. If the detainee refuses, the custody officer will be obliged to ascertain what property they have in accordance with paragraph 4.1.

4B   Paragraph 4.4 does not require the custody officer to record on the custody record property in the detainee's possession on arrest if, by virtue of its nature, quantity or size, it is not practicable to remove it to the police station.

4C   Paragraph 4.4 does not require items of clothing worn by the person be recorded unless withheld by the custody offices as in paragraph 4.2.

5   Right not to be held incommunicado

(a) Action

5.1   Any person arrested and held in custody at a police station or other premises may, on request, have one person known to them or likely to take an interest in their welfare informed at public expense of their whereabouts as soon as practicable. If the person cannot be contacted the detainee may choose up to two alternatives. If they cannot be contacted, the person in charge of detention or the investigation has discretion to allow further attempts until the information has been conveyed. See Notes 5C and 5D

5.2   The exercise of the above right in respect of each person nominated may be delayed only in accordance with Annex B.

5.3   The above right may be exercised each time a detainee is taken to another police station.

5.4   The detainee may receive visits at the custody officer's discretion. See Note 5B

5.5   If a friend, relative or person with an interest in the detainee's welfare enquires about their whereabouts, this information shall be given if the suspect agrees and *Annex B* does not apply. See Note 5D

5.6   The detainee shall be given writing materials, on request, and allowed to telephone one person for a reasonable time, see Notes 5A and 5E. Either or both these privileges may be denied or delayed if an officer of inspector rank or above considers sending a letter or making a telephone call may result in any of the consequences in:

(a) Annex B paragraphs 1 and 2 and the person is detained in connection with an arrestable or serious arrestable offence; or

(b) Annex B paragraphs 8 and 9 and the person is detained under the Terrorism Act 2000, Schedule 7 or section 41

For the purposes of this paragraph, any reference to a serious arrestable offence in Annex B includes an arrestable offence. However, nothing in this paragraph permits the restriction or denial of the rights in paragraphs 5.1 and 6.1.

5.7   Before any letter or message is sent, or telephone call made, the detainee shall be informed that what they say in any letter, call or message (other than in a communication to a solicitor) may be read or listened to and may be given in evidence. A telephone call may be terminated if it is being abused. The costs can be at public expense at the custody officer's discretion.

(b) Documentation

5.8   A record must be kept of any:

(a) request made under this section and the action taken;

(b) letters, messages or telephone calls made or received or visit received;

(c) refusal by the detainee to have information about them given to an outside enquirer. The detainee must be asked to countersign the record accordingly and any refusal recorded.

Notes for Guidance

5A   A person may request an interpreter to interpret a telephone call or translate a letter.

5B   At the custody officer's discretion, visits should be allowed when possible, subject to having sufficient personnel to supervise a visit and any possible hindrance to the investigation.

5C   If the detainee does not know anyone to contact for advice or support or cannot contact a friend or relative, the custody officer should bear in mind any local voluntary bodies or other organisations who might be able to help. Paragraph 6.1 applies if legal advice is required.

5D   In some circumstances it may not be appropriate to use the telephone to disclose information under paragraphs 5.1 and 5.5.

5E   The telephone call at paragraph 5.6 is in addition to any communication under paragraphs 5.1 and 6.1.

6   Right to legal advice

(a) Action

6.1   Unless Annex B applies, all detainees must be informed that they may at any time consult and communicate privately with a solicitor, whether in person, in writing or by telephone, and that free independent legal advice is available from the duty solicitor. See paragraph 3.1, Note 6B and Note 6J

6.2   Not Used

6.3   A poster advertising the right to legal advice must be prominently displayed in the charging area of every police station. See Note 6H

6.4   No police officer should, at any time, do or say anything with the intention of dissuading a detainee from obtaining legal advice.

6.5   The exercise of the right of access to legal advice may be delayed only as in Annex B. Whenever legal advice is requested, and unless Annex B applies, the custody officer must act without delay to secure the provision of such advice. If, on being informed or reminded of this right, the detainee declines to speak to a solicitor in person, the officer should point out that the right includes the right to speak with a solicitor on the telephone. If the detainee continues to waive this right the officer should ask them why and any reasons should be recorded on the custody record or the interview record as appropriate. Reminders of the right to legal advice must be given as in paragraphs 3.5, 11.2, 15.4, 16.4 and 16.5 and Code D, paragraphs 3.17(ii) and 6.3. Once it is clear a detainee does not want to speak to a solicitor in person or by telephone they should cease to be asked their reasons. See Note 6K

6.6   A detainee who wants legal advice may not be interviewed or continue to be interviewed until they have received such advice unless:

(a) Annex B applies, when the restriction on drawing adverse inferences from silence in Annex C will apply because the detainee is not allowed an opportunity to consult a solicitor; or

(b) an officer of superintendent rank or above has reasonable grounds for believing that:

    (i) the consequent delay might:

- lead to interference with, or harm to, evidence connected with an offence;
- lead to interference with, or physical harm to, other people;
- lead to serious loss of, or damage to, property;
- lead to alerting other people suspected of having committed an offence but not yet arrested for it;
- hinder the recovery of property obtained in consequence of the commission of an offence.

    (ii) when a solicitor, including a duty solicitor, has been contacted and has agreed to attend, awaiting their arrival would cause unreasonable delay to the process of investigation.

Note: In these cases the restriction on drawing adverse inferences from silence in Annex C will apply because the detainee is not allowed an opportunity to consult a solicitor;

(c) the solicitor the detainee has nominated or selected from a list:

    (i)   cannot be contacted;

    (ii) has previously indicated they do not wish to be contacted; or

    (iii) having been contacted, has declined to attend; and

          the detainee has been advised of the Duty Solicitor Scheme but has declined to ask for the duty solicitor.

          In these circumstances the interview may be started or continued without further delay provided an officer of inspector rank or above has agreed to the interview proceeding.

Note: The restriction on drawing adverse inferences from silence in Annex C will not apply because the detainee is allowed an opportunity to consult the duty solicitor;

(d) the detainee changes their mind, about wanting legal advice.

          In these circumstances the interview may be started or continued without delay provided that:

    (i) the detainee agrees to do so, in writing or on tape; and

    (ii) an officer of inspector rank or above has inquired about the detainee's reasons for their change of mind and gives authority for the interview to proceed.

Confirmation of the detainee's agreement, their change of mind, the reasons for it if given and, subject to paragraph 2.6A, the name of the authorising officer shall be recorded in the taped or written interview record. See Note 61. Note: In these circumstances the restriction on drawing adverse inferences from silence in Annex C will not apply because the detainee is allowed an opportunity to consult a solicitor if they wish.

6.7   If paragraph 6.6(b)(i) applies, once sufficient information has been obtained to avert the risk, questioning must cease until the detainee has received legal advice unless paragraph 6.6(a), (b)(ii), (c) or (d) applies.

6.8   A detainee who has been permitted to consult a solicitor shall be entitled on request to have the solicitor present when they are interviewed unless one of the exceptions in paragraph 6.6 applies.

6.9   The solicitor may only be required to leave the interview if their conduct is such that the interviewer is unable properly to put questions to the suspect. See Notes 6D and 6E

6.10   If the interviewer considers a solicitor is acting in such a way, they will stop the interview and consult an officer not below superintendent rank, if one is readily available, and otherwise an officer not below inspector rank not connected with the investigation. After speaking to the solicitor, the officer consulted will decide if the interview should continue in the presence of that solicitor. If they decide it should not, the suspect will be given the opportunity to consult another solicitor before the interview continues and that solicitor given an opportunity to be present at the interview. See Note 6E

6.11   The removal of a solicitor from an interview is a serious step and, if it occurs, the officer of superintendent rank or above who took the decision will consider if the incident should be reported to the Law Society. If the decision to remove the solicitor has been taken by an officer below superintendent rank, the facts must be reported to an officer of superintendent rank or above who will similarly consider whether a report to the Law Society would be appropriate. When the solicitor concerned is a duty solicitor, the report should be both to the Law Society and to the Legal Services Commission.

6.12   'Solicitor' in this Code means:
- a solicitor who holds a current practising certificate;
- a trainee solicitor;
- a duty solicitor representative;
- an accredited representative included on the register of representatives maintained by the Legal Services Commission.

6.12A   A non-accredited or probationary representative sent to provide advice by, and on behalf of, a solicitor shall be admitted to the police station for this purpose unless an officer of inspector rank or above considers such a visit will hinder the investigation and directs otherwise. Hindering the investigation does not include giving proper legal advice to a detainee as in Note 6D. Once admitted to the police station, paragraphs 6.6 to 6.10 apply.

6.13   In exercising their discretion under paragraph 6.12A, the officer should take into account in particular:
- whether:
  - ~ the identity and status of the non-accredited or probationary representative have been satisfactorily established;
  - ~ they are of suitable character to provide legal advice, e.g. a person with a criminal record is unlikely to be suitable unless the conviction was for a minor offence and not recent.
- any other matters in any written letter of authorisation provided by the solicitor on whose behalf the person is attending the police station. See Note 6F

6.14   If the inspector refuses access to a non-accredited or probationary representative or a decision is taken that such a person should not be permitted to remain at an interview, the inspector must notify the solicitor on whose behalf the representative was acting and give them an opportunity to make alternative arrangements. The detainee must be informed and the custody record noted.

6.15   If a solicitor arrives at the station to see a particular person, that person must, unless Annex B applies, be so informed whether or not they are being interviewed and asked if they would like to see the solicitor. This applies even if the detainee has declined legal advice or, having requested it, subsequently agreed to be interviewed without receiving advice. The solicitor's attendance and the detainee's decision must be noted in the custody record.

(b) Documentation

6.16   Any request for legal advice and the action taken shall be recorded.

6.17   A record shall be made in the interview record if a detainee asks for legal advice and an interview is begun either in the absence of a solicitor or their representative, or they have been required to leave an interview.

Notes for Guidance

6A   In considering if paragraph 6.6(b) applies, the officer should, if practicable, ask the solicitor for an estimate of how long it will take to come to the station and relate this to the time detention is permitted, the time of day (i.e. whether the rest period under paragraph 12.2

is imminent) and the requirements of other investigations. If the solicitor is on their way or is to set off immediately, it will not normally be appropriate to begin an interview before they arrive. If it appears necessary to begin an interview before the solicitor's arrival, they should be given an indication of how long the police would be able to wait before 6.6(b) applies so there is an opportunity to make arrangements for someone else to provide legal advice.

6B   A detainee who asks for legal advice should be given an opportunity to consult a specific solicitor or another solicitor from that solicitor's firm or the duty solicitor. If advice is not available by these means, or they do not want to consult the duty solicitor, the detainee should be given an opportunity to choose a solicitor from a list of those willing to provide legal advice. If this solicitor is unavailable, they may choose up to two alternatives. If these attempts are unsuccessful, the custody officer has discretion to allow further attempts until a solicitor has been contacted and agrees to provide legal advice. Apart from carrying out these duties, an officer must not advise the suspect about any particular firm of solicitors.

6C   Not Used

6D   A detainee has a right to free legal advice and to be represented by a solicitor. The solicitor's only role in the police station is to protect and advance the legal rights of their client. On occasions this may require the solicitor to give advice which has the effect of the client avoiding giving evidence which strengthens a prosecution case. The solicitor may intervene in order to seek clarification, challenge an improper question to their client or the manner in which it is put, advise their client not to reply to particular questions, or if they wish to give their client further legal advice. Paragraph 6.9 only applies if the solicitor's approach or conduct prevents or unreasonably obstructs proper questions being put to the suspect or the suspect's response being recorded. Examples of unacceptable conduct include answering questions on a suspect's behalf or providing written replies for the suspect to quote.

6E   An officer who takes the decision to exclude a solicitor must be in a position to satisfy the court the decision was properly made. In order to do this they may need to witness what is happening.

6F   If an officer of at least inspector rank considers a particular solicitor or firm of solicitors is persistently sending non-accredited or probationary representatives who are unsuited to provide legal advice, they should inform an officer of at least superintendent rank, who may wish to take the matter up with the Law Society.

6G   Subject to the constraints of Annex B, a solicitor may advise more than one client in an investigation if they wish. Any question of a conflict of interest is for the solicitor under their professional code of conduct. If, however, waiting for a solicitor to give advice to one client may lead to unreasonable delay to the interview with another, the provisions of paragraph 6.6(b) may apply.

6H   In addition to a poster in English, a poster or posters containing translations into Welsh, the main minority ethnic languages and the principal European languages should be displayed wherever they are likely to be helpful and it is practicable to do so.

6I   Paragraph 6.6(d) requires the authorisation of an officer of inspector rank or above to the continuation of an interview when a detainee who wanted legal advice changes their mind. It is permissible for such authorisation to be given over the telephone, if the authorising officer is able to satisfy themselves about the reason for the detainee's change of mind and is satisfied it is proper to continue the interview in those circumstances.

6J   Whenever a detainee exercises their right to legal advice by consulting or communicating with a solicitor, they must be allowed to do so in private. This right to consult or communicate in private is fundamental. Except as allowed by the Terrorism Act 2000, Schedule 8, paragraph 9, if the requirement for privacy is compromised because what is said or written by the detainee or solicitor for the purpose of giving and receiving legal advice is overheard, listened to, or read by others without the informed consent of the detainee, the right will effectively have been denied. When a detainee chooses to speak to a solicitor on the telephone, they should be allowed to do so in private unless this is impractical because of the design and layout of the custody area or the location of telephones. However, the normal expectation should be that facilities will be available, unless they are being used, at all police stations to enable detainees to speak in private to a solicitor either face to face or over the telephone.

6K   A detainee is not obliged to give reasons for declining legal advice and should not be pressed to do so.

7   Citizens of independent Commonwealth countries or foreign nationals

(a) Action

7.1   Any citizen of an independent Commonwealth country or a national of a foreign country, including the Republic of Ireland, may communicate at any time with the appropriate High Commission, Embassy or Consulate. The detainee must be informed as soon as practicable of:
* this right;
* their right, upon request, to have their High Commission, Embassy or Consulate told of their whereabouts and the grounds for their detention. Such a request should be acted upon as soon as practicable.

7.2   If a detainee is a citizen of a country with which a bilateral consular convention or agreement is in force requiring notification of arrest, the appropriate High Commission, Embassy or Consulate shall be informed as soon as practicable, subject to paragraph 7.4. The countries to which this applies as at 1st April 2003 are listed in Annex F.

7.3   Consular officers may visit one of their nationals in police detention to talk to them and, if required, to arrange for legal advice. Such visits shall take place out of the hearing of a police officer.

7.4   Notwithstanding the provisions of consular conventions, if the detainee is a political refugee whether for reasons of race, nationality, political opinion or religion, or is seeking political asylum, consular officers shall not be informed of the arrest of one of their nationals or given access or information about them except at the detainee's express request.

(b) Documentation

7.5   A record shall be made when a detainee is informed of their rights under this section and of any communications with a High Commission, Embassy or Consulate.

Note for Guidance

7A   The exercise of the rights in this section may not be interfered with even though Annex B applies.

8   Conditions of detention

(a) Action

8.1   So far as it is practicable, not more than one detainee should be detained in each cell.

8.2   Cells in use must be adequately heated, cleaned and ventilated. They must be adequately lit, subject to such dimming as is compatible with safety and security to allow people detained overnight to sleep. No additional restraints shall be used within a locked cell unless absolutely necessary and then only restraint equipment, approved for use in that force by the Chief Officer, which is reasonable and necessary in the circumstances having regard to the detainee's demeanour and with a view to ensuring their safety and the safety of others. If a detainee is deaf, mentally disordered or otherwise mentally vulnerable, particular care must be taken when deciding whether to use any form of approved restraints.

8.3   Blankets, mattresses, pillows and other bedding supplied shall be of a reasonable standard and in a clean and sanitary condition. See Note 8A

8.4   Access to toilet and washing facilities must be provided.

8.5   If it is necessary to remove a detainee's clothes for the purposes of investigation, for hygiene, health reasons or cleaning, replacement clothing of a reasonable standard of comfort and cleanliness shall be provided. A detainee may not be interviewed unless adequate clothing has been offered.

8.6   At least two light meals and one main meal should be offered in any 24 hour period. See Note 8B. Drinks should be provided at meal times and upon reasonable request between meals. Whenever necessary, advice shall be sought from the appropriate health care professional, see Note 9A, on medical and dietary matters. As far as practicable, meals provided shall offer a varied diet and meet any specific dietary needs or religious beliefs the detainee may have. The detainee may, at the custody officer's discretion, have meals supplied by their family or friends at their expense. See Note 8A

8.7   Brief outdoor exercise shall be offered daily if practicable.

8.8   A juvenile shall not be placed in a police cell unless no other secure accommodation is available and the custody officer considers it is not practicable to supervise them if they are not placed in a cell or that a cell provides more comfortable accommodation than other secure accommodation in the station. A juvenile may not be placed in a cell with a detained adult.

(b) Documentation

8.9   A record must be kept of replacement clothing and meals offered.

8.10   If a juvenile is placed in a cell, the reason must be recorded.

8.11   The use of any restraints on a detainee whilst in a cell, the reasons for it and, if appropriate, the arrangements for enhanced supervision of the detainee whilst so restrained, shall be recorded. See paragraph 3.9

Notes for Guidance

8A   The provisions in paragraph 8.3 and 8.6 respectively are of particular importance in the case of a person detained under the Terrorism Act 2000, immigration detainees and others likely to be detained for an extended period. In deciding whether to allow meals to be supplied by family or friends, the custody officer is entitled to take account of the risk of items being concealed in any food or package and the officer's duties and responsibilities under food handling legislation.

8B   Meals should, so far as practicable, be offered at recognised meal times, or at other times that take account of when the detainee last had a meal.

9   Care and treatment of detained persons

(a) General

9.1   Nothing in this section prevents the police from calling the police surgeon or, if appropriate, some other health care professional, to examine a detainee for the purposes of obtaining evidence relating to any offence in which the detainee is suspected of being involved. See Note 9A

9.2   If a complaint is made by, or on behalf of, a detainee about their treatment since their arrest, or it comes to notice that a detainee may have been treated improperly, a report must be made as soon as practicable to an officer of inspector rank or above not connected with the investigation. If the matter concerns a possible assault or the possibility of the unnecessary or unreasonable use of force, an appropriate health care professional must also be called as soon as practicable.

9.3   Detainees should be visited at least every hour. If no reasonably foreseeable risk was identified in a risk assessment, see paragraphs 3.6–3.10, there is no need to wake a sleeping detainee. Those suspected of being intoxicated through drink or drugs or whose level of consciousness causes concern must, subject to any clinical directions given by the appropriate health care professional, see paragraph 9.13:

- be visited and roused at least every half hour;
- have their condition assessed as in Annex H;
- and clinical treatment arranged if appropriate.

See Notes 9B, 9C and 9H

9.4   When arrangements are made to secure clinical attention for a detainee, the custody officer must make sure all relevant information which might assist in the treatment of the detainee's condition is made available to the responsible health care professional. This applies whether or not the health care professional asks for such information. Any officer or civilian support staff with relevant information must inform the custody officer as soon as practicable.

(b) Clinical treatment and attention

9.5   The custody officer must make sure a detainee receives appropriate clinical attention as soon as reasonably practicable if the person:

    (a) appears to be suffering from physical illness; or

    (b) is injured; or

    (c) appears to be suffering from a mental disorder; or

    (d) appears to need clinical attention.

This applies even if the detainee makes no request for clinical attention and whether or not they have already received clinical attention elsewhere. If the need for attention appears urgent, e.g. when indicated as in Annex H, the nearest available health care professional or an ambulance must be called immediately. See Note 9C

9.6   Paragraph 9.5 is not meant to prevent or delay the transfer to a hospital if necessary of a person detained under the Mental Health Act 1983, section 136. See Note 9D. When an assessment under that Act takes place at a police station, see paragraph 3.16, the custody officer must consider whether an appropriate health care professional should be called to conduct an initial clinical check on the detainee. This applies particularly when there is likely to be any significant delay in the arrival of a suitably qualified medical practitioner.

9.7   If it appears to the custody officer, or they are told, that a person brought to a station under arrest may be suffering from an infectious disease or condition, the custody officer must take reasonable steps to safeguard the health of the detainee and others at the station. In deciding what action to take, advice must be sought from an appropriate health care professional. See Note 9E. The custody officer has discretion to isolate the person and their property until clinical directions have been obtained.

9.8   If a detainee requests a clinical examination, an appropriate health care professional must be called as soon as practicable to assess the detainee's clinical needs. If a safe and appropriate care plan cannot be provided, the police surgeon's advice must be sought. The detainee may also be examined by a medical practitioner of their choice at their expense.

9.9   If a detainee is required to take or apply any medication in compliance with clinical directions prescribed before their detention, the custody officer must consult the appropriate health care professional before the use of the medication. Subject to the restrictions in paragraph 9.10, the custody officer is responsible for the safekeeping of any medication and for making sure the detainee is given the opportunity to take or apply prescribed or approved medication. Any such consultation and its outcome shall be noted in the custody record.

9.10   No police officer may administer or supervise the self-administration of controlled drugs of the types and forms listed in the Misuse of Drugs Regulations 2001, Schedule 1, 2 or 3. A detainee may only self-administer such drugs under the personal supervision of the registered medical practitioner authorising their use. Drugs listed in Schedule 4 or 5 may be distributed by the custody officer for selfadministration if they have consulted the registered medical practitioner authorising their use, this may be done by telephone, and both parties are satisfied selfadministration will not expose the detainee, police officers or anyone else to the risk of harm or injury.

9.11   When appropriate health care professionals administer drugs or other medications, or supervise their self-administration, it must be within current medicines legislation and the scope of practice as determined by their relevant professional body.

9.12   If a detainee has in their possession, or claims to need, medication relating to a heart condition, diabetes, epilepsy or a condition of comparable potential seriousness then, even though paragraph 9.5 may not apply, the advice of the appropriate health care professional must be obtained.

9.13   Whenever the appropriate health care professional is called in accordance with this section to examine or treat a detainee, the custody officer shall ask for their opinion about:

- any risks or problems which police need to take into account when making decisions about the detainee's continued detention;
- when to carry out an interview if applicable; and
- the need for safeguards.

9.14   When clinical directions are given by the appropriate health care professional, whether orally or in writing, and the custody officer has any doubts or is in any way uncertain about any aspect of the directions, the custody officer shall ask for clarification. It is particularly important that directions concerning the frequency of visits are clear, precise and capable of being implemented. See Note 9F.

(c) Documentation

9.15   A record must be made in the custody record of:

(a) the arrangements made for an examination by an appropriate health care professional under paragraph 9.2 and of any complaint reported under that paragraph together with any relevant remarks by the custody officer;

(b) any arrangements made in accordance with paragraph 9.5;

(c) any request for a clinical examination under paragraph 9.8 and any arrangements made in response;

(d) the injury, ailment, condition or other reason which made it necessary to make the arrangements in (a) to (c), see Note 9G;

(e) any clinical directions and advice, including any further clarifications, given to police by a health care professional concerning the care and treatment of the detainee in connection with any of the arrangements made in (a) to (c), see Note 9F;

(f) if applicable, the responses received when attempting to rouse a person using the procedure in Annex H, see Note 9H.

9.16   If a health care professional does not record their clinical findings in the custody record, the record must show where they are recorded. See Note 9G. However, information which is necessary to custody staff to ensure the effective ongoing care and well being of the detainee must be recorded openly in the custody record, see paragraph 3.8 and Annex G, paragraph 7.

9.17   Subject to the requirements of section 4, the custody record shall include:

- a record of all medication a detainee has in their possession on arrival at the police station;
- a note of any such medication they claim to need but do not have with them.

Notes for Guidance

9A   A 'health care professional' means a clinically qualified person working within the scope of practice as determined by their relevant professional body. Whether a health care professional is 'appropriate' depends on the circumstances of the duties they carry out at the time.

9B   Whenever possible juveniles and mentally vulnerable detainees should be visited more frequently.

9C   A detainee who appears drunk or behaves abnormally may be suffering from illness, the effects of drugs or may have sustained injury, particularly a head injury which is not apparent. A detainee needing or dependent on certain drugs, including alcohol, may experience harmful effects within a short time of being deprived of their supply. In these circumstances, when there is any doubt, police should always act urgently to call an appropriate health care professional or an ambulance. Paragraph 9.5 does not apply to minor ailments or injuries which do not need attention. However, all such ailments or injuries must be recorded in the custody record and any doubt must be resolved in favour of calling the appropriate health care professional.

9D   Whenever practicable, arrangements should be made for persons detained for assessment under the Mental Health Act 1983, section 136 to be taken to a hospital. There is no power under that Act to transfer a person detained under section 136 from one place of safety to another place of safety for assessment.

9E   It is important to respect a person's right to privacy and information about their health must be kept confidential and only disclosed with their consent or in accordance with clinical advice when it is necessary to protect the detainee's health or that of others who come into contact with them.

9F   The custody officer should always seek to clarify directions that the detainee requires constant observation or supervision and should ask the appropriate health care professional to explain precisely what action needs to be taken to implement such directions.

9G   Paragraphs 9.15 and 9.16 do not require any information about the cause of any injury, ailment or condition to be recorded on the custody record if it appears capable of providing evidence of an offence.

9H   The purpose of recording a person's responses when attempting to rouse them using the procedure in Annex H is to enable any change in the individual's consciousness level to be noted and clinical treatment arranged if appropriate.

10 Cautions

(a) When a caution must be given

10.1   A person whom there are grounds to suspect of an offence, see Note 10A, must be cautioned before any questions about an offence, or further questions if the answers provide the grounds for suspicion, are put to them if either the suspect's answers or silence, (i.e. failure or refusal to answer or answer satisfactorily) may be given in evidence to a court in a prosecution. A person need not be cautioned if questions are for other necessary purposes, e.g.:

(a) solely to establish their identity or ownership of any vehicle;
(b) to obtain information in accordance with any relevant statutory requirement, see paragraph 10.9;
(c) in furtherance of the proper and effective conduct of a search, e.g. to determine the need to search in the exercise of powers of stop and search or to seek co-operation while carrying out a search;
(d) to seek verification of a written record as in paragraph 11.13;
(e) when examining a person in accordance with the Terrorism Act 2000, Schedule 7 and the Code of Practice for Examining Officers issued under that Act, Schedule 14, paragraph 6.

10.2   Whenever a person not under arrest is initially cautioned, or reminded they are under caution, that person must at the same time be told they are not under arrest and are free to leave if they want to. See Note 10C

10.3   A person who is arrested, or further arrested, must be informed at the time, or as soon as practicable thereafter, that they are under arrest and the grounds for their arrest, see Note 10B.

10.4   A person who is arrested, or further arrested, must also be cautioned unless:

(a) it is impracticable to do so by reason of their condition or behaviour at the time;
(b) they have already been cautioned immediately prior to arrest as in paragraph 10.1.

(b) Terms of the cautions

10.5   The caution which must be given on:

(a) arrest;

(b) all other occasions before a person is charged or informed they may be prosecuted, see section 16,

should, unless the restriction on drawing adverse inferences from silence applies, see *Annex C*, be in the following terms:

'You do not have to say anything. But it may harm your defence if you do not mention when questioned something which you later rely on in Court. Anything you do say may be given in evidence.'

See Note 10G

10.6   Annex C, paragraph 2 sets out the alternative terms of the caution to be used when the restriction on drawing adverse inferences from silence applies.

10.7   Minor deviations from the words of any caution given in accordance with this Code do not constitute a breach of this Code, provided the sense of the relevant caution is preserved. See Note 10D

10.8   After any break in questioning under caution, the person being questioned must be made aware they remain under caution. If there is any doubt the relevant caution should be given again in full when the interview resumes. See Note 10E

10.9   When, despite being cautioned, a person fails to co-operate or to answer particular questions which may affect their immediate treatment, the person should be informed of any relevant consequences and that those consequences are not affected by the caution. Examples are when a person's refusal to provide:

- their name and address when charged may make them liable to detention;
- particulars and information in accordance with a statutory requirement, e.g. under the Road Traffic Act 1988, may amount to an offence or may make the person liable to a further arrest.

(c) Special warnings under the Criminal Justice and Public Order Act 1994, sections 36 and 37

10.10   When a suspect interviewed at a police station or authorised place of detention after arrest fails or refuses to answer certain questions, or to answer satisfactorily, after due warning, see Note 10F, a court or jury may draw such inferences as appear proper under the Criminal Justice and Public Order Act 1994, sections 36 and 37. Such inferences may only be drawn when:

(a) the restriction on drawing adverse inferences from silence, see Annex C, does not apply; and

(b) the suspect is arrested by a constable and fails or refuses to account for any objects, marks or substances, or marks on such objects found:

- on their person;
- in or on their clothing or footwear;
- otherwise in their possession; or
- in the place they were arrested;

(c) the arrested suspect was found by a constable at a place at or about the time the offence for which that officer has arrested them is alleged to have been committed, and the suspect fails or refuses to account for their presence there.

When the restriction on drawing adverse inferences from silence applies, the suspect may still be asked to account for any of the matters in (b) or (c) but the special warning described in paragraph 10.11 will not apply and must not be given.

10.11   For an inference to be drawn when a suspect fails or refuses to answer a question about one of these matters or to answer it satisfactorily, the suspect must first be told in ordinary language:

(a) what offence is being investigated;

(b) what fact they are being asked to account for;

(c) this fact may be due to them taking part in the commission of the offence;

(d) a court may draw a proper inference if they fail or refuse to account for this fact;

(e) a record is being made of the interview and it may be given in evidence if they are brought to trial.

(d) Juveniles and persons who are mentally disordered or otherwise mentally vulnerable

10.12   If a juvenile or a person who is mentally disordered or otherwise mentally vulnerable is cautioned in the absence of the appropriate adult, the caution must be repeated in the adult's presence.

(e) Documentation

10.13   A record shall be made when a caution is given under this section, either in the interviewer's pocket book or in the interview record.

Notes for Guidance

10A   There must be some reasonable, objective grounds for the suspicion, based on known facts or information which are relevant to the likelihood the offence has been committed and the person to be questioned committed it.

10B   An arrested person must be given sufficient information to enable them to understand they have been deprived of their liberty and the reason they have been arrested, e.g. when a person is arrested on suspicion of committing an offence they must be informed of the suspected offence's nature, when and where it was committed. If the arrest is made under the general arrest conditions in PACE, section 25, the grounds for arrest must include an explanation of the conditions which make the arrest necessary. Vague or technical language should be avoided.

10C   The restriction on drawing inferences from silence, see Annex C, paragraph 1, does not apply to a person who has not been detained and who therefore cannot be prevented from seeking legal advice if they want, see paragraph 3.21.

10D   If it appears a person does not understand the caution, the person giving it should explain it in their own words.

10E   It may be necessary to show to the court that nothing occurred during an interview break or between interviews which influenced the suspect's recorded evidence. After a break in an interview or at the beginning of a subsequent interview, the interviewing officer should summarise the reason for the break and confirm this with the suspect.

10F   The Criminal Justice and Public Order Act 1994, sections 36 and 37 apply only to suspects who have been arrested by a constable or Customs and Excise officer and are given the relevant warning by the police or customs officer who made the arrest or who is investigating the offence. They do not apply to any interviews with suspects who have not been arrested.

10G   Nothing in this Code requires a caution to be given or repeated when informing a person not under arrest they may be prosecuted for an offence. However, a court will not be able to draw any inferences under the Criminal Justice and Public Order Act 1994, section 34, if the person was not cautioned.

11   Interviews – general

(a) Action

11.1A   An interview is the questioning of a person regarding their involvement or suspected involvement in a criminal offence or offences which, under paragraph 10.1, must be carried out under caution. Whenever a person is interviewed they must be informed of the nature of the offence, or further offence. Procedures under the Road Traffic Act 1988, section 7 or the Transport and Works Act 1992, section 31 do not constitute interviewing for the purpose of this Code.

11.1   Following a decision to arrest a suspect, they must not be interviewed about the relevant offence except at a police station or other authorised place of detention, unless the consequent delay would be likely to:

(a) lead to:
- interference with, or harm to, evidence connected with an offence;
- interference with, or physical harm to, other people; or
- serious loss of, or damage to, property;

(b) lead to alerting other people suspected of committing an offence but not yet arrested for it; or

(c) hinder the recovery of property obtained in consequence of the commission of an offence.

Interviewing in any of these circumstances shall cease once the relevant risk has been averted or the necessary questions have been put in order to attempt to avert that risk.

11.2   Immediately prior to the commencement or re-commencement of any interview at a police station or other authorised place of detention, the interviewer should remind the suspect of their entitlement to free legal advice and that the interview can be delayed for legal advice to be obtained, unless one of the exceptions in paragraph 6.6 applies. It is the interviewer's responsibility to make sure all reminders are recorded in the interview record.

11.3   Not Used

11.4   At the beginning of an interview the interviewer, after cautioning the suspect, see section 10, shall put to them any significant statement or silence which occurred in the presence and hearing of a police officer or civilian interviewer before the start of the interview and which have not been put to the suspect in the course of a previous interview. See Note 11A. The interviewer shall ask the suspect whether they confirm or deny that earlier statement or silence and if they want to add anything.

11.4A   A significant statement is one which appears capable of being used in evidence against the suspect, in particular a direct admission of guilt. A significant silence is a failure or refusal to answer a question or answer satisfactorily when under caution, which might, allowing for the restriction on drawing adverse inferences from silence, see Annex C, give rise to an inference under the Criminal Justice and Public Order Act 1994, Part III.

11.5   No interviewer may try to obtain answers or elicit a statement by the use of oppression. Except as in paragraph 10.9, no interviewer shall indicate, except to answer a direct question, what action will be taken by the police if the person being questioned answers questions, makes a statement or refuses to do either. If the person asks directly what action will be taken if they answer questions, make a statement or refuse to do either, the interviewer may inform them what action the police propose to take provided that action is itself proper and warranted.

11.6   The interview or further interview of a person about an offence with which that person has not been charged or for which they have not been informed they may be prosecuted, must cease when the officer in charge of the investigation:

(a) is satisfied all the questions they consider relevant to obtaining accurate and reliable information about the offence have been put to the suspect, this includes allowing the suspect an opportunity to give an innocent explanation and asking questions to test if the explanation is accurate and reliable, e.g. to clear up ambiguities or clarify what the suspect said;

(b) has taken account of any other available evidence; and

(c) the officer in charge of the investigation, or in the case of a detained suspect, the custody officer, see paragraph 16.1, reasonably believes there is sufficient evidence to provide a realistic prospect of conviction for that offence if the person was prosecuted for it. See Note 11B

This paragraph does not prevent officers in revenue cases or acting under the confiscation provisions of the Criminal Justice Act 1988 or the Drug Trafficking Act 1994 from inviting suspects to complete a formal question and answer record after the interview is concluded.

(b) Interview records

11.7 (a) An accurate record must be made of each interview, whether or not the interview takes place at a police station

(b) The record must state the place of interview, the time it begins and ends, any interview breaks and, subject to paragraph 2.6A, the names of all those present; and must be made on the forms provided for this purpose or in the interviewer's pocket book or in accordance with the Codes of Practice E or F;

(c) Any written record must be made and completed during the interview, unless this would not be practicable or would interfere with the conduct of the interview, and must constitute either a verbatim record of what has been said or, failing this, an account of the interview which adequately and accurately summarises it.

11.8 If a written record is not made during the interview it must be made as soon as practicable after its completion.

11.9 Written interview records must be timed and signed by the maker.

11.10 If a written record is not completed during the interview the reason must be recorded in the interview record.

11.11 Unless it is impracticable, the person interviewed shall be given the opportunity to read the interview record and to sign it as correct or to indicate how they consider it inaccurate. If the person interviewed cannot read or refuses to read the record or sign it, the senior interviewer present shall read it to them and ask whether they would like to sign it as correct or make their mark or to indicate how they consider it inaccurate. The interviewer shall certify on the interview record itself what has occurred. See Note 11E

11.12 If the appropriate adult or the person's solicitor is present during the interview, they should also be given an opportunity to read and sign the interview record or any written statement taken down during the interview.

11.13 A written record shall be made of any comments made by a suspect, including unsolicited comments, which are outside the context of an interview but which might be relevant to the offence. Any such record must be timed and signed by the maker. When practicable the suspect shall be given the opportunity to read that record and to sign it as correct or to indicate how they consider it inaccurate. See Note 11E

11.14 Any refusal by a person to sign an interview record when asked in accordance with this Code must itself be recorded.

(c) Juveniles and mentally disordered or otherwise mentally vulnerable people

11.15 A juvenile or person who is mentally disordered or otherwise mentally vulnerable must not be interviewed regarding their involvement or suspected involvement in a criminal offence or offences, or asked to provide or sign a written statement under caution or record of interview, in the absence of the appropriate adult unless paragraphs 11.1, 11.18 to 11.20 apply. See Note 11C

11.16 Juveniles may only be interviewed at their place of education in exceptional circumstances and only when the principal or their nominee agrees. Every effort should be made to notify the parent(s) or other person responsible for the juvenile's welfare and the appropriate adult, if this is a different person, that the police want to interview the juvenile and reasonable time should be allowed to enable the appropriate adult to be present at the interview. If awaiting the appropriate adult would cause unreasonable delay, and unless the juvenile is suspected of an offence against the educational establishment, the principal or their nominee can act as the appropriate adult for the purposes of the interview.

11.17 If an appropriate adult is present at an interview, they shall be informed:
- they are not expected to act simply as an observer; and
- the purpose of their presence is to:
  - ~ advise the person being interviewed;

~ observe whether the interview is being conducted properly and fairly;
~ facilitate communication with the person being interviewed.

(d) Vulnerable suspects – urgent interviews at police stations

11.18. The following persons may not be interviewed unless an officer of super-intendent rank or above considers delay will lead to the consequences in paragraph 11.1(a) to (c), and is satisfied the interview would not significantly harm the person's physical or mental state (see Annex G):

(a) a juvenile or person who is mentally disordered or otherwise mentally vulnerable if at the time of the interview the appropriate adult is not present;
(b) anyone other than in (a) who at the time of the interview appears unable to:
  • appreciate the significance of questions and their answers; or
  • understand what is happening because of the effects of drink, drugs or any illness, ailment or condition;
(c) a person who has difficulty understanding English or has a hearing disability, if at the time of the interview an interpreter is not present.

11.19   These interviews may not continue once sufficient information has been obtained to avert the consequences in paragraph 11.1(a) to (c).

11.20   A record shall be made of the grounds for any decision to interview a person under paragraph 11.18.

Notes for Guidance

11A Paragraph 11.4 does not prevent the interviewer from putting significant state-ments and silences to a suspect again at a later stage or a further interview.

11B The Criminal Procedure and Investigations Act 1996 Code of Practice, paragraph 3.4 states 'In conducting an investigation, the investigator should pursue all reasonable lines of enquiry, whether these point towards or away from the suspect. What is reasonable will depend on the particular circumstances.' Interviewers should keep this in mind when deciding what questions to ask in an interview.

11C Although juveniles or people who are mentally disordered or otherwise mentally vulnerable are often capable of providing reliable evidence, they may, without knowing or wishing to do so, be particularly prone in certain circumstances to provide information that may be unreliable, misleading or self-incriminating. Special care should always be taken when questioning such a person, and the appropriate adult should be involved if there is any doubt about a person's age, mental state or capacity. Because of the risk of unreliable evidence it is also important to obtain corroboration of any facts admitted whenever possible.

11D Juveniles should not be arrested at their place of education unless this is unavoid-able. When a juvenile is arrested at their place of education, the principal or their nominee must be informed.

11E Significant statements described in paragraph 11.4 will always be relevant to the offence and must be recorded. When a suspect agrees to read records of interviews and other comments and sign them as correct, they should be asked to endorse the record with, e.g. 'I agree that this is a correct record of what was said' and add their signature. If the suspect does not agree with the record, the interviewer should record the details of any disagreement and ask the suspect to read these details and sign them to the effect that they accurately reflect their disagreement. Any refusal to sign should be recorded.

12   Interviews in police stations

(a) Action

12.1   If a police officer wants to interview or conduct enquiries which require the presence of a detainee, the custody officer is responsible for deciding whether to deliver the detainee into the officer's custody.

12.2   Except as below, in any period of 24 hours a detainee must be allowed a continuous period of at least 8 hours for rest, free from questioning, travel or any interruption in connection with the investigation concerned. This period should normally be at night or other appropriate time which takes account of when the detainee last slept or rested. If a detainee is arrested at a police station after going there voluntarily, the period of 24 hours runs from the time of their arrest and not the time of arrival at the police station. The period may not be interrupted or delayed, except:

(a)   when there are reasonable grounds for believing not delaying or interrupting the period would:
   (i)   involve a risk of harm to people or serious loss of, or damage to, property;
   (ii)   delay unnecessarily the person's release from custody;
   (iii) otherwise prejudice the outcome of the investigation;
(b)   at the request of the detainee, their appropriate adult or legal representative;
(c)   when a delay or interruption is necessary in order to:
   (i)   comply with the legal obligations and duties arising under section 15;
   (ii)   to take action required under section 9 or in accordance with medical advice.

If the period is interrupted in accordance with (a), a fresh period must be allowed. Interruptions under (b) and (c), do not require a fresh period to be allowed.

12.3   Before a detainee is interviewed the custody officer, in consultation with the officer in charge of the investigation and appropriate health care professionals as necessary, shall assess whether the detainee is fit enough to be interviewed. This means determining and considering the risks to the detainee's physical and mental state if the interview took place and determining what safeguards are needed to allow the interview to take place. See Annex G. The custody officer shall not allow a detainee to be interviewed if the custody officer considers it would cause significant harm to the detainee's physical or mental state. Vulnerable suspects listed at paragraph 11.18 shall be treated as always being at some risk during an interview and these persons may not be interviewed except in accordance with paragraphs 11.18 to 11.20.

12.4   As far as practicable interviews shall take place in interview rooms which are adequately heated, lit and ventilated.

12.5   A suspect whose detention without charge has been authorised under PACE, because the detention is necessary for an interview to obtain evidence of the offence for which they have been arrested, may choose not to answer questions but police do not require the suspect's consent or agreement to interview them for this purpose. If a suspect takes steps to prevent themselves being questioned or further questioned, e.g. by refusing to leave their cell to go to a suitable interview room or by trying to leave the interview room, they shall be advised their consent or agreement to interview is not required. The suspect shall be cautioned as in section 10, and informed' if they fail or refuse to co-operate, the interview may take place in the cell and that their failure or refusal to co-operate may be given in evidence. The suspect shall then be invited to co-operate and go into the interview room.

12.6   People being questioned or making statements shall not be required to stand.

12.7   Before the interview commences each interviewer shall, subject to paragraph 2.6A, identify themselves and any other persons present to the interviewee.

12.8   Breaks from interviewing should be made at recognised meal times or at other times that take account of when an interviewee last had a meal. Short refreshment breaks shall be provided at approximately two hour intervals, subject to the interviewer's discretion to delay a break if there are reasonable grounds for believing it would:

(i)   involve a:
   •   risk of harm to people;
   •   serious loss of, or damage to, property;

(ii)   unnecessarily delay the detainee's release;

(iii) otherwise prejudice the outcome of the investigation.

See Note 12B

12.9   If during the interview a complaint is made by or on behalf of the interviewee concerning the provisions of this Code, the interviewer should:

(i)   record it in the interview record;

(ii)   inform the custody officer, who is then responsible for dealing with it as in section 9.

(b)   Documentation

12.10   A record must be made of the:

- time a detainee is not in the custody of the custody officer, and why
- reason for any refusal to deliver the detainee out of that custody

12.11   A record shall be made of:

(a)   the reasons it was not practicable to use an interview room; and

(b)   any action taken as in paragraph 12.5.

The record shall be made on the custody record or in the interview record for action taken whilst an interview record is being kept, with a brief reference to this effect in the custody record.

12.12   Any decision to delay a break in an interview must be recorded, with reasons, in the interview record.

12.13   All written statements made at police stations under caution shall be written on forms provided for the purpose.

12.14   All written statements made under caution shall be taken in accordance with Annex D. Before a person makes a written statement under caution at a police station they shall be reminded about the right to legal advice. See Note 12A

Notes for Guidance

12A   It is not normally necessary to ask for a written statement if the interview was recorded or taped at the time and the record signed by the interviewee in accordance with paragraph 11.11. Statements under caution should normally be taken in these circumstances only at the person's express wish. A person may however be asked if they want to make such a statement.

12B   Meal breaks should normally last at least 45 minutes and shorter breaks after two hours should last at least 15 minutes. If the interviewer delays a break in accordance with paragraph 12.8 and prolongs the interview, a longer break should be provided. If there is a short interview, and another short interview is contemplated, the length of the break may be reduced if there are reasonable grounds to believe this is necessary to avoid any of the consequences in paragraph 12.8(1) to (iii).

13   Interpreters

(a) General

13.1   Chief officers are responsible for making sure appropriate arrangements are in place for provision of suitably qualified interpreters for people who:

- are deaf;
- do not understand English.

(b) Foreign languages

13.2   Unless paragraphs 11.1, 11.18 to 11.20 apply, a person must not be interviewed in the absence of a person capable of interpreting if:

(a)   they have difficulty understanding English;

(b)   the interviewer cannot speak the person's own language;

(c)   the person wants an interpreter present.

13.3   The interviewer shall make sure the interpreter makes a note of the interview at the time in the person's language for use in the event of the interpreter being called to give evidence, and certifies its accuracy. The interviewer should allow sufficient time for the interpreter to note each question and answer after each is put, given and interpreted. The person should be allowed to read the record or have it read to them and sign it as correct or indicate the respects in which they consider it inaccurate. If the interview is tape-recorded or visually recorded, the arrangements in Code E or F apply.

13.4   In the case of a person making a statement other than in English:
    (a)   the interpreter shall record the statement in the language it is made;
    (b)   the person shall be invited to sign it;
    (c)   an official English translation shall be made in due course.

(c) Deaf people and people with speech difficulties

13.5   If a person appears to be deaf or there is doubt about their hearing or speaking ability, they must not be interviewed in the absence of an interpreter unless they agree in writing to being interviewed without one or paragraphs 11.1, 11.18 to 11.20 apply.

13.6   An interpreter should also be called if a juvenile is interviewed and the parent or guardian present as the appropriate adult appears to be deaf or there is doubt about their hearing or speaking ability, unless they agree in writing to the interview proceeding without one or paragraphs 11.1, 11.18 to 11.20 apply.

13.7   The interviewer shall make sure the interpreter is allowed to read the interview record and certify its accuracy in the event of the interpreter being called to give evidence. If the interview is tape-recorded or visually recorded, the arrangements in Code E or F apply.

(d) Additional rules for detained persons

13.8   All reasonable attempts should be made to make the detainee understand that interpreters will be provided at public expense.

13.9   If paragraph 6.1 applies and the detainee cannot communicate with the solicitor because of language, hearing or speech difficulties, an interpreter must be called. The interpreter may not be a police officer or civilian support staff when interpretation is needed for the purposes of obtaining legal advice. In all other cases a police officer or civilian support staff may only interpret if the detainee and the appropriate adult, if applicable, give their agreement in writing or if the interview is tape-recorded or visually recorded as in Code E or F.

13.10   When the custody officer cannot establish effective communication with a person charged with an offence who appears deaf or there is doubt about their ability to hear, speak or to understand English, arrangements must be made as soon as practicable for an interpreter to explain the offence and any other information given by the custody officer.

(e) Documentation

13.11   Action taken to call an interpreter under this section and any agreement to be interviewed in the absence of an interpreter must be recorded.

14   Questioning – special restrictions

14.1   If a person is arrested by one police force on behalf of another and the lawful period of detention in respect of that offence has not yet commenced in accordance with PACE, section 41 no questions may be put to them about the offence while they are in transit between the forces except to clarify any voluntary statement they make.

14.2   If a person is in police detention at a hospital they may not be questioned without the agreement of a responsible doctor. See Note 14A

Note for Guidance

14A   If questioning takes place at a hospital under paragraph 14.2, or on the way to or from a hospital, the period of questioning concerned counts towards the total period of detention permitted.

15   Reviews and extensions of detention

(a) Persons detained under PACE

15.1   The review officer is responsible under PACE, section 40 for periodically determining if a person's detention, before or after charge, continues to be necessary. This requirement continues throughout the detention period and except as in paragraph 15.10, the review officer must be present at the police station holding the detainee. See Notes 15A and 15B

15.2   Under PACE, section 42, an officer of superintendent rank or above who is responsible for the station holding the detainee may give authority any time after the second review to extend the maximum period the person may be detained without charge by up to 12 hours. Further detention without charge may be authorised only by a magistrates' court in accordance with PACE, sections 43 and 44. See Notes 15C, 15D and 15E

15.3   Before deciding whether to authorise continued detention the officer responsible under paragraphs 15.1 or 15.2 shall give an opportunity to make representations about the detention to:

(a)   the detainee, unless in the case of a review as in paragraph 15.1, the detainee is asleep;

(b)   the detainee's solicitor if available at the time; and

(c)   the appropriate adult if available at the time.

15.3A   Other people having an interest in the detainee's welfare may also make representations at the authorising officer's discretion.

15.3B   Subject to paragraph 15.10, the representations may be made orally in person or by telephone or in writing. The authorising officer may, however, refuse to hear oral representations from the detainee if the officer considers them unfit to make representations because of their condition or behaviour. See Note 15C

15.4   Before conducting a review or determining whether to extend the maximum period of detention without charge, the officer responsible must make sure the detainee is reminded of their entitlement to free legal advice, see paragraph 6.5, unless in the case of a review the person is asleep.

15.5   If, after considering any representations, the officer decides to keep the detainee in detention or extend the maximum period they may be detained without charge, any comment made by the detainee shall be recorded. If applicable, the officer responsible under paragraph 15.1 or 15.2 shall be informed of the comment as soon as practicable. See also paragraphs 11.4 and 11.13

15.6   No officer shall put specific questions to the detainee:

- regarding their involvement in any offence; or
- in respect of any comments they may make;
  - ~   when given the opportunity to make representations; or
  - ~   in response to a decision to keep them in detention or extend the maximum period of detention.

Such an exchange could constitute an interview as in paragraph 11.1A and would be subject to the associated safeguards in section 11 and, in respect of a person who has been charged, paragraph 16.5. See also paragraph 11.13

15.7   A detainee who is asleep at a review, see paragraph 15.1, and whose continued detention is authorised must be informed about the decision and reason as soon as practicable after waking.

(b) Persons detained under the Terrorism Act 2000

15.8   In terrorism cases:

(a)   the powers and duties of the review officer are in the Terrorism Act 2000, Schedule 8, Part II;

(b)   a police officer of at least superintendent rank may apply to a judicial authority for a warrant of further detention under the Terrorism Act 2000, Schedule 8, Part III.

(c) Telephone review of detention

15.9   PACE, section 40A provides that the officer responsible under section 40 for reviewing the detention of a person who has not been charged, need not attend the police station holding the detainee and may carry out the review by telephone if:

(a) it is not reasonably practicable for the officer to be present;

(b) PACE, section 45A, in respect of the use of video conferencing facilities, does not apply or it is not reasonably practicable to use such facilities.

See Note 15F

15.10   When a telephone review is carried out, an officer at the station holding the detainee shall be required by the review officer to fulfil that officer's obligations under PACE section 40 or this Code by:

(a) making any record connected with the review in the detainee's custody record;

(b) if applicable, making a record in (a) in the presence of the detainee; and

(c) giving the detainee information about the review.

15.11   When a telephone review is carried out, the requirement in paragraph 15.3 will be satisfied:

(a) if facilities exist for the immediate transmission of written representations to the review officer, e.g. fax or email message, by giving the detainee an opportunity to make representations:

(i)   orally by telephone; or

(ii) in writing using those facilities; and

(b) in all other cases, by giving the detainee an opportunity to make their representations orally by telephone.

(d) Documentation

15.12   It is the officer's responsibility to make sure all reminders given under paragraph 15.4 are noted in the custody record.

15.13   The grounds for, and extent of, any delay in conducting a review shall be recorded.

15.14   When a telephone review is carried out, a record shall be made of:

(a) the reason the review officer did not attend the station holding the detainee;

(b) the place the review officer was;

(c) the method representations, oral or written, were made to the review officer, see paragraph 15.11.

15.15   Any written representations shall be retained.

15.16   A record shall be made as soon as practicable about the outcome of each review or determination whether to extend the maximum detention period without charge or an application for a warrant of further detention or its extension. If paragraph 15.7 applies, a record shall also be made of when the person was informed and by whom. If an authorisation is given under PACE, section 42, the record shall state the number of hours and minutes by which the detention period is extended or further extended. If a warrant for further detention, or extension, is granted under section 43 or 44, the record shall state the detention period authorised by the warrant and the date and time it was granted.

Notes for Guidance

15A   Review officer for the purposes of:

• PACE, sections 40 and 40A means, in the case of a person arrested but not charged, an officer of at least inspector rank not directly involved in the investigation and, if a person has been arrested and charged, the custody officer;

• the Terrorism Act 2000, means an officer not directly involved in the investigation connected with the detention and of at least inspector rank, for reviews within 24 hours of the detainee's arrest or superintendent for all other reviews.

15B   The detention of persons in police custody not subject to the statutory review requirement in paragraph 15.1 should still be reviewed periodically as a matter of good practice. The purpose of such reviews is to check the particular power under which a detainee is held continues to apply, any associated conditions are complied with and to make sure appropriate action is taken to deal with any changes. This includes the detainee's prompt release when the power no longer applies, or their transfer if the power requires the detainee be taken elsewhere as soon as the necessary arrangements are made. Examples include persons:

    (a) arrested on warrant because they failed to answer bail to appear at court;

    (b) arrested under the Bail Act 1976, section 7(3) for breaching a condition of bail granted after charge;

    (c) in police custody for specific purposes and periods under the Crime (Sentences) Act 1997, Schedule 1;

    (d) convicted, or remand prisoners, held in police stations on behalf of the Prison Service under the Imprisonment (Temporary Provisions) Act 1980, section 6;

    (e) being detained to prevent them causing a breach of the peace;

    (f) detained at police stations on behalf of the Immigration Service.

The detention of persons remanded into police detention by order of a court under the Magistrates' Courts Act 1980, section 128 is subject to a statutory requirement to review that detention. This is to make sure the detainee is taken back to court no later than the end of the period authorised by the court or when the need for their detention by police ceases, whichever is the sooner.

15C   In the case of a review of detention, but not an extension, the detainee need not be woken for the review. However, if the detainee is likely to be asleep, e.g. during a period of rest allowed as in paragraph 12.2, at the latest time a review or authorisation to extend detention may take place, the officer should, if the legal obligations and time constraints permit, bring forward the procedure to allow the detainee to make representations. A detainee not asleep during the review must be present when the grounds for their continued detention are recorded and must at the same time be informed of those grounds unless the review officer considers the person is incapable of understanding what is said, violent or likely to become violent or in urgent need of medical attention.

15D   An application to a Magistrates' Court under PACE, section 43 or 44 for a warrant of further detention or its extension should be made between 10am and 9pm, and if possible during normal court hours. It will not usually be practicable to arrange for a court to sit specially outside the hours of 10am to 9pm. If it appears a special sitting may be needed outside normal court hours but between 10am and 9pm, the clerk to the justices should be given notice and informed of this possibility, while the court is sitting if possible.

15E   In paragraph 15.2, the officer responsible for the station holding the detainee includes a superintendent or above who, in accordance with their force operational policy or police regulations, is given that responsibility on a temporary basis whilst the appointed long-term holder is off duty or otherwise unavailable.

15F   The provisions of PACE, section 40A allowing telephone reviews do not apply to reviews of detention after charge by the custody officer or to reviews under the Terrorism Act 2000, Schedule 8, Part II in terrorism cases. When video conferencing is not required, they allow the use of a telephone to carry out a review of detention before charge if it is not reasonably practicable for the review officer to attend the station holding the detainee, e.g. when severe weather conditions or an unforeseen operational emergency prevent the review officer from attending. The procedure under PACE, section 42 must be done in person.

16   Charging detained persons

(a) Action

16.1   When the officer in charge of the investigation reasonably believes there is sufficient evidence to provide a realistic prospect of the detainee's conviction, see paragraph 11.6, they shall without delay, and subject to the following qualification, inform the custody officer who will be responsible for considering whether the detainee should be charged. See Notes 11B and 16A. When a person is detained in respect of more than one offence it is permissible to delay informing the custody officer until the above conditions are satisfied in respect of all the offences, but see paragraph 11.6. If the detainee is a juvenile, mentally disordered or otherwise mentally vulnerable, any resulting action shall be taken in the presence of the appropriate adult if they are present at the time. See Notes 16B and 16C

16.2   When a detainee is charged with or informed they may be prosecuted for an offence, see Note 16B, they shall, unless the restriction on drawing adverse inferences from silence applies, see Annex C, be cautioned as follows:

'You do not have to say anything. But it may harm your defence if you do not mention now something which you later rely on in court. Anything you do say may be given in evidence.'

Annex C, paragraph 2 sets out the alternative terms of the caution to be used when the restriction on drawing adverse inferences from silence applies.

16.3   When a detainee is charged they shall be given a written notice showing particulars of the offence and, subject to paragraph 2.6A, the officer's name and the case reference number. As far as possible the particulars of the charge shall be stated in simple terms, but they shall also show the precise offence in law with which the detainee is charged. The notice shall begin:

'You are charged with the offence(s) shown below.' Followed by the caution.

If the detainee is a juvenile, mentally disordered or otherwise mentally vulnerable, the notice should be given to the appropriate adult.

16.4   If, after a detainee has been charged with or informed they may be prosecuted for an offence, an officer wants to tell them about any written statement or interview with another person relating to such an offence, the detainee shall either be handed a true copy of the written statement or the content of the interview record brought to their attention. Nothing shall be done to invite any reply or comment except to:

(a) caution the detainee, *'You do not have to say anything, but anything you do say may be given in evidence.'*; and

(b) remind the detainee about their right to legal advice.

16.4A   If the detainee:

- cannot read, the document may be read to them
- is a juvenile, mentally disordered or otherwise mentally vulnerable, the appropriate adult shall also be given a copy, or the interview record shall be brought to their attention

16.5   A detainee may not be interviewed about an offence after they have been charged with, or informed they may be prosecuted for it, unless the interview is necessary:

- to prevent or minimise harm or loss to some other person, or the public
- to clear up an ambiguity in a previous answer or statement
- in the interests of justice for the detainee to have put to them, and have an opportunity to comment on, information concerning the offence which has come to light since they were charged or informed they might be prosecuted

Before any such interview, the interviewer shall:

(a) caution the detainee, *'You do not have to say anything, but anything you do say may be given in evidence.'*;

(b) remind the detainee about their right to legal advice.

See Note 16B

16.6   The provisions of paragraphs 16.2 to 16.5 must be complied with in the appropriate adult's presence if they are already at the police station. If they are not at the police station then these provisions must be complied with again in their presence when they arrive unless the detainee has been released.

See Note 16C

16.7   When a juvenile is charged with an offence and the custody officer authorises their continued detention after charge, the custody officer must try to make arrangements for the juvenile to be taken into the care of a local authority to be detained pending appearance in court unless the custody officer certifies it is impracticable to do so or, in the case of a juvenile of at least 12 years old, no secure accommodation is available and there is a risk to the public of serious harm from that juvenile, in accordance with PACE, section 38(6). See Note 16D

(b) Documentation
16.8   A record shall be made of anything a detainee says when charged.

16.9   Any questions put in an interview after charge and answers given relating to the offence shall be recorded in full during the interview on forms for that purpose and the record signed by the detainee or, if they refuse, by the interviewer and any third parties present. If the questions are tape recorded or visually recorded the arrangements in Code E or F apply.

16.10   If it is not practicable to make arrangements for a juvenile's transfer into local authority care as in paragraph 16.7, the custody officer must record the reasons and complete a certificate to be produced before the court with the juvenile. See Note 16D

Notes for Guidance
16A   The custody officer must take into account alternatives to prosecution under the Crime and Disorder Act 1998, reprimands and warning applicable to persons under 18, and in national guidance on the cautioning of offenders, for persons aged 18 and over.

16B   The giving of a warning or the service of the Notice of Intended Prosecution required by the Road Traffic Offenders Act 1988, section 1 does not amount to informing a detainee they may be prosecuted for an offence and so does not preclude further questioning in relation to that offence.

16C   There is no power under PACE to detain a person and delay action under paragraphs 16.2 to 16.5 solely to await the arrival of the appropriate adult. After charge, bail cannot be refused, or release on bail delayed, simply because an appropriate adult is not available, unless the absence of that adult provides the custody officer with the necessary grounds to authorise detention after charge under PACE, section 38.

16D   Except as in paragraph 16.7, neither a juvenile's behaviour nor the nature of the offence provides grounds for the custody officer to decide it is impracticable to arrange the juvenile's transfer to local authority care. Similarly, the lack of secure local authority accommodation does not make it impracticable to transfer the juvenile. The availability of secure accommodation is only a factor in relation to a juvenile aged 12 or over when the local authority accommodation would not be adequate to protect the public from serious harm from them. The obligation to transfer a juvenile to local authority accommodation applies as much to a juvenile charged during the daytime as to a juvenile to be held overnight, subject to a requirement to bring the juvenile before a court under PACE, section 46.

ANNEX A   INTIMATE AND STRIP SEARCHES

A   Intimate search
1.   An intimate search consists of the physical examination of a person's body orifices other than the mouth. The intrusive nature of such searches means the actual and potential risks associated with intimate searches must never be underestimated.

(a) Action
2.   Body orifices other than the mouth may be searched only if authorised by an officer of inspector rank or above who has reasonable grounds for believing that:
    (a)   the person may have concealed on themselves
        (i)   anything which they could and might use to cause physical injury to themself or others at the station; or

(ii) a Class A drug which they intended to supply to another or to export; and

(b) an intimate search is the only means of removing those items.

2A.   The reasons an intimate search is considered necessary shall be explained to the person before the search begins.

3.   An intimate search may only be carried out by a registered medical practitioner or registered nurse, unless an officer of at least inspector rank considers this is not practicable and the search is to take place under paragraph 2(a)(i), in which case a police officer may carry out the search. See Notes A1 to A5

3A.   Any proposal for a search under paragraph 2(a)(i) to be carried out by someone other than a registered medical practitioner or registered nurse must only be considered as a last resort and when the authorising officer is satisfied the risks associated with allowing the item to remain with the detainee outweigh the risks associated with removing it. See Notes A1 to A5

4.   An intimate search under:

- paragraph 2(a)(i) may take place only at a hospital, surgery, other medical premises or police station;
- paragraph 2(a)(ii) may take place only at a hospital, surgery or other medical premises and must be carried out by a registered medical practitioner or a registered nurse.

5.   An intimate search at a police station of a juvenile or mentally disordered or otherwise mentally vulnerable person may take place only in the presence of an appropriate adult of the same sex, unless the detainee specifically requests a particular adult of the opposite sex who is readily available. In the case of a juvenile the search may take place in the absence of the appropriate adult only if the juvenile signifies in the presence of the appropriate adult they do not want the adult present during the search and the adult agrees. A record shall be made of the juvenile's decision and signed by the appropriate adult.

6.   When an intimate search under paragraph 2(a)(i) is carried out by a police officer, the officer must be of the same sex as the detainee. A minimum of two people, other than the detainee, must be present during the search. Subject to paragraph 5, no person of the opposite sex who is not a medical practitioner or nurse shall be present, nor shall anyone whose presence is unnecessary. The search shall be conducted with proper regard to the sensitivity and vulnerability of the detainee.

(b) Documentation

7.   In the case of an intimate search the custody officer shall as soon as practicable, record:

- which parts of the detainee's body were searched;
- who carried out the search;
- who was present;
- the reasons for the search including the reasons to believe the article could not otherwise be removed;
- the result.

8.   If an intimate search is carried out by a police officer, the reason why it was impracticable for a registered medical practitioner or registered nurse to conduct it must be recorded.

B   Strip search

9.   A strip search is a search involving the removal of more than outer clothing. In this Code, outer clothing includes shoes and socks.

(a) Action

10.   A strip search may take place only if it is considered necessary to remove an article which a detainee would not be allowed to keep, and the officer reasonably considers the detainee might have concealed such an article. Strip searches shall not be routinely carried out if there is no reason to consider that articles are concealed.

The conduct of strip searches

11. When strip searches are conducted:

(a) a police officer carrying out a strip search must be the same sex as the detainee;

(b) the search shall take place in an area where the detainee cannot be seen by anyone who does not need to be present, nor by a member of the opposite sex except an appropriate adult who has been specifically requested by the detainee;

(c) except in cases of urgency, where there is risk of serious harm to the detainee or to others, whenever a strip search involves exposure of intimate body parts, there must be at least two people present other than the detainee, and if the search is of a juvenile or mentally disordered or otherwise mentally vulnerable person, one of the people must be the appropriate adult. Except in urgent cases as above, a search of a juvenile may take place in the absence of the appropriate adult only if the juvenile signifies in the presence of the appropriate adult that they do not want the adult to be present during the search and the adult agrees. A record shall be made of the juvenile's decision and signed by the appropriate adult. The presence of more than two people, other than an appropriate adult, shall be permitted only in the most exceptional circumstances;

(d) the search shall be conducted with proper regard to the sensitivity and vulnerability of the detainee in these circumstances and every reasonable effort shall be made to secure the detainee's co-operation and minimise embarrassment. Detainees who are searched shall not normally be required to remove all their clothes at the same time, e.g. a person should be allowed to remove clothing above the waist and redress before removing further clothing;

(e) if necessary to assist the search, the detainee may be required to hold their arms in the air or to stand with their legs apart and bend forward so a visual examination may be made of the genital and anal areas provided no physical contact is made with any body orifice;

(f) if articles are found, the detainee shall be asked to hand them over. If articles are found within any body orifice other than the mouth, and the detainee refuses to hand them over, their removal would constitute an intimate search, which must be carried out as in Part A;

(g) a strip search shall be conducted as quickly as possible, and the detainee allowed to dress as soon as the procedure is complete.

(b) Documentation

12. A record shall be made on the custody record of a strip search including the reason it was considered necessary, those present and any result.

Notes for Guidance

A1   Before authorising any intimate search, the authorising officer must make every reasonable effort to persuade the detainee to hand the article over without a search. If the detainee agrees, a registered medical practitioner or registered nurse should whenever possible be asked to assess the risks involved and, if necessary, attend to assist the detainee.

A2   If the detainee does not agree to hand the article over without a search, the authorising officer must carefully review all the relevant factors before authorising an intimate search. In particular, the officer must consider whether the grounds for believing an article may be concealed are reasonable.

A3   If authority is given for a search under paragraph 2(a)(i), a registered medical practitioner or registered nurse shall be consulted whenever possible. The presumption should be that the search will be conducted by the registered medical practitioner or registered nurse and the authorising officer must make every reasonable effort to persuade the detainee to allow the medical practitioner or nurse to conduct the search.

A4   A constable should only be authorised to carry out a search as a last resort and when all other approaches have failed. In these circumstances, the authorising officer must be satisfied the detainee might use the article for one or more of the purposes in paragraph 2(a)(i) and the physical injury likely to be caused is sufficiently severe to justify authorising a constable to carry out the search.

A5   If an officer has any doubts whether to authorise an intimate search by a constable, the officer should seek advice from an officer of superintendent rank or above.

ANNEX B   DELAY IN NOTIFYING ARREST OR ALLOWING ACCESS TO LEGAL ADVICE

A   Persons detained under PACE

1.   The exercise of the rights in Section 5 or Section 6, or both, may be delayed if the person is in police detention, as in PACE, section 118(2), in connection with a serious arrestable offence, has not yet been charged with an offence and an officer of superintendent rank or above, or inspector rank or above only for the rights in Section 5, has reasonable grounds for believing their exercise will:

(i)   lead to:
  • interference with, or harm to, evidence connected with a serious arrestable offence; or
  • interference with, or physical harm to, other people; or

(ii) lead to alerting other people suspected of having committed a serious arrestable offence but not yet arrested for it; or

(iii) hinder the recovery of property obtained in consequence of the commission of such an offence.

2.   These rights may also be delayed if the serious arrestable offence is:

(i)   a drug trafficking offence and the officer has reasonable grounds for believing the detainee has benefited from drug trafficking, and the recovery of the value of the detainee's proceeds from drug trafficking will be hindered by the exercise of either right;

(ii) an offence to which the Criminal Justice Act 1988, Part VI (confiscation orders) applies and the officer has reasonable grounds for believing the detainee has benefited from the offence, and the exercise of either right will hinder the recovery of the value of the:
  • property obtained by the detainee from or in connection with the offence;
  • pecuniary advantage derived by the detainee from or in connection with it.

3.   Authority to delay a detainee's right to consult privately with a solicitor may be given only if the authorising officer has reasonable grounds to believe the solicitor the detainee wants to consult will, inadvertently or otherwise, pass on a message from the detainee or act in some other way which will have any of the consequences specified under paragraphs 1 or 2. In these circumstances the detainee must be allowed to choose another solicitor. See Note B3

4.   If the detainee wishes to see a solicitor, access to that solicitor may not be delayed on the grounds they might advise the detainee not to answer questions or the solicitor was initially asked to attend the police station by someone else. In the latter case the detainee must be told the solicitor has come to the police station at another person's request, and must be asked to sign the custody record to signify whether they want to see the solicitor.

5.   The fact the grounds for delaying notification of arrest may be satisfied does not automatically mean the grounds for delaying access to legal advice will also be satisfied.

6.   These rights may be delayed only for as long as grounds exist and in no case beyond 36 hours after the relevant time as in PACE, section 41. If the grounds cease to apply within

this time, the detainee must, as soon as practicable, be asked if they want to exercise either right, the custody record must be noted accordingly, and action taken in accordance with the relevant section of the Code.

7.   A detained person must be permitted to consult a solicitor for a reasonable time before any court hearing.

B   Persons detained under the Terrorism Act 2000

8.   The rights as in section 5 or 6, may be delayed if the person is detained under the Terrorism Act 2000, section 41 or Schedule 7, has not yet been charged with an offence and an officer of superintendent rank or above has reasonable grounds for believing the exercise of either right will:

- (i)   lead to:
  - interference with, or harm to, evidence connected with a serious arrestable offence;
  - interference with, or physical harm to, other people; or
- (ii)   lead to the alerting of other people suspected of having committed a serious arrestable offence but not yet arrested for it; or
- (iii)   hinder the recovery of property:
  - obtained in consequence of the commission of such an offence; or
  - in respect of which a forfeiture order could be made under that Act, section 23;
- (iv)   lead to interference with the gathering of information about the commission, preparation or instigation of acts of terrorism; or
- (v)   by alerting any person, make it more difficult to prevent an act of terrorism or secure the apprehension, prosecution or conviction of any person in connection with the commission, preparation or instigation of an act of terrorism.

9.   These rights may also be delayed if the officer has reasonable grounds for believing:

- (a)   the detainee:
  - (i)   has committed an offence to which the Criminal Justice Act 1988, Part VI (confiscation orders) applies;
  - (ii)   has benefited from the offence; and
- (b)   the exercise of either right will hinder the recovery of the value of that benefit.

10.   In these cases paragraphs 3 (with regards to the consequences specified at paragraphs 8 and 9), 4 and 5 apply.

11.   These rights may be delayed only for as long as is necessary but not beyond 48 hours from the time of arrest if arrested under section 41, or if detained under the Terrorism Act 2000, Schedule 7 when arrested under section 41, from the beginning of their examination. If the above grounds cease to apply within this time the detainee must as soon as practicable be asked if they wish to exercise either right, the custody record noted accordingly, and action taken in accordance with the relevant section of this Code.

12.   In this case paragraph 7 applies.

C   Documentation

13.   The grounds for action under this Annex shall be recorded and the detainee informed of them as soon as practicable.

14.   Any reply given by a detainee under paragraph 6 or 11 must be recorded and the detainee asked to endorse the record in relation to whether they want to receive legal advice at this point.

D   Cautions and special warnings

When a suspect detained at a police station is interviewed during any period for which access to legal advice has been delayed under this Annex, the court or jury may not draw adverse inferences from their silence.

Notes for Guidance

B1 Even if Annex B applies in the case of a juvenile, or a person who is mentally disordered or otherwise mentally vulnerable, action to inform the appropriate adult and the person responsible for a juvenile's welfare if that is a different person, must nevertheless be taken as in paragraph 3.13 and 3.15.

B2 In the case of Commonwealth citizens and foreign nationals, see Note 7A.

B3 A decision to delay access to a specific solicitor is likely to be a rare occurrence and only when it can be shown the suspect is capable of misleading that particular solicitor and there is more than a substantial risk that the suspect will succeed in causing information to be conveyed which will lead to one or more of the specified consequences.

ANNEX C   RESTRICTION ON DRAWING ADVERSE INFERENCES FROM SILENCE AND TERMS OF THE CAUTION WHEN THE RESTRICTION APPLIES

(a) The restriction on drawing adverse inferences from silence

1. The Criminal Justice and Public Order Act 1994, sections 34, 36 and 37 as amended by the Youth Justice and Criminal Evidence Act 1999, section 58 describe the conditions under which adverse inferences may be drawn from a person's failure or refusal to say any-thing about their involvement in the offence when interviewed, after being charged or informed they may be prosecuted. These provisions are subject to an overriding restriction on the ability of a court or jury to draw adverse inferences from a person's silence. This restriction applies:

(a) to any detainee at a police station, see Note 10C who, before being interviewed, see section 11 or being charged or informed they may be prosecuted, see section 16, has:

(i) asked for legal advice, see section 6, paragraph 6.1;

(ii) not been allowed an opportunity to consult a solicitor, including the duty solicitor, as in this Code: and

(iii) not changed their mind about wanting legal advice, see section 6, paragraph 6.6(d)

Note the condition in (ii) will

~ apply when a detainee who has asked for legal advice is interviewed before speaking to a solicitor as in section 6, paragraph 6.6(a) or (b).

~ not apply if the detained person declines to ask for the duty solicitor, see section 6, paragraphs 6.6(c) and (d);

(b) to any person charged with, or informed they may be prosecuted for, an offence who:

(i) has had brought to their notice a written statement made by another person or the content of an interview with another person which relates to that offence, see section 16, paragraph 16.4;

(ii) is interviewed about that offence, see section 16, paragraph 16.5; or

(iii) makes a written statement about that offence, see Annex D paragraphs 4 and 9.

(b) Terms of the caution when the restriction applies

2. When a requirement to caution arises at a time when the restriction on drawing adverse inferences from silence applies, the caution shall be:

'*You do not have to say anything, but anything you do say may be given in evidence.*'

3. Whenever the restriction either begins to apply or ceases to apply after a caution has already been given, the person shall be re-cautioned in the appropriate terms. The changed

position on drawing inferences and that the previous caution no longer applies shall also be explained to the detainee in ordinary language. See Note C2

Notes for Guidance

C1   The restriction on drawing inferences from silence does not apply to a person who has not been detained and who therefore cannot be prevented from seeking legal advice if they want to, see paragraphs 10.2 and 3.15.

C2   The following is suggested as a framework to help explain changes in the position on drawing adverse inferences if the restriction on drawing adverse inferences from silence:

(a) begins to apply:
'The caution you were previously given no longer applies. This is because after that caution:
  (i)   you asked to speak to a solicitor but have not yet been allowed an opportunity to speak to a solicitor.' See paragraph 1(a); or
  (ii) you have been charged with/informed you may be prosecuted.' See paragraph 1(b).
    'This means that from now on, adverse inferences cannot be drawn at court and your defence will not be harmed just because you choose to say nothing. Please listen carefully to the caution I am about to give you because it will apply from now on. You will see that it does not say anything about your defence being harmed.'

(b) ceases to apply before or at the time the person is charged or informed they may be prosecuted, see paragraph 1(a);
    'The caution you were previously given no longer applies. This is because after that caution you have been allowed an opportunity to speak to a solicitor. Please listen carefully to the caution I am about to give you because it will apply from now on. It explains how your defence at court may be affected if you choose to say nothing.'

ANNEX D   WRITTEN STATEMENTS UNDER CAUTION

(a) Written by a person under caution

1.   A person shall always be invited to write down what they want to say.

2.   A person who has not been charged with, or informed they may be prosecuted for, any offence to which the statement they want to write relates, shall:

(a) unless the statement is made at a time when the restriction on drawing adverse inferences from silence applies, see Annex C, be asked to write out and sign the following before writing what they want to say:
    '*I make this statement of my own free will. I understand that I do not have to say anything but that it may harm my defence if I do not mention when questioned something which I later rely on in court. This statement may be given in evidence.*';

(b) if the statement is made at a time when the restriction on drawing adverse inferences from silence applies, be asked to write out and sign the following before writing what they want to say;
    '*I make this statement of my own free will. I understand that I do not have to say anything. This statement may be given in evidence.*'

3.   When a person, on the occasion of being charged with or informed they may be prosecuted for any offence, asks to make a statement which relates to any such offence and wants to write it they shall:

(a) unless the restriction on drawing adverse inferences from silence, see Annex C, applied when they were so charged or informed they may be prosecuted, be asked to write out and sign the following before writing what they want to say:

'I make this statement of my own free will. I understand that I do not have to say anything but that it may harm my defence if I do not mention when questioned something which I later rely on in court. This statement may be given in evidence.';

(b) if the restriction on drawing adverse inferences from silence applied when they were so charged or informed they may be prosecuted, be asked to write out and sign the following before writing what they want to say:

'I make this statement of my own free will. I understand that I do not have to say anything. This statement may be given in evidence.'

4. When a person, who has already been charged with or informed they may be prosecuted for any offence, asks to make a statement which relates to any such offence and wants to write it they shall be asked to write out and sign the following before writing what they want to say:

'I make this statement of my own free will. I understand that I do not have to say anything. This statement may be given in evidence.';

5. Any person writing their own statement shall be allowed to do so without any prompting except a police officer or civilian interviewer may indicate to them which matters are material or question any ambiguity in the statement.

(b) Written by a police officer or civilian interviewer

6. If a person says they would like someone to write the statement for them, a police officer, or civilian interviewer shall write the statement.

7. If the person has not been charged with, or informed they may be prosecuted for, any offence to which the statement they want to make relates they shall, before starting, be asked to sign, or make their mark, to the following:

(a) unless the statement is made at a time when the restriction on drawing adverse inferences from silence applies, see Annex C:

'I, ..., wish to make a statement. I want someone to write down what I say. I understand that I do not have to say anything but that it may harm my defence if I do not mention when questioned something which I later rely on in court. This statement may be given in evidence.';

(b) if the statement is made at a time when the restriction on drawing adverse inferences from silence applies:

'I, ..., wish to make a statement. I want someone to write down what I say. This statement may be given in evidence.'

8. If, on the occasion of being charged with or informed they may be prosecuted for any offence, the person asks to make a statement which relates to any such offence they shall before starting be asked to sign, or make their mark to, the following:

(a) unless the restriction on drawing adverse inferences from silence applied, see Annex C, when they were so charged or informed they may be prosecuted:

'I, ..., wish to make a statement. I want someone to write down what I say. I understand that I do not have to say anything but that it may harm my defence if I do not mention when questioned something which I later rely on in court. This statement may be given in evidence.';

(b) if the restriction on drawing adverse inferences from silence applied when they were so charged or informed they may be prosecuted:

'I, ..., wish to make a statement. I want someone to write down what I say. This statement may be given in evidence.'

9. If, having already been charged with or informed they may be prosecuted for any offence, a person asks to make a statement which relates to any such offence they shall before starting, be asked to sign, or make their mark to:

'I, ..., wish to make a statement. I want someone to write down what I say. This statement may be given in evidence.'

10.   The person writing the statement must take down the exact words spoken by the person making it and must not edit or paraphrase it. Any questions that are necessary, e.g. to make it more intelligible, and the answers given must be recorded at the same time on the statement form.

11.   When the writing of a statement is finished the person making it shall be asked to read it and to make any corrections, alterations or additions they want. When they have finished reading they shall be asked to write and sign or make their mark on the following certificate at the end of the statement:

'I have read the above statement, and I have been able to correct, alter or add anything I wish. This statement is true. I have made it of my own free will.'

12.   If the person making the statement cannot read, or refuses to read it, or to write the above mentioned certificate at the end of it or to sign it, the person taking the statement shall read it to them and ask them if they would like to correct, alter or add anything and to put their signature or make their mark at the end. The person taking the statement shall certify on the statement itself what has occurred.

ANNEX E – SUMMARY OF PROVISIONS RELATING TO MENTALLY DISORDERED AND OTHERWISE MENTALLY VULNERABLE PEOPLE

1.   If an officer has any suspicion, or is told in good faith, that a person of any age may be mentally disordered or otherwise mentally vulnerable, or mentally incapable of understanding the significance of questions or their replies that person shall be treated as mentally disordered or otherwise mentally vulnerable for the purposes of this Code. See paragraph 1.4

2.   In the case of a person who is mentally disordered or otherwise mentally vulnerable, 'the appropriate adult' means:
   (a) a relative, guardian or other person responsible for their care or custody;
   (b) someone experienced in dealing with mentally disordered or mentally vulnerable people but who is not a police officer or employed by the police;
   (c) failing these, some other responsible adult aged 18 or over who is not a police officer or employed by the police.

See paragraph 1.7(b) and Note 1 D

3.   If the custody officer authorises the detention of a person who is mentally vulnerable or appears to be suffering from a mental disorder, the custody officer must as soon as practicable inform the appropriate adult of the grounds for detention and the person's whereabouts, and ask the adult to come to the police station to see them. If the appropriate adult:
   • is already at the station when information is given as in paragraphs 3.1 to 3.5 the information must be given in their presence
   • is not at the station when the provisions of paragraph 3.1 to 3.5 are complied with these provisions must be complied with again in their presence once they arrive.

See paragraphs 3.15 to 3.17

4.   If the appropriate adult, having been informed of the right to legal advice, considers legal advice should be taken, the provisions of section 6 apply as if the mentally disordered or otherwise mentally vulnerable person had requested access to legal advice. See paragraph 3.19 and Note E1

5.   The custody officer must make sure a person receives appropriate clinical attention as soon as reasonably practicable if the person appears to be suffering from a mental disorder or in urgent cases immediately call the nearest health care professional or an ambulance. It is not intended these provisions delay the transfer of a detainee to a place of safety under the Mental Health Act 1983, section 136 if that is applicable. If an assessment under that Act is to take place at a police station, the custody officer must consider whether an appropriate health

care professional should be called to conduct an initial clinical check on the detainee. See paragraphs 9.5 and 9.6

6.   It is imperative a mentally disordered or otherwise mentally vulnerable person detained under the Mental Health Act 1983, section 136 be assessed as soon as possible. If that assessment is to take place at the police station, an approved social worker and registered medical practitioner shall be called to the station as soon as possible in order to interview and examine the detainee. Once the detainee has been interviewed, examined and suitable arrangements been made for their treatment or care, they can no longer be detained under section 136. A detainee should be immediately discharged from detention if a registered medical practitioner having examined them, concludes they are not mentally disordered within the meaning of the Act. See paragraph 3.16

7.   If a mentally disordered or otherwise mentally vulnerable person is cautioned in the absence of the appropriate adult, the caution must be repeated in the appropriate adult's presence. See paragraph 10.12

8.   A mentally disordered or otherwise mentally vulnerable person must not be interviewed or asked to provide or sign a written statement in the absence of the appropriate adult unless the provisions of paragraphs 11.1 or 11.18 to 11.20 apply. Questioning in these circumstances may not continue in the absence of the appropriate adult once sufficient information to avert the risk has been obtained. A record shall be made of the grounds for any decision to begin an interview in these circumstances. See paragraphs 11.1, 11.15 and 11.18 to 11.20

9.   If the appropriate adult is present at an interview, they shall be informed they are not expected to act simply as an observer and the purposes of their presence are to:
   •   advise the interviewee;
   •   observe whether or not the interview is being conducted properly and fairly;
   •   facilitate communication with the interviewee.
See paragraph 11.17

10.   If the detention of a mentally disordered or otherwise mentally vulnerable person is reviewed by a review officer or a superintendent, the appropriate adult must, if available at the time, be given an opportunity to make representations to the officer about the need for continuing detention. See paragraph 15.3

11.   If the custody officer charges a mentally disordered or otherwise mentally vulnerable person with an offence or takes such other action as is appropriate when there is sufficient evidence for a prosecution this must be done in the presence of the appropriate adult. The written notice embodying any charge must be given to the appropriate adult. See paragraphs 16.1 to 16.4A

12.   An intimate or strip search of a mentally disordered or otherwise mentally vulnerable person may take place only in the presence of the appropriate adult of the same sex, unless the detainee specifically requests the presence of a particular adult of the opposite sex. A strip search may take place in the absence of an appropriate adult only in cases of urgency when there is a risk of serious harm to the detainee or others. See Annex A, paragraphs 5 and 11(c)

13.   Particular care must be taken when deciding whether to use any form of approved restraints on a mentally disordered or otherwise mentally vulnerable person in a locked cell. See paragraph 8.2

Notes for Guidance

E1   The purpose of the provision at paragraph 3.19 is to protect the rights of a mentally disordered or otherwise mentally vulnerable detained person who does not understand the significance of what is said to them. If the detained person wants to exercise the right to legal advice, the appropriate action should be taken and not delayed until the appropriate adult arrives. A mentally disordered or otherwise mentally vulnerable detained person should always be given an opportunity, when an appropriate adult is called to the police station, to consult privately with a solicitor in the absence of the appropriate adult if they want.

E2   Although people who are mentally disordered or otherwise mentally vulnerable are often capable of providing reliable evidence, they may, without knowing or wanting to do so, be particularly prone in certain circumstances to provide information that may be unreliable, misleading or self-incriminating. Special care should always be taken when questioning such a person, and the appropriate adult should be involved if there is any doubt about a person's mental state or capacity. Because of the risk of unreliable evidence, it is important to obtain corroboration of any facts admitted whenever possible.

E3   Because of the risks referred to in Note E2, which the presence of the appropriate adult is intended to minimise, officers of superintendent rank or above should exercise their discretion to authorise the commencement of an interview in the appropriate adult's absence only in exceptional cases, if it is necessary to avert an immediate risk of serious harm. See paragraphs 11.1, 11.18 to 11.20

ANNEX F   COUNTRIES WITH WHICH BILATERAL CONSULAR CONVENTIONS OR AGREEMENTS REQUIRING NOTIFICATION OF THE ARREST AND DETENTION OF THEIR NATIONAL ARE IN FORCE AS AT 1 APRIL 2003

Armenia
Austria
Azerbaijan
Belarus
Belgium
Bosnia-Herzegovina
Bulgaria
China*
Croatia
Cuba
Czech Republic
Denmark
Egypt
France
Georgia
German Federal Republic
Greece
Hungary
Italy
Japan

Kazakhstan
Macedonia
Mexico
Moldova
Mongolia
Norway
Poland
Romania
Russia
Slovak Republic
Slovenia
Spain
Sweden
Tajikistan
Turkmenistan
Ukraine
USA
Uzbekistan
Yugoslavia

* Police are required to inform Chinese officials of arrest/detention in the Manchester consular district only. This comprises Derbyshire, Durham, Greater Manchester, Lancashire, Merseyside, North South and West Yorkshire, and Tyne and Wear.

ANNEX G   FITNESS TO BE INTERVIEWED

1.   This Annex contains general guidance to help police officers and health care professionals assess whether a detainee might be at risk in an interview.

2.   A detainee may be at risk in an interview if it is considered that:

   (a)   conducting the interview could significantly harm the detainee's physical or mental state;

   (b)   anything the detainee says in the interview about their involvement or suspected involvement in the offence about which they are being interviewed might be considered unreliable in subsequent court proceedings because of their physical or mental state.

3.   In assessing whether the detainee should be interviewed, the following must be considered:

> (a) how the detainee's physical or mental state might affect their ability to understand the nature and purpose of the interview, to comprehend what is being asked and to appreciate the significance of any answers given and make rational decisions about whether they want to say anything;
>
> (b) the extent to which the detainee's replies may be affected by their physical or mental condition rather than representing a rational and accurate explanation of their involvement in the offence;
>
> (c) how the nature of the interview, which could include particularly probing questions, might affect the detainee.

4.   It is essential health care professionals who are consulted consider the functional ability of the detainee rather than simply relying on a medical diagnosis, e.g. it is possible for a person with severe mental illness to be fit for interview.

5.   Health care professionals should advise on the need for an appropriate adult to be present, whether reassessment of the person's fitness for interview may be necessary if the interview lasts beyond a specified time, and whether a further specialist opinion may be required.

6.   When health care professionals identify risks they should be asked to quantify the risks. They should inform the custody officer:

- whether the person's condition:
  - ~ is likely to improve;
  - ~ will require or be amenable to treatment; and
- indicate how long it may take for such improvement to take effect.

7.   The role of the health care professional is to consider the risks and advise the custody officer of the outcome of that consideration. The health care professional's determination and any advice or recommendations should be made in writing and form part of the custody record.

8.   Once the health care professional has provided that information, it is a matter for the custody officer to decide whether or not to allow the interview to go ahead and if the interview is to proceed, to determine what safeguards are needed. Nothing prevents safeguards being provided in addition to those required under the Code. An example might be to have an appropriate health care professional present during the interview, in addition to an appropriate adult, in order constantly to monitor the person's condition and how it is being affected by the interview.

ANNEX H   DETAINED PERSON: OBSERVATION LIST

1.   If any detainee fails to meet any of the following criteria, an appropriate health care professional or an ambulance must be called.

2.   When assessing the level of rousability, consider:

Rousability – can they be woken?

- go into the cell;
- call their name;
- shake gently.

Response to questions – can they give appropriate answers to questions such as:

- What's your name?
- Where do you live?
- Where do you think you are?

Response to commands – can they respond appropriately to commands such as:

- Open your eyes!
- Lift one arm, now the other arm!

3. Remember to take into account the possibility or presence of other illnesses, injury, or mental condition, a person who is drowsy and smells of alcohol may also have the following:

- Diabetes;
- Epilepsy;
- Head injury;
- Drug intoxication or overdose;
- Stroke.

Code of Practice for the Identification of Persons by Police Officers (Code D)

1 Introduction

1.1 This Code of Practice concerns the principal methods used by police to identify people in connection with the investigation of offences and the keeping of accurate and reliable criminal records.

1.2 Identification by witnesses arises, e.g., if the offender is seen committing the crime and a witness is given an opportunity to identify the suspect in a video identification, identification parade or similar procedure. The procedures are designed to:

- test the witness' ability to identify the person they saw on a previous occasion
- provide safeguards against mistaken identification.

While this Code concentrates on visual identification procedures, it does not preclude the police making use of aural identification procedures such as a 'voice identification parade', where they judge that appropriate.

1.3 Identification by fingerprints applies when a person's fingerprints are taken to:

- compare with fingerprints found at the scene of a crime
- check and prove convictions
- help to ascertain a person's identity.

1.4 Identification by body samples and impressions includes taking samples such as blood or hair to generate a DNA profile for comparison with material obtained from the scene of a crime, or a victim.

1.5 Taking photographs of arrested people applies to recording and checking identity and locating and tracing persons who:

- are wanted for offences
- fail to answer their bail.

1.6 Another method of identification involves searching and examining detained suspects to find, e.g., marks such as tattoos or scars which may help establish their identity or whether they have been involved in committing an offence.

1.7 The provisions of the Police and Criminal Evidence Act 1984 (PACE) and this Code are designed to make sure fingerprints, samples, impressions and photographs are taken, used and retained, and identification procedures carried out, only when justified and necessary for preventing, detecting or investigating crime. If these provisions are not observed, the application of the relevant procedures in particular cases may be open to question.

2 General

2.1 This Code must be readily available at all police stations for consultation by:

- police officers;
- detained persons;
- members of the public;

2.2   The provisions of this Code:
- include the *Annexes*;
- do not include the *Notes for Guidance*.

2.3   Code C, paragraph 1.4, regarding a person who may be mentally disordered or otherwise mentally vulnerable and the Notes for guidance applicable to those provisions apply to this Code.

2.4   Code C, paragraph 1.5, regarding a person who appears to be under the age of 17 applies to this Code.

2.5   Code C, paragraph 1.6, regarding a person who appears blind, seriously visually impaired, deaf, unable to read or speak or has difficulty orally because of a speech impediment applies to this Code.

2.6   In this Code:
- 'appropriate adult' means the same as in Code C, paragraph 1.7,
- 'solicitor' means the same as in Code C, paragraph 6.12

and the *Notes for Guidance* applicable to those provisions apply to this Code.

2.7   References to custody officers include those performing the functions of custody officer.

2.8   When a record of any action requiring the authority of an officer of a specified rank is made under this Code, subject to paragraph 2.18, the officer's name and rank must be recorded.

2.9   When this Code requires the prior authority or agreement of an officer of at least inspector or superintendent rank, that authority may be given by a sergeant or chief inspector who has been authorised to perform the functions of the higher rank under PACE, section 107.

2.10   Subject to paragraph 2.18, all records must be timed and signed by the maker.

2.11   Records must be made in the custody record, unless otherwise specified. References to 'pocket book' include any official report book issued to police officers or civilian support staff.

2.12   If any procedure in this Code requires a person's consent, the consent of a:
- mentally disordered or otherwise mentally vulnerable person is only valid if given in the presence of the appropriate adult
- juvenile, is only valid if their parent's or guardian's consent is also obtained unless the juvenile is under 14, when their parent's or guardian's consent is sufficient in its own right. If the only obstacle to an identification procedure in section 3 is that a juvenile's parent or guardian refuses consent or reasonable efforts to obtain it have failed, the identification officer may apply the provisions of paragraph 3.21. See Note 2A

2.13   If a person is blind, seriously visually impaired or unable to read, the custody officer or identification officer shall make sure their solicitor, relative, appropriate adult or some other person likely to take an interest in them and not involved in the investigation is available to help check any documentation. When this Code requires written consent or signing, the person assisting may be asked to sign instead, if the detainee prefers. This paragraph does not require an appropriate adult to be called solely to assist in checking and signing documentation for a person who is not a juvenile, or mentally disordered or otherwise mentally vulnerable (see Note 2B and Code C paragraph 3.15).

2.14   If any procedure in this Code requires information to be given to or sought from a suspect, it must be given or sought in the appropriate adult's presence if the suspect is mentally disordered, otherwise mentally vulnerable or a juvenile. If the appropriate adult is not present when the information is first given or sought, the procedure must be repeated in the presence of the appropriate adult when they arrive. If the suspect appears deaf or there is doubt about their hearing or speaking ability or ability to understand English, and effective communication cannot be established, the information must be given or sought through an interpreter.

2.15   Any procedure in this Code involving the participation of a person (whether as a suspect or a witness) who is mentally disordered, otherwise mentally vulnerable or a juvenile, must take place in the presence of the appropriate adult. However, the adult must not be allowed to prompt any identification of a suspect by a witness.

2.16   References to:

- 'taking a photograph', include the use of any process to produce a single, still, visual image
- 'photographing a person', should be construed accordingly
- 'photographs', 'films', 'negatives' and 'copies' include relevant visual images recorded, stored, or reproduced through any medium
- 'destruction' includes the deletion of computer data relating to such images or making access to that data impossible.

2.17   Except as described, nothing in this Code affects the powers and procedures:

   (i)   for requiring and taking samples of breath, blood and urine in relation to driving offences, etc, when under the influence of drink, drugs or excess alcohol under the:

- Road Traffic Act 1988, sections 4 to 11;
- Road Traffic Offenders Act 1988, sections 15 and 16;
- Transport and Works Act 1992, sections 26 to 38;

   (ii)   under the Immigration Act 1971, Schedule 2, paragraph 18, for taking photographs and fingerprints from persons detained under that Act, Schedule 2, paragraph 16 (Administrative Controls as to Control on Entry etc.); for taking fingerprints in accordance with the Immigration and Asylum Act 1999; sections 141 and 142(3), or other methods for collecting information about a person's external physical characteristics provided for by regulations made under that Act, section 144;

   (iii)   under the Terrorism Act 2000, Schedule 8, for taking photographs, fingerprints, skin impressions, body samples or impressions from people:

- arrested under that Act, section 41;
- detained for the purposes of examination under that Act, Schedule 7, and to whom the Code of Practice issued under that Act, Schedule 14, paragraph 6, applies ('the terrorism provisions');

   See Note 2C;

   (iv)   for taking photographs, fingerprints, skin impressions, body samples or impressions from people who have been:

- arrested on warrants issued in Scotland, by officers exercising powers under the Criminal Justice and Public Order Act 1994, section 136(2);
- arrested or detained without warrant by officers from a police force in Scotland exercising their powers of arrest or detention under the Criminal Justice and Public Order Act 1994, section 137(2), (Cross Border powers of arrest etc.).

   Note: In these cases, police powers and duties and the person's rights and entitlements whilst at a police station in England and Wales are the same as if the person had been arrested in Scotland by a Scottish police officer.

2.18   Nothing in this Code requires the identity of officers or civilian support staff to be recorded or disclosed:

   (a)   in the case of enquiries linked to the investigation of terrorism;
   (b)   if the officers or civilian support staff reasonably believe recording or disclosing their names might put them in danger.

In these cases, they shall use warrant or other identification numbers and the name of their police station. See Note 2D

2.19   In this Code:

(a) 'designated person' means a person other than a police officer, designated under the Police Reform Act 2002, Part 4, who has specified powers and duties of police officers conferred or imposed on them;

(b) any reference to a police officer includes a designated person acting in the exercise or performance of the powers and duties conferred or imposed on them by their designation.

2.20   If a power conferred on a designated person:

(a) allows reasonable force to be used when exercised by a police officer, a designated person exercising that power has the same entitlement to use force;

(b) includes power to use force to enter any premises, that power is not exercisable by that designated person except:

(i) in the company, and under the supervision, of a police officer; or

(ii) for the purpose of:

- saving life or limb; or
- preventing serious damage to property.

2.21   Nothing in this Code prevents the custody officer, or other officer given custody of the detainee, from allowing civilian support staff who are not designated persons to carry out individual procedures or tasks at the police station if the law allows. However, the officer remains responsible for making sure the procedures and tasks are carried out correctly in accordance with the Codes of Practice. Any such civilian must be:

(a) a person employed by a police authority maintaining a police force and under the control and direction of the Chief Officer of that force;

(b) employed by a person with whom a police authority has a contract for the provision of services relating to persons arrested or otherwise in custody.

2.22   Designated persons and other civilian support staff must have regard to any relevant provisions of the Codes of Practice.

Notes for Guidance

2A   For the purposes of paragraph 2.12, the consent required from a parent or guardian may, for a juvenile in the care of a local authority or voluntary organisation, be given by that authority or organisation. In the case of a juvenile, nothing in paragraph 2.12 requires the parent, guardian or representative of a local authority or voluntary organisation to be present to give their consent, unless they are acting as the appropriate adult under paragraphs 2.14 or 2.15. However, it is important that a parent or guardian not present is fully informed before being asked to consent. They must be given the same information about the procedure and the juvenile's suspected involvement in the offence as the juvenile and appropriate adult. The parent or guardian must also be allowed to speak to the juvenile and the appropriate adult if they wish. Provided the consent is fully informed and is not withdrawn, it may be obtained at any time before the procedure takes place.

2B   People who are seriously visually impaired or unable to read may be unwilling to sign police documents. The alternative, i.e. their representative signing on their behalf, seeks to protect the interests of both police and suspects.

2C   Photographs, fingerprints, samples and impressions may be taken from a person detained under the terrorism provisions to help determine whether they are, or have been, involved in terrorism, as well as when there are reasonable grounds for suspecting their involvement in a particular offence.

2D   The purpose of paragraph 2.18(b) is to protect those involved in serious organised crime investigations or arrests of particularly violent suspects when there is reliable information that those arrested or their associates may threaten or cause harm to the officers. In cases of doubt, an officer of inspector rank or above should be consulted.

3   Identification by witnesses

3.1   A record shall be made of the suspect's description as first given by a potential witness. This record must:

(a) be made and kept in a form which enables details of that description to be accurately produced from it, in a visible and legible form, which can be given to the suspect or the suspect's solicitor in accordance with this Code; and

(b) unless otherwise specified, be made before the witness takes part in any identification procedures under paragraphs 3.5 to 3.10, 3.21 or 3.23.

A copy of the record shall where practicable, be given to the suspect or their solicitor before any procedures under paragraphs 3.5 to 3.10, 3.21 or 3.23 are carried out. See Note 3E

(a) Cases when the suspect's identity is not known

3.2   In cases when the suspect's identity is not known, a witness may be taken to a particular neighbourhood or place to see whether they can identify the person they saw. Although the number, age, sex, race, general description and style of clothing of other people present at the location and the way in which any identification is made cannot be controlled, the principles applicable to the formal procedures under paragraphs 3.5 to 3.10 shall be followed as far as practicable. For example:

(a) where it is practicable to do so, a record should be made of the witness' description of the suspect, as in paragraph 3.1(a), before asking the witness to make an identification;

(b) care must be taken not to direct the witness' attention to any individual unless, taking into account all the circumstances, this cannot be avoided. However, this does not prevent a witness being asked to look carefully at the people around at the time or to look towards a group or in a particular direction, if this appears necessary to make sure that the witness does not overlook a possible suspect simply because the witness is looking in the opposite direction and also to enable the witness to make comparisons between any suspect and others who are in the area; See Note 3F

(c) where there is more than one witness, every effort should be made to keep them separate and witnesses should be taken to see whether they can identify a person independently;

(d) once there is sufficient information to justify the arrest of a particular individual for suspected involvement in the offence, e.g., after a witness makes a positive identification, the provisions set out from paragraph 3.4 onwards shall apply for any other witnesses in relation to that individual. Subject to paragraphs 3.12 and 3.13, it is not necessary for the witness who makes such a positive identification to take part in a further procedure;

(e) the officer or civilian support staff accompanying the witness must record, in their pocket book, the action taken as soon as, and in as much detail, as possible. The record should include: the date, time and place of the relevant occasion the witness claims to have previously seen the suspect; where any identification was made; how it was made and the conditions at the time (e.g., the distance the witness was from the suspect, the weather and light); if the witness's attention was drawn to the suspect; the reason for this; and anything said by the witness or the suspect about the identification or the conduct of the procedure.

3.3   A witness must not be shown photographs, computerised or artist's composite likenesses or similar likenesses or pictures (including 'E-fit' images) if the identity of the suspect is known to the police and the suspect is available to take part in a video identification, an identification parade or a group identification. If the suspect's identity is not known, the showing of such images to a witness to obtain identification evidence must be done in accordance with Annex E.

(b) Cases when the suspect is known and available

3.4   If the suspect's identity is known to the police and they are available, the identification procedures set out in paragraphs 3.5 to 3.10 may be used. References in this section to a suspect being 'known' mean there is sufficient information known to the police to justify the arrest of a particular person for suspected involvement in the offence. A suspect being 'available' means they are immediately available or will be within a reasonably short time and willing to take an effective part in at least one of the following which it is practicable to arrange;

- video identification;
- identification parade; or
- group identification.

Video identification

3.5   A 'video identification' is when the witness is shown moving images of a known suspect, together with similar images of others who resemble the suspect. See paragraph 3.21 for circumstances in which still images may be used.

3.6   Video identifications must be carried out in accordance with Annex A.

Identification parade

3.7   An 'identification parade' is when the witness sees the suspect in a line of others who resemble the suspect.

3.8   Identification parades must be carried out in accordance with Annex B.

Group identification

3.9   A 'group identification' is when the witness sees the suspect in an informal group of people.

3.10   Group identifications must be carried out in accordance with Annex C.

Arranging identification procedures

3.11   Except for the provisions in paragraph 3.19, the arrangements for, and conduct of, the identification procedures in paragraphs 3.5 to 3.10 and circumstances in which an identification procedures must be held shall be the responsibility of an officer not below inspector rank who is not involved with the investigation, 'the identification officer'. Unless otherwise specified, the identification officer may allow another officer or civilian support staff, see paragraph 2.21, to make arrangements for, and conduct, any of these identification procedures. In delegating these procedures, the identification officer must be able to supervise effectively and either intervene or be contacted for advice. No officer or any other person involved with the investigation of the case against the suspect, beyond the extent required by these procedures, may take any part in these procedures or act as the identification officer. This does not prevent the identification officer from consulting the officer in charge of the investigation to determine which procedure to use. When an identification procedure is required, in the interest of fairness to suspects and witnesses, it must be held as soon as practicable.

Circumstances in which an identification procedure must be held

3.12   Whenever:
- (i)   a witness has identified a suspect or purported to have identified them prior to any identification procedure set out in paragraphs 3.5 to 3.10 having been held; or
- (ii)   there is a witness available, who expresses an ability to identify the suspect, or where there is a reasonable chance of the witness being able to do so, and they have not been given an opportunity to identify the suspect in any of the procedures set out in paragraphs 3.5 to 3.10,

and the suspect disputes being the person the witness claims to have seen, an identification procedure shall be held unless it is not practicable or it would serve no useful purpose in proving or disproving whether the suspect was involved in committing the offence. For example, when it is not disputed that the suspect is already well known to the witness who claims to have seen them commit the crime.

3.13   Such a procedure may also be held if the officer in charge of the investigation considers it would be useful.

Selecting an identification procedure

3.14   If, because of paragraph 3.12, an identification procedure is to be held, the suspect shall initially be offered either a video identification or identification unless:

    (a) a video identification is not practicable; or

    (b) an identification parade is both practicable and more suitable than a video identification; or

    (c) paragraph 3.16 applies.

The identification officer and the officer in charge of the investigation shall consult each other to determine which option is to be offered. An identification parade may not be practicable because of factors relating to the witnesses, such as their number, state of health, availability and travelling requirements. A video identification would normally be more suitable if it could be arranged and completed sooner than an identification parade.

3.15   A suspect who refuses the identification procedure first offered shall be asked to state their reason for refusing and may get advice from their solicitor and/or if present, their appropriate adult. The suspect, solicitor and/or appropriate adult shall be allowed to make representations about why another procedure should be used. A record should be made of the reasons for refusal and any representations made. After considering any reasons given, and representations made, the identification officer shall, if appropriate, arrange for the suspect to be offered an alternative which the officer considers suitable and practicable. If the officer decides it is not suitable and practicable to offer an alternative identification procedure, the reasons for that decision shall be recorded.

3.16   A group identification may initially be offered if the officer in charge of the investigation considers it is more satisfactory than a video identification or an identification parade and the identification officer considers it practicable to arrange.

Notice to suspect

3.17   Unless paragraph 3.20 applies, before a video identification, an identification parade or group identification is arranged, the following shall be explained to the suspect:

    (i)   the purposes of the video identification, identification parade or group identification;

    (ii)   their entitlement to free legal advice; see Code C, paragraph 6.5;

    (iii) the procedures for holding it, including their right to have a solicitor or friend present;

    (iv)   that they do not have to consent to or co-operate in a video identification, identification parade or group identification;

    (v)   that if they do not consent to, and co-operate in, a video identification, identification parade or group identification, their refusal may be given in evidence in any subsequent trial and police may proceed covertly without their consent or make other arrangements to test whether a witness can identify them, see paragraph 3.21

    (vi)   whether, for the purposes of the video identification procedure, images of them have previously been obtained, see paragraph 3.20, and if so, that they may co-operate in providing further, suitable images to be used instead;

    (vii) if appropriate, the special arrangements for juveniles;

(viii) if appropriate, the special arrangements for mentally disordered or otherwise mentally vulnerable people;

(ix) that if they significantly alter their appearance between being offered an identification procedure and any attempt to hold an identification procedure, this may be given in evidence if the case comes to trial, and the identification officer may then consider other forms of identification, see paragraph 3.21 and Note 3C;

(x) that a moving image or photograph may be taken of them when they attend for any identification procedure;

(xi) whether, before their identity became known, the witness was shown photographs, a computerised or artist's composite likeness or similar likeness or image by the police; see Note 3B

(xii) that if they change their appearance before an identification parade, it may not be practicable to arrange one on the day or subsequently and, because of the appearance change, the identification officer may consider alternative methods of identification; see Note 3C

(xiii) that they or their solicitor will be provided with details of the description of them as first given by any witnesses who are to attend the video identification, identification parade, group identification or confrontation, see paragraph 3.1.

3.18   This information must also be recorded in a written notice handed to the suspect. The suspect must be given a reasonable opportunity to read the notice, after which, they should be asked to sign a second copy to indicate if they are willing to co-operate with the making of a video or take part in the identification parade or group identification. The signed copy shall be retained by the identification officer.

3.19   The duties of the identification officer under paragraphs 3.17 and 3.18 may be performed by the custody officer or other officer not involved in the investigation if:

(a) it is proposed to hold an identification procedure at a later date, e.g., if the suspect is to be bailed to attend an identification parade; and

(b) an inspector is not available to act as the identification officer, see paragraph 3.11, before the suspect leaves the station.

The officer concerned shall inform the identification officer of the action taken and give them the signed copy of the notice. See Note 3C

3.20   If the identification officer and officer in charge of the investigation suspect, on reasonable grounds that if the suspect was given the information and notice as in paragraphs 3.17 and 3.18, they would then take steps to avoid being seen by a witness in any identification procedure, the identification officer may arrange for images of the suspect suitable for use in a video identification procedure to be obtained before giving the information and notice. If suspect's images are obtained in these circumstances, the suspect may, for the purposes of a video identification procedure, co-operate in providing suitable new images to be used instead, see paragraph 3.17(vi).

(c) Cases when the suspect is known but not available

3.21   When a known suspect is not available or has ceased to be available, see paragraph 3.4, the identification officer may make arrangements for a video identification (see Annex A). If necessary, the identification officer may follow the video identification procedures but using still images. Any suitable moving or still images may be used and these may be obtained covertly if necessary. Alternatively, the identification officer may make arrangements for a group identification. See Note 3D. These provisions may also be applied to juveniles where the consent of their parent or guardian is either refused or reasonable efforts to obtain that consent have failed (see paragraph 2.12).

3.22   Any covert activity should be strictly limited to that necessary to test the ability of the witness to identify the suspect.

3.23   The identification officer may arrange for the suspect to be confronted by the witness if none of the options referred to in paragraphs 3.5 to 3.10 or 3.21 are practicable. A 'confrontation' is when the suspect is directly confronted by the witness. A confrontation does not require the suspect's consent. Confrontations must be carried out in accordance with Annex D.

3.24   Requirements for information to be given to, or sought from, a suspect or for the suspect to be given an opportunity to view images before they are shown to a witness, do not apply if the suspect's lack of co-operation prevents the necessary action.

(d) Documentation

3.25   A record shall be made of the video identification, identification parade, group identification or confrontation on forms provided for the purpose.

3.26   If the identification officer considers it is not practicable to hold a video identification or identification parade requested by the suspect, the reasons shall be recorded and explained to the suspect.

3.27   A record shall be made of a person's failure or refusal to co-operate in a video identification, identification parade or group identification and, if applicable, of the grounds for obtaining images in accordance with paragraph 3.20.

(e) Showing films and photographs of incidents and information released to the media

3.28   Nothing in this Code inhibits showing films or photographs to the public through the national or local media, or to police officers for the purposes of recognition and tracing suspects. However, when such material is shown to potential witnesses, including police officers, see Note 3A, to obtain identification evidence, it shall be shown on an individual basis to avoid any possibility of collusion, and, as far as possible, the showing shall follow the principles for video identification if the suspect is known, see Annex A, or identification by photographs if the suspect is not known, see Annex E.

3.29   When a broadcast or publication is made, see paragraph 3.28, a copy of the relevant material released to the media for the purposes of recognising or tracing the suspect, shall be kept. The suspect or their solicitor shall be allowed to view such material before any procedures under paragraphs 3.5 to 3.10, 3.21 or 3.23 are carried out, provided it is practicable and would not unreasonably delay the investigation. Each witness involved in the procedure shall be asked, after they have taken part, whether they have seen any broadcast or published films or photographs relating to the offence or any description of the suspect and their replies shall be recorded. This paragraph does not affect any separate requirement under the Criminal Procedure and Investigations Act 1996 to retain material in connection with criminal investigations.

(f) Destruction and retention of photographs and images taken or used in identification procedures

3.30   PACE, section 64A, provides powers to take photographs of suspects detained at police stations and allows these photographs to be used or disclosed only for purposes related to the prevention or detection of crime, the investigation of offences or the conduct of prosecutions by, or on behalf of, police or other law enforcement and prosecuting authorities inside and outside the United Kingdom. After being so used or disclosed, they may be retained but can only be used or disclosed for the same purposes.

3.31   Subject to paragraph 3.33, the photographs (and all negatives and copies), of suspects not detained and any moving images, (and copies), of suspects whether or not they have been detained which are taken for the purposes of, or in connection with, the identification procedures in paragraphs 3.5 to 3.10, 3.21 or 3.23 must be destroyed unless the suspect:

(a) is charged with, or informed they may be prosecuted for, a recordable offence;

(b) is prosecuted for a recordable offence;

(c) is cautioned for a recordable offence or given a warning or reprimand in accordance with the Crime and Disorder Act 1998 for a recordable offence; or

(d) gives informed consent, in writing, for the photograph or images to be retained for purposes described in paragraph 3.30.

3.32 When paragraph 3.31 requires the destruction of any photograph or images, the person must be given an opportunity to witness the destruction or to have a certificate confirming the destruction if they request one within five days of being informed that the destruction is required.

3.33 Nothing in paragraph 3.31 affects any separate requirement under the Criminal Procedure and Investigations Act 1996 to retain material in connection with criminal investigations.

Notes for Guidance

3A Except for the provisions of Annex E, paragraph 1, a police officer who is a witness for the purposes of this part of the Code is subject to the same principles and procedures as a civilian witness.

3B When a witness attending an identification procedure has previously been shown photographs, or been shown or provided with computerised or artist's composite likenesses, or similar likenesses or pictures, it is the officer in charge of the investigation's responsibility to make the identification officer aware of this.

3C The purpose of paragraph 3.19 is to avoid or reduce delay in arranging identification procedures by enabling the required information and warnings, see sub-paragraphs 3.17(ix) and 3.17(xii), to be given at the earliest opportunity.

3D Paragraph 3.21 would apply when a known suspect deliberately makes themself 'unavailable' in order to delay or frustrate arrangements for obtaining identification evidence. It also applies when a suspect refuses or fails to take part in a video identification, an identification parade or a group identification, or refuses or fails to take part in the only practicable options from that list. It enables any suitable images of the suspect, moving or still, which are available or can be obtained, to be used in an identification procedure.

3E When it is proposed to show photographs to a witness in accordance with Annex E, it is the responsibility of the officer in charge of the investigation to confirm to the officer responsible for supervising and directing the showing, that the first description of the suspect given by that witness has been recorded. If this description has not been recorded, the procedure under Annex E must be postponed. See Annex E paragraph 2

3F The admissibility and value of identification evidence obtained when carrying out the procedure under paragraph 3.2 may be compromised if:

(a) before a person is identified, the witness' attention is specifically drawn to that person; or

(b) the suspect's identity becomes known before the procedure.

4 Identification by fingerprints

(A) Taking fingerprints in connection with a criminal investigation

(a) General

4.1 References to 'fingerprints' means any record, produced by any method, of the skin pattern and other physical characteristics or features of a person's:

(i) fingers; or

(ii) palms.

(b) Action

4.2 A person's fingerprints may be taken in connection with the investigation of an offence only with their consent or if paragraph 4.3 applies. If the person is at a police station consent must be in writing.

4.3 PACE, section 61, provides powers to take fingerprints without consent from any person over the age of ten years:

(a) under section 61(3)(a), from a detainee at a police station if authorised by an officer of at least inspector rank who has reasonable grounds for suspecting that person is involved in a criminal offence and for believing their fingerprints will tend to confirm or disprove involvement, or assist in establishing their identity (including showing that they are not a particular person), or both. However, authority may not be given solely to establish the person's identity unless they have refused to identify themselves or the authorising officer has reasonable grounds to suspect the person is not who they claim to be.

(b) under section 61(3)(b), from a detainee at a police station who has been charged with a recordable offence, see Note 4A, or informed they will be reported for such an offence if, in the course of the investigation of that offence:
   (i) they have not had their fingerprints taken; or
   (ii) the fingerprints taken do not constitute a complete set of their fingerprints or some, or all, of the fingerprints are not of sufficient quality to allow satisfactory analysis, comparison or matching;

(c) under section 61(4A), from a person who has been bailed to appear at a court or police station if the person:
   (i) has answered to bail for a person whose fingerprints were taken previously and there are reasonable grounds for believing they are not the same person; or
   (ii) who has answered to bail claims to be a different person from a person whose fingerprints were previously taken;
   and in either case, the court or an officer of inspector rank or above, authorises the fingerprints to be taken at the court or police station;

(d) under section 61(6), from a person who has been:
   (i) convicted of a recordable offence;
   (ii) given a caution in respect of a recordable offence which, at the time of the caution, the person admitted; or
   (iii) warned or reprimanded under the Crime and Disorder Act 1998, section 65, for a recordable offence.

4.4   PACE, section 27, provides power to:

(a) require the person as in paragraph 4.3(d) to attend a police station to have their fingerprints taken if the:
   (i) person has not been in police detention for the offence and has not had their fingerprints taken in the course of the investigation of that offence; or
   (ii) fingerprints that were taken from the person in the course of the investigation of that offence, do not constitute a complete set or some, or all, of the fingerprints are not of sufficient quality to allow satisfactory analysis, comparison or matching; and

(b) arrest, without warrant, a person who fails to comply with the requirement.

Note: The requirement must be made within one month of the date the person is convicted, cautioned, warned or reprimanded and the person must be given a period of at least 7 days within which to attend. This 7 day period need not fall during the month allowed for making the requirement.

4.5   A person's fingerprints may be taken, as above, electronically.

4.6   Reasonable force may be used, if necessary, to take a person's fingerprints without their consent under the powers as in paragraphs 4.3 and 4.4.

4.7   Before any fingerprints are taken with, or without, consent as above, the person must be informed:

(a) of the reason their fingerprints are to be taken;
(b) of the grounds on which the relevant authority has been given if the powers mentioned in paragraph 4.3(a) or (c) apply;

(c) that their fingerprints may be retained and may be subject of a speculative search against other fingerprints, see Note 4B, unless destruction of the fingerprints is required in accordance with Annex F, Part (a); and

(d) that if their fingerprints are required to be destroyed, they may witness their destruction as provided for in Annex F, Part (a).

(c) Documentation

4.8   A record must be made as soon as possible, of the reason for taking a person's fingerprints without consent. If force is used, a record shall be made of the circumstances and those present.

4.9   A record shall be made when a person has been informed under the terms of paragraph 4.7(c), of the possibility that their fingerprints may be subject of a speculative search.

(B) Taking fingerprints in connection with immigration enquiries

Action

4.10   A person's fingerprints may be taken for the purposes of Immigration Service enquiries in accordance with powers and procedures other than under PACE and for which the Immigration Service (not the police) are responsible, only with the person's consent in writing or if paragraph 4.11 applies.

4.11   Powers to take fingerprints for these purposes without consent are given to police and immigration officers under the:

(a) Immigration Act 1971, Schedule 2, paragraph 18(2), when it is reasonably necessary for the purposes of identifying a person detained under the Immigration Act 1971, Schedule 2, paragraph 16 (Detention of person liable to examination or removal);

(b) Immigration and Asylum Act 1999, section 141(7)(a), from a person who fails to produce, on arrival, a valid passport with a photograph or some other document satisfactorily establishing their identity and nationality if an immigration officer does not consider the person has a reasonable excuse for the failure;

(c) Immigration and Asylum Act 1999, section 141(7)(b), from a person who has been refused entry to the UK but has been temporarily admitted if an immigration officer reasonably suspects the person might break a condition imposed on them relating to residence or reporting to a police or immigration officer, and their decision is confirmed by a chief immigration officer;

(d) Immigration and Asylum Act 1999, section 141(7)(c), when directions are given to remove a person:
   • as an illegal entrant,
   • liable to removal under the Immigration and Asylum Act 1999, section 10,
   • who is the subject of a deportation order from the UK;

(e) Immigration and Asylum Act 1999, section 141(7)(d), from a person arrested under UK immigration laws under the Immigration Act 1971, Schedule 2, paragraph 17;

(f) Immigration and Asylum Act 1999, section 141(7)(e), from a person who has made a claim:
   • for asylum
   • under Article 3 of the European Convention on Human Rights; or

(g) Immigration and Asylum Act 1999, section 141(7)(f), from a person who is a dependant of someone who falls into (b) to (f) above.

4.12   The Immigration and Asylum Act 1999, section 142(3), gives a police and immigration officer power to arrest, without warrant, a person who fails to comply with a requirement imposed by the Secretary of State to attend a specified place for fingerprinting.

4.13   Before any fingerprints are taken, with or without consent, the person must be informed:
  (a) of the reason their fingerprints are to taken;
  (b) the fingerprints, and all copies of them, will be destroyed in accordance with Annex F, Part B.

4.14   Reasonable force may be used, if necessary, to take a person's fingerprints without their consent under powers as in paragraph 4.11.

4.15   Paragraphs 4.1 and 4.8 apply.

Notes for Guidance

4A   References to 'recordable offences' in this Code relate to those offences for which convictions, cautions, reprimands and warnings may be recorded in national police records. See PACE, section 27(4). The recordable offences current at the time when this Code was prepared, are any offences which carry a sentence of imprisonment on conviction (irrespective of the period, or the age of the offender or actual sentence passed) as well as the non-imprisonable offences under the Street Offences Act 1959, section 1 (loitering or soliciting for purposes of prostitution), the Telecommunications Act 1984, section 43 (improper use of public telecommunications systems), the Road Traffic Act 1988, section 25 (tampering with motor vehicles), the Malicious Communications Act 1988, section 1 (sending letters, etc. with intent to cause distress or anxiety) and others listed in the National Police Records (Recordable Offences) Regulations 2000.

4B   Fingerprints or a DNA sample (and the information derived from it) taken from a person arrested on suspicion of being involved in a recordable offence, or charged with such an offence, or informed they will be reported for such an offence, may be subject of a speculative search. This means the fingerprints or DNA sample may be checked against other fingerprints and DNA records held by, or on behalf of, the police and other law enforcement authorities in, or outside, the UK, or held in connection with, or as a result of, an investigation of an offence inside or outside the UK. Fingerprints and samples taken from a person suspected of committing a recordable offence but not arrested, charged or informed they will be reported for it, may be subject to a speculative search only if the person consents in writing. The following is an example of a basic form of words:

'I consent to my fingerprints and DNA sample and information derived from it being retained and used only for purposes related to the prevention and detection of a crime, the investigation of an offence or the conduct of a prosecution either nationally or internationally.

I understand that my fingerprints or this sample may be checked against other fingerprint and DNA records held by or on behalf of relevant law enforcement authorities, either nationally or internationally.

I understand that once I have given my consent for the sample to be retained and used I cannot withdraw this consent.'

See Annex F regarding the retention and use of fingerprints taken with consent for elimination purposes.

5   Examinations to establish identity and the taking of photographs

(A) Detainees at police stations

(a) Searching or examination of detainees at police stations

5.1   PACE, section 54A (1), allows a detainee at a police station to be searched or examined or both, to establish:
  (a) whether they have any marks, features or injuries that would tend to identify them as a person involved in the commission of an offence and to photograph any identifying marks, see paragraph 5.5; or
  (b) their identity, see Note 5A.

A person detained at a police station to be searched under a stop and search power, see Code A, is not a detainee for the purposes of these powers.

5.2   A search and/or examination to find marks under section 54A (1) (a) may be carried out without the detainee's consent, see paragraph 2.12, only if authorised by an officer of at least inspector rank when consent has been withheld or it is not practicable to obtain consent, see Note 5D.

5.3   A search or examination to establish a suspect's identity under section 54A (1) (b) may be carried out without the detainee's consent, see paragraph 2.12, only if authorised by an officer of at least inspector rank when the detainee has refused to identify themselves or the authorising officer has reasonable grounds for suspecting the person is not who they claim to be.

5.4   Any marks that assist in establishing the detainee's identity, or their identification as a person involved in the commission of an offence, are identifying marks. Such marks may be photographed with the detainee's consent, see paragraph 2.12; or without their consent if it is withheld or it is not practicable to obtain it, see Note 5D.

5.5   A detainee may only be searched, examined and photographed under section 54A, by a police officer of the same sex.

5.6   Any photographs of identifying marks, taken under section 54A, may be used or disclosed only for purposes related to the prevention or detection of crime, the investigation of offences or the conduct of prosecutions by, or on behalf of, police or other law enforcement and prosecuting authorities inside, and outside, the UK. After being so used or disclosed, the photograph may be retained but must not be used or disclosed except for these purposes, see Note 5B.

5.7   The powers, as in paragraph 5.1, do not affect any separate requirement under the Criminal Procedure and Investigations Act 1996 to retain material in connection with criminal investigations.

5.8   Authority for the search and/or examination for the purposes of paragraphs 5.2 and 5.3 may be given orally or in writing. If given orally, the authorising officer must confirm it in writing as soon as practicable. A separate authority is required for each purpose which applies.

5.9   If it is established a person is unwilling to co-operate sufficiently to enable a search and/or examination to take place or a suitable photograph to be taken, an officer may use reasonable force to:

(a)   search and/or examine a detainee without their consent; and

(b)   photograph any identifying marks without their consent.

5.10   The thoroughness and extent of any search or examination carried out in accordance with the powers in section 54A must be no more than the officer considers necessary to achieve the required purpose. Any search or examination which involves the removal of more than the person's outer clothing shall be conducted in accordance with Code C, Annex A, paragraph 11.

5.11   An intimate search may not be carried out under the powers in section 54A.

(b) Photographing detainees at police stations

5.12   Under PACE, section 64A, an officer may photograph a detainee at a police station:

(a)   with their consent; or

(b)   without their consent if it is:

(i)   withheld; or

(ii)   not practicable to obtain their consent.

See Note 5E

and paragraph 5.6 applies to the retention and use of photographs taken under this section as it applies to the retention and use of photographs taken under section 54A, see Note 5B.

5.13   The officer proposing to take a detainee's photograph may, for this purpose, require the person to remove any item or substance worn on, or over, all, or any part of, their head or face. If they do not comply with such a requirement, the officer may remove the item or substance.

5.14   If it is established the detainee is unwilling to co-operate sufficiently to enable a suitable photograph to be taken and it is not reasonably practicable to take the photograph covertly, an officer may use reasonable force:

(a) to take their photograph without their consent; and

(b) for the purpose of taking the photograph, remove any item or substance worn on, or over, all, or any part of, the person's head or face which they have failed to remove when asked.

5.15   For the purposes of this Code, a photograph may be obtained without the person's consent by making a copy of an image of them taken at any time on a camera system installed anywhere in the police station.

(c) Information to be given

5.16   When a person is searched, examined or photographed under the provisions as in paragraphs 5.1 and 5.12, or their photograph obtained as in paragraph 5.15, they must be informed of the:

(a) purpose of the search, examination or photograph;

(b) grounds on which the relevant authority, if applicable, has been given; and

(c) purposes for which the photograph may be used, disclosed or retained.

This information must be given before the search or examination commences or the photograph is taken, except if the photograph is:

(i)   to be taken covertly;

(ii) obtained as in paragraph 5.15, in which case the person must be informed as soon as practicable after the photograph is taken or obtained.

(d) Documentation

5.17   A record must be made when a detainee is searched, examined, or a photograph of the person, or any identifying marks found on them, are taken. The record must include the:

(a) identity, subject to paragraph 2.18, of the officer carrying out the search, examination or taking the photograph;

(b) purpose of the search, examination or photograph and the outcome;

(c) detainee's consent to the search, examination or photograph, or the reason the person was searched, examined or photographed without consent;

(d) giving of any authority as in paragraphs 5.2 and 5.3, the grounds for giving it and the authorising officer.

5.18   If force is used when searching, examining or taking a photograph in accordance with this section, a record shall be made of the circumstances and those present.

(B) Persons at police stations not detained

5.19   When there are reasonable grounds for suspecting the involvement of a person in a criminal offence, but that person is at a police station voluntarily and not detained, the provisions of paragraphs 5.1 to 5.18 should apply, subject to the modifications in the following paragraphs.

5.20   References to the 'person being detained' and to the powers mentioned in paragraph 5.1 which apply only to detainees at police stations shall be omitted.

5.21   Force may not be used to:

(a) search and/or examine the person to:

(i)   discover whether they have any marks that would tend to identify them as a person involved in the commission of an offence; or

(ii) establish their identity, see Note 5A;

(b) take photographs of any identifying marks, see paragraph 5.4; or

(c) take a photograph of the person.

5.22   Subject to paragraph 5.24, the photographs or images, of persons not detained, or of their identifying marks, must be destroyed (together with any negatives and copies) unless the person:

(a) is charged with, or informed they may be prosecuted for, a recordable offence;

(b) is prosecuted for a recordable offence;

(c) is cautioned for a recordable offence or given a warning or reprimand in accordance with the Crime and Disorder Act 1998 for a recordable offence; or

(d) gives informed consent, in writing, for the photograph or image to be retained as in paragraph 5.6.

5.23   When paragraph 5.22 requires the destruction of any photograph or image, the person must be given an opportunity to witness the destruction or to have a certificate confirming the destruction provided they so request the certificate within five days of being informed the destruction is required.

5.24   Nothing in paragraph 5.22 affects any separate requirement under the Criminal Procedure and Investigations Act 1996 to retain material in connection with criminal investigations.

Notes for Guidance

5A   The conditions under which fingerprints may be taken to assist in establishing a person's identity, are described in section 4.

5B   Examples of purposes related to the prevention or detection of crime, the investigation of offences or the conduct of prosecutions include:

(a) checking the photograph against other photographs held in records or in connection with, or as a result of, an investigation of an offence to establish whether the person is liable to arrest for other offences;

(b) when the person is arrested at the same time as other people, or at a time when it is likely that other people will be arrested, using the photograph to help establish who was arrested, at what time and where;

(c) when the real identity of the person is not known and cannot be readily ascertained or there are reasonable grounds for doubting a name and other personal details given by the person, are their real name and personal details. In these circumstances, using or disclosing the photograph to help to establish or verify their real identity or determine whether they are liable to arrest for some other offence, e.g. by checking it against other photographs held in records or in connection with, or as a result of, an investigation of an offence;

(d) when it appears any identification procedure in section 3 may need to be arranged for which the person's photograph would assist;

(e) when the person's release without charge may be required, and if the release is:

(i) on bail to appear at a police station, using the photograph to help verify the person's identity when they answer their bail and if the person does not answer their bail, to assist in arresting them; or

(ii) without bail, using the photograph to help verify their identity or assist in locating them for the purposes of serving them with a summons to appear at court in criminal proceedings;

(f) when the person has answered to bail at a police station and there are reasonable grounds for doubting they are the person who was previously granted bail, using the photograph to help establish or verify their identity;

(g) when the person arrested on a warrant claims to be a different person from the person named on the warrant and a photograph would help to confirm or disprove their claim;

(h) when the person has been charged with, reported for, or convicted of, a recordable offence and their photograph is not already on record as a result of (a) to (f) or their photograph is on record but their appearance has changed since it was taken and the person has not yet been released or brought before a court.

5C   There is no power to arrest a person convicted of a recordable offence solely to take their photograph. The power to take photographs in this section applies only where the person is in custody as a result of the exercise of another power, e.g. arrest for fingerprinting under PACE, section 27.

5D   Examples of when it would not be practicable to obtain a detainee's consent, see paragraph 2.12, to a search, examination or the taking of a photograph of an identifying mark include:

(a) when the person is drunk or otherwise unfit to give consent;
(b) when there are reasonable grounds to suspect that if the person became aware a search or examination was to take place or an identifying mark was to be photographed, they would take steps to prevent this happening, e.g. by violently resisting, covering or concealing the mark etc and it would not otherwise be possible to carry out the search or examination or to photograph any identifying mark;
(c) in the case of a juvenile, if the parent or guardian cannot be contacted in sufficient time to allow the search or examination to be carried out or the photograph to be taken.

5E   Examples of when it would not be practicable to obtain the person's consent, see paragraph 2.12, to a photograph being taken include:

(a) when the person is drunk or otherwise unfit to give consent;
(b) when there are reasonable grounds to suspect that if the person became aware a photograph, suitable to be used or disclosed for the use and disclosure described in paragraph 5.6, was to be taken, they would take steps to prevent it being taken, e.g. by violently resisting, covering or distorting their face etc, and it would not otherwise be possible to take a suitable photograph;
(c) when, in order to obtain a suitable photograph, it is necessary to take it covertly; and
(d) in the case of a juvenile, if the parent or guardian cannot be contacted in sufficient time to allow the photograph to be taken.

6   Identification by body samples and impressions

(A) General

6.1   References to:

(a) an 'intimate sample' mean a dental impression or sample of blood, semen or any other tissue fluid, urine, or pubic hair, or a swab taken from a person's body orifice other than the mouth;
(b) a 'non-intimate sample' means:
  (i) a sample of hair, other than pubic hair, which includes hair plucked with the root, see Note 6A;
  (ii) a sample taken from a nail or from under a nail;
  (iii) a swab taken from any part of a person's body including the mouth but not any other body orifice;
  (iv) saliva;
  (v) a skin impression which means any record, other than a fingerprint, which is a record, in any form and produced by any method, of the skin pattern and other physical characteristics or features of the whole, or any part of, a person's foot or of any other part of their body.

(B) Action

(a) Intimate samples

    6.2   PACE, section 62, provides that intimate samples may be taken under:

      (a) section 62(1), from a person in police detention only:

        (i) if a police officer of inspector rank or above has reasonable grounds to believe such an impression or sample will tend to confirm or disprove the suspect's involvement in a recordable offence, see Note 4A, and gives authorisation for a sample to be taken; and

        (ii) with the suspect's written consent;

      (b) section 62(1A), from a person not in police detention but from whom two or more non-intimate samples have been taken in the course of an investigation of an offence and the samples, though suitable, have proved insufficient if:

        (i) a police officer of inspector rank or above authorises it to be taken; and

        (ii) the person concerned gives their written consent. See Notes 6B and 6C.

    6.3   Before a suspect is asked to provide an intimate sample, they must be warned that if they refuse without good cause, their refusal may harm their case if it comes to trial, see Note 6D. If the suspect is in police detention and not legally represented, they must also be reminded of their entitlement to have free legal advice, see Code C, paragraph 6.5, and the reminder noted in the custody record. If paragraph 6.2(b) applies and the person is attending a station voluntarily, their entitlement to free legal advice as in Code C, paragraph 3.21 shall be explained to them.

    6.4   Dental impressions may only be taken by a registered dentist. Other intimate samples, except for samples of urine, may only be taken by a registered medical practitioner or registered health care professional.

(b) Non-intimate samples

    6.5   A non-intimate sample may be taken from a detainee only with their written consent or if paragraph 6.6 applies.

    6.6   A non-intimate sample may be taken from a person without consent in accordance with PACE. The principal circumstances provided for are as follows:

      (a) under section 63(3), from a person in police detention, or police custody on the authority of a court, if a police officer of inspector rank or above has reasonable grounds to believe the sample will tend to confirm or disprove the suspect's involvement in a recordable offence, see Note 4A, and gives authorisation for a sample to be taken. However, the officer may not give authorisation to take a non-intimate sample consisting of a skin impression if a skin impression of the same part of the body has already been taken from that person in the course of the investigation of the offence and the impression previously taken is not one that has proved insufficient;

      (b) under section 63(3A), from a person charged with a recordable offence or informed they will be reported for such an offence: and

        (i) that person has not had a non-intimate sample taken from them in the course of the investigation; or

        (ii) if they have had a sample taken, it proved unsuitable or insufficient for the same form of analysis, see Note 6B; or

      (c) under section 63(3B), from a person convicted of a recordable offence after the date on which that provision came into effect. PACE, section 63A, describes the circumstances in which a police officer may require a person convicted of a recordable offence to attend a police station for a non-intimate sample to be taken.

    6.7   Reasonable force may be used, if necessary, to take a non-intimate sample from a person without their consent under the powers mentioned in paragraph 6.6.

6.8   Before any intimate sample is taken with consent or non-intimate sample is taken with, or without, consent, the person must be informed:

    (a) of the reason for taking the sample;

    (b) of the grounds on which the relevant authority has been given, including, if appropriate, the nature of the suspected offence;

    (c) that the sample or information derived from the sample may be retained and subject of a speculative search, see Note 6E, unless their destruction is required as in Annex F, Part A.

6.9   When clothing needs to be removed in circumstances likely to cause embarrassment to the person, no person of the opposite sex who is not a registered medical practitioner or registered health care professional shall be present, (unless in the case of a juvenile, mentally disordered or mentally vulnerable person, that person specifically requests the presence of an appropriate adult of the opposite sex who is readily available) nor shall anyone whose presence is unnecessary. However, in the case of a juvenile, this is subject to the overriding proviso that such a removal of clothing may take place in the absence of the appropriate adult only if the juvenile signifies, in their presence, that they prefer the adult's absence and they agree.

(c) Documentation

6.10   A record of the reasons for taking a sample or impression and, if applicable, of its destruction must be made as soon as practicable. If force is used, a record shall be made of the circumstances and those present. If written consent is given to the taking of a sample or impression, the fact must be recorded in writing.

6.11   A record must be made of a warning given as required by paragraph 6.3.

6.12   A record shall be made of the fact that a person has been informed as in paragraph 6.8(c) that samples may be subject of a speculative search.

Notes for Guidance

6A   When hair samples are taken for the purpose of DNA analysis (rather than for other purposes such as making a visual match), the suspect should be permitted a reasonable choice as to what part of the body the hairs are taken from. When hairs are plucked, they should be plucked individually, unless the suspect prefers otherwise and no more should be plucked than the person taking them reasonably considers necessary for a sufficient sample.

6B   (a) An insufficient sample is one which is not sufficient either in quantity or quality to provide information for a particular form of analysis, such as DNA analysis. A sample may also be insufficient if enough information cannot be obtained from it by analysis because of loss, destruction, damage or contamination of the sample or as a result of an earlier, unsuccessful attempt at analysis.

    (b) An unsuitable sample is one which, by its nature, is not suitable for a particular form of analysis.

6C   Nothing in paragraph 6.2 prevents intimate samples being taken for elimination purposes with the consent of the person concerned but the provisions of paragraph 2.12 relating to the role of the appropriate adult, should be applied. Paragraph 6.2(b) does not, however, apply where the non-intimate samples were previously taken under the Terrorism Act 2000, Schedule 8, paragraph 10.

6D   In warning a person who is asked to provide an intimate sample as in paragraph 6.3, the following form of words may be used:

'You do not have to provide this sample/allow this swab or impression to be taken, but I must warn you that if you refuse without good cause, your refusal may harm your case if it comes to trial.'

6E   Fingerprints or a DNA sample and the information derived from it taken from a person arrested on suspicion of being involved in a recordable offence, or charged with such an offence, or informed they will be reported for such an offence, may be subject of a speculative search. This means they may be checked against other fingerprints and DNA records held by, or on behalf of, the police and other law enforcement authorities in or outside the UK or held in connection with, or as a result of, an investigation of an offence inside or outside the UK. Fingerprints and samples taken from any other person, e.g. a person suspected of committing a recordable offence but who has not been arrested, charged or informed they will be reported for it, may be subject to a speculative search only if the person consents in writing to their fingerprints being subject of such a search. The following is an example of a basic form of words:

> *'I consent to my fingerprints/DNA sample and information derived from it being retained and used only for purposes related to the prevention and detection of a crime, the investigation of an offence or the conduct of a prosecution either nationally or internationally.*

> *I understand that this sample may be checked against other fingerprint/DNA records held by or on behalf of relevant law enforcement authorities, either nationally or internationally.*

> *I understand that once I have given my consent for the sample to be retained and used I cannot withdraw this consent.'*

See Annex F regarding the retention and use of fingerprints and samples taken with consent for elimination purposes.

ANNEX A   VIDEO IDENTIFICATION

(a) General

1. The arrangements for obtaining and ensuring the availability of a suitable set of images to be used in a video identification must be the responsibility of an identification officer, who has no direct involvement with the case.

2. The set of images must include the suspect and at least eight other people who, so far as possible, resemble the suspect in age, height, general appearance and position in life. Only one suspect shall appear in any set unless there are two suspects of roughly similar appearance, in which case they may be shown together with at least twelve other people.

3. The images used to conduct a video identification shall, as far as possible, show the suspect and other people in the same positions or carrying out the same sequence of movements. They shall also show the suspect and other people under identical conditions unless the identification officer reasonably believes:

> (a) because of the suspect's failure or refusal to co-operate or other reasons, it is not practicable for the conditions to be identical; and
>
> (b) any difference in the conditions would not direct a witness' attention to any individual image.

4. The reasons identical conditions are not practicable shall be recorded on forms provided for the purpose.

5. Provision must be made for each person shown to be identified by number.

6. If police officers are shown, any numerals or other identifying badges must be concealed. If a prison inmate is shown, either as a suspect or not, then either all, or none of, the people shown should be in prison clothing.

7. The suspect or their solicitor, friend, or appropriate adult must be given a reasonable opportunity to see the complete set of images before it is shown to any witness. If the suspect has a reasonable objection to the set of images or any of the participants, the suspect shall be asked to state the reasons for the objection. Steps shall, if practicable, be taken to remove the grounds for objection. If this is not practicable, the suspect and/or their representative shall be told why their objections cannot be met and the objection, the reason given for it and why it cannot be met shall be recorded on forms provided for the purpose.

8. Before the images are shown in accordance with paragraph 7, the suspect or their

solicitor shall be provided with details of the first description of the suspect by any witnesses who are to attend the video identification. When a broadcast or publication is made, as in *paragraph 3.28*, the suspect or their solicitor must also be allowed to view any material released to the media by the police for the purpose of recognising or tracing the suspect, provided it is practicable and would not unreasonably delay the investigation.

9.   The suspect's solicitor, if practicable, shall be given reasonable notification of the time and place the video identification is to be conducted so a representative may attend on behalf of the suspect. If a solicitor has not been instructed, this information shall be given to the suspect. The suspect may not be present when the images are shown to the witness(es). In the absence of the suspect's representative, the viewing itself shall be recorded on video. No unauthorised people may be present.

(b) Conducting the video identification

10.   The identification officer is responsible for making the appropriate arrangements to make sure, before they see the set of images, witnesses are not able to communicate with each other about the case or overhear a witness who has already seen the material. There must be no discussion with the witness about the composition of the set of images and they must not be told whether a previous witness has made any identification.

11.   Only one witness may see the set of images at a time. Immediately before the images are shown, the witness shall be told that the person they saw on a specified earlier occasion may, or may not, appear in the images they are shown and that if they cannot make a positive identification, they should say so. The witness shall be advised that at any point, they may ask to see a particular part of the set of images or to have a particular image frozen for them to study. Furthermore, it should be pointed out to the witness that there is no limit on how many times they can view the whole set of images or any part of them. However, they should be asked not to make any decision as to whether the person they saw is on the set of images until they have seen the whole set at least twice.

12.   Once the witness has seen the whole set of images at least twice and has indicated that they do not want to view the images, or any part of them, again, the witness shall be asked to say whether the individual they saw in person on a specified earlier occasion has been shown and, if so, to identify them by number of the image. The witness will then be shown that image to confirm the identification, see paragraph 17.

13.   Care must be taken not to direct the witness' attention to any one individual image or give any indication of the suspect's identity. Where a witness has previously made an identification by photographs, or a computerised or artist's composite or similar likeness, the witness must not be reminded of such a photograph or composite likeness once a suspect is available for identification by other means in accordance with this Code. Nor must the witness be reminded of any description of the suspect.

14.   After the procedure, each witness shall be asked whether they have seen any broadcast or published films or photographs, or any descriptions of suspects relating to the offence and their reply shall be recorded.

(c) Image security and destruction

15.   Arrangements shall be made for all relevant material containing sets of images used for specific identification procedures to be kept securely and their movements accounted for. In particular, no-one involved in the investigation shall be permitted to view the material prior to it being shown to any witness.

16.   As appropriate, paragraph 33 or 31 applies to the destruction or retention of relevant sets of images.

(d) Documentation

17.   A record must be made of all those participating in, or seeing, the set of images whose names are known to the police.

18.   A record of the conduct of the video identification must be made on forms provided for the purpose. This shall include anything said by the witness about any identifications or the conduct of the procedure and any reasons it was not practicable to comply with any of the provisions of this Code governing the conduct of video identifications.

ANNEX B   IDENTIFICATION PARADES

(a) General

1.   A suspect must be given a reasonable opportunity to have a solicitor or friend present, and the suspect shall be asked to indicate on a second copy of the notice whether or not they wish to do so.

2.   An identification parade may take place either in a normal room or one equipped with a screen permitting witnesses to see members of the identification parade without being seen. The procedures for the composition and conduct of the identification parade are the same in both cases, subject to paragraph 8 (except that an identification parade involving a screen may take place only when the suspect's solicitor, friend or appropriate adult is present or the identification parade is recorded on video).

3.   Before the identification parade takes place, the suspect or their solicitor shall be provided with details of the first description of the suspect by any witnesses who are attending the identification parade. When a broadcast or publication is made as in paragraph 3.28, the suspect or their solicitor should also be allowed to view any material released to the media by the police for the purpose of recognising or tracing the suspect, provided it is practicable to do so and would not unreasonably delay the investigation.

(b) Identification parades involving prison inmates

4.   If a prison inmate is required for identification, and there are no security problems about the person leaving the establishment, they may be asked to participate in an identification parade or video identification.

5.   An identification parade may be held in a Prison Department establishment but shall be conducted, as far as practicable under normal identification parade rules. Members of the public shall make up the identification parade unless there are serious security, or control, objections to their admission to the establishment. In such cases, or if a group or video identification is arranged within the establishment, other inmates may participate. If an inmate is the suspect, they are not required to wear prison clothing for the identification parade unless the other people taking part are other inmates in similar clothing, or are members of the public who are prepared to wear prison clothing for the occasion.

(c) Conduct of the identification parade

6.   Immediately before the identification parade, the suspect must be reminded of the procedures governing its conduct and cautioned in the terms of Code C, paragraphs 10.5 or 10.6, as appropriate.

7.   All unauthorised people must be excluded from the place where the identification parade is held.

8.   Once the identification parade has been formed, everything afterwards, in respect of it, shall take place in the presence and hearing of the suspect and any interpreter, solicitor, friend or appropriate adult who is present (unless the identification parade involves a screen, in which case everything said to, or by, any witness at the place where the identification parade is held, must be said in the hearing and presence of the suspect's solicitor, friend or appropriate adult or be recorded on video).

9. The identification parade shall consist of at least eight people (in addition to the suspect) who, so far as possible, resemble the suspect in age, height, general appearance and position in life. Only one suspect shall be included in an identification parade unless there are

two suspects of roughly similar appearance, in which case they may be paraded together with at least twelve other people. In no circumstances shall more than two suspects be included in one identification parade and where there are separate identification parades, they shall be made up of different people.

10.   If the suspect has an unusual physical feature, e.g., a facial scar, tattoo or distinctive hairstyle or hair colour which cannot be replicated on other members of the identification parade, steps may be taken to conceal the location of that feature on the suspect and the other members of the identification parade if the suspect and their solicitor, or appropriate adult, agree. For example, by use of a plaster or a hat, so that all members of the identification parade resemble each other in general appearance.

11.   When all members of a similar group are possible suspects, separate identification parades shall be held for each unless there are two suspects of similar appearance when they may appear on the same identification parade with at least twelve other members of the group who are not suspects. When police officers in uniform form an identification parade any numerals or other identifying badges shall be concealed.

12.   When the suspect is brought to the place where the identification parade is to be held, they shall be asked if they have any objection to the arrangements for the identification parade or to any of the other participants in it and to state the reasons for the objection. The suspect may obtain advice from their solicitor or friend, if present, before the identification parade proceeds. If the suspect has a reasonable objection to the arrangements or any of the participants, steps shall, if practicable, be taken to remove the grounds for objection. When it is not practicable to do so, the suspect shall be told why their objections cannot be met and the objection, the reason given for it and why it cannot be met, shall be recorded on forms provided for the purpose.

13.   The suspect may select their own position in the line, but may not otherwise interfere with the order of the people forming the line. When there is more than one witness, the suspect must be told, after each witness has left the room, that they can, if they wish, change position in the line. Each position in the line must be clearly numbered, whether by means of a number laid on the floor in front of each identification parade member or by other means.

14.   Appropriate arrangements must be made to make sure, before witnesses attend the identification parade, they are not able to:

    (i)   communicate with each other about the case or overhear a witness who has already seen the identification parade;

    (ii) see any member of the identification parade;

    (iii) see, or be reminded of, any photograph or description of the suspect or be given any other indication as to the suspect's identity; or

    (iv) see the suspect before or after the identification parade.

15.   The person conducting a witness to an identification parade must not discuss with them the composition of the identification parade and, in particular, must not disclose whether a previous witness has made any identification.

16.   Witnesses shall be brought in one at a time. Immediately before the witness inspects the identification parade, they shall be told the person they saw on a specified earlier occasion may, or may not, be present and if they cannot make a positive identification, they should say so. The witness must also be told they should not make any decision about whether the person they saw is on the identification parade until they have looked at each member at least twice.

17.   When the officer or civilian support staff (see paragraph 3.11) conducting the identification procedure is satisfied the witness has properly looked at each member of the identification parade, they shall ask the witness whether the person they saw on a specified earlier occasion is on the identification parade and, if so, to indicate the number of the person concerned, see paragraph 28.

18.   If the witness wishes to hear any identification parade member speak, adopt any specified posture or move, they shall first be asked whether they can identify any person(s) on the identification parade on the basis of appearance only. When the request is to hear members of the identification parade speak, the witness shall be reminded that the participants in the identification parade have been chosen on the basis of physical appearance only. Members of the identification parade may then be asked to comply with the witness' request to hear them speak, see them move or adopt any specified posture.

19.   If the witness requests that the person they have indicated remove anything used for the purposes of paragraph 10 to conceal the location of an unusual physical feature, that person may be asked to remove it.

20.   If the witness makes an identification after the identification parade has ended, the suspect and, if present, their solicitor, interpreter or friend shall be informed. When this occurs, consideration should be given to allowing the witness a second opportunity to identify the suspect.

21.   After the procedure, each witness shall be asked whether they have seen any broadcast or published films or photographs or any descriptions of suspects relating to the offence and their reply shall be recorded.

22.   When the last witness has left, the suspect shall be asked whether they wish to make any comments on the conduct of the identification parade.

(d) Documentation

23.   A video recording must normally be taken of the identification parade. If that is impracticable, a colour photograph must be taken. A copy of the video recording or photograph shall be supplied, on request, to the suspect or their solicitor within a reasonable time.

24.   As appropriate, paragraph 3.30 or 3.31, should apply to any photograph or video taken as in paragraph 23.

25.   If any person is asked to leave an identification parade because they are interfering with its conduct, the circumstances shall be recorded.

26.   A record must be made of all those present at an identification parade whose names are known to the police.

27.   If prison inmates make up an identification parade, the circumstances must be recorded.

28.   A record of the conduct of any identification parade must be made on forms provided for the purpose. This shall include anything said by the witness or the suspect about any identifications or the conduct of the procedure, and any reasons it was not practicable to comply with any of this Code's provisions.

ANNEX C   GROUP IDENTIFICATION

(a) General

1.   The purpose of this Annex is to make sure, as far as possible, group identifications follow the principles and procedures for identification parades so the conditions are fair to the suspect in the way they test the witness' ability to make an identification.

2.   Group identifications may take place either with the suspect's consent and cooperation or covertly without their consent.

3.   The location of the group identification is a matter for the identification officer, although the officer may take into account any representations made by the suspect, appropriate adult, their solicitor or friend.

4.   The place where the group identification is held should be one where other people are either passing by or waiting around informally, in groups such that the suspect is able to join them and be capable of being seen by the witness at the same time as others in the group.

For example people leaving an escalator, pedestrians walking through a shopping centre, passengers on railway and bus stations, waiting in queues or groups or where people are standing or sitting in groups in other public places.

5. If the group identification is to be held covertly, the choice of locations will be limited by the places where the suspect can be found and the number of other people present at that time. In these cases, suitable locations might be along regular routes travelled by the suspect, including buses or trains or public places frequented by the suspect.

6. Although the number, age, sex, race and general description and style of clothing of other people present at the location cannot be controlled by the identification officer, in selecting the location the officer must consider the general appearance and numbers of people likely to be present. In particular, the officer must reasonably expect that over the period the witness observes the group, they will be able to see, from time to time, a number of others whose appearance is broadly similar to that of the suspect.

7. A group identification need not be held if the identification officer believes, because of the unusual appearance of the suspect, none of the locations it would be practicable to use satisfy the requirements of paragraph 6 necessary to make the identification fair.

8. Immediately after a group identification procedure has taken place (with or without the suspect's consent), a colour photograph or video should be taken of the general scene, if practicable, to give a general impression of the scene and the number of people present. Alternatively, if it is practicable, the group identification may be video recorded.

9. If it is not practicable to take the photograph or video in accordance with paragraph 8, a photograph or film of the scene should be taken later at a time determined by the identification officer if the officer considers it practicable to do so.

10. An identification carried out in accordance with this Code remains a group identification even though, at the time of being seen by the witness, the suspect was on their own rather than in a group.

11. Before the group identification takes place, the suspect or their solicitor shall be provided with details of the first description of the suspect by any witnesses who are to attend the identification. When a broadcast or publication is made, as in paragraph 3.28, the suspect or their solicitor should also be allowed to view any material released by the police to the media for the purposes of recognising or tracing the suspect, provided that it is practicable and would not unreasonably delay the investigation.

12. After the procedure, each witness shall be asked whether they have seen any broadcast or published films or photographs or any descriptions of suspects relating to the offence and their reply recorded.

(b) Identification with the consent of the suspect

13. A suspect must be given a reasonable opportunity to have a solicitor or friend present. They shall be asked to indicate on a second copy of the notice whether or not they wish to do so.

14. The witness, the person carrying out the procedure and the suspect's solicitor, appropriate adult, friend or any interpreter for the witness, may be concealed from the sight of the individuals in the group they are observing, if the person carrying out the procedure considers this assists the conduct of the identification.

15. The person conducting a witness to a group identification must not discuss with them the forthcoming group identification and, in particular, must not disclose whether a previous witness has made any identification.

16. Anything said to, or by, the witness during the procedure about the identification should be said in the presence and hearing of those present at the procedure.

17. Appropriate arrangements must be made to make sure, before witnesses attend the group identification, they are not able to:

(i)   communicate with each other about the case or overhear a witness who has already been given an opportunity to see the suspect in the group;

(ii) see the suspect; or

(iii) see, or be reminded of, any photographs or description of the suspect or be given any other indication of the suspect's identity.

18.   Witnesses shall be brought one at a time to the place where they are to observe the group. Immediately before the witness is asked to look at the group, the person conducting the procedure shall tell them that the person they saw may, or may not, be in the group and that if they cannot make a positive identification, they should say so. The witness shall be asked to observe the group in which the suspect is to appear. The way in which the witness should do this will depend on whether the group is moving or stationary.

Moving group

19.   When the group in which the suspect is to appear is moving, e.g. leaving an escalator, the provisions of paragraphs 20 to 24 should be followed.

20.   If two or more suspects consent to a group identification, each should be the subject of separate identification procedures. These may be conducted consecutively on the same occasion.

21.   The person conducting the procedure shall tell the witness to observe the group and ask them to point out any person they think they saw on the specified earlier occasion.

22.   Once the witness has been informed as in paragraph 21 the suspect should be allowed to take whatever position in the group they wish.

23.   When the witness points out a person as in paragraph 21 they shall, if practicable, be asked to take a closer look at the person to confirm the identification. If this is not practicable, or they cannot confirm the identification, they shall be asked how sure they are that the person they have indicated is the relevant person.

24.   The witness should continue to observe the group for the period which the person conducting the procedure reasonably believes is necessary in the circumstances for them to be able to make comparisons between the suspect and other individuals of broadly similar appearance to the suspect as in paragraph 6.

Stationary groups

25.   When the group in which the suspect is to appear is stationary, e.g. people waiting in a queue, the provisions of paragraphs 26 to 29 should be followed.

26.   If two or more suspects consent to a group identification, each should be subject to separate identification procedures unless they are of broadly similar appearance when they may appear in the same group. When separate group identifications are held, the groups must be made up of different people.

27.   The suspect may take whatever position in the group they wish. If there is more than one witness, the suspect must be told, out of the sight and hearing of any witness, that they can, if they wish, change their position in the group.

28.   The witness shall be asked to pass along, or amongst, the group and to look at each person in the group at least twice, taking as much care and time as possible according to the circumstances, before making an identification. Once the witness has done this, they shall be asked whether the person they saw on the specified earlier occasion is in the group and to indicate any such person by whatever means the person conducting the procedure considers appropriate in the circumstances. If this is not practicable, the witness shall be asked to point out any person they think they saw on the earlier occasion.

29.   When the witness makes an indication as in paragraph 28, arrangements shall be made, if practicable, for the witness to take a closer look at the person to confirm the identification. If this is not practicable, or the witness is unable to confirm the identification, they shall be asked how sure they are that the person they have indicated is the relevant person.

All cases

30. If the suspect unreasonably delays joining the group, or having joined the group, deliberately conceals themselves from the sight of the witness, this may be treated as a refusal to co-operate in a group identification.

31. If the witness identifies a person other than the suspect, that person should be informed what has happened and asked if they are prepared to give their name and address. There is no obligation upon any member of the public to give these details. There shall be no duty to record any details of any other member of the public present in the group or at the place where the procedure is conducted.

32. When the group identification has been completed, the suspect shall be asked whether they wish to make any comments on the conduct of the procedure.

33. If the suspect has not been previously informed, they shall be told of any identifications made by the witnesses.

(c) Identification without the suspect's consent

34. Group identifications held covertly without the suspect's consent should, as far as practicable, follow the rules for conduct of group identification by consent.

35. A suspect has no right to have a solicitor, appropriate adult or friend present as the identification will take place without the knowledge of the suspect.

36. Any number of suspects may be identified at the same time.

(d) Identifications in police stations

37. Group identifications should take place in police stations only for reasons of safety, security or because it is not practicable to hold them elsewhere.

38. The group identification may take place either in a room equipped with a screen permitting witnesses to see members of the group without being seen, or anywhere else in the police station that the identification officer considers appropriate.

39. Any of the additional safeguards applicable to identification parades should be followed if the identification officer considers it is practicable to do so in the circumstances.

(e) Identifications involving prison inmates

40. A group identification involving a prison inmate may only be arranged in the prison or at a police station.

41. When a group identification takes place involving a prison inmate, whether in a prison or in a police station, the arrangements should follow those in paragraphs 37 to 39. If a group identification takes place within a prison, other inmates may participate. If an inmate is the suspect, they do not have to wear prison clothing for the group identification unless the other participants are wearing the same clothing.

(f) Documentation

42. When a photograph or video is taken as in paragraph 8 or 9, a copy of the photograph or video shall be supplied on request to the suspect or their solicitor within a reasonable time.

43. Paragraph 3.30 or 3.31, as appropriate, shall apply when the photograph or film taken in accordance with paragraph 8 or 9 includes the suspect.

44. A record of the conduct of any group identification must be made on forms provided for the purpose. This shall include anything said by the witness or suspect about any identifications or the conduct of the procedure and any reasons why it was not practicable to comply with any of the provisions of this Code governing the conduct of group identifications.

ANNEX D   CONFRONTATION BY A WITNESS

1.   Before the confrontation takes place, the witness must be told that the person they saw may, or may not, be the person they are to confront and that if they are not that person, then the witness should say so.

2.   Before the confrontation takes place the suspect or their solicitor shall be provided with details of the first description of the suspect given by any witness who is to attend. When a broadcast or publication is made, as in paragraph 3.28, the suspect or their solicitor should also be allowed to view any material released to the media for the purposes of recognising or tracing the suspect, provided it is practicable to do so and would not unreasonably delay the investigation.

3.   Force may not be used to make the suspect's face visible to the witness.

4.   Confrontation must take place in the presence of the suspect's solicitor, interpreter or friend unless this would cause unreasonable delay.

5.   The suspect shall be confronted independently by each witness, who shall be asked 'Is this the person?'. If the witness identifies the person but is unable to confirm the identification, they shall be asked how sure they are that the person is the one they saw on the earlier occasion.

6.   The confrontation should normally take place in the police station, either in a normal room or one equipped with a screen permitting a witness to see the suspect without being seen. In both cases, the procedures are the same except that a room equipped with a screen may be used only when the suspect's solicitor, friend or appropriate adult is present or the confrontation is recorded on video.

7.   After the procedure, each witness shall be asked whether they have seen any broadcast or published films or photographs or any descriptions of suspects relating to the offence and their reply shall be recorded.

ANNEX E   SHOWING PHOTOGRAPHS

(a) Action

1.   An officer of sergeant rank or above shall be responsible for supervising and directing the showing of photographs. The actual showing may be done by another officer or civilian support staff, see paragraph 3.11.

2.   The supervising officer must confirm the first description of the suspect given by the witness has been recorded before they are shown the photographs. If the supervising officer is unable to confirm the description has been recorded they shall postpone showing the photographs.

3.   Only one witness shall be shown photographs at any one time. Each witness shall be given as much privacy as practicable and shall not be allowed to communicate with any other witness in the case.

4.   The witness shall be shown not less than twelve photographs at a time, which shall, as far as possible, all be of a similar type.

5.   When the witness is shown the photographs, they shall be told the photograph of the person they saw may, or may not, be amongst them and if they cannot make a positive identification, they should say so. The witness shall also be told they should not make a decision until they have viewed at least twelve photographs. The witness shall not be prompted or guided in any way but shall be left to make any selection without help.

6.   If a witness makes a positive identification from photographs, unless the person identified is otherwise eliminated from enquiries or is not available, other witnesses shall not be shown photographs. But both they, and the witness who has made the identification, shall be asked to attend a video identification, an identification parade or group identification unless there is no dispute about the suspect's identification.

7.   If the witness makes a selection but is unable to confirm the identification, the person showing the photographs shall ask them how sure they are that the photograph they have indicated is the person they saw on the specified earlier occasion.

8.   When the use of a computerised or artist's composite or similar likeness has led to there being a known suspect who can be asked to participate in a video identification, appear on an identification parade or participate in a group identification, that likeness shall not be shown to other potential witnesses.

9.   When a witness attending a video identification, an identification parade or group identification has previously been shown photographs or computerised or artist's composite or similar likeness (and it is the responsibility of the officer in charge of the investigation to make the identification officer aware that this is the case), the suspect and their solicitor must be informed of this fact before the identification procedure takes place.

10.   None of the photographs shown shall be destroyed, whether or not an identification is made, since they may be required for production in court. The photographs shall be numbered and a separate photograph taken of the frame or part of the album from which the witness made an identification as an aid to reconstituting it.

(b) Documentation

11.   Whether or not an identification is made, a record shall be kept of the showing of photographs on forms provided for the purpose. This shall include anything said by the witness about any identification or the conduct of the procedure, any reasons it was not practicable to comply with any of the provisions of this Code governing the showing of photographs and the name and rank of the supervising officer.

12.   The supervising officer shall inspect and sign the record as soon as practicable.

ANNEX F   FINGERPRINTS AND SAMPLES— DESTRUCTION AND SPECULATIVE SEARCHES

(a) Fingerprints and samples taken in connection with a criminal investigation

1.   When fingerprints or DNA samples are taken from a person in connection with an investigation and the person is not suspected of having committed the offence, see Note F1, they must be destroyed as soon as they have fulfilled the purpose for which they were taken unless:

(a)   they were taken for the purposes of an investigation of an offence for which a person has been convicted; and

(b)   fingerprints or samples were also taken from the convicted person for the purposes of that investigation.

However, subject to paragraph 2, the fingerprints and samples, and the information derived from samples, may not be used in the investigation of any offence or in evidence against the person who is, or would be, entitled to the destruction of the fingerprints and samples, see Note F2.

2.   The requirement to destroy fingerprints and DNA samples, and information derived from samples, and restrictions on their retention and use in paragraph 1 do not apply if the person gives their written consent for their fingerprints or sample to be retained and used after they have fulfilled the purpose for which they were taken, see Note F1.

3.   When a person's fingerprints or sample are to be destroyed:

(a)   any copies of the fingerprints must also be destroyed;

(b)   the person may witness the destruction of their fingerprints or copies if they ask to do so within five days of being informed destruction is required;

(c)   access to relevant computer fingerprint data shall be made impossible as soon as it is practicable to do so and the person shall be given a certificate to this effect within three months of asking; and

(d) neither the fingerprints, the sample, or any information derived from the sample, may be used in the investigation of any offence or in evidence against the person who is, or would be, entitled to its destruction.

4.   Fingerprints or samples, and the information derived from samples, taken in connection with the investigation of an offence which are not required to be destroyed, may be retained after they have fulfilled the purposes for which they were taken but may be used only for purposes related to the prevention or detection of crime, the investigation of an offence or the conduct of a prosecution in, as well as outside, the UK and may also be subject to a speculative search. This includes checking them against other fingerprints and DNA records held by, or on behalf of, the police and other law enforcement authorities in, as well as outside, the UK.

(b) Fingerprints taken in connection with Immigration Service enquiries

5.   Fingerprints taken for Immigration Service enquiries in accordance with powers and procedures other than under PACE and for which the Immigration Service, not the police, are responsible, must be destroyed as follows:

(a) fingerprints and all copies must be destroyed as soon as practicable if the person from whom they were taken proves they are a British or Commonwealth citizen who has the right of abode in the UK under the Immigration Act 1971, section 2(1)(b);

(b) fingerprints taken under the power as in paragraph 4.11(g) from a dependant of a person in 4.11 (b) to (f) must be destroyed when that person's fingerprints are to be destroyed;

(c) fingerprints taken from a person under any power as in paragraph 4.11 or with the person's consent which have not already been destroyed as above, must be destroyed within ten years of being taken or within such period specified by the Secretary of State under the Immigration and Asylum Act 1999, section 143(5).

Notes for Guidance

F1   Fingerprints and samples given voluntarily for the purposes of elimination play an important part in many police investigations. It is, therefore, important to make sure innocent volunteers are not deterred from participating and their consent to their fingerprints and DNA being used for the purposes of a specific investigation is fully informed and voluntary. If the police or volunteer seek to have the sample or fingerprints retained for use after the specific investigation ends, it is important the volunteer's consent to this is also fully informed and voluntary.

Examples of consent for:

- DNA/fingerprints – to be used only for the purposes of a specific investigation;
- DNA/fingerprints – to be used in the specific investigation and retained by the police for future use.

To minimise the risk of confusion, each consent should be physically separate and the volunteer should be asked to sign one or the other, not both.

(a) DNA:

(i) DNA sample taken for the purposes of elimination or as part of an intelligence-led screen and to be used only for the purposes of that investigation and destroyed afterwards:

'I consent to my DNA/mouth swab being taken for forensic analysis. I understand that the sample will be destroyed at the end of the case and that my profile will only be compared to the crime stain profile from this enquiry. I have been advised that the person taking the sample may be required to give evidence and/or provide a written statement to the police in relation to the taking of it'.

(ii) DNA sample to be retained on the National DNA database and used in the future:

'I consent to my DNA sample and information derived from it being retained and used only for purposes related to the prevention and detection of a crime, the investigation of an offence or the conduct of a prosecution either nationally or internationally.'

'I understand that this sample may be checked against other DNA records held by, or on behalf of, relevant law enforcement authorities, either nationally or internationally'.

'I understand that once I have given my consent for the sample to be retained and used I cannot withdraw this consent.'

(b) Fingerprints:

(i) Fingerprints taken for the purposes of elimination or as part of an intelligence-led screen and to be used only for the purposes of that investigation and destroyed afterwards:

'I consent to my fingerprints being taken for elimination purposes. I understand that the fingerprints will be destroyed at the end of the case and that my fingerprints will only be compared to the fingerprints from this enquiry. I have been advised that the person taking the fingerprints may be required to give evidence and/or provide a written statement to the police in relation to the taking of it.'

(ii) Fingerprints to be retained for future use:

'I consent to my fingerprints being retained and used only for purposes related to the prevention and detection of a crime, the investigation of an offence or the conduct of a prosecution either nationally or internationally'.

'I understand that my fingerprints may be checked against other records held by, or on behalf of, relevant law enforcement authorities, either nationally or internationally.'

'I understand that once I have given my consent for my fingerprints to be retained and used I cannot withdraw this consent.'

F2   The provisions for the retention of fingerprints and samples in paragraph 1 allow for all fingerprints and samples in a case to be available for any subsequent miscarriage of justice investigation.

Code of Practice on Tape Recording Interviews with Suspects (Code E)

1   General

1.1   This Code of Practice must be readily available for consultation by:
- police officers
- detained persons
- members of the public.

1.2   The *Notes for Guidance* included are not provisions of this Code.

1.3   Nothing in this Code shall detract from the requirements of Code C, the Code of Practice for the detention, treatment and questioning of persons by police officers.

1.4   This Code does not apply to those people listed in Code C, paragraph 1.12.

1.5   The term:
- 'appropriate adult' has the same meaning as in Code C, paragraph 1.7
- 'solicitor' has the same meaning as in Code C, paragraph 6.12.

1.6   In this Code:

(a) 'designated person' means a person other than a police officer, designated under the Police Reform Act 2002, Part 4 who has specified powers and duties of police officers conferred or imposed on them;

(b) any reference to a police officer includes a designated person acting in the exercise or performance of the powers and duties conferred or imposed on them by their designation.

1.7   If a power conferred on a designated person:

(a) allows reasonable force to be used when exercised by a police officer, a designated person exercising that power has the same entitlement to use force;

(b) includes power to use force to enter any premises, that power is not exercisable by that designated person except:

(i)   in the company, and under the supervision, of a police officer; or

(ii) for the purpose of:

• saving life or limb; or

• preventing serious damage to property.

1.8   Nothing in this Code prevents the custody officer, or other officer given custody of the detainee, from allowing civilian support staff who are not designated persons to carry out individual procedures or tasks at the police station if the law allows. However, the officer remains responsible for making sure the procedures and tasks are carried out correctly in accordance with these Codes. Any such civilian must be:

(a) a person employed by a police authority maintaining a police force and under the control and direction of the Chief Officer of that force; or

(b) employed by a person with whom a police authority has a contract for the provision of services relating to persons arrested or otherwise in custody.

1.9   Designated persons and other civilian support staff must have regard to any relevant provisions of the Codes of Practice.

1.10   References to pocket book include any official report book issued to police officers or civilian support staff.

1.11   References to a custody officer include those performing the functions of a custody officer.

2   Recording and sealing master tapes

2.1   Tape recording of interviews shall be carried out openly to instil confidence in its reliability as an impartial and accurate record of the interview.

2.2   One tape, the master tape, will be sealed in the suspect's presence. A second tape will be used as a working copy. The master tape is either of the two tapes used in a twin deck machine or the only tape in a single deck machine. The working copy is either the second/third tape used in a twin/triple deck machine or a copy of the master tape made by a single deck machine. See Notes 2A and 2B

2.3   Nothing in this Code requires the identity of officers or civilian support staff conducting interviews to be recorded or disclosed:

(a) in the case of enquiries linked to the investigation of terrorism; or

(b) if the interviewer reasonably believes recording or disclosing their name might put them in danger.

In these cases interviewers should use warrant or other identification numbers and the name of their police station. See Note 2C

Notes for Guidance

2A   The purpose of sealing the master tape in the suspect's presence is to show the tape's integrity is preserved. If a single deck machine is used the working copy of the master tape must be made in the suspect's presence and without the master tape leaving their sight. The working copy shall be used for making further copies if needed.

2B   Reference to 'tapes' includes 'tape', if a single deck machine is used.

2C   The purpose of paragraph 2.3(b) is to protect those involved in serious organised crime investigations or arrests of particularly violent suspects when there is reliable information that those arrested or their associates may threaten or cause harm to those involved. In cases of doubt, an officer of inspector rank or above should be consulted.

3   Interviews to be tape recorded

3.1   Subject to paragraphs 3.3 and 3.4, tape recording shall be used at police stations for any interview:

(a) with a person cautioned under Code C, section 10 in respect of any indictable offence, including an offence triable either way; see Note 3A

(b) which takes place as a result of an interviewer exceptionally putting further questions to a suspect about an offence described in paragraph 3.1(a) after they have been charged with, or told they may be prosecuted for, that offence, see Code C, paragraph 16.5

(c) when an interviewer wants to tell a person, after they have been charged with, or informed they may be prosecuted for, an offence described in paragraph 3.1(a), about any written statement or interview with another person, see Code C, paragraph 16.4.

3.2   The Terrorism Act 2000 makes separate provision for a Code of Practice for the tape recording of interviews of those arrested under Section 41 or detained under Schedule 7 of the Act. The provisions of this Code do not apply to such interviews.

3.3   The custody officer may authorise the interviewer not to tape record the interview when it is:

(a) not reasonably practicable because of equipment failure or the unavailability of a suitable interview room or recorder and the authorising officer considers, on reasonable grounds, that the interview should not be delayed; or

(b) clear from the outset there will not be a prosecution.

Note: In these cases the interview should be recorded in writing in accordance with Code C, section 11. In all cases the custody officer shall record the specific reasons for not tape recording. See Note 3B

3.4   If a person refuses to go into or remain in a suitable interview room, see Code C paragraph 12.5, and the custody officer considers, on reasonable grounds, that the interview should not be delayed the interview may, at the custody officer's discretion, be conducted in a cell using portable recording equipment or, if none is available, recorded in writing as in Code C, section 11. The reasons for this shall be recorded.

3.5   The whole of each interview shall be tape recorded, including the taking and reading back of any statement.

Notes for Guidance

3A   Nothing in this Code is intended to preclude tape recording at police discretion of interviews at police stations with people cautioned in respect of offences not covered by paragraph 3.1, or responses made by persons after they have been charged with, or told they may be prosecuted for, an offence, provided this Code is complied with.

3B   A decision not to tape record an interview for any reason may be the subject of comment in court. The authorising officer should be prepared to justify that decision.

4   The interview

(a) General

4.1   The provisions of Code C:

• sections 10 and 11, and the applicable *Notes for Guidance* apply to the conduct of interviews to which this Code applies

• paragraphs 11.7 to 11.14 apply only when a written record is needed.

4.2   Code C, paragraphs 10.10, 10.11 and Annex C describe the restriction on drawing adverse inferences from a suspect's failure or refusal to say anything about their involvement in the offence when interviewed or after being charged or informed they may be prosecuted, and how it affects the terms of the caution and determines if and by whom a special warning under sections 36 and 37 can be given.

(b) Commencement of interviews

4.3   When the suspect is brought into the interview room the interviewer shall, without delay but in the suspect's sight, load the recorder with clean tapes and set it to record. The tapes must be unwrapped or opened in the suspect's presence.

4.4   The interviewer should tell the suspect about the tape recording. The interviewer shall:

(a) say the interview is being tape recorded;
(b) subject to paragraph 2.3, give their name and rank and that of any other interviewer present;
(c) ask the suspect and any other party present, e.g. a solicitor, to identify themselves;
(d) state the date, time of commencement and place of the interview;
(e) state the suspect will be given a notice about what will happen to the tapes.

See Note 4A

4.5   The interviewer shall:

• caution the suspect, see Code C, section 10;
• remind the suspect of their entitlement to free legal advice, see Code C, paragraph 11.2.

4.6   The interviewer shall put to the suspect any significant statement or silence; see Code C, paragraph 11.4.

(c) Interviews with deaf persons

4.7   If the suspect is deaf or is suspected of having impaired hearing, the interviewer shall make a written note of the interview in accordance with Code C, at the same time as tape recording it in accordance with this Code. See Notes 4B and 4C

(d) Objections and complaints by the suspect

4.8   If the suspect objects to the interview being tape recorded at the outset, during the interview or during a break, the interviewer shall explain that the interview is being tape recorded and that this Code requires the suspect's objections be recorded on tape. When any objections have been tape recorded or the suspect has refused to have their objections recorded, the interviewer shall say they are turning off the recorder, give their reasons and turn it off. The interviewer shall then make a written record of the interview as in Code C, section 11. If, however, the interviewer reasonably considers they may proceed to question the suspect with the tape still on, the interviewer may do so. See Note 4D

4.9   If in the course of an interview a complaint is made by or on behalf of the person being questioned concerning the provisions of this Code or Code C, the interviewer shall act as in Code C, paragraph 12.9. See Notes 4E and 4F

4.10   If the suspect indicates they want to tell the interviewer about matters not directly connected with the offence and they are unwilling for these matters to be tape recorded, the suspect should be given the opportunity to tell the interviewer at the end of the formal interview.

(e) Changing tapes

4.11   When the recorder shows the tapes have only a short time left, the interviewer shall tell the suspect the tapes are coming to an end and round off that part of the interview. If the interviewer leaves the room for a second set of tapes, the suspect shall not be left unattended. The interviewer will remove the tapes from the tape recorder and insert the new tapes which shall be unwrapped or opened in the suspect's presence. The tape recorder should be set to record on the new tapes. To avoid confusion between the tapes, the interviewer shall mark the tapes with an identification number immediately they are removed from the tape recorder.

(f) Taking a break during interview

4.12   When a break is taken, the fact that a break is to be taken, the reason for it and the time shall be recorded on tape.

4.12A   When the break is taken and the interview room vacated by the suspect, the tapes shall be removed from the tape recorder and the procedures for the conclusion of an interview followed; see paragraph 4.18.

4.13   When a break is a short one and both the suspect and an interviewer remain in the interview room, the tape recorder may be turned off. There is no need to remove the tapes and when the interview recommences the tape recording should continue on the same tapes. The time the interview recommences shall be recorded on tape.

4.14   After any break in the interview the interviewer must, before resuming the interview, remind the person being questioned that they remain under caution or, if there is any doubt, give the caution in full again. See Note 4G

(g) Failure of recording equipment

4.15   If there is an equipment failure which can be rectified quickly, e.g. by inserting new tapes, the interviewer shall follow the appropriate procedures as in paragraph 4.11. When the recording is resumed the interviewer shall explain what happened and record the time the interview recommences. If, however, it will not be possible to continue recording on that tape recorder and no replacement recorder is readily available, the interview may continue without being tape recorded. If this happens, the interviewer shall seek the custody officer's authority as in paragraph 3.3. See Note 4H

(h) Removing tapes from the recorder

4.16   When tapes are removed from the recorder during the interview, they shall be retained and the procedures in paragraph 4.18 followed.

(i) Conclusion of interview

4.17   At the conclusion of the interview, the suspect shall be offered the opportunity to clarify anything he or she has said and asked if there is anything they want to add.

4.18   At the conclusion of the interview, including the taking and reading back of any written statement, the time shall be recorded and the tape recorder switched off. The interviewer shall seal the master tape with a master tape label and treat it as an exhibit in accordance with force standing orders. The interviewer shall sign the label and ask the suspect and any third party present during the interview to sign it. If the suspect or third party refuse to sign the label an officer of at least inspector rank, or if not available the custody officer, shall be called into the interview room and asked, subject to paragraph 2.3, to sign it.

4.19   The suspect shall be handed a notice which explains:

- how the tape recording will be used;
- the arrangements for access to it;
- that if the person is charged or informed they will be prosecuted, a copy of the tape will be supplied as soon as practicable or as otherwise agreed between the suspect and the police.

Notes for Guidance

4A   For the purpose of voice identification the interviewer should ask the suspect and any other people present to identify themselves.

4B   This provision is to give a person who is deaf or has impaired hearing equivalent rights of access to the full interview record as far as this is possible using audio recording.

4C   The provisions of Code C, section 13 on interpreters for deaf persons or for interviews with suspects who have difficulty understanding English continue to apply. However, in a tape recorded interview the requirement on the interviewer to make sure the interpreter makes a separate note of the interview applies only to paragraph 4.7 (interviews with deaf persons).

4D   The interviewer should remember that a decision to continue recording against the wishes of the suspect may be the subject of comment in court.

4E   If the custody officer is called to deal with the complaint, the tape recorder should, if possible, be left on until the custody officer has entered the room and spoken to the person being interviewed. Continuation or termination of the interview should be at the interviewer's discretion pending action by an inspector under Code C, paragraph 9.2.

4F   If the complaint is about a matter not connected with this Code or Code C, the decision to continue is at the interviewer's discretion. When the interviewer decides to continue the interview, they shall tell the suspect the complaint will be brought to the custody officer's attention at the conclusion of the interview. When the interview is concluded the interviewer must, as soon as practicable, inform the custody officer about the existence and nature of the complaint made.

4G   The interviewer should remember that it may be necessary to show to the court that nothing occurred during a break or between interviews which influenced the suspect's recorded evidence. After a break or at the beginning of a subsequent interview, the interviewer should consider summarising on tape the reason for the break and confirming this with the suspect.

4H   If one of the tapes snaps during the interview it should be sealed as a master tape in the suspect's presence and the interview resumed where it left off. The unbroken tape should be copied and the original sealed as a master tape in the suspect's presence, if necessary after the interview. If equipment for copying the unbroken tape is not readily available, both tapes should be sealed in the suspect's presence and the interview begun again. If the tape breaks when a single deck machine is being used and the machine is one where a broken tape cannot be copied on available equipment, the tape should be sealed as a master tape in the suspect's presence and the interview begun again.

5   After the interview

5.1   The interviewer shall make a note in their pocket book that the interview has taken place, was tape recorded, its time, duration and date and the master tape's identification number.

5.2   If no proceedings follow in respect of the person whose interview was recorded, the tapes must be kept securely as in *paragraph 6.1* and *Note 6A*.

Note for Guidance

5A   Any written record of a tape recorded interview should be made in accordance with national guidelines approved by the Secretary of State.

6   Tape security

6.1   The officer in charge of each police station at which interviews with suspects are recorded shall make arrangements for master tapes to be kept securely and their movements accounted for on the same basis as material which may be used for evidential purposes, in accordance with force standing orders. See Note 6A

6.2   A police officer has no authority to break the seal on a master tape required for criminal trial or appeal proceedings. If it is necessary to gain access to the master tape, the police officer shall arrange for its seal to be broken in the presence of a representative of the Crown Prosecution Service. The defendant or their legal adviser should be informed and given a reasonable opportunity to be present. If the defendant or their legal representative is present they shall be invited to reseal and sign the master tape. If either refuses or neither is present this should be done by the representative of the Crown Prosecution Service. See Notes 6B and 6C

6.3   If no criminal proceedings result or the criminal trial and, if applicable, appeal proceedings to which the interview relates have been concluded, the chief officer of police is responsible for establishing arrangements for breaking the seal on the master tape, if necessary.

6.4   When the master tape seal is broken, a record must be made of the procedure followed, including the date, time, place and persons present.

Notes for Guidance

6A   This section is concerned with the security of the master tape sealed at the conclusion of the interview. Care must be taken of working copies of tapes because their loss or destruction may lead to the need to access master tapes.

6B   If the tape has been delivered to the crown court for their keeping after committal for trial the crown prosecutor will apply to the chief clerk of the crown court centre for the release of the tape for unsealing by the crown prosecutor.

6C   Reference to the Crown Prosecution Service or to the crown prosecutor in this part of the Code should be taken to include any other body or person with a statutory responsibility for prosecution for whom the police conduct any tape recorded interviews.

Code of Practice on Visual Recordings with Sound of Interviews with Suspects (Code F)

1   General

1.1   This code of practice must be readily available for consultation by police officers, detained persons and members of the public.

1.2   The notes for guidance included are not provisions of this code. They form guidance to police officers and others about its application and interpretation.

1.3   Nothing in this code shall be taken as detracting in any way from the requirements of the Code of Practice for the Detention, Treatment and Questioning of Persons by Police Officers (Code C). [See Note 1A]

1.4   The interviews to which this Code applies are set out in paragraph 3.1–3.3.

1.5   In this code, the term 'appropriate adult', 'solicitor' and 'interview' have the same meaning as those set out in Code C. The corresponding provisions and Notes for Guidance in Code C applicable to those terms shall also apply where appropriate.

1.6   Any reference in this code to visual recording shall be taken to mean visual recording with sound.

1.7   References to 'pocket book' in this Code include any official report book issued to police officers.

Note for Guidance

1A   As in Code C, references to custody officers include those carrying out the functions of a custody officer.

2   Recording and sealing of master tapes

2.1   The visual recording of interviews shall be carried out openly to instill confidence in its reliability as an impartial and accurate record of the interview. [See Note 2A]

2.2   The camera(s) shall be placed in the interview room so as to ensure coverage of as much of the room as is practicably possible whilst the interviews are taking place.

2.3   The certified recording medium will be of a high quality, new and previously unused. When the certified recording medium is placed in the recorder and switched on to record, the correct date and time, in hours, minutes and seconds will be superimposed automatically, second by second, during the whole recording. [See Note 2B]

2.4   One copy of the certified recording medium, referred to in this code as the master copy, will be sealed before it leaves the presence of the suspect. A second copy will be used as a working copy. [See Note 2C and 2D]

2.5   Nothing in this code requires the identity of an officer to be recorded or disclosed if:

(a) the interview or record relates to a person detained under the Terrorism Act 2000; or

(b) otherwise where the officer reasonably believes that recording or disclosing their name might put them in danger.

In these cases, the officer will have their back to the camera and shall use their warrant or other identification number and the name of the police station to which they are attached. Such instances and the reasons for them shall be recorded in the custody record. [See Note 2E]

Notes for Guidance

2A   Interviewing officers will wish to arrange that, as far as possible, visual recording arrangements are unobtrusive. It must be clear to the suspect, however, that there is no opportunity to interfere with the recording equipment or the recording media.

2B   In this context, the certified recording media will be of either a VHS or digital CD format and should be capable of having an image of the date and time superimposed upon them as they record the interview.

2C   The purpose of sealing the master copy before it leaves the presence of the suspect is to establish their confidence that the integrity of the copy is preserved.

2D   The recording of the interview is not to be used for any identification purpose.

2E   The purpose of the (sic) paragraph 2.5 is to protect police officers and others involved in the investigation of serious organised crime or the arrest of particularly violent suspects when there is reliable information that those arrested or their associates may threaten or cause harm to the officers, their families or their personal property.

3   Interviews to be visually recorded

3.1   Subject to paragraph 3.2 below, visual recording shall be used for any interview:

(a) with a suspect in respect of an indictable offence (including an offence triable either way) [See Notes 3A and 3B];

(b) which takes place as a result of an interviewer exceptionally putting further questions to a suspect about an offence described in sub-paragraph (a) above after they have been charged with, or informed they may be prosecuted for, that offence [see Note 3C];

(c) in which an interviewer wishes to bring to the notice of a person, after that person has been charged with, or informed they may be prosecuted for an offence described in sub-paragraph (a) above, any written statement made by another person, or the content of an interview with another person [see Note 3D];

(d) with, or in the presence of, a deaf or deaf/blind or speech impaired person who uses sign language to communicate;

(e) with, or in the presence of anyone who requires an 'appropriate adult'; or

(f) in any case where the suspect or their representative requests that the interview be recorded visually.

3.2   The Terrorism Act 2000 makes separate provision for a code of practice for the video recording of interviews in a police station of those detained under Schedule 7 or section 41 of the Act. The provisions of this code do not therefore apply to such interviews [see Note 3E].

3.3   The custody officer may authorise the interviewing officer not to record the interview visually:

(a) where it is not reasonably practicable to do so because of failure of the equipment, or the non-availability of a suitable interview room, or recorder and the authorising officer considers on reasonable grounds that the interview should not be delayed until the failure has been rectified or a suitable room or recorder becomes available. In such cases the custody officer may authorise the interviewing officer to audio record the interview in accordance with the guidance set out in Code E;

(b) where it is clear from the outset that no prosecution will ensue; or

(c) where it is not practicable to do so because at the time the person resists being taken to a suitable interview room or other location which would enable the interview to be recorded, or otherwise fails or refuses to go into such a room or location, and the authorising officer considers on reasonable grounds that the interview should not be delayed until these conditions cease to apply.

In all cases the custody officer shall make a note in the custody records of the reason for not taking a visual record. [See Note 3F]

3.4   When a person who is voluntarily attending the police station is required to be cautioned in accordance with Code C prior to being interviewed, the subsequent interview shall be recorded, unless the custody officer gives authority in accordance with the provisions of paragraph 3.3 above for the interview not to be so recorded.

3.5   The whole of each interview shall be recorded visually, including the taking and reading back of any statement.

3.6   A visible illuminated sign or indicator will light and remain on at all times when the recording equipment is activated or capable of recording or transmitting any signal or information.

Notes for Guidance

3A   Nothing in the code is intended to preclude visual recording at police discretion of interviews at police stations with people cautioned in respect of offences not covered by paragraph 3.1, or responses made by interviewees after they have been charged with or informed they may be prosecuted for, an offence, provided that this code is complied with.

3B   Attention is drawn to the provisions set out in Code C about the matters to be considered when deciding whether a detained person is fit to be interviewed.

3C   Code C sets out the circumstances in which a suspect may be questioned about an offence after being charged with it.

3D   Code C sets out the procedures to be followed when a person's attention is drawn after charge, to a statement made by another person. One method of bringing the content of an interview with another person to the notice of a suspect may be to play him a recording of that interview.

3E   When it only becomes clear during the course of an interview which is being visually recorded that the interviewee may have committed an offence to which paragraph 3.2 applies, the interviewing officer should turn off the recording equipment and the interview should continue in accordance with the provisions of the Terrorism Act 2000.

3F   A decision not to record an interview visually for any reason may be the subject of comment in court. The authorising officer should therefore be prepared to justify their decision in each case.

4   The interview

(a) General

4.1   The provisions of Code C in relation to cautions and interviews and the Notes for Guidance applicable to those provisions shall apply to the conduct of interviews to which this Code applies.

4.2   Particular attention is drawn to those parts of Code C that describe the restrictions on drawing adverse inferences from a suspect's failure or refusal to say anything about their involvement in the offence when interviewed, or after being charged or informed they may be prosecuted and how those restrictions affect the terms of the caution and determine whether a special warning under Sections 36 and 37 of the Criminal Justice and Public Order Act 1994 can be given.

(b) Commencement of interviews

4.3   When the suspect is brought into the interview room the interviewer shall without delay, but in sight of the suspect, load the recording equipment and set it to record. The recording media must be unwrapped or otherwise opened in the presence of the suspect [See Note 4A]

4.4   The interviewer shall then tell the suspect formally about the visual recording. The interviewer shall:

    (a)   explain the interview is being visually recorded;

    (b)   subject to paragraph 2.5, give his or her name and rank, and that of any other interviewer present;

    (c)   ask the suspect and any other party present (e.g. his solicitor) to identify themselves;

    (d)   state the date, time of commencement and place of the interview; and

    (e)   state that the suspect will be given a notice about what will happen to the recording.

4.5   The interviewer shall then caution the suspect, which should follow that set out in Code C, and remind the suspect of their entitlement to free and independent legal advice and that they can speak to a solicitor on the telephone.

4.6   The interviewer shall then put to the suspect any significant statement or silence (i.e. failure or refusal to answer a question or to answer it satisfactorily) which occurred before the start of the interview, and shall ask the suspect whether they wish to confirm or deny that earlier statement or silence or whether they wish to add anything. The definition of a 'significant' statement or silence is the same as that set out in Code C.

(c) Interviews with the deaf

4.7   If the suspect is deaf or there is doubt about their hearing ability, the provisions of Code C on interpreters for the deaf or for interviews with suspects who have difficulty in understanding English continue to apply.

(d) Objections and complaints by the suspect

4.8   If the suspect raises objections to the interview being visually recorded either at the outset or during the interview or during a break in the interview, the interviewer shall explain the fact that the interview is being visually recorded and that the provisions of this code require that the suspect's objections shall be recorded. The suspect's objections shall be noted.

4.9   If in the course of an interview a complaint is made by the person being questioned, or on their behalf, concerning the provisions of this code or of Code C, then the interviewer shall act in accordance with Code C, record it in the interview record and inform the custody officer. [See 4B and 4C]

4.10   If the suspect indicates that they wish to tell the interviewer about matters not directly connected with the offence of which they are suspected and that they are unwilling for these matters to be recorded, the suspect shall be given the opportunity to tell the interviewer about these matters after the conclusion of the formal interview.

(e) Changing the recording media

4.11   In instances where the recording medium is not of sufficient length to record all of the interview with the suspect, further certified recording medium will be used. When the recording equipment indicates that the recording medium has only a short time left to run, the interviewer shall advise the suspect and round off that part of the interview. If the interviewer wishes to continue the interview but does not already have further certified recording media with him, they shall obtain a set. The suspect should not be left unattended in the interview room. The interviewer will remove the recording media from the recording equipment and insert the new ones which have been unwrapped or otherwise opened in the suspect's presence. The recording equipment shall then be set to record. Care must be taken, particularly when a number of sets of recording media have been used, to ensure that there is no confusion between them. This could be achieved by marking the sets of recording media with consecutive identification numbers.

(f) Taking a break during the interview

4.12   When a break is to be taken during the course of an interview and the interview room is to be vacated by the suspect, the fact that a break is to be taken, the reason for it and the time shall be recorded. The recording equipment must be turned off and the recording media removed. The procedures for the conclusion of an interview set out in paragraph 4.19, below, should be followed.

4.13   When a break is to be a short one, and both the suspect and a police officer are to remain in the interview room, the fact that a break is to be taken, the reasons for it and the time shall be recorded on the recording media. The recording equipment may be turned off, but there is no need to remove the recording media. When the interview is recommenced the recording shall continue on the same recording media and the time at which the interview recommences shall be recorded.

4.14   When there is a break in questioning under caution, the interviewing officer must ensure that the person being questioned is aware that they remain under caution. If there is any doubt the caution must be given again in full when the interview resumes. [See Note 4D and 4E]

(g) Failure of recording equipment

4.15   If there is a failure of equipment which can be rectified quickly, the appropriate procedures set out in paragraph 4.12 shall be followed. When the recording is resumed the interviewer shall explain what has happened and record the time the interview recommences. If, however, it is not possible to continue recording on that particular recorder and no alternative equipment is readily available, the interview may continue without being recorded visually. In such circumstances, the procedures set out in paragraph 3.3 of this code for seeking the authority of the custody officer will be followed. [See Note 4F]

(h) Removing used recording media from recording equipment

4.16   Where used recording media are removed from the recording equipment during the course of an interview, they shall be retained and the procedures set out in paragraph 4.18 below followed.

(i) Conclusion of interview

4.17   Before the conclusion of the interview, the suspect shall be offered the opportunity to clarify anything he or she has said and asked if there is anything that they wish to add.

4.18   At the conclusion of the interview, including the taking and reading back of any written statement, the time shall be recorded and the recording equipment switched off. The master tape or CD shall be removed from the recording equipment, sealed with a master copy label and treated as an exhibit in accordance with the force standing orders. The interviewer shall sign the label and also ask the suspect and any appropriate adults or other third party present during the interview to sign it. If the suspect or third party refuses to sign the label, an officer of at least the rank of inspector, or if one is not available, the custody officer, shall be called into the interview room and asked to sign it.

4.19   The suspect shall be handed a notice which explains the use which will be made of the recording and the arrangements for access to it. The notice will also advise the suspect that a copy of the tape shall be supplied as soon as practicable if the person is charged or informed that he will be prosecuted.

Notes for Guidance

4A   The interviewer should attempt to estimate the likely length of the interview and ensure that an appropriate quantity of certified recording media and labels with which to seal the master copies are available in the interview room.

4B   Where the custody officer is called immediately to deal with the complaint, wherever possible the recording equipment should be left to run until the custody officer has entered the interview room and spoken to the person being interviewed. Continuation or termination of the interview should be at the discretion of the interviewing officer pending action by an inspector as set out in Code C.

4C   Where the complaint is about a matter not connected with this code of practice or Code C, the decision to continue with the interview is at the discretion of the interviewing officer. Where the interviewing officer decides to continue with the interview, the person being interviewed shall be told that the complaint will be brought to the attention of the custody officer at the conclusion of the interview. When the interview is concluded, the interviewing officer must, as soon as practicable, inform the custody officer of the existence and nature of the complaint made.

4D   In considering whether to caution again after a break, the officer should bear in mind that he may have to satisfy a court that the person understood that he was still under caution when the interview resumed.

4E   The officer should bear in mind that it may be necessary to satisfy the court that nothing occurred during a break in an interview or between interviews which influenced the suspect's recorded evidence. On the re-commencement of an interview, the officer should consider summarising on the tape or CD the reason for the break and confirming this with the suspect.

4F   If any part of the recording media breaks or is otherwise damaged during the interview, it should be sealed as a master copy in the presence of the suspect and the interview resumed where it left off. The undamaged part should be copied and the original sealed as a master tape in the suspect's presence, if necessary after the interview. If equipment for copying is not readily available, both parts should be sealed in the suspect's presence and the interview begun again.

5   After the interview

5.1   The interviewer shall make a note in his or her pocket book of the fact that the interview has taken place and has been recorded, its time, duration and date and the identification number of the master copy of the recording media.

5.2   Where no proceedings follow in respect of the person whose interview was recorded, the recording media must nevertheless be kept securely in accordance with paragraph 6.1 and Note 6A.

Note for Guidance

5A   Any written record of a recorded interview shall be made in accordance with national guidelines approved by the Secretary of State, and with regard to the advice contained in the Manual of Guidance for the preparation, processing and submission of files.

6   Tape security

(a) General

6.1   The officer in charge of the police station at which interviews with suspects are recorded shall make arrangements for the master copies to be kept securely and their movements accounted for on the same basis as other material which may be used for evidential purposes, in accordance with force standing orders. [See Note 6A]

(b) Breaking master copy seal for criminal proceedings

6.2   A police officer has no authority to break the seal on a master copy which is required for criminal trial or appeal proceedings. If it is necessary to gain access to the master copy, the police officer shall arrange for its seal to be broken in the presence of a representative of the Crown Prosecution Service. The defendant or their legal adviser shall be informed and given a reasonable opportunity to be present. If the defendant or their legal representative is present they shall be invited to reseal and sign the master copy. If either refuses or neither is present, this shall be done by the representative of the Crown Prosecution Service. [See Notes 6B and 6C]

(c) Breaking master copy seal: other cases

6.3   The chief officer of police is responsible for establishing arrangements for breaking the seal of the master copy where no criminal proceedings result, or the criminal proceedings, to which the interview relates, have been concluded and it becomes necessary to break the seal. These arrangements should be those which the chief officer considers are reasonably necessary to demonstrate to the person interviewed and any other party who may wish to use or refer to the interview record that the master copy has not been tampered with and that the interview record remains accurate. [See Note 6D]

6.4   Subject to paragraph 6.6, a representative of each party must be given a reasonable opportunity to be present when the seal is broken, the master copy copied and re-sealed.

6.5   If one or more of the parties is not present when the master copy seal is broken because they cannot be contacted or refuse to attend or paragraph 6.6 applies, arrangements should be made for an independent person such as a custody visitor, to be present. Alternatively, or as an additional safeguard, arrangement should be made for a film or photographs to be taken of the procedure.

6.6   Paragraph 6.5 does not require a person to be given an opportunity to be present when:

(a)   it is necessary to break the master copy seal for the proper and effective further investigation of the original offence or the investigation of some other offence; and

(b)   the officer in charge of the investigation has reasonable grounds to suspect that allowing an opportunity might prejudice any such an investigation or criminal proceedings which may be brought as a result or endanger any person. [See Note 6E]

(e) Documentation

6.7   When the master copy seal is broken, copied and re-sealed, a record must be made of the procedure followed, including the date time and place and persons present.

Notes for Guidance

6A   This section is concerned with the security of the master copy which will have been sealed at the conclusion of the interview. Care should, however, be taken of working copies since their loss or destruction may lead unnecessarily to the need to have access to master copies.

6B   If the master copy has been delivered to the Crown Court for their keeping after committal for trial the Crown Prosecutor will apply to the Chief Clerk of the Crown Court Centre for its release for unsealing by the Crown Prosecutor.

6C   Reference to the Crown Prosecution Service or to the Crown Prosecutor in this part of the code shall be taken to include any other body or person with a statutory responsibility for prosecution for whom the police conduct any recorded interviews.

6D   The most common reasons for needing access to master copies that are not required for criminal proceedings arise from civil actions and complaints against police and civil actions between individuals arising out of allegations of crime investigated by police.

6E   Paragraph 6.6 could apply, for example, when one or more of the outcomes or likely outcomes of the investigation might be; (i) the prosecution of one or more of the original suspects, (ii) the prosecution of someone previously not suspected, including someone who was originally a witness; and (iii) any original suspect being treated as a prosecution witness and when premature disclosure of any police action, particularly through contact with any parties involved, could lead to a real risk of compromising the investigation and endangering witnesses.

Road Traffic Regulation Act 1984
(1984, c. 27)

89   Speeding offences generally

(1) A person who drives a motor vehicle on a road at a speed exceeding a limit imposed by or under any enactment to which this section applies shall be guilty of an offence.

(2) A person prosecuted for such an offence shall not be liable to be convicted solely on the evidence of one witness to the effect that, in the opinion of the witness, the person prosecuted was driving the vehicle at a speed exceeding a specified limit.

(3) The enactments to which this section applies are—

    (a) any enactment contained in this Act except section 17(2);

    (b) section 2 of the Parks Regulation (Amendment) Act 1926; and

    (c) any enactment not contained in this Act, but passed after 1st September 1960, whether before or after the passing of this Act.

If a person who employs other persons to drive motor vehicles on roads publishes or issues any time-table or schedule, or gives any directions, under which any journey, or any stage or part of any journey, is to be completed within some specified time, and it is not practicable in the circumstances of the case of that journey (or that stage or part of it) to be completed in the specified time without the commission of such an offence as is mentioned in subsection (1) above, the publication or issue of the time-table or schedule, or the giving of the directions may be produced as prima facie evidence that the employer procured or (as the case may be) incited the persons employed by him to drive the vehicles to commit such an offence.

Prosecution of Offences Act 1985
(1985, c. 23)

25   Consents to prosecutions etc.

(1) This section applies to any enactment which prohibits the institution or carrying on of proceedings for any offence except—

    (a) with the consent (however expressed) of a Law Officer of the Crown or the Director; or

    (b) where the proceedings are instituted or carried on by or on behalf of a Law Officer of the Crown or the Director;

and so applies whether or not there are other exceptions to the prohibition (and in particular whether or not the consent is an alternative to the consent of any other authority or person).

(2) An enactment to which this section applies—

    (a) shall not prevent the arrest without warrant, or the issue or execution of a warrant for the arrest, of a person for any offence, or the remand in custody or on bail of a person charged with any offence; and

    (b) shall be subject to any enactment concerning the apprehension or detention of children or young persons.

(3) In this section 'enactment' includes any provision having effect under or by virtue of any Act; and this section applies to enactments whenever passed or made.

26   Consents to be admissible in evidence
Any document purporting to be the consent of a Law Officer of the Crown, the Director or a Crown Prosecutor for, or to—
>   (a) the institution of any criminal proceedings; or
>   (b) the institution of criminal proceedings in any particular form;

and to be signed by a Law Officer of the Crown, the Director or, as the case may be, a Crown Prosecutor shall be admissible as prima facie evidence without further proof.

Public Order Act 1986
(1986, c. 64)

5   Harassment, alarm or distress
(1) A person is guilty of an offence if he—
>   (a) uses threatening, abusive or insulting words or behaviour, or disorderly behaviour, or
>   (b) displays any writing, sign or other visible representation which is threatening, abusive or insulting, within the hearing or sight of a person likely to be caused harassment, alarm or distress thereby.

(2) An offence under this section may be committed in a public or a private place, except that no offence is committed where the words or behaviour are used, or the writing, sign or other visible representation is displayed, by a person inside a dwelling and the other person is also inside that or another dwelling.

(3) It is a defence for the accused to prove—
>   (a) that he had no reason to believe that there was any person within hearing or sight who was likely to be caused harassment, alarm or distress, or
>   (b) that he was inside a dwelling and had no reason to believe that the words or behaviour used, or the writing, sign or other visible representation displayed, would be heard or seen by a person outside that or any other dwelling, or
>   (c) that his conduct was reasonable.

(4) A constable may arrest a person without warrant if—
>   (a) he engages in offensive conduct which a constable warns him to stop, and
>   (b) he engages in further offensive conduct immediately or shortly after the warning.

(5) In subsection (4) 'offensive conduct' means conduct the constable reasonably suspects to constitute an offence under this section, and the conduct mentioned in paragraph (a) and the further conduct need not be of the same nature.

(6) A person guilty of an offence under this section is liable on summary conviction to a fine not exceeding level 3 on the standard scale.

Criminal Justice Act 1987
(1987, c. 38)

1   The Serious Fraud Office
(1) A Serious Fraud Office shall be constituted for England and Wales and Northern Ireland.

(2) The Attorney General shall appoint a person to be the Director of the Serious Fraud Office (referred to in this Part of this Act as 'the Director'), and he shall discharge his functions under the superintendence of the Attorney General.

(3) The Director may investigate any suspected offence which appears to him on reasonable grounds to involve serious or complex fraud.

(4) The Director may, if he thinks fit, conduct any such investigation in conjunction either with the police or with any other person who is, in the opinion of the Director, a proper person to be concerned in it.

(5) The Director may—
    (a) institute and have the conduct of any criminal proceedings which appear to him to relate to such fraud; and
    (b) take over the conduct of any such proceedings at any stage.

(6) The Director shall discharge such other functions in relation to fraud as may from time to time be assigned to him by the Attorney General.

(7) The Director may designate for the purposes of subsection (5) above any member of the Serious Fraud Office who is—
    (a) a barrister in England and Wales or Northern Ireland;
    (b) a solicitor of the Supreme Court; or
    (c) a solicitor of the Supreme Court of Judicature of Northern Ireland.

(8) Any member so designated shall, without prejudice to any functions which may have been assigned to him in his capacity as a member of that Office, have all the powers of the Director as to the institution and conduct of proceedings but shall exercise those powers under the direction of the Director.

(12) Any member so designated who is a barrister in Northern Ireland or a solicitor of the Supreme Court of Judicature of Northern Ireland shall have—
    (a) in any court the rights of audience enjoyed by solicitors of the Supreme Court of Judicature of Northern Ireland and, in the Crown Court in Northern Ireland, such additional rights of audience as may be given by virtue of subsection (14) below; and
    (b) in the Crown Court in Northern Ireland, the rights of audience enjoyed by barristers employed by the Director of Public Prosecutions for Northern Ireland.

(13) Subject to subsection (14) below, the reference in subsection (12)(a) above to rights of audience enjoyed by solicitors of the Supreme Court of Judicature of Northern Ireland is a reference to such rights enjoyed in the Crown Court in Northern Ireland as restricted by any direction given by the Lord Chief Justice of Northern Ireland under section 50 of the Judicature (Northern Ireland) Act 1978.

(14) For the purpose of giving any member so designated who is a barrister in Northern Ireland or a solicitor of the Supreme Court of Judicature of Northern Ireland additional rights of audience in the Crown Court in Northern Ireland, the Lord Chief Justice of Northern Ireland may direct that any direction given by him under the said section 50 shall not apply to such members.

(15) Schedule 1 to this Act shall have effect.

(16) For the purposes of this section (including that Schedule) references to the conduct of any proceedings include references to the proceedings being discontinued and to the taking of any steps (including the bringing of appeal and making of representations in respect of applications for bail) which may be taken in relation to them.

(17) In the application of this section (including that Schedule) to Northern Ireland references to the Attorney General are to be construed as references to him in his capacity as Attorney General for Northern Ireland.

2   Director's investigation powers

(1) The powers of the Director under this section shall be exercisable, but only for the purposes of an investigation under section 1 above, for, on a request made by the authority entitled to make such a request,] in any case in which it appears to him that there is good

reason to do so for the purpose of investigating the affairs, or any aspect of the affairs, of any person.

(1A) The authorities entitled to request the Director to exercise his powers under this section are—

(a) the Attorney-General of the Isle of Man, Jersey or Guernsey, acting under legislation corresponding to section 1 of this Act and having effect in the Island whose Attorney-General makes the request; and

(b) the Secretary of State acting under under section 15(2) of the Crime (International Co-operation Act) 2003, in response to a request received by him from a person mentioned in section 13(2) of that Act (an "overseas authority").

(1B) The Director shall not exercise his powers on a request from the Secretary of State acting in response to a request received from an overseas authority within subsection (1A)(b) above unless it appears to the Director on reasonable grounds that the offence in respect of which he has been requested to obtain evidence involves serious or complex fraud.

(2) The Director may by notice in writing require the person whose affairs are to be investigated ('the person under the investigation') or any other person whom he has reason to believe has relevant information to [answer questions or otherwise furnish information with respect to any matter relevant to the investigation at a specified place and either at a specified time or forthwith].

(3) The Director may by notice in writing require the person under investigation or any other person to produce at [such place as may be specified in the notice and either forthwith or at such time as may be so specified] any specified documents which appear to the Director to relate to any matter relevant to the investigation or any documents of a specified [description] which appear to him so to relate; and—

(a) if any such documents are produced, the Director may—
  (i) take copies or extracts from them;
  (ii) require the person producing them to provide an explanation of any of them;

(b) if any such documents are not produced, the Director may require the person who was required to produce them to state, to the best of his knowledge and belief, where they are.

(4) Where, on information on oath laid by a member of the Serious Fraud Office, a justice of the peace if satisfied, in relation to any documents, that there are reasonable grounds for believing—

(a) that—
  (i)   a person has failed to comply with an obligation under this section to produce them;
  (ii) it is not practicable to serve a notice under subsection (3) above in relation to them; or
  (iii) the service of such a notice in relation to them might seriously prejudice the investigation; and

(b) that they are on premises specified in the information, he may issue such a warrant as is mentioned in subsection (5) below.

(5) the warrant referred to above is a warrant authorising any constable—

(a) to enter (using such force as is reasonably necessary for the purpose) and search the premises, and

(b) to take possession of any documents appearing to be documents of the description specified in the information or to take in relation to any documents so appearing any other steps which may appear to be necessary for preserving them and preventing interference with them.

(6) Unless it is not practicable in the circumstances, a constable executing a warrant issued under subsection (4) above shall be accompanied by an appropriate person.

(6A) Where an appropriate person accompanies a constable, he may exercise the powers conferred by subsection (5) but only in the company, and under the supervision, of the constable.

(7) In this section 'appropriate person' means—

(a) a member of the Serious Fraud Office; or

(b) some person who is not a member of that Office but whom the Director has authorised to accompany the constable.

(8) A statement by a person in response to a requirement imposed by virtue of this section may only be used in evidence against him—

(a) on a prosecution for an offence under subsection (14) below; or

(b) on a prosecution for some other offence where in giving evidence he makes a statement inconsistent with it.

(8A) Any evidence obtained by the Director for use by an overseas authority shall be given to the overseas authority which requested it or given to the Secretary of State for forwarding to that overseas authority.

(8AA) However, the statement may not be used against that person by virtue of paragraph (b) of subsection (8) unless evidence relating to it is adduced, or a question relating to it is asked, by or on behalf of that person in the proceedings arising out of the prosecution.

(8B) . . .

(8C) Where any evidence obtained by the Director for use by an overseas authority consists of a document the original or a copy shall be forwarded, and where it consists of any other article the article itself or a description, photograph or other representation of it shall be forwarded, as may be necessary in order to comply with the request of the overseas authority.

(8D) The references in subsections (8A) to (8C) above to evidence obtained by the Director include references to evidence obtained by him by virtue of the exercise by a constable or by an appropriate person, in the course of a search authorised by a warrant issued under subsection (4) above, of powers conferred by *section 50* of the Criminal Justice and Police Act 2001.

(9) A person shall not under this section be required to disclose information or produce any document which he would be entitled to refuse to disclose or produce on grounds of legal professional privilege in proceedings in the High Court, except that a lawyer may be required to furnish the name and address of his client.

(10) A person shall not under this section be required to disclose any information or produce any document in respect of which he owes an obligation of confidence by virtue of carrying on any banking business unless—

(a) the person to whom the obligation of confidence is owed consents to the disclosure or production; or

(b) the Director has authorised the making of the requirement or, if it is impracticable for him to act personally, a member of the Serious Fraud Office designated by him for the purposes of this subsection has done so.

(11) Without prejudice to the power of the Director to assign functions to members of the Serious Fraud Office, the Director may authorise any competent investigator (other than a constable) who is not a member of that Office to exercise on his behalf all or any of the powers conferred by this section, but no such authority shall be granted except for the purpose of investigating the affairs, or any aspect of the affairs, of a person specified in the authority.

(12) No person shall be bound to comply with any requirement imposed by a person exercising powers by virtue of any authority granted under subsection (11) above unless he has, if required to do so, produced evidence of his authority.

(13) Any person who without reasonable excuse fails to comply with a requirement imposed on him under this section shall be guilty of an offence and liable on summary

conviction to imprisonment for a term not exceeding six months or to a fine not exceeding level 5 on the standard scale or to both.

(14) A person who, in purported compliance with a requirement under this section—

(a) makes a statement which he knows to be false or misleading in a material particular; or

(b) recklessly makes a statement which is false or misleading in a material particular, shall be guilty of an offence.

(15) A person guilty of an offence under subsection (14) above shall—

(a) on conviction on indictment, be liable to imprisonment for a term, not exceeding two years or to a fine or to both; and

(b) on summary conviction, be liable to imprisonment for a term not exceeding six months or to a fine not exceeding the statutory maximum, or to both.

(16) Where any person—

(a) knows or suspects that an investigation by the police or the Serious Fraud Office into serious or complex fraud is being or is likely to be carried out; and

(b) falsifies, conceals, destroys or otherwise disposes of, or causes or permits the falsification, concealment, destruction or disposal of documents which he knows or suspects are or would be relevant to such an investigation, he shall be guilty of an offence unless he proves that he had no intention of concealing the facts disclosed by the documents from persons carrying out such an investigation.

(17) A person guilty of an offence under subsection (16) above shall—

(a) on conviction on indictment, be liable to imprisonment for a term not exceeding 7 years or to a fine or to both; and

(b) on summary conviction, be liable to imprisonment for a term not exceeding 6 months or to a fine not exceeding the statutory maximum or to both.

(18) In this section, 'documents' includes information recorded in any form and, in relation to information recorded otherwise than in legible form, references to its production include references to producing a copy of the information in legible form; and 'evidence' (in relation to subsection (1A)(b), (8A), and (8C) above) includes documents and other articles.

Criminal Justice Act 1988

(1988, c. 33)

PART III   OTHER PROVISIONS ABOUT EVIDENCE IN CRIMINAL PROCEEDINGS

30 Expert reports

(1) An expert report shall be admissible as evidence in criminal proceedings, whether or not the person making it attends to give oral evidence in those proceedings.

(2) If it is proposed that the person making the report shall not give oral evidence, the report shall only be admissible with the leave of the court.

(3) For the purpose of determining whether to give leave the court shall have regard—

(a) to the contents of the report;

(b) to the reasons why it is proposed that the person making the report shall not give oral evidence;

(c) to any risk, having regard in particular to whether it is likely to be possible to controvert statements in the report if the person making it does not attend to give oral evidence in the proceedings, that its admission or exclusion will result in unfairness to the accused or, if there is more than one, to any of them; and

(d) to any other circumstances that appear to the court to be relevant.

(4) An expert report, when admitted, shall be evidence of any fact or opinion of which the person making it could have given oral evidence.

(4A) . . .

(5) In this section 'expert report' means a written report by a person dealing wholly or mainly with matters on which he is (or would if living be) qualified to give expert evidence.

31   Form of evidence and glossaries

For the purpose of helping members of juries to understand complicated issues of fact or technical terms Crown Court Rules may make provision:

(a) as to the furnishing of evidence in any form, notwithstanding the existence of admissible material from which the evidence to be given in that form would be derived; and

(b) as to the furnishing of glossaries for such purposes as may be specified; in any case where the court gives leave for, or requires, evidence or a glossary to be so furnished.

This section shall not apply to proceedings before a magistrates' court inquiring into an offence as examining justices.

32   Evidence through television links

(1) A person other than the accused may give evidence through a live television link in proceedings to which subsection (1A) below applies if—

(a) the witness is outside the United Kingdom;

but evidence may not be so given without the leave of the court.

(1A) This subsection applies—

(a) to trials on indictment, appeals to the criminal division of the Court of Appeal and hearings of references under section 9 of the Criminal Appeal Act 1995; and

(b) to proceedings in youth courts, appeals to the Crown Court arising out of such proceedings and hearings of references under section 11 of the Criminal Appeal Act 1995 so arising'..

(2) This subsection applies—

(a) to an offence which involves an assault on, or injury or a threat of injury to, a person;

(b) to an offence under section 1 of the Children and Young Persons Act 1933 (cruelty to persons under 16);

(c) to an offence under the Protection of Children Act 1978 or Part 1 of the Sexual Offences Act 2003; and

(d) to an offence which consists of attempting or conspiring to commit, or of aiding, abetting, counselling, procuring or inciting the commission of, an offence falling within paragraph (a), (b) or (c) above.

(3) A statement made on oath by a witness outside the United Kingdom and given in evidence through a link by virtue of this section shall be treated for the purposes of section 1 of the Perjury Act 1911 as having been made in the proceedings in which it is given in evidence.

(4) Without prejudice to the generality of any enactment conferring power to make rules to which this subsection applies, such rules may make such provision as appears to the authority making them to be necessary or expedient for the purposes of this section.

(5) The rules to which subsection (4) above applies are:

Magistrates' Courts Rules, Crown Court Rules and Criminal Appeal Rules.

34   Abolition of requirement of corroboration for unsworn evidence of children

(2) Any requirement whereby at a trial on indictment it is obligatory for the court to give the jury a warning about convicting the accused on the uncorroborated evidence of a child is abrogated.

(3) Unsworn evidence admitted by virtue of section 56 of the Youth Justice and Criminal Evidence Act 1999 may corroborate evidence (sworn or unsworn) given by any other person.

Road Traffic Offenders Act 1988
(1988, c. 53)

11 Evidence by certificate as to driver, user or owner

(1) In any proceedings in England and Wales for an offence to which this section applies, a certificate in the prescribed form, purporting to be signed by a constable and certifying that a person specified in the certificate stated to the constable—

(a) that a particular mechanically propelled vehicle was being driven or used by, or belonged to, that person on a particular occasion, or

(b) that a particular mechanically propelled vehicle on a particular occasion was used by, or belonged to, a firm and that he was, at the time of the statement, a partner in that firm, or

(c) that a particular mechanically propelled vehicle on a particular occasion was used by, or belonged to, a corporation and that he was, at the time of the statement, a director, officer or employee of that corporation, shall be admissible as evidence for the purpose of determining by whom the vehicle was being driven or used, or to whom it belonged, as the case may be, on that occasion.

(2) Nothing in subsection (1) above makes a certificate admissible as evidence in proceedings for an offence except in a case where and to the like extent to which oral evidence to the like effect would have been admissible in those proceedings.

(3) Nothing in subsection (1) above makes a certificate admissible as evidence in proceedings for an offence—

(a) unless a copy of it has, not less than seven days before the hearing or trial, been served in the prescribed manner on the person charged with the offence, or

(b) if that person, not later than three days before the hearing or trial or within such further time as the court in special circumstances allow, serves a notice in the prescribed form and manner on the prosecutor requiring the attendance at the trial of the person who signed the certificate.

12 Proof, in summary proceedings, of identity of driver of vehicle

(1) Where on the summary trial in England and Wales of an information for an offence to which this subsection applies—

(a) it is proved to the satisfaction of the court, on oath or in manner prescribed by rules made under section 144 of the Magistrates' Courts Act 1980, that a requirement under section 172(2) of the Road Traffic Act 1988 to give information as to the identity of the driver of a particular vehicle on the particular occasion to which the information relates has been served on the accused by post, and

(b) a statement in writing is produced to the court purporting to be signed by the accused that the accused was the driver of that vehicle on that occasion, the court may accept that statement as evidence that the accused was the driver of that vehicle on that occasion.

(2) Schedule 1 to this Act shows the offences to which subsection (1) above applies.

(3) Where on the summary trial in England and Wales of an information for an offence to which section 112 of the Road Traffic Regulation Act 1984 applies—

(a) it is proved to the satisfaction of the court, on oath or in manner prescribed by rules made under section 144 of the Magistrates' Courts Act 1980, that a requirement under section 112(2) of the Road Traffic Regulation Act 1984 to give information as to the identity of the driver of a particular vehicle on the particular occasion to which the information relates has been served on the accused by post, and

(b) a statement in writing is produced to the court purporting to be signed by the accused that the accused was the driver of that vehicle on that occasion, the court may accept that statement as evidence that the accused was the driver of that vehicle on that occasion.

(4) In summary proceedings in Scotland . . .

13   Admissibility of records as evidence

(1) This section applies to a statement contained in a document purporting to be—

(a) a part of the records maintained by the Secretary of State in connection with any functions exercisable by him by virtue of Part III of the Road Traffic Act 1988 or a part of any other records maintained by the Secretary of State with respect to vehicles, or

(b) a copy of a document forming part of those records, or

(c) a note of any information contained in those records,

and to be authenticated by a person authorised in that behalf by the Secretary of State.

(2) A statement to which this section applies shall be admissible in any proceedings as evidence (in Scotland, sufficient evidence) of any fact stated in it to the same extent as oral evidence of that fact is admissible in those proceedings.

(3) In the preceding subsections, except in Scotland—

'copy', in relation to a document, means anything onto which information recorded in the document has been copied, by whatever means and whether directly or indirectly;

'document' means anything in which information of any description is recorded; and

'statement' means any representation of fact, however made.

[(3A) In any case where—

(a) a person is convicted by a magistrates' court of a summary offence under the Traffic Acts or the Road Traffic (Driver Licensing and Information Systems) Act 1989,

(b) a statement to which this section applies is produced to the court in the proceedings,

(c) the statement specifies an alleged previous conviction of the accused of an offence involving obligatory endorsment or an order made on the conviction, and

(d) the accused is not present in person before the court when the statement is produced, the court may take account of the previous conviction or order as if the accused had appeared and admitted it.

(3B) Section 104 of the Magistrates' Courts Act 1980 (under which the previous convictions may be adduced in the absence of the accused after giving him seven days' notice of them) does not limit the effect of subsection (3A) above.]

(4) In any case where—

(a) a statement to which this section applies is produced to a magistrates' court in any proceedings for an offence involving obligatory or discretionary disqualification [other than a summary offence under any of the enactments mentioned in subsection (3A) above],

(b) the statement specifies an alleged previous conviction of an accused person of any such offence or any order made on the conviction,

(c) it is proved to the satisfaction of the court, on oath or in such manner as may be prescribed by rules under section 144 of the Magistrates' Courts Act 1980, that not less than seven days before the statement is so produced a notice was served on the accused, in such form and manner as may be so prescribed, specifying the previous conviction or order and stating that it is proposed to bring it to the notice of the court in the event of or, as the case may be, in view of his conviction, and

(d) the accused is not present in person before the court when the statement is so produced, the court may take account of the previous conviction or order as if the accused had appeared and admitted it.

(5) Nothing in the preceding provisions of this section enables evidence to be given in respect of any matter other than a matter of a description prescribed by regulations made by the Secretary of State.

(6) The power to make regulations under this section shall be exercisable by statutory instrument, which shall be subject to annulment in pursuance of a resolution of either House of Parliament.

16 Documentary evidence as to specimens in such proceedings

(1) Evidence of the proportion of alcohol or a drug in a specimen of breath, blood or urine may, subject to subsections (3) and (4) below and to section 15(5) of this Act, be given by the production of a document or documents purporting to be whichever of the following is appropriate, that is to say—

(a) a statement automatically produced by the device by which the proportion of alcohol in a specimen of breath was measured and a certificate signed by a constable (which may but need not be contained in the same document as the statement) that the statement relates to a specimen provided by the accused at the date and time shown in the statement, and

(b) a certificate signed by an authorised analyst as to the proportion of alcohol or any drug found in a specimen of blood or urine identified in the certificate.

(2) Subject to subsections (3) and (4) below, evidence that a specimen of blood was taken from the accused with his consent by a medical practitioner may be given by the production of a document purporting to certify that fact and to be signed by a medical practitioner.

(3) Subject to subsection (4) below—

(a) a document purporting to be such a statement or such a certificate (or both such a statement and such a certificate) as is mentioned in subsection (1)(a) above is admissible in evidence on behalf of the prosecution in pursuance of this section only if a copy of it either has been handed to the accused when the document was produced or has been served on him not later than seven days before the hearing, and

(b) any other document is so admissible only if a copy of it has been served on the accused not later than seven days before the hearing.

(4) A document purporting to be a certificate (or so much of a document as purports to be a certificate) is not so admissible if the accused, not later than three days before the hearing or within such further time as the court may in special circumstances allow, has served notice on the prosecutor requiring the attendance at the hearing of the person by whom the document purports to be signed.

(5) (*Applies to Scotland only.*)

(6) A copy of a certificate required by this section to be served on the accused or a notice required by this section to be served on the prosecutor may be served personally or sent by registered post or recorded delivery service.

(7) In this section 'authorised analyst' means—

(a) any person possessing the qualifications prescribed by regulations made under section 27 of the Food Safety Act 1990 as qualifying persons for appointment as public analysts under those Acts, and

(b) any other person authorised by the Secretary of State to make analyses for the purposes of this section.

18   Evidence by certificate as to registration of driving instructors and licences to give instruction

(1) A certificate signed by the Registrar and stating that, on any date—

(a) a person's name was, or was not, in the register,

(b) the entry of a person's name was made in the register or a person's name was removed from it,

(c) a person was, or was not, the holder of a current licence under section 129 of the Road Traffic Act 1988, or

(d) a licence under that section granted to a person came into force or ceased to be in force, shall be evidence, and in Scotland sufficient evidence, of the facts stated in the certificate in pursuance of this section.

(2) A certificate so stating and purporting to be signed by the Registrar shall be deemed to be so signed unless the contrary is proved.

(3) In this section 'current licence', 'Registrar' and 'register' have the same meanings as in Part V of the Road Traffic Act 1988.

20   Speeding offences etc.: admissibility of certain evidence

(1) Evidence (which in Scotland shall be sufficient evidence) of a fact relevant to proceedings for an offence to which this section applies may be given by the production of—

(a) a record produced by a prescribed device, and

(b) (in the same or another document) a certificate as to the circumstances in which the record was produced signed by a constable or by a person authorised by or on behalf of the chief officer of police for the police area in which the offence is alleged to have been committed;

but subject to the following provisions of this section.

(2) This section applies to—

(a) an offence under section 16 of the Road Traffic Regulation Act 1984 consisting in the contravention of a restriction on the speed of vehicles imposed under section 14 of that Act;

(b) an offence under subsection (4) of section 17 of that Act consisting in the contravention of a restriction on the speed of vehicles imposed under that section;

(c) an offence under section 88(7) of that Act (temporary minimum speed limits);

(d) an offence under section 89(1) of that Act (speeding offences generally);

(e) an offence under section 36(1) of the Road Traffic Act 1988 consisting in the failure to comply with an indication given by a light signal that vehicular traffic is not to proceed.

(3) The Secretary of State may by order amend subsection (2) above by making additions to or deletions from the list of offences for the time being set out there; and an order under this subsection may make such transitional provision as appears to him to be necessary or expedient.

(4) A record produced or measurement made by a prescribed device shall not be admissible as evidence of a fact relevant to proceedings for an offence to which this section applies unless—

(a) the device is of a type approved by the Secretary of State, and

(b) any conditions subject to which the approval was given are satisfied.

(5) Any approval given by the Secretary of State for the purposes of this section may be given subject to conditions as to the purposes for which, and the manner and other circumstances in which, any device of the type concerned is to be used.

(6) In proceedings for an offence to which this section applies, evidence (which in Scotland shall be sufficient evidence)—

(a) of a measurement made by a device, or of the circumstances in which it was made, or

(b) that a device was of a type approved for the purposes of this section, or that any conditions subject to which an approval was given were satisfied,

may be given by the production of a document which is signed as mentioned in subsection (1) above and which, as the case may be, gives particulars of the measurement or of the circumstances in which it was made, or states that the device was of such a type or that, to the best of the knowledge and belief of the person making the statement, all such conditions were satisfied.

(7) For the purposes of this section a document purporting to be a record of the kind mentioned in subsection (1) above, or to be a certificate or other document signed as mentioned in that subsection or in subsection (6) above, shall be deemed to be such a record, or to be so signed, unless the contrary is proved.

(8) Nothing in subsection (1) or (6) above makes a document admissible as evidence in proceedings for an offence unless a copy of it has, not less than seven days before the hearing or trial, been served on the person charged with the offence; and nothing in those subsections makes a document admissible as evidence of anything other than the matters shown on a record produced by a prescribed device if that person, not less than three days before the hearing or trial or within such further time as the court may in special circumstances allow, serves a notice on the prosecutor requiring attendance at the hearing or trial of the person who signed the document.

(9) In this section 'prescribed device' means device of a description specified in an order made by the Secretary of State.

(10) The powers to make orders under subsections (3) and (9) above shall be exercisable by statutory instrument, which shall be subject to annulment in pursuance of a resolution of either House of Parliament.

172　Duty to give information as to identity of driver etc. in certain circumstances

(1) This section applies—
  (a) to any offence under the preceding provisions of this Act except—
      (i) an offence under Part V, or
      (ii) an offence under section 13, 16, 51(2), 61(4), 67(9), 68(4), 96 or 120, and to an offence under section 178 of this Act,
  (b) to any offence under sections 25, 26 or 27 of the Road Traffic Offenders Act 1988,
  (c) to any offence against any other enactment relating to the use of vehicles on roads, except an offence under paragraph 8 of Schedule 1 to the Road Traffic (Driver Licensing and Information Systems) Act 1989, and
  (d) to manslaughter, or in Scotland culpable homicide, by the driver of a motor vehicle.

(2) Where the driver of a vehicle is alleged to be guilty of an offence to which this section applies—
  (a) the person keeping the vehicle shall give such information as to the identity of the driver as he may be required to give by or on behalf of a chief officer of police, and
  (b) any other person shall if required as stated above give any information which it is in his power to give and may lead to identification of the driver.

(3) Subject to the following provisions, a person who fails to comply with a requirement under subsection (2) above shall be guilty of an offence.

(4) A person shall not be guilty of an offence by virtue of paragraph (a) of subsection (2) above if he shows that he did not know and could not with reasonable diligence have ascertained who the driver of the vehicle was.

(5) Where a body corporate is guilty of an offence under this section and the offence is proved to have been committed with the consent or connivance of, or to be attributable to neglect on the part of, a director, manager, secretary or other similar officer of the body

corporate, or a person who was purporting to act in any such capacity, he, as well as the body corporate, is guilty of that offence and liable to be proceeded against and punished accordingly.

(6) Where the alleged offender is a body corporate, or in Scotland a partnership or an unincorporated association, or the proceedings are brought against him by virtue of sub-section (5) above or subsection (11) below, subsection (4) above shall not apply unless, in addition to the matters there mentioned, the alleged offender shows that no record was kept of the persons who drove the vehicle and that the failure to keep a record was reasonable.

(7) A requirement under subsection (2) may be made by written notice served by post; and where it is so made—

    (a) it shall have effect as a requirement to give the information within the period of 28 days beginning with the day on which the notice is served, and

    (b) the person on whom the notice is served shall not be guilty of an offence under this section if he shows either that he gave the information as soon as reasonably practicable after the end of that period or that it has not been reasonably practicable for him to give it.

(8) Where the person on whom a notice under subsection (7) above is to be served is a body corporate, the notice is duly served if it is served on the secretary or clerk of that body.

(9) For the purposes of section 7 of the Interpretation Act 1978 as it applies for the purposes of this section the proper address of any person in relation to the service on him of a notice under subsection (7) above is—

    (a) in the case of the secretary or clerk of a body corporate, that of the registered or principal office of that body or (if the body corporate is the registered keeper of the vehicle concerned) the registered address, and

    (b) in any other case, his last known address at the time of service.

(10) in this section—

'registered address', in relation to the registered keeper of a vehicle, means the address recorded in the record kept under the Vehicles (Excise) Act 1971 with respect to that vehicle as being that person's address, and

'registered keeper', in relation to a vehicle, means the person in whose name the vehicle is registered under that Act;

and references to the driver of a vehicle include references to the rider of a cycle.

(11) *(Applies to Scotland only.)*

Children Act 1989

(1989, c. 41)

96   Evidence given by, or with respect to, children

(1) Subsection (2) applies where a child who is called as a witness in any civil proceedings does not, in the opinion of the court, understand the nature of an oath.

(2) The child's evidence may be heard by the court if, in its opinion—

    (a) he understands that it is his duty to speak the truth; and

    (b) he has sufficient understanding to justify his evidence being heard.

(3) The Lord Chancellor may by order make provision for the admissibility of evidence which would otherwise be inadmissible under any rule of law relating to hearsay.

(4) An order under subsection (3) may only be made with respect to—

    (a) civil proceedings in general or such civil proceedings, or class of civil proceedings, as may be prescribed; and

    (b) evidence in connection with the upbringing, maintenance or welfare of a child.

(5) An order under subsection (3)—

(a) may, in particular, provide for the admissibility of statements which are made orally or in a prescribed form or which are recorded by any prescribed method of recording;

(b) may make different provision for different purposes and in relation to different descriptions of court; and

(c) may make such amendments and repeals in any enactment relating to evidence (other than in this Act) as the Lord Chancellor considers necessary or expedient in consequence of the provision made by the order.

(6) Subsection (5)(b) is without prejudice to section 104(4).

(7) In this section—

'civil proceedings' means civil proceedings, before any tribunal, in relation to which the strict rules of evidence apply, whether as a matter of law or agreement between the parties, and reference to 'the court' shall be construed accordingly; and

'prescribed' means prescribed by an order under subsection (3).

98   Self-incrimination

(1) In any proceedings in which a court is hearing an application for an order under Part IV or V, no person shall be excused from—

(a) giving evidence on any matter; or

(b) answering any question put to him in the course of his giving evidence,

on the ground that doing so might incriminate him or his spouse of an offence.

(2) A statement or admission made in such proceedings shall not be admissible in evidence against the person making it or his spouse in proceedings for an offence other than perjury.

Criminal Justice (International Co-operation) Act 1990

(1990, c. 5)

PART I   CRIMINAL PROCEEDINGS AND INVESTIGATIONS

Mutual service of process

5   Transfer of United Kingdom prisoner to give evidence or assist investigation overseas

(1) The Secretary of State may, if he thinks fit, issue a warrant providing for any person ('a prisoner') serving a sentence in a prison or other institution to which the Prison Act 1952 . . . applies to be transferred to a country or territory outside the United Kingdom for the purpose—

(a) of giving evidence in criminal proceedings there; or

(b) of being identified in, or otherwise by his presence assisting, such proceedings or the investigation of an offence.

(2) No warrant shall be issued under this section in respect of any prisoner unless he has consented to being transferred as mentioned in subsection (1) above and that consent may be given either—

(a) by the prisoner himself; or

(b) in circumstances in which it appears to the Secretary of State inappropriate, by reason of the prisoner's physical or mental condition or his youth, for him to act for himself, by a person appearing to the Secretary of State to be an appropriate person to act on his behalf;

but a consent once given shall not be capable of being withdrawn after the issue of the warrant.

(3) The effect of a warrant under this section shall be to authorise—

(a) the taking of the prisoner to a place in the United Kingdom and his delivery at a place of departure from the United Kingdom into the custody of a person representing the appropriate authority of the country or territory to which the prisoner is to be transferred; and

(b) the bringing of the prisoner back to the United Kingdom and his transfer in custody to the place where he is liable to be detained under the sentence to which he is subject.

(3A) A warrant under this section has effect in spite of section 127(1) of the Army Act 1955, section 127(1) of the Air Force Act 1955 or section 82A(1) of the Naval Discipline Act 1957 (restriction on removing persons out of the United Kingdom who are serving military sentences).

(4) Where a warrant has been issued in respect of a prisoner under this section he shall be deemed to be in legal custody at any time when, being in the United Kingdom or on board a British ship, British aircraft or British hovercraft, he is being taken under the warrant to or from any place or being kept in custody under the warrant.

(5) A person authorised by or for the purposes of the warrant to take the prisoner to or from any place or to keep him in custody shall have all the powers, authority, protection and privileges—

(a) of a constable in the part of the United Kingdom in which that person is for the time being; or

(b) if he is outside the United Kingdom, of a constable in the part of the United Kingdom to or from which the prisoner is to be taken under the warrant.

(6) If the prisoner escapes or is unlawfully at large, he may be arrested without warrant by a constable and taken to any place to which he may be taken under the warrant issued under this section.

(7) In subsection (4) above—

'British aircraft' means a British-controlled aircraft within the meaning of section 92 of the Civil Aviation Act 1982 (application of criminal law to aircraft) or one of Her Majesty's aircraft;

'British hovercraft' means a British-controlled hovercraft within the meaning of that section as applied in relation to hovercraft by virtue of provisions made under the Hovercraft Act 1968 or one of Her Majesty's hovercraft;

'British ship' means a British ship for the purposes of the Merchant Shipping Acts 1894 to 1988 or one of Her Majesty's ships;

and in this subsection references to Her Majesty's aircraft, hovercraft or ships are references to aircraft, hovercraft or, as the case may be, ships belonging to or exclusively employed in the service of Her Majesty in right of the Government of the United Kingdom.

(8) In subsection (6) above 'constable', in relation to any part of the United Kingdom, means any person who is a constable in that or any other part of the United Kingdom or any person who, at the place in question has, under any enactment including subsection (5) above, the powers of a constable in that or any other part of the United Kingdom.

(9) The section applies to a person in custody awaiting trial or sentence and a person committed to prison for default in paying a fine as it applies to a prisoner and the reference in subsection (3)(b) above to a sentence shall be construed accordingly.

(10) (*Applies to Northern Ireland.*)

6 Transfer of overseas prisoner to give evidence or assist investigation in the United Kingdom

(1) This section has effect where—

(a) a witness order has been made or a witness summons or citation issued in criminal proceedings in the United Kingdom in respect of a person ('a prisoner') who is detained in custody in a country or territory outside the United Kingdom by virtue of a sentence or order of a court or tribunal exercising criminal jurisdiction in that country or territory; or

(b) it appears to the Secretary of State that it is desirable for a prisoner to be identified in, or otherwise by his presence to assist, such proceedings or the investigation in the United Kingdom of an offence.

(2) If the Secretary of State is satisfied that the appropriate authority in the country or territory where the prisoner is detained will make arrangements for him to come to the United Kingdom to give evidence pursuant to the witness order, witness summons or citation or, as the case may be, for the purpose mentioned in subsection (1)(b) above, he may issue a warrant under this section.

(3) No warrant shall be issued under this section in respect of any prisoner unless he has consented to being brought to the United Kingdom to give evidence as aforesaid or, as the case may be, for the purpose mentioned in subsection (1)(b) above but a consent once given shall not be capable of being withdrawn after the issue of the warrant.

(4) The effect of the warrant shall be to authorise—

(a) the bringing of the prisoner to the United Kingdom;

(b) the taking of the prisoner to, and his detention in custody at, such place or places in the United Kingdom as are specified in the warrant; and

(c) the returning of the prisoner to the country or territory from which he has come.

(5) Subsection (4) to (8) of section 5 above shall have effect in relation to a warrant issued under this section as they have effect in relation to a warrant issued under that section.

(6) A person shall not be subject to the Immigration Act 1971 in respect of his entry into or presence in the United Kingdom in pursuance of a warrant under this section but if the warrant ceases to have effect while he is still in the United Kingdom—

(a) he shall be treated for the purposes of that Act as if he has then illegally entered the United Kingdom; and

(b) the provisions of Schedule 2 to that Act shall have effect accordingly except that paragraph 20(1) (liability of carrier for expenses of custody etc. of illegal entrant) shall not have effect in relation to directions for his removal given by virtue of this subsection.

(7) This section applies to a person detained in custody in a country or territory outside the United Kingdom in consequence of having been transferred there—

(a) from the United Kingdom under the Repatriation of Prisoners Act 1984; or

(b) under any similar provision or arrangement from any other country or territory, as it applies to a person detained as mentioned in subsection (1) above.

Additional co-operation powers

(9) (*Applies to Northern Ireland.*)

9   Enforcement of overseas forfeiture orders

(1) Her Majesty may by Order in Council provide for the enforcement in the United Kingdom of any order which—

(a) is made by a court in a country or territory outside the United Kingdom designated for the purposes of this section by the Order in Council; and

(b) is for the forfeiture and destruction, or the forfeiture and other disposal, of anything in respect of which an offence to which this section applies has been committed or which was used in connection with the commission of such an offence.

(2) Without prejudice to the generality of subsection (1) above an Order in Council under this section may provide for the registration by a court in the United Kingdom of any order as a condition of its enforcement and prescribe requirements to be satisfied before an order can be registered.

(3) An Order in Council under this section may include such supplementary and incidental provisions as appear to Her Majesty to be necessary or expedient and may apply for the purposes of the Order (with such modification as appear to Her Majesty to be appropriate) any provisions relating to confiscation or forfeiture orders under any other enactment.

(4) An Order in Council under this section may make different provision for different cases.

(5) No Order in Council shall be made under this section unless a draft of it has been laid before and approved by a resolution of each House of Parliament.

(6) This section applies to any offence which corresponds to or is similar to an offence under the Misuse of Drugs Act 1971, a drug trafficking offence as defined in section 1(3) of the Drug Trafficking Act 1994, . . . relates or an offence to which Part VI of the Criminal Justice Act 1988 applies.

Supplementary

10   Rules of court

(1) Provision may be made by rules of court for any purpose for which it appears to the authority having power to make the rules that it is necessary or expedient that provision should be made in connection with any of the provisions of this Part of this Act.

(2) Rules made for the purposes of Schedule 1 to this Act may, in particular, make provision with respect to the persons entitled to appear or take part in the proceedings to which that Schedule applies and for excluding the public from any such proceedings.

(3) An Order in Council under section 9 above may authorise the making of rules of court for any purpose specified in the Order.

(4) (*Applies to Scotland.*)

(5) This section is without prejudice to the generality of any existing power to make rules.

PART IV   GENERAL

30   Expenses and receipts

(1) Any expenses incurred by the Secretary of State under this Act shall be defrayed out of money provided by Parliament.

(2) Any money representing cash forfeited under Part III of this Act or accrued interest thereon shall be paid into the Consolidated Fund.

31   Consequential and other amendments, repeals and revocation

(1) The enactments and instruments mentioned in Schedule 4 to this Act shall have effect with the amendments there specified, being amendments consequential on or otherwise relating to the provisions of this Act.

(2) For the avoidance of doubt it is hereby declared that the amendment by that Schedule of the definition of 'drug trafficking offence' in section 38(1) of the Drug Trafficking Offences Act 1986 applies to that definition as applied by any other enactment, including this Act.

(3) The enactments mentioned in Schedule 5 to this Act are hereby repealed to the extent specified in the third column of that Schedule.

(4) (*Applies to Northern Ireland.*)

32   Short title, commencement and extent

(1) This Act may be cited as the Criminal Justice (International Co-operation) Act 1990.

(2) This Act shall come into force on such day as may be appointed by the Secretary of State by an order made by statutory instrument and different days may be appointed for different provisions and different purposes and for different parts of the United Kingdom.

(3) (*Applies to Northern Ireland.*)

(4) . . .

SCHEDULES
Section 4(6)   SCHEDULE 1   UNITED KINGDOM EVIDENCE
FOR USE OVERSEAS: PROCEEDINGS OF NOMINATED COURT

Securing attendance of witnesses

1. The court shall have the like powers for securing the attendance of a witness for the purpose of the proceedings as it has for the purpose of other proceedings before the court.

2. (*Applies to Scotland.*)

Power to administer oaths

3. The court may in the proceedings take evidence on oath.

Privilege of witnesses

4.—(1) A person shall not be compelled to give in the proceedings any evidence which he could not be compelled to give—

   (a) in criminal proceedings in the part of the United Kingdom in which the nominated court exercises jurisdiction; or

   (b) subject to sub-paragraph (2) below, in criminal proceedings in the country or territory from which the request for the evidence has come.

(2) Sub-paragraph (1)(b) above shall not apply unless the claim of the person questioned to be exempt from giving the evidence is conceded by the court, tribunal or authority which made the request.

(3) Where such a claim made by any person is not conceded as aforesaid he may (subject to the other provisions of this paragraph) be required to give the evidence to which the claim relates but the evidence shall not be transmitted to the court, tribunal or authority which requested it if a court in the country or territory in question, on the matter being referred to it, upholds the claim.

(4) Without prejudice to sub-paragraph (1) above a person shall not be compelled under this Schedule to give any evidence if his doing so would be prejudicial to the security of the United Kingdom; and a certificate signed by or on behalf of the Secretary of State . . . to the effect that it would be so prejudicial for that person to do so shall be conclusive evidence of that fact.

(5) Without prejudice to sub-paragraph (1) above a person shall not be compelled under this Schedule to give any evidence in his capacity as an officer or servant of the Crown.

(6) In this paragraph references to giving evidence include references to answering any question and to producing any document or other article and the reference in sub-paragraph (3) above to the transmission of evidence given by a person shall be construed accordingly.

Transmission of evidence

5.—(1) The evidence received by the court shall be furnished to the Secretary of State . . . for transmission to the court, tribunal or authority that made the request.

(2) If in order to comply with the request it is necessary for the evidence to be accompanied by any certificate, affidavit or other verifying document, the court shall also furnish for transmission such document of that nature as may be specified in the notice nominating the court.

(3) Where the evidence consists of a document the original or a copy shall be transmitted, and where it consists of any other article the article itself or a description, photograph or other representation of it shall be transmitted, as may be necessary in order to comply with the request.

Supplementary

6. For the avoidance of doubt it is hereby declared that the Bankers Books' Evidence Act 1879 applies to the proceedings as it applies to other proceedings before the court.

7. No order for costs shall be made in the proceedings.

Sexual Offences (Amendment) Act 1992
(1992, c. 34)

1 Anonymity of victims of certain offences

(1) Where an allegation has been made that an offence to which this Act applies has been committed against a person, no matter relating to that person shall during that person's lifetime be included in any publication.

(2) Where a person is accused of an offence to which this Act applies, no matter likely to lead members of the public to identify a person as the person against whom the offence is alleged to have been committed ('the complainant') shall during the complainant's lifetime be included in any publication.

(3) This section—

    (a) does not apply in relation to a person by virtue of subsection (1) at any time after a person has been accused of the offence, and

    (b) in its application in relation to a person by virtue of subsection (2), has effect subject to any direction given under section 3.

(3A) The matters relating to a person in relation to which the restrictions imposed by subsection (1) or (2) apply (if their inclusion in any publication is likely to have the result mentioned in that subsection) include in particular—

    (a) the person's name,

    (b) the person's address,

    (c) the identity of any school or other educational establishment attended by the person,

    (d) the identity of any place of work, and

    (e) any still or moving picture of the person.

(4) Nothing in this section prohibits the inclusion in a publication of matter consisting only of a report of criminal proceedings other than proceedings at, or intended to lead to, or on an appeal arising out of, a trial at which the accused is charged with the offence.

2 Offences to which this Act applies

(1) This Act applies to the following offences against the law of England and Wales—

    (a) any offence under any of the provisions of the Sexual Offences Act 1956 mentioned in subsection (2);

    (aa) rape;

    (ab) burglary with intent to rape;

    (b) any offence under section 128 of the Mental Health Act 1959 (intercourse with mentally handicapped person by hospital staff etc.);

    (c) any offence under section 1 of the Indecency with Children Act 1960 (indecent conduct towards young child);

    (d) any offence under section 54 of the Criminal Law Act 1977 (incitement by man of his grand-daughter, daughter or sister under the age of 16 to commit incest with him);

(da) any offence under any of the provisions of Part 1 of the Sexual Offences Act 2003 except section 64, 65, 69 or 71;

(e) any attempt to commit any of the offences mentioned in paragraphs (aa) to (d);

(f) any conspiracy to commit any of those offences;

(g) any incitement of another to commit any of those offences;

(h) aiding, abetting, counselling or procuring the commission of any of the offences mentioned in paragraphs (aa) to (e) and (g).

(2) The provisions of the Act of 1956 are—

(a) section 2 (procurement of a woman by threats);

(b) section 3 (procurement of a woman by false pretences);

(c) section 4 (administering drugs to obtain intercourse with a woman);

(d) section 5 (intercourse with a girl under the age of 13);

(e) section 6 (intercourse with a girl between the ages of 13 and 16);

(f) section 7 (intercourse with a mentally handicapped person);

(g) section 9 (procurement of a mentally handicapped person);

(h) section 10 (incest by a man);

(i) section 11 (incest by a woman);

(j) section 12 (buggery);

(k) section 14 (indecent assault on a woman);

(l) section 15 (indecent assault on a man);

(m) section 16 (assault with intent to commit buggery);

(n) section 17 (abduction of women by force).

(3) This Act applies to the following offences against the law of Northern Ireland—

(a) rape;

(b) burglary with intent to rape;

(c) any offence under any of the following provisions of the Offences against the Person Act 1861—

    (i) section 52 (indecent assault on a female);

    (ii) section 53 so far as it relates to abduction of a woman against her will;

    (iii) section 61 (buggery);

    (iv) section 62 (attempt to commit buggery, assault with intent to commit buggery or indecent assault on a male);

(d) any offence under any of the following provisions of the Criminal Law Amendment Act 1885—

    (i) section 3 (procuring unlawful carnal knowledge of woman by threats, false pretences or administering drugs);

    (ii) section 4 (unlawful carnal knowledge, or attempted unlawful carnal knowledge, of a girl under 14);

    (iii) section 5 (unlawful carnal knowledge of a girl under 17);

(e) any offence under any of the following provisions of the Punishment of Incest Act 1908—

    (i) section 1 (incest, attempted incest by males);

    (ii) section 2 (incest by females over 16);

(f) (*Applies to Northern Ireland only.*)

(g) (*Applies to Northern Ireland only.*)

(h) (*Applies to Northern Ireland only.*)

(i) any attempt to commit any of the offences mentioned in paragraphs (a) to (e);

(j) any conspiracy to commit any of those offences;

(k) any incitement of another to commit any of those offences;

(l) aiding, abetting, counselling or procuring the commission of any of the offences mentioned in paragraphs (a) to (e) and (k).

3   Power to displace section 1

(1) If, before the commencement of a trial at which a person is charged with an offence to which this Act applies, he or another person against whom the complainant may be expected to give evidence at the trial, applies to the judge for a direction under this subsection and satisfies the judge—

(a) that the direction is required for the purpose of inducing persons who are likely to be needed as witnesses at the trial to come forward; and

(b) that the conduct of the applicant's defence at the trial is likely to be substantially prejudiced if the direction is not given,

the judge shall direct that section 1 shall not, by virtue of the accusation alleging the offence in question, apply in relation to the complainant.

(2) If at a trial the judge is satisfied—

(a) that the effect of section 1 is to impose a substantial and unreasonable restriction upon the reporting of proceedings at the trial, and

(b) that it is in the public interest to remove or relax the restriction,

he shall direct that that section shall not apply to such matter as is specified in the direction.

(3) A direction shall not be given under subsection (2) by reason only of the outcome of the trial.

(4) If a person who has been convicted of an offence and has given notice of appeal against the conviction, or notice of an application for leave so to appeal, applies to the appellate court for a direction under this subsection and satisfies the court—

(a) that the direction is required for the purpose of obtaining evidence in support of the appeal; and

(b) that the applicant is likely to suffer substantial injustice if the direction is not given,

the court shall direct that section 1 shall not, by virtue of an accusation which alleges an offence to which this Act applies and is specified in the direction, apply in relation to a complainant so specified.

(5) A direction given under any provision of this section does not affect the operation of section 1 at any time before the direction is given.

(6) In subsections (1) and (2), 'judge' means—

(a) in the case of an offence which is to be tried summarily or for which the mode of trial has not been determined, any justice of the peace acting for the petty sessions area concerned; and

(b) in any other case, any judge of the Crown Court in England and Wales.

(6A) (*Applies to Northern Ireland only.*)

(7) If, after the commencement of a trial at which a person is charged with an offence to which this Act applies, a new trial of the person for that offence is ordered, the commencement of any previous trial shall be disregarded for the purposes of subsection (1).

4   Special rules for cases of incest or buggery

(1) In this section—

'section 10 offence' means an offence under section 10 of the Sexual Offences Act 1956 (incest by a man) or an attempt to commit that offence;

'section 11 offence' means an offence under section 11 of that Act (incest by a woman) or an attempt to commit that offence;

'section 12 offence' means an offence under section 12 of that Act (buggery) or an attempt to commit that offence.

(2) Section 1 does not apply to a woman against whom a section 10 offence is alleged to have been committed if she is accused of having committed a section 11 offence against the man who is alleged to have committed the section 10 offence against her.

(3) Section 1 does not apply to a man against whom a section 11 offence is alleged to have been committed if he is accused of having committed a section 10 offence against the woman who is alleged to have committed the section 11 offence against him.

(4) Section 1 does not apply to a person against whom a section 12 offence is alleged to have been committed if that person is accused of having committed a section 12 offence against the person who is alleged to have committed the section 12 offence against him.

(5) Subsection (2) does not affect the operation of this Act in relation to anything done at any time before the woman is accused.

(6) Subsection (3) does not affect the operation of this Act in relation to anything done at any time before the man is accused.

(7) Subsection (4) does not affect the operation of this Act in relation to anything done at any time before the person mentioned first in that subsection is accused.

(8) (*Applies to Northern Ireland only.*)

5   Offences

(1) If any matter is included in a publication in contravention of section 1, the following persons shall be guilty of an offence and liable on summary conviction to a fine not exceeding level 5 on the standard scale—

    (a) where the publication is a newspaper or periodical, any proprietor, any editor and any publisher of the newspaper or periodical;

    (b) where the publication is a relevant programme—

        (i) any body corporate engaged in providing the programme service in which the programme is included; and

        (ii) any person having functions in relation to the programme corresponding to those of an editor of a newspaper;

    (c) in the case of any other publication, any person publishing it.

(2) Where a person is charged with an offence under this section in respect of the inclusion of any matter in a publication, it shall be a defence, subject to subsection (3), to prove that the publication in which the matter appeared was one in respect of which the person against whom the offence mentioned in section 1 is alleged to have been committed had given written consent to the appearance of matter of that description.

(3) Written consent is not a defence if it is proved that any person interfered unreasonably with the peace or comfort of the person giving the consent, with intent to obtain it, or that person was under the age of 16 at the time when it was given.

(4) Proceedings for an offence under this section shall not be instituted except by or with the consent of the Attorney General, if the offence is alleged to have been committed in England and Wales. . . .

(5) Where a person is charged with an offence under this section it shall be a defence to prove that at the time of the alleged offence he was not aware, and neither suspected nor had reason to suspect, that the publication included the matter in question.

(5A) Where—

    (a) a person is charged with an offence under this section, and

    (b) the offence relates to the inclusion of any matter in a publication in contravention of section 1(1),

it shall be a defence to prove that at the time of the alleged offence he was not aware, and neither suspected nor had reason to suspect, that the allegation in question had been made.

254254254

Sexual Offences (Amendment) Act 1992

(6) Where an offence under this section committed by a body corporate is proved to have been committed with the consent or connivance of, or to be attributable to any neglect on the part of—

    (a) a director, manager, secretary or other similar officer of the body corporate, or

    (b) a person purporting to act in any such capacity,

he as well as the body corporate shall be guilty of the offence and liable to be proceeded against and punished accordingly.

(7) In relation to a body corporate whose affairs are managed by its members 'director', in subsection (6), means a member of the body corporate.

(8) (*Applies to Scotland only.*)

6 Interpretation etc.

(1) In this Act—

'complainant' has the meaning given in section 1(2);

'picture' includes a likeness however produced;

'publication' includes any speech, writing, relevant programme or other communication on whatever form, which is addressed to the public at large or any section of the public (and for this purpose every relevant programme shall be taken to be so addressed), but does not include an indictment or other document prepared for use in particular legal proceedings;

'relevant programme' means a programme included in a programme service, within the meaning of the Broadcasting Act 1990.

(2) For the purposes of this Act—

    (a) where it is alleged that an offence to which this Act applies has been committed, the fact that any person has consented to an act which, on any prosecution for that offence, would fall to be proved by the prosecution, does not prevent that person from being regarded as a person against whom the alleged offence was committed; and

    (b) where a person is accused of an offence of incest or buggery, the other party to the act in question shall be taken to be a person against whom the offence was committed even though he consented to that act.

(2A) For the purposes of this Act, where it is alleged or there is an accusation—

    (a) that an offence of conspiracy or incitement of another to commit an offence mentioned in section 2(1) (aa) to (d) or (3)(a) to (h) has been committed, or

    (b) that an offence of aiding, abetting, counselling or procuring the commission of an offence of incitement of another to commit an offence mentioned in section 2(1)(aa) to (d) or (3)(a) to (h) has been committed, the person against whom the substantive offence is alleged to have been intended to be committed shall be regarded as the person against whom the conspiracy or incitement is alleged to have been committed.

In this subsection, 'the substantive offence' means the offence to which the alleged conspiracy or incitement related; and

    (b) in subsection (3), after the words 'references in' there shall be inserted the words 'subsection (2A) and in'.

(3) For the purposes of this Act, a person is accused of an offence if—

    (a) an information is laid, . . . alleging that he has committed the offence,

    (b) he appears before a court charged with the offence,

    (c) a court before which he is appearing sends him to the Crown Court for trial on a new charge alleging the offence, or

    (d) a bill of indictment charging him with the offence is preferred before a court in which he may lawfully be indicted for the offence,

and references in section 3 to an accusation alleging an offence shall be construed accordingly.

(4) Nothing in this Act affects any prohibition or restriction imposed by virtue of any other enactment upon a publication or upon matter included in a relevant programme.

7 Courts-martial

(1) This Act shall have effect with the modifications set out in subsection (2) in any case where, in pursuance of any provision of the Army Act 1955, the Air Force Act 1955 or the Naval Discipline Act 1957, a person is charged with an offence to which this Act applies by virtue of section 2(1).

(2) The modifications are—

    (a) any reference to a trial shall be read as a reference to a trial by court-martial;

    (c) in section 3(1) any reference to a judge, in relation to the person charged with the offence, shall be read as a reference to the judge advocate appointed to conduct proceedings under section 3(1) relating to the offence (whether or not also appointed to conduct other preliminary proceedings relating to the offence);

    (d) in section 3(2), any reference to a judge shall be read as a reference to the judge advocate appointed to be a member of the court-martial; and

    (f) for section 6(3)(a) to (d) there shall be substituted 'he is charged, in pursuance of any provision of the Army Act 1955, the Air Force Act 1955 or the Naval Discipline Act 1957, with an offence to which this Act applies'.

(4) In section 36(1) of the Courts-Martial (Appeals) Act 1968 (which provides that certain powers of the Courts-Martial Appeal Court may be exercised by a single judge) after the words 'section 5(1)(d) of that Act' there shall be inserted 'or section 3(4) of the Sexual Offences (Amendment) Act 1992'.

8 Short title, commencement and extent, etc.

(1) This Act may be cited as the Sexual Offences (Amendment) Act 1992.

(2) This Act and the Sexual Offences Acts 1956 to 1976 may be cited together as the Sexual Offences Acts 1956 to 1992.

(3) This section comes into force on the passing of this Act but otherwise this act comes into force on such date as may be appointed by order made by the Secretary of State.

(4) The power to make an order under subsection (3) shall be exercisable by statutory instrument.

(5) Different dates may be appointed for different provisions of this Act and for different purposes.

(6) . . .

(7) This Act, so far as it relates to proceedings before a court-martial or the Courts-Martial Appeal Court, applies to such proceedings wherever they may take place (whether in the United Kingdom or elsewhere)

Vehicle Excise and Registration Act 1994
(1994, c. 22)

Evidence

51 Admissions

(1) This section applies where in any proceedings in England and Wales . . . for an offence under section 29, 34 or 43A—

    (a) it is appropriately proved that there has been served on the accused by post a requirement under section 46(1) or (2) to give information as to the identity of—

      (i) the driver of, or a person who used, a particular vehicle, or

      (ii) the person who kept a particular vehicle on a road,

on the particular occasion on which the offence is alleged to have been committed, and

    (b) a statement in writing is produced to the court purporting to be signed by the accused that he was—

      (i) the driver of, or a person who used, that vehicle, or

      (ii) the person who kept that vehicle on a road,

on that occasion.

(2) Where this section applies, the court may accept the statement as evidence that the accused was—

    (a) the driver of, or a person who used, that vehicle, or

    (b) the person who kept that vehicle on a road,

on that occasion.

(3) In subsection (1) 'appropriately proved' means proved to the satisfaction of the court—

    (a) on oath, or

    (b) in the manner prescribed—

      (i) in England and Wales, by rules under section 144 of the Magistrates' Courts Act 1980, or

      (ii) *(Applies to Northern Ireland only.)*

[51A Admissions: offences under regulations

(1) Subsection (2) applies in relation to any proceedings in England, Wales or Northern Ireland against a person for an offence on the grounds that—

    (a) a vehicle has been sold or disposed of by, through or to him and he has failed to furnish particulars prescribed by regulations made by virtue of section 22(1)(d);

    (b) a vehicle has been sold or disposed of by or through him and he has failed to furnish a document prescribed by regulations made by virtue of section 22(1)(dd); or

    (c) he has surrendered, or not renewed, a vehicle licence or is keeping an unlicensed vehicle and has failed to furnish any particulars or make a declaration prescribed by regulations made by virtue of section 22(1D).

(2) If—

    (a) it is appropriately proved that there has been served on the accused by post a requirement under section 46A to give information as to the identity of the person keeping the vehicle at a particular time, and

    (b) a statement in writing is produced to the court purporting to be signed by the accused that he was keeping the vehicle at that time, the court may accept the statement as evidence that the accused was keeping the vehicle at that time.

(3) In subsection (2) 'appropriately proved' has the same meaning as in section 51.]

52   Records

(1) A statement to which this section applies is admissible in any proceedings as evidence
... of any fact stated in it with respect to matters prescribed by regulations made by the
Secretary of State to the same extent as oral evidence of that fact is admissible in the
proceedings.

(2) This section applies to a statement contained in a document purporting to be—

(a) a part of the records maintained by the Secretary of State in connection with any
functions exercisable by him under or by virtue of this Act,

(b) a copy of a document forming part of those records, or

(c) a note of any information contained in those records,

and to be authenticated by a person authorised to do so by the Secretary of State.

'(3) In this section . . .—

"document" means anything in which information of any description is recorded;

"copy", in relation to a document, means anything onto which information recorded
in the document has been copied, by whatever means and whether directly or indirectly;
and

"statement" means any representation of fact, however made'.

(6) Nothing in subsection (4) or (5) limits to civil proceedings the references to
proceedings in subsection (1).'.

53   Burden of proof

Where in any proceedings for an offence under section 29, 34, 37 or 45 any question arises
as to—

(a) the number of vehicles used,

(b) the character, weight or cylinder capacity of a vehicle,

(c) the seating capacity of a vehicle, or

(d) the purpose for which a vehicle has been used,

the burden of proof in respect of the matter lies on the accused.

...

55   Guilty plea by absent accused.

(1) This section applies where, under section 12(2) of the Magistrates' Courts Act 1980
..., a person is convicted in his absence of [an offence under section 29 or 35A] and it is
appropriately proved that a relevant notice was served on the accused with the summons.

(2) In subsection (1) 'appropriately proved' means—

(a) ..., proved to the satisfaction of the court—

(i) on oath, or

(ii) in the manner prescribed by rules under section 144 of the Magistrates' Courts
Act 1980, and

(b) (*Applies to Northern Ireland only.*)

(3) In this section 'relevant notice', in relation to an accused, means a notice stating that,
in the event of his being convicted of the offence, it will be alleged that an order requiring him
to pay an amount specified in the notice falls to be made by the court—

(a) in a case within subsection (1)(a), under section 30, or

(b) in a case within subsection (1)(b), under section 36.

(4) Where this section applies, the court shall proceed under section 30, or section 36, as
if the amount specified in the relevant notice were the amount calculated in accordance with
that section.

(5) The court shall not so proceed if it is stated in the notification purporting to be given
by or on behalf of the accused under—

(a) section 12(2) of the Magistrates' Courts Act 1980, or

(b) (*Applies to Northern Ireland only.*)

that the amount specified in the relevant notice is inappropriate.

Criminal Justice and Public Order Act 1994
(1994, c. 33)

Corroboration

32   Abolition of corroboration rules

(1) Any requirement whereby at a trial on indictment it is obligatory for the court to give the jury a warning about convicting the accused on the uncorroborated evidence of a person merely because that person is—

    (a) an alleged accomplice of the accused, or

    (b) where the offence charged is a sexual offence, the person in respect of whom it is alleged to have been committed,

is hereby abrogated.

(2) In section 34(2) of the Criminal Justice Act 1988 (abolition of requirement of corroboration warning in respect of evidence of a child) the words from 'in relation to' to the end shall be omitted.

(3) Any requirement that—

    (a) is applicable at the summary trial of a person for an offence, and

    (b) corresponds to the requirement mentioned in subsection (1) above or that mentioned in section 34(2) of the Criminal Justice Act 1988,

is hereby abrogated.

(4) Nothing in this section applies in relation to—

    (a) any trial, or

    (b) any proceedings before a magistrates' court as examining justices,

which began before the commencement of this section.

33   Abolition of corroboration requirements under Sexual Offences Act 1956

(1) The following provisions of the Sexual Offences Act 1956 (which provide that a person shall not be convicted of the offence concerned on the evidence of one witness only unless the witness is corroborated) are hereby repealed—

    (a) section 2(2) (procurement of woman by threats),

    (b) section 3(2) (procurement of woman by false pretences),

    (c) section 4(2) (administering drugs to obtain or facilitate intercourse),

    (d) section 22(2) (causing prostitution of women), and

    (e) section 23(2) (procuration of girl under twenty-one).

(2) Nothing in this section applies in relation to—

    (a) any trial, or

    (b) any proceedings before a magistrates' court as examining justices,

which began before the commencement of this section.

Inferences from accused's silence

34   Effect of accused's failure to mention facts when questioned or charged

(1) Where, in any proceedings against a person for an offence, evidence is given that the accused—

    (a) at any time before he was charged with the offence, on being questioned under caution by a constable trying to discover whether or by whom the offence had been committed, failed to mention any fact relied on in his defence in those proceedings; or

    (b) on being charged with the offence or officially informed that he might be prosecuted for it, failed to mention any such fact, being a fact which in the circumstances existing at the time the accused could reasonably have been expected to mention when so questioned, charged or informed, as the case may be, subsection (2) below applies.

(2) Where this subsection applies—

    (a) ...

    (b) a judge, in deciding whether to grant an application made by the accused under—

        (i) paragraph 2 of Schedule 3 to the Crime and Disorder Act 1998;

    (c) the court, in determining whether there is a case to answer; and

    (d) the court or jury, in determining whether the accused is guilty of the offence charged,

may draw such inferences from the failure as appear proper.

(2A) Where the accused was at an authorised place of detention at the time of failure, subsections (1) and (2) above do not apply if he had not been allowed an opportunity to consult a solicitor prior to being questioned, charged or informed as mentioned in subsection (1) above.

(3) Subject to any directions by the court, evidence tending to establish the failure may be given before or after evidence tending to establish the fact which the accused is alleged to have failed to mention.

(4) This section applies in relation to questioning by persons (other than constables) charged with the duty of investigating offences or charging offenders as it applies in relation to questioning by constables; and in subsection (1) above 'officially informed' means informed by a constable or any such person.

(5) This section does not—

    (a) prejudice the admissibility in evidence of the silence or other reaction of the accused in the face of anything said in his presence relating to the conduct in respect of which he is charged, in so far as evidence thereof would be admissible apart from this section; or

    (b) preclude the drawing of any inference from any such silence or other reaction of the accused which could properly be drawn apart from this section.

(6) This section does not apply in relation to a failure to mention a fact if the failure occurred before the commencement of this section.

35 Effect of accused's silence at trial

(1) At the trial of any person for an offence, subsections (2) and (3) below apply unless—

    (a) the accused's guilt is not in issue; or

    (b) it appears to the court that the physical or mental condition of the accused makes it undesirable for him to give evidence;

but subsection (2) below does not apply if, at the conclusion of the evidence for the prosecution, his legal representative informs the court that the accused will give evidence or, where he is unrepresented, the court ascertains from him that he will give evidence.

(2) Where this subsection applies, the court shall, at the conclusion of the evidence for the prosecution, satisfy itself (in the case of proceedings on indictment with a jury, in the presence of the jury) that the accused is aware that the stage has been reached at which evidence can be given for the defence and that he can, if he wishes, give evidence and that, if he chooses not to give evidence, or having been sworn, without good cause refuses to answer any question, it will be permissible for the court or jury to draw such inferences as appear proper from his failure to give evidence or his refusal, without good cause, to answer any question.

(3) Where this subsection applies, the court or jury, in determining whether the accused is guilty of the offence charged, may draw such inferences as appear proper from the failure of the accused to give evidence or his refusal, without good cause, to answer any question.

(4) This section does not render the accused compellable to give evidence on his own behalf, and he shall accordingly not be guilty of contempt of court by reason of a failure to do so.

(5) For the purposes of this section a person who, having been sworn, refuses to answer any question shall be taken to do so without good cause unless—
- (a) he is entitled to refuse to answer the question by virtue of any enactment, whenever passed or made, or on the ground of privilege; or
- (b) the court in the exercise of its general discretion excuses him from answering it.

(7) This section applies—
- (a) in relation to proceedings on indictment for an offence, only if the person charged with the offence is arraigned on or after the commencement of this section;
- (b) in relation to proceedings in a magistrates' court, only if the time when the court begins to receive evidence in the proceedings falls after the commencement of this section.

36 Effect of accused's failure or refusal to account for objects, substances or marks

(1) Where—
- (a) a person is arrested by a constable, and there is—
  - (i) on his person; or
  - (ii) in or on his clothing or footwear; or
  - (iii) otherwise in his possession; or
  - (iv) in any place in which he is at the time of his arrest,

any object, substance or mark, or there is any mark on any such object; and
- (b) that or another constable investigating the case reasonably believes that the presence of the object, substance or mark may be attributable to the participation of the person arrested in the commission of an offence specified by the constable; and
- (c) the constable informs the person arrested that he so believes, and requests him to account for the presence of the object, substance or mark; and
- (d) the person fails or refuses to do so,

then if, in any proceedings against the person for the offence so specified, evidence of those matters is given, subsection (2) below applies.

(2) Where this subsection applies—
- (a) ...
- (b) a judge, in deciding whether to grant an application made by the accused under—
  - (i) paragraph 2 of Schedule 3 to the Crime and Disorder Act 1998;
- (c) the court, in determining whether there is a case to answer; and
- (d) the court or jury, in determining whether the accused is guilty of the offence charged,

may draw such inferences from the failure or refusal as appear proper.

(3) Subsections (1) and (2) above apply to the condition of clothing or footwear as they apply to a substance or mark thereon.

(4) Subsections 1 and 2 above do not apply unless the accused was told in ordinary language by the constable when making the request mentioned in subsection (1)(c) above what the effect of this section would be if he failed or refused to comply with the request.

(4A) Where the accused was at an authorised place of detention at the time of the failure or refusal, subsections (1) and (2) above do not apply if he had not been allowed an opportunity to consult a solicitor prior to the request being made.

(5) This section applies in relation to officers of customs and excise as it applies in relation to constables.

(6) This section does not preclude the drawing of any inference from a failure or refusal of the accused to account for the presence of an object, substance or mark or from the condition of clothing or footwear which could properly be drawn apart from this section.

(7) This section does not apply in relation to a failure or refusal which occurred before the commencement of this section.

37 Effect of accused's failure or refusal to account for presence at a particular place

(1) Where—

    (a) a person arrested by a constable was found by him at a place at or about the time the offence for which he was arrested is alleged to have been committed; and

    (b) that or another constable investigating the offence reasonably believes that the presence of the person at that place and at that time may be attributable to his participation in the commission of the offence; and

    (c) the constable informs the person that he so believes, and requests him to account for that presence; and

    (d) the person fails or refuses to do so, then if, in any proceedings against the person for the offence, evidence of those matters is given, subsection (2) below applies.

(2) Where this subsection applies—

    (a) . . .

    (b) a judge, in deciding whether to grant an application made by the accused under—

        (i) paragraph 2 of Schedule 3 to the Crime and Disorder Act 1998;

    (c) the court, in determining whether there is a case to answer, and

    (d) the court or jury, in determining whether the accused is guilty of the offence charged,

may draw such inferences from the failure or refusal as appear proper.

(3) Subsections (1) and (2) do not apply unless the accused was told in ordinary language by the constable when making the request mentioned in subsection (1)(c) above what the effect of this section would be if he failed or refused to comply with the request.

(3A) Where the accused was at an authorised place of detention at the time of the failure or refusal, subsections (1) and (2) do not apply if he had not been allowed an opportunity to consult a solicitor prior to the request being made.

(4) This section applies in relation to officers of customs and excise as it applies in relation to constables.

(5) This section does not preclude the drawing of any inference from a failure or refusal of the accused to account for his presence at a place which could properly be drawn apart from this section.

(6) This section does not apply in relation to a failure or refusal which occurred before the commencement of this section.

38 Interpretation and savings for sections 34, 35, 36 and 37

(1) In sections 34, 35, 36 and 37 of this Act—

'legal representative' means an authorised advocate or authorised litigator, as defined by section 119(1) of the Courts and Legal Services Act 1990; and

'place' includes any building or part of a building, any vehicle, vessel, aircraft or hovercraft and any other place whatsoever.

(2) In sections 34(2), 35(3), 36(2) and 37(2), references to an offence charged include references to any other offence of which the accused could lawfully be convicted on that charge.

(2A) In each of sections 34(2A), 36(4A) and 37(3A) 'authorised place of detention' means—

    (a) a police station; or

    (b) any other place prescribed for the purpose of that provision by the Secretary of State;

and the power to make an order under this subsection shall be exercisable by statutory instrument which shall be subject to annulment on pursuance of a resolution of either House of Parliament.

(3) A person shall not have the proceedings against him transferred to the Crown Court for trial, have a case to answer or be convicted of an offence solely on an inference drawn from such a failure or refusal as is mentioned in section 34(2), 35(3), 36(2) or 37(2).

(4) A judge shall not refuse to grant such an application as is mentioned in section 34(2)(b), 36(2)(b) and 37(2)(b) solely on an inference drawn from such a failure as is mentioned in section 34(2), 36(2) or 37(2).

(5) Nothing in sections 34, 35, 36 or 37 prejudices the operation of a provision of an enactment which provides (in whatever words) that any answer or evidence given by a person in specified circumstances shall not be admissible in evidence against him or some other person in any proceedings or class of proceedings (however described, and whether civil or criminal).

In this subsection, the reference to giving evidence is a reference to giving evidence in any manner, whether by furnishing information, making discovery, producing documents or otherwise.

(6) Nothing in sections 34, 35, 36 or 37 prejudices any power of a court, in any proceedings, to exclude evidence (whether by preventing questions being put or otherwise) at its discretion.

39 Power to apply sections 34 to 38 to armed forces

(1) The Secretary of State may by order direct that any provision of sections 34 to 38 of this Act shall apply, subject to such modifications as he may specify, to any proceedings to which this section applies.

(2) This section applies—

- (a) to proceedings whereby a charge is dealt with summarily under Part II of the Army Act 1955;
- (b) to proceedings whereby a charge is dealt with summarily under Part II of the Air Force Act 1955;
- (c) to proceedings whereby a charge is summarily tried under Part II of the Naval Discipline Act 1957;
- (d) to proceedings before a court martial constituted under the Army Act 1955;
- (e) to proceedings before a court martial constituted under the Air Force Act 1955;
- (f) to proceedings before a court martial constituted under the Naval Discipline Act 1957;
- (g) to proceedings before a disciplinary court constituted under section 52G of the Naval Discipline Act 1957;
- (h) to proceedings before the Courts-Martial Appeal Court;
- (i) to proceedings before a Standing Civilian Court;

and it applies wherever the proceedings take place.

(3) An order under this section shall be made by statutory instrument and shall be subject to annulment in pursuance of a resolution of either House of Parliament.

Criminal Appeal Act 1995

(1995, c. 35)

8 The commission

(1) There shall be a body corporate to be known as the Criminal Cases Review Commission.

(2) The Commission shall not be regarded as the servant or agent of the Crown or as enjoying any status, immunity or privilege of the Crown; and the Commission's property shall not be regarded as property of, or held on behalf of, the Crown.

(3) The Commission shall consist of not fewer than eleven members.

(4) The members of the Commission shall be appointed by Her Majesty on the recommendation of the Prime Minister.

(5) At least one third of the members of the Commission shall be persons who are legally qualified; and for this purpose a person is legally qualified if—

    (a) he has a ten year general qualification, within the meaning of section 71 of the Courts and Legal Services Act 1990, or

    (b) he is a member of the Bar of Northern Ireland, or solicitor of the Supreme Court of Northern Ireland, of at least ten years' standing.

(6) At least two thirds of the members of the Commission shall be persons who appear to the Prime Minister to have knowledge or experience of any aspect of the criminal justice system and of them at least one shall be a person who appears to him to have knowledge or experience of any aspect of the criminal justice system in Northern Ireland; and for the purposes of this subsection the criminal justice system includes, in particular, the investigation of offences and the treatment of offenders.

(7) Schedule 1 (further provisions with respect to the Commission) shall have effect.

References to court

9   Cases dealt with on indictment in England and Wales

(1) Where a person has been convicted of an offence on indictment in England and Wales, the Commission—

    (a) may at any time refer the conviction to the Court of Appeal, and

    (b) (whether or not they refer the conviction) may at any time refer to the Court of Appeal any sentence (not being a sentence fixed by law) imposed on, or in subsequent proceedings relating to, the conviction.

(2) A reference under subsection (1) of a person's conviction shall be treated for all purposes as an appeal by the person under section 1 of the 1968 Act against the conviction.

(3) A reference under subsection (1) of a sentence imposed on, or in subsequent proceedings relating to, a person's conviction on an indictment shall be treated for all purposes as an appeal by the person under section 9 of the 1968 Act against—

    (a) the sentence, and

    (b) any other sentence (not being a sentence fixed by law) imposed on, or in subsequent proceedings relating to, the conviction or any other conviction on the indictment.

(4) On a reference under subsection (1) of a person's conviction on an indictment the Commission may give notice to the Court of Appeal that any other conviction on the indictment which is specified in the notice is to be treated as referred to the Court of Appeal under subsection (1).

(5) Where a verdict of not guilty by reason of insanity has been returned in England and Wales in the case of a person, the Commission may at any time refer the verdict to the Court of Appeal; and a reference under this subsection shall be treated for all purposes as an appeal by the person under section 12 of the 1968 Act against the verdict.

(6) Where a jury in England and Wales has returned findings that a person is under a disability and that he did the act or made the omission charged against him, the Commission may at any time refer either or both of those findings to the Court of Appeal; and a reference under this subsection shall be treated for all purposes as an appeal by the person under section 15 of the 1968 Act against the finding or findings referred.

10   (*Applies to Northern Ireland only.*)

11   Cases dealt with summarily in England and Wales

(1) Where a person has been convicted of an offence by a magistrates' court in England and Wales, the Commission—

(a) may at any time refer the conviction to the Crown Court, and

(b) (whether or not they refer the conviction) may at any time refer to the Crown Court any sentence imposed on, or in subsequent proceedings relating to, the conviction.

(2) A reference under subsection (1) of a person's conviction shall be treated for all purposes as an appeal by the person under section 108(1) of the Magistrates' Courts Act 1980 against the conviction (whether or not he pleaded guilty).

(3) A reference under subsection (1) of a sentence imposed on, or in subsequent proceedings relating to, a person's conviction shall be treated for all purposes as an appeal by the person under section 108(1) of the Magistrates' Courts Act 1980 against—

(a) the sentence, and

(b) any other sentence imposed on, or in subsequent proceedings relating to, the conviction or any related conviction.

(4) On a reference under subsection (1) of a person's conviction the Commission may give notice to the Crown Court that any related conviction which is specified in the notice is to be treated as referred to the Crown Court under subsection (1).

(5) For the purposes of this section convictions are related if they are convictions of the same person by the same court on the same day.

(6) On a reference under this section the Crown Court may not award any punishment more severe than that awarded by the court whose decision is referred.

(7) The Crown Court may grant bail to a person whose conviction or sentence has been referred under this section; and any time during which he is released on bail shall not count as part of any term of imprisonment or detention under his sentence.

12   (*Applies to Northern Ireland only.*)

13   Conditions for making of references

(1) A reference of a conviction, verdict, finding or sentence shall not be made under any of sections 9 to 12 unless—

(a) the Commission consider that there is a real possibility that the conviction, verdict, finding or sentence would not be upheld were the reference to be made,

(b) the Commission so consider—

(i) in the case of a conviction, verdict or finding, because of an argument, or evidence, not raised in the proceedings which led to it or on any appeal or application for leave to appeal against it, or

(ii) in the case of a sentence, because of an argument on a point of law, or information, not so raised, and

(c) an appeal against the conviction, verdict, finding or sentence has been determined or leave to appeal against it has been refused.

(2) Nothing in subsection (1)(b)(i) or (c) shall prevent the making of a reference if it appears to the Commission that there are exceptional circumstances which justify making it.

14   Further provisions about references

(1) A reference of a conviction, verdict, finding or sentence may be made under any of sections 9 to 12 either after an application has been made by or on behalf of the person to whom it relates or without an application having been so made.

(2) In considering whether to make a reference of a conviction, verdict, finding or sentence under any of sections 9 to 12 the Commission shall have regard to—

(a) any application or representations made to the Commission by or on behalf of the person to whom it relates,

(b) any other representations made to the Commission in relation to it, and

(c) any other matters which appear to the Commission to be relevant.

(3) In considering whether to make a reference under section 9 or 10 the Commission may at any time refer any point on which they desire the assistance of the Court of Appeal to that Court for the Court's opinion on it; and on a reference under this subsection the Court of Appeal shall consider the point referred and furnish the Commission with the Court's opinion on the point.

(4) Where the Commission make a reference under any of sections 9 to 12 the Commission shall—

    (a) give the court to which the reference is made a statement of the Commission's reasons for making the reference, and

    (b) send a copy of the statement to every person who appears to the Commission to be likely to be a party to any proceedings on the appeal arising from the reference.

(5) Where a reference under any of sections 9 to 12 is treated as an appeal against any conviction, verdict, finding or sentence, the appeal may be on any ground relating to the conviction, verdict, finding or sentence (whether or not the ground is related to any reason given by the Commission for making the reference).

(6) In every case in which—

    (a) an application has been made to the Commission by or on behalf of any person for the reference under any of sections 9 to 12 of any conviction, verdict, finding or sentence, but

    (b) the Commission decide not to make a reference of the conviction, verdict, finding or sentence,

the Commission shall give a statement of the reasons for their decision to the person who made the application.

Investigations and assistance

15 Investigations for Court of Appeal

(1) Where a direction is given by the Court of Appeal under section 23A(1) of the 1968 Act or section 25A(1) of the 1980 Act the Commission shall investigate the matter specified in the direction in such manner as the Commission think fit.

(2) Where, in investigating a matter specified in such a direction, it appears to the Commission that—

    (a) another matter (a 'related matter') which is relevant to the determination of the case by the Court of Appeal ought, if possible, to be resolved before the case is determined by that Court, and

    (b) an investigation of the related matter is likely to result in the Court's being able to resolve it,

the Commission may also investigate the related matter.

(3) The Commission shall—

    (a) keep the Court of Appeal informed as to the progress of the investigation of any matter specified in a direction under section 23A(1) of the 1968 Act or section 25A(1) of the 1980 Act, and

    (b) if they decide to investigate any related matter, notify the Court of Appeal of their decision and keep the Court informed as to the progress of the investigation.

(4) The Commission shall report to the Court of Appeal on the investigation of any matter specified in direction under section 23A(1) of the 1968 Act or section 25A(1) of the 1980 Act when—

    (a) they complete the investigation of that matter and of any related matter investigated by them, or

    (b) they are directed to do so by the Court of Appeal,

whichever happens first.

266   Criminal Appeal Act 1995
(5) A report under subsection (4) shall include details of any inquiries made by or for the Commission in the investigation of the matter specified in the direction or any related matter investigated by them.

(6) Such a report shall be accompanied—

(a) by any statements and opinions received by the Commission in the investigation of the matter specified in the direction or any related matter investigated by them, and

(b) subject to subsection (7), by any reports so received.

(7) Such a report need not be accompanied by any reports submitted to the Commission under section 20(6) by an investigating officer.

16 Assistance in connection with prerogative of mercy

(1) Where the Secretary of State refers to the Commission any matter which arises in the consideration of whether to recommend the exercise of Her Majesty's prerogative of mercy in relation to a conviction and on which he desires their assistance, the Commission shall—

(a) consider the matter referred, and

(b) give to the Secretary of State a statement of their conclusions on it;

and the Secretary of State shall, in considering whether so to recommend, treat the Commission's statement as conclusive of the matter referred.

(2) Where in any case the Commission are of the opinion that the Secretary of State should consider whether to recommend the exercise of Her Majesty's prerogative of mercy in relation to the case they shall give him the reasons for their opinion.

Supplementary powers

17 Power to obtain documents etc.

(1) This section applies where the Commission believe that a person serving in a public body has possession or control of a document or other material which may assist the Commission in the exercise of any of their functions.

(2) Where it is reasonable to do so, the Commission may require the person who is the appropriate person in relation to the public body—

(a) to produce the document or other material to the Commission or to give the Commission access to it, and

(b) to allow the Commission to take away the document or other material or to make and take away a copy of it in such form as they think appropriate,

and may direct that person that the document or other material must not be destroyed, damaged or altered before the direction is withdrawn by the Commission.

(3) The documents and other material covered by this section include, in particular, any document or other material obtained or created during any investigation or proceedings relating to—

(a) the case in relation to which the Commission's function is being or may be exercised, or

(b) any other case which may be in any way connected with that case (whether or not any function of the Commission could be exercised in relation to that other case).

(4) The duty to comply with a requirement under this section is not affected by any obligation of secrecy or other limitation on disclosure (including any such obligation or limitation imposed by or by virtue of any enactment) which would otherwise prevent the production of the document or other material to the Commission or the giving of access to it to the Commission.

18 Government documents etc. relating to current or old cases

(1) Section 17 does not apply to any document or other material in the possession or control of a person serving in a government department if the document or other material—

(a) is relevant to a case to which this subsection applies, and

(b) is in the possession or control of the person in consequence of the Secretary of State's consideration of the case.

(2) Subsection (1) applies to a case if the Secretary of State—

(a) is, immediately before the day on which the repeal by this Act of section 17 of the 1968 Act or of section 14 of the 1980 Act comes into force, considering the case with a view to deciding whether to make a reference under that section or whether to recommend the exercise of Her Majesty's prerogative of mercy in relation to a conviction by a magistrates' court, or

(b) has at any earlier time considered the case with a view to deciding whether to make such a reference or whether so to recommend.

(3) The Secretary of State shall give to the Commission any document or other material which—

(a) contains representations made to him in relation to any case to which this subsection applies, or

(b) was received by him in connection with any such case otherwise than from a person serving in a government department,

and may give to the Commission any document or other material which is relevant to any such case but does not fall within paragraph (a) or (b).

(4) Subsection (3) applies to a case if—

(a) the Secretary of State is, immediately before the day on which the repeal by this Act of section 17 of the 1968 Act or of section 14 of the 1980 Act comes into force, considering the case with a view to deciding whether to make a reference under that section or whether to recommend the exercise of Her Majesty's prerogative of mercy in relation to a conviction by a magistrates' court, or

(b) the Secretary of State has at any earlier time considered the case with a view to deciding whether to make such a reference, or whether so to recommend, and the Commission at any time notify him that they wish subsection (3) to apply to the case.

19 Power to require appointment of investigating officers

(1) Where the Commission believe that inquiries should be made for assisting them in the exercise of any of their functions in relation to any case they may require the appointment of an investigating officer to carry out the inquiries.

(2) Where any offence to which the case relates was investigated by persons serving in a public body, a requirement under this section may be imposed—

(a) on the person who is the appropriate person in relation to the public body, or

(b) where the public body has ceased to exist, on any chief officer to police or on the person who is the appropriate person in relation to any public body which appears to the Commission to have functions which consist of or include functions similar to any of those of the public body which has ceased to exist.

(3) Where no offence to which the case relates was investigated by persons serving in a public body, a requirement under this section may be imposed on any chief officer of police.

(4) A requirement under this section imposed on a chief officer of police may be—

(a) a requirement to appoint a person serving in the police force in relation to which he is the chief officer of police, or

(b) a requirement to appoint a person serving in another police force selected by the chief officer.

(5) A requirement under this section imposed on a person who is the appropriate person in relation to a public body other than a police force may be—

(a) a requirement to appoint a person serving in the public body, or

(b) a requirement to appoint a person serving in a police force, or in a public body (other than a police force) having functions which consist of or include the investigation of offences, selected by the appropriate person.

(6) The Commission may direct—

(a) that a person shall not be appointed, or

(b) that a police force or other public body shall not be selected,

under subsection (4) or (5) without the approval of the Commission.

(7) Where an appointment is made under this section by the person who is the appropriate person in relation to any public body, that person shall inform the Commission of the appointment; and if the Commission are not satisfied with the person appointed they may direct that—

(a) the person who is the appropriate person in relation to the public body shall, as soon as is reasonably practicable, select another person in his place and notify the Commission of the proposal to appoint the other person, and

(b) the other person shall not be appointed without the approval of the Commission.

20 Inquiries by investigating officers

(1) A person appointed as the investigating officer in relation to a case shall undertake such inquiries as the Commission may from time to time reasonably direct him to undertake in relation to the case.

(2) A person appointed as an investigating officer shall be permitted to act as such by the person who is the appropriate person in relation to the public body in which he is serving.

(3) Where the chief officer of an England and Wales police force appoints a member of the Royal Ulster Constabulary as an investigating officer, the member appointed shall have in England and Wales the same powers and privileges as a member of the police force has there as a constable; and where the Chief Constable of the Royal Ulster Constabulary appoints a member of an England and Wales police force as an investigating officer, the member appointed shall have in Northern Ireland the same powers and privileges as a member of the Royal Ulster Constabulary has there as a constable.

(4) The Commission may take any steps which they consider appropriate for supervising the undertaking of inquiries by an investigating officer.

(5) The Commission may at any time direct that a person appointed as the investigating officer in relation to a case shall cease to act as such; but the making of such a direction shall not prevent the Commission from imposing a requirement under section 19 to appoint another investigating officer in relation to the case.

(6) When a person appointed as the investigating officer in relation to a case has completed the inquiries which he has been directed by the Commission to undertake in relation to the case, he shall—

(a) prepare a report of his findings,

(b) submit it to the Commission, and

(c) send a copy of it to the person by whom he was appointed.

(7) When a person appointed as the investigating officer in relation to a case submits to the Commission a report of his findings he shall also submit to them any statements, opinions and reports received by him in connection with the inquiries which he was directed to undertake in relation to the case.

21 Other powers

(1) Sections 17 to 20 are without prejudice to the taking by the Commission of any steps which they consider appropriate for assisting them in the exercise of any of their functions including, in particular—

(a) undertaking, or arranging for others to undertake, inquiries, and

(b) obtaining, or arranging for others to obtain, statements, opinions and reports.

22   Meaning of 'public body' etc.

(1) In sections 17, 19 and 20 and this section 'public body' means—

(a) any police force,

(b) any government department, local authority or other body constituted for purposes of the public service, local government or the administration of justice, or

(c) any other body whose members are appointed by Her Majesty, any Minister or any government department or whose revenues consist wholly or mainly of money provided by Parliament or appropriated by Measure of the Northern Ireland Assembly.

(2) In sections 19 and 20 and this section—

(a) 'police force' includes the Royal Ulster Constabulary and the Royal Ulster Constabulary Reserve, the National Crime Squad and any body of constables maintained otherwise than by a police authority,

(b) references to the chief officer of police—

(i)   in relation to the Royal Ulster Constabulary and the Royal Ulster Constabulary Reserve, are to the Chief Constable of the Constabulary,

(ii) in relation to the National Crime Squad, are to the Director General of the Squad, and

(iii) in relation to any other police force maintained otherwise than by a police authority, are to the chief constable.

(c) references to an England and Wales police force are to a police force maintained under section 2 of the Police Act 1996, the metropolitan police force or the City of London police force, or the National Crime Squad,

(d) 'police authority' includes the Service Authority for the National Crime Squad, and

(e) references to a person serving in a police force or to a member of a police force, in relation to the National Crime Squad, mean a police member of that Squad appointed under section 55(1)(b) of the Police Act 1997.

(3) In section 18 and this section—

(a) references to a government department include a Northern Ireland department and the Office of the Director of Public Prosecutions for Northern Ireland, and

(b) 'Minister' means a Minister of the Crown as defined by section 8 of the Ministers of the Crown Act 1975 but also includes the head of a Northern Ireland department.

(4) In sections 17, 19 and 20 'the appropriate person' means—

(a)   in relation to a police force, the chief officer of police,

(aa) in relation to the National Crime Intelligence Service, the Director General of that service,

(b)   in relation to the Crown Prosecution Service, the Director of Public Prosecutions,

(c)   in relation to the Office of the Director of Public Prosecutions for Northern Ireland, that Director,

(d)   in relation to the Serious Fraud Office, the Director of the Serious Fraud Office,

(e)   in relation to the Inland Revenue, the Commissioners of Inland Revenue,

(f)   in relation to the Customs and Excise, the Commissioners of Customs and Excise,

(g)   in relation to any government department not within any of the preceding paragraphs, the Minister in charge of the department, and

(h)   in relation to any public body not within any of the preceding paragraphs, the public body itself (if it is a body corporate) or the person in charge of the public body (if it is not).

Disclosure of information

23   Offence of disclosure

(1) A person who is or has been a member or employee of the Commission shall not disclose any information obtained by the Commission in the exercise of any of their functions unless the disclosure of the information is excepted from this section by section 24.

(2) A person who is or has been an investigating officer shall not disclose any information obtained by him in his inquiries unless the disclosure of the information is excepted from this section by section 24.

(3) A member of the Commission shall not authorise—

(a) the disclosure by an employee of the Commission of any information obtained by the Commission in the exercise of any of their functions, or

(b) the disclosure by an investigating officer of any information obtained by him in his inquiries,

unless the authorisation of the disclosure of the information is excepted from this section by section 24.

(4) A person who contravenes this section is guilty of an offence and liable on summary conviction to a fine of an amount not exceeding level 5 on the standard scale.

24   Exceptions from obligations of non-disclosure

(1) The disclosure of information, or the authorisation of the disclosure of information, is expected from section 23 by this section if the information is disclosed, or is authorised to be disclosed—

(a) for the purposes of any criminal, disciplinary or civil proceedings,

(b) in order to assist in dealing with an application made to the Secretary of State for compensation for a miscarriage of justice,

(c) by a person who is a member or an employee of the Commission either to another person who is a member or an employee of the Commission or to an investigating officer,

(d) by an investigating officer to a member or an employee of the Commission,

(e) in any statement or report required by this Act,

(f) in or in connection with the exercise of any function under this Act, or

(g) in any circumstances in which the disclosure of information is permitted by an order made by the Secretary of State.

(2) The disclosure of information is also excepted from section 23 by this section if the information is disclosed by an employee of the Commission, or an investigating officer, who is authorised to disclose the information by a member of the Commission.

(3) The disclosure of information, or the authorisation of the disclosure of information, is also excepted from section 23 by this section if the information is disclosed, or is authorised to be disclosed, for the purposes of—

(a) the investigation of an offence, or

(b) deciding whether to prosecute a person for an offence,

unless the disclosure is or would be prevented by an obligation of secrecy or other limitation on disclosure (including any such obligation or limitation imposed by or by virtue of an enactment) arising otherwise than under that section.

(4) Where the disclosure of information is excepted from section 23 by subsection (1) or (2), the disclosure of the information is not prevented by any obligation of secrecy or other limitation on disclosure (including any such obligation or limitation imposed by or by virtue of an enactment) arising otherwise than under that section.

(5) The power to make an order under subsection (1)(g) is excercisable by statutory instrument which shall be subject to annulment in pursuance of a resolution of either House of Parliament.

25   Consent to disclosure

(1) Where a person on whom a requirement is imposed under section 17 notifies the Commission that any information contained in any document or other material to which the requirement relates is not to be disclosed by the Commission without his prior consent, the Commission shall not disclose the information without such consent.

(2) Such consent may not be withheld unless—

(a) (apart from section 17) the person would have been prevented by any obligation of secrecy or other limitation on disclosure from disclosing the information to the Commission, and

(b) it is reasonable for the person to withhold his consent to disclosure of the information by the Commission.

(3) An obligation of secrecy or other limitation on disclosure which applies to a person only where disclosure is not authorised by another person shall not be taken for the purposes of subsection (2)(a) to prevent the disclosure by the person of information to the Commission unless—

(a) reasonable steps have been taken to obtain the authorisation of the other person, or

(b) such authorisation could not reasonably be expected to be obtained.

PART IV   SUPPLEMENTARY

30   Interpretation

(1) In this Act—

'the 1968 Act' means the Criminal Appeal Act 1968,

'the 1980 Act' means the Criminal Appeal (Northern Ireland) Act 1980,

'the Commission' means the Criminal Cases Review Commission,

'enactment' includes an enactment comprised in Northern Ireland legislation, and

'investigating officer' means a person appointed under section 19 to carry out inquiries.

(2) In this Act 'sentence'—

(a) in section 9 has the same meaning as in the 1968 Act,

(b) in section 10 has the same meaning as in Part I of the 1980 Act,

(c) in section 11 has the same meaning as in section 108 of the Magistrates' Courts Act 1980, and

(d) in section 12 has the same meaning as in Article 140(1) of the Magistrates' Courts (Northern Ireland) Order 1981.

33   Extent

(1) The provisions of Part I and III and of Schedules 2 and 3 have the same extent as the enactments which they amend or repeal.

(2) Section 8 and Schedule 1 and sections 13 to 25 extend only to England and Wales and Northern Ireland.

(3) Section 9 and 11 extend only to England and Wales.

(4) . . .

Section 8   **SCHEDULE 1**

Evidence

7.   A document purporting to be—

(a) duly executed under the seal of the Commission, or

(b) signed on behalf of the Commission,

shall be received in evidence and, unless the contrary is proved, taken to be so executed or signed.

Criminal Evidence (Amendment) Act 1997
(1997, c. 17)

Extension of power to take non-intimate body samples without consent

1   Persons imprisoned or detained by virtue of pre-existing conviction for sexual offence etc.

(1) This section has effect for removing, in relation to persons to whom this section applies, the restriction on the operation of section 63(3B) of the Police and Criminal Evidence Act 1984 (power to take non-intimate samples without the appropriate consent from persons convicted of recordable offences)—

    (a) which is imposed by the subsection (10) inserted in section 63 by section 55(6) of the Criminal Justice and Public Order Act 1994, and

    (b) by virtue of which section 63(3B) does not apply to persons convicted before 10 April 1995.

(3) This section applies to a person who was convicted of a recordable offence before 10 April 1995 if—

    (a) that offence was one of the offences listed in Schedule 1 to this Act (which lists certain sexual, violent and other offences), and

    (b) at the relevant time he is serving a sentence of imprisonment in respect of that offence.

(4) This section also applies to a person who was convicted of a recordable offence before 10 April 1995 if—

    (a) that offence was one of the offences listed in Schedule 1 to this Act, and

    (b) at the relevant time he is detained under Part III of the Mental Health Act 1983 in pursuance of—

        (i) a hospital order or interim hospital order made following that conviction, or

        (ii) a transfer direction given at a time when he was serving a sentence of imprisonment in respect of that offence.

Expressions used in this subsection and in the Mental Health Act 1983 have the same meaning as in that Act.

(5) Where a person convicted of a recordable offence before 10 April 1995 was, following his conviction for that and any other offence or offences, sentenced to two or more terms of imprisonment (whether taking effect consecutively or concurrently), he shall be treated for the purposes of this section as serving a sentence of imprisonment in respect of that offence at any time when serving any of those terms.

(6) For the purposes of this section, references to a person serving a sentence of imprisonment include references—

    (a) to his being detained in any institution to which the Prison Act 1952 applies in pursuance of any other sentence or order for detention imposed by a court in criminal proceedings, or

    (b) to his being detained (otherwise than in any such institution) in pursuance of directions of the Secretary of State under section 53 of the Children and Young Persons Act 1933;

and any reference to a term of imprisonment shall be construed accordingly.

2   Persons detained following acquittal on grounds of insanity or finding of unfitness to plead

(1) This section has effect for enabling non-intimate samples to be taken from persons under section 63 of the 1984 Act without the appropriate consent where they are persons to whom this section applies.

(3) This section applies to a person if—

    (a) at the relevant time he is detained under Part III of the Mental Health Act 1983 in pursuance of an order made under—

        (i) section 5(2)(a) of the Criminal Procedure (Insanity) Act 1964 or section 6 or 14 of the Criminal Appeal Act 1968 (finding of insanity or unfitness to plead), or

        (ii) section 37(3) of the Mental Health Act 1983 (power of magistrates' court to make hospital order without convicting accused); and

    (b) that order was made on or after the date of the passing of this Act in respect of a recordable offence.

(4) This section also applies to a person if—

    (a) at the relevant time he is detained under Part III of the Mental Health Act 1983 in pursuance of an order made under—

        (i) any of the provisions mentioned in subsection (3)(a), or

        (ii) section 5(1) of the Criminal Procedure (Insanity) Act 1964 as originally enacted; and

    (b) that order was made before the date of the passing of this Act in respect of any offence listed in Schedule 1 to this Act.

(5) Subsection (4)(a)(i) does not apply to any order made under section 14(2) of the Criminal Appeal Act 1968 as originally enacted.

(6) For the purposes of this section an order falling within subsection (3) or (4) shall be treated as having been made in respect of an offence of a particular description—

    (a) if, where the order was made following—

        (i) a finding of not guilty by reason of insanity, or

        (ii) a finding that the person in question was under a disability and did the act or made the omission charged against him, or

        (iii) a finding for the purposes of section 37(3) of the Mental Health Act 1983 that the person in question did the act or made the omission charged against him, or

        (iv) (in the case of an order made under section 5(1) of the Criminal Procedure (Insanity) Act 1964 as originally enacted) a finding that he was under a disability,

    that finding was recorded in respect of an offence of that description; or

    (b) if, where the order was made following the Court of Appeal forming such opinion as is mentioned in section 6(1) or 14(1) of the Criminal Appeal Act 1968, that opinion was formed on an appeal brought in respect of an offence of that description.

(7) In this section any reference to an Act 'as originally enacted' is a reference to that Act as it had effect without any of the amendments made by the Criminal Procedure (Insanity and Unfitness to Plead) Act 1991.

Supplementary

5 Interpretation

In this Act—

    'the 1984 Act' means the Police and Criminal Evidence Act 1984;

    'appropriate consent' has the meaning given by section 65 of the 1984 Act;

    'non-intimate sample' has the meaning given by section 65 of the 1984 Act;

    'recordable offence' means any offence to which regulations under section 27 of the 1984 Act (fingerprinting) apply;

    'the relevant time' means, in relation to the exercise of any power to take a non-intimate sample from a person, the time when it is sought to take the sample.

6 Short title, repeal and extent

(1) This Act may be cited as the Criminal Evidence (Amendment) Act 1997.

(2) . . .

(3) Section 55(6) of the Criminal Justice and Public Order Act 1994 is repealed.

(4) This Act extends to England and Wales only.

SCHEDULE 1   LIST OF OFFENCES

Sexual offences and offences of indecency

1.   Any offence under the Sexual Offences Act 1956, other than an offence under section 30, 31 or 33 to 36 of that Act.

2.   Any offence under section 128 of the Mental Health Act 1959 (intercourse with mentally handicapped person by hospital staff etc.).

3.   Any offence under section 1 of the Indecency with Children Act 1960 (indecent conduct towards young child).

4.   Any offence under section 54 of the Criminal Law Act 1977 (incitement by man of his grand-daughter, daughter or sister under the age of 16 to commit incest with him).

5.   Any offence under section 1 of the Protection of Children Act 1978.

Violent and other offences

6.   Any of the following offences—

(a) murder;

(b) manslaughter;

(c) false imprisonment; and

(d) kidnapping.

7.   Any offence under any of the following provisions of the Offences Against the Person Act 1861—

(a) section 4 (conspiring or soliciting to commit murder);

(b) section 16 (threats to kill);

(c) section 18 (wounding with intent to cause grievous bodily harm);

(d) section 20 (causing grievous bodily harm);

(e) section 21 (attempting to choke etc. in order to commit or assist in the committing of any indictable offence);

(f) section 22 (using chloroform etc. to commit or assist in the committing of any indictable offence);

(g) section 23 (maliciously administering poison etc. so as to endanger life or inflict grievous bodily harm);

(h) section 24 (maliciously administering poison etc. with intent to injure etc.); and

(i) section 47 (assault occasioning actual bodily harm).

8.   Any offence under either of the following provisions of the Explosive Substances Act 1883—

(a) section 2 (causing explosion likely to endanger life or property); and

(b) section 3 (attempt to cause explosion, or making or keeping explosive with intent to endanger life or property).

9.   Any offence under section 1 of the Children and Young Persons Act 1933 (cruelty to person under 16).

10.   Any offence under section 4(1) of the Criminal Law Act 1967 (assisting offender) committed in relation to the offence of murder.

11.   Any offence under any of the following provisions of the Firearms Act 1968—

(a) section 16 (possession of firearm with intent to injure);

(b) section 17 (use of firearm to resist arrest); and

(c) section 18 (carrying firearm with criminal intent).

12.   Any offence under either of the following provisions of the Theft Act 1968—

(a) section 9 (burglary); and

(b) section 10 (aggravated burglary);

and any offence under section 12A of that Act (aggravated vehicle-taking) involving an accident which caused the death of any person.

13.   Any offence under section 1 of the Criminal Damage Act 1971 (destroying or damaging property) required to be charged as arson.

14.   Any offence under section 2 of the Child Abduction Act 1984 (abduction of child by person other than parent).

Conspiracy, incitement and attempts

15.   Any offence under section 1 of the Criminal Law Act 1977 of conspiracy to commit any of the offences mentioned in paragraphs 1 to 14.

16.   Any offence under section 1 of the Criminal Attempts Act 1981 of attempting to commit any of those offences.

17.   Any offence of inciting another to commit any of those offences.

Human Rights Act 1998

(1998, c. 42)

Introduction

1   The Convention Rights

(1) In this Act 'the Convention rights' means the rights and fundamental freedoms set out in—

(a) Articles 2 to 12 and 14 of the Convention,

(b) Articles 1 to 3 of the First Protocol, and

(c) Articles 1 and 2 of the Sixth Protocol,

as read with Articles 16 to 18 of the Convention.

(2) Those Articles are to have effect for the purposes of this Act subject to any designated derogation or reservation (as to which see sections 14 and 15).

(3) The Articles are set out in Schedule 1.

(4) The Secretary of State may by order make such amendments to this Act as he considers appropriate to reflect the effect, in relation to the United Kingdom, of a protocol.

(5) In subsection (4) 'protocol' means a protocol to the Convention—

(a) which the United Kingdom has ratified; or

(b) which the United Kingdom has signed with a view to ratification.

(6) No amendment may be made by an order under subsection (4) so as to come into force before the protocol concerned is in force in relation to the United Kingdom.

2   Interpretation of Convention rights

(1) A court or tribunal determining a question which has arisen in connection with a Convention right must take into account any—

(a) judgment, decision, declaration or advisory opinion of the European Court of Human Rights,

(b) opinion of the Commission given in a report adopted under Article 31 of the Convention,

(c) decision of the Commission in connection with Article 26 or 27(2) of the Convention, or

(d) decision of the Committee of Ministers taken under Article 46 of the Convention,

whenever made or given, so far as, in the opinion of the court or tribunal, it is relevant to the proceedings in which that question has arisen.

(2) Evidence of any judgment, decision, declaration or opinion of which account may have to be taken under this section is to be given in proceedings before any court or tribunal in such manner as may be provided by rules.

(3) In this section 'rules' means rules of court or, in the case of proceedings before a tribunal, rules made for the purposes of this section—

(a) by the Lord Chancellor or the Secretary of State, in relation to any proceedings outside Scotland;

(b) by the Secretary of State, in relation to proceedings in Scotland; or

(c) by a Northern Ireland department, in relation to proceedings before a tribunal in Northern Ireland—

(i) which deals with transferred matters; and

(ii) for which no rules made under paragraph (a) are in force.

Legislation

3   Interpretation of legislation

(1) So far as it is possible to do so, primary legislation and subordinate legislation must be read and given effect in a way which is compatible with the Convention rights.

(2) This section—

(a) applies to primary legislation and subordinate legislation whenever enacted;

(b) does not affect the validity, continuing operation or enforcement of any incompatible primary legislation; and

(c) does not affect the validity, continuing operation or enforcement of any incompatible subordinate legislation if (disregarding any possibility of revocation) primary legislation prevents removal of the incompatibility.

4   Declaration of incompatibility

(1) Subsection (2) applies in any proceedings in which a court determines whether a provision of primary legislation is compatible with a Convention right.

(2) If the court is satisfied that the provision is incompatible with a Convention right, it may make a declaration of that incompatibility.

(3) Subsection (4) applies in any proceedings in which a court determines whether a provision of subordinate legislation, made in the exercise of a power conferred by primary legislation, is compatible with a Convention right.

(4) If the court is satisfied—

(a) that the provision is incompatible with a Convention right, and

(b) that (disregarding any possibility of revocation) the primary legislation concerned prevents removal of the incompatibility,

it may make a declaration of that incompatibility.

(5) In this section 'court' means—

(a) the House of Lords;

(b) the Judicial Committee of the Privy Council;

(c) the Courts-Martial Appeal Court;

(d) in Scotland, the High Court of Justiciary sitting otherwise than as a trial court or the Court of Session;

(e) in England and Wales or Northern Ireland, the High Court or the Court of Appeal.

(6) A declaration under this section ('a declaration of incompatibility')—

    (a) does not affect the validity, continuing operation or enforcement of the provision in respect of which it is given; and

    (b) is not binding on the parties to the proceedings in which it is made.

5   Right of Crown to intervene

(1) Where a court is considering whether to make a declaration of incompatibility, the Crown is entitled to notice in accordance with rules of court.

(2) In any case to which subsection (1) applies—

    (a) a Minister of the Crown (or a person nominated by him),

    (b) a member of the Scottish Executive,

    (c) a Northern Ireland Minister,

    (d) a Northern Ireland department,

is entitled, on giving notice in accordance with rules of court, to be joined as a party to the proceedings.

(3) Notice under subsection (2) may be given at any time during the proceedings.

(4) A person who has been made a party to criminal proceedings (other than in Scotland) as the result of a notice under subsection (2) may, with leave, appeal to the House of Lords against any declaration of incompatibility made in the proceedings.

(5) In subsection (4)—

'criminal proceedings' includes all proceedings before the Courts-Martial Appeal Court; and

'leave' means leave granted by the court making the declaration of incompatibility or by the House of Lords.

Public authorities

6   Acts of public authorities

(1) It is unlawful for a public authority to act in a way which is incompatible with a Convention right.

(2) Subsection (1) does not apply to an act if—

    (a) as the result of one or more provisions of primary legislation, the authority could not have acted differently; or

    (b) in the case of one or more provisions of, or made under, primary legislation which cannot be read or given effect in a way which is compatible with the Convention rights, the authority was acting so as to give effect to or enforce those provisions.

(3) In this section 'public authority' includes—

    (a) a court or tribunal, and

    (b) any person certain of whose functions are functions of a public nature,

but does not include either House of Parliament or a person exercising functions in connection with proceedings in Parliament.

(4) In subsection (3) 'Parliament' does not include the House of Lords in its judicial capacity.

(5) In relation to a particular act, a person is not a public authority by virtue only of subsection (3)(b) if the nature of the act is private.

(6) 'An act' includes a failure to act but does not include a failure to—

    (a) introduce in, or lay before, Parliament a proposal for legislation; or

    (b) make any primary legislation or remedial order.

7   Proceedings

(1) A person who claims that a public authority has acted (or proposes to act) in a way which is made unlawful by section 6(1) may—

    (a) bring proceedings against the authority under this Act in the appropriate court or tribunal, or

    (b) rely on the Convention right or rights concerned in any legal proceedings, but only if he is (or would be) a victim of the unlawful act.

(2) In subsection (1)(a) 'appropriate court or tribunal' means such court or tribunal as may be determined in accordance with rules; and proceedings against an authority include a counterclaim or similar proceeding.

(3) If the proceedings are brought on an application for judicial review, the applicant is to be taken to have a sufficient interest in relation to the unlawful act only if he is, or would be, a victim of that act.

(4) (*Applies to Scotland only.*)

(5) Proceedings under subsection (1)(a) must be brought before the end of—

    (a) the period of one year beginning with the date on which the act complained of took place; or

    (b) such longer period as the court or tribunal considers equitable having regard to all the circumstances,

but that is subject to any rule imposing a stricter time limit in relation to the procedure in question.

(6) In subsection (1)(b) 'legal proceedings' includes—

    (a) proceedings brought by or at the instigation of a public authority; and

    (b) an appeal against the decision of a court or tribunal.

(7) For the purposes of this section, a person is a victim of an unlawful act only if he would be a victim for the purposes of Article 34 of the Convention if proceedings were brought in the European Court of Human Rights in respect of that act.

(8) Nothing in this Act creates a criminal offence.

(9) In this section 'rules' means—

    (a) in relation to proceedings before a court or tribunal outside Scotland, rules made by the Lord Chancellor or the Secretary of State for the purposes of this section or rules of court,

    (b) (*Applies to Scotland only.*)

    (c) (*Applies to Northern Ireland only.*)

and includes provision made by order under section 1 of the Courts and Legal Services Act 1990.

(10) In making rules, regard must be had to section 9.

(11) The Minister who has power to make rules in relation to a particular tribunal may, to the extent he considers it necessary to ensure that the tribunal can provide an appropriate remedy in relation to an act (or proposed act) of a public authority which is (or would be) unlawful as a result of section 6(1), by order add to—

    (a) the relief or remedies which the tribunal may grant; or

    (b) the grounds on which it may grant any of them.

(12) An order made under subsection (11) may contain such incidental, supplemental, consequential or transitional provision as the Minister making it considers appropriate.

(13) 'The Minister' includes the Northern Ireland department concerned.

8 Judicial remedies

(1) In relation to any act (or proposed act) of a public authority which the court finds is (or would be) unlawful, it may grant such relief or remedy, or make such order, within its powers as it considers just and appropriate.

(2) But damages may be awarded only by a court which has power to award damages, or to order the payment of compensation, in civil proceedings.

(3) No award of damages is to be made unless, taking account of all the circumstances of the case, including—

(a) any other relief or remedy granted, or order made, in relation to the act in question (by that or any other court), and

(b) the consequences of any decision (of that or any other court) in respect of that act,

the court is satisfied that the award is necessary to afford just satisfaction to the person in whose favour it is made.

(4) In determining—

(a) whether to award damages, or

(b) the amount of an award,

the court must take into account the principles applied by the European Court of Human Rights in relation to the award of compensation under Article 41 of the Convention.

(5) A public authority against which damages are awarded is to be treated—

(a) (*Applies to Scotland only.*)

(b) for the purposes of the Civil Liability (Contribution) Act 1978 as liable in respect of damage suffered by the person to whom the award is made.

(6) In this section—

'court' includes a tribunal;

'damages' means damages for an unlawful act of a public authority; and

'unlawful' means unlawful under section 6(1).

9   Judicial acts

(1) Proceedings under section 7(1)(a) in respect of a judicial act may be brought only—

(a) by exercising a right of appeal;

(b) on an application . . . for judicial review; or

(c) in such other forum as may be prescribed by rules.

(2) That does not affect any rule of law which prevents a court from being the subject of judicial review.

(3) In proceedings under this Act in respect of a judicial act done in good faith, damages may not be awarded otherwise than to compensate a person to the extent required by Article 5(5) of the Convention.

(4) An award of damages permitted by subsection (3) is to be made against the Crown; but no award may be made unless the appropriate person, if not a party to the proceedings, is joined.

(5) In this section—

'appropriate person' means the Minister responsible for the court concerned, or a person or government department nominated by him;

'court' includes a tribunal;

'judge' includes a member of a tribunal, a justice of the peace and a clerk or other officer entitled to exercise the jurisdiction of a court;

'judicial act' means a judicial act of a court and includes an act done on the instructions, or on behalf, of a judge; and

'rules' has the same meaning as in section 7(9).

Remedial action

10   Power to take remedial action

(1) This section applies if—

(a) a provision of legislation has been declared under section 4 to be incompatible with a Convention right and, if an appeal lies—

(i) all persons who may appeal have stated in writing that they do not intend to do so;

(ii) the time for bringing an appeal has expired and no appeal has been brought within that time; or

(iii) an appeal brought within that time has been determined or abandoned; or

(b) it appears to a Minister of the Crown or Her Majesty in Council that, having regard to a finding of the European Court of Human Rights made after the coming into force of this section in proceedings against the United Kingdom, a provision of legislation is incompatible with an obligation of the United Kingdom arising from the Convention.

(2) If a Minister of the Crown considers that there are compelling reasons for proceeding under this section, he may by order make such amendments to the legislation as he considers necessary to remove the incompatibility.

(3) If, in the case of subordinate legislation, a Minister of the Crown considers—

(a) that it is necessary to amend the primary legislation under which the subordinate legislation in question was made, in order to enable the incompatibility to be removed, and

(b) that there are compelling reasons for proceeding under this section,

he may by order make such amendments to the primary legislation as he considers necessary.

(4) This section also applies where the provision in question is in subordinate legislation and has been quashed, or declared invalid, by reason of incompatibility with a Convention right and the Minister proposes to proceed under paragraph 2(b) of Schedule 2.

(5) If the legislation is an Order in Council, the power conferred by subsection (2) or (3) is exercisable by Her Majesty in Council.

(6) In this section 'legislation' does not include a Measure of the Church Assembly or of the General Synod of the Church of England.

(7) Schedule 2 makes further provision about remedial orders.

21   Interpretation etc.

(1) In this Act—

'amend' includes repeal and apply (with or without modifications);

'the appropriate Minister' means the Minister of the Crown having charge of the appropriate authorised government department (within the meaning of the Crown Proceedings Act 1947);

'the Commission' means the European Commission of Human Rights;

'the Convention' means the Convention for the Protection of Human Rights and Fundamental Freedoms, agreed by the Council of Europe at Rome on 4th November 1950 as it has effect for the time being in relation to the United Kingdom;

'declaration of incompatibility' means a declaration under section 4;

'Minister of the Crown' has the same meaning as in the Ministers of the Crown Act 1975;

'primary legislation' means any—

(a) public general Act;

(b) local and personal Act;

(c) private Act;

(d) Measure of the Church Assembly;

(e) Measure of the General Synod of the Church of England;

(f) Order in Council—

(i) made in exercise of Her Majesty's Royal Prerogative;

(ii) (*Applies to Northern Ireland only.*)

(iii) amending an Act of a kind mentioned in paragraph (a), (b) or (c);

and includes an order or other instrument made under primary legislation . . . to the extent to which it operates to bring one or more provisions of that legislation into force or amends any primary legislation;

'the First Protocol' means the protocol to the Convention agreed at Paris on 20th March 1952;

'the Sixth Protocol' means the protocol to the Convention agreed at Strasbourg on 28th April 1983;

'the Eleventh Protocol' means the protocol to the Convention (restructuring the control machinery established by the Convention) agreed at Strasbourg on 11th May 1994;

'remedial order' means an order under section 10;

'subordinate legislation' means any—

    (a) Order in Council other than one—

        (i)   made in exercise of Her Majesty's Royal Prerogative;

        (ii) *(Applies to Northern Ireland only.)*

        (iii) amending an Act of a kind mentioned in the definition of primary legislation;

    (b) ...

    (c) ...

    (d) ...

    (e) ...

    (f) order, rules, regulations, scheme, warrant, byelaw or other instrument made under primary legislation (except to the extent to which it operates to bring one or more provisions of that legislation into force or amends any primary legislation);

    (g) ...

    (h) ...

'tribunal' means any tribunal in which legal proceedings may be brought.

(2) The references in paragraphs (b) and (c) of section 2(1) to Articles are to Articles of the Convention as they had effect immediately before the coming into force of the Eleventh Protocol.

(3) The reference in paragraph (d) of section 2(1) to Article 46 includes a reference to Articles 32 and 54 of the Convention as they had effect immediately before the coming into force of the Eleventh Protocol.

(4) The references in section 2(1) to a report or decision of the Commission or a decision of the Committee of Ministers include references to a report or decision made as provided by paragraphs 3, 4 and 6 of Article 5 of the Eleventh Protocol (transitional provisions).

(5) Any liability under the Army Act 1955, the Air Force Act 1955 or the Naval Discipline Act 1957 to suffer death for an offence is replaced by a liability to imprisonment for life or any less punishment authorised by those Acts; and those Acts shall accordingly have effect with the necessary modifications.

22   Short title, commencement, application and extent

(1) This Act may be cited as the Human Rights Act 1998.

(2) Section 18, 20 and 21(5) and this section come into force on the passing of this Act.

(3) The other provisions of this Act come into force on such day as the Secretary of State may by order appoint; and different days may be appointed for different purposes.

(4) Paragraph (b) of subsection (1) of section 7 applies to proceedings brought by or at the instigation of a public authority whenever the act in question took place; but otherwise that subsection does not apply to an act taking place before the coming into force of that section.

(5) This Act binds the Crown.

(6) ...

(7) Section 21(5), so far as it relates to any provision contained in the Army Act 1955, the Air Force Act 1955 or the Naval Discipline Act 1957, extends to any place to which that provision extends.

Youth Justice and Criminal Evidence Act 1999
(1999, c. 23)

PART II   GIVING OF EVIDENCE OR INFORMATION FOR
PURPOSES OF CRIMINAL PROCEEDINGS

CHAPTER I   SPECIAL MEASURES DIRECTIONS IN CASE OF
VULNERABLE AND INTIMIDATED WITNESSES

Preliminary

16   Witnesses eligible for assistance on grounds of age or incapacity

(1) For the purposes of this Chapter a witness in criminal proceedings (other than the accused) is eligible for assistance by virtue of this section—

(a) if under the age of 17 at the time of the hearing; or

(b) if the court considers that the quality of evidence given by the witness is likely to be diminished by reason of any circumstances falling within subsection (2).

(2) The circumstances falling within this subsection are—

(a) that the witness—

(i)   suffers from mental disorder within the meaning of the Mental Health Act 1983, or

(ii) otherwise has a significant impairment of intelligence and social functioning;

(b) that the witness has a physical disability or is suffering from a physical disorder.

(3) In subsection (1)(a) 'the time of the hearing', in relation to a witness, means the time when it falls to the court to make a determination for the purposes of section 19(2) in relation to the witness.

(4) In determining whether a witness falls within subsection (1)(b) the court must consider any views expressed by the witness.

(5) In this Chapter references to the quality of a witness's evidence are to its quality in terms of completeness, coherence and accuracy; and for this purpose 'coherence' refers to a witness's ability in giving evidence to give answers which address the questions put to the witness and can be understood both individually and collectively.

17   Witnesses eligible for assistance on grounds of fear or distress about testifying

(1) For the purposes of this Chapter a witness in criminal proceedings (other than the accused) is eligible for assistance by virtue of this subsection if the court is satisfied that the quality of evidence given by the witness is likely to be diminished by reason of fear or distress on the part of the witness in connection with testifying in the proceedings.

(2) In determining whether a witness falls within subsection (1) the court must take into account, in particular—

(a) the nature and alleged circumstances of the offence to which the proceedings relate;

(b) the age of the witness;

(c) such of the following matters as appear to the court to be relevant, namely—

(i)   the social and cultural background and ethnic origins of the witness,

(ii) the domestic and employment circumstances of the witness, and

(iii) any religious beliefs or political opinions of the witness;

(d) any behaviour towards the witness on the part of—

(i)   the accused,

(ii) members of the family or associates of the accused, or

(iii) any other person who is likely to be an accused or a witness in the proceedings.

(3) In determining that question the court must in addition consider any views expressed by the witness.

(4) Where the complainant in respect of a sexual offence is a witness in proceedings relating to that offence (or to that offence and any other offences), the witness is eligible for assistance in relation to those proceedings by virtue of this subsection unless the witness has informed the court of the witness's wish not to be so eligible by virtue of this subsection.

18 Special measures available to eligible witnesses

(1) For the purposes of this Chapter—

    (a) the provision which may be made by a special measures direction by virtue of each of sections 23 to 30 is a special measure available in relation to a witness eligible for assistance by virtue of section 16; and

    (b) the provision which may be made by such a direction by virtue of each of sections 23 to 28 is a special measure available in relation to a witness eligible for assistance by virtue of section 17;

but this subsection has effect subject to subsection (2).

(2) Where (apart from this subsection) a special measure would, in accordance with subsection (1)(a) or (b), be available in relation to a witness in any proceedings, it shall not be taken by a court to be available in relation to the witness unless—

    (a) the court has been notified by the Secretary of State that relevant arrangements may be made available in the area in which it appears to the court that the proceedings will take place, and

    (b) the notice has not been withdrawn.

(3) In subsection (2) 'relevant arrangements' means arrangements for implementing the measure in question which cover the witness and the proceedings in question.

(4) The withdrawal of a notice under that subsection relating to a special measure shall not affect the availability of that measure in relation to a witness if a special measures direction providing for that measure to apply to the witness's evidence has been made by the court before the notice is withdrawn.

(5) The Secretary of State may by order make such amendments of this Chapter as he considers appropriate for altering the special measures which, in accordance with subsection (1)(a) or (b), are available in relation to a witness eligible for assistance by virtue of section 16 or (as the case may be) section 17, whether—

    (a) by modifying the provisions relating to any measure for the time being available in relation to such a witness,

    (b) by the addition—

        (i) (with or without modifications) of any measure which is for the time being available in relation to a witness eligible for assistance virtue of the other of those sections, or

        (ii) of any new measure, or

    (c) by the removal of any measure.

Special measures directions

19 Special measures direction relating to eligible witness

(1) This section applies where in any criminal proceedings—

    (a) a party to the proceedings makes an application for the court to give a direction under this section in relation to a witness in the proceedings other than the accused, or

    (b) the court of its own motion raises the issue whether such a direction should be given.

(2) Where the court determines that the witness is eligible for assistance by virtue of section 16 or 17, the court must then—

(a) determine whether any of the special measures available in relation to the witness (or any combination of them) would, in its opinion, be likely to improve the quality of evidence given by the witness; and
(b) if so—
  (i) determine which of those measures (or combination of them) would, in its opinion, be likely to maximise so far as practicable the quality of such evidence; and
  (ii) give a direction under this section providing for the measure or measures so determined to apply to evidence given by the witness.

(3) In determining for the purposes of this Chapter whether any special measure or measures would or would not be likely to improve, or to maximise so far as practicable, the quality of evidence given by the witness, the court must consider all the circumstances of the case, including in particular—
(a) any views expressed by the witness; and
(b) whether the measure or measures might tend to inhibit such evidence being effectively tested by a party to the proceedings.

(4) A special measures direction must specify particulars of the provision made by the direction in respect of each special measure which is to apply to the witness's evidence.

(5) In this Chapter 'special measures direction' means a direction under this section.

(6) Nothing in this Chapter is to be regarded as affecting any power of a court to make an order or give leave of any description (in the exercise of its inherent jurisdiction or otherwise)—
(a) in relation to a witness who is not an eligible witness, or
(b) in relation to an eligible witness where (as, for example, in a case where a foreign language interpreter is to be provided) the order is made or the leave is given otherwise than by reason of the fact that the witness is an eligible witness.

20 Further provisions about directions: general
(1) Subject to subsection (2) and section 21(8), a special measures direction has binding effect from the time it is made until the proceedings for the purposes of which it is made are either—
(a) determined (by acquittal, conviction or otherwise), or
(b) abandoned,
in relation to the accused or (if there is more than one) in relation to each of the accused.

(2) The court may discharge or vary (or further vary) a special measures direction if it appears to the court to be in the interests of justice to do so, and may do so either—
(a) on an application made by a party to the proceedings, if there has been a material change of circumstances since the relevant time, or
(b) of its own motion.

(3) In subsection (2) 'the relevant time' means—
(a) the time when the direction was given, or
(b) if a previous application has been made under that subsection, the time when the application (or last application) was made.

(4) Nothing in section 24(2) and (3), 27(4) to (7) or 28(4) to (6) is to be regarded as affecting the power of the court to vary or discharge a special measures direction under subsection (2).

(5) The court must state in open court its reasons for—
(a) giving or varying,
(b) refusing an application for, or for the variation or discharge of, or
(c) discharging,
a special measures direction and, if it is a magistrates' court, must cause them to be entered in the register of its proceedings.

(6) Rules of court may make provision—
    (a) for uncontested applications to be determined by the court without a hearing;
    (b) for preventing the renewal of an unsuccessful application for a special measures direction except where there has been a material change of circumstances;
    (c) for expert evidence to be given in connection with an application for, or for varying or discharging, such a direction;
    (d) for the manner in which confidential or sensitive information is to be treated in connection with such an application and in particular as to its being disclosed to, or withheld from, a party to the proceedings.

21   Special provisions relating to child witnesses

(1) For the purposes of this section—
    (a) a witness in criminal proceedings is a 'child witness' if he is an eligible witness by reason of section 16(1)(a) (whether or not he is an eligible witness by reason of any other provision of section 16 or 17);
    (b) a child witness is 'in need of special protection' if the offence (or any of the offences) to which the proceedings relate is—
        (i)   an offence falling within section 35(3)(a) (sexual offences etc.), or
        (ii) an offence falling within section 35(3)(b), (c) or (d) (kidnapping, assaults etc.);
        and
    (c) a 'relevant recording', in relation to a child witness, is a video recording of an interview of the witness made with a view to its admission as evidence in chief of the witness.

(2) Where the court, in making a determination for the purposes of section 19(2), determines that a witness in criminal proceedings is a child witness, the court must—
    (a) first have regard to subsections (3) to (7) below; and
    (b) then have regard to section 19(2);
and for the purposes of section 19(2), as it then applies to the witness, any special measures required to be applied in relation to him by virtue of this section shall be treated as if they were measures determined by the court, pursuant to section 19(2)(a) and (b)(i), to be ones that (whether on their own or with any other special measures) would be likely to maximise, so far as practicable, the quality of his evidence.

(3) The primary rule in the case of a child witness is that the court must give a special measures direction in relation to the witness which complies with the following requirements—
    (a) it must provide for any relevant recording to be admitted under section 27 (video recorded evidence in chief); and
    (b) it must provide for any evidence given by the witness in the proceedings which is not given by means of a video recording (whether in chief or otherwise) to be given by means of a live link in accordance with section 24.

(4) The primary rule is subject to the following limitations—
    (a) the requirement contained in subsection (3)(a) or (b) has effect subject to the availability (within the meaning of section 18(2)) of the special measure in question in relation to the witness;
    (b) the requirement contained in subsection (2)(a) also has effect subject to section 27(2); and
    (c) the rule does not apply to the extent that the court is satisfied that compliance with it would not be likely to maximise the quality of the witness's evidence so far as practicable (whether because the application to that evidence of one or more other special measures available in relation to the witness would have that result or for any other reason).

(5) However, subsection (4)(c) does not apply in relation to a child witness in need of special protection.

(6) Where a child witness is in need of special protection by virtue of subsection (1)(b)(i), any special measures direction given by the court which complies with the requirement contained in subsection (3)(a) must in addition provide for the special measure available under section 28 (video recorded cross-examination or re-examination) to apply in relation to—

(a) any cross-examination of the witness otherwise than by the accused in person, and

(b) any subsequent re-examination.

(7) The requirement contained in subsection (6) has effect subject to the following limitations—

(a) it has effect subject to the availability (within the meaning of section 18(2)) of that special measure in relation to the witness; and

(b) it does not apply if the witness has informed the court that he does not want that special measure to apply in relation to him.

(8) Where a special measures direction is given in relation to a child witness who is an eligible witness by reason only of section 16(1)(a), then—

(a) subject to subsection (9) below, and

(b) except where the witness has already begun to give evidence in the proceedings, the direction shall cease to have effect at the time when the witness attains the age of 17.

(9) Where a special measures direction is given in relation to a child witness who is an eligible witness by reason only of section 16(1)(a) and—

(a) the direction provides—

(i) for any relevant recording to be admitted under section 27 as evidence in chief of the witness, or

(ii) for the special measure available under section 28 to apply in relation to the witness, and

(b) if it provides for that special measure to so apply, the witness is still under the age of 17 when the video recording is made for the purposes of section 28,

then, so far as it provides as mentioned in paragraph (a)(i) or (ii) above, the direction shall continue to have effect in accordance with section 20(1) even though the witness subsequently attains that age.

22 Extension of provisions of section 21 to certain witness over 17

(1) For the purposes of this section—

(a) a witness in criminal proceedings (other than the accused) is a 'qualifying witness' if he—

(i) is not an eligible witness at the time of the hearing (as defined by section 16(3)), but

(ii) was under the age of 17 when a relevant recording was made;

(b) a qualifying witness is 'in need of special protection' if the offence (or any of the offences) to which the proceedings relate is—

(i) an offence falling within section 35(3)(a) (sexual offences etc.), or

(ii) an offence falling within section 35(3)(b), (c) or (d) (kidnapping, assaults etc.); and

(c) a 'relevant recording', in relation to a witness, is a video recording of an interview of the witness made with a view to its admission as evidence in chief of the witness.

(2) Subsections (2) to (7) of section 21 shall apply as follows in relation to a qualifying witness—

(a) subsections (2) to (4), so far as relating to the giving of a direction complying with the requirement contained in subsection (3)(a), shall apply to a qualifying witness in respect of the relevant recording as they apply to a child witness (within the meaning of that section);

(b) subsection (5), so far as relating to the giving of such a direction, shall apply to a qualifying witness in need of special protection as it applies to a child witness in need of special protection (within the meaning of that section); and

(c) subsection (6) and (7) shall apply to a qualifying witness in need of special protection by virtue of subsection (1)(b)(i) above as they apply to such a child witness as is mentioned in subsection (6).

Special measures

23   Screening witness from accused

(1) A special measures direction may provide for the witness, while giving testimony or being sworn in court, to be prevented by means of a screen or other arrangement from seeing the accused.

(2) But the screen or other arrangement must not prevent the witness from being able to see, and to be seen by—

(a) the judge or justices (or both) and the jury (if there is one);

(b) legal representatives acting in the proceedings; and

(c) any interpreter or other person appointed (in pursuance of the direction or otherwise) to assist the witness.

(3) Where two or more legal representatives are acting for a party to the proceedings, subsection (2)(b) is to be regarded as satisfied in relation to those representatives if the witness is able to all material times to see and be seen by at least one of them.

24   Evidence by live link

(1) A special measures direction may provide for the witness to give evidence by means of a live link.

(2) Where a direction provides for the witness to give evidence by means of a live link, the witness may not give evidence in any other way without the permission of the court.

(3) The court may give permission for the purposes of subsection (2) if it appears to the court to be in the interests of justice to do so, and may do so either—

(a) on an application by a party to the proceedings, if there has been a material change of circumstances since the relevant time, or

(b) of its own motion.

(4) In subsection (3) 'the relevant time' means—

(a) the time when the direction was given, or

(b) if a previous application has been made under that subsection, the time when the application (or last application) was made.

(8) In this Chapter 'live link' means a live television link or other arrangement whereby a witness, while absent from the courtroom or other place where the proceedings are being held, if able to see and hear a person there and to be such and heard by the persons specified in section 23(2)(a) to (c).

25   Evidence given in private

(1) A special measures direction may provide for the exclusion from the court, during the giving of the witness's evidence, of persons of any description specified in the direction.

(2) The persons who may be so excluded do not include—
  (a) the accused,
  (b) legal representatives acting in the proceedings, or
  (c) any interpreter or other person appointed (in pursuance of the direction or otherwise) to assist the witness.

(3) A special measures direction providing for representatives of news gathering or reporting organisations to be so excluded shall be expressed not to apply to one named person who—
  (a) is a representative of such an organisation, and
  (b) has been nominated for the purpose by one or more such organisations,
unless it appears to the court that no such nomination has been made.

(4) A special measures direction may only provide for the exclusion of persons under this section where—
  (a) the proceedings relate to a sexual offence; or
  (b) it appears to the court that there are reasonable grounds for believing that any person other than the accused has sought, or will seek, to intimidate the witness in connection with testifying in the proceedings.

(5) Any proceedings from which persons are excluded under this section (whether or not those persons include representatives of news gathering or reporting organisations) shall nevertheless be taken to be held in public for the purposes of any privilege or exemption from liability available in respect of fair, accurate and contemporaneous reports of legal proceedings held in public.

26   Removal of wigs and gowns

A special measures direction may provide for the wearing of wigs or gowns to be dispensed with during the giving of the witness's evidence.

27   Video recorded evidence in chief

(1) A special measures direction may provide for a video recording of an interview of the witness to be admitted as evidence in chief of the witness.

(2) A special measures direction may, however, not provide for a video recording, or a part of such a recording, to be admitted under this section if the court is of the opinion, having regard to all the circumstances of the case, that in the interests of justice the recording, or that part of it, should not be so admitted.

(3) In considering for the purposes of subsection (2) whether any part of a recording should not be admitted under this section, the court must consider whether any prejudice to the accused which might result from that part being so admitted is outweighed by the desirability of showing the whole, or substantially the whole, of the recorded interview.

(4) Where a special measures direction provides for a recording to be admitted under this section, the court may nevertheless subsequently direct that it is not to be so admitted if—
  (a) it appears to the court that—
    (i) the witness will not be available for cross-examination (whether conducted in the ordinary way or in accordance with any such direction), and
    (ii) the parties to the proceedings have not agreed that there is no need for the witness to be so available; or
  (b) any rules of court requiring disclosure of the circumstances in which the recording was made have not been complied with to the satisfaction of the court.

(5) Where a recording is admitted under this section—
  (a) the witness must be called by the party tendering it in evidence, unless—
    (i) a special measures direction provides for the witness's evidence on cross-examination to be given otherwise than by testimony in court, or
    (ii) the parties to the proceedings have agreed as mentioned in subsection (4)(a)(ii); and

(b) the witness may not give evidence in chief otherwise than by means of the recording—

   (i) as to any matter which, in the opinion of the court, has been dealt with adequately in the witness's recorded testimony, or

   (ii) without the permission of the court, as to any other matter which, in the opinion of the court, is dealt with in that testimony.

(6) Where in accordance with subsection (2) a special measures direction provides for part only of a recording to be admitted under this section, references in subsection (4) and (5) to the recording or to the witness's recorded testimony are references to the part of the recording or testimony which is to be so admitted.

(7) The court may give permission for the purposes of subsection (5)(b)(ii) if it appears to the court to be in the interests of justice to do so, and may do so either—

(a) on an application by a party to the proceedings, if there has been a material change of circumstances since the relevant time, or

(b) of its own motion.

(8) In subsection (7) 'the relevant time' means—

(a) the time when the direction was given, or

(b) if a previous application has been made under that subsection, the time when the application (or last application) was made.

(9) The court may, in giving permission for the purposes of subsection (5)(b)(ii), direct that the evidence in question is to be given by the witness by means of a live link; and, if the court so directs, subsections (5) to (7) of section 24 shall apply in relation to that evidence as they apply in relation to evidence which is to be given in accordance with a special measures direction.

(11) Nothing in this section affects the admissibility of any video recording which would be admissible apart from this section.

28   Video recorded cross-examination or re-examination

(1) Where a special measures direction provides for a video recording to be admitted under section 27 as evidence in chief of the witness, the direction may also provide—

(a) for any cross-examination of the witness, and any re-examination, to be recorded by means of a video recording; and

(b) for such a recording to be admitted, so far as it relates to any such cross-examination or re-examination, as evidence of the witness under cross-examination or on re-examination, as the case may be.

(2) Such a recording must be made in the presence of such persons as rules of court or the direction may provide and in the absence of the accused, but in circumstances in which—

(a) the judge or justices (or both) and legal representatives acting in the proceedings are able to see and hear the examination of the witness and to communicate with the persons in whose presence the recording is being made, and

(b) the accused is able to see and hear any such examination and to communicate with any legal representative acting for him.

(3) Where two or more legal representatives are acting for a party to the proceedings, subsection (2)(a) and (b) are to be regarded as satisfied in relation to those representatives if at all material times they are satisfied in relation to at least one of them.

(4) Where a special measures direction provides for a recording to be admitted under this section, the court may nevertheless subsequently direct that it is not to be so admitted if any requirement of subsection (2) or rules of court or the direction has not been complied with to the satisfaction of the court.

(5) Where in pursuance of subsection (1) a recording has been made of any examination of the witness, the witness may not be subsequently cross-examined or re-examined in

respect of any evidence given by the witness in the proceedings (whether in any recording admissible under section 27 or this section or otherwise than in such a recording) unless the court gives a further special measures direction making such provision as is mentioned in subsection (1)(a) and (b) in relation to any subsequent cross-examination, and re-examination, of the witness.

(6) The court may only give such a further direction if it appears to the court—

(a) that the proposed cross-examination is sought by a party to the proceedings as a result of that party having become aware, since the time when the original recording was made in pursuance of subsection (1), of a matter which that party could not with reasonable diligence have ascertained by then, or

(b) that for any other reason it is in the interests of justice to give the further direction.

(7) Nothing in this section shall be read as applying in relation to any cross-examination of the witness by the accused in person (in a case where the accused is to be able to conduct any such cross-examination).

29 Examination of witness through intermediary

(1) A special measures direction may provide for any examination of the witness (how-ever and wherever conducted) to be conducted through an interpreter or other person approved by the court for the purposes of this section ('an intermediary').

(2) The function of an intermediary is to communicate—

(a) to the witness, questions put to the witness, and

(b) to any person asking such questions, the answers given by the witness in reply to them,

and to explain such questions or answers so far as necessary to enable them to be understood by the witness or person in question.

(3) Any examination of the witness in pursuance of subsection (1) must take place in the presence of such persons as rules of court or the direction may provide, but in circumstances in which—

(a) the judge or justices (or both) and legal representatives acting in the proceedings are able to see and hear the examination of the witness and to communicate with the intermediary, and

(b) (except in the case of a video recorded examination) the jury (if there is one) are able to see and hear the examination of the witness.

(4) Where two or more legal representatives are acting for a party to the proceedings, subsection (3)(a) is to be regarded as satisfied in relation to those representatives if at all material times it is satisfied in relation to at least one of them.

(5) A person may not act as an intermediary in a particular case except after making a declaration, in such form as may be prescribed by rules of court, that he will faithfully perform his function as intermediary.

(6) Subsection (1) does not apply to an interview of the witness which is recorded by means of a video recording with a view to its admission as evidence in chief of the witness; but a special measures direction may provide for such a recording to be admitted under section 27 if the interview was conducted through an intermediary and—

(a) that person complied with subsection (5) before the interview began, and

(b) the court's approval for the purposes of this action is given before the direction is given.

(7) Section 1 of the Perjury Act 1911 (perjury) shall apply in relation to a person acting as an intermediary as it applies in relation to a person lawfully sworn as an interpreter in a judicial proceeding; and for this purpose, where a person acts as an intermediary in any proceeding which is not a judicial proceeding for the purposes of that section, that pro-ceeding shall be taken to be part of the judicial proceeding in which the witness's evidence is given.

30   Aids to communication

A special measures direction may provide for the witness, while giving evidence (whether by testimony in court or otherwise), to be provided with such device as the court considers appropriate with a view to enabling questions or answers to be communicated to or by the witness despite any disability or disorder or other impairment which the witness has or suffers form.

Supplementary

31   Status of evidence given under Chapter 1.

(1) Subsections (2) to (4) apply to a statement made by a witness in criminal proceedings which, in accordance with a special measures direction, is not made by the witness in direct oral testimony in court but forms part of the witness's evidence in those proceedings.

(2) The statement shall be treated as if made by the witness in direct oral testimony in court; and accordingly—

    (a) it is admissible evidence of any fact of which such testimony from the witness would be admissible;

    (b) it is not capable of corroborating any other evidence given by the witness.

(3) Subsection (2) applies to a statement admitted under section 27 or 28 which is not made by the witness on oath even though it would have been required to be made on oath if made by the witness in direct oral testimony in court.

(4) In estimating the weight (if any) to be attached to the statement, the court must have regard to all the circumstances from which an inference can reasonably be drawn (as to the accuracy of the statement or otherwise).

(5) Nothing in this Chapter (apart from subsection (3)) affects the operation of any rule of law relating to evidence in criminal proceedings.

(6) Where any statement made by a person on oath in any proceeding which is not a judicial proceeding for the purposes of section 1 of the Perjury Act 1911 (perjury) is received in evidence in pursuance of a special measures direction, that proceeding shall be taken for the purposes of that section to be part of the judicial proceeding in which the statement is so received in evidence.

(7) Where in any proceeding which is not a judicial proceeding for the purposes of that Act—

    (a) a person wilfully makes a false statement otherwise than on oath which is subsequently received in evidence in pursuance of a special measures direction, and

    (b) the statement is made in such circumstances that had it been given on oath in any such judicial proceeding that person would have been guilty of perjury, he shall be guilty of an offence and liable to any punishment which might be imposed on conviction of an offence under section 57(2) (giving of false unsworn evidence in criminal proceedings).

(8) In this section 'statement' includes any representation of fact, whether made in words or otherwise.

32   Warning to jury

Where on a trial on indictment with a jury evidence has been given in accordance with a special measures direction, the judge must give the jury such warning (if any) as the judge considers necessary to ensure that the fact that the direction was given in relation to the witness does not prejudice the accused.

33   Interpretation etc. of Chapter 1

(1) In this Chapter—

'eligible witness' means a witness eligible for assistance by virtue of section 16 or 17;

'livelink' has the meaning given by section 24(8);

'quality', in relation to the evidence of a witness, shall be construed in accordance with section 16(5);

'special measures direction' means (in accordance with section 19(5)) a direction under section 19.

(2) In this Chapter references to the special measures available in relation to a witness shall be construed in accordance with section 18.

(3) In this Chapter references to a person being able to see or hear, or be seen or heard by, another person are to be read as not applying to the extent that either of them is unable to see or hear by reason of any impairment of eyesight or hearing.

(4) In the case of any proceedings in which there is more than one accused—

    (a) any reference to the accused in sections 23 to 28 may be taken by a court, in connection with the giving of a special measures direction, as a reference to all or any of the accused, as the court may determine, and

    (b) any such direction may be given on the basis of any such determination.

CHAPTER II   PROTECTION OF WITNESSES FROM CROSS-EXAMINATION BY ACCUSED IN PERSON

General prohibitions

34 Complainants in proceedings for sexual offences

No person charged with a sexual offence may in any criminal proceedings cross-examine in person a witness who is the complainant, either—

    (a) in connection with that offence, or

    (b) in connection with any other offence (or whatever nature) with which that person is charged in the proceedings.

35 Child complainants and other child witnesses

(1) No person charged with an offence to which this section applies may in any criminal proceedings cross-examine in person a protected witness, either—

    (a) in connection with that offence, or

    (b) in connection with any other offence (of whatever nature) with which that person is charged in the proceedings.

(2) For the purposes of subsection (1) a 'protected witness' is a witness who—

    (a) either is the complainant or is alleged to have been a witness to the commission of the offence to which this section applies, and

    (b) either is a child or falls to be cross-examined after giving evidence in chief (whether wholly or in part)—

        (i) by means of a video recording made (for the purposes of section 27) at a time when the witness was a child, or

        (ii) in any other way at any such time.

(3) the offences to which this section applies are—

    (a) any offence under—

        (i) . . .

        (ii) . . .

        (iii) . . .

        (iv) . . .

        (v) the Protection of Children Act 1978; or

        (vi) Part I of the Sexual Offences Act 2003.

    (b) kidnapping, false imprisonment or an offence under section 1 or 2 of the Child Abduction Act 1984;

    (c) any offence under section 1 of the Children and Young Persons Act 1933;

(d) any offence (not within any of the preceding paragraphs) which involves an assault on, or injury or a threat of injury to, any person.

(4) In this section 'child' means—

  (a) where the offence falls within subsection (3)(a), a person under the age of 17; or

  (b) where the offence falls within subsection (3)(b), (c) or (d), a person under the age of 14.

(5) For the purposes of this section 'witness' includes a witness who is charged with an offence in the proceedings.

Prohibition imposed by court

36 Direction prohibiting accused from cross-examining particular witness

(1) This section applies where, in a case where neither of sections 34 and 35 operates to prevent an accused in any criminal proceedings from cross-examining a witness in person—

  (a) the prosecutor makes an application for the court to give a direction under this section in relation to the witness, or

  (b) the court of its own motion raises the issue whether such a direction should be given.

(2) If it appears to the court—

  (a) that the quality of evidence given by the witness on cross-examination—

    (i) is likely to be diminished if the cross-examination (or further cross-examination) is conducted by the accused in person, and

    (ii) would be likely to be improved if a direction were given under this section, and

  (b) that it would not be contrary to the interests of justice to give such a direction,

the court may give a direction prohibiting the accused from cross-examining (or further cross-examining) the witness in person.

(3) In determining whether subsection (2)(a) applies in the case of a witness the court must have regard, in particular, to—

  (a) any views expressed by the witness as to whether or not the witness is content to be cross-examined by the accused in person;

  (b) the nature of the questions likely to be asked, having regard to the issues in the proceedings and the defence case advanced so far (if any);

  (c) any behaviour on the part of the accused at any stage of the proceedings, both generally and in relation to the witness;

  (d) any relationship (of whatever nature) between the witness and the accused;

  (e) whether any person (other than the accused) is or has at any time been charged in the proceedings with a sexual offence or an offence to which section 35 applies, and (if so) whether section 34 or 35 operates or would have operated to prevent that person from cross-examining the witness in person;

  (f) any direction under section 19 which the court has given, or proposes to give, in relation to the witness.

(4) For the purposes of this section—

  (a) 'witness', in relation to an accused, does not include any other person who is charged with an offence in the proceedings; and

  (b) any reference to the quality of a witness's evidence shall be construed in accordance with section 16(5).

37 Further provisions about directions under section 36

(1) Subject to subsection (2), a direction has binding effect from the time it is made until the witness to whom it applies is discharged.

In this section 'direction' means a direction under section 36.

(2) The court may discharge a direction if it appears to the court to be in the interests of justice to do so, and may do so either—

    (a) on an application made by a party to the proceedings, if there has been a material change of circumstances since the relevant time, or

    (b) of its own motion.

(3) In subsection (2) 'the relevant time' means—

    (a) the time when the direction was given, or

    (b) if a previous application has been made under that subsection, the time when the application (or last application) was made.

(4) The court must state in open court its reasons for—

    (a) giving, or

    (b) refusing an application for, or for the discharge of, or

    (c) discharging,

a direction and, if it is a magistrates' court, must cause them to be entered in the register of its proceedings.

(5) Rules of court may make provision—

    (a) for uncontested applications to be determined by the court without a hearing;

    (b) for preventing the renewal of an unsuccessful application for a direction except where there has been a material change of circumstances;

    (c) for expert evidence to be given in connection with an application for, or for discharging, a direction;

    (d) for the manner in which confidential or sensitive information is to be treated in connection with such an application and in particular as to its being disclosed to, or withheld from, a party to the proceedings.

Cross-examination on behalf of accused

38　Defence representation for purposes of cross-examination

(1) This section applies where an accused is prevented from cross-examining a witness in person by virtue of section 34, 35 or 36.

(2) Where it appears to the court that this section applies, it must—

    (a) invite the accused to arrange for a legal representative to act for him for the purpose of cross-examining the witness; and

    (b) require the accused to notify the court, by the end of such period as it may specify, whether a legal representative is to act for him for that purpose.

(3) If by the end of the period mentioned in subsection (2)(b) either—

    (a) the accused has notified the court that no legal representative is to act for him for the purpose of cross-examining the witness, or

    (b) no notification has been received by the court and it appears to the court that no legal representative is to so act,

the court must consider whether it is necessary in the interests of justice for the witness to be cross-examined by a legal representative appointed to represent the interests of the accused.

(4) If the court decides that it is necessary in the interests of justice for the witness to be so cross-examined, the court must appoint a qualified legal representative (chosen by the court) to cross-examine the witness in the interests of the accused.

(5) A person so appointed shall not be responsible to the accused.

(6) Rules of court may make provision—

    (a) as to the time when, and the manner in which, subsection (2) is to be complied with;

    (b) in connection with the appointment of a legal representative under subsection (4), and in particular for securing that a person so appointed is provided with evidence or other material relating to the proceedings.

(7) Rules of court made in pursuance of subsection (6)(b) may make provision for the application, with such modifications as are specified in the rules, of any of the provisions of—

(a) Part I of the Criminal Procedure and Investigations Act 1996 (disclosure of material in connection with criminal proceedings), or

(b) the Sexual Offences (Protected Material) Act 1997.

(8) For the purposes of this section—

(a) any reference to cross-examination includes (in a case where a direction is given under section 36 after the accused has begun cross-examining the witness) a reference to further cross-examination; and

(b) 'qualified legal representative' means a legal representative who has a right of audience (within the meaning of the Courts and Legal Services Act 1990) in relation to the proceedings before the court.

39 Warning to jury

(1) Where on a trial on indictment with a jury an accused is prevented from cross-examining a witness in person by virtue of section 34, 35 or 36, the judge must give the jury such warning (if any) as the judge considers necessary to ensure that the accused is not prejudiced—

(a) by any inferences that might be drawn from the fact that the accused has been prevented from cross-examining the witness in person;

(b) where the witness has been cross-examined by a legal representative appointed under section 38(4), by the fact that the cross-examination was carried out by such a legal representative and not by a person acting as the accused's own legal representative.

(2) Subsection (8)(a) of section 38 applies for the purposes of this section as it applies for the purposes of section 38.

CHAPTER III PROTECTION OF COMPLAINANTS IN PROCEEDINGS
FOR SEXUAL OFFENCES

41 Restriction on evidence or questions about complainant's sexual history

(1) If at a trial a person is charged with a sexual offence, then, except with the leave of the court—

(a) no evidence may be adduced, and

(b) no question may be asked in cross-examination,

by or on behalf of any accused at the trial, about any sexual behaviour of the complainant.

(2) The court may give leave in relation to any evidence or question only on an application made by or on behalf of an accused, and may not give such leave unless it is satisfied—

(a) that subsection (3) or (5) applies, and

(b) that a refusal of leave might have the result of rendering unsafe a conclusion of the jury or (as the case may be) the court on any relevant issue in the case.

(3) This subsection applies if the evidence or question relates to a relevant issue in the case and either—

(a) that issue is not an issue of consent; or

(b) it is an issue of consent and the sexual behaviour of the complainant to which the evidence or question relates is alleged to have taken place at or about the same time as the event which is the subject matter of the charge against the accused; or

(c) it is an issue of consent and the sexual behaviour of the complainant to which the evidence or question relates is alleged to have been, in any respect, so similar—

(i)   to any sexual behaviour of the complainant which (according to evidence adduced or to be adduced by or on behalf of the accused) took place as part of the event which is the subject matter of the charge against the accused, or

(ii) to any other sexual behaviour of the complainant which (according to such evidence) took place at or about the same time as the event, that the similarity cannot reasonably be explained as a coincidence.

(4) For the purposes of subsection (3) no evidence or question shall be regarded as relating to a relevant issue in the case if it appears to the court to be reasonable to assume that the purpose (or main purpose) for which it would be adduced or asked is to establish or elicit material for impugning the credibility of the complainant as a witness.

(5) This subsection applies if the evidence or question—

(a)   relates to any evidence adduced by the prosecution about any sexual behaviour of the complainant; and

(b)   in the opinion of the court, would go no further than is necessary to enable the evidence adduced by the prosecution to be rebutted or explained by or on behalf of the accused.

(6) For the purposes of subsections (3) and (5) the evidence or question must relate to a specific instance (or specific instances) of alleged sexual behaviour on the part of the complainant (and accordingly nothing in those subsections is capable of applying in relation to the evidence or question to the extent that it does not so relate).

(7) Where this section applies in relation to a trial by virtue of the fact that one or more of a number of persons charged in the proceedings is or are charged with a sexual offence—

(a)   it shall cease to apply in relation to the trial if the prosecutor decides not to proceed with the case against that person or those persons in respect of that charge; but

(b)   it shall not cease to do so in the event of that person or those persons pleading guilty to, or being convicted of, that charge.

(8) Nothing in this section authorises any evidence to be adduced or any question to be asked which cannot be adduced or asked apart from this section.

42   Interpretation and application of section 41

(1) In section 41—

(a)   'relevant issue in the case' means any issue falling to be proved by the prosecution or defence in the trial of the accused;

(b)   'issue of consent' means any issue whether the complainant in fact consented to the conduct constituting the offence with which the accused is charged (and accordingly does not include any issue as to the belief of the accused that the complainant so consented);

(c)   'sexual behaviour' means any sexual behaviour or other sexual experience, whether or not involving any accused or other person, but excluding (except in section 41(3)(c)(i) and (5)(a)) anything alleged to have taken place as part of the event which is the subject matter of the charge against the accused; and

(d)   subject to any other made under subsection (2), 'sexual offence' shall be construed in accordance with section 62.

(2) The Secretary of State may by order make such provision as he considers appropriate for adding or removing, for the purposes of section 41, any offence to or from the offences which are sexual offences for the purposes of this Act by virtue of section 62.

(3) Section 41 applies in relation to the following proceedings as it applies to a trial, namely—

(c) the hearing of an application under paragraph 2(1) of Schedule 3 to the Crime and Disorder Act 1998 (application to dismiss charge by person sent for trial under section 51 or 51A of that Act),

(d) any hearing held, between conviction and sentencing, for the purpose of determining matters relevant to the court's decision as to how the accused is to be dealt with, and

(e) the hearing of an appeal,

and references (in section 41 or this section) to a person charged with an offence accordingly include a person convicted of an offence.

43 Procedure on applications under section 41

(1) An application for leave shall be heard in private and in the absence of the complainant.

In this section 'leave' means leave under section 41.

(2) Where such an application has been determined, the court must state in open court (but in the absence of the jury, if there is one)—

(a) its reasons for giving, or refusing, leave, and

(b) if it gives leave, the extent to which evidence may be adduced or questions asked in pursuance of the leave,

and, if it is a magistrates' court, must cause those matters to be entered in the register of its proceedings.

(3) Rules of court may make provision—

(a) requiring applications for leave to specify, in relation to each item of evidence or question to which they relate, particulars of the grounds on which it is asserted that leave should be given by virtue of subsection (3) or (5) or section 41;

(b) enabling the court to request a party to the proceedings to provide the court with information which it considers would assist it in determining an application for leave;

(c) for the manner in which confidential or sensitive information is to be treated in connection with such an application, and in particular as to its being disclosed to, or withheld from, parties to the proceedings.

CHAPTER IV   REPORTING RESTRICTIONS

Reports relating to persons under 18

44 Restrictions on reporting alleged offences involving persons under 18

(1) This section applies (subject to subsection (3)) where a criminal investigation has begun in respect of—

(a) an alleged offence against the law of—

(i)   England and Wales, or

(ii) . . .

(b) an alleged civil offence (other than an offence falling within paragraph (a)) committed (whether or not in the United Kingdom) by a person subject to service law.

(2) No matter relating to any person involved in the offence shall while he is under the age of 18 be included in any publication if it is likely to lead members of the public to identify him as a person involved in the offence.

(3) The restrictions imposed by subsection (2) cease to apply once there are proceedings in a court (whether a court in England and Wales, a service court . . .) in respect of the offence.

(4) For the purposes of subsection (2) any reference to a person involved in the offence is to—

(a) a person by whom the offence is alleged to have been committed; or

(b) if this paragraph applies to the publication in question by virtue of subsection (5)—

    (i) a person against or in respect of whom the offence is alleged to have been committed, or

    (ii) a person who is alleged to have been a witness to the commission of the offence;

except that paragraph (b)(i) does not include a person in relation to whom section 1 of the Sexual Offences (Amendment) Act 1992 (anonymity of victims of certain sexual offences) applies in connection with the offence.

(5) Subsection (4)(b) applies to a publication if—

(a) where it is a relevant programme, it is transmitted, or

(b) in the case of any other publication, it is published,

on or after such date as may be specified in an order made by the Secretary of State.

(6) The matters relating to a person in relation to which the restrictions imposed by subsection (2) apply (if their inclusion in any publication is likely to have the result mentioned in that subsection) include in particular—

(a) his name,

(b) his address,

(c) the identity of an school or other educational establishment attended by him,

(d) the identity of any place of work, and

(e) any still or moving picture of him.

(7) Any appropriate criminal court may by order dispense, to any extent specified in the order, with the restrictions imposed by subsection (2) in relation to a person if it is satisfied that it is necessary in the interests of justice to do so.

(8) However, when deciding whether to make such an order dispensing (to any extent) with the restrictions imposed by subsection (2) in relation to a person, the court shall have regard to the welfare of that person.

(9) In subsection (7) 'appropriate criminal court' means—

(a) in a case where this section applies by virtue of subsection (1)(a)(i) or (ii), any court in England and Wales ... which has any jurisdiction in, or in relation to, any criminal proceedings (but not a service court unless the offence is alleged to have been committed by a person subject to service law);

(b) in a case where this section applies by virtue of subsection (1)(b), any court falling within paragraph (a) or a service court.

(10) The power under subsection (7) of a magistrates' court in England and Wales may be exercised by a single justice.

(11) In the case of a decision of a magistrates' court ... to make or refuse to make an order under subsection (7), the following persons, namely—

(a) any person who was a party to the proceedings on the application for the order, and

(b) with the leave of the Crown Court, any other person,

may, in accordance with rules of court, appeal to the Crown Court against that decision or appear or be represented at the hearing of such an appeal.

(12) On such an appeal the Crown Court—

(a) may make such order as is necessary to give effect to its determination of the appeal; and

(b) may also make such incidental or consequential orders as appear to it to be just.

(13) In this section—

(a) 'civil offence' means an act or omission which, if committed in England and Wales, would be an offence against the law of England and Wales;

(b) any reference to a criminal investigation, in relation to an alleged offence, is to an investigation conducted by police officers, or other persons charged with the duty of investigation offences, with a view to it being ascertained whether a person should be charged with the offence;

(c) any reference to a person subject to service law is to—
  (i) a person subject to military law, air-force law or the Naval Discipline Act 1957, or
  (ii) any other person to whom provisions of Part II of the Army Act 1955, Part II of the Air Force Act 1955 or Parts I and II of the Naval Discipline Act 1957 apply (whether with or without any modifications).

45 Power to restrict reporting of criminal proceedings involving persons under 18

(1) This section applies (subject to subsection (2)) in relation to—
  (a) any criminal proceedings in any court (other than a service court) . . .; and
  (b) any proceedings (whether in the United Kingdom or elsewhere) in any service court.

(2) This section does not apply in relation to any proceedings to which section 49 of the Children and Young Persons Act 1933 applies.

(3) The court may direct that no matter relating to any person concerned in the proceedings shall while he is under the age of 18 be included in any publication if it is likely to lead members of the public to identify him as a person concerned in the proceedings.

(4) The court or an appellate court may by direction ('an excepting direction') dispense, to any extent specified in the excepting direction, with the restrictions imposed by a direction under subsection (3) if it is satisfied that it is necessary in the interests of justice to do so.

(5) The court or an appellate court may also by direction ('an excepting direction') dispense, to any extent specified in the excepting direction, with the restrictions imposed by a direction under subsection (3) if it is satisfied—
  (a) that their effect is to impose a substantial and unreasonable restriction on the reporting of the proceedings, and
  (b) that it is in the public interest to remove or relax that restriction;
but no excepting direction shall be given under this subsection by reason only of the fact that the proceedings have been determined in any way or have been abandoned.

(6) When deciding whether to make—
  (a) a direction under subsection (3) in relation to a person, or
  (b) an expecting direction under subsection (4) or (5) by virtue of which the restrictions imposed by a direction under subsection (3) would be dispensed with (to any extent) in relation to a person,
the court or (as the case may be) the appellate court shall have regard to the welfare of that person.

(7) For the purposes of subsection (3) any reference to a person concerned in the proceedings is to a person—
  (a) against or in respect of whom the proceedings are taken, or
  (b) who is a witness in the proceedings.

(8) the matters relating to a person in relation to which the restrictions imposed by a direction under subsection (3) apply (if their inclusion in any publication is likely to have the result mentioned in that subsection) include in particular—
  (a) his name,
  (b) his address,
  (c) the identity of any school or other educational establishment attended by him,
  (d) the identity of any place of work, and
  (e) any still or moving picture of him.

(9) A direction under subsection (3) may be revoked by the court or an appellate court.

(10) An excepting direction—

    (a) may be given at the time the direction under subsection (3) is given or subsequently; and

    (b) may be varied or revoked by the court or an appellate court.

(11) In this section 'appellate court', in relation to any proceedings in a court, means a court dealing with an appeal (including an appeal by way of case stated) arising out of the proceedings or with any further appeal.

Reports relating to adult witnesses

46 Power to restrict reports about certain adult witnesses in criminal proceedings

(1) This section applies where—

    (a) in any criminal proceedings in any court (other than a service court) or

    (b) in any proceedings (whether in the United Kingdom or elsewhere) in any service court,

a party to the proceedings makes an application for the court to give a reporting direction in relation to a witness in the proceedings (other than the accused) who has attained the age of 18.

In this section 'reporting direction' has the meaning given by subsection (6).

(2) If the court determines—

    (a) that the witness is eligible for protection, and

    (b) that giving a reporting direction in relation to the witness is likely to improve—

        (i) the quality of evidence given by the witness, or

        (ii) the level of co-operation given by the witness to any party to the proceedings in connection with that party's preparation of its case,

the court may give a reporting direction in relation to the witness.

(3) For the purposes of this section a witness is eligible for protection if the court is satisfied—

    (a) that the quality of evidence given by the witness, or

    (b) the level of co-operation given by the witness to any party to the proceedings in connection with that party's preparation of its case,

is likely to be diminished by reason of fear or distress on the part of the witness in connection with being identified by members of the public as a witness in the proceedings.

(4) In determining whether a witness is eligible for protection the court must take into account, in particular—

    (a) the nature and alleged circumstances of the offence to which the proceedings relate;

    (b) the age of the witness;

    (c) such of the following matters as appear to the court to be relevant, namely—

        (i) the social and cultural background and ethnic origins of the witness,

        (ii) the domestic and employment circumstances of the witness, and

        (iii) any religious beliefs or political opinions of the witness;

    (d) any behaviour towards the witness on the part of—

        (i) the accused,

        (ii) members of the family or associates of the accused, or

        (iii) any other person who is likely to be an accused or a witness in the proceedings.

(5) In determining that question the court must in addition consider any views expressed by the witness.

(6) For the purposes of this section a reporting direction in relation to a witness is a direction that no matter relating to the witness shall during the witness's lifetime be included

in any publication if it is likely to lead members of the public to identify him as being a witness in the proceedings.

(7) The matters relating to a witness in relation to which the restrictions imposed by a reporting direction apply (if their inclusion in any publication is likely to have the result mentioned in subsection (6)) include in particular—

(a) the witness's name,

(b) the witness's address,

(c) the identity of any educational establishment attended by the witness,

(d) the identity of any place of work, and

(e) any still or moving picture of the witness.

(8) In determining whether to give a reporting direction the court shall consider—

(a) whether it would be in the interests of justice to do so, and

(b) the public interest in avoiding the imposition of a substantial and unreasonable restriction on the reporting of the proceedings.

(9) The court or an appellate court may by direction ('an excepting direction') dispense, to any extent specified in the excepting direction, with the restrictions imposed by a reporting direction if—

(a) it is satisfied that it is necessary in the interests of justice to do so, or

(b) it is satisfied—

(i) that the effect of those restrictions is to impose a substantial and unreasonable restriction on the reporting of the proceedings, and

(ii) that it is in the public interest to remove or relax that restriction;

but no excepting direction shall be given under paragraph (b) by reason only of the fact that the proceedings have been determined in any way or have been abandoned.

(10) A reporting direction may be revoked by the court or an appellate court.

(11) An expecting direction—

(a) may be given at the time the reporting direction is given or subsequently; and

(b) may be varied or revoked by the court or an appellate court.

(12) In this section—

(a) 'appellate court', in relation to any proceedings in a court, means a court dealing with an appeal (including an appeal by way of case stated) arising out of the proceedings or with any further appeal;

(b) references to the quality of a witness's evidence are to its quality in terms of completeness, coherence and accuracy (and for this purpose 'coherence' refers to a witness's ability in giving evidence to give answers which address the questions put to the witness and can be understood both individually and collectively);

(c) references to the preparation of the case of a party to any proceedings include, where the party is the prosecution, the carrying out of investigations into any offence at any time charged in the proceedings.

Reports relating to directions under Chapter I or II

47   Restrictions on reporting directions under Chapter I or II

(1) Except as provided by this section, no publication shall include a report of a matter falling within subsection (2).

(2) The matters falling within this subsection are—

(a) a direction under section 19 or 36 or an order discharging, or (in the case of a direction under section 19) varying, such a direction;

(b) proceedings—

(i) on an application for such a direction or order, or

(ii) where the court acts of its own motion to determine whether to give or make any such direction or order.

302 Youth Justice and Criminal Evidence Act 1999

(3) The court dealing with a matter falling within subsection (2) may order that subsection (1) is not to apply, or is not to apply to a specified extent, to a report of that matter.

(4) Where—

(a) there is only one accused in the relevant proceedings, and

(b) he objects to the making of an order under subsection (3),

the court shall make the order if (and only if) satisfied after hearing the representations of the accused that it is in the interests of justice to do so; and if the order is made it shall not apply to the extent that a report deals with any such objections or representations.

(5) Where—

(a) there are two or more accused in the relevant proceedings, and

(b) one or more of them object to the making of an order under subsection (3),

the court shall make the order if (and only if) satisfied after hearing the representations of each of the accused that it is in the interests of justice to do so; and if the order is made it shall not apply to the extent that a report deals with any such objections or representations.

(6) Subsection (1) does not apply to the inclusion in a publication of a report of matters after the relevant proceedings are either—

(a) determined (by acquittal, conviction or otherwise), or

(b) abandoned,

in relation to the accused or (if there is more than one) in relation to each of the accused.

(7) In this section 'the relevant proceedings' means the proceedings to which any such direction as is mentioned in subsection (2) relates or would relate.

(8) Nothing in this section affects any prohibition or restriction by virtue of any other enactment on the inclusion of matter in a publication.

Other restrictions

48 Amendments relating to other reporting restrictions

Schedule 2, which contains amendments relating to reporting restrictions under—

(a) the Children and Young Persons Act 1933,

(b) the Sexual Offences (Amendment) Act 1976,

(c) the Sexual Offences (Northern Ireland) Order 1978,

(d) the Sexual Offences (Amendment) Act 1992, and

(e) the Criminal Justice (Northern Ireland) Order 1994,

shall have effect.

Offences

49 Offences under Chapter IV

(1) This section applies if a publication—

(a) includes any matter in contravention of section 44(2) or of a direction under section 45(3) or 46(2); or

(b) includes a report in a contravention of section 47.

(2) Where the publication is a newspaper or periodical, any proprietor, any editor and any publisher of the newspaper or periodical is guilty of an offence.

(3) Where the publication is a relevant programme—

(a) any body corporate . . . engaged in providing the programme service in which the programme is included, and

(b) any person having functions in relation to the programme corresponding to those of an editor of a newspaper,

is guilty of an offence.

(4) In the case of any other publication, any person publishing it is guilty of an offence.

(5) A person guilty of an offence under this section is liable on summary conviction to a fine not exceeding level 5 on the standard scale.

(6) Proceedings for an offence under this section in respect of a publication falling within subsection (1)(b) may not be instituted—

    (a) in England and Wales otherwise than by or with the consent of the Attorney General, or

    (b) *(Applies to Northern Ireland only.)*

50 Defences

(1) Where a person is charged with an offence under section 49 it shall be a defence to prove that at the time of the alleged offence he was not aware, and neither suspected nor had reason to suspect, that the publication included in the matter or report in question.

(2) Where—

    (a) a person is charged with an offence under section 49, and

    (b) the offence relates to the inclusion of any matter in a publication in contravention of section 44(2),

it shall be a defence to prove that at the time of the alleged offence he was not aware, and neither suspected nor had reason to suspect, that the criminal investigation in question had begun.

(3) Where—

    (a) paragraphs (a) and (b) or subsection (2) apply, and

    (b) the contravention of section 44(2) does not relate to either—

        (i) the person by whom the offence mentioned in that provision is alleged to have been committed, or

        (ii) (where that offence is one in relation to which section 1 of the Sexual Offences (Amendment) Act 1992 applies) a person who is alleged to be a witness to the commission of the offence,

it shall be a defence to show to the satisfaction of the court that the inclusion in the publication of the matter in question was in the public interest on the ground that, to the extent that they operated to prevent that matter from being so included, the effect of the restrictions imposed by section 44(2) was to impose a substantial and unreasonable restriction on the reporting of matters connected with that offence.

(4) Subsection (5) applies where—

    (a) paragraphs (a) and (b) of subsection (2) apply, and

    (b) the contravention of section 44(2) relates to a person ('the protected person') who is neither—

        (i) the person mentioned in subsection (3)(b)(i), nor

        (ii) a person within subsection (3)(b)(ii) who is under the age of 16.

(5) In such a case it shall be a defence, subject to subsection (6), to prove that written consent to the inclusion of the matter in question in the publication had been given—

    (a) by an appropriate person, if at the time when the consent was given the protected person was under the age of 16, or

    (b) by the protected person, if that person was aged 16 or 17 at that time,

and (where the consent was given by an appropriate person) that written notice had been previously given to that person drawing to his attention the need to consider the welfare of the protected person when deciding whether to give consent.

(6) The defence provided by subsection (5) is not available if—

    (a) (where the consent was given by an appropriate person) it is proved that written or other notice withdrawing the consent—

        (i) was given to the appropriate recipient by any other appropriate person or by the protected person, and

        (ii) was so given in sufficient time to enable the inclusion in the publication of the matter in question to be prevented; or

    (b) subsection (8) applies.

(7) Where—

    (a) a person is charged with an offence under section 49, and

    (b) the offence relates to the inclusion of any matter in a publication in contravention of a direction under section 46(2),

it shall be a defence, unless subsection (8) applies, to prove that the person in relation to whom the direction was given had given written consent to the inclusion of that matter in the publication.

(8) Written consent is not a defence if it is proved that any person interfered—

    (a) with the peace or comfort of the person giving the consent, or

    (b) (where the consent was given by an appropriate person) with the peace or comfort of either that person or the protected person,

with intent to obtain the consent.

(9) In this section—

'an appropriate person' means (subject to subsections (10) to (12))—

    (a) . . ., a person who is a parent or guardian of the protected person, or

    (b) (*Applies to Scotland only.*)

'guardian', in relation to the protected person, means any person who is not a parent of the protected person but who has parental responsibility for the protected person within the meaning of—

    (a) . . . the Children Act 1989, or

    (b) . . .

(10) Where the protected person is (within the meaning of the Children Act 1989) a child who is looked after by a local authority, 'an appropriate person' means a person who is—

    (a) a representative of that authority, or

    (b) a parent or guardian of the protected person with whom the protected person is allowed to live.

(11) (*Applies to Northern Ireland only.*)

(12) (*Applies to Scotland only.*)

(13) However, no person by whom the offence mentioned in section 44(2) is alleged to have been committed is, by virtue of subsection (9) to (10), an appropriate person for the purposes of this section.

(14) In this section 'the appropriate recipient', in relation to a notice under subsection (6)(a), means—

    (a) the person to whom the notice giving consent was given,

    (b) (if different) the person by whom the matter in question was published, or

    (c) any other person exercising, on behalf of the person mentioned in paragraph (b), any responsibility in relation to the publication of that matter;

and for this purpose 'person' includes a body of persons and a partnership.

51   Offences committed by bodies corporate [or Scottish partnerships]

(1) If an offence under section 49 committed by a body corporate is proved—

    (a) to have been committed with the consent or connivance of, or

    (b) to be attributable to any neglect on the part of,

an officer, the officer as well as the body corporate is guilty of the offence and liable to be proceeded against and punished accordingly.

(2) In subsection (1) 'officer' means a director, manager, secretary or other similar officer of the body, or a person purporting to act in any such capacity.

(3) If the affairs of a body corporate are managed by its members, 'director' in subsection (2) means a member of that body.

(4) (*Applies to Scotland only.*)

Supplementary

52   Decisions as to public interest for purposes of Chapter IV

(1) Where for the purposes of any provision of this Chapter it falls to a court to determine whether anything is (or, as the case may be, was) in the public interest, the court must have regard, in particular, to the matters referred to in subsection (2) (so far as relevant).

(2) Those matters are—

  (a) the interest in each of the following—
    (i)   the open reporting of crime,
    (ii) the open reporting of matters relating to human health or safety, and
    (iii) the prevention and exposure of miscarriages of justice;
  (b) the welfare of any person in relation to whom the relevant restrictions imposed by or under this Chapter apply or would apply (or, as the case may be, applied); and
  (c) any views expressed—
    (i)   by an appropriate person on behalf of a person within paragraph (b) who is under the age of 16 ('the protected person'), or
    (ii) by a person within that paragraph who has attained that age.

(3) In subsection (2) 'an appropriate person', in relation to the protected person, has the same meaning as it has for the purposes of section 50.

CHAPTER V   COMPETENCE OF WITNESSES AND CAPACITY TO BE SWORN

Competence of witnesses

53   Competence of witnesses to give evidence

(1) At every stage in criminal proceedings all persons are (whatever their age) competent to give evidence.

(2) Subsection (1) has effect subject to subsections (3) and (4).

(3) A person is not competent to give evidence in criminal proceedings if it appears to the court that he is not a person who is able to—

  (a) understand questions put to him as a witness, and
  (b) give answers to them which can be understood.

(4) A person charged in criminal proceedings is not competent to give evidence in the proceedings for the prosecution (whether he is the only person, or is one of two or more persons, charged in the proceedings).

(5) In subsection (4) the reference to a person charged in criminal proceedings does not include a person who is not, or is no longer, liable to be convicted of any offence in the proceedings (whether as a result of pleading guilty or for any other reason).

54   Determining competence of witnesses

(1) Any question whether a witness in criminal proceedings is competent to give evidence in the proceedings, whether raised—

  (a) by a party to the proceedings, or
  (b) by the court of its own motion,

shall be determined by the court in accordance with this section.

(2) It is for the party calling the witness to satisfy the court that, on a balance of probabilities, the witness is competent to give evidence in the proceedings.

(3) In determining the question mentioned in subsection (1) the court shall treat the witness as having the benefit of any directions under section 19 which the court has given, or proposes to give, in relation to the witness.

(4) Any proceedings held for the determination of the question shall take place in the absence of the jury (if there is one).

(5) Expert evidence may be received on the question.

(6) Any questioning of the witness (where the court considers that necessary) shall be conducted by the court in the presence of the parties.

Giving of sworn or unsworn evidence

55 Determining whether witness to be sworn

(1) Any question whether a witness in criminal proceedings may be sworn for the purpose of giving evidence on oath, whether raised—

    (a) by a party to the proceedings, or

    (b) by the court of its own motion,

shall be determined by the court in accordance with this section.

(2) The witness may not be sworn for that purpose unless—

    (a) he has attained the age of 14, and

    (b) he has a sufficient appreciation of the solemnity of the occasion and of the particular responsibility to tell the truth which is involved in taking an oath.

(3) The witness shall, if he is able to give intelligible testimony, be presumed to have a sufficient appreciation of those matters if no evidence tending to show the contrary is adduced (by any party).

(4) If any such evidence is adduced, it is for the party seeking to have the witness sworn to satisfy the court that, on a balance of probabilities, the witness has attained the age of 14 and has a sufficient appreciation of the matters mentioned in subsection (2)(b).

(5) Any proceedings held for the determination of the question mentioned in subsection (1) shall take place in the absence of the jury (if there is one).

(6) Expert evidence may be received on the question.

(7) Any questioning of the witness (where the court considers that necessary) shall be conducted by the court in the presence of the parties.

(8) For the purposes of this section a person is able to give intelligible testimony if he is able to—

    (a) understand questions put to him as a witness, and

    (b) give answers to them which can be understood.

56 Reception of unsworn evidence

(1) Subsections (2) and (3) apply to a person (of any age) who—

    (a) is competent to give evidence in criminal proceedings, but

    (b) (by virtue of section 55(2)) is not permitted to be sworn for the purpose of giving evidence on oath in such proceedings.

(2) The evidence in criminal proceedings of a person to whom this subsection applies shall be given unsworn.

(3) A deposition of unsworn evidence given by a person to whom this subsection applies may be taken for the purposes of criminal proceedings as if that evidence had been given on oath.

(4) A court in criminal proceedings shall accordingly receive in evidence any evidence given unsworn in pursuance of subsection (2) or (3).

(5) Where a person ('the witness') who is competent to give evidence in criminal proceedings gives evidence in such proceedings unsworn, no conviction, verdict or finding in those proceedings shall be taken to be unsafe for the purposes of any of sections 2(1), 13(1) and 16(1) of the Criminal Appeal Act 1968 (grounds for allowing appeals) by reason only that it appears to the Court of Appeal that the witness was a person falling within section 55(2) (and should accordingly have given his evidence on oath).

57 Penalty for giving false unsworn evidence

(1) This section applies where a person gives unsworn evidence in criminal proceedings in pursuance of section 56(2) or (3).

(2) If such a person wilfully gives false evidence in such circumstances that, had the evidence been given on oath, he would have been guilty of perjury, he shall be guilty of an offence and liable on summary conviction to—

(a) imprisonment for a term not exceeding 6 months, or

(b) a fine not exceeding £1,000,

or both.

(3) In relation to a person under the age of 14, subsection (2) shall have effect as if for the words following 'on summary conviction' there were substituted 'to a fine not exceeding £250'.

59 Restriction on use of answers etc. obtained under compulsion

Schedule 3, which amends enactments providing for the use of answers and statements given under compulsion so as to restrict in criminal proceedings their use in evidence against the persons giving them, shall have effect.

CHAPTER VII   GENERAL

61 Application of Part II to service courts

(1) The Secretary of State may by order direct that any provision of—

(a) Chapters I to III and V, or

(b) sections 62, 63 and 65 so far as having effect for the purposes of any of those Chapters,

shall apply, subject to such modifications as he may specify, to any proceedings before a service court.

(2) Chapter IV (and sections 62, 63 and 65 so far as having effect for the purposes of that Chapter) shall have effect for the purposes of proceedings before a service court subject to any modifications which the Secretary of State may by order specify.

(3) The power to make an order under section 39 of the Criminal Justice and Public Order Act 1994 (power to apply sections 34 to 38 to the armed forces) in relation to any provision of sections 34 to 38 of that Act shall be exercisable in relation to any provision of those sections as amended by section 58 above.

62 Meaning of 'sexual offence' and other references to offences

(1) In this Part 'sexual offence' means any offence under Part 1 of the Sexual Offences Acct 2003.

(2) In this part any reference (including a reference having effect by virtue of this subsection) to an offence of any description ('the substantive offence') is to be taken to include a reference to an offence which consists of attempting or conspiring to commit, or of aiding, abetting, counselling, procuring or inciting the commission of, the substantive offence.

63 General interpretation etc. of Part II

(1) In this Part (except where the context otherwise requires)—

'accused', in relation to any criminal proceedings, means any person charged with an offence to which the proceedings relate (whether or not he has been convicted);

'the complainant', in relation to any offence (or alleged offence), means a person against or in relation to whom the offence was (or is alleged to have been) committed;

'court' (except in Chapter IV or V or subsection (2)) means a magistrates' court, the Crown Court or criminal division of the Court of Appeal;

'legal representative' means any authorised advocate or authorised litigator (as defined by section 119(1) of the Courts and Legal Services Act 1990);

'picture' includes a likeness however produced;

'the prosecutor' means any person acting as prosecutor, whether an individual or body;

'publication' includes any speech, writing, relevant programme or other communication in whatever form, which is addressed to the public at large or any section of the public (and for this purpose every relevant programme shall be taken to be so addressed), but does not include an indictment or other document prepared for use in particular legal proceedings;

'relevant programme' means a programme included in a programme service, within the meaning of the Broadcasting Act 1990;

'service court' means—

(a) a court-martial constituted under the Army Act 1955, the Air Force Act 1955 or the Naval Discipline Act 1957 or a disciplinary court constituted under section 52G of the Naval Discipline Act 1957,

(b) the Courts-Martial Appeal Court, or

(b) the Courts-Martial Appeal Court, or

(c) a Standing Civilian Court;

'video recording' means any recording, on any medium, from which a moving image may by any means be produced, and includes the accompanying sound-track;

'witness', in relation to any criminal proceedings, means any person called, or proposed to be called, to give evidence in the proceedings.

(2) Nothing in this Part shall affect any power of a court to exclude evidence at its discretion (whether by preventing questions being put or otherwise) which is exercisable apart from this Part.

Criminal Cases Review (Insanity) Act 1999
(1999, c. 25)

1   Reference of former verdict of guilty but insane

(1) Where a verdict was returned in England and Wales or Northern Ireland to the effect that a person was guilty of the act or omission charged against him but was insane at the time, the Criminal Cases Review Commission may at any time refer the verdict to the Court of Appeal if subsection (2) below applies.

(2) This subsection applies if the commission consider that there is a real possibility that the verdict would not be upheld were the reference to be made and either—

(a) the Commission so consider because of an argument, or evidence, not raised in the proceedings which led to the verdict, or

(b) it appears to the Commission that there are exceptional circumstances which justify the making of the reference.

(3) Section 14 of the Criminal Appeal Act 1995 (supplementary provision about the reference of a verdict) shall apply in relation to a reference under subsection (1) above as it applies in relation to references under section 9 or 10 of that Act.

2   Reference treated as appeal: England and Wales

(1) A reference under section 1(1) above of a verdict returned in England and Wales in the case of a person shall be treated for all purposes as an appeal by the person under section 12 of the Criminal Appeal Act 1968.

(2) In their application to such a reference by virtue of subsection (1) above, sections 13 and 14 of that Act shall have effect—

(a) as if references to the verdict of not guilty by reason of insanity were to the verdict referred under section 1(1) above, and

(b) as if, in section 14(1)(b), for the words from the beginning to 'that he' there were substituted 'the accused was under a disability and'.

3   (*Applies to Northern Ireland only.*)

4   Extent and short title

(1) ...

(2) ...

(3) ...

(4) This Act may be cited as the Criminal Cases Review (Insanity) Act 1999.

Terrorism Act 2000
(1996, c. 25)

PART V   COUNTER-TERRORIST POWERS

Suspected terrorists

40 Terrorist: interpretation

(1) In this Part "terrorist" means a person who—

(a) has committed an offence under any of sections 11, 12, 15 to 18, 54 and 56 to 63, or

(b) is or has been concerned in the commission, preparation or instigation of acts of terrorism.

(2) The reference in subsection (1)(b) to a person who has been concerned in the commission, preparation or instigation of acts of terrorism includes a reference to a person who has been, whether before or after the passing of this Act, concerned in the commission, preparation or instigation of acts of terrorism within the meaning given by section 1.

41 Arrest without warrant

(1) A constable may arrest without a warrant a person whom he reasonably suspects to be a terrorist.

(2) Where a person is arrested under this section the provisions of Schedule 8 (detention: treatment, review and extension) shall apply.

(3) Subject to subsections (4) to (7), a person detained under this section shall (unless detained under any other power) be released not later than the end of the period of 48 hours beginning—

(a) with the time of his arrest under this section, or

(b) if he was being detained under Schedule 7 when he was arrested under this section, with the time when his examination under that Schedule began.

(4) If on a review of a person's detention under Part II of Schedule 8 the review officer does not authorise continued detention, the person shall (unless detained in accordance with subsection (5) or (6) or under any other power) be released.

(5) Where a police officer intends to make an application for a warrant under paragraph 29 of Schedule 8 extending a person's detention, the person may be detained pending the making of the application.

(6) Where an application has been made under paragraph 29 or 36 of Schedule 8 in respect of a person's detention, he may be detained pending the conclusion of proceedings on the application.

(7) Where an application under paragraph 29 or 36 of Schedule 8 is granted in respect of a person's detention, he may be detained, subject to paragraph 37 of that Schedule, during the period specified in the warrant.

(8) The refusal of an application in respect of a person's detention under paragraph 29 or 36 of Schedule 8 shall not prevent his continued detention in accordance with this section.

(9) A person who has the powers of a constable in one Part of the United Kingdom may exercise the power under subsection (1) in any Part of the United Kingdom.

42 Search of premises

(1) A justice of the peace may on the application of a constable issue a warrant in relation to specified premises if he is satisfied that there are reasonable grounds for suspecting that a person whom the constable reasonably suspects to be a person falling within section 40(1)(b) is to be found there.

(2) A warrant under this section shall authorise any constable to enter and search the specified premises for the purpose of arresting the person referred to in subsection (1) under section 41.

(3) [Scotland]

43   Search of persons

(1) A constable may stop and search a person whom he reasonably suspects to be a terrorist to discover whether he has in his possession anything which may constitute evidence that he is a terrorist.

(2) A constable may search a person arrested under section 41 to discover whether he has in his possession anything which may constitute evidence that he is a terrorist.

(3) A search of a person under this section must be carried out by someone of the same sex.

(4) A constable may seize and retain anything which he discovers in the course of a search of a person under subsection (1) or (2) and which he reasonably suspects may constitute evidence that the person is a terrorist.

(5) A person who has the powers of a constable in one Part of the United Kingdom may exercise a power under this section in any Part of the United Kingdom.

Power to stop and search

44   Authorisations

(1) An authorisation under this subsection authorises any constable in uniform to stop a vehicle in an area or at a place specified in the authorisation and to search—

    (a) the vehicle;

    (b) the driver of the vehicle;

    (c) a passenger in the vehicle;

    (d) anything in or on the vehicle or carried by the driver or a passenger.

(2) An authorisation under this subsection authorises any constable in uniform to stop a pedestrian in an area or at a place specified in the authorisation and to search—

    (a) the pedestrian;

    (b) anything carried by him.

(3) An authorisation under subsection (1) or (2) may be given only if the person giving it considers it expedient for the prevention of acts of terrorism.

(4) An authorisation may be given—

    (a) where the specified area or place is the whole or part of a police area outside Northern Ireland other than one mentioned in paragraph (b) or (c), by a police officer for the area who is of at least the rank of assistant chief constable;

    (b) where the specified area or place is the whole or part of the metropolitan police district, by a police officer for the district who is of at least the rank of commander of the metropolitan police;

    (c) where the specified area or place is the whole or part of the City of London, by a police officer for the City who is of at least the rank of commander in the City of London police force;

    (d) where the specified area or place is the whole or part of Northern Ireland, by a member of the Royal Ulster Constabulary who is of at least the rank of assistant chief constable.

(5) If an authorisation is given orally, the person giving it shall confirm it in writing as soon as is reasonably practicable.

45   Exercise of power

(1) The power conferred by an authorisation under section 44(1) or (2)—

(a) may be exercised only for the purpose of searching for articles of a kind which could be used in connection with terrorism, and

(b) may be exercised whether or not the constable has grounds for suspecting the presence of articles of that kind.

(2) A constable may seize and retain an article which he discovers in the course of a search by virtue of section 44(1) or (2) and which he reasonably suspects is intended to be used in connection with terrorism.

(3) A constable exercising the power conferred by an authorisation may not require a person to remove any clothing in public except for headgear, footwear, an outer coat, a jacket or gloves.

(4) Where a constable proposes to search a person or vehicle by virtue of section 44(1) or (2) he may detain the person or vehicle for such time as is reasonably required to permit the search to be carried out at or near the place where the person or vehicle is stopped.

(5) Where—

(a) a vehicle or pedestrian is stopped by virtue of section 44(1) or (2), and

(b) the driver of the vehicle or the pedestrian applies for a written statement that the vehicle was stopped, or that he was stopped, by virtue of section 44(1) or (2),

the written statement shall be provided.

(6) An application under subsection (5) must be made within the period of 12 months beginning with the date on which the vehicle or pedestrian was stopped.

46   Duration of authorisation

(1) An authorisation under section 44 has effect, subject to subsections (2) to (7), during the period—

(a) beginning at the time when the authorisation is given, and

(b) ending with a date or at a time specified in the authorisation.

(2) The date or time specified under subsection (1)(b) must not occur after the end of the period of 28 days beginning with the day on which the authorisation is given.

(3) The person who gives an authorisation shall inform the Secretary of State as soon as is reasonably practicable.

(4) If an authorisation is not confirmed by the Secretary of State before the end of the period of 48 hours beginning with the time when it is given—

(a) it shall cease to have effect at the end of that period, but

(b) its ceasing to have effect shall not affect the lawfulness of anything done in reliance on it before the end of that period.

(5) Where the Secretary of State confirms an authorisation he may substitute an earlier date or time for the date or time specified under subsection (1)(b).

(6) The Secretary of State may cancel an authorisation with effect from a specified time.

(7) An authorisation may be renewed in writing by the person who gave it or by a person who could have given it; and subsections (1) to (6) shall apply as if a new authorisation were given on each occasion on which the authorisation is renewed.

47   Offences

(1) A person commits an offence if he—

(a) fails to stop a vehicle when required to do so by a constable in the exercise of the power conferred by an authorisation under section 44(1);

(b) fails to stop when required to do so by a constable in the exercise of the power conferred by an authorisation under section 44(2);

(c) wilfully obstructs a constable in the exercise of the power conferred by an authorisation under section 44(1) or (2).

(2) A person guilty of an offence under this section shall be liable on summary conviction to—

(a) imprisonment for a term not exceeding six months,

(b) a fine not exceeding level 5 on the standard scale, or

(c) both.

PART VIII   GENERAL

114   Police powers

(1) A power conferred by virtue of this Act on a constable—

(a) is additional to powers which he has at common law or by virtue of any other enactment, and

(b) shall not be taken to affect those powers.

(2) A constable may if necessary use reasonable force for the purpose of exercising a power conferred on him by virtue of this Act (apart from paragraphs 2 and 3 of Schedule 7).

(3) Where anything is seized by a constable under a power conferred by virtue of this Act, it may (unless the contrary intention appears) be retained for so long as is necessary in all the circumstances.

115   Officers' powers

Schedule 14 (which makes provision about the exercise of functions by authorised officers for the purposes of sections 25 to 31 and examining officers for the purposes of Schedule 7) shall have effect.

116   Powers to stop and search

(1) A power to search premises conferred by virtue of this Act shall be taken to include power to search a container.

(2) A power conferred by virtue of this Act to stop a person includes power to stop a vehicle (other than an aircraft which is airborne).

(3) A person commits an offence if he fails to stop a vehicle when required to do so by virtue of this section.

(4) A person guilty of an offence under subsection (3) shall be liable on summary conviction to—

(a) imprisonment for a term not exceeding six months,

(b) a fine not exceeding level 5 on the standard scale, or

(c) both.

117   Consent to prosecution

(1) This section applies to an offence under any provision of this Act other than an offence under—

(a) section 36,

(b) section 51,

(c) paragraph 18 of Schedule 7,

(d) paragraph 12 of Schedule 12, or

(e) Schedule 13.

(2) Proceedings for an offence to which this section applies—

(a) shall not be instituted in England and Wales without the consent of the Director of Public Prosecutions, and

(b) (*Applies to Northern Ireland only.*)

(3) Where it appears to the Director of Public Prosecutions . . . that an offence to which this section applies is committed for a purpose connected with the affairs of a country other than the United Kingdom—

(a) subsection (2) shall not apply, and

(b) proceedings for the offence shall not be instituted without the consent of the Attorney General. . . .

118 Defences

(1) Subsection (2) applies where in accordance with a provision mentioned in subsection (5) it is a defence for a person charged with an offence to prove a particular matter.

(2) If the person adduces evidence which is sufficient to raise an issue with respect to the matter the court or jury shall assume that the defence is satisfied unless the prosecution proves beyond reasonable doubt that it is not.

(3) Subsection (4) applies where in accordance with a provision mentioned in subsection (5) a court—

(a) may make an assumption in relation to a person charged with an offence unless a particular matter is proved, or

(b) may accept a fact as sufficient evidence unless a particular matter is proved.

(4) If evidence is adduced which is sufficient to raise an issue with respect to the matter mentioned in subsection (3)(a) or (b) the court shall treat it as proved unless the prosecution disproves it beyond reasonable doubt.

(5) The provisions in respect of which subsections (2) and (4) apply are—

(a) sections 12(4), 39(5)(a), 54, 57, 58, 77 and 103 of this Act, and

(b) (*Applies to Northern Ireland only.*)

120 Evidence

(1) A document which purports to be—

(a) a notice or direction given or order made by the Secretary of State for the purposes of a provision of this Act, and

(b) signed by him or on his behalf,

shall be received in evidence and shall, until the contrary is proved, be deemed to have been given or made by the Secretary of State.

(2) A document bearing a certificate which—

(a) purports to be signed by or on behalf of the Secretary of State, and

(b) states that the document is a true copy of a notice or direction given or order made by the Secretary of State for the purposes of a provision of this Act,

shall be evidence . . . of the document in legal proceedings.

(3) In subsections (1) and (2) a reference to an order does not include a reference to an order made by statutory instrument.

(4) The Documentary Evidence Act 1868 shall apply to an authorisation given in writing by the Secretary of State for the purposes of this Act as it applies to an order made by him.

SCHEDULE 8   DETENTION
PART I   TREATMENT OF PERSONS DETAINED
UNDER SECTION 41 OR SCHEDULE 7

Place of detention

1.—(1) The Secretary of State shall designate places at which persons may be detained under Schedule 7 or section 41.

(2) In this Schedule a reference to a police station includes a reference to any place which the Secretary of State has designated under sub-paragraph (1) as a place where a person may be detained under section 41.

(3) Where a person is detained under Schedule 7, he may be taken in the custody of an examining officer or of a person acting under an examining officer's authority to and from any place where his attendance is required for the purpose of—

(a) his examination under that Schedule,

(b) establishing his nationality or citizenship, or

(c) making arrangements for his admission to a country or territory outside the United Kingdom.

(4) A constable who arrests a person under section 41 shall take him as soon as is reasonably practicable to the police station which the constable considers the most appropriate.

(5) In this paragraph "examining officer" has the meaning given in Schedule 7.

(6) Where a person is arrested in one Part of the United Kingdom and all or part of his detention takes place in another Part, the provisions of this Schedule which apply to detention in a particular Part of the United Kingdom apply in relation to him while he is detained in that Part.

Identification

2.—(1) An authorised person may take any steps which are reasonably necessary for—
  (a) photographing the detained person,
  (b) measuring him, or
  (c) identifying him.

(2) In sub-paragraph (1) "authorised person" means any of the following—
  (a) a constable,
  (b) a prison officer,
  (c) a person authorised by the Secretary of State, and
  (d) in the case of a person detained under Schedule 7, an examining officer (within the meaning of that Schedule).

(3) This paragraph does not confer the power to take—
  (a) fingerprints, non-intimate samples or intimate samples (within the meaning given by paragraph 15 below), or
  (b) [Scotland]

Audio and video recording of interviews

3.—(1) The Secretary of State shall—
  (a) issue a code of practice about the audio recording of interviews to which this paragraph applies, and
  (b) make an order requiring the audio recording of interviews to which this paragraph applies in accordance with any relevant code of practice under paragraph (a).

(2) The Secretary of State may make an order requiring the video recording of—
  (a) interviews to which this paragraph applies;
  (b) interviews to which this paragraph applies which take place in a particular Part of the United Kingdom.

(3) An order under sub-paragraph (2) shall specify whether the video recording which it requires is to be silent or with sound.

(4) Where an order is made under sub-paragraph (2)—
  (a) the Secretary of State shall issue a code of practice about the video recording of interviews to which the order applies, and
  (b) the order shall require the interviews to be video recorded in accordance with any relevant code of practice under paragraph (a).

(5) Where the Secretary of State has made an order under sub-paragraph (2) requiring certain interviews to be video recorded with sound—
  (a) he need not make an order under sub-paragraph (1)(b) in relation to those interviews, but
  (b) he may do so.

(6) This paragraph applies to any interview by a constable of a person detained under Schedule 7 or section 41 if the interview takes place in a police station.

(7) A code of practice under this paragraph—

    (a) may make provision in relation to a particular Part of the United Kingdom;

    (b) may make different provision for different Parts of the United Kingdom.

4.—(1) This paragraph applies to a code of practice under paragraph 3.

(2) Where the Secretary of State proposes to issue a code of practice he shall—

    (a) publish a draft,

    (b) consider any representations made to him about the draft, and

    (c) if he thinks it appropriate, modify the draft in the light of any representations made to him.

(3) The Secretary of State shall lay a draft of the code before Parliament.

(4) When the Secretary of State has laid a draft code before Parliament he may bring it into operation by order.

(5) The Secretary of State may revise a code and issue the revised code; and sub-paragraphs (2) to (4) shall apply to a revised code as they apply to an original code.

(6) The failure by a constable to observe a provision of a code shall not of itself make him liable to criminal or civil proceedings.

(7) A code—

    (a) shall be admissible in evidence in criminal and civil proceedings, and

    (b) shall be taken into account by a court or tribunal in any case in which it appears to the court or tribunal to be relevant.

Status

5.   A detained person shall be deemed to be in legal custody throughout the period of his detention.

Rights: England, Wales and Northern Ireland

6.—(1) Subject to paragraph 8, a person detained under Schedule 7 or section 41 at a police station in England, Wales [or Northern Ireland] shall be entitled, if he so requests, to have one named person informed as soon as is reasonably practicable that he is being detained there.

(2) The person named must be—

    (a) a friend of the detained person,

    (b) a relative, or

    (c) a person who is known to the detained person or who is likely to take an interest in his welfare.

(3) Where a detained person is transferred from one police station to another, he shall be entitled to exercise the right under this paragraph in respect of the police station to which he is transferred.

7.—(1) Subject to paragraphs 8 and 9, a person detained under Schedule 7 or section 41 at a police station in England, Wales [or Northern Ireland] shall be entitled, if he so requests, to consult a solicitor as soon as is reasonably practicable, privately and at any time.

(2) Where a request is made under sub-paragraph (1), the request and the time at which it was made shall be recorded.

8.—(1) Subject to sub-paragraph (2), an officer of at least the rank of superintendent may authorise a delay—

    (a) in informing the person named by a detained person under paragraph 6;

    (b) in permitting a detained person to consult a solicitor under paragraph 7.

(2) But where a person is detained under section 41 he must be permitted to exercise his rights under paragraphs 6 and 7 before the end of the period mentioned in subsection (3) of that section.

(3) Subject to sub-paragraph (5), an officer may give an authorisation under sub-paragraph (1) only if he has reasonable grounds for believing—

    (a) in the case of an authorisation under sub-paragraph (1)(a), that informing the named person of the detained person's detention will have any of the consequences specified in sub-paragraph (4), or

    (b) in the case of an authorisation under sub-paragraph (1)(b), that the exercise of the right under paragraph 7 at the time when the detained person desires to exercise it will have any of the consequences specified in sub-paragraph (4).

(4) Those consequences are—

    (a) interference with or harm to evidence of a serious arrestable offence,

    (b) interference with or physical injury to any person,

    (c) the alerting of persons who are suspected of having committed a serious arrestable offence but who have not been arrested for it,

    (d) the hindering of the recovery of property obtained as a result of a serious arrestable offence or in respect of which a forfeiture order could be made under section 23,

    (e) interference with the gathering of information about the commission, preparation or instigation of acts of terrorism,

    (f) the alerting of a person and thereby making it more difficult to prevent an act of terrorism, and

    (g) the alerting of a person and thereby making it more difficult to secure a person's apprehension, prosecution or conviction in connection with the commission, preparation or instigation of an act of terrorism.

'(5) An officer may also give an authorisation under sub-paragraph (1) if he has reasonable grounds for believing that—

    (a) the detained person has benefited from his criminal conduct, and

    (b) the recovery of the value of the property constituting the benefit will be hindered by—

        (i) informing the named person of the detained person's detention (in the case of an authorisation under subparagraph (1)(a)), or

        (ii) the exercise of the right under paragraph 7 (in the case of an authorisation under sub-paragraph (1)(b)).

(5A) For the purpose of sub-paragraph (5) the question whether a person has benefited from his criminal conduct is to be decided in accordance with Part 2 of the Proceeds of Crime Act 2002.'

(6) If an authorisation under sub-paragraph (1) is given orally, the person giving it shall confirm it in writing as soon as is reasonably practicable.

(7) Where an authorisation under sub-paragraph (1) is given—

    (a) the detained person shall be told the reason for the delay as soon as is reasonably practicable, and

    (b) the reason shall be recorded as soon as is reasonably practicable.

(8) Where the reason for authorising delay ceases to subsist there may be no further delay in permitting the exercise of the right in the absence of a further authorisation under sub-paragraph (1).

(9) In this paragraph 'serious arrestable offence' has the meaning given by section 116 of the Police and Criminal Evidence Act 1984 (in relation to England and Wales) . . .; but it also includes—

    (a) an offence under any of the provisions mentioned in section 40(1)(a) of this Act, and

    (b) an attempt or conspiracy to commit an offence under any of the provisions mentioned in section 40(1)(a).

9.—(1) A direction under this paragraph may provide that a detained person who wishes to exercise the right under paragraph 7 may consult a solicitor only in the sight and hearing of a qualified officer.

(2) A direction under this paragraph may be given—

(a) where the person is detained at a police station in England or Wales, by an officer of at least the rank of Commander or Assistant Chief Constable, or

(b) (*Applies to Northern Ireland only.*)

(3) A direction under this paragraph may be given only if the officer giving it has reasonable grounds for believing that, unless the direction is given, the exercise of the right by the detained person will have any of the consequences specified in paragraph 8(4) or the consequence specified in paragraph 8(5)(c).

(4) In this paragraph 'a qualified officer' means a police officer who—

(a) is of at least the rank of inspector,

(b) is of the uniformed branch of the force of which the officer giving the direction is a member, and

(c) in the opinion of the officer giving the direction, has no connection with the detained person's case.

(5) A direction under this paragraph shall cease to have effect once the reason for giving it ceases to subsist.

10.—(1) This paragraph applies where a person is detained in England, Wales [or Northern Ireland] under Schedule 7 or section 41.

(2) Fingerprints may be taken from the detained person only if they are taken by a constable—

(a) with the appropriate consent given in writing, or

(b) without that consent under sub-paragraph (4).

(3) A non-intimate sample may be taken from the detained person only if it is taken by a constable—

(a) with the appropriate consent given in writing, or

(b) without that consent under sub-paragraph (4).

(4) Fingerprints or a non-intimate sample may be taken from the detained person without the appropriate consent only if—

(a) he is detained at a police station and a police officer of at least the rank of superintendent authorises the fingerprints or sample to be taken, or

(b) he has been convicted of a recordable offence and, where a non-intimate sample is to be taken, he was convicted of the offence on or after 10th April 1995. . . .

(5) An intimate sample may be taken from the detained person only if—

(a) he is detained at a police station,

(b) the appropriate consent is given in writing,

(c) a police officer of at least the rank of superintendent authorises the sample to be taken, and

(d) subject to paragraph 13(2) and (3), the sample is taken by a constable.

(6) An officer may give an authorisation under sub-paragraph (4)(a) or (5)(c) only if—

(a) in the case of a person detained under section 41, the officer reasonably suspects that the person has been involved in an offence under any of the provisions mentioned in section 40(1)(a), and the officer reasonably believes that the fingerprints or sample will tend to confirm or disprove his involvement, or

(b) in any case, the officer is satisfied that the taking of the fingerprints or sample from the person is necessary in order to assist in determining whether he falls within section 40(1)(b).

(6A) An officer may also give an authorisation under sub-paragraph (4)(a) for the taking of fingerprints if—

(a) he is satisfied that the fingerprints of the detained person will facilitate the ascertainment of that person's identity; and

(b) that person has refused to identify himself or the officer has resonable grounds for suspecting that that person is not who he claims to be.

(6B) In this paragraph references to ascertaining a person's identity include references to showing that he is not a particular person.

(7) If an authorisation under sub-paragraph (4)(a) or (5)(c) is given orally, the person giving it shall confirm it in writing as soon as is reasonably practicable.

11.—(1) Before fingerprints or a sample are taken from a person under paragraph 10, he shall be informed—

(a) that the fingerprints or sample may be used for the purposes of paragraph 14(4), section 63A(1) of the Police and Criminal Evidence Act 1984 . . . and

(b) where the fingerprints or sample are to be taken under paragraph 10(2)(a), (3)(a) or (4)(b), of the reason for taking the fingerprints or sample.

(2) Before fingerprints or a sample are taken from a person upon an authorisation given under paragraph 10(4)(a) or (5)(c), he shall be informed—

(a) that the authorisation has been given,

(b) of the grounds upon which it has been given, and

(c) where relevant, of the nature of the offence in which it is suspected that he has been involved.

(3) After fingerprints or a sample are taken under paragraph 10, there shall be recorded as soon as is reasonably practicable any of the following which apply—

(a) the fact that the person has been informed in accordance with subparagraphs (1) and (2),

(b) the reason referred to in sub-paragraph (1)(b),

(c) the authorisation given under paragraph 10(4)(a) or (5)(c),

(d) the grounds upon which that authorisation has been given, and

(e) the fact that the appropriate consent has been given.

12.—(1) This paragraph applies where—

(a) two or more non-intimate samples suitable for the same means of analysis have been taken from a person under paragraph 10,

(b) those samples have proved insufficient, and

(c) the person has been released from detention.

(2) An intimate sample may be taken from the person if—

(a) the appropriate consent is given in writing,

(b) a police officer of at least the rank of superintendent authorises the sample to be taken, and

(c) subject to paragraph 13(2) and (3), the sample is taken by a constable.

(3) Paragraphs 10(6) and (7) and 11 shall apply in relation to the taking of an intimate sample under this paragraph; and a reference to a person detained under section 41 shall be taken as a reference to a person who was detained under section 41 when the non-intimate samples mentioned in sub-paragraph (1)(a) were taken.

13.—(1) Where appropriate written consent to the taking of an intimate sample from a person under paragraph 10 or 12 is refused without good cause, in any proceedings against that person for an offence—

(a) the court, in determining whether to commit him for trial or whether there is a case to answer, may draw such inferences from the refusal as appear proper, and

(b) the court or jury, in determining whether that person is guilty of the offence charged, may draw such inferences from the refusal as appear proper.

(2) An intimate sample other than a sample of urine or a dental impression may be taken under paragraph 10 or 12 only by a registered medical practitioner acting on the authority of a constable.

(3) An intimate sample which is a dental impression may be taken under paragraph 10 or 12 only by a registered dentist acting on the authority of a constable.

(4) Where a sample of hair other than pubic hair is to be taken under paragraph 10 the sample may be taken either by cutting hairs or by plucking hairs with their roots so long as no more are plucked than the person taking the sample reasonably considers to be necessary for a sufficient sample.

14.—(1) This paragraph applies to—

    (a) fingerprints or samples taken under paragraph 10 or 12, and

    (b) information derived from those samples.

(2) The fingerprints, samples or information may be used only for the purpose of a terrorist investigation.

(3) In particular, a check may not be made against them under—

    (a) section 63A(1) of the Police and Criminal Evidence Act 1984 (checking of fingerprints and samples)

    (b) (*Applies to Northern Ireland only.*)

except for the purpose of a terrorist investigation.

(4) The fingerprints, samples or information may be checked, subject to sub-paragraph (2), against—

    (a) other fingerprints or samples taken under paragraph 10 or 12 or information derived from those samples,

    (b) relevant physical data or samples taken by virtue of paragraph 20,

    (c) any of the fingerprints, samples and information mentioned in section 63A(1)(a) and (b) of the Police and Criminal Evidence Act 1984 (checking of fingerprints and samples),

    (d) (*Applies to Northern Ireland only.*) and

    (e) fingerprints or samples taken under section 15(9) of, or paragraph 7(5) of Schedule 5 to, the Prevention of Terrorism (Temporary Provisions) Act 1989 or information derived from those samples.

(4A) In this paragraph—

    (a) a reference to crime includes a reference to any conduct which—

      (i) constitutes one or more criminal offences (whether under the law of a part of the United Kingdom or of a country or territory outside the United Kingdom); or

      (ii) is, or corresponds to, any conduct which, if it all took place in any one part of the United Kingdom, would constitute one or more criminal offences; and

    (b) the references to an investigation and to a prosecution include references, respectively, to any investigation outside the United Kingdom of any crime or suspected crime and to a prosecution brought in respect of any crime in a country or territory outside the United Kingdom.

(5) This paragraph (other than sub-paragraph (4)) shall apply to fingerprints or samples taken under section 15(9) of, or paragraph 7(5) of Schedule 5 to, the Prevention of Terrorism (Temporary Provisions) Act 1989 and information derived from those samples as it applies to fingerprints or samples taken under paragraph 10 or 12 and the information derived from those samples.

15.—(1) In the application of paragraphs 10 to 14 in relation to a person detained in England or Wales the following expressions shall have the meaning given by section 65 of the Police and Criminal Evidence Act 1984 (Part V definitions)—

    (a) 'appropriate consent',

    (b) 'fingerprints',

    (c) 'insufficient',

    (d) 'intimate sample',

    (e) 'non-intimate sample',
    (f) 'registered dentist', and
    (g) 'sufficient'.
(2) (*Applies to Northern Ireland only.*)
(3) In paragraph 10 'recordable offence' shall have—
    (a) in relation to a person detained in England or Wales, the meaning given by section 118(1) of the Police and Criminal Evidence Act 1984 (general interpretation), and
    (b) (*Applies to Northern Ireland only.*)

PART II   REVIEW OF DETENTION UNDER SECTION 41

Requirement

21.—(1) A person's detention shall be periodically reviewed by a review officer.
(2) The first review shall be carried out as soon as is reasonably practicable after the time of the person's arrest.
(3) Subsequent reviews shall, subject to paragraph 22, be carried out at intervals of not more than 12 hours.
(4) No review of a person's detention shall be carried out after a warrant extending his detention has been issued under Part III.

Postponement

22.—(1) A review may be postponed if at the latest time at which it may be carried out in accordance with paragraph 21—
    (a) the detained person is being questioned by a police officer and an officer is satisfied that an interruption of the questioning to carry out the review would prejudice the investigation in connection with which the person is being detained,
    (b) no review officer is readily available, or
    (c) it is not practicable for any other reason to carry out the review.
(2) Where a review is postponed it shall be carried out as soon as is reasonably practicable.
(3) For the purposes of ascertaining the time within which the next review is to be carried out, a postponed review shall be deemed to have been carried out at the latest time at which it could have been carried out in accordance with paragraph 21.

Grounds for continued detention

23.—(1) A review officer may authorise a person's continued detention only if satisfied that it is necessary—
    (a) to obtain relevant evidence whether by questioning him or otherwise,
    (b) to preserve relevant evidence,
    (c) pending a decision whether to apply to the Secretary of State for a deportation notice to be served on the detained person,
    (d) pending the making of an application to the Secretary of State for a deportation notice to be served on the detained person,
    (e) pending consideration by the Secretary of State whether to serve a deportation notice on the detained person, or
    (f) pending a decision whether the detained person should be charged with an offence.

(2) The reveiw officer shall not authorise continued detention by virtue of sub-paragraph (1)(a) or (b) unless he is satisfied that the investigation in connection with which the person is detained is being conducted diligently and expeditiously.

(3) The review officer shall not authorise continued detention by virtue of sub-paragraph (1)(c) to (f) unless he is satisfied that the process pending the completion of which detention is necessary is being conducted diligently and expeditiously.

(4) In sub-paragraph (1)(a) and (b) "relevant evidence" means evidence which—

    (a) relates to the commission by the detained person of an offence under any of the provisions mentioned in section 40(1)(a), or

    (b) indicates that the detained person falls within section 40(1)(b).

(5) In sub-paragraph (1) "deportation notice" means notice of a decision to make a deportation order under the Immigration Act 1971.

Review officer

24.—(1) The review officer shall be an officer who has not been directly involved in the investigation in connection with which the person is detained.

(2) In the case of a review carried out within the period of 24 hours beginning with the time of arrest, the review officer shall be an officer of at least the rank of inspector.

(3) In the case of any other review, the review officer shall be an officer of at least the rank of superintendent.

25.—(1) This paragraph applies where—

    (a) the review officer is of a rank lower than superintendent,

    (b) an officer of higher rank than the review officer gives directions relating to the detained person, and

    (c) those directions are at variance with the performance by the review officer of a duty imposed on him under this Schedule.

(2) The review officer shall refer the matter at once to an officer of at least the rank of superintendent.

Representations

26.—(1) Before determining whether to authorise a person's continued detention, a review officer shall give either of the following persons an opportunity to make representations about the detention—

    (a) the detained person, or

    (b) a solicitor representing him who is available at the time of the review.

(2) Representations may be oral or written.

(3) A review officer may refuse to hear oral representations from the detained person if he considers that he is unfit to make representations because of his condition or behaviour.

Rights

27.—(1) Where a review officer authorises continued detention he shall inform the detained person—

    (a) of any of his rights under paragraphs 6 and 7 which he has not yet exercised, and

    (b) if the exercise of any of his rights under either of those paragraphs is being delayed in accordance with the provisions of paragraph 8, of the fact that it is being so delayed.

(2) Where a review of a person's detention is being carried out at a time when his exercise of a right under either of those paragraphs is being delayed—

(a) the review officer shall consider whether the reason or reasons for which the delay was authorised continue to subsist, and

(b) if in his opinion the reason or reasons have ceased to subsist, he shall inform the officer who authorised the delay of his opinion (unless he was that officer).

Record

28.—(1) A review officer carrying out a review shall make a written record of the outcome of the review and of any of the following which apply—

(a) the grounds upon which continued detention is authorised,

(b) the reason for postponement of the review,

(c) the fact that the detained person has been informed as required under paragraph 27(1),

(d) the officer's conclusion on the matter considered under paragraph 27(2)(a),

(e) the fact that he has taken action under paragraph 27(2)(b), and

(f) the fact that the detained person is being detained by virtue of section 41(5) or (6).

(2) The review officer shall—

(a) make the record in the presence of the detained person, and

(b) inform him at that time whether the review officer is authorising continued detention, and if he is, of his grounds.

(3) Sub-paragraph (2) shall not apply where, at the time when the record is made, the detained person is—

(a) incapable of understanding what is said to him,

(b) violent or likely to become violent, or

(c) in urgent need of medical attention.

PART III   EXTENSION OF DETENTION UNDER SECTION 41

Warrants of further detention

29.—(1) A police officer of at least the rank of superintendent may apply to a judicial authority for the issue of a warrant of further detention under this Part.

(2) A warrant of further detention—

(a) shall authorise the further detention under section 41 of a specified person for a specified period, and

(b) shall state the time at which it is issued.

(3) Subject to paragraph 36(3A), the specified period in relation to a person shall end not later than the end of the period of seven days beginning—

(a) with the time of his arrest under section 41, or

(b) if he was being detained under Schedule 7 when he was arrested under section 41, with the time when his examination under that Schedule began.

(4) In this Part "judicial authority" means—

(a) ..., a District Judge (Magistrates' Courts) who is designated for the purpose of this Part by the Lord Chancellor,

(b) (*Applies to Scotland only.*)

(c) (*Applies to Northern Ireland only.*)

Time limit

30.—(1) An application for a warrant shall be made—

(a) during the period mentioned in section 41(3), or

(b) within six hours of the end of that period.

(2) The judicial authority hearing an application made by virtue of sub-paragraph (1)(b) shall dismiss the application if he considers that it would have been reasonably practicable to make it during the period mentioned in section 41(3).

(3) For the purposes of this Schedule, an application for a warrant is made when written or oral notice of an intention to make the application is given to a judicial authority.

Notice

31.   An application for a warrant may not be heard unless the person to whom it relates has been given a notice stating—

(a) that the application has been made,

(b) the time at which the application was made,

(c) the time at which it is to be heard, and

(d) the grounds upon which further detention is sought.

Grounds for extension

32.—(1) A judicial authority may issue a warrant of further detention only if satisfied that—

(a) there are reasonable grounds for believing that the further detention of the person to whom the application relates is necessary to obtain relevant evidence whether by questioning him or otherwise or to preserve relevant evidence, and

(b) the investigation in connection with which the person is detained is being conducted diligently and expeditiously.

(2) In sub-paragraph (1) "relevant evidence" means, in relation to the person to whom the application relates, evidence which—

(a) relates to his commission of an offence under any of the provisions mentioned in section 40(1)(a), or

(b) indicates that he is a person falling within section 40(1)(b).

Representation

33.—(1) The person to whom an application relates shall—

(a) be given an opportunity to make oral or written representations to the judicial authority about the application, and

(b) subject to sub-paragraph (3), be entitled to be legally represented at the hearing.

(2) A judicial authority shall adjourn the hearing of an application to enable the person to whom the application relates to obtain legal representation where—

(a) he is not legally represented,

(b) he is entitled to be legally represented, and

(c) he wishes to be so represented.

(3) A judicial authority may exclude any of the following persons from any part of the hearing—

(a) the person to whom the application relates;

(b) anyone representing him.

Information

34.—(1) The officer who has made an application for a warrant may apply to the judicial authority for an order that specified information upon which he intends to rely be withheld from—

    (a) the person to whom the application relates, and

    (b) anyone representing him.

  (2) Subject to sub-paragraph (3), a judicial authority may make an order under sub-paragraph (1) in relation to specified information only if satisfied that there are reasonable grounds for believing that if the information were disclosed—

    (a) evidence of an offence under any of the provisions mentioned in section 40(1)(a) would be interfered with or harmed,

    (b) the recovery of property obtained as a result of an offence under any of those provisions would be hindered,

    (c) the recovery of property in respect of which a forfeiture order could be made under section 23 would be hindered,

    (d) the apprehension, prosecution or conviction of a person who is suspected of falling within section 40(1)(a) or (b) would be made more difficult as a result of his being alerted,

    (e) the prevention of an act of terrorism would be made more difficult as a result of a person being alerted,

    (f) the gathering of information about the commission, preparation or instigation of an act of terrorism would be interfered with, or

    (g) a person would be interfered with or physically injured.

  '(3) A judicial authority may also make an order under subparagraph (1) in relation to specified information if satisfied that there are reasonable grounds for believing that—

    (a) the detained person has benefited from his criminal conduct, and

    (b) the recovery of the value of the property constituting the benefit would be hindered if the information were disclosed.

  (3A) For the purposes of sub-paragraph (3) the question whether a person has benefited from his criminal conduct is to be decided in accordance with Part 2 or 3 of the Proceeds of Crime Act 2002.'

  (4) The judicial authority shall direct that the following be excluded from the hearing of the application under this paragraph—

    (a) the person to whom the application for a warrant relates, and

    (b) anyone representing him.

Adjournments

  35.—(1) A judicial authority may adjourn the hearing of an application for a warrant only if the hearing is adjourned to a date before the expiry of the period mentioned in section 41(3).

  (2) This paragraph shall not apply to an adjournment under paragraph 33(2).

Extensions of warrants

  36.—(1) A police officer of at least the rank of superintendent may apply to a judicial authority for the extension or further extension of the period specified in a warrant of further detention.

  (2) Where the period specified is extended, the warrant shall be endorsed with a note stating the new specified period.

  (3) Subject to paragraph (3A), the specified period shall end not later than the end of the period of seven days beginning with the relevant time.

  (3A) Where the period specified in a warrant of further detention—

    (a) ends at the end of the period of seven days beginning with the relevant time, or

    (b) by virtue of a previous extension (or further extension) under this sub-paragraph, ends after the end of that period, the specified period may, on an application under this paragraph, be extended or further extended to a period ending not later than the end of the period of fourteen days beginning with the relevant time.

(3B) In this paragraph "the relevant time", in relation to a person, means—

    (a) the time of his arrest under section 41, or

    (b) if he was being detained under Schedule 7 when he was arrested under section 41, the time when his examination under that Schedule began."

(4) Paragraphs 30(3) and 31 to 34 shall apply to an application under this paragraph as they apply to an application for a warrant of further detention.

(5) A judicial authority may adjourn the hearing of an application under sub-paragraph (1) only if the hearing is adjourned to a date before the expiry of the period specified in the warrant.

(6) Sub-paragraph (5) shall not apply to an adjournment under paragraph 33(2).

Detention—conditions

37.   A person detained by virtue of a warrant issued under this Part shall (unless detained in accordance with section 41(5) or (6) or under any other power) be released immediately if the officer having custody of him becomes aware that any of the grounds under paragraph 32(1)(a) and (b) upon which the judicial authority authorised his further detention have ceased to apply.

Code of Practice Under Paragraph 3(1) of Schedule 8 to the Terrorism Act 2000 Governing the Audio Recording of Police Interviews in a Police Station of persons detained under Section 41 of or Schedule 7 to the Terrorism Act 2000

Commencement—Transitional Arrangements

This code applies to an interview, or any part of an interview, carried out after midnight on 18 February 2001, except where a person is detained and section 129(1) of the Terrorism Act 2000 applies.

SECTION 1   GENERAL

1.1   This code of practice applies to the audio recording of police interviews in a police station of persons detained under section 41 of or Schedule 7 to the Terrorism Act 2000 ('the Act').

1.2   The code must be readily available at all police stations for consultation by police officers, arrested or detained persons, members of the public, appropriate adults and solicitors.

1.3   In this code reference to a 'police station' includes any place which is designated by the Secretary of State under paragraph 1(1) of Schedule 8 to the Act as a place at which persons may be detained under section 41.

1.4   The notes for guidance included are not provisions of this code. They form guidance to police officers and others about its application and interpretation.

1.5   Nothing in this code shall be taken as detracting in any way from the legal responsibilities of interviewing officers in conducting an interview with a detained person.

1.6   In this code 'appropriate adult' means:
  (i)   in the case of a juvenile . . . a child:
      (a)   his parent or guardian (where they are not involved in the case); or; if he is in care, the care authority or voluntary organisation. The term 'in care' is used in this code to cover all cases in which a juvenile is 'looked after' by a local authority under the terms of the Children Act 1989 . . .;
      (b)   a social worker; or
      (c)   failing either of the above, another responsible adult aged 18 or over who is not a police officer or employed by the police.
  (ii) in the case of a person who is mentally disordered or mentally handicapped:
      (a)   a relative, guardian or other person responsible for his care or custody;
      (b)   someone who has experience of dealing with mentally disordered or mentally handicapped people but who is not a police officer or employed by the police; or
      (c)   failing either of the above, some other responsible adult aged 18 or over who is not a police officer or employed by the police. (*See Note 1A*).

'Mental disorder' is a generic term which has the meaning given to it in section 1(2) of the Mental Health Act 1983, that is, 'mental illness, arrested or incomplete development of mind, psychopathic disorder and any other disorder or disability of mind' and which includes reference to 'mental handicap' as defined in Article 3(1) of the Mental Health (Northern Ireland) Order 1986 as 'a state of arrested or incomplete development of mind which includes significant impairment of intelligence and social functioning.

1.7   In this code 'solicitor' means (*see Note 1C*)
    . . . a solicitor who holds a current practising certificate, a trainee solicitor, a duty solicitor representative or an accredited representative included on the register of representatives maintained by the Legal Aid Board.

1.8   In this code the term 'relevant prosecuting authority' includes the Director of Public Prosecutions in England & Wales . . . and any other body or person, other than the police, with a statutory responsibility for prosecution and to whom the police report the investigation of any criminal offence.

1.9   If anyone appears to be under the age of 17 then he shall be treated as a juvenile for the purposes of this code.

1.10   Only officers who have been trained for the purpose can carry out tape-recorded interviews under this code.

Notes for guidance

1A   In the case of people who are mentally disordered or mentally handicapped, it may in certain circumstances be more satisfactory for all concerned if the appropriate adult is someone who has experience or training in their care rather than a relative lacking such qualifications. But if the person himself prefers a relative to a better-qualified stranger or objects to a particular person as the appropriate adult, his wishes should if practicable be respected.

1B   It is important to bear in mind that, although juveniles or people who are mentally disordered or mentally handicapped are often capable of providing reliable evidence, they may, without knowing or wishing to do so, be particularly prone in certain circumstances to provide information which is unreliable, misleading or self incriminating. Special care should therefore always be exercised in questioning such a person, and the appropriate adult should always be involved, if there is any doubt about a person's age, mental state or capacity. Because of the risk of unreliable evidence it is also important to obtain corroboration of any facts admitted wherever possible.

1C   Reasonable effort should be made to allow access to a solicitor from an outside jurisdiction provided there is entitlement to practice.

SECTION 2   RECORDING AND SEALING OF MASTER TAPES

2.1   The audio recording of interviews shall be carried out openly so as to instill confidence in the integrity of the tape as an impartial and accurate record of the interview. (*See Note 2A*).

2.2   One tape, referred to in this code as the master tape, will be sealed before it leaves the presence of the detained person. A second tape will be used as a working copy. The master tape is either one of the tapes used in the twin or triple deck tape-recorder or the only tape used in single deck machines. The working copy is either the second tape used in a twin or triple deck machine or a copy of the master tape made by a single deck machine. (*See Note 2B*).

Notes for guidance

2A.   Interviewing officers will wish to ensure that, as far as possible, audio recording arrangements are unobtrusive. It must be clear to the detained person, however, that there is no opportunity to interfere with the recording equipment or the tapes.

2B.   The purpose of sealing the master tape before it leaves the presence of the detained person is to establish his confidence that the integrity of the tape is preserved. Where a single deck machine is used the working copy of the master tape must be made in the presence of the suspect without the master tape having left his sight. The working copy shall be used for making further copies where the need arises. The recorder will be capable of recording voices and will have a time coding or other security device.

SECTION 3   INTERVIEWS TO BE AUDIO RECORDED

When audio recording is required

3.1   Subject to paragraph 3.5 below, audio recording shall be used for any police interview in a police station of a person detained under section 41 of or Schedule 7 to the Act. (*See Note 3A*).

3.2   Audio recording shall also be used in an interview with a person suspected on reasonable grounds of an offence under section 1 of the Official Secrets Act 1911 (offences prejudicial to the safety or interests of the State).

3.3   The whole of each interview shall be audio recorded, including the taking and reading back of any statement.

When audio recording is not required

3.4   Audio recording is *not* required for people being examined under Schedule 7 to the Act unless they are detained at a police station.

3.5   A uniformed officer not below the rank of inspector who is not involved with the investigation (the authorising officer) may authorise the interviewing officer not to audio record the interview where it is not reasonably practicable to do so because of failure of the equipment or the non-availability of a suitable interview room or recorder, and the authorising officer considers on reasonable grounds that the interview should not be delayed until the failure has been rectified or a suitable room or recorder becomes available. In such cases the interview shall be recorded verbatim in writing. In all cases the authorising officer shall make a note in specific terms of the reasons for not audio recording. (*See Note 3B*).

Notes for guidance

3A   No person who is unfit through drink or drugs to the extent that they are unable to appreciate the significance of questions put to them or of their answers may be questioned in that condition. A medical officer or medical practitioner can give advice about whether or not a person is fit to be interviewed.

3B   A decision not to audio record an interview for any reason may be the subject of comment if a case comes to court. The authorising officer should therefore be prepared to justify his decision in each case.

SECTION 4   THE INTERVIEW

(a) Commencement of interview

4.1   When the detained person is brought into the interview room the interviewing officer (the police officer conducting the interview or any of such officers, if there are more than one) shall, without delay, but in the sight of the detained person, load the recorder with previously unused tapes and set it to record. The tapes must be unwrapped or otherwise opened in the presence of the detained person. (*See Note 4A*).

4.2 (i) The interviewing officer shall then tell the detained person formally about the audio recording. He shall state:

    (a)   that the interview is being audio recorded;

    (b)   the date, time of commencement and place of the interview;

    (c)   his name (or his warrant or other identification numbers) and rank and the name (or warrant or other identification numbers) and rank of any other police officer present;

    (d)   the name of the detained person and any other person present (eg solicitor); and

    (e)   that the detained person will be given a notice about what will happen to the tapes.

  (ii)   When the interviewing officer identifies himself and his rank in accordance with sub-paragraph 4.2(i)(c) above, any other police officer present shall then also state his name (or warrant or other identification number) and rank.

 (iii)   When the interviewing officer states the name of the detained person and any other person present, in accordance with sub-paragraph 4.2(i)(d) above, he shall invite each such person to identify himself for the purpose of the tape. (*See Note 4B*).

 (iv)   Any person entering the interview room after the interview has commenced shall be invited by the interviewing officer to identify himself for the purpose of the tape and state the reason for which he has entered the interview room.

(b) Interviews under section 41

4.3   Unless in accordance with paragraphs 8 and 16 of Schedule 8 of the Act access to independent legal advice has been delayed (the reasons for which should be communicated to the detained person and recorded as soon as is reasonably practicable), the interviewing officer shall remind the detained person of his right to free and independent legal advice and that he can speak to a solicitor privately. Immediately prior to the commencement or recommencement of any interview at a police station, the interviewing officer should remind the detained person of his entitlement to legal advice and that the interview can be delayed for this purpose.

4.4   The interviewing officer shall then advise the detained person in the following terms:

'you do not have to say anything. But it may harm your defence if you do not mention when questioned something which you later rely on in court. Anything you do say may be given in evidence'

Further cautions may be appropriate during the course of the interview where, for example, fresh evidence suggests further offences may have been committed.

4.5   Minor deviations from the form of words set out in the above paragraphs do not constitute a breach of this code provided that the sense is preserved.

(c) Special warnings under Sections 36 and 37 of the Criminal Justice and Public Order Act 1994 (England and Wales) . . .

4.6   When a suspect who is interviewed after arrest fails or refuses to answer certain questions, or to answer them satisfactorily, after due warning, a court or jury may draw a proper inference from this silence under sections 36 and 37 of the Criminal Justice and Public Order Act 1994. This applies when:

    (a)   a suspect is arrested by a constable and there is found on his person, or in or on his clothing or footwear, or otherwise in his possession, or in the place where he was arrested, any objects, marks or substances, or marks on such objects, and the person fails or refuses to account for the objects, marks or substances found; or

    (b)   an arrested person was found by a constable at a place or at about the time the offence for which he was arrested is alleged to have been committed, and the person fails or refuses to account for his presence at that place.

4.7   For an inference to be drawn from a suspect's failure or refusal to answer a question about one of these matters or to answer it satisfactorily, the interviewing officer must first tell him in ordinary language:

    (a)   what offence he is investigating;

    (b)   what fact he is asking the suspect to account for;

    (c)   that he believes this fact may be due to the suspect's taking part in the commission of the offence in question;

    (d)   that a court may draw a proper inference from his silence if he fails or refuses to account for the fact about which he is being questioned;

    (e)   that a record is being made of the interview and may be given in evidence if he is brought to trial.

(d) Interviews of those detained at a police station under Schedule 7 of the Act

4.8   The interviewing officer shall inform the detained person that he is *not* under arrest or caution but that he is being detained under the provisions of Schedule 7 to the Act. He will explain that this in itself does not mean that the interviewer suspects that the detained person is or has been concerned in the commission, preparation or instigation of acts of terrorism and that the purpose of the questioning is to enable the interviewer to determine whether the detained person appears to be such a person.

4.9   The interviewer shall advise the detained person that, in accordance with paragraph 5 of Schedule 7 to the Act, he has a duty to give the interviewer all the information in his possession which the interviewer requests in connection with his determining whether the person is or has been concerned in the commission, preparation or instigation of acts of terrorism.

4.10   He shall also advise the detained person that if he deliberately fails to comply with the interviewer's request he may be guilty of an offence under paragraph 18(1) of Schedule 7 to the Act.

4.11   The interviewer shall inform the detained person that he may, if he wishes, at public expense, inform a relative or someone close to him, or known to him, or someone who is likely to take an interest in his welfare that he is being questioned and where he is. The interviewers shall also advise the detained person that he can, if he wishes, also consult a solicitor, either in person, in writing or by telephone and that the interview can be delayed for this purpose.

(e) Interviews with the deaf or with those who do not understand English

4.12   If a person appears to be deaf or there is doubt about his hearing or speaking ability, he must not be interviewed in the absence of an interpreter unless he agrees in writing to be interviewed without one or unless an officer of the rank of superintendent or above considers that delaying the interview would be likely:

     (a) to lead to interference with or harm to evidence connected with an offence or interference with or physical harm to other people;

     (b) to lead to the alerting of other people suspected of having committed an offence but not yet arrested for it; or

     (c) to hinder the recovery of property obtained in consequence of the commission of an offence.

Questioning in these circumstances may not continue once sufficient information to avert the immediate risk has been obtained. A record shall be made of the grounds for any decision to interview a person under this paragraph.

    4.13 If the detained person is deaf, or there is doubt about his hearing ability, the interviewing officer shall take a verbatim contemporaneous note of the interview, in addition to audio recording it in accordance with the provisions of this code. (*See Note 4C*).

    4.14 Except where an officer of the rank of superintendent or above believes that (a), (b) or (c) in paragraph 4.12 above applies, a person must not be interviewed in the absence of a person capable of acting as interpreter if:

     (a) he has difficulty in understanding English;

     (b) the interviewing officer cannot understand the person's own language; and

     (c) the person wishes an interpreter to be present.

    4.15 Where paragraph 4.3 applies and the person concerned cannot communicate with the solicitor, whether because of language, hearing or speech difficulties, the interpreter must be called. The interpreter may be a police officer except where interpretation is needed for the purposes of obtaining legal advice.

(f) Objections and complaints by the detained person

    4.16 If the detained person raises objections to the interview being audio recorded either at the outset or during the interview or during a break in the interview, the interviewing officer shall remind him (see sub-paragraph 4.2(i)(a) above) that the interview is being audio recorded and that his objections are being recorded on tape. When any objections have been recorded or the detained person has refused to have his objections recorded, the interviewing officer shall, before turning off the recorder, give his reasons for doing so and then turn it off. He shall then make a verbatim written record of the interview. If the interviewing officer reasonably considers that he should proceed to put questions to the detained person with the recorder still on, he may do so. The detained person's attention shall be drawn to the fact that the recorder is still operating. (*See Note 4D*).

    4.17 If in the course of an interview a complaint is made by the person being questioned, or on his behalf, about his detention, treatment and questioning or if the complaint is that the provisions of this code have not been observed, then the interviewing officer shall record it in the interview record and inform the custody officer, or those carrying out the functions of a custody officer, who is then responsible for dealing with the complaint in accordance with recognised procedures. (*See Note 4E*).

    4.18 If the detained person indicates that he wishes to tell a police officer about matters not directly connected with the matter about which he is being interviewed and that he is unwilling for these matters to be audio recorded, he shall be given the opportunity to tell a police officer about these matters after the conclusion of the interview. Consideration should be given as to whether a separate caution is appropriate in those circumstances.

(g) Changing tapes

    4.19 When the recorder indicates that the tapes have only a short time left to run, the interviewing officer shall tell the detained person that the tapes are coming to an end and round off that part of the interview. If the officer wishes to continue the interview but does not already have a second set of tapes, he shall obtain a set. The detained person shall not be left unattended in the interview room. The interviewing officer shall remove the tapes from the recorder and insert the new tapes which shall be unwrapped or otherwise opened in the detained person's presence. The recorder shall then be set to record on the new tapes. When more than one set of tapes has been used, care must be taken to ensure there is no confusion between the sets of tapes. This must be done by marking each set of tapes with the same identification number immediately it is removed from the recorder.

(h) Taking a break during interview

4.20   When a break is to be taken during the course of an interview and the interview room is to be vacated by the detained person, the fact that a break is to be taken, the reason for it and the time shall be audio recorded. The tapes shall then be removed from the recorder and the procedures for the conclusion of an interview set out below shall be followed.

4.21   When a break is to be a short one and both the detained person and the interviewing officer are to remain in the interview room the fact that a break is to be taken, the reason for it and the time shall be audio recorded. The recorder may be turned off: there is, however, no need to remove the tape and when the interview is recommenced the recording shall be continued on the same tape. The time at which the interview recommences shall be audio recorded.

4.22   When there is a break in questioning *under caution* the interviewing officer must ensure that the person being questioned is reminded of their right to legal advice and also that he is aware that he remains under caution. If there is any doubt the caution must be given again in full when the interview resumes. (*See Notes 4F and 4G*).

(i) Failure of recording equipment

4.23   If there is a failure of equipment which can be rectified quickly, for example by inserting new tapes, the procedures set out in paragraph 4.19 shall be followed, and when the recording is resumed the interviewing officer shall explain what has happened and audio record the time the interview recommences. If, however, it is not possible to continue recording on that particular recorder and no replacement recorder or other suitably equipped interview room is readily available, the interview may continue without being audio recorded. In such circumstances the authorisation procedures in paragraph 3.5 above shall be followed. (*See Note 4H*).

(j) Removing tapes from the recorder

4.24   Where tapes are removed from the recorder in the course of an interview, they shall be retained and the procedures set out in paragraph 4.26 below followed.

(k) Conclusion of interview

4.25   At the conclusion of the interview, the detained person shall be offered the opportunity to clarify anything he has said and to add anything he may wish.

4.26   At the conclusion of the interview, including the taking and reading back of any written statement, the time shall be recorded and the recorder switched off. The master tape, as selected by the detained person, shall be sealed with a master tape label and treated as an exhibit. The interviewing officer shall sign the label (a warrant or other identification number may be used) and ask the detained person and any other third party present to sign it also. If the detained person or third party refuses to sign the label, an officer not below the rank of inspector, who is not involved with the investigation, or if one is not available, the custody officer shall be called into the interview room and asked to sign it. (*See Note 41*).

4.27   The detained person or an appropriate adult or an interpreter shall be handed a notice at the end of the first interview which explains:

the use which will be made of the tape-recording;

the arrangements for access to the tape;

that a copy of the tape shall be supplied upon request as soon as practicable if the detained person is charged or informed that he will be prosecuted;

the period of retention of the tape;

the arrangements for the destruction of the tape. (See Note 4J and the Annex).

Notes for guidance

4A   The interviewing officer should attempt to estimate the likely length of the interview and ensure the appropriate number of unused tapes, and labels with which to seal the master tapes are available in the interview room.

4B   It is necessary, for the purpose of voice identification in the recording, for the interviewing officer to ask the detained person and any other persons present to identify themselves.

4C   Paragraph 4.13 is intended to give the deaf equivalent rights of first hand access to the full interview record.

4D   The interviewing officer should bear in mind that his decision to continue recording against the wishes of the detained person may be the subject of comment if the case comes to court. He may wish to consider, however, reminding the interviewee that audio-recording is an added safeguard in the interview process and, where appropriate, seek a view from the interviewee's legal representative before switching off the tape recorder.

4E   Where the custody officer is called immediately to deal with the complaint, wherever possible the tape recorder should be left to run until the custody officer has entered the interview room and spoken to the person being interviewed. Continuation or termination of the interview should be at the discretion of the interviewing officer pending the instigation of recognised complaints procedures. Where the complaint concerns a matter not connected with this code or with the detained person's detention, treatment or questioning, the decision to continue with the interview is at the discretion of the interviewing officer. Where the interviewing officer decides to continue with the interview the person being interviewed shall be told that the complaint will be brought to the attention of the custody officer at the conclusion of the interview. When the interview is concluded the interviewing officer must, as soon as practicable, inform the custody officer of the existence and nature of the complaint made.

4F   In considering whether to caution again after a break in an interview, the interviewing officer should bear in mind that he may have to satisfy a court that the detained person understood he was still under caution when the interview resumed (or during the course of the interview itself).

4G   The officer should bear in mind that it may be necessary to show to the court that nothing occurred during a break in an interview or between interviews which influenced the detained person's recorded evidence. The officer should consider, therefore, after a break in an interview or at the beginning of a subsequent interview summarising on tape the reason for the break and confirming this with the detained person.

4H   If one of the tapes breaks during the interview it should be sealed as a master tape in the presence of the detained person and the interview resumed where it left off. The unbroken tape should be copied and the original sealed as a master tape in the detained person's presence, if necessary after the interview. If equipment for copying the unbroken tape is not readily available, both tapes should be sealed in the presence of the detained person and the interview begun again.

4I   Where the detained person refuses to sign the label, they should be given an opportunity to place their reasons for so doing on record.

4J   Only one notice is required to be served on the detained person, or an appropriate adult or an interpreter; and this should be carried out at the end of the first interview.

SECTION 5   INTERVIEW RECORDS OF INTERVIEWS UNDER SECTIONS 3.5, 4.13 AND 4.16 ABOVE

5.1   An accurate record must be made of each interview with a detained person, carried out at a police station under paragraphs 3.5, 4.13 or 4.16 above.

5.2   The record must state the place of the interview, the time it begins and ends, the time the record is made (if different), any breaks in the interview and the names (or warrant or other identification number) and duty station of such officers and all those present; and must be made on the forms provided for this purpose or in the officer's pocket book.

5.3   The record must be made during the course of the interview, unless in the investigating officer's view this would not be practicable or would interfere with the conduct of the interview, and must constitute either a verbatim record of what was said or, failing this, an account of the interview which adequately and accurately summarises it.

5.4   If an interview record is not made during the course of the interview it must be made as soon as practicable after its completion.

5.5   Written interview records must be timed and signed by the maker.

5.6   If an interview record is not completed in the course of the interview the reason must be recorded in the officer's pocket book.

5.7   Unless it is impracticable the person interviewed must be given the opportunity under tape recorded conditions to read the interview record and to sign it as correct or to indicate the respects in which he considers it inaccurate. If the person concerned cannot read or refuses to read the record or to sign it, the senior officer present shall read it to him and ask him whether he would like to sign it as correct (or make his mark) or to indicate the respects in which he considers it inaccurate. The police officer shall then certify on the interview record itself what has occurred. (*See Note 5A*).

5.8   If an appropriate adult or person's solicitor is present during the interview, he shall also be given the opportunity to read and sign the interview record (or any written statement taken down by a police officer).

5.9   A written record shall also be made of any comments made by a suspected person, including unsolicited comments which are outside the context of an interview but which might be relevant to the offence. Any such record must be timed and signed by the maker. Where practicable the person should be given the opportunity to read and sign it as correct or to indicate the respects in which he considers it inaccurate. (*See Note 5B*).

5.10   Where an interview has been conducted under paragraph 3.5 or 4.16 and the detained person is someone to which paragraph 4.14 of the code refers, the interviewing officer shall ensure that the interpreter makes a note of the interview at the time in the language of the person being interviewed for use in the event of his being called to give evidence, and certifies its accuracy. He shall allow sufficient time for the interpreter to make a note of each question and answer after each has been put or given and interpreted. The person shall be given an opportunity to read it or have it read to him and sign it as correct or to indicate the respects in which he considers it inaccurate.

5.11   In the case of a person making a statement in a language other than English:

    (a)   the interpreter shall take down the statement in the language in which it is made;

    (b)   the person making the statement shall be invited to sign it; and

    (c)   an official English translation shall be made in due course.

Notes for guidance

5A   Where a suspect agrees to read the records of interviews and other comments and to sign them as correct, he should be asked to endorse the records with words such as 'I agree that this is a correct record of what was said' and add his signature. Where the suspect does not agree with the record, the officer should record details of any disagreements and then ask the suspect to read these details and then sign them to the effect that they accurately reflect his disagreement. Any refusal to sign when asked to do so shall be recorded.

5B   Interviewing officers will wish to consider whether unsolicited relevant comments made during the course of interview should be brought into the interview to assist in establishing them as evidence.

SECTION 6   AFTER THE INTERVIEW UNDER SECTION 4 ABOVE

6.1   The interviewing officer shall make a written record of the fact that the interview has taken place, that it has been recorded on audio tape, its time, duration and date. The times during which the recorder has been operating and the identification number of the master tape will be included in the written record.

6.2   Where no further action, including arrest and/or criminal proceedings follow in respect of the person whose interview has been recorded the tapes must nevertheless be kept securely in accordance with section 7.

6.3   Subject as mentioned at paragraph 6.6, where criminal proceedings do follow or are under consideration, the interviewing officer shall prepare, or have prepared on his behalf, a full transcript of the interview or a summary of the interview, which shall be signed by the interviewing officer (*see Notes 6A, 6B and 6C*).

6.4   Any written statement of evidence prepared by the interviewing officer in relation to what took place at the interview shall refer to the fact that the interview was audio recorded and refer to the master tape as an exhibit to the statement.

6.5   Subject to paragraph 6.6, the full transcript of the interview or a summary of the interview shall be exhibited to any such written statement of evidence prepared by the interviewing officer under paragraph 6.4. If a full transcript or a summary of the interview, as the case may be, is prepared by a person other than the interviewing officer, the interviewing officer must check that the full transcript or summary of the interview is correct before he signs it, and his written statement must contain a reference to the fact that he has been shown the full transcript or summary of interview, checked it, found it to be correct and signed it.

6.6   The Chief Officer of the Police Force concerned or, where applicable, the relevant prosecuting authority may direct that, in circumstances which he shall specify, neither a full transcript of the interview or a summary of the interview will be required to be included in files submitted for the decision of the relevant Chief Officer or, where applicable, the relevant prosecuting authority. Accordingly, where the specified circumstances arise, paragraphs 6.3 and 6.5 shall not apply unless the Chief Officer or, where applicable, the relevant prosecuting authority after receipt of the file directs that a full transcript of the interview be prepared or a summary of it be prepared in that individual case. (*See Note 6D*).

6.7   The court shall be made aware of any transcript of the audio-recorded interview which has been made.

Notes for guidance

6A   Prior to preparing the summary of the interview or to checking a summary of interview which has been prepared on his behalf by another person, the interviewing officer may refresh his memory by listening to the working copy of the tape.

6B   A person preparing a summary of interview on behalf of the interviewing officer should be a police officer, or other person who has received appropriate training in the preparation of summaries of interview. He should prepare the summary after listening to the tape and if necessary after consultation with the interviewing officer.

6C   The summary of interview should be prepared on the basis that it will be exhibited to the interviewing officer's statement of evidence and that it will be used for the following purposes:

to enable the Chief Officer or the relevant prosecuting authority to make informed decisions about the case on the basis of what was said at the interview;

for use pursuant to any rule of law permitting the admission of written statements as evidence in court;

where applicable, for use as a basis for the conduct of the case by the prosecution, the defence and the court without the necessity for the master tape to be played in court.

The summary should, therefore, comprise a balanced account of the interview, including points in mitigation and/or defence made by the detained person. Where an admission is made the question as well as the answer containing the admission should be recorded verbatim in the summary. Care should be taken to bring to the attention of the Chief Officer and/or relevant prosecuting authority, by means of a covering report, any material on the tape which might be regarded by a court as prejudicial or inadmissible.

6D   Where, in the interviewing officer's view, a significant interview occurs, for example, an admission is made, an explanation is provided, inferences may be drawn from a failure to answer questions or there are ambiguous answers, a full transcript will normally be provided. In cases of doubt early consultation with the relevant prosecuting authority is desirable.

SECTION 7   TAPE SECURITY

7.1   The officer in charge of each police station at which interviews with detained persons are recorded shall make arrangements for all master tapes to be kept securely and their movements accounted for on the same basis as any material which may be used for evidential purposes, in accordance with Force Standing Orders. (*See Note 7A*).

7.2   A police officer has no authority to break the seal on a master tape which is required for criminal proceedings. If it is necessary to gain access to the master tape the police shall request the relevant prosecuting authority to seek the authority of the appropriate court for the seal to be broken, the tape copied, and resealed in the presence of an official appointee of the court. Where no court proceedings have been commenced, but are contemplated or are under consideration, the seal shall be broken, and the tape copied and resealed, in the presence of a legally qualified representative of the relevant prosecuting authority. In either case the detained person or his solicitor shall be informed and given a reasonable opportunity to be present. If the detained person or his solicitor is present he shall be invited to reseal and sign the master tape. If this offer is refused, or neither the detained person nor his solicitor is present, this shall be done by the official appointee of the court or representative of the relevant prosecuting authority, as applicable. (*See Note 7B*).

7.3   Where no further action including criminal proceedings results, or is under consideration, or where criminal proceedings have been concluded, it is the responsibility of the Chief Officer to establish arrangements for the breaking of the seal on the master tape, where this becomes necessary.

Notes for guidance

7A   This section is concerned with the security of the master tape which will have been sealed at the conclusion of the interview. Care should, however, be taken of working copies of tapes since their loss or destruction may lead unnecessarily to the need to have access to master tapes.

7B   "Legally qualified representative of a relevant prosecuting authority" shall be taken to mean a barrister or solicitor employed by the relevant prosecuting authority or instructed by him to represent him in regard to any matter referred to in paragraph 7.2 above.

SECTION 8   TAPE DESTRUCTION

8.1   At the conclusion of criminal proceedings, or in the event of a direction not to prosecute, the contents of a working copy of the tape shall be completely erased. Such tapes shall not be reissued for the purpose of recording interviews.

8.2   Unless the provisions of the Criminal Procedure and Investigations Act 1996, code of practice, apply, or unless civil proceedings have been instigated or it is clear that none will be, master tapes will be destroyed six years after the date of the interview.

ANNEX

[Name of Police Force]

AUDIO RECORDING OF INTERVIEW

Notice to persons arrested under section 41 OR detained under Schedule 7 to the Terrorism Act 2000 whose interview has been audio recorded.

This notice explains how the audio recording will be used and how you or your solicitor can, if you wish, arrange to listen to it if you are prosecuted.

The use which will be made of the audio recording

The interview has been audio recorded using a single, twin or triple deck tape recorder. One of the tapes has been sealed in your presence and will be kept securely in case it is needed in court (this tape is known as the "master tape"). The other tape will be a working copy to which the police and you or your solicitor may listen if you wish. Both tapes are protected against tampering.

Arrangements to access the tape

If you wish, you or your solicitor may listen to the audio recording by applying to the Police Officer in charge of the area or Police Commander for the area where this interview took place.

When a copy of the tape will be supplied

If you are charged, or informed that you will be prosecuted, a copy of the tape shall be supplied upon request to you or your solicitor as soon as practicable. Your solicitor can obtain a copy of the tape by applying to the Police Officer in charge of the area.

Retention of audio tapes

The master tape has been sealed and will be retained at least until you are acquitted or convicted, or the prosecutor decides not to proceed with the case. You should note that if no further action is taken against you including if criminal proceedings are not instigated against you, and if by the end of six years from the date of your interview a complaint has not been received, or civil proceedings have not been instigated and it is clear that none will be, the master tape of your interview will be destroyed. In all cases, the retention periods as set out in the Criminal Procedure and Investigations Act 1996, Code of Practice, paragraph 5(b), will be followed.

Destruction of audio tapes

You or your solicitor may be present to witness the destruction of the master tape. You will be notified of the date and time that the destruction of the master tape will take place.

Important Note
You are entitled to make a complaint about your treatment in police custody at any time.

Code of Practice for Authorised Officers under the Terrorism Act 2000

General

1.   This code of practice applies to the exercise by an authorised officer of functions under Part III of the Terrorism Act 2000 ('the Act'). The code is issued under paragraph 6(1) of Schedule 14 to the Act.

2.   'Authorised officer' for the purpose of this code has the same meaning as in Section 24 of the Act. It therefore applies to an immigration officer and a customs officer when exercising functions under Part III of the Act as well as to a police officer exercising these functions. The code does not apply in other circumstances in which seizure, detention or forfeiture powers under the Act or any other legislation are exercised. Nor does the code apply where a customs officer or police officer exercises powers of seizure and detention of cash under the Drug Trafficking Act 1994 (DTA) because the cash directly or indirectly represents proceeds from drug trafficking, even though it may also be cash which would be liable to seizure under Section 25 of the Act.

3.   'Cash' has the same meaning as in Section 24(2) of the Act.

'Port' has the same meaning as in Schedule 7 to the Act.

Reference to an officer's rank includes an officer acting temporarily in that rank.

4.   The code should be available at all police stations for consultation by the police and members of the public. It should also be available at police offices at ports where the powers are, or are likely to be used. The code should also form part of the published instructions or guidance for immigration officers and customs officers.

Authority to seize cash

5.   Any decision to seize cash under the Act must be authorised
— where seizure is undertaken by a police constable, by a police officer of the rank of Inspector or above;
— where seizure is undertaken by an immigration officer, by a Chief Immigration Officer;
— where seizure is undertaken by a customs officer, by a Customs Officer Pay Band 7 or above.

Authorisation to seize cash should be obtained prior to actual seizure of the cash itself. Verbal authorisation should be supported by written authorisation as soon as is reasonably practicable.

Use of the powers by immigration and customs officers

6.   The powers to seize and detain cash under the Act should only be exercised by an immigration officer or customs officer exceptionally. If such an officer develops a suspicion in the course of exercising his/her powers under the Immigration Act 1971 or the Customs and Excise Management Act 1979 that cash found is liable to be seized under the Act he/she should alert a police officer at the earliest opportunity in order to continue any investigation. The person or persons carrying the cash should be informed of the suspicion and of the action taken (or proposed) to inform the police.

Scope

7.   There is no minimum or maximum limit on the amount of cash which may be seized.

8.   The authorised officer may seize and detain cash (for up to 48 hours), where he/she has reasonable grounds for suspecting that:

(a)
  — it is intended to be used for the purposes of terrorism;
  — it forms the whole or part of the resources of a proscribed organisation; or
  — it is terrorist property within the meaning given in Section 14(1)(b) (proceeds of the commission of acts of terrorism) or (c) (proceeds of acts carried out for the purposes of terrorism) of the Act;

and

(b) the cash
  — is being imported into or exported from the United Kingdom,
  — is being brought to any place in the United Kingdom for the purpose of being exported from the United Kingdom,
  — is being brought to Northern Ireland from Great Britain, or to Great Britain from Northern Ireland,
  — is being brought to any place in Northern Ireland for the purpose of being brought to Great Britain, or
  — is being brought to any place in Great Britain for the purpose of being brought to Northern Ireland.

9.   If therefore the authorised officer does not believe that a condition under (a) above applies to cash being brought or carried by a person no attempt should be made to seize it under Section 25 of the Act. Similarly, even if the authorised officer believes that one or more of the provisions in (a) above apply but that none of the provisions in (b) above covering the movement of the cash apply he/she should not attempt seizure under the Act.

10.   In Great Britain these powers will normally be exercised only at a port which, under Schedule 7 para. 1(2), includes an airport and a hoverport. There may, however, be occasions when authorised officers are clear that cash not at a port is nonetheless cash which falls within the criteria set out under paragraph 8(b) above, for example cash that is in the postal system.

Seizure of cash

11.   'Reasonable grounds for suspecting' are likely to depend upon particular circumstances and the authorised officer should take into account such factors as how the cash was discovered, the amount involved, its origins, intended movement, destination, reasons given for a cash as opposed to normal banking transaction, whether the courier(s) and/or the owners of the cash (if different) have any links with terrorists or terrorist groups, whether here or overseas. Where the authorised officer has suspicions about the cash he/she should give the person who has possession of it a reasonable opportunity to provide an explanation on the details of its ownership, origins, purpose, destination and reasons for moving the amount in this way and to provide the authorised officer with supporting documentation. The authorised officer should make clear to the person that anything said will be noted and used in the event that the cash is seized and an application made to the court for its detention or forfeiture.

12.   If the authorised officer believes the person has committed an offence and/or is to be arrested he or she should be cautioned and questioned in the normal way. A customs or immigration officer acting in the capacity of an authorised officer may wish or need to refer the matter to a police officer in such instances.

13.   The cash should be counted in the presence of the person and another officer. Cash should not be taken out of sight of the person carrying it unless and until it is seized.

14.   Where cash is seized, the authorised officer should inform the person carrying it that he suspects that it is cash within one or more of the provision(s) of Section 25 of the Act and the reasons for suspecting this.

15.   The authorised officer should physically seize the cash and give a written notification (see Annex) to the person from whom the cash is seized. (This includes the sender and intended recipient of unattended parcels and other containers). This notification explains that an application may be made for detention of the cash within 48 hours of seizure and provides details of the court to which the application will be made. It also advises the person that he or she is entitled to appear at the court hearing either in person or represented by a solicitor. It advises finally that cash will be released no later than the end of the period of 48 hours from the time of seizure unless an order for its further detention is granted.

16.   Where the cash seized is not in sterling, the figure should be entered in the relevant currency. The authorised officer should not attempt to convert the currency into sterling. Similarly, where the cash is in different forms (for example, travellers cheques, bank notes or postal orders) a description and their value should be recorded on the written notification and receipt.

17.   The authorised officer should explain the contents of the notification to the person from whom the cash has been taken and what he or she has to do in order to try to get it back. The authorised officer should make every reasonable effort to ensure that the person concerned understands. The person should be asked to sign the statement in the written notification that the content of the notice has been read and understood and the authorised officer should give a copy of the notification to him. If the person refuses to sign the authorised officer should endorse the form 'refused to sign' and initial the endorsement.

18.   If the person does not appear to understand what is being said or the authorised officer has doubts as to the person's ability to speak English the officer should make every reasonable effort to communicate so as to be satisfied that the person understands what is required of him or her, where necessary using someone who can act as an interpreter.

Detention of cash seized

19.   The authorised officer should record in the written notification the time and date when the cash is first seized. He must release the cash and return it to the person unless a court order is obtained *no later than 48 hours* after the cash has been first seized.

20.   The authorised officer should apply in writing without delay to the relevant court for an order to detain the cash. A copy of the written application should be given to the person from whom the cash has been seized, wherever practicable at the time of the seizure in order to give him/her the maximum time in which to make an application to the court to contest seizure and secure the release of the cash. An application for the detention of cash should be authorised by a police officer of the rank of Inspector or above.

21.   Where cash is deposited in an interest bearing account in accordance with Section 27(1) of the Act, the authorised officer should ensure a central record is kept of the details of the account and when the cash was deposited. To ensure interest accrued is accurately accounted, separate accounts for each cash seizure should be opened.

22.   When an order to detain cash has been granted *and where no application for forfeiture has been made to and is under consideration by a court* the authorised officer should keep under review whether continued detention of the cash is justified. If for any reason the authorised officer considers he is no longer justified in detaining the cash he/she should release it and return it to the person from whom it was seized (although authorised officers should bear in mind that, notwithstanding the lack of any forfeiture proceedings, the cash cannot be released while other proceedings, whether in the United Kingdom or elsewhere, which relate to the cash have not been concluded). Where detained cash is released, the authorised officer should inform the court without delay. A decision to release the cash should be authorised by a police officer of the rank of Inspector or above.

23.   An application to renew an order to detain cash beyond 6 months and up to the maximum limit of 2 years (beginning with the date when the first order was made), should be authorised by a police officer of the rank of superintendent or above.

Forfeiture

24.   Any application under Section 28 of the Act by or on behalf of the authorised officer for the forfeiture of cash must be authorised by a police officer of the rank of superintendent or above who, prior to any application being made, should review the facts in order to be satisfied on the balance of probabilities that the cash is of the kind mentioned in Section 25(1)(a), (b) or (c) of the Act and that section 25(3) applies.

Security of cash seized

25.   Any cash seized or received by a police officer under the Act should be handled in accordance with any standing instructions or orders in force. Without prejudice to any such instructions or orders the authorised officer who seizes cash should ensure that it is held in a safe, secure place until either released or lodged in an interest accruing account under Section 27 of the Act following a detention order under Section 26.

26.   Cash seized by an immigration officer or a customs officer must be handed at the earliest opportunity to the police officer with responsibility for investigating whether an application for its continued detention is to be made. The amount delivered to the police officer should be agreed and a receipt given for it by the police officer receiving it.

ANNEX

Notification of Cash Seizure under Section 25 of the Terrorism Act 2000

Under section 25 of the Terrorism Act 2000, cash to the value of in (currency)*/postal orders*/ travellers' cheques*/bankers' drafts* was seized on .... (date) at .... (place).

Any application for continued detention of the cash under section 26 of the Terrorism Act must be made not later than the period of 48 hours from the period beginning with the time when it was seized.

An application will be made *by an authorised officer (a constable, customs officer or immigration officer) to the magistrates' court at /*by the procurator fiscal to the sheriff's court at ....

You will receive a copy of the written application to the court with notification of the hearing. You are entitled to appear in court at the hearing, either in person or represented by a solicitor.

If no application for continued detention of the cash is made within the period of 48 hours mentioned above, the cash seized must be released.

Signed ....

Time ....

Date ....

I ....acknowledge that cash to the value of ....in (currency)*/postal orders*/traveller's cheques*/bankers' drafts* has been seized from me and that I have read and understood this notification.

Signed ....

Time ....

Date ....

*Delete as necessary.

International Criminal Court Act 2001
(2001, c. 17)

OTHER FORMS OF ASSISTANCE

Introduction

27 Provision of assistance
(1) The powers conferred by this Part on the Secretary of State are exercisable for the purpose of providing assistance to the ICC in relation to investigations or prosecutions where—
  (a) an investigation has been initiated by the ICC, and
  (b) the investigation and any proceedings arising out of it have not been concluded.
(2) Where facsimile transmission is used—
  (a) for the making of a request by the ICC or the transmission of any supporting documents, or
  (b) for the transmission of any document in consequence of such a request, this Part applies as if the documents so sent were the originals of the documents so transmitted.
Any such document shall be receivable in evidence accordingly.
(3) Nothing in this Part shall be read as preventing the provision of assistance to the ICC otherwise than under this Part.

Forms of assistance

28 Questioning
(1) This section applies where the Secretary of State receives a request from the ICC for assistance in questioning a person being investigated or prosecuted.
(2) The person concerned shall not be questioned in pursuance of the request unless—
  (a) he has been informed of his rights under article 55, and
  (b) he consents to be interviewed.
(3) The provisions of article 55 are set out in Schedule 3 to this Act.
(4) Consent for the purposes of subsection (2)(b) may be given—
  (a) by the person himself, or
  (b) in circumstances in which it is inappropriate for the person to act for himself, by reason of his physical or mental condition or his youth, by an appropriate person acting on his behalf.
(5) Such consent may be given orally or in writing, but if given orally it shall be recorded in writing as soon as is reasonably practicable.

29 Taking or production of evidence

(1) This section applies where the Secretary of State receives a request from the ICC for assistance in the taking or production of evidence.
For this purpose "evidence" includes documents and other articles.

(2) The Secretary of State may nominate a court in England and Wales to receive the evidence to which the request relates.

(3) For this purpose the nominated court—

    (a) has the same powers with respect to securing the attendance of witnesses and the production of documents or other articles as it has for the purpose of other proceedings before the court; and

    (b) may take evidence on oath.

(4) A person shall not be compelled to give evidence or produce anything in proceedings under this section that he could not be compelled to give or produce in criminal proceedings in the part of the United Kingdom in which the nominated court has jurisdiction.

(5) If in order to comply with the request it is necessary for the evidence received by the court to be verified in any manner, the notice nominating the court shall specify the nature of the verification required.

(6) No order for costs shall be made in proceedings under this section.

30 Taking or production of evidence: further provisions

(1) The following provisions apply in relation to proceedings before a nominated court under section 29 and the evidence received in the proceedings.

(2) The court may, if it thinks it necessary in order to protect—

    (a) victims and witnesses, or a person alleged to have committed an ICC crime, or

    (b) confidential or sensitive information,

direct that the public be excluded from the court.

(3) The court shall ensure that a register is kept of the proceedings that indicates, in particular—

    (a) which persons with an interest in the proceedings were present,

    (b) which of those persons were represented and by whom, and

    (c) whether any of those persons was denied the opportunity of cross-examining a witness as to any part of his testimony.

(4) The register shall not be open to inspection except as authorised by the Secretary of State or with the leave of the court.

(5) A copy of the register of the proceedings shall be sent to the Secretary of State for transmission to the ICC.

31 Service of process

(1) This section applies where the Secretary of State receives from the ICC a summons or other document together with a request for it to be served on a person in England, Wales [or Northern Ireland].

(2) The Secretary of State may direct the chief officer of police for the area in which the person appears to be to cause the document to be personally served on him.

(3) If the document is so served, the chief officer of police shall forthwith inform the Secretary of State when and how it was served.

(4) If it does not prove possible to serve the document, the chief officer of police shall forthwith inform the Secretary of State of that fact and of the reason.

(5) (*Applies to Northern Ireland only.*)

32 Transfer of prisoner to give evidence or assist in investigation

(1) This section applies where the Secretary of State receives a request from the ICC for the temporary transfer of a prisoner to the ICC for purposes of identification or for obtaining testimony or other assistance.

(2) Where the prisoner is detained in Scotland, the Secretary of State shall transmit the request to the Scottish Ministers.

(3) The relevant Minister may issue a warrant (a 'transfer warrant') requiring the prisoner to be delivered up, in accordance with arrangements made by the relevant Minister with the ICC, into the custody of the ICC.

(4) A transfer warrant shall not be issued unless the prisoner consents to the transfer, but consent may not be withdrawn after the issue of the warrant.

(5) The following provisions of Part 2 of this Act apply in relation to a transfer warrant under this section as they apply in relation to a delivery order under that Part—
section 15 (effect of delivery order), and
section 24 and Schedule 2 (delivery up of persons subject to criminal proceedings, &c.).

(6) In this section 'prisoner' means—
  (a) a person serving a sentence in a prison to which the Prison Act 1952 (c. 52) . . . applies,
  (b) (*Applies to Scotland only.*)
  (c) a person serving a sentence of detention or imprisonment imposed by a service court,
  (d) a person detained in custody otherwise than in pursuance of a sentence, including in particular—
    (i) a person in custody awaiting trial or sentence,
    (ii) a person committed to prison for contempt or for default in paying a fine,
    (iii) a person in custody in connection with proceedings to which Part 2 or 3 of Schedule 2 applies (extradition or other delivery proceedings),
    (iv) a person detained under any provision of the Immigration Act 1971 (c. 77).

(7) For the purposes of the Immigration Acts (within the meaning of the Immigration and Asylum Act 1999 (c. 33)) a person detained under any provision of the Immigration Act 1971 is not to be regarded as having left the United Kingdom at any time when a transfer warrant is in force in respect of him (including any time when he is in the custody of the ICC).

(8) In this section, 'the relevant Minister' means—
  (a) . . . the Secretary of State;
  (b) (*Applies to Scotland only.*)

33 Entry, search and seizure

(1) This section applies where the Secretary of State receives from the ICC a request for assistance which appears to him to require the exercise of any of the powers conferred by Part 2 of the Police and Criminal Evidence Act 1984 (c. 60). . . .

(2) The Secretary of State may direct a constable to apply for a warrant or order under the relevant Part, which shall apply in relation to an ICC crime as it applies to a serious arrestable offence.

34 Taking of fingerprints or non-intimate sample

(1) The provisions of Schedule 4 have effect with respect to the taking of fingerprints or a non-intimate sample in response to a request from the ICC for assistance in obtaining evidence as to the identity of a person.

(2) In subsection (1) and that Schedule 'fingerprints' and 'non-intimate sample' have the meaning given by section 65 of the Police and Criminal Evidence Act 1984. . . .

35 Orders for exhumation

Proceedings before the ICC in respect of an ICC crime are criminal proceedings for the purposes of section 23 of the Coroners Act 1988 (c. 13). . . .

36 Provision of records and documents

(1) This section applies where the Secretary of State receives a request from the ICC for the provision of records and documents relating to—

    (a) the evidence given in any proceedings in England and Wales [or Northern Ireland] in respect of conduct that would constitute an ICC crime, or

    (b) the results of any investigation of such conduct with a view to such proceedings.

(2) The Secretary of State shall take such steps as appear to him to be appropriate to obtain the records and documents requested, and on their being produced to him he shall transmit them to the ICC.

37 Investigation of proceeds of ICC crime

(1) Where the Secretary of State receives a request from the ICC for assistance—

    (a) in ascertaining whether a person has benefited from an ICC crime, or

    (b) in identifying the extent or whereabouts of property derived directly or indirectly from an ICC crime,

the Secretary of State may direct a constable to apply for an order or warrant under Schedule 5.

(2) In that Schedule—

Part 1 makes provision for production or access orders,

Part 2 makes provision for the issuing of search warrants, and

Part 3 contains supplementary provisions.

38 Freezing orders in respect of property liable to forfeiture

Where the Secretary of State receives a request from the ICC for assistance in the freezing or seizure of proceeds, property and assets or instrumentalities of crime for the purpose of eventual forfeiture, he may—

    (a) authorise a person to act on behalf of the ICC for the purposes of applying for a freezing order, and

    (b) direct that person to apply for such an order under Schedule 6.

National security

39 Production or disclosure prejudicial to national security

(1) Nothing in any of the provisions of this Part . . . requires or authorises the production of documents, or the disclosure of information, which would be prejudicial to the security of the United Kingdom.

(2) For the purposes of any such provision a certificate signed by or on behalf of the Secretary of State to the effect that it would be prejudicial to the security of the United Kingdom for specified documents to be produced, or for specified information to be disclosed, is conclusive evidence of that fact.

Supplementary provisions

40 Verification of material

If in order to comply with a request of the ICC it is necessary for any evidence or other material obtained under this Part to be verified in any manner, the Secretary of State may give directions as to the nature of the verification required.

41 Transmission of material to the ICC

(1) Any evidence or other material obtained under this Part by a person other than the Secretary of State, together with any requisite verification, shall be sent to the Secretary of State for transmission to the ICC.

(2) Where any evidence or other material is to be transmitted to the ICC, there shall be transmitted—

    (a) where the material consists of a document, the original or a copy, and

    (b) where the material consists of any other article, the article itself or a photograph or other description of it,

as may be necessary to comply with the request of the ICC.

Crime (International Co-operation) Act 2003
(2003, c. 32)

CHAPTER 2   MUTUAL PROVISION OF EVIDENCE

Assistance in obtaining evidence abroad

7   Requests for assistance in obtaining evidence abroad

(1) If it appears to a judicial authority in the United Kingdom on an application made by a person mentioned in subsection (3)—

   (a) that an offence has been committed or that there are reasonable grounds for suspecting that an offence has been committed, and

   (b) that proceedings in respect of the offence have been instituted or that the offence is being investigated,

the judicial authority may request assistance under this section.

(2) The assistance that may be requested under this section is assistance in obtaining outside the United Kingdom any evidence specified in the request for use in the proceedings or investigation.

(3) The application may be made—

   (a) in relation to England and Wales . . . by a prosecuting authority,

   (b) . . .

   (c) where proceedings have been instituted, by the person charged in those proceedings.

(4) The judicial authorities are—

   (a) in relation to England and Wales, any judge or justice of the peace,

   (b) . . .

   (c) . . .

(5) In relation to England and Wales . . . a designated prosecuting authority may itself request assistance under this section if—

   (a) it appears to the authority that an offence has been committed or that there are reasonable grounds for suspecting that an offence has been committed, and

   (b) the authority has instituted proceedings in respect of the offence in question or it is being investigated.

   "Designated" means designated by an order made by the Secretary of State.

(6) . . .

(7) If a request for assistance under this section is made in reliance on Article 2 of the 2001 Protocol (requests for information on banking transactions) in connection with the investigation of an offence, the request must state the grounds on which the person making the request considers the evidence specified in it to be relevant for the purposes of the investigation.

8   Sending requests for assistance

(1) A request for assistance under section 7 may be sent—

   (a) to a court exercising jurisdiction in the place where the evidence is situated, or

   (b) to any authority recognised by the government of the country in question as the appropriate authority for receiving requests of that kind.

(2) Alternatively, if it is a request by a judicial authority or a designated prosecuting authority it may be sent to the Secretary of State . . . for forwarding to a court or authority mentioned in subsection (1).

(3) In cases of urgency, a request for assistance may be sent to—

   (a) the International Criminal Police Organisation, or

(b) any body or person competent to receive it under any provisions adopted under the Treaty on European Union,

for forwarding to any court or authority mentioned in subsection (1).

9 Use of evidence obtained

(1) This section applies to evidence obtained pursuant to a request for assistance under section 7.

(2) The evidence may not without the consent of the appropriate overseas authority be used for any purpose other than that specified in the request.

(3) When the evidence is no longer required for that purpose (or for any other purpose for which such consent has been obtained), it must be returned to the appropriate overseas authority, unless that authority indicates that it need not be returned.

(4) ...

(5) ...

(6) In this section, the appropriate overseas authority means the authority recognised by the government of the country in question as the appropriate authority for receiving requests of the kind in question.

10 Domestic freezing orders

(1) If it appears to a judicial authority in the United Kingdom, on an application made by a person mentioned in subsection (4)—

(a) that proceedings in respect of a listed offence have been instituted or such an offence is being investigated,

(b) that there are reasonable grounds to believe that there is evidence in a participating country which satisfies the requirements of subsection (3), and

(c) that a request has been made, or will be made, under section 7 for the evidence to be sent to the authority making the request,

the judicial authority may make a domestic freezing order in respect of the evidence.

(2) A domestic freezing order is an order for protecting evidence which is in the participating country pending its transfer to the United Kingdom.

(3) The requirements are that the evidence—

(a) is on premises specified in the application in the participating country,

(b) is likely to be of substantial value (whether by itself or together with other evidence) to the proceedings or investigation,

(c) is likely to be admissible in evidence at a trial for the offence, and

(d) does not consist of or include items subject to legal privilege.

(4) The application may be made—

(a) in relation to England and Wales and Northern Ireland, by a constable,

(b) ...

(5) The judicial authorities are—

(a) in relation to England and Wales, any judge or justice of the peace,

(b) ...

(c) ....

(6) This section does not prejudice the generality of the power to make a request for assistance under section 7.

11 Sending freezing orders

(1) A domestic freezing order made in England and Wales . . . is to be sent to the Secretary of State for forwarding to—

(a) a court exercising jurisdiction in the place where the evidence is situated, or

(b) any authority recognised by the government of the country in question as the appropriate authority for receiving orders of that kind.

(2) ...

(3) The judicial authority is to send the order to the Secretary of State . . . before the end of the period of 14 days beginning with its being made.

(4) The order must be accompanied by a certificate giving the specified information and, unless the certificate indicates when the judicial authority expects such a request to be made, by a request under section 7 for the evidence to be sent to the authority making the request.

(5) The certificate must include a translation of it into an appropriate language of the participating country (if that language is not English).

(6) The certificate must be signed by or on behalf of the judicial authority who made the order and must include a statement as to the accuracy of the information given in it.

The signature may be an electronic signature.

12   Variation or revocation of freezing orders

(1) The judicial authority that made a domestic freezing order may vary or revoke it on an application by a person mentioned below.

(2) The persons are—
  (a) the person who applied for the order,
  (b) in relation to England and Wales . . . a prosecuting authority,
  (c) . . . ,
  (d) any other person affected by the order.

Assisting overseas authorities to obtain evidence in the UK

13   Requests for assistance from overseas authorities

(1) Where a request for assistance in obtaining evidence in a part of the United Kingdom is received by the territorial authority for that part, the authority may—
  (a) if the conditions in section 14 are met, arrange for the evidence to be obtained under section 15, or
  (b) . . ..

(2) The request for assistance may be made only by—
  (a) a court exercising criminal jurisdiction, or a prosecuting authority, in a country outside the United Kingdom,
  (b) any other authority in such a country which appears to the territorial authority to have the function of making such requests for assistance,
  (c) any international authority mentioned in subsection (3).

(3) The international authorities are—
  (a) the International Criminal Police Organisation,
  (b) any other body or person competent to make a request of the kind to which this section applies under any provisions adopted under the Treaty on European Union.

14   Powers to arrange for evidence to be obtained

(1) The territorial authority may arrange for evidence to be obtained under section 15 if the request for assistance in obtaining the evidence is made in connection with—
  (a) criminal proceedings or a criminal investigation, being carried on outside the United Kingdom,
  (b) administrative proceedings, or an investigation into an act punishable in such proceedings, being carried on there,
  (c) clemency proceedings, or proceedings on an appeal before a court against a decision in administrative proceedings, being carried on, or intended to be carried on, there.

(2) In a case within subsection (1)(a) or (b), the authority may arrange for the evidence to be so obtained only if the authority is satisfied—

(a) that an offence under the law of the country in question has been committed or that there are reasonable grounds for suspecting that such an offence has been committed, and

(b) that proceedings in respect of the offence have been instituted in that country or that an investigation into the offence is being carried on there.

An offence includes an act punishable in administrative proceedings.

(3) The territorial authority is to regard as conclusive a certificate as to the matters mentioned in subsection (2)(a) and (b) issued by any authority in the country in question which appears to him to be the appropriate authority to do so.

(4) If it appears to the territorial authority that the request for assistance relates to a fiscal offence in respect of which proceedings have not yet been instituted, the authority may not arrange for the evidence to be so obtained unless—

(a) the request is from a country which is a member of the Commonwealth or is made pursuant to a treaty to which the United Kingdom is a party, or

(b) the authority is satisfied that if the conduct constituting the offence were to occur in a part of the United Kingdom, it would constitute an offence in that part.

15 Nominating a court etc. to receive evidence

(1) Where the evidence is in England and Wales . . . the Secretary of State may by a notice nominate a court to receive any evidence to which the request relates which appears to the court to be appropriate for the purpose of giving effect to the request.

(2) But if it appears to the Secretary of State that the request relates to an offence involving serious or complex fraud, he may refer the request (or any part of it) to the Director of the Serious Fraud Office for the Director to obtain any evidence to which the request or part relates which appears to him to be appropriate for the purpose of giving effect to the request or part.

(3) . . .

(4) . . .

(5) Schedule 1 is to have effect in relation to proceedings before a court nominated under this section.

16 Extension of statutory search powers in England and Wales . . .

(1) Part 2 of the Police and Criminal Evidence Act 1984 (c. 60) (powers of entry, search and seizure) is to have effect as if references to serious arrestable offences in section 8 of, and Schedule 1 to, that Act included any conduct which—

(a) constitutes an offence under the law of a country outside the United Kingdom, and

(b) would, if it occurred in England and Wales, constitute a serious arrestable offence.

(2) But an application for a warrant or order by virtue of subsection (1) may be made only—

(a) in pursuance of a direction given under section 13, or

(b) if it is an application for a warrant or order under section 8 of, or Schedule 1 to, that Act by a constable for the purposes of an investigation by an international joint investigation team of which he is a member.

(3) . . .

(4) . . .

(5) In this section, "international joint investigation team" has the meaning given by section 88(7) of the Police Act 1996 (c. 16).

17 Warrants in England and Wales . . .

(1) A justice of the peace may issue a warrant under this section if he is satisfied, on an application made by a constable, that the following conditions are met.

(2) But an application for a warrant under subsection (1) may be made only in pursuance of a direction given under section 13.

(3) The conditions are that—

    (a) criminal proceedings have been instituted against a person in a country outside the United Kingdom or a person has been arrested in the course of a criminal investigation carried on there,

    (b) the conduct constituting the offence which is the subject of the proceedings or investigation would, if it occurred in England and Wales ... constitute an arrestable offence, and

    (c) there are reasonable grounds for suspecting that there is on premises in England and Wales ... occupied or controlled by that person evidence relating to the offence.

"Arrestable offence" has the same meaning as in the Police and Criminal Evidence Act 1984 (c. 60) ....

(4) A warrant under this section may authorise a constable—

    (a) to enter the premises in question and search the premises to the extent reasonably required for the purpose of discovering any evidence relating to the offence,

    (b) to seize and retain any evidence for which he is authorised to search.

19 Seized evidence

(1) Any evidence seized by a constable under or by virtue of section 16, 17 or 18 is to be sent to the court or authority which made the request for assistance or to the territorial authority for forwarding to that court or authority.

(2) So far as may be necessary in order to comply with the request for assistance—

    (a) where the evidence consists of a document, the original or a copy is to be sent, and

    (b) where the evidence consists of any other article, the article itself or a description, photograph or other representation of it is to be sent.

(3) This section does not apply to evidence seized under or by virtue of section 16(2)(b) or (4)(b) or 18(2)(b).

CHAPTER 3   HEARING EVIDENCE THROUGH TELEVISION LINKS
OR BY TELEPHONE

29 Hearing witnesses abroad through television links

(1) The Secretary of State may by order provide for section 32(1A) of the Criminal Justice Act 1988 (c. 33) ... (proceedings in which evidence may be given through television link) to apply to any further description of criminal proceedings, or to all criminal proceedings.

(2) ....

30 Hearing witnesses in the UK through television links

(1) This section applies where the Secretary of State receives a request, from an authority mentioned in subsection (2) ("the external authority"), for a person in the United Kingdom to give evidence through a live television link in criminal proceedings before a court in a country outside the United Kingdom.

Criminal proceedings include any proceedings on an appeal before a court against a decision in administrative proceedings.

(2) The authority referred to in subsection (1) is the authority in that country which appears to the Secretary of State to have the function of making requests of the kind to which this section applies.

(3) Unless he considers it inappropriate to do so, the Secretary of State must by notice in writing nominate a court in the United Kingdom where the witness may be heard in the proceedings in question through a live television link.

(4) Anything done by the witness in the presence of the nominated court which, if it were done in proceedings before the court, would constitute contempt of court is to be treated for that purpose as done in proceedings before the court.

(5) Any statement made on oath by a witness giving evidence in pursuance of this section is to be treated for the purposes of—

(a) section 1 of the Perjury Act 1911 (c. 6),

(b) . . .

(c) . . .

as made in proceedings before the nominated court.

(6) Part 1 of Schedule 2 (evidence given by television link) is to have effect.

(7) Subject to subsections (4) and (5) and the provisions of that Schedule, evidence given pursuant to this section is not to be treated for any purpose as evidence given in proceedings in the United Kingdom.

(8) . . .

31 Hearing witnesses in the UK by telephone

(1) This section applies where the Secretary of State receives a request, from an authority mentioned in subsection (2) ("the external authority") in a participating country, for a person in the United Kingdom to give evidence by telephone in criminal proceedings before a court in that country.

Criminal proceedings include any proceedings on an appeal before a court against a decision in administrative proceedings.

(2) The authority referred to in subsection (1) is the authority in that country which appears to the Secretary of State to have the function of making requests of the kind to which this section applies.

(3) A request under subsection (1) must—

(a) specify the court in the participating country,

(b) give the name and address of the witness,

(c) state that the witness is willing to give evidence by telephone in the proceedings before that court.

(4) Unless he considers it inappropriate to do so, the Secretary of State must by notice in writing nominate a court in the United Kingdom where the witness may be heard in the proceedings in question by telephone.

(5) Anything done by the witness in the presence of the nominated court which, if it were done in proceedings before the court, would constitute contempt of court is to be treated for that purpose as done in proceedings before the court.

(6) Any statement made on oath by a witness giving evidence in pursuance of this section is to be treated for the purposes of—

(a) section 1 of the Perjury Act 1911 (c. 6),

(b) . . .

(c) . . .

as made in proceedings before the nominated court.

(7) Part 2 of Schedule 2 (evidence given by telephone link) is to have effect.

(8) Subject to subsections (5) and (6) and the provisions of that Schedule, evidence given in pursuance of this section is not to be treated for any purpose as evidence given in proceedings in the United Kingdom.

(9) . . . .

Sexual Offences Act 2003

(2003, c. 42)

75 Evidential presumptions about consent

(1) If in proceedings for an offence to which this section applies it is proved—

    (a) that the defendant did the relevant act,

    (b) that any of the circumstances specified in subsection (2) existed, and

    (c) that the defendant knew that those circumstances existed,

the complainant is to be taken not to have consented to the relevant act unless sufficient evidence is adduced to raise an issue as to whether he consented, and the defendant is to be taken not to have reasonably believed that the complainant consented unless sufficient evidence is adduced to raise an issue as to whether he reasonably believed it.

    (2) The circumstances are that—

    (a) any person was, at the time of the relevant act or immediately before it began, using violence against the complainant or causing the complainant to fear that immediate violence would be used against him;

    (b) any person was, at the time of the relevant act or immediately before it began, causing the complainant to fear that violence was being used, or that immediate violence would be used, against another person;

    (c) the complainant was, and the defendant was not, unlawfully detained at the time of the relevant act;

    (d) the complainant was asleep or otherwise unconscious at the time of the relevant act;

    (e) because of the complainant's physical disability, the complainant would not have been able at the time of the relevant act to communicate to the defendant whether the complainant consented;

    (f) any person had administered to or caused to be taken by the complainant, without the complainant's consent, a substance which, having regard to when it was administered or taken, was capable of causing or enabling the complainant to be stupefied or overpowered at the time of the relevant act.

    (3) In subsection (2)(a) and (b), the reference to the time immediately before the relevant act began is, in the case of an act which is one of a continuous series of sexual activities, a reference to the time immediately before the first sexual activity began.

76 Conclusive presumptions about consent

    (1) If in proceedings for an offence to which this section applies it is proved that the defendant did the relevant act and that any of the circumstances specified in subsection (2) existed, it is to be conclusively presumed—

    (a) that the complainant did not consent to the relevant act, and

    (b) that the defendant did not believe that the complainant consented to the relevant act.

    (2) The circumstances are that—

    (a) the defendant intentionally deceived the complainant as to the nature or purpose of the relevant act;

    (b) the defendant intentionally induced the complainant to consent to the relevant act by impersonating a person known personally to the complainant.

77 Sections 75 and 76: relevant acts

    In relation to an offence to which sections 75 and 76 apply, references in those sections to the relevant act and to the complainant are to be read as follows—

Offence

Relevant Act

An offence under section 1 (rape).

    The defendant intentionally penetrating, with his penis, the vagina, anus or mouth of another person ("the complainant").

An offence under section 2 (assault by penetration).

The defendant intentionally penetrating, with a part of his body or anything else, the vagina or anus of another person ("the complainant"), where the penetration is sexual.

An offence under section 3 (sexual assault).

The defendant intentionally touching another person ("the complainant"), where the touching is sexual.

An offence under section 4 (causing a person to engage in sexual activity without consent).

The defendant intentionally causing another person ("the complainant") to engage in an activity, where the activity is sexual.

78   "Sexual"

For the purposes of this Part (except section 71), penetration, touching or any other activity is sexual if a reasonable person would consider that—

    (a) whatever its circumstances or any person's purpose in relation to it, it is because of its nature sexual, or

    (b) because of its nature it may be sexual and because of its circumstances or the purpose of any person in relation to it (or both) it is sexual.

79   Part 1: general interpretation

(1) The following apply for the purposes of this Part.

(2) Penetration is a continuing act from entry to withdrawal.

(3) References to a part of the body include references to a part surgically constructed (in particular, through gender reassignment surgery).

(4) "Image" means a moving or still image and includes an image produced by any means and, where the context permits, a three-dimensional image.

(5) References to an image of a person include references to an image of an imaginary person.

(6) "Mental disorder" has the meaning given by section 1 of the Mental Health Act 1983 (c. 20).

(7) References to observation (however expressed) are to observation whether direct or by looking at an image.

(8) Touching includes touching—

    (a) with any part of the body,

    (b) with anything else,

    (c) through anything,

and in particular includes touching amounting to penetration.

(9) "Vagina" includes vulva.

(10) In relation to an animal, references to the vagina or anus include references to any similar part.

Criminal Justice Act 2003
(2003, c. 44)

PART 8   LIVE LINKS

51   Live links in criminal proceedings

(1) A witness (other than the defendant) may, if the court so directs, give evidence through a live link in the following criminal proceedings.

(2) They are—

(a) a summary trial,

(b) an appeal to the Crown Court arising out of such a trial,

(c) a trial on indictment,

(d) an appeal to the criminal division of the Court of Appeal,

(e) the hearing of a reference under section 9 or 11 of the Criminal Appeal Act 1995 (c. 35),

(f) a hearing before a magistrates' court or the Crown Court which is held after the defendant has entered a plea of guilty, and

(g) a hearing before the Court of Appeal under section 80 of this Act.

(3) A direction may be given under this section—

(a) on an application by a party to the proceedings, or

(b) of the court's own motion.

(4) But a direction may not be given under this section unless-

(a) the court is satisfied that it is in the interests of the efficient or effective administration of justice for the person concerned to give evidence in the proceedings through a live link,

(b) it has been notified by the Secretary of State that suitable facilities for receiving evidence through a live link are available in the area in which it appears to the court that the proceedings will take place, and

(c) that notification has not been withdrawn.

(5) The withdrawal of such a notification is not to affect a direction given under this section before that withdrawal.

(6) In deciding whether to give a direction under this section the court must consider all the circumstances of the case.

(7) Those circumstances include in particular—

(a) the availability of the witness,

(b) the need for the witness to attend in person,

(c) the importance of the witness's evidence to the proceedings,

(d) the views of the witness,

(e) the suitability of the facilities at the place where the witness would give evidence through a live link,

(f) whether a direction might tend to inhibit any party to the proceedings from effectively testing the witness's evidence.

(8) The court must state in open court its reasons for refusing an application for a direction under this section and, if it is a magistrates' court, must cause them to be entered in the register of its proceedings.

52   Effect of, and rescission of, direction

(1) Subsection (2) applies where the court gives a direction under section 51 for a person to give evidence through a live link in particular proceedings.

(2) The person concerned may not give evidence in those proceedings after the direction is given otherwise than through a live link (but this is subject to the following provisions of this section).

(3) The court may rescind a direction under section 51 if it appears to the court to be in the interests of justice to do so.

(4) Where it does so, the person concerned shall cease to be able to give evidence in the proceedings through a live link, but this does not prevent the court from giving a further direction under section 51 in relation to him.

(5) A direction under section 51 may be rescinded under subsection (3)—

(a) on an application by a party to the proceedings, or

(b) of the court's own motion.

(6) But an application may not be made under subsection (5)(a) unless there has been a material change of circumstances since the direction was given.

(7) The court must state in open court its reasons—

    (a) for rescinding a direction under section 51, or

    (b) for refusing an application to rescind such a direction,

and, if it is a magistrates' court, must cause them to be entered in the register of its proceedings.

53   Magistrates' courts permitted to sit at other locations

(1) This section applies where—

    (a) a magistrates' court is minded to give a direction under section 51 for evidence to be given through a live link in proceedings before the court, and

    (b) suitable facilities for receiving such evidence are not available at any petty-sessional court-house in which the court can (apart from subsection (2)) lawfully sit.

(2) The court may sit for the purposes of the whole or any part of the proceedings at any place at which such facilities are available and which has been appointed for the purposes of this section by the justices acting for the petty sessions area for which the court acts.

(3) A place appointed under subsection (2) may be outside the petty sessions area for which it is appointed; but (if so) it shall be deemed to be in that area for the purpose of the jurisdiction of the justices acting for that area.

54   Warning to jury

(1) This section applies where, as a result of a direction under section 51, evidence has been given through a live link in proceedings before the Crown Court.

(2) The judge may give the jury (if there is one) such direction as he thinks necessary to ensure that the jury gives the same weight to the evidence as if it had been given by the witness in the courtroom or other place where the proceedings are held.

55   Rules of court

(1) Rules of court may make such provision as appears to the authority making them to be necessary or expedient for the purposes of this Part.

(2) Rules of court may in particular make provision—

    (a) as to the procedure to be followed in connection with applications under section 51 or 52, and

    (b) as to the arrangements or safeguards to be put in place in connection with the operation of live links.

(3) The provision which may be made by virtue of subsection (2)(a) includes provision—

    (a) for uncontested applications to be determined by the court without a hearing,

    (b) for preventing the renewal of an unsuccessful application under section 51 unless there has been a material change of circumstances,

    (c) for the manner in which confidential or sensitive information is to be treated in connection with an application under section 51 or 52 and in particular as to its being disclosed to, or withheld from, a party to the proceedings.

(4) Nothing in this section is to be taken as affecting the generality of any enactment conferring power to make rules of court.

56   Interpretation of part 8

(1) In this Part—

"legal representative" means an authorised advocate or authorised litigator (as defined by section 119(1) of the Courts and Legal Services Act 1990 (c. 41)),

"petty-sessional court-house" has the same meaning as in the Magistrates' Courts Act 1980 (c. 43),

"petty sessions area" has the same meaning as in the Justices of the Peace Act 1997 (c. 25), "rules of court" means Magistrates' Courts Rules, Crown Court Rules or Criminal Appeal Rules,

"witness", in relation to any criminal proceedings, means a person called, or proposed to be called, to give evidence in the proceedings.

(2) In this Part "live link" means a live television link or other arrangement by which a witness, while at a place in the United Kingdom which is outside the building where the proceedings are being held, is able to see and hear a person at the place where the proceedings are being held and to be seen and heard by the following persons.

(3) They are—

    (a) the defendant or defendants,

    (b) the judge or justices (or both) and the jury (if there is one),

    (c) legal representatives acting in the proceedings, and

    (d) any interpreter or other person appointed by the court to assist the witness.

(4) The extent (if any) to which a person is unable to see or hear by reason of any impairment of eyesight or hearing is to be disregarded for the purposes of subsection (2).

(5) Nothing in this Part is to be regarded as affecting any power of a court—

    (a) to make an order, give directions or give leave of any description in relation to any witness (including the defendant or defendants), or

    (b) to exclude evidence at its discretion (whether by preventing questions being put or otherwise).

PART 9   PROSECUTION APPEALS

Introduction

57   Introduction

(1) In relation to a trial on indictment, the prosecution is to have the rights of appeal for which provision is made by this Part.

(2) But the prosecution is to have no right of appeal under this Part in respect of—

    (a) a ruling that a jury be discharged, or

    (b) a ruling from which an appeal lies to the Court of Appeal by virtue of any other enactment.

(3) An appeal under this Part is to lie to the Court of Appeal.

(4) Such an appeal may be brought only with the leave of the judge or the Court of Appeal.

General right of appeal in respect of rulings

58   General right of appeal in respect of rulings

(1) This section applies where a judge makes a ruling in relation to a trial on indictment at an applicable time and the ruling relates to one or more offences included in the indictment.

(2) The prosecution may appeal in respect of the ruling in accordance with this section.

(3) The ruling is to have no effect whilst the prosecution is able to take any steps under subsection (4).

(4) The prosecution may not appeal in respect of the ruling unless-

    (a) following the making of the ruling, it—

        (i) informs the court that it intends to appeal, or

        (ii) requests an adjournment to consider whether to appeal, and

    (b) if such an adjournment is granted, it informs the court following the adjournment that it intends to appeal.

(5) If the prosecution requests an adjournment under subsection (4)(a)(ii), the judge may grant such an adjournment.

(6) Where the ruling relates to two or more offences-

(a) any one or more of those offences may be the subject of the appeal, and
(b) if the prosecution informs the court in accordance with subsection (4) that it intends to appeal, it must at the same time inform the court of the offence or offences which are the subject of the appeal.

(7) Where—
(a) the ruling is a ruling that there is no case to answer, and
(b) the prosecution, at the same time that it informs the court in accordance with subsection (4) that it intends to appeal, nominates one or more other rulings which have been made by a judge in relation to the trial on indictment at an applicable time and which relate to the offence or offences which are the subject of the appeal,

that other ruling, or those other rulings, are also to be treated as the subject of the appeal.

(8) The prosecution may not inform the court in accordance with subsection (4) that it intends to appeal, unless, at or before that time, it informs the court that it agrees that, in respect of the offence or each offence which is the subject of the appeal, the defendant in relation to that offence should be acquitted of that offence if either of the conditions mentioned in subsection (9) is fulfilled.

(9) Those conditions are—
(a) that leave to appeal to the Court of Appeal is not obtained, and
(b) that the appeal is abandoned before it is determined by the Court of Appeal.

(10) If the prosecution informs the court in accordance with subsection (4) that it intends to appeal, the ruling mentioned in subsection (1) is to continue to have no effect in relation to the offence or offences which are the subject of the appeal whilst the appeal is pursued.

(11) If and to the extent that a ruling has no effect in accordance with this section—
(a) any consequences of the ruling are also to have no effect,
(b) the judge may not take any steps in consequence of the ruling, and
(c) if he does so, any such steps are also to have no effect.

(12) Where the prosecution has informed the court of its agreement under subsection (8) and either of the conditions mentioned in subsection (9) is fulfilled, the judge or the Court of Appeal must order that the defendant in relation to the offence or each offence concerned be acquitted of that offence.

(13) In this section "applicable time", in relation to a trial on indictment, means any time (whether before or after the commencement of the trial) before the start of the judge's summing-up to the jury.

59   Expedited and non-expedited appeals

(1) Where the prosecution informs the court in accordance with section 58(4) that it intends to appeal, the judge must decide whether or not the appeal should be expedited.

(2) If the judge decides that the appeal should be expedited, he may order an adjournment.

(3) If the judge decides that the appeal should not be expedited, he may-
(a) order an adjournment, or
(b) discharge the jury (if one has been sworn).

(4) If he decides that the appeal should be expedited, he or the Court of Appeal may subsequently reverse that decision and, if it is reversed, the judge may act as mentioned in subsection (3)(a) or (b).

60   Continuation of proceedings for offences not affected by ruling

(1) This section applies where the prosecution informs the court in accordance with section 58(4) that it intends to appeal.

(2) Proceedings may be continued in respect of any offence which is not the subject of the appeal.

61   Determination of appeal by court of appeal

(1) On an appeal under section 58, the Court of Appeal may confirm, reverse or vary any ruling to which the appeal relates.

(2) Subsections (3) to (5) apply where the appeal relates to a single ruling.

(3) Where the Court of Appeal confirms the ruling, it must, in respect of the offence or each offence which is the subject of the appeal, order that the defendant in relation to that offence be acquitted of that offence.

(4) Where the Court of Appeal reverses or varies the ruling, it must, in respect of the offence or each offence which is the subject of the appeal, do any of the following—

  (a) order that proceedings for that offence may be resumed in the Crown Court,

  (b) order that a fresh trial may take place in the Crown Court for that offence,

  (c) order that the defendant in relation to that offence be acquitted of that offence.

(5) But the Court of Appeal may not make an order under subsection (4)(a) or (b) in respect of an offence unless it considers it necessary in the interests of justice to do so.

(6) Subsections (7) and (8) apply where the appeal relates to a ruling that there is no case to answer and one or more other rulings.

(7) Where the Court of Appeal confirms the ruling that there is no case to answer, it must, in respect of the offence or each offence which is the subject of the appeal, order that the defendant in relation to that offence be acquitted of that offence.

(8) Where the Court of Appeal reverses or varies the ruling that there is no case to answer, it must in respect of the offence or each offence which is the subject of the appeal, make any of the orders mentioned in subsection (4)(a) to (c) (but subject to subsection (5)).

Right of appeal in respect of evidentiary rulings

62   Right of appeal in respect of evidentiary rulings

(1) The prosecution may, in accordance with this section and section 63, appeal in respect of—

  (a) a single qualifying evidentiary ruling, or

  (b) two or more qualifying evidentiary rulings.

(2) A "qualifying evidentiary ruling" is an evidentiary ruling of a judge in relation to a trial on indictment which is made at any time (whether before or after the commencement of the trial) before the opening of the case for the defence.

(3) The prosecution may not appeal in respect of a single qualifying evidentiary ruling unless the ruling relates to one or more qualifying offences (whether or not it relates to any other offence).

(4) The prosecution may not appeal in respect of two or more qualifying evidentiary rulings unless each ruling relates to one or more qualifying offences (whether or not it relates to any other offence).

(5) If the prosecution intends to appeal under this section, it must before the opening of the case for the defence inform the court—

  (a) of its intention to do so, and

  (b) of the ruling or rulings to which the appeal relates.

(6) In respect of the ruling, or each ruling, to which the appeal relates—

  (a) the qualifying offence, or at least one of the qualifying offences, to which the ruling relates must be the subject of the appeal, and

  (b) any other offence to which the ruling relates may, but need not, be the subject of the appeal.

(7) The prosecution must, at the same time that it informs the court in accordance with subsection (5), inform the court of the offence or offences which are the subject of the appeal.

(8) For the purposes of this section, the case for the defence opens when, after the conclusion of the prosecution evidence, the earliest of the following events occurs—

(a) evidence begins to be adduced by or on behalf of a defendant,
(b) it is indicated to the court that no evidence will be adduced by or on behalf of a defendant,
(c) a defendant's case is opened, as permitted by section 2 of the Criminal Procedure Act 1865 (c. 18).

(9) In this section—

"evidentiary ruling" means a ruling which relates to the admissibility or exclusion of any prosecution evidence,

"qualifying offence" means an offence described in Part 1 of Schedule 4.

(10) The Secretary of State may by order amend that Part by doing any one or more of the following—

(a) adding a description of offence,
(b) removing a description of offence for the time being included,
(c) modifying a description of offence for the time being included.

(11) Nothing in this section affects the right of the prosecution to appeal in respect of an evidentiary ruling under section 58.

63 Condition that evidentiary ruling significantly weakens prosecution case

(1) Leave to appeal may not be given in relation to an appeal under section 62 unless the judge or, as the case may be, the Court of Appeal is satisfied that the relevant condition is fulfilled.

(2) In relation to an appeal in respect of a single qualifying evidentiary ruling, the relevant condition is that the ruling significantly weakens the prosecution's case in relation to the offence or offences which are the subject of the appeal.

(3) In relation to an appeal in respect of two or more qualifying evidentiary rulings, the relevant condition is that the rulings taken together significantly weaken the prosecution's case in relation to the offence or offences which are the subject of the appeal.

64 Expedited and non-expedited appeals

(1) Where the prosecution informs the court in accordance with section 62(5), the judge must decide whether or not the appeal should be expedited.

(2) If the judge decides that the appeal should be expedited, he may order an adjournment.

(3) If the judge decides that the appeal should not be expedited, he may—

(a) order an adjournment, or
(b) discharge the jury (if one has been sworn).

(4) If he decides that the appeal should be expedited, he or the Court of Appeal may subsequently reverse that decision and, if it is reversed, the judge may act as mentioned in subsection (3)(a) or (b).

65 Continuation of proceedings for offences not affected by ruling

(1) This section applies where the prosecution informs the court in accordance with section 62(5).

(2) Proceedings may be continued in respect of any offence which is not the subject of the appeal.

66 Determination of appeal by court of appeal

(1) On an appeal under section 62, the Court of Appeal may confirm, reverse or vary any ruling to which the appeal relates.

(2) In addition, the Court of Appeal must, in respect of the offence or each offence which is the subject of the appeal, do any of the following—

(a) order that proceedings for that offence be resumed in the Crown Court,
(b) order that a fresh trial may take place in the Crown Court for that offence,
(c) order that the defendant in relation to that offence be acquitted of that offence.

(3) But no order may be made under subsection (2)(c) in respect of an offence unless the prosecution has indicated that it does not intend to continue with the prosecution of that offence.

67 Reversal of rulings

The Court of Appeal may not reverse a ruling on an appeal under this Part unless it is satisfied—

    (a) that the ruling was wrong in law,

    (b) that the ruling involved an error of law or principle, or

    (c) that the ruling was a ruling that it was not reasonable for the judge to have made.

Miscellaneous and supplemental

71 Restrictions on reporting

(1) Except as provided by this section no publication shall include a report of—

    (a) anything done under section 58, 59, 62, 63 or 64,

    (b) an appeal under this Part,

    (c) an appeal under Part 2 of the 1968 Act in relation to an appeal under this Part, or

    (d) an application for leave to appeal in relation to an appeal mentioned in paragraph (b) or (c).

(2) The judge may order that subsection (1) is not to apply, or is not to apply to a specified extent, to a report of—

    (a) anything done under section 58, 59, 62, 63 or 64, or

    (b) an application to the judge for leave to appeal to the Court of Appeal under this Part.

(3) The Court of Appeal may order that subsection (1) is not to apply, or is not to apply to a specified extent, to a report of—

    (a) an appeal to the Court of Appeal under this Part,

    (b) an application to that Court for leave to appeal to it under this Part, or

    (c) an application to that Court for leave to appeal to the House of Lords under Part 2 of the 1968 Act.

(4) The House of Lords may order that subsection (1) is not to apply, or is not to apply to a specified extent, to a report of—

    (a) an appeal to that House under Part 2 of the 1968 Act, or

    (b) an application to that House for leave to appeal to it under Part 2 of that Act.

(5) Where there is only one defendant and he objects to the making of an order under subsection (2), (3) or (4)—

    (a) the judge, the Court of Appeal or the House of Lords are to make the order if (and only if) satisfied, after hearing the representations of the defendant, that it is in the interests of justice to do so, and

    (b) the order (if made) is not to apply to the extent that a report deals with any such objection or representations.

(6) Where there are two or more defendants and one or more of them object to the making of an order under subsection (2), (3) or (4)—

    (a) the judge, the Court of Appeal or the House of Lords are to make the order if (and only if) satisfied, after hearing the representations of each of the defendants, that it is in the interests of justice to do so, and

    (b) the order (if made) is not to apply to the extent that a report deals with any such objection or representations.

(7) Subsection (1) does not apply to the inclusion in a publication of a report of—

    (a) anything done under section 58, 59, 62, 63 or 64,

    (b) an appeal under this Part,

(c) an appeal under Part 2 of the 1968 Act in relation to an appeal under this Part, or

(d) an application for leave to appeal in relation to an appeal mentioned in paragraph (b) or (c),

at the conclusion of the trial of the defendant or the last of the defendants to be tried.

(8) Subsection (1) does not apply to a report which contains only one or more of the following matters—

(a) the identity of the court and the name of the judge,

(b) the names, ages, home addresses and occupations of the defendant or defendants and witnesses,

(c) the offence or offences, or a summary of them, with which the defendant or defendants are charged,

(d) the names of counsel and solicitors in the proceedings,

(e) where the proceedings are adjourned, the date and place to which they are adjourned,

(f) any arrangements as to bail,

(g) whether a right to representation funded by the Legal Services Commission as part of the Criminal Defence Service was granted to the defendant or any of the defendants.

(9) The addresses that may be included in a report by virtue of subsection (8) are addresses—

(a) at any relevant time, and

(b) at the time of their inclusion in the publication.

(10) Nothing in this section affects any prohibition or restriction by virtue of any other enactment on the inclusion of any matter in a publication.

(11) In this section—

"programme service" has the same meaning as in the Broadcasting Act 1990 (c. 42),

"publication" includes any speech, writing, relevant programme or other communication in whatever form, which is addressed to the public at large or any section of the public (and for this purpose every relevant programme is to be taken to be so addressed), but does not include an indictment or other document prepared for use in particular legal proceedings,

"relevant time" means a time when events giving rise to the charges to which the proceedings relate are alleged to have occurred,

"relevant programme" means a programme included in a programme service.

72 Offences in connection with reporting

(1) This section applies if a publication includes a report in contravention of section 71.

(2) Where the publication is a newspaper or periodical, any proprietor, editor or publisher of the newspaper or periodical is guilty of an offence.

(3) Where the publication is a relevant programme—

(a) any body corporate or Scottish partnership engaged in providing the programme service in which the programme is included, and

(b) any person having functions in relation to the programme corresponding to those of an editor of a newspaper,

is guilty of an offence.

(4) In the case of any other publication, any person publishing it is guilty of an offence.

(5) If an offence under this section committed by a body corporate is proved—

(a) to have been committed with the consent or connivance of, or

(b) to be attributable to any neglect on the part of, an officer, the officer as well as the body corporate is guilty of the offence and liable to be proceeded against and punished accordingly.

(6) In subsection (5), "officer" means a director, manager, secretary or other similar officer of the body, or a person purporting to act in any such capacity.

(7) If the affairs of a body corporate are managed by its members, "director" in subsection (6) means a member of that body.

(8) Where an offence under this section is committed by a Scottish partnership and is proved to have been committed with the consent or connivance of a partner, he as well as the partnership shall be guilty of the offence and shall be liable to be proceeded against and punished accordingly.

(9) A person guilty of an offence under this section is liable on summary conviction to a fine not exceeding level 5 on the standard scale.

(10) Proceedings for an offence under this section may not be instituted—

(a) in England and Wales otherwise than by or with the consent of the Attorney General, or

(b) in Northern Ireland otherwise than by or with the consent of-

(i)   before the relevant date, the Attorney General for Northern Ireland, or

(ii) on or after the relevant date, the Director of Public Prosecutions for Northern Ireland.

(11) In subsection (10) "the relevant date" means the date on which section 22(1) of the Justice (Northern Ireland) Act 2002 (c. 26) comes into force.

73   Rules of court

(1) Rules of court may make such provision as appears to the authority making them to be necessary or expedient for the purposes of this Part.

(2) Without limiting subsection (1), rules of court may in particular make provision—

(a) for time limits which are to apply in connection with any provisions of this Part,

(b) as to procedures to be applied in connection with this Part,

(c) enabling a single judge of the Court of Appeal to give leave to appeal under this Part or to exercise the power of the Court of Appeal under section 58(12).

(3) Nothing in this section is to be taken as affecting the generality of any enactment conferring powers to make rules of court.

74   Interpretation of part 9

(1) In this Part—

"programme service" has the meaning given by section 71(11),

"publication" has the meaning given by section 71(11),

"qualifying evidentiary ruling" is to be construed in accordance with section 62(2),

"the relevant condition" is to be construed in accordance with section 63(2) and (3),

"relevant programme" has the meaning given by section 71(11),

"ruling" includes a decision, determination, direction, finding, notice, order, refusal, rejection or requirement,

"the 1968 Act" means the Criminal Appeal Act 1968 (c. 19).

(2) Any reference in this Part (other than section 73(2)(c)) to a judge is a reference to a judge of the Crown Court.

(3) There is to be no right of appeal under this Part in respect of a ruling in relation to which the prosecution has previously informed the court of its intention to appeal under either section 58(4) or 62(5).

(4) Where a ruling relates to two or more offences but not all of those offences are the subject of an appeal under this Part, nothing in this Part is to be regarded as affecting the ruling so far as it relates to any offence which is not the subject of the appeal.

(5) Where two or more defendants are charged jointly with the same offence, the provisions of this Part are to apply as if the offence, so far as relating to each defendant, were a separate offence (so that, for example, any reference in this Part to a ruling which relates to one or more offences includes a ruling which relates to one or more of those separate offences).

(6) Subject to rules of court made under section 53(1) of the Supreme Court Act 1981 (c. 54) (power by rules to distribute business of Court of Appeal between its civil and criminal divisions)—

> (a) the jurisdiction of the Court of Appeal under this Part is to be exercised by the criminal division of that court, and
>
> (b) references in this Part to the Court of Appeal are to be construed as references to that division.

PART 10   RETRIAL FOR SERIOUS OFFENCES

Cases that may be retried

75   Cases that may be retried

(1) This Part applies where a person has been acquitted of a qualifying offence in proceedings—

> (a) on indictment in England and Wales,
>
> (b) on appeal against a conviction, verdict or finding in proceedings on indictment in England and Wales, or
>
> (c) on appeal from a decision on such an appeal.

(2) A person acquitted of an offence in proceedings mentioned in subsection (1) is treated for the purposes of that subsection as also acquitted of any qualifying offence of which he could have been convicted in the proceedings because of the first-mentioned offence being charged in the indictment, except an offence—

> (a) of which he has been convicted,
>
> (b) of which he has been found not guilty by reason of insanity, or
>
> (c) in respect of which, in proceedings where he has been found to be under a disability (as defined by section 4 of the Criminal Procedure (Insanity) Act 1964 (c. 84)), a finding has been made that he did the act or made the omission charged against him.

(3) References in subsections (1) and (2) to a qualifying offence do not include references to an offence which, at the time of the acquittal, was the subject of an order under section 77(1) or (3).

(4) This Part also applies where a person has been acquitted, in proceedings elsewhere than in the United Kingdom, of an offence under the law of the place where the proceedings were held, if the commission of the offence as alleged would have amounted to or included the commission (in the United Kingdom or elsewhere) of a qualifying offence.

(5) Conduct punishable under the law in force elsewhere than in the United Kingdom is an offence under that law for the purposes of subsection (4), however it is described in that law.

(6) This Part applies whether the acquittal was before or after the passing of this Act.

(7) References in this Part to acquittal are to acquittal in circumstances within subsection (1) or (4).

(8) In this Part "qualifying offence" means an offence listed in Part 1 of Schedule 5.

Application for retrial

76   Application to court of appeal

(1) A prosecutor may apply to the Court of Appeal for an order—

> (a) quashing a person's acquittal in proceedings within section 75(1), and
>
> (b) ordering him to be retried for the qualifying offence.

(2) A prosecutor may apply to the Court of Appeal, in the case of a person acquitted elsewhere than in the United Kingdom, for—

(a) a determination whether the acquittal is a bar to the person being tried in England and Wales for the qualifying offence, and

(b) if it is, an order that the acquittal is not to be a bar.

(3) A prosecutor may make an application under subsection (1) or (2) only with the written consent of the Director of Public Prosecutions.

(4) The Director of Public Prosecutions may give his consent only if satisfied that—

(a) there is evidence as respects which the requirements of section 78 appear to be met,

(b) it is in the public interest for the application to proceed, and

(c) any trial pursuant to an order on the application would not be inconsistent with obligations of the United Kingdom under Article 31 or 34 of the Treaty on European Union relating to the principle of *ne bis in idem*.

(5) Not more than one application may be made under subsection (1) or (2) in relation to an acquittal.

77 Deterination by court of appeal

(1) On an application under section 76(1), the Court of Appeal—

(a) if satisfied that the requirements of sections 78 and 79 are met, must make the order applied for;

(b) otherwise, must dismiss the application.

(2) Subsections (3) and (4) apply to an application under section 76(2).

(3) Where the Court of Appeal determines that the acquittal is a bar to the person being tried for the qualifying offence, the court—

(a) if satisfied that the requirements of sections 78 and 79 are met, must make the order applied for;

(b) otherwise, must make a declaration to the effect that the acquittal is a bar to the person being tried for the offence.

(4) Where the Court of Appeal determines that the acquittal is not a bar to the person being tried for the qualifying offence, it must make a declaration to that effect.

78 New and compelling evidence

(1) The requirements of this section are met if there is new and compelling evidence against the acquitted person in relation to the qualifying offence.

(2) Evidence is new if it was not adduced in the proceedings in which the person was acquitted (nor, if those were appeal proceedings, in earlier proceedings to which the appeal related).

(3) Evidence is compelling if—

(a) it is reliable,

(b) it is substantial, and

(c) in the context of the outstanding issues, it appears highly probative of the case against the acquitted person.

(4) The outstanding issues are the issues in dispute in the proceedings in which the person was acquitted and, if those were appeal proceedings, any other issues remaining in dispute from earlier proceedings to which the appeal related.

(5) For the purposes of this section, it is irrelevant whether any evidence would have been admissible in earlier proceedings against the acquitted person.

79 Interests of justice

(1) The requirements of this section are met if in all the circumstances it is in the interests of justice for the court to make the order under section 77.

(2) That question is to be determined having regard in particular to—

(a) whether existing circumstances make a fair trial unlikely;

(b) for the purposes of that question and otherwise, the length of time since the qualifying offence was allegedly committed;

    (c) whether it is likely that the new evidence would have been adduced in the earlier proceedings against the acquitted person but for a failure by an officer or by a prosecutor to act with due diligence or expedition;

    (d) whether, since those proceedings or, if later, since the commencement of this Part, any officer or prosecutor has failed to act with due diligence or expedition.

(3) In subsection (2) references to an officer or prosecutor include references to a person charged with corresponding duties under the law in force elsewhere than in England and Wales.

(4) Where the earlier prosecution was conducted by a person other than a prosecutor, subsection (2)(c) applies in relation to that person as well as in relation to a prosecutor.

80   Procedure and evidence

(1) A prosecutor who wishes to make an application under section 76(1) or (2) must give notice of the application to the Court of Appeal.

(2) Within two days beginning with the day on which any such notice is given, notice of the application must be served by the prosecutor on the person to whom the application relates, charging him with the offence to which it relates or, if he has been charged with it in accordance with section 87(4), stating that he has been so charged.

(3) Subsection (2) applies whether the person to whom the application relates is in the United Kingdom or elsewhere, but the Court of Appeal may, on application by the prosecutor, extend the time for service under that subsection if it considers it necessary to do so because of that person's absence from the United Kingdom.

(4) The Court of Appeal must consider the application at a hearing.

(5) The person to whom the application relates-

    (a) is entitled to be present at the hearing, although he may be in custody, unless he is in custody elsewhere than in England and Wales or Northern Ireland, and

    (b) is entitled to be represented at the hearing, whether he is present or not.

(6) For the purposes of the application, the Court of Appeal may, if it thinks it necessary or expedient in the interests of justice—

    (a) order the production of any document, exhibit or other thing, the production of which appears to the court to be necessary for the determination of the application, and

    (b) order any witness who would be a compellable witness in proceedings pursuant to an order or declaration made on the application to attend for examination and be examined before the court.

(7) The Court of Appeal may at one hearing consider more than one application (whether or not relating to the same person), but only if the offences concerned could be tried on the same indictment.

81   Appeals

(1) The Criminal Appeal Act 1968 (c. 19) is amended as follows.

(2) In section 33 (right of appeal to House of Lords), after subsection (1A) there is inserted—

"(1B) An appeal lies to the House of Lords, at the instance of the acquitted person or the prosecutor, from any decision of the Court of Appeal on an application under section 76(1) or (2) of the Criminal Justice Act 2003 (retrial for serious offences)."

(3) At the end of that section there is inserted—

"(4) In relation to an appeal under subsection (1B), references in this Part to a defendant are references to the acquitted person."

(4) In section 34(2) (extension of time for leave to appeal), after "defendant" there is inserted "or, in the case of an appeal under section 33(1B), by the prosecutor".

(5) In section 38 (presence of defendant at hearing), for "has been convicted of an offence and" substitute "has been convicted of an offence, or in whose case an order under section 77

of the Criminal Justice Act 2003 or a declaration under section 77(4) of that Act has been made, and who".

82   Restrictions on publication in the interests of justice

(1) Where it appears to the Court of Appeal that the inclusion of any matter in a publication would give rise to a substantial risk of prejudice to the administration of justice in a retrial, the court may order that the matter is not to be included in any publication while the order has effect.

(2) In subsection (1) "retrial" means the trial of an acquitted person for a qualifying offence pursuant to any order made or that may be made under section 77.

(3) The court may make an order under this section only if it appears to it necessary in the interests of justice to do so.

(4) An order under this section may apply to a matter which has been included in a publication published before the order takes effect, but such an order—

  (a) applies only to the later inclusion of the matter in a publication (whether directly or by inclusion of the earlier publication), and

  (b) does not otherwise affect the earlier publication.

(5) After notice of an application has been given under section 80(1) relating to the acquitted person and the qualifying offence, the court may make an order under this section only—

  (a) of its own motion, or

  (b) on the application of the Director of Public Prosecutions.

(6) Before such notice has been given, an order under this section—

  (a) may be made only on the application of the Director of Public Prosecutions, and

  (b) may not be made unless, since the acquittal concerned, an investigation of the commission by the acquitted person of the qualifying offence has been commenced by officers.

(7) The court may at any time, of its own motion or on an application made by the Director of Public Prosecutions or the acquitted person, vary or revoke an order under this section.

(8) Any order made under this section before notice of an application has been given under section 80(1) relating to the acquitted person and the qualifying offence must specify the time when it ceases to have effect.

(9) An order under this section which is made or has effect after such notice has been given ceases to have effect, unless it specifies an earlier time—

  (a) when there is no longer any step that could be taken which would lead to the acquitted person being tried pursuant to an order made on the application, or

  (b) if he is tried pursuant to such an order, at the conclusion of the trial.

(10) Nothing in this section affects any prohibition or restriction by virtue of any other enactment on the inclusion of any matter in a publication or any power, under an enactment or otherwise, to impose such a prohibition or restriction.

(11) In this section—

"programme service" has the same meaning as in the Broadcasting Act 1990 (c. 42),

"publication" includes any speech, writing, relevant programme or other communication in whatever form, which is addressed to the public at large or any section of the public (and for this purpose every relevant programme is to be taken to be so addressed), but does not include an indictment or other document prepared for use in particular legal proceedings,

"relevant programme" means a programme included in a programme service.

83   Offences in connection with publication restrictions

(1) This section applies if—

  (a) an order under section 82 is made, whether in England and Wales or Northern Ireland, and

    (b) while the order has effect, any matter is included in a publication, in any part of the United Kingdom, in contravention of the order.

(2) Where the publication is a newspaper or periodical, any proprietor, editor or publisher of the newspaper or periodical is guilty of an offence.

(3) Where the publication is a relevant programme—

    (a) any body corporate or Scottish partnership engaged in providing the programme service in which the programme is included, and

    (b) any person having functions in relation to the programme corresponding to those of an editor of a newspaper,

is guilty of an offence.

(4) In the case of any other publication, any person publishing it is guilty of an offence.

(5) If an offence under this section committed by a body corporate is proved—

    (a) to have been committed with the consent or connivance of, or

    (b) to be attributable to any neglect on the part of,

an officer, the officer as well as the body corporate is guilty of the offence and liable to be proceeded against and punished accordingly.

(6) In subsection (5), "officer" means a director, manager, secretary or other similar officer of the body, or a person purporting to act in any such capacity.

(7) If the affairs of a body corporate are managed by its members, "director" in subsection (6) means a member of that body.

(8) Where an offence under this section is committed by a Scottish partnership and is proved to have been committed with the consent or connivance of a partner, he as well as the partnership shall be guilty of the offence and shall be liable to be proceeded against and punished accordingly.

(9) A person guilty of an offence under this section is liable on summary conviction to a fine not exceeding level 5 on the standard scale.

(10) Proceedings for an offence under this section may not be instituted—

    (a) in England and Wales otherwise than by or with the consent of the Attorney General, or

    (b) in Northern Ireland otherwise than by or with the consent of—

        (i) before the relevant date, the Attorney General for Northern Ireland, or

        (ii) on or after the relevant date, the Director of Public Prosecutions for Northern Ireland.

(11) In subsection (10)"the relevant date" means the date on which section 22(1)of the Justice (Northern Ireland) Act 2002 (c. 26) comes into force.

Retrial

84 Retrial

(1) Where a person—

    (a) is tried pursuant to an order under section 77(1), or

    (b) is tried on indictment pursuant to an order under section 77(3),

the trial must be on an indictment preferred by direction of the Court of Appeal.

(2) After the end of 2 months after the date of the order, the person may not be arraigned on an indictment preferred in pursuance of such a direction unless the Court of Appeal gives leave.

(3) The Court of Appeal must not give leave unless satisfied that—

    (a) the prosecutor has acted with due expedition, and

    (b) there is a good and sufficient cause for trial despite the lapse of time since the order under section 77.

(4) Where the person may not be arraigned without leave, he may apply to the Court of Appeal to set aside the order and—

(a) for any direction required for restoring an earlier judgment and verdict of acquittal of the qualifying offence, or

(b) in the case of a person acquitted elsewhere than in the United Kingdom, for a declaration to the effect that the acquittal is a bar to his being tried for the qualifying offence.

(5) An indictment under subsection (1)may relate to more than one offence, or more than one person, and may relate to an offence which, or a person who, is not the subject of an order or declaration under section 77.

(6) Evidence given at a trial pursuant to an order under section 77(1) or (3) must be given orally if it was given orally at the original trial, unless—

(a) all the parties to the trial agree otherwise,

(b) section 116 applies, or

(c) the witness is unavailable to give evidence, otherwise than as mentioned in subsection (2) of that section, and section 114(1)(d) applies.

(7) At a trial pursuant to an order under section 77(1), paragraph 5 of Schedule 3 to the Crime and Disorder Act 1998 (c. 37) (use of depositions) does not apply to a deposition read as evidence at the original trial.

Investigations

85   Authorisation of investigations

(1) This section applies to the investigation of the commission of a qualifying offence by a person—

(a) acquitted in proceedings within section 75(1) of the qualifying offence, or

(b) acquitted elsewhere than in the United Kingdom of an offence the commission of which as alleged would have amounted to or included the commission (in the United Kingdom or elsewhere) of the qualifying offence.

(2) Subject to section 86, an officer may not do anything within subsection (3) for the purposes of such an investigation unless the Director of Public Prosecutions—

(a) has certified that in his opinion the acquittal would not be a bar to the trial of the acquitted person in England and Wales for the qualifying offence, or

(b) has given his written consent to the investigation (whether before or after the start of the investigation).

(3) The officer may not, either with or without the consent of the acquitted person—

(a) arrest or question him,

(b) search him or premises owned or occupied by him,

(c) search a vehicle owned by him or anything in or on such a vehicle,

(d) seize anything in his possession, or

(e) take his fingerprints or take a sample from him.

(4) The Director of Public Prosecutions may only give his consent on a written application, and such an application may be made only by an officer who—

(a) if he is an officer of the metropolitan police force or the City of London police force, is of the rank of commander or above, or

(b) in any other case, is of the rank of assistant chief constable or above.

(5) An officer may make an application under subsection (4) only if—

(a) he is satisfied that new evidence has been obtained which would be relevant to an application under section 76(1) or (2) in respect of the qualifying offence to which the investigation relates, or

(b) he has reasonable grounds for believing that such new evidence is likely to be obtained as a result of the investigation.

(6) The Director of Public Prosecutions may not give his consent unless satisfied that—

(a) there is, or there is likely as a result of the investigation to be, sufficient new evidence to warrant the conduct of the investigation, and

(b) it is in the public interest for the investigation to proceed.

(7) In giving his consent, the Director of Public Prosecutions may recommend that the investigation be conducted otherwise than by officers of a specified police force or specified team of customs and excise officers.

86   Urgent investigative steps

(1) Section 85 does not prevent an officer from taking any action for the purposes of an investigation if—

(a) the action is necessary as a matter of urgency to prevent the investigation being substantially and irrevocably prejudiced,

(b) the requirements of subsection (2) are met, and

(c) either—

(i)   the action is authorised under subsection (3), or

(ii) the requirements of subsection (5) are met.

(2) The requirements of this subsection are met if—

(a) there has been no undue delay in applying for consent under section 85(2),

(b) that consent has not been refused, and

(c) taking into account the urgency of the situation, it is not reasonably practicable to obtain that consent before taking the action.

(3) An officer of the rank of superintendent or above may authorise the action if—

(a) he is satisfied that new evidence has been obtained which would be relevant to an application under section 76(1) or (2) in respect of the qualifying offence to which the investigation relates, or

(b) he has reasonable grounds for believing that such new evidence is likely to be obtained as a result of the investigation.

(4) An authorisation under subsection (3) must—

(a) if reasonably practicable, be given in writing;

(b) otherwise, be recorded in writing by the officer giving it as soon as is reasonably practicable.

(5) The requirements of this subsection are met if—

(a) there has been no undue delay in applying for authorisation under subsection (3),

(b) that authorisation has not been refused, and

(c) taking into account the urgency of the situation, it is not reasonably practicable to obtain that authorisation before taking the action.

(6) Where the requirements of subsection (5) are met, the action is nevertheless to be treated as having been unlawful unless, as soon as reasonably practicable after the action is taken, an officer of the rank of superintendent or above certifies in writing that he is satisfied that, when the action was taken—

(a) new evidence had been obtained which would be relevant to an application under section 76(1) or (2) in respect of the qualifying offence to which the investigation relates, or

(b) the officer who took the action had reasonable grounds for believing that such new evidence was likely to be obtained as a result of the investigation.

Arrest, custody and bail

87   Arrest and charge

(1) Where section 85 applies to the investigation of the commission of an offence by any person and no certification has been given under subsection (2) of that section—

(a) a justice of the peace may issue a warrant to arrest that person for that offence only if satisfied by written information that new evidence has been obtained which would be relevant to an application under section 76(1) or (2) in respect of the commission by that person of that offence, and

(b) that person may not be arrested for that offence except under a warrant so issued.

(2) Subsection (1) does not affect section 89(3)(b) or 91(3), or any other power to arrest a person, or to issue a warrant for the arrest of a person, otherwise than for an offence.

(3) Part 4 of the 1984 Act (detention) applies as follows where a person—

(a) is arrested for an offence under a warrant issued in accordance with subsection (1)(a), or

(b) having been so arrested, is subsequently treated under section 34(7) of that Act as arrested for that offence.

(4) For the purposes of that Part there is sufficient evidence to charge the person with the offence for which he has been arrested if, and only if, an officer of the rank of superintendent or above (who has not been directly involved in the investigation) is of the opinion that the evidence available or known to him is sufficient for the case to be referred to a prosecutor to consider whether consent should be sought for an application in respect of that person under section 76.

(5) For the purposes of that Part it is the duty of the custody officer at each police station where the person is detained to make available or known to an officer at that police station of the rank of superintendent or above any evidence which it appears to him may be relevant to an application under section 76(1) or (2) in respect of the offence for which the person has been arrested, and to do so as soon as practicable—

(a) after the evidence becomes available or known to him, or

(b) if later, after he forms that view.

(6) Section 37 of that Act (including any provision of that section as applied by section 40(8) of that Act) has effect subject to the following modifications—

(a) in subsection (1)—

(i) for "determine whether he has before him" there is substituted "request an officer of the rank of superintendent or above (who has not been directly involved in the investigation) to determine, in accordance with section 87(4) of the Criminal Justice Act 2003, whether there is";

(ii) for "him to do so" there is substituted "that determination to be made";

(b) in subsection (2)—

(i) for the words from "custody officer determines" to "before him" there is substituted "officer determines that there is not such sufficient evidence";

(ii) the word "custody" is omitted from the second place where it occurs;

(c) in subsection (3)—

(i) the word "custody" is omitted;

(ii) after "may" there is inserted "direct the custody officer to";

(d) in subsection (7) for the words from "the custody officer" to the end of that subsection there is substituted "an officer of the rank of superintendent or above (who has not been directly involved in the investigation) determines, in accordance with section 87(4) of the Criminal Justice Act 2003, that there is sufficient evidence to charge the person arrested with the offence for which he was arrested, the person arrested shall be charged.";

(e) subsections (7A), (7B) and (8) do not apply;

(f) after subsection (10) there is inserted-

"(10A) The officer who is requested by the custody officer to make a determination under subsection (1) above shall make that determination as soon as practicable after the request is made.".

(7) Section 40 of that Act has effect as if in subsections (8) and (9) of that section after "(6)" there were inserted "and (10A)".

(8) Section 42 of that Act has effect as if in subsection (1) of that section for the words from "who" to "detained" there were substituted "(who has not been directly involved in the investigation)".

88 Bail and custody before application

(1) In relation to a person charged in accordance with section 87(4)—
- (a) section 38 of the 1984 Act (including any provision of that section as applied by section 40(10) of that Act) has effect as if, in subsection (1), for "either on bail or without bail" there were substituted "on bail",
- (b) section 47(3) of that Act does not apply and references in section 38 of that Act to bail are references to bail subject to a duty to appear before the Crown Court at such place as the custody officer may appoint and at such time, not later than 24 hours after the person is released, as that officer may appoint, and
- (c) section 43B of the Magistrates' Courts Act 1980 (c. 43) does not apply.

(2) Where such a person is, after being charged—
- (a) kept in police detention, or
- (b) detained by a local authority in pursuance of arrangements made under section 38(6) of the 1984 Act,

he must be brought before the Crown Court as soon as practicable and, in any event, not more than 24 hours after he is charged, and section 46 of the 1984 Act does not apply.

(3) For the purpose of calculating the period referred to in subsection (1) or (2), the following are to be disregarded—
- (a) Sunday,
- (b) Christmas Day,
- (c) Good Friday, and
- (d) any day which is a bank holiday under the Banking and Financial Dealings Act 1971 (c. 80) in the part of the United Kingdom where the person is to appear before the Crown Court as mentioned in subsection (1) or, where subsection (2) applies, is for the time being detained.

(4) Where a person appears or is brought before the Crown Court in accordance with subsection (1) or (2), the Crown Court may either—
- (a) grant bail for the person to appear, if notice of an application is served on him under section 80(2), before the Court of Appeal at the hearing of that application, or
- (b) remand the person in custody to be brought before the Crown Court under section 89(2).

(5) If the Crown Court grants bail under subsection (4), it may revoke bail and remand the person in custody as referred to in subsection (4)(b).

(6) In subsection (7) the "relevant period", in relation to a person granted bail or remanded in custody under subsection (4), means—
- (a) the period of 42 days beginning with the day on which he is granted bail or remanded in custody under that subsection, or
- (b) that period as extended or further extended under subsection (8).

(7) If at the end of the relevant period no notice of an application under section 76(1) or (2) in relation to the person has been given under section 80(1), the person—
- (a) if on bail subject to a duty to appear as mentioned in subsection (4)(a), ceases to be subject to that duty and to any conditions of that bail, and
- (b) if in custody on remand under subsection (4)(b) or (5), must be released immediately without bail.

(8) The Crown Court may, on the application of a prosecutor, extend or further extend the period mentioned in subsection (6)(a) until a specified date, but only if satisfied that—

(a) the need for the extension is due to some good and sufficient cause, and

(b) the prosecutor has acted with all due diligence and expedition.

89 Bail and custody before hearing

(1) This section applies where notice of an application is given under section 80(1).

(2) If the person to whom the application relates is in custody under section 88(4)(b) or (5), he must be brought before the Crown Court as soon as practicable and, in any event, within 48 hours after the notice is given.

(3) If that person is not in custody under section 88(4)(b) or (5), the Crown Court may, on application by the prosecutor—

(a) issue a summons requiring the person to appear before the Court of Appeal at the hearing of the application, or

(b) issue a warrant for the person's arrest,

and a warrant under paragraph (b) may be issued at any time even though a summons has previously been issued.

(4) Where a summons is issued under subsection (3)(a), the time and place at which the person must appear may be specified either—

(a) in the summons, or

(b) in a subsequent direction of the Crown Court.

(5) The time or place specified may be varied from time to time by a direction of the Crown Court.

(6) A person arrested under a warrant under subsection (3)(b) must be brought before the Crown Court as soon as practicable and in any event within 48 hours after his arrest, and section 81(5) of the Supreme Court Act 1981 (c. 54) does not apply.

(7) If a person is brought before the Crown Court under subsection (2) or (6) the court must either—

(a) remand him in custody to be brought before the Court of Appeal at the hearing of the application, or

(b) grant bail for him to appear before the Court of Appeal at the hearing.

(8) If bail is granted under subsection (7)(b), the Crown Court may revoke the bail and remand the person in custody as referred to in subsection (7)(a).

(9) For the purpose of calculating the period referred to in subsection (2) or (6), the following are to be disregarded—

(a) Sunday,

(b) Christmas Day,

(c) Good Friday, and

(d) any day which is a bank holiday under the Banking and Financial Dealings Act 1971 (c. 80) in the part of the United Kingdom where the person is for the time being detained.

90 Bail and custody during and after hearing

(1) The Court of Appeal may, at any adjournment of the hearing of an application under section 76(1) or (2)—

(a) remand the person to whom the application relates on bail, or

(b) remand him in custody.

(2) At a hearing at which the Court of Appeal—

(a) makes an order under section 77,

(b) makes a declaration under subsection (4) of that section, or

(c) dismisses the application or makes a declaration under subsection (3) of that section, if it also gives the prosecutor leave to appeal against its decision or the prosecutor gives notice that he intends to apply for such leave,

the court may make such order as it sees fit for the custody or bail of the acquitted person pending trial pursuant to the order or declaration, or pending determination of the appeal.

(3) For the purpose of subsection (2), the determination of an appeal is pending—

    (a) until any application for leave to appeal is disposed of, or the time within which it must be made expires;

    (b) if leave to appeal is granted, until the appeal is disposed of.

(4) Section 4 of the Bail Act 1976 (c. 63) applies in relation to the grant of bail under this section as if in subsection (2) the reference to the Crown Court included a reference to the Court of Appeal.

(5) The court may at any time, as it sees fit—

    (a) revoke bail granted under this section and remand the person in custody, or

    (b) vary an order under subsection (2).

91   Revocation of bail

(1) Where—

    (a) a court revokes a person's bail under this Part, and

    (b) that person is not before the court when his bail is revoked,

the court must order him to surrender himself forthwith to the custody of the court.

(2) Where a person surrenders himself into the custody of the court in compliance with an order under subsection (1), the court must remand him in custody.

(3) A person who has been ordered to surrender to custody under subsection (1) may be arrested without a warrant by an officer if he fails without reasonable cause to surrender to custody in accordance with the order.

(4) A person arrested under subsection (3) must be brought as soon as practicable, and, in any event, not more than 24 hours after he is arrested, before the court and the court must remand him in custody.

(5) For the purpose of calculating the period referred to in subsection (4), the following are to be disregarded—

    (a) Sunday,

    (b) Christmas Day,

    (c) Good Friday,

    (d) any day which is a bank holiday under the Banking and Financial Dealings Act 1971 (c. 80) in the part of the United Kingdom where the person is for the time being detained.

Part 10: supplementary

92   Functions of the dpp

(1) Section 1(7) of the Prosecution of Offences Act 1985 (c. 23) (DPP's functions exercisable by Crown Prosecutor) does not apply to the provisions of this Part other than section 85(2)(a).

(2) In the absence of the Director of Public Prosecutions, his functions under those provisions may be exercised by a person authorised by him.

(3) An authorisation under subsection (2)—

    (a) may relate to a specified person or to persons of a specified description, and

    (b) may be general or relate to a specified function or specified circumstances.

93   Rules of court

(1) Rules of court may make such provision as appears to the authority making them to be necessary or expedient for the purposes of this Part.

(2) Without limiting subsection (1), rules of court may in particular make provision as to procedures to be applied in connection with sections 76 to 82, 84 and 88 to 90.

(3) Nothing in this section is to be taken as affecting the generality of any enactment conferring power to make rules of court.

95 Interpretation of part 10

(1) In this Part—

"the 1984 Act" means the Police and Criminal Evidence Act 1984 (c. 60),

"acquittal" and related expressions are to be read in accordance with section 75(7),

"customs and excise officer" means an officer as defined by section 1(1) of the Customs and Excise Management Act 1979 (c. 2), or a person to whom section 8(2) of that Act applies,

"new evidence" is to be read in accordance with section 78(2),

"officer", except in section 83, means an officer of a police force or a customs and excise officer,

"police force" has the meaning given by section 3(3) of the Prosecution of Offences Act 1985 (c. 23),

"prosecutor" means an individual or body charged with duties to conduct criminal prosecutions,

"qualifying offence" has the meaning given by section 75(8).

(2) Subject to rules of court made under section 53(1) of the Supreme Court Act 1981 (c. 54) (power by rules to distribute business of Court of Appeal between its civil and criminal divisions)—

(a) the jurisdiction of the Court of Appeal under this Part is to be exercised by the criminal division of that court, and

(b) references in this Part to the Court of Appeal are to be construed as references to that division.

(3) References in this Part to an officer of a specified rank or above are, in the case of a customs and excise officer, references to an officer of such description as—

(a) appears to the Commissioners of Customs and Excise to comprise officers of equivalent rank or above, and

(b) is specified by the Commissioners for the purposes of the provision concerned.

97 Application of criminal appeal acts to proceedings under part 10

Subject to the provisions of this Part, the Secretary of State may make an order containing provision, in relation to proceedings before the Court of Appeal under this Part, which corresponds to any provision, in relation to appeals or other proceedings before that court, which is contained in the Criminal Appeal Act 1968 (c. 19) or the Criminal Appeal (Northern Ireland) Act 1980 (c. 47) (subject to any specified modifications).

PART 11

CHAPTER 1   EVIDENCE OF BAD CHARACTER

Introductory

98 "Bad character"

References in this Chapter to evidence of a person's "bad character" are to evidence of, or of a disposition towards, misconduct on his part, other than evidence which—

(a) has to do with the alleged facts of the offence with which the defendant is charged, or

(b) is evidence of misconduct in connection with the investigation or prosecution of that offence.

99 Abolition of common law rules

(1) The common law rules governing the admissibility of evidence of bad character in criminal proceedings are abolished.

(2) Subsection (1) is subject to section 118(1) in so far as it preserves the rule under which in criminal proceedings a person's reputation is admissible for the purposes of proving his bad character.

Persons other than defendants

100 Non-defendant's bad character

(1) In criminal proceedings evidence of the bad character of a person other than the defendant is admissible if and only if—

    (a) it is important explanatory evidence,

    (b) it has substantial probative value in relation to a matter which—

        (i)   is a matter in issue in the proceedings, and

        (ii) is of substantial importance in the context of the case as a whole,

    or

    (c) all parties to the proceedings agree to the evidence being admissible.

(2) For the purposes of subsection (1)(a) evidence is important explanatory evidence if—

    (a) without it, the court or jury would find it impossible or difficult properly to understand other evidence in the case, and

    (b) its value for understanding the case as a whole is substantial.

(3) In assessing the probative value of evidence for the purposes of subsection (1)(b) the court must have regard to the following factors (and to any others it considers relevant)—

    (a) the nature and number of the events, or other things, to which the evidence relates;

    (b) when those events or things are alleged to have happened or existed;

    (c) where—

        (i)   the evidence is evidence of a person's misconduct, and

        (ii) it is suggested that the evidence has probative value by reason of similarity between that misconduct and other alleged misconduct,

    the nature and extent of the similarities and the dissimilarities between each of the alleged instances of misconduct;

    (d) where—

        (i)   the evidence is evidence of a person's misconduct,

        (ii) it is suggested that that person is also responsible for the misconduct charged, and

        (iii) the identity of the person responsible for the misconduct charged is disputed,

    the extent to which the evidence shows or tends to show that the same person was responsible each time.

(4) Except where subsection (1)(c) applies, evidence of the bad character of a person other than the defendant must not be given without leave of the court.

Defendants

101 Defendant's bad character

(1) In criminal proceedings evidence of the defendant's bad character is admissible if, but only if—

    (a) all parties to the proceedings agree to the evidence being admissible,

    (b) the evidence is adduced by the defendant himself or is given in answer to a question asked by him in cross-examination and intended to elicit it,

    (c) it is important explanatory evidence,

    (d) it is relevant to an important matter in issue between the defendant and the prosecution,

    (e) it has substantial probative value in relation to an important matter in issue between the defendant and a co-defendant,

    (f) it is evidence to correct a false impression given by the defendant, or

    (g) the defendant has made an attack on another person's character.

(2) Sections 102 to 106 contain provision supplementing subsection (1).

(3) The court must not admit evidence under subsection (1)(d) or (g) if, on an application by the defendant to exclude it, it appears to the court that the admission of the evidence would have such an adverse effect on the fairness of the proceedings that the court ought not to admit it.

(4) On an application to exclude evidence under subsection (3) the court must have regard, in particular, to the length of time between the matters to which that evidence relates and the matters which form the subject of the offence charged.

102 "Important explanatory evidence"
For the purposes of section 101(1)(c) evidence is important explanatory evidence if—
  (a) without it, the court or jury would find it impossible or difficult properly to understand other evidence in the case, and
  (b) its value for understanding the case as a whole is substantial.

103 "Matter in issue between the defendant and the prosecution"
(1) For the purposes of section 101(1)(d) the matters in issue between the defendant and the prosecution include—
  (a) the question whether the defendant has a propensity to commit offences of the kind with which he is charged, except where his having such a propensity makes it no more likely that he is guilty of the offence;
  (b) the question whether the defendant has a propensity to be untruthful, except where it is not suggested that the defendant's case is untruthful in any respect.

(2) Where subsection (1)(a) applies, a defendant's propensity to commit offences of the kind with which he is charged may (without prejudice to any other way of doing so) be established by evidence that he has been convicted of—
  (a) an offence of the same description as the one with which he is charged, or
  (b) an offence of the same category as the one with which he is charged.

(3) Subsection (2) does not apply in the case of a particular defendant if the court is satisfied, by reason of the length of time since the conviction or for any other reason, that it would be unjust for it to apply in his case.

(4) For the purposes of subsection (2)—
  (a) two offences are of the same description as each other if the statement of the offence in a written charge or indictment would, in each case, be in the same terms;
  (b) two offences are of the same category as each other if they belong to the same category of offences prescribed for the purposes of this section by an order made by the Secretary of State.

(5) A category prescribed by an order under subsection (4)(b) must consist of offences of the same type.

(6) Only prosecution evidence is admissible under section 101(1)(d).

104 "Matter in issue between the defendant and a co-defendant"
(1) Evidence which is relevant to the question whether the defendant has a propensity to be untruthful is admissible on that basis under section 101(1)(e) only if the nature or conduct of his defence is such as to undermine the co-defendant's defence.

(2) Only evidence—
  (a) which is to be (or has been) adduced by the co-defendant, or
  (b) which a witness is to be invited to give (or has given) in cross-examination by the co-defendant,
is admissible under section 101(1)(e).

105 **"Evidence to correct a false impression"**

(1) For the purposes of section 101(1)(f)—

(a) the defendant gives a false impression if he is responsible for the making of an express or implied assertion which is apt to give the court or jury a false or misleading impression about the defendant;

(b) evidence to correct such an impression is evidence which has probative value in correcting it.

(2) A defendant is treated as being responsible for the making of an assertion if—

(a) the assertion is made by the defendant in the proceedings (whether or not in evidence given by him),

(b) the assertion was made by the defendant—

(i) on being questioned under caution, before charge, about the offence with which he is charged, or

(ii) on being charged with the offence or officially informed that he might be prosecuted for it,

and evidence of the assertion is given in the proceedings,

(c) the assertion is made by a witness called by the defendant,

(d) the assertion is made by any witness in cross-examination in response to a question asked by the defendant that is intended to elicit it, or is likely to do so, or

(e) the assertion was made by any person out of court, and the defendant adduces evidence of it in the proceedings.

(3) A defendant who would otherwise be treated as responsible for the making of an assertion shall not be so treated if, or to the extent that, he withdraws it or disassociates himself from it.

(4) Where it appears to the court that a defendant, by means of his conduct (other than the giving of evidence) in the proceedings, is seeking to give the court or jury an impression about himself that is false or misleading, the court may if it appears just to do so treat the defendant as being responsible for the making of an assertion which is apt to give that impression.

(5) In subsection (4) "conduct" includes appearance or dress.

(6) Evidence is admissible under section 101(1)(f) only if it goes no further than is necessary to correct the false impression.

(7) Only prosecution evidence is admissible under section 101(1)(f).

106 **"Attack on another person's character"**

(1) For the purposes of section 101(1)(g) a defendant makes an attack on another person's character if—

(a) he adduces evidence attacking the other person's character,

(b) he (or any legal representative appointed under section 38(4) of the Youth Justice and Criminal Evidence Act 1999 (c. 23) to cross-examine a witness in his interests) asks questions in cross-examination that are intended to elicit such evidence, or are likely to do so, or

(c) evidence is given of an imputation about the other person made by the defendant—

(i) on being questioned under caution, before charge, about the offence with which he is charged, or

(ii) on being charged with the offence or officially informed that he might be prosecuted for it.

(2) In subsection (1) "evidence attacking the other person's character" means evidence to the effect that the other person—

(a) has committed an offence (whether a different offence from the one with which the defendant is charged or the same one), or

(b) has behaved, or is disposed to behave, in a reprehensible way;
and "imputation about the other person" means an assertion to that effect.

(3) Only prosecution evidence is admissible under section 101(1)(g).

107 Stopping the case where evidence contaminated

(1) If on a defendant's trial before a judge and jury for an offence—
   (a) evidence of his bad character has been admitted under any of paragraphs (c) to (g) of section 101(1), and
   (b) the court is satisfied at any time after the close of the case for the prosecution that—
      (i)   the evidence is contaminated, and
      (ii) the contamination is such that, considering the importance of the evidence to the case against the defendant, his conviction of the offence would be unsafe,
the court must either direct the jury to acquit the defendant of the offence or, if it considers that there ought to be a retrial, discharge the jury.

(2) Where—
   (a) a jury is directed under subsection (1) to acquit a defendant of an offence, and
   (b) the circumstances are such that, apart from this subsection, the defendant could if acquitted of that offence be found guilty of another offence,
the defendant may not be found guilty of that other offence if the court is satisfied as mentioned in subsection (1)(b) in respect of it.

(3) If—
   (a) a jury is required to determine under section 4A(2) of the Criminal Procedure (Insanity) Act 1964 (c. 84) whether a person charged on an indictment with an offence did the act or made the omission charged,
   (b) evidence of the person's bad character has been admitted under any of paragraphs (c) to (g) of section 101(1), and
   (c) the court is satisfied at any time after the close of the case for the prosecution that—
      (i)   the evidence is contaminated, and
      (ii) the contamination is such that, considering the importance of the evidence to the case against the person, a finding that he did the act or made the omission would be unsafe,
   the court must either direct the jury to acquit the defendant of the offence or, if it considers that there ought to be a rehearing, discharge the jury.

(4) This section does not prejudice any other power a court may have to direct a jury to acquit a person of an offence or to discharge a jury.

(5) For the purposes of this section a person's evidence is contaminated where—
   (a) as a result of an agreement or understanding between the person and one or more others, or
   (b) as a result of the person being aware of anything alleged by one or more others whose evidence may be, or has been, given in the proceedings,
the evidence is false or misleading in any respect, or is different from what it would otherwise have been.

108 Offences committed by defendant when a child

(1) Section 16(2) and (3) of the Children and Young Persons Act 1963 (c. 37) (offences committed by person under 14 disregarded for purposes of evidence relating to previous convictions) shall cease to have effect.

(2) In proceedings for an offence committed or alleged to have been committed by the defendant when aged 21 or over, evidence of his conviction for an offence when under the age of 14 is not admissible unless—

(a) both of the offences are triable only on indictment, and

(b) the court is satisfied that the interests of justice require the evidence to be admissible.

(3) Subsection (2) applies in addition to section 101.

General

109   Assumption of truth in assessment of relevance or probative value

(1) Subject to subsection (2), a reference in this Chapter to the relevance or probative value of evidence is a reference to its relevance or probative value on the assumption that it is true.

(2) In assessing the relevance or probative value of an item of evidence for any purpose of this Chapter, a court need not assume that the evidence is true if it appears, on the basis of any material before the court (including any evidence it decides to hear on the matter), that no court or jury could reasonably find it to be true.

110   Court's duty to give reasons for rulings

(1) Where the court makes a relevant ruling—

(a) it must state in open court (but in the absence of the jury, if there is one) its reasons for the ruling;

(b) if it is a magistrates' court, it must cause the ruling and the reasons for it to be entered in the register of the court's proceedings.

(2) In this section "relevant ruling" means—

(a) a ruling on whether an item of evidence is evidence of a person's bad character;

(b) a ruling on whether an item of such evidence is admissible under section 100 or 101 (including a ruling on an application under section 101(3));

(c) a ruling under section 107.

111   Rules of court

(1) Rules of court may make such provision as appears to the appropriate authority to be necessary or expedient for the purposes of this Act; and the appropriate authority is the authority entitled to make the rules.

(2) The rules may, and, where the party in question is the prosecution, must, contain provision requiring a party who—

(a) proposes to adduce evidence of a defendant's bad character, or

(b) proposes to cross-examine a witness with a view to eliciting such evidence,

to serve on the defendant such notice, and such particulars of or relating to the evidence, as may be prescribed.

(3) The rules may provide that the court or the defendant may, in such circumstances as may be prescribed, dispense with a requirement imposed by virtue of subsection (2).

(4) In considering the exercise of its powers with respect to costs, the court may take into account any failure by a party to comply with a requirement imposed by virtue of subsection (2) and not dispensed with by virtue of subsection (3).

(5) The rules may—

(a) limit the application of any provision of the rules to prescribed circumstances;

(b) subject any provision of the rules to prescribed exceptions;

(c) make different provision for different cases or circumstances.

(6) Nothing in this section prejudices the generality of any enactment conferring power to make rules of court; and no particular provision of this section prejudices any general provision of it.

(7) In this section—

"prescribed" means prescribed by rules of court;

"rules of court" means—

(a) Crown Court Rules;

(b) Criminal Appeal Rules;

(c) rules under section 144 of the Magistrates' Courts Act 1980 (c. 43).

112 Interpretation of Chapter 1

(1) In this Chapter—

"bad character" is to be read in accordance with section 98;

"criminal proceedings" means criminal proceedings in relation to which the strict rules of evidence apply;

"defendant", in relation to criminal proceedings, means a person charged with an offence in those proceedings; and "co-defendant", in relation to a defendant, means a person charged with an offence in the same proceedings;

"important matter" means a matter of substantial importance in the context of the case as a whole;

"misconduct" means the commission of an offence or other reprehensible behaviour;

"offence" includes a service offence;

"probative value", and "relevant" (in relation to an item of evidence), are to be read in accordance with section 109;

"prosecution evidence" means evidence which is to be (or has been) adduced by the prosecution, or which a witness is to be invited to give (or has given) in cross-examination by the prosecution;

"service offence" means an offence under the Army Act 1955 (3 & 4 Eliz. 2 c. 18), the Air Force Act 1955 (3 & 4 Eliz. 2 c. 19) or the Naval Discipline Act 1957 (c. 53);

"written charge" has the same meaning as in section 29 and also includes an information.

(2) Where a defendant is charged with two or more offences in the same criminal proceedings, this Chapter (except section 101(3)) has effect as if each offence were charged in separate proceedings; and references to the offence with which the defendant is charged are to be read accordingly.

(3) Nothing in this Chapter affects the exclusion of evidence—

(a) under the rule in section 3 of the Criminal Procedure Act 1865 (c. 18) against a party impeaching the credit of his own witness by general evidence of bad character,

(b) under section 41 of the Youth Justice and Criminal Evidence Act 1999 (c. 23) (restriction on evidence or questions about complainant's sexual history), or

(c) on grounds other than the fact that it is evidence of a person's bad character.

114 Admissibility of hearsay evidence

(1) In criminal proceedings a statement not made in oral evidence in the proceedings is admissible as evidence of any matter stated if, but only if—

(a) any provision of this Chapter or any other statutory provision makes it admissible,

(b) any rule of law preserved by section 118 makes it admissible,

(c) all parties to the proceedings agree to it being admissible, or

(d) the court is satisfied that it is in the interests of justice for it to be admissible.

(2) In deciding whether a statement not made in oral evidence should be admitted under subsection (1)(d), the court must have regard to the following factors (and to any others it considers relevant)—

(a) how much probative value the statement has (assuming it to be true) in relation to a matter in issue in the proceedings, or how valuable it is for the understanding of other evidence in the case;

(b) what other evidence has been, or can be, given on the matter or evidence mentioned in paragraph (a);

(c) how important the matter or evidence mentioned in paragraph (a) is in the context of the case as a whole;

(d) the circumstances in which the statement was made;

(e) how reliable the maker of the statement appears to be;

(f) how reliable the evidence of the making of the statement appears to be;

(g) whether oral evidence of the matter stated can be given and, if not, why it cannot;

(h) the amount of difficulty involved in challenging the statement;

(i) the extent to which that difficulty would be likely to prejudice the party facing it.

(3) Nothing in this Chapter affects the exclusion of evidence of a statement on grounds other than the fact that it is a statement not made in oral evidence in the proceedings.

115   Statements and matters stated

(1) In this Chapter references to a statement or to a matter stated are to be read as follows.

(2) A statement is any representation of fact or opinion made by a person by whatever means; and it includes a representation made in a sketch, photofit or other pictorial form.

(3) A matter stated is one to which this Chapter applies if (and only if) the purpose, or one of the purposes, of the person making the statement appears to the court to have been—

(a) to cause another person to believe the matter, or

(b) to cause another person to act or a machine to operate on the basis that the matter is as stated.

Principal categories of admissibility

116   Cases where a witness is unavailable

(1) In criminal proceedings a statement not made in oral evidence in the proceedings is admissible as evidence of any matter stated if—

(a) oral evidence given in the proceedings by the person who made the statement would be admissible as evidence of that matter,

(b) the person who made the statement (the relevant person) is identified to the court's satisfaction, and

(c) any of the five conditions mentioned in subsection (2) is satisfied.

(2) The conditions are—

(a) that the relevant person is dead;

(b) that the relevant person is unfit to be a witness because of his bodily or mental condition;

(c) that the relevant person is outside the United Kingdom and it is not reasonably practicable to secure his attendance;

(d) that the relevant person cannot be found although such steps as it is reasonably practicable to take to find him have been taken;

(e) that through fear the relevant person does not give (or does not continue to give) oral evidence in the proceedings, either at all or in connection with the subject matter of the statement, and the court gives leave for the statement to be given in evidence.

(3) For the purposes of subsection (2)(e) "fear" is to be widely construed and (for example) includes fear of the death or injury of another person or of financial loss.

(4) Leave may be given under subsection (2)(e) only if the court considers that the statement ought to be admitted in the interests of justice, having regard—

(a) to the statement's contents,

(b) to any risk that its admission or exclusion will result in unfairness to any party to the proceedings (and in particular to how difficult it will be to challenge the statement if the relevant person does not give oral evidence),

(c) in appropriate cases, to the fact that a direction under section 19 of the Youth

Justice and Criminal Evidence Act 1999 (c. 23) (special measures for the giving of evidence by fearful witnesses etc) could be made in relation to the relevant person, and

(d) to any other relevant circumstances.

(5) A condition set out in any paragraph of subsection (2) which is in fact satisfied is to be treated as not satisfied if it is shown that the circumstances described in that paragraph are caused—

(a) by the person in support of whose case it is sought to give the statement in evidence, or

(b) by a person acting on his behalf,

in order to prevent the relevant person giving oral evidence in the proceedings (whether at all or in connection with the subject matter of the statement).

117 Business and other documents

(1) In criminal proceedings a statement contained in a document is admissible as evidence of any matter stated if—

(a) oral evidence given in the proceedings would be admissible as evidence of that matter,

(b) the requirements of subsection (2) are satisfied, and

(c) the requirements of subsection (5) are satisfied, in a case where subsection (4) requires them to be.

(2) The requirements of this subsection are satisfied if—

(a) the document or the part containing the statement was created or received by a person in the course of a trade, business, profession or other occupation, or as the holder of a paid or unpaid office,

(b) the person who supplied the information contained in the statement (the relevant person) had or may reasonably be supposed to have had personal knowledge of the matters dealt with, and

(c) each person (if any) through whom the information was supplied from the relevant person to the person mentioned in paragraph (a) received the information in the course of a trade, business, profession or other occupation, or as the holder of a paid or unpaid office.

(3) The persons mentioned in paragraphs (a) and (b) of subsection (2) may be the same person.

(4) The additional requirements of subsection (5) must be satisfied if the statement—

(a) was prepared for the purposes of pending or contemplated criminal proceedings, or for a criminal investigation, but

(b) was not obtained pursuant to a request under section 7 of the Crime (International Co-operation) Act 2003 (c. 32) or an order under paragraph 6 of Schedule 13 to the Criminal Justice Act 1988 (c. 33) (which relate to overseas evidence).

(5) The requirements of this subsection are satisfied if—

(a) any of the five conditions mentioned in section 116(2) is satisfied (absence of relevant person etc), or

(b) the relevant person cannot reasonably be expected to have any recollection of the matters dealt with in the statement (having regard to the length of time since he supplied the information and all other circumstances).

(6) A statement is not admissible under this section if the court makes a direction to that effect under subsection (7).

(7) The court may make a direction under this subsection if satisfied that the statement's reliability as evidence for the purpose for which it is tendered is doubtful in view of—

(a) its contents,

(b) the source of the information contained in it,

(c) the way in which or the circumstances in which the information was supplied or received, or

(d) the way in which or the circumstances in which the document concerned was created or received.

118 Preservation of certain common law categories of admissibility

(1) The following rules of law are preserved.

Public information etc

1. Any rule of law under which in criminal proceedings—

(a) published works dealing with matters of a public nature (such as histories, scientific works, dictionaries and maps) are admissible as evidence of facts of a public nature stated in them,

(b) public documents (such as public registers, and returns made under public authority with respect to matters of public interest) are admissible as evidence of facts stated in them,

(c) records (such as the records of certain courts, treaties, Crown grants, pardons and commissions) are admissible as evidence of facts stated in them, or

(d) evidence relating to a person's age or date or place of birth may be given by a person without personal knowledge of the matter.

Reputation as to character

2. Any rule of law under which in criminal proceedings evidence of a person's reputation is admissible for the purpose of proving his good or bad character.

Note

The rule is preserved only so far as it allows the court to treat such evidence as proving the matter concerned.

Reputation or family tradition

3. Any rule of law under which in criminal proceedings evidence of reputation or family tradition is admissible for the purpose of proving or disproving—

(a) pedigree or the existence of a marriage,

(b) the existence of any public or general right, or

(c) the identity of any person or thing.

Note

The rule is preserved only so far as it allows the court to treat such evidence as proving or disproving the matter concerned.

Res gestae

4. Any rule of law under which in criminal proceedings a statement is admissible as evidence of any matter stated if—

(a) the statement was made by a person so emotionally overpowered by an event that the possibility of concoction or distortion can be disregarded,

(b) the statement accompanied an act which can be properly evaluated as evidence only if considered in conjunction with the statement, or

(c) the statement relates to a physical sensation or a mental state (such as intention or emotion).

Confessions etc

5. Any rule of law relating to the admissibility of confessions or mixed statements in criminal proceedings.

Admissions by agents etc

6. Any rule of law under which in criminal proceedings—
    (a) an admission made by an agent of a defendant is admissible against the defendant as evidence of any matter stated, or
    (b) a statement made by a person to whom a defendant refers a person for information is admissible against the defendant as evidence of any matter stated.

Common enterprise

7. Any rule of law under which in criminal proceedings a statement made by a party to a common enterprise is admissible against another party to the enterprise as evidence of any matter stated.

Expert evidence

8. Any rule of law under which in criminal proceedings an expert witness may draw on the body of expertise relevant to his field.

(2) With the exception of the rules preserved by this section, the common law rules governing the admissibility of hearsay evidence in criminal proceedings are abolished.

119 Inconsistent statements

(1) If in criminal proceedings a person gives oral evidence and—
    (a) he admits making a previous inconsistent statement, or
    (b) a previous inconsistent statement made by him is proved by virtue of section 3, 4 or 5 of the Criminal Procedure Act 1865 (c. 18),
the statement is admissible as evidence of any matter stated of which oral evidence by him would be admissible.

(2) If in criminal proceedings evidence of an inconsistent statement by any person is given under section 124(2)(c), the statement is admissible as evidence of any matter stated in it of which oral evidence by that person would be admissible.

120 Other previous statements of witnesses

(1) This section applies where a person (the witness) is called to give evidence in criminal proceedings.

(2) If a previous statement by the witness is admitted as evidence to rebut a suggestion that his oral evidence has been fabricated, that statement is admissible as evidence of any matter stated of which oral evidence by the witness would be admissible.

(3) A statement made by the witness in a document—
    (a) which is used by him to refresh his memory while giving evidence,
    (b) on which he is cross-examined, and
    (c) which as a consequence is received in evidence in the proceedings,
is admissible as evidence of any matter stated of which oral evidence by him would be admissible.

(4) A previous statement by the witness is admissible as evidence of any matter stated of which oral evidence by him would be admissible, if—
    (a) any of the following three conditions is satisfied, and
    (b) while giving evidence the witness indicates that to the best of his belief he made the statement, and that to the best of his belief it states the truth.

(5) The first condition is that the statement identifies or describes a person, object or place.

(6) The second condition is that the statement was made by the witness when the matters stated were fresh in his memory but he does not remember them, and cannot reasonably be expected to remember them, well enough to give oral evidence of them in the proceedings.

(7) The third condition is that—

    (a) the witness claims to be a person against whom an offence has been committed,

    (b) the offence is one to which the proceedings relate,

    (c) the statement consists of a complaint made by the witness (whether to a person in authority or not) about conduct which would, if proved, constitute the offence or part of the offence,

    (d) the complaint was made as soon as could reasonably be expected after the alleged conduct,

    (e) the complaint was not made as a result of a threat or a promise, and

    (f) before the statement is adduced the witness gives oral evidence in connection with its subject matter.

(8) For the purposes of subsection (7) the fact that the complaint was elicited (for example, by a leading question) is irrelevant unless a threat or a promise was involved.

Supplementary

121   Additional requirement for admissibility of multiple hearsay

(1) A hearsay statement is not admissible to prove the fact that an earlier hearsay statement was made unless—

    (a) either of the statements is admissible under section 117, 119 or 120,

    (b) all parties to the proceedings so agree, or

    (c) the court is satisfied that the value of the evidence in question, taking into account how reliable the statements appear to be, is so high that the interests of justice require the later statement to be admissible for that purpose.

(2) In this section "hearsay statement" means a statement, not made in oral evidence, that is relied on as evidence of a matter stated in it.

122   Documents produced as exhibits

(1) This section applies if on a trial before a judge and jury for an offence—

    (a) a statement made in a document is admitted in evidence under section 119 or 120, and

    (b) the document or a copy of it is produced as an exhibit.

(2) The exhibit must not accompany the jury when they retire to consider their verdict unless—

    (a) the court considers it appropriate, or

    (b) all the parties to the proceedings agree that it should accompany the jury.

123   Capability to make statement

(1) Nothing in section 116, 119 or 120 makes a statement admissible as evidence if it was made by a person who did not have the required capability at the time when he made the statement.

(2) Nothing in section 117 makes a statement admissible as evidence if any person who, in order for the requirements of section 117(2) to be satisfied, must at any time have supplied or received the information concerned or created or received the document or part concerned—

    (a) did not have the required capability at that time, or

    (b) cannot be identified but cannot reasonably be assumed to have had the required capability at that time.

(3) For the purposes of this section a person has the required capability if he is capable of—

    (a) understanding questions put to him about the matters stated, and

    (b) giving answers to such questions which can be understood.

(4) Where by reason of this section there is an issue as to whether a person had the required capability when he made a statement—

    (a) proceedings held for the determination of the issue must take place in the absence of the jury (if there is one);

    (b) in determining the issue the court may receive expert evidence and evidence from any person to whom the statement in question was made;

    (c) the burden of proof on the issue lies on the party seeking to adduce the statement, and the standard of proof is the balance of probabilities.

124   Credibility

(1) This section applies if in criminal proceedings—

    (a) a statement not made in oral evidence in the proceedings is admitted as evidence of a matter stated, and

    (b) the maker of the statement does not give oral evidence in connection with the subject matter of the statement.

(2) In such a case—

    (a) any evidence which (if he had given such evidence) would have been admissible as relevant to his credibility as a witness is so admissible in the proceedings;

    (b) evidence may with the court's leave be given of any matter which (if he had given such evidence) could have been put to him in cross-examination as relevant to his credibility as a witness but of which evidence could not have been adduced by the cross-examining party;

    (c) evidence tending to prove that he made (at whatever time) any other statement inconsistent with the statement admitted as evidence is admissible for the purpose of showing that he contradicted himself.

(3) If as a result of evidence admitted under this section an allegation is made against the maker of a statement, the court may permit a party to lead additional evidence of such description as the court may specify for the purposes of denying or answering the allegation.

(4) In the case of a statement in a document which is admitted as evidence under section 117 each person who, in order for the statement to be admissible, must have supplied or received the information concerned or created or received the document or part concerned is to be treated as the maker of the statement for the purposes of subsections (1) to (3) above.

125   Stopping the case where evidence is unconvincing

(1) If on a defendant's trial before a judge and jury for an offence the court is satisfied at any time after the close of the case for the prosecution that—

    (a) the case against the defendant is based wholly or partly on a statement not made in oral evidence in the proceedings, and

    (b) the evidence provided by the statement is so unconvincing that, considering its importance to the case against the defendant, his conviction of the offence would be unsafe,

the court must either direct the jury to acquit the defendant of the offence or, if it considers that there ought to be a retrial, discharge the jury.

(2) Where—

    (a) a jury is directed under subsection (1) to acquit a defendant of an offence, and

    (b) the circumstances are such that, apart from this subsection, the defendant could if acquitted of that offence be found guilty of another offence,

the defendant may not be found guilty of that other offence if the court is satisfied as mentioned in subsection (1) in respect of it.

(3) If—

  (a) a jury is required to determine under section 4A(2) of the Criminal Procedure (Insanity) Act 1964 (c. 84) whether a person charged on an indictment with an offence did the act or made the omission charged, and

  (b) the court is satisfied as mentioned in subsection (1) above at any time after the close of the case for the prosecution that—

    (i) the case against the defendant is based wholly or partly on a statement not made in oral evidence in the proceedings, and

    (ii) the evidence provided by the statement is so unconvincing that, considering its importance to the case against the person, a finding that he did the act or made the omission would be unsafe,

the court must either direct the jury to acquit the defendant of the offence or, if it considers that there ought to be a rehearing, discharge the jury.

(4) This section does not prejudice any other power a court may have to direct a jury to acquit a person of an offence or to discharge a jury.

126   Court's general discretion to exclude evidence

(1) In criminal proceedings the court may refuse to admit a statement as evidence of a matter stated if—

  (a) the statement was made otherwise than in oral evidence in the proceedings, and

  (b) the court is satisfied that the case for excluding the statement, taking account of the danger that to admit it would result in undue waste of time, substantially outweighs the case for admitting it, taking account of the value of the evidence.

(2) Nothing in this Chapter prejudices—

  (a) any power of a court to exclude evidence under section 78 of the Police and Criminal Evidence Act 1984 (c. 60) (exclusion of unfair evidence), or

  (b) any other power of a court to exclude evidence at its discretion (whether by preventing questions from being put or otherwise).

Miscellaneous

127   Expert evidence: preparatory work

(1) This section applies if—

  (a) a statement has been prepared for the purposes of criminal proceedings,

  (b) the person who prepared the statement had or may reasonably be supposed to have had personal knowledge of the matters stated,

  (c) notice is given under the appropriate rules that another person (the expert) will in evidence given in the proceedings orally or under section 9 of the Criminal Justice Act 1967 (c. 80) base an opinion or inference on the statement, and

  (d) the notice gives the name of the person who prepared the statement and the nature of the matters stated.

(2) In evidence given in the proceedings the expert may base an opinion or inference on the statement.

(3) If evidence based on the statement is given under subsection (2) the statement is to be treated as evidence of what it states.

(4) This section does not apply if the court, on an application by a party to the proceedings, orders that it is not in the interests of justice that it should apply.

(5) The matters to be considered by the court in deciding whether to make an order under subsection (4) include—

  (a) the expense of calling as a witness the person who prepared the statement;

  (b) whether relevant evidence could be given by that person which could not be given by the expert;

(c) whether that person can reasonably be expected to remember the matters stated well enough to give oral evidence of them.

(6) Subsections (1) to (5) apply to a statement prepared for the purposes of a criminal investigation as they apply to a statement prepared for the purposes of criminal proceedings, and in such a case references to the proceedings are to criminal proceedings arising from the investigation.

(7) The appropriate rules are rules made—

(a) under section 81 of the Police and Criminal Evidence Act 1984 (advance notice of expert evidence in Crown Court), or

(b) under section 144 of the Magistrates' Courts Act 1980 (c. 43) by virtue of section 20(3) of the Criminal Procedure and Investigations Act 1996 (c. 25) (advance notice of expert evidence in magistrates' courts).

128 Confessions

(1) ... [Refers to section 76A Police and Criminal Evidence Act 1984]

(2) Subject to subsection (1), nothing in this Chapter makes a confession by a defendant admissible if it would not be admissible under section 76 of the Police and Criminal Evidence Act 1984 (c. 60).

(3) In subsection (2) "confession" has the meaning given by section 82 of that Act.

129 Representations other than by a person

(1) Where a representation of any fact—

(a) is made otherwise than by a person, but

(b) depends for its accuracy on information supplied (directly or indirectly) by a person,

the representation is not admissible in criminal proceedings as evidence of the fact unless it is proved that the information was accurate.

(2) Subsection (1) does not affect the operation of the presumption that a mechanical device has been properly set or calibrated.

131 Evidence at retrial

For paragraphs 1 and 1A of Schedule 2 to the Criminal Appeal Act 1968 (c. 19) (oral evidence and use of transcripts etc at retrials under that Act) there is substituted—

"1 *Evidence*

(1) Evidence given at a retrial must be given orally if it was given orally at the original trial, unless—

(a) all the parties to the retrial agree otherwise;

(b) section 116 of the Criminal Justice Act 2003 applies (admissibility of hearsay evidence where a witness is unavailable); or

(c) the witness is unavailable to give evidence, otherwise than as mentioned in subsection (2) of that section, and section 114(1)(d) of that Act applies (admission of hearsay evidence under residual discretion).

(2) Paragraph 5 of Schedule 3 to the Crime and Disorder Act 1998 (use of depositions) does not apply at a retrial to a deposition read as evidence at the original trial."

General

132 Rules of court

(1) Rules of court may make such provision as appears to the appropriate authority to be necessary or expedient for the purposes of this Chapter; and the appropriate authority is the authority entitled to make the rules.

(2) The rules may make provision about the procedure to be followed and other conditions to be fulfilled by a party proposing to tender a statement in evidence under any provision of this Chapter.

(3) The rules may require a party proposing to tender the evidence to serve on each party to the proceedings such notice, and such particulars of or relating to the evidence, as may be prescribed.

(4) The rules may provide that the evidence is to be treated as admissible by agreement of the parties if—

    (a) a notice has been served in accordance with provision made under subsection (3), and

    (b) no counter-notice in the prescribed form objecting to the admission of the evidence has been served by a party.

(5) If a party proposing to tender evidence fails to comply with a prescribed requirement applicable to it—

    (a) the evidence is not admissible except with the court's leave;

    (b) where leave is given the court or jury may draw such inferences from the failure as appear proper;

    (c) the failure may be taken into account by the court in considering the exercise of its powers with respect to costs.

(6) In considering whether or how to exercise any of its powers under subsection (5) the court shall have regard to whether there is any justification for the failure to comply with the requirement.

(7) A person shall not be convicted of an offence solely on an inference drawn under subsection (5)(b).

(8) Rules under this section may—

    (a) limit the application of any provision of the rules to prescribed circumstances;

    (b) subject any provision of the rules to prescribed exceptions;

    (c) make different provision for different cases or circumstances.

(9) Nothing in this section prejudices the generality of any enactment conferring power to make rules of court; and no particular provision of this section prejudices any general provision of it.

(10) In this section—

"prescribed" means prescribed by rules of court;

"rules of court" means—

    (a) Crown Court Rules;

    (b) Criminal Appeal Rules;

    (c) rules under section 144 of the Magistrates' Courts Act 1980 (c. 43).

133   Proof of statements in documents

Where a statement in a document is admissible as evidence in criminal proceedings, the statement may be proved by producing either—

    (a) the document, or

    (b) (whether or not the document exists) a copy of the document or of the material part of it,

authenticated in whatever way the court may approve.

134   Interpretation of Chapter 2

(1) In this Chapter—

"copy", in relation to a document, means anything on to which information recorded in the document has been copied, by whatever means and whether directly or indirectly;

"criminal proceedings" means criminal proceedings in relation to which the strict rules of evidence apply;

"defendant", in relation to criminal proceedings, means a person charged with an offence in those proceedings;

"document" means anything in which information of any description is recorded;

"oral evidence" includes evidence which, by reason of any disability, disorder or other impairment, a person called as a witness gives in writing or by signs or by way of any device;

"statutory provision" means any provision contained in, or in an instrument made under, this or any other Act, including any Act passed after this Act.

(2) Section 115 (statements and matters stated) contains other general interpretative provisions.

(3) Where a defendant is charged with two or more offences in the same criminal proceedings, this Chapter has effect as if each offence were charged in separate proceedings.

CHAPTER 3   MISCELLANEOUS AND SUPPLEMENTAL

137   Evidence by video recording

(1) This section applies where—

    (a) a person is called as a witness in proceedings for an offence triable only on indictment, or for a prescribed offence triable either way,

    (b) the person claims to have witnessed (whether visually or in any other way)—

        (i) events alleged by the prosecution to include conduct constituting the offence or part of the offence, or

        (ii) events closely connected with such events,

    (c) he has previously given an account of the events in question (whether in response to questions asked or otherwise),

    (d) the account was given at a time when those events were fresh in the person's memory (or would have been, assuming the truth of the claim mentioned in paragraph (b)),

    (e) a video recording was made of the account,

    (f) the court has made a direction that the recording should be admitted as evidence in chief of the witness, and the direction has not been rescinded, and

    (g) the recording is played in the proceedings in accordance with the direction.

(2) If, or to the extent that, the witness in his oral evidence in the proceedings asserts the truth of the statements made by him in the recorded account, they shall be treated as if made by him in that evidence.

(3) A direction under subsection (1)(f)—

    (a) may not be made in relation to a recorded account given by the defendant;

    (b) may be made only if it appears to the court that-

        (i) the witness's recollection of the events in question is likely to have been significantly better when he gave the recorded account than it will be when he gives oral evidence in the proceedings, and

        (ii) it is in the interests of justice for the recording to be admitted, having regard in particular to the matters mentioned in subsection (4).

(4) Those matters are—

    (a) the interval between the time of the events in question and the time when the recorded account was made;

    (b) any other factors that might affect the reliability of what the witness said in that account;

    (c) the quality of the recording;

    (d) any views of the witness as to whether his evidence in chief should be given orally or by means of the recording.

(5) For the purposes of subsection (2) it does not matter if the statements in the recorded account were not made on oath.

(6) In this section "prescribed" means of a description specified in an order made by the Secretary of State.

138   Video evidence: further provisions

(1) Where a video recording is admitted under section 137, the witness may not give evidence in chief otherwise than by means of the recording as to any matter which, in the opinion of the court, has been dealt with adequately in the recorded account.

(2) The reference in subsection (1)(f) of section 137 to the admission of a recording includes a reference to the admission of part of the recording; and references in that section and this one to the video recording or to the witness's recorded account shall, where appropriate, be read accordingly.

(3) In considering whether any part of a recording should be not admitted under section 137, the court must consider—

    (a) whether admitting that part would carry a risk of prejudice to the defendant, and

    (b) if so, whether the interests of justice nevertheless require it to be admitted in view of the desirability of showing the whole, or substantially the whole, of the recorded interview.

(4) A court may not make a direction under section 137(1)(f) in relation to any proceedings unless—

    (a) the Secretary of State has notified the court that arrangements can be made, in the area in which it appears to the court that the proceedings will take place, for implementing directions under that section, and

    (b) the notice has not been withdrawn.

(5) Nothing in section 137 affects the admissibility of any video recording which would be admissible apart from that section.

139   Use of documents to refresh memory

(1) A person giving oral evidence in criminal proceedings about any matter may, at any stage in the course of doing so, refresh his memory of it from a document made or verified by him at an earlier time if—

    (a) he states in his oral evidence that the document records his recollection of the matter at that earlier time, and

    (b) his recollection of the matter is likely to have been significantly better at that time than it is at the time of his oral evidence.

(2) Where—

    (a) a person giving oral evidence in criminal proceedings about any matter has previously given an oral account, of which a sound recording was made, and he states in that evidence that the account represented his recollection of the matter at that time,

    (b) his recollection of the matter is likely to have been significantly better at the time of the previous account than it is at the time of his oral evidence, and

    (c) a transcript has been made of the sound recording,

he may, at any stage in the course of giving his evidence, refresh his memory of the matter from that transcript.

140   Interpretation of chapter 3

In this Chapter—

"criminal proceedings" means criminal proceedings in relation to which the strict rules of evidence apply;

"defendant", in relation to criminal proceedings, means a person charged with an offence in those proceedings;

"document" means anything in which information of any description is recorded, but not including any recording of sounds or moving images;

"oral evidence" includes evidence which, by reason of any disability, disorder or other impairment, a person called as a witness gives in writing or by signs or by way of any device;

"video recording" means any recording, on any medium, from which a moving image may by any means be produced, and includes the accompanying sound-track.

SCHEDULE 4
QUALIFYING OFFENCES FOR PURPOSES OF SECTION 62

PART 1   LIST OF OFFENCES

Section 62

Offences against the person

Murder
    1. Murder.

Attempted murder
    2. An offence under section 1 of the Criminal Attempts Act 1981 (c. 47) of attempting to commit murder.

Soliciting murder
    3. An offence under section 4 of the Offences against the Person Act 1861 (c. 100).

Manslaughter
    4. Manslaughter.

Wounding or causing grievous bodily harm with intent
    5. An offence under section 18 of the Offences against the Person Act 1861 (c. 100).

Kidnapping
    6. Kidnapping.

Sexual offences

Rape
    7. An offence under section 1 of the Sexual Offences Act 1956 (c. 69) or section 1 of the Sexual Offences Act 2003 (c. 42).

Attempted rape
    8. An offence under section 1 of the Criminal Attempts Act 1981 (c. 47) of attempting to commit an offence under section 1 of the Sexual Offences Act 1956 or section 1 of the Sexual Offences Act 2003.

Intercourse with a girl under thirteen
    9. An offence under section 5 of the Sexual Offences Act 1956.

Incest by a man with a girl under thirteen
    10. An offence under section 10 of the Sexual Offences Act 1956 alleged to have been committed with a girl under thirteen.

Assault by penetration
    11. An offence under section 2 of the Sexual Offences Act 2003.

Causing a person to engage in sexual activity without consent
    12. An offence under section 4 of the Sexual Offences Act 2003 where it is alleged that the activity caused involved penetration within subsection (4)(a) to (d) of that section.

Rape of a child under thirteen
    13. An offence under section 5 of the Sexual Offences Act 2003.

Attempted rape of a child under thirteen
14.   An offence under section 1 of the Criminal Attempts Act 1981 of attempting to commit an offence under section 5 of the Sexual Offences Act 2003.

Assault of a child under thirteen by penetration
15.   An offence under section 6 of the Sexual Offences Act 2003.

Causing a child under thirteen to engage in sexual activity
16.   An offence under section 8 of the Sexual Offences Act 2003 (c. 42) where it is alleged that an activity involving penetration within subsection (2)(a) to (d) of that section was caused.

Sexual activity with a person with a mental disorder impeding choice
17.   An offence under section 30 of the Sexual Offences Act 2003 where it is alleged that the touching involved penetration within subsection (3)(a) to (d) of that section.

Causing or inciting a person with a mental disorder impeding choice to engage in sexual activity
18.   An offence under section 31 of the Sexual Offences Act 2003 where it is alleged that an activity involving penetration within subsection (3)(a) to (d) of that section was caused.

Drugs offences

Unlawful importation of Class A drug
19.   An offence under section 50(2) of the Customs and Excise Management Act 1979 (c. 2) alleged to have been committed in respect of a Class A drug (as defined by section 2 of the Misuse of Drugs Act 1971 (c. 38)).

Unlawful exportation of Class A drug
20.   An offence under section 68(2) of the Customs and Excise Management Act 1979 alleged to have been committed in respect of a Class A drug (as defined by section 2 of the Misuse of Drugs Act 1971).

Fraudulent evasion in respect of Class A drug
21.   An offence under section 170(1) or (2) of the Customs and Excise Management Act 1979 alleged to have been committed in respect of a Class A drug (as defined by section 2 of the Misuse of Drugs Act 1971).

Producing or being concerned in production of Class A drug
22.   An offence under section 4(2) of the Misuse of Drugs Act 1971 alleged to have been committed in relation to a Class A drug (as defined by section 2 of that Act).

Supplying or offering to supply Class A drug
23.   An offence under section 4(3) of the Misuse of Drugs Act 1971 alleged to have been committed in relation to a Class A drug (as defined by section 2 of that Act).

Theft offences

Robbery
24.   An offence under section 8(1) of the Theft Act 1968 (c. 60) where it is alleged that, at some time during the commission of the offence, the defendant had in his possession a firearm or imitation firearm (as defined by section 57 of the Firearms Act 1968 (c. 27)).

Criminal damage offences

Arson endangering life
25.   An offence under section 1(2) of the Criminal Damage Act 1971 (c. 48) alleged to have been committed by destroying or damaging property by fire.

Causing explosion likely to endanger life or property
    26.   An offence under section 2 of the Explosive Substances Act 1883 (c. 3).

Intent or conspiracy to cause explosion likely to endanger life or property
    27.   An offence under section 3(1)(a) of the Explosive Substances Act 1883.

War crimes and terrorism

Genocide, crimes against humanity and war crimes
    28.   An offence under section 51 or 52 of the International Criminal Court Act 2001 (c. 17).

Grave breaches of the geneva conventions
    29.   An offence under section 1 of the Geneva Conventions Act 1957 (c. 52).

Directing terrorist organisation
    30.   An offence under section 56 of the Terrorism Act 2000 (c. 11).

Hostage-taking
    31.   An offence under section 1 of the Taking of Hostages Act 1982 (c. 28).

Hijacking and other offences relating to aviation, maritime and rail security

Hijacking of aircraft
    32.   An offence under section 1 of the Aviation Security Act 1982 (c. 36).

Destroying, damaging or endangering the safety of an aircraft
    33.   An offence under section 2 of the Aviation Security Act 1982.

Hijacking of ships
    34.   An offence under section 9 of the Aviation and Maritime Security Act 1990 (c. 31).

Seizing or exercising control of fixed platforms
    35.   An offence under section 10 of the Aviation and Maritime Security Act 1990.

Destroying ships or fixed platforms or endangering their safety
    36.   An offence under section 11 of the Aviation and Maritime Security Act 1990.

Hijacking of channel tunnel trains
    37.   An offence under article 4 of the Channel Tunnel (Security) Order 1994 (S.I.1994/570).

Seizing or exercising control of the channel tunnel system
    38.   An offence under article 5 of the Channel Tunnel (Security) Order 1994 (S.I.1994/570).

Conspiracy

Conspiracy
    39.   An offence under section 1 of the Criminal Law Act 1977 (c. 45) of conspiracy to commit an offence listed in this Part of this Schedule.

PART 2   SUPPLEMENTARY

    40.   A reference in Part 1 of this Schedule to an offence includes a reference to an offence of aiding, abetting, counselling or procuring the commission of the offence.

41.   A reference in Part 1 of this Schedule to an enactment includes a reference to the enactment as enacted and as amended from time to time.

SCHEDULE 5

SECTION 75   QUALIFYING OFFENCES FOR PURPOSES OF PART 10
PART 1   LIST OF OFFENCES FOR ENGLAND AND WALES

Offences against the person

Murder
   1.   Murder.

Attempted murder
   2.   An offence under section 1 of the Criminal Attempts Act 1981 (c. 47) of attempting to commit murder.

Soliciting murder
   3.   An offence under section 4 of the Offences against the Person Act 1861 (c. 100).

Manslaughter
   4.   Manslaughter.

Kidnapping
   5.   Kidnapping.

Sexual offences

Rape
   6.   An offence under section 1 of the Sexual Offences Act 1956 (c. 69) or section 1 of the Sexual Offences Act 2003 (c. 42).

Attempted rape
   7.   An offence under section 1 of the Criminal Attempts Act 1981 of attempting to commit an offence under section 1 of the Sexual Offences Act 1956 or section 1 of the Sexual Offences Act 2003.

Intercourse with a girl under thirteen
   8.   An offence under section 5 of the Sexual Offences Act 1956.

Incest by a man with a girl under thirteen
   9.   An offence under section 10 of the Sexual Offences Act 1956 alleged to have been committed with a girl under thirteen.

Assault by penetration
   10.   An offence under section 2 of the Sexual Offences Act 2003 (c. 42).

Causing a person to engage in sexual activity without consent
   11.   An offence under section 4 of the Sexual Offences Act 2003 where it is alleged that the activity caused involved penetration within subsection (4)(a) to (d) of that section.

Rape of a child under thirteen
   12.   An offence under section 5 of the Sexual Offences Act 2003.

Attempted rape of a child under thirteen
   13.   An offence under section 1 of the Criminal Attempts Act 1981 (c. 47) of attempting to commit an offence under section 5 of the Sexual Offences Act 2003.

Assault of a child under thirteen by penetration
    14.   An offence under section 6 of the Sexual Offences Act 2003.

Causing a child under thirteen to engage in sexual activity
    15.   An offence under section 8 of the Sexual Offences Act 2003 where it is alleged that an activity involving penetration within subsection (2)(a) to (d) of that section was caused.

Sexual activity with a person with a mental disorder impeding choice
    16.   An offence under section 30 of the Sexual Offences Act 2003 where it is alleged that the touching involved penetration within subsection (3)(a) to (d) of that section.

Causing a person with a mental disorder impeding choice to engage in sexual activity
    17.   An offence under section 31 of the Sexual Offences Act 2003 where it is alleged that an activity involving penetration within subsection (3)(a) to (d) of that section was caused.

Drugs offences

Unlawful importation of class a drug
    18.   An offence under section 50(2) of the Customs and Excise Management Act 1979 (c. 2) alleged to have been committed in respect of a Class A drug (as defined by section 2 of the Misuse of Drugs Act 1971 (c. 38)).

Unlawful exportation of class a drug
    19.   An offence under section 68(2) of the Customs and Excise Management Act 1979 alleged to have been committed in respect of a Class A drug (as defined by section 2 of the Misuse of Drugs Act 1971).

Fraudulent evasion in respect of class a drug
    20.   An offence under section 170(1) or (2) of the Customs and Excise Management Act 1979 (c. 2) alleged to have been committed in respect of a Class A drug (as defined by section 2 of the Misuse of Drugs Act 1971 (c. 38)).

Producing or being concerned in production of class a drug
    21.   An offence under section 4(2) of the Misuse of Drugs Act 1971 alleged to have been committed in relation to a Class A drug (as defined by section 2 of that Act).

Criminal damage Offences

Arson endangering life
    22.   An offence under section 1(2) of the Criminal Damage Act 1971 (c. 48) alleged to have been committed by destroying or damaging property by fire.

Causing explosion likely to endanger life or property
    23.   An offence under section 2 of the Explosive Substances Act 1883 (c. 3).

Intent or conspiracy to cause explosion likely to endanger life or property
    24.   An offence under section 3(1)(a) of the Explosive Substances Act 1883.

War crimes and terrorism

Genocide, crimes against humanity and war crimes
    25.   An offence under section 51 or 52 of the International Criminal Court Act 2001 (c. 17).

Grave breaches of the geneva conventions
    26.   An offence under section 1 of the Geneva Conventions Act 1957 (c. 52).

Directing terrorist organisation
    27.   An offence under section 56 of the Terrorism Act 2000 (c. 11).

Hostage-taking

 28. An offence under section 1 of the Taking of Hostages Act 1982 (c. 28).

Conspiracy

Conspiracy

 29. An offence under section 1 of the Criminal Law Act 1977 (c. 45) of conspiracy to commit an offence listed in this Part of this Schedule.

PART B

Rules and Guidelines

Practice Direction (Submission of No Case)
[1962] 1 WLR 227

LORD PARKER CJ Those of us who sit in the Divisional Court have the distinct impression that Justices today are being persuaded all too often to uphold a submission of no case. In the result, this court has had on many occasions to send the case back to the Justices for the hearing to be continued with inevitable delay and increased expenditure. Without attempting to lay down any principle of law, we think that as a matter of practice Justices should be guided by the following considerations.

A submission that there is no case to answer may properly be made and upheld: (a) when there has been no evidence to prove an essential element in the alleged offence; (b) when the evidence adduced by the prosecution has been so discredited as a result of cross-examination or is so manifestly unreliable that no reasonable tribunal could safely convict upon it.

Apart from these two situations a tribunal should not in general be called upon to reach a decision as to conviction or acquittal until the whole of the evidence which either side wishes to tender has been placed before it. If however a submission is made that there is no case to answer, the decision should depend not so much on whether the adjudicating tribunal (if compelled to do so) would at that stage convict or acquit but on whether the evidence is such that a reasonable tribunal might convict. If a reasonable tribunal might convict on the evidence so far laid before it, there is a case to answer.

Appendix 7 Disclosure: Criminal Procedure and Investigations Act 1996: Code of Practice under Part II

Introduction

1.1   This code of practice is issued under Part II of the Criminal Procedure and Investigations Act 1996 ('the Act'). It applies in respect of criminal investigations conducted by police officers which begin on or after the day on which this code comes into effect. Persons other than police officers who are charged with the duty of conducting an investigation as defined in the Act are to have regard to the relevant provisions of the code, and should take these into account in applying their own operating procedures.

1.2   This code does not apply to persons who are not charged with the duty of conducting an investigation as defined in the Act.

1.3   Nothing in this code applies to material intercepted in obedience to a warrant issued under section 2 of the Interception of Communications Act 1985, or to any copy of that material as defined in section 10 of that Act.

1.4   ...

Definitions

2.1   In this code:

— a *criminal investigation* is an investigation conducted by police officers with a view to it being ascertained whether a person should be charged with an offence, or whether a person charged with an offence is guilty of it. This will include:

— investigations into crimes that have been committed;

— investigations whose purpose is to ascertain whether a crime has been committed, with a view to the possible institution of criminal proceedings; and

— investigations which begin in the belief that a crime may be committed, for example when the police keep premises or individuals under observation for a period of time, with a view to the possible institution of criminal proceedings;

— charging a person with an offence includes prosecution by way of summons;

— an *investigator* is any police officer involved in the conduct of a criminal investigation. All investigators have a responsibility for carrying out the duties imposed on them under this code, including in particular recording information, and retaining records of information and other material;

— the *officer in charge of an investigation* is the police officer responsible for directing a criminal investigation. He is also responsible for ensuring that proper procedures are in place for recording information, and retaining records of information and other material, in the investigation;

— the *disclosure officer* is the person responsible for examining material retained by the police during the investigation; revealing material to the prosecutor during the investigation and any criminal proceedings resulting from it, and certifying that he has done this; and disclosing material to the accused at the request of the prosecutor;

— the *prosecutor* is the authority responsible for the conduct of criminal proceedings on behalf of the Crown. Particular duties may in practice fall to individuals acting on behalf of the prosecuting authority;

— *material* is material of any kind, including information and objects, which is obtained in the course of a criminal investigation and which may be relevant to the investigation;

— material may be *relevant to an investigation* if it appears to an investigator, or to the officer in charge of an investigation, or to the disclosure officer, that it has some bearing on any offence under investigation or any person being investigated, or on the surrounding circumstances of the case, unless it is incapable of having any impact on the case;

— *sensitive material* is material which the disclosure officer believes, after consulting the officer in charge of the investigation, it is not in the public interest to disclose;

— references to *primary prosecution disclosure* are to the duty of the prosecutor under section 3 of the Act to disclose material which is in his possession or which he has inspected in pursuance of this code, and which in his opinion might undermine the case against the accused;

— references to *secondary prosecution disclosure* are to the duty of the prosecutor under section 7 of the Act to disclose material which is in his possession or which he has inspected in pursuance of this code, and which might reasonably be expected to assist the defence disclosed by the accused in a defence statement given under the Act;

— references to the disclosure of material to a person accused of an offence include references to the disclosure of material to his legal representative;

— references to police officers and to the chief officer of police include those employed in a police force as defined in section 3(3) of the Prosecution of Offences Act 1985.

General responsibilities

3.1   The functions of the investigator, the officer in charge of an investigation and the disclosure officer are separate. Whether they are undertaken by one, two or more persons will depend on the complexity of the case and the administrative arrangements within each police force. Where they are undertaken by more than one person, close consultation between them is essential to the effective performance of the duties imposed by this code.

3.2   The chief officer of police for each police force is responsible for putting in place arrangements to ensure that in every investigation the identity of the officer in charge of an investigation and the disclosure officer is recorded.

3.3   The officer in charge of an investigation may delegate tasks to another investigator or to civilians employed by the police force, but he remains responsible for ensuring that these have been carried out and for accounting for any general policies followed in the investigation. In particular, it is an essential part of his duties to ensure that all material which may be relevant to an investigation is retained, and either made available to the disclosure officer or (in exceptional circumstances) revealed directly to the prosecutor.

3.4   In conducting an investigation, the investigator should pursue all reasonable lines of inquiry, whether these point towards or away from the suspect. What is reasonable in each case will depend on the particular circumstances.

3.5   If the officer in charge of an investigation believes that other persons may be in possession of material that may be relevant to the investigation, and if this has not been obtained under paragraph 3.4 above, he should ask the disclosure officer to inform them of the existence of the investigation and to invite them to retain the material in case they receive a request for its disclosure. The disclosure officer should inform the prosecutor that they may have such material. However, the officer in charge of an investigation is not required to make speculative enquiries of other persons: there must be some reason to believe that they may have relevant material. That reason may come from information provided to the police by the accused or from other inquiries made or from some other source.

3.6   If, during a criminal investigation, the officer in charge of an investigation or disclosure officer for any reason no longer has responsibility for the functions falling to him, either his supervisor or the police officer in charge of criminal investigations for the police force concerned must assign someone else to assume that responsibility. That person's identity must be recorded, as with those initially responsible for these functions in each investigation.

Recording of information

4.1   If material which may be relevant to the investigation consists of information which is not recorded in any form, the officer in charge of an investigation must ensure that it is recorded in a durable or retrieval form (whether in writing, on video or audio tape, or on computer disk).

4.2   Where it is not practicable to retain the initial record of information because it forms part of a larger record which is to be destroyed, its contents should be transferred as a true record to a durable and more easily-stored form before that happens.

4.3   Negative information is often relevant to an investigation. If it may be relevant it must be recorded. An example might be a number of people present in a particular place at a particular time who state that they saw nothing unusual.

4.4   Where information which may be relevant is obtained, it must be recorded at the time it is obtained or as soon as practicable after that time. This includes, for example, information obtained in house-to-house enquiries, although the requirement to record information promptly does not require an investigator to take a statement from a potential witness where it would not otherwise be taken.

Retention of material

(a) Duty to retain material

5.1   The investigator must retain material obtained in a criminal investigation which may be relevant to the investigation. This includes not only material coming into the possession of the investigator (such as documents seized in the course of searching premises) but also material generated by him (such as interview records). Material may be photographed, or retained in the form of a copy rather than the original, if the original is perishable, or was supplied to the investigator rather than generated by him and is to be returned to its owner.

5.2   Where material has been seized in the exercise of the powers of seizure conferred by the Police and Criminal Evidence Act 1984, the duty to retain it under this code is subject to the provisions on the retention of seized material in section 22 of that Act.

5.3   If the officer in charge of an investigation becomes aware as a result of developments in the case that material previously examined but not retained (because it was not thought to be relevant) may now be relevant to the investigation, he should, wherever practicable, take steps to obtain it or ensure that it is retained for further inspection or for production in court if required.

5.4   The duty to retain material includes in particular the duty to retain material falling into the following categories, where it may be relevant to the investigation:

— crime reports (including crime report forms, relevant parts of incident report books or police officers' notebooks);
— custody records;
— records which are derived from tapes of telephone messages (for example, 999 calls) containing descriptions of an alleged offence or offender;
— final versions of witness statements (and draft versions where their content differs from the final version), including any exhibits mentioned (unless these have been returned to their owner on the understanding that they will be produced in court if required);
— interview records (written records, or audio or video tapes, of interviews with actual or potential witnesses or suspects);
— communications between the police and experts such as forensic scientists, reports of work carried out by experts, and schedules of scientific material prepared by the expert for the investigator, for the purposes of criminal proceedings;
— any material casting doubt on the reliability of a confession;
— any material casting doubt on the reliability of a witness;
— any other material which may fall within the test for primary prosecution disclosure in the Act.

5.5   The duty to retain material falling into these categories does not extend to items which are purely ancillary to such material and possess no independent significance (for example, duplicate copies of records or reports).

(b) Length of time for which material is to be retained

5.6   All material which may be relevant to the investigation must be retained until a decision is taken whether to institute proceedings against a person for an offence.

5.7   If a criminal investigation results in proceedings being instituted, all material which may be relevant must be retained at least until the accused is acquitted or convicted or the prosecutor decides not to proceed with the case.

5.8   Where the accused is convicted after a not guilty plea, all material which may be relevant must be retained for the following minimum periods after the date of conviction:

— one year, in respect of a conviction at a summary trial;
— three years, in respect of a conviction at a trial on indictment.

5.9   If an appeal against conviction is in progress at the end of the periods specified in paragraph 5.8, all material which may be relevant must be retained until the appeal is determined.

5.10   Material need not be retained by the police for the duration of the periods specified in paragraph 5.8 in these circumstances:

— it was seized and is to be returned to its owner;
— the material is not durable and deteriorates so much that it has no evidential value;
— copies of the material are held by another criminal justice agency, and it is agreed in writing between the police and that agency that the agency will retain these for the minimum periods specified above.

Preparation of material for prosecutor

(a) Introduction

6.1   The officer in charge of the investigation, the disclosure officer or an investigator may seek advice from the prosecutor about whether any particular item of material may be relevant to the investigation.

6.2   Material which may be relevant to an investigation, which has been retained in accordance with this code, and which the disclosure officer believes will not form part of the prosecution case, must be listed on a schedule.

6.3   Material which the disclosure officer does not believe is sensitive must be listed on a schedule of non-sensitive material. The schedule must include a statement that the disclosure officer does not believe the material is sensitive.

6.4   Any material which is believed to be sensitive must be either listed on a schedule of sensitive material or, in exceptional circumstances, revealed to the prosecutor separately.

6.5   Paragraphs 6.6 to 6.11 below apply to both sensitive and non-sensitive material. Paragraphs 6.12 to 6.14 apply to sensitive material only.

(b) Circumstances in which a schedule is to be prepared

6.6   The disclosure officer must ensure that a schedule is prepared in the following circumstances:

— the accused is charged with an offence which is triable only on indictment;
— the accused is charged with an offence which is triable either way, and it is considered either that the case is likely to be tried on indictment or that the accused is likely to plead not guilty at a summary trial;
— the accused is charged with a summary offence, and it is considered that he is likely to plead not guilty.

6.7   In respect of either way and summary offences, a schedule may not be needed if a person has admitted the offence, or if a police officer witnessed the offence and that person has not denied it.

6.8   If it is believed that the accused is likely to plead guilty at a summary trial, it is not necessary to prepare a schedule in advance. If, contrary to this belief, the accused pleads not guilty at a summary trial, or the offence is to be tried on indictment, the disclosure officer must ensure that a schedule is prepared as soon as is reasonably practicable after that happens.

(c) Way in which material is to be listed on schedule

6.9   The disclosure officer should ensure that each item of material is listed separately on the schedule, and is numbered consecutively. The description of each item should make clear the nature of the item and should contain sufficient detail to enable the prosecutor to decide whether he needs to inspect the material before deciding whether or not it should be disclosed.

6.10   In some enquiries it may not be practicable to list each item of material separately. For example, there may be many items of a similar or repetitive nature. These may be listed in a block and described by quantity and generic title.

6.11   Even if some material is listed in a block, the disclosure officer must ensure that any items among that material which might meet the test for primary prosecution disclosure are listed and described individually.

(d) Treatment of sensitive material

6.12   Subject to paragraph 6.13 below, the disclosure officer must list on a sensitive schedule any material which he believes it is not in the public interest to disclose, and the reason for that belief. The schedule must include a statement that the disclosure officer believes the material is sensitive. Depending on the circumstances, examples of such material may include the following among others:

— material relating to national security;
— material received from the intelligence and security agencies;
— material relating to intelligence from foreign sources which reveals sensitive intelligence gathering methods;
— material given in confidence;
— material which relates to the use of a telephone system and which is supplied to an investigator for intelligence purposes only;
— material relating to the identity or activities of informants, or under-cover police officers, or other persons supplying information to the police who may be in danger if their identities are revealed;
— material revealing the location of any premises or other place used for police surveillance, or the identity of any person allowing a police officer to use them for surveillance;
— material revealing, either directly or indirectly, techniques and methods relied upon by a police officer in the course of a criminal investigation, for example covert surveillance techniques, or other methods of detecting crime;
— material whose disclosure might facilitate the commission of other offences or hinder the prevention and detection of crime;
— internal police communications such as management minutes;
— material upon the strength of which search warrants were obtained;
— material containing details of persons taking part in identification parades;
— material supplied to an investigator during a criminal investigation which has been generated by an official of a body concerned with the regulation or supervision of bodies corporate or of persons engaged in financial activities, or which has been generated by a person retained by such a body;
— material supplied to an investigator during a criminal investigation which relates to a child or young person and which has been generated by a local authority Social services department, an Area Child Protection Committee or other party contacted by an investigator during the investigation.

6.13   In exceptional circumstances, where an investigator considers that material is so sensitive that its revelation to the prosecutor by means of an entry on the sensitive schedule is inappropriate, the existence of the material must be revealed to the prosecutor separately. This will apply where compromising the material would be likely to lead directly to the loss of life, or directly threaten national security.

6.14   In such circumstances, the responsibility for informing the prosecutor lies with the investigator who knows the detail of the sensitive material. The investigator should act as soon as is reasonably practicable after the file containing the prosecution case is sent to the prosecutor. The investigator must also ensure that the prosecutor is able to inspect the material so that he can assess whether it needs to be brought before a court for a ruling on disclosure.

Revelation of material to prosecutor

7.1   The disclosure officer must give the schedules to the prosecutor. Wherever practicable this should be at the same time as he gives him the file containing the material for the prosecution case (or as soon as is reasonably practicable after the decision on mode of trial or the plea, in cases to which paragraph 6.8 applies).

7.2   The disclosure officer should draw the attention of the prosecutor to any material an investigator has retained (whether or not listed on a schedule) which may fall within the test for primary prosecution disclosure in the Act, and should explain why he has come to that view.

7.3   At the same time as complying with the duties in paragraphs 7.1 and 7.2, the disclosure officer must give the prosecutor a copy of any material which falls into the following categories (unless such material has already been given to the prosecutor as part of the file containing the material for the prosecution case):

— records of the first description of a suspect given to the police by a potential witness, whether or not the description differs from that of the alleged offender;
— information provided by an accused person which indicates an explanation for the offence with which he has been charged;
— any material casting doubt on the reliability of a confession;
— any material casting doubt on the reliability of a witness;
— any other material which the investigator believes may fall within the test for primary prosecution disclosure in the Act.

7.4   If the prosecutor asks to inspect material which has not already been copied to him, the disclosure officer must allow him to inspect it. If the prosecutor asks for a copy of material which has not already been copied to him, the disclosure officer must give him a copy. However, this does not apply where the disclosure officer believes, having consulted the officer in charge of the investigation, that the material is too sensitive to be copied and can only be inspected.

7.5   If material consists of information which is recorded other than in writing, whether it should be given to the prosecutor in its original form as a whole, or by way of relevant extracts recorded in the same form, or in the form of a transcript, is a matter for agreement between the disclosure officer and the prosecutor.

Subsequent action by disclosure officer

8.1   At the time a schedule of non-sensitive material is prepared, the disclosure officer may not know exactly what material will form the case against the accused, and the prosecutor may not have given advice about the likely relevance of particular items of material. Once these matters have been determined, the disclosure officer must give the prosecutor, where necessary, an amended schedule listing any additional material:

— which may be relevant to the investigation,
— which does not form part of the case against the accused,
— which is not already listed on the schedule, and
— which he believes is not sensitive,

unless he is informed in writing by the prosecutor that the prosecutor intends to disclose the material to the defence.

8.2   After a defence statement has been given, the disclosure officer must look again at the material which has been retained and must draw the attention of the prosecutor to any material which might reasonably be expected to assist the defence disclosed by the accused; and he must reveal it to him in accordance with paragraphs 7.4 and 7.5 above.

8.3   Section 9 of the Act imposes a continuing duty on the prosecutor, for the duration of criminal proceedings against the accused, to disclose material which meets the tests for disclosure (subject to public interest considerations). To enable him to do this, any new material coming to light should be treated in the same way as the earlier material.

Certification by disclosure officer

9.1   The disclosure officer must certify to the prosecutor that, to the best of his knowledge and belief, all material which has been retained and made available to him has been revealed to the prosecutor in accordance with this code. He must sign and date the certificate. It will be necessary to certify not only at the time when the schedule and accompanying material is submitted to the prosceutor, but also when material which has been retained is reconsidered after the accused has given a defence statement.

Disclosure of material to accused

10.1   If material has not already been copied to the prosecutor, and he requests its disclosure to the accused on the ground that:

— it falls within the test for primary or secondary prosecution disclosure, or

— the court has ordered its disclosure after considering an application from the accused, the disclosure officer must disclose it to the accused.

10.2   If material has been copied to the prosecutor, and it is to be disclosed, whether it is disclosed by the prosecutor or the disclosure officer is a matter for agreement between the two of them.

10.3   The disclosure officer must disclose material to the accused either by giving him a copy or by allowing him to inspect it. If the accused person asks for a copy of any material which he has been allowed to inspect, the disclosure officer must give it to him, unless in the opinion of the disclosure officer that is either not practicable (for example because the material consists of an object which cannot be copied, or because the volume of material is so great), or not desirable (for example because the material is a statement by a child witness in relation to a sexual offence).

10.4   If material which the accused has been allowed to inspect consists of information which is recorded other than in writing, whether it should be given to the accused in its original form or in the form of a transcript is a matter for the discretion of the disclosure officer. If the material is transcribed, the disclosure officer must ensure that the transcript is certified to the accused as a true record of the material which has been transcribed.

10.5   If a court concludes that it is in the public interest that an item of sensitive material must be disclosed to the accused, it will be necessary to disclose the material if the case is to proceed. This does not mean that sensitive documents must always be disclosed in their original form: for example, the court may agree that sensitive details still requiring protection should be blocked out, or that documents may be summarised, or that the prosecutor may make an admission about the substance of the material under section 10 of the Criminal Justice Act 1967.

Attorney-General's Guidelines on Disclosure of Information in Criminal Proceedings
Issued 29 November 2000

Introduction

1.   Every accused person has a right to a fair trial, a right long embodied in our law and guaranteed under Article 6 of the European Convention on Human Rights. A fair trial is the proper object and expectation of all participants in the trial process. Fair disclosure to an accused is an inseparable part of a fair trial.

2.   The scheme set out in the Criminal Procedure and Investigations Act 1996 (the Act) is designed to ensure that there is fair disclosure of material which may be relevant to an investigation and which does not form part of the prosecution case. Disclosure under the Act

should assist the accused in the timely preparation and presentation of their case and assist the court to focus on all the relevant issues in the trial. Disclosure which does not meet these objectives risks preventing a fair trial taking place.

3.   Fairness does however, recognise that there are other interests that need to be protected, including those of victims and witnesses who might otherwise be exposed to harm. The scheme of the Act protects those interests. It should also ensure that material is not disclosed which overburdens the participants in the trial process, diverts attention from the relevant issues, leads to unjustifiable delay, and is wasteful of resources.

4.   These guidelines build upon the existing law to help to ensure that the legislation is operated more effectively. In some areas guidance is given which goes beyond the requirements of the legislation, where experience has suggested that such guidance is desirable.

General principles

Investigators and disclosure officers

5.   Investigators and disclosure officers must be fair and objective and must work together with prosecutors to ensure that disclosure obligations are met. A failure to take action leading to proper disclosure may result in a wrongful conviction. It may alternatively lead to a successful abuse of process argument or an acquittal against the weight of the evidence.

6.   In discharging their obligations under the statute, code, common law and any operational instructions, investigators should always err on the side of recording and retaining material where they have any doubt as to whether it may be relevant.

7.   An individual must not be appointed as disclosure officer, or continue in that role, if that is likely to result in a conflict of interest, for instance, if the disclosure officer is the victim of the alleged crime which is the subject of criminal proceedings. The advice of a more senior officer must always be sought if there is doubt as to whether a conflict of interest precludes an individual acting as the disclosure officer. If thereafter the doubt remains, the advice of a prosecutor should be sought.

8.   Disclosure officers, or their deputies, must inspect, view or listen to all material that has been retained by the investigator, and the disclosure officer must provide a personal declaration to the effect that this task has been done. The obligation does not apply, however, in the circumstances set out in paragraph 9 below.

9.   In some cases, out of an abundance of caution, investigators seize large volumes of material which may, not, because of its source, general nature or other reasons, seem likely ever to be relevant. In such circumstances, the investigator may consider that it is not an appropriate use of resources to examine such large volumes of material seized on a precautionary basis. If such material is not examined by the investigator or disclosure officer, and it is not intended to examine it, but the material is nevertheless retained, its existence should be made known to the accused in general terms at the primary stage and permission granted for its inspection by him or his legal advisers. A section 9 statement will be completed by the investigating officer or disclosure officer describing the material by general category and justifying it not having been examined. This statement will itself be listed as unused material and automatically disclosed to the defence.

10.   In meeting the obligations in paragraph 6.9 and 8.1 of the Code, it is crucial that descriptions by disclosure officers in non-sensitive schedules are detailed, clear and accurate. The descriptions may require a summary of the contents of the retained material to assist the prosecutor to make an informed decision on disclosure. The same applies to sensitive schedules, to the extent possible without compromising the confidentiality of the information.

11.   Disclosure officers must specifically draw material to the attention of the prosecutor for consideration where they have any doubt as to whether it might undermine the prosecution case or might reasonably be expected to assist the defence disclosed by the accused.

12.   Disclosure officers must seek the advice and assistance of prosecutors when in doubt as to their responsibility, and must deal expeditiously with requests by the prosecutor for further information on material which may lead to disclosure.

Prosecutors generally

13.   Prosecutors must do all that they can to facilitate proper disclosure, as part of their general and personal professional responsibility to act fairly and impartially, in the interests of justice. Prosecutors must also be alert to the need to provide advice to disclosure officers on disclosure issues and to advise on disclosure procedure generally.

14.   Prosecutors must review schedules prepared by disclosure officers thoroughly and must be alert to the possibility that material may exist which has not been revealed to them. If no schedules have been provided, or there are apparent omissions from the schedules, or documents or other items are insufficiently described or are unclear, the prosecutor must at once take action to obtain properly completed schedules. If, following this, prosecutors remain dissatisfied with the quality or content of the schedules they must raise the matter with a senior officer, and if necessary, persist, with a view to resolving the matter satisfactorily.

15.   Where prosecutors have reason to believe that the disclosure officer has not discharged the obligation in paragraph 8 to inspect, view or listen to material, they must at once raise the matter with the disclosure officer and, if it is believed that the officer has not inspected, viewed or listened to the material, request that it be done.

16.   When the prosecutor or disclosure officer believes that material might undermine the prosecution case or assist the defence case, for instance in the case of records of previous statements by witnesses, prosecutors must always inspect, view or listen to the material and satisfy themselves that the prosecution can properly be continued. Their judgement as to what other material to inspect, view or listen to will depend on the circumstances of each case.

17.   Prosecutors should inform the investigator if, in their view, reasonable and relevant lines of further inquiry exist.

18.   Prosecutors should not adduce evidence of the contents of a defence statement other than in the circumstances envisaged by section 11 of the Act or to rebut alibi evidence. Where evidence may be adduced in these circumstances, this can be done through cross-examination as well as through the introduction of evidence. There may be occasions when a defence statement points the prosecution to other lines of inquiry. Further investigation in these circumstances is possible and evidence obtained as a result of inquiring into a defence statement may be used as part of the prosecution case or to rebut the defence.

19.   Prosecutors must ensure that they record in writing all actions and decisions they make in discharging their disclosure responsibilities, and this information is to be made available to the prosecution advocate if requested or if relevant to an issue.

20.   In deciding what material should be disclosed (at any stage of the proceedings) prosecutors should resolve any doubt they may have in favour of disclosure, unless the material is on the sensitive schedule and will be placed before the court for the issue of disclosure to be determined.

21.   If prosecutors are satisfied that a fair trial cannot take place because of a failure to disclose which cannot or will not be remedied, they must not continue with the case.

Prosecution advocates

22.   Prosecution advocates should use their best endeavours to ensure that all material that ought properly to be made available is either presented by the prosecution or disclosed to the defence. However, the prosecution cannot be expected to disclose material if they are not aware of its existence. As far as is possible, prosecution advocates must place themselves in a fully informed position to enable them to make decisions on disclosure.

23.   Upon receipt of instructions, prosecution advocates should consider as a priority all the information provided regarding disclosure of material. Prosecution advocates should

consider, in every case, whether they can be satisfied that they are in possession of all relevant documentation and that they have been instructed fully regarding disclosure matters. Decisions already made regarding disclosure should be reviewed. If as a result the advocate considers that further information or action is required, written advice should be promptly provided setting out the aspects that need clarification or action. If necessary and where appropriate a conference should be held to determine what is required.

24. The prosecution advocate must continue to keep under review until the conclusion of the trial decisions regarding disclosure. The prosecution advocate must in every case specifically consider whether he or she can satisfactorily discharge the duty of continuing review on the basis of the material supplied already, or whether it is necessary to inspect further material or to reconsider material already inspected.

25. Prior to the commencement of a trial, the prosecuting advocate should always make decisions on disclosure in consultation with those instructing him and it is desirable that the disclosure officer should also be consulted. After a trial has started, it is recognised that in practice consultation on disclosure issues may not be practicable; it continues to be desirable, however, whenever this can be achieved without affecting unduly the conduct of the trial.

26. The practice of 'counsel to counsel' disclosure should cease: it is inconsistent with the requirement of transparency in the prosecution process.

Defence practitioners
27. A defence statement should set out the nature of the defence, the matters on which issue is taken and the reasons for taking issue. A comprehensive defence statement assists the participants in the trial to ensure that it is fair. It provides information that the prosecutor needs to identify any remaining material that fails to be disclosed at the secondary stage. The more detail a defence statement contains the more likely it is that the prosecutor will make a properly informed decision about whether any remaining material might assist the defence case, or whether to advise the investigator to undertake further inquiries. It also helps in the management of the trial by narrowing down and focussing the issues in dispute. It may result in the prosecution discontinuing the case. Defence practitioners should be aware of these considerations in advising their clients.

28. Defence solicitors should ensure that statements are agreed by the accused before being served. Wherever possible, the accused should sign the defence statement to evidence his or her agreement.

Involvement of other agencies

(a) Material held by government departments or other crown bodies
29. Where it appears to an investigator, disclosure officer or prosecutor that a Government department or other Crown body has material that may be relevant to an issue in the case, reasonable steps should be taken to identify and consider such material. Although what is reasonable will vary from case to case, prosecutors should inform the department or other body of the nature of its case and of relevant issues in the case in respect of which the department or body might possess material, and ask whether it has any such material. Departments in England and Wales have established Enquiry Points to deal with issues concerning the disclosure of information in criminal proceedings. Further guidance for prosecutors and investigators seeking information (including documents) from Government departments or other Crown bodies may be found in the pamphlet 'Giving Evidence or Information about suspected crimes: Guidance for Departments and Investigators' (March, 1997, Cabinet Office).

(b) Material held by other agencies
30. There may be cases where the investigator, disclosure officer or prosecutor suspects that a non-government agency or other third party (for example, a local authority, a social

services department, a hospital, a doctor, a school, providers of forensic services) has material or information which might be disclosable if it were in the possession of the prosecution. In such cases consideration should be given as to whether it is appropriate to seek access to the material or information and if so, steps should be taken by the prosecution to obtain such material or information. It will be important to do so if the material or information is likely to undermine the prosecution case, or assist a known defence.

31.   If the investigator, disclosure officer or prosecutor seeks access to the material or information but the third party declines or refuses to allow access to it, the matter should not be left. If despite any reasons offered by the third party it is still believed that it is reasonable to seek production of the material or information, and the requirements of section 2 of the Criminal Procedure (Attendance of Witnesses) Act 1965 or as appropriate section 97 of the Magistrates Courts Act 1980[1] are satisfied, then the prosecutor or investigator should apply for a witness summons causing a representative of the third party to produce the material to the Court.

32.   Information which might be disclosable if it were in the possession of the prosecution which comes to the knowledge of investigators or prosecutors as a result of liaison with third parties should be recorded by the investigator or prosecutor in a durable or retrievable form (for example potentially relevant information revealed in discussions at a child protection conference attended by police officers).

33.   Where information comes into the possession of the prosecution in the circumstances set out in paragraphs 30–32 above, consultation with the other agency should take place before disclosure is made: there may be public interest reasons which justify witholding disclosure and which would require the issue of disclosure of the information to be placed before the court.

Disclosure prior to primary disclosure under the CPIA 1996

34.   Prosecutors must always be alive to the need, in the interests of justice and fairness in the particular circumstances of any case, to make disclosure of material after the commencement of proceedings but before the prosecutor's duty arises under the Act. For instance, disclosure ought to be made of significant information that might affect a bail decision or that might enable the defence to contest the committal proceedings.

35.   Where the need for such disclosure is not apparent to the prosecutor, any disclosure will depend on what the defendant chooses to reveal about the defence. Clearly, such disclosure will not normally exceed that which is obtainable after the duties under the 'Act' arise.

Primary disclosure

36.   Generally, material can be considered to potentially undermine the prosecution case if it has an adverse effect on the strength of the prosecution case. This will include anything that tends to show a fact inconsistent with the elements of the case that must be proved by the prosecution. Material can have an adverse effect on the strength of the prosecution case:
  (a) by the use made of it in cross-examination; and
  (b) by its capacity to suggest any potential submissions that could lead to:
       (i)   the exclusion of evidence;
       (ii) a stay of proceedings;
       (iii) a court or tribunal finding that any public authority had acted incompatibly with the defendant's rights under the ECHR.

37.   In deciding what material might undermine the prosecution case, the prosecution should pay particular attention to material that has potential to weaken the prosecution case or is inconsistent with it. Examples are:

---

[1] The equivalent legislation in Northern Ireland is section 51A of the Judicature (Northern Ireland) Act 1978 and Article 118 of the Magistrates' Courts (Northern Ireland) Order 1981.

(i)   Any material casting doubt upon the accuracy of any prosecution evidence.

(ii)   Any material which may point to another person, whether charged or not (including a co-accused) having involvement in the commission of the offence.

(iii) Any material which may cast doubt upon the reliability of a confession.

(iv)   Any material that might go to the credibility of a prosecution witness.

(v)   Any material that might support a defence that is either raised by the defence or apparent from the prosecution papers. If the material might undermine the prosecution case it should be disclosed at this stage even though it suggests a defence inconsistent with or alternative to one already advanced by the accused or his solicitor.

(vi)   Any material which may have a bearing on the admissibility of any prosecution evidence.

It should also be borne in mind that while items of material viewed in isolation may not be considered to potentially undermine the prosecution case, several items together can have that effect.

38.   Experience suggests that any item which relates to the defendant's mental or physical health, his intellectual capacity, or to any ill-treatment which the defendant may have suffered when in the investigator's custody is likely to have the potential for casting doubt on the reliability of an accused's purported confession, and prosecutors should pay particular attention to any such item in the possession of the prosecution.

Secondary disclosure

39.   Prosecutors should be open, alert and promptly responsive to requests for disclosure of material supported by the comprehensive defence statement. Conversely, if no defence statement has been served or if the prosecutor considers that the defence statement is lacking specific and/or clarity, a letter should be sent to the defence indicating that secondary disclosure will not take place or will be limited (as appropriate), and inviting the defence to specify and/or clarify the accused's case. The prosecutor should consider raising the issue at a preliminary hearing if the position is not resolved satisfactorily to enable the court to give directions.

40.   Experience suggests that material of the description set out below might reasonably be expected to be disclosed to the defence where it relates to the defence being put forward. Accordingly, following the delivery of a defence statement and on receipt of a request specifically linking the material sought with the defence being put forward, such linked material should be disclosed unless there is good reason not to do so. However, if defences put forward in a defence statement are inconsistent within the meaning of section 11 of the Act, then the preceding guidance set out in this paragraph will not apply. Conversely, if material of the description set out below might undermine the prosecution case, and does not justify an application to the court to withhold disclosure, prosecutors must disclose it at the primary stage. The material is:

(i)   Those recorded scientific or scenes of crime findings retained by the investigator which:
— relate to the defendant; and
— are linked to the point at issue; and
— have not previously been disclosed.

(ii)   where identification is or may be in issue, all previous descriptions of suspects, however recorded, together with all records of identification procedures in respect of the offence(s) and photographs of the accused taken by the investigator around the time of his arrest;

(iii) Information that any prosecution witness has received, has been promised or has requested any payment or reward in connection with the case;

(iv)   Plans of crime scenes or video recordings made by investigators of crime scenes;

(v)   Names, within the knowledge of investigators, of individuals who may have relevant information and whom investigators do not intend to interview;

(vi) Records which the investigator has made of information which may be relevant, provided by any individual (such information would include, but not be limited to, records of conversation and interviews with any such person).

Disclosure of video recordings or scientific findings by means of supplying copies may well involve delay or otherwise not be practicable or desirable, in which case the investigator should make reasonable arrangements for the video, recordings or scientific findings to be viewed by the defence.

Applications for non-disclosure in the public interest

41.   Before making an application to the court to withhold material which would otherwise fall to be disclosed, on the basis that to disclose would not be in the public interest, a prosecutor should aim to disclose as much of the material as he properly can (by giving the defence redacted or edited copies of summaries).

42.   Prior to or at the hearing, the court must be provided with full and accurate information. The prosecution advocate must examine all material which is the subject matter of the application and make any necessary enquiries of the prosecutor and/or investigator. The prosecutor (or representative) and/or investigator should attend such applications.

Summary trial

43.   The prosecutor should, in addition to complying with the obligations under the CPIA, provide to the defence all evidence upon which the Crown proposes to rely in a summary trial. Such provision should allow the accused or their legal advisers sufficient time properly to consider the evidence before it is called. Exceptionally, statements may be withheld for the protection of witnesses or to avoid interference with the course of justice.

Material relevant to sentence

44.   In all cases the prosecutor must consider disclosing in the interests of justice any material which is relevant to sentence (eg. information which might mitigate the seriousness of the offence or assist the accused to lay blame in whole or in part upon a co-accused or another person).

Applicability of these guidelines

45.   These guidelines should be adopted with immediate effect in relation to all cases submitted in future to the prosecuting authorities in receipt of these guidelines. They should also be adopted as regards cases already submitted to which the Act applies, so far as they relate to stages in the proceedings that have not yet been reached.

Crown Court Rules 1982

Evidence through television link where witness is a child or is to be cross-examined after admission of a video recording

23A.—(1) Any party may apply for leave under section 32(1) of the Criminal Justice Act 1988 for evidence to be given through a live television link where—

(a)   the offence charged is one to which section 32(2) applies; and

(b)   the evidence is to be given by a witness who is either—

(i)   in the case of an offence falling within section 32(2)(a) or (b), under the age of 14; or

(ii) in the case of an offence falling within section 32(2)(c), under the age of 17; or

(iii) a person who is to be cross-examined following the admission under section 32A of that Act of a video recording of testimony from him;

and references in this rule to an offence include references to attempting or conspiring to commit, or aiding, abetting, counselling, procuring or inciting the commission of, that offence,

(2) An application under paragraph (1) shall be made by giving notice in writing, which shall be in the form prescribed in Schedule 5 or a form to the like effect.

(3) An application under paragraph (1) shall be made within 28 days after the date of the committal of the defendant, or of the consent to the preferment of a bill of indictment in relation to the case, or of the service of notice of transfer under section 53 of the Criminal Justice Act 1991, or of the service of copies of the documents containing the evidence on which the charge or charges are based under paragraph 1 of Schedule 3 to the Crime and Disorder Act 1998, or of the service of Notice of Appeal from a decision of a youth court or magistrates' court, as the case may be.

(4) The notice under paragraph (2) shall be sent to the appropriate officer of the Crown Court and at the same time a copy thereof shall be sent by the applicant to every other party to the proceedings.

(5) A party who receives a copy of a notice under paragraph (2) and who wishes to oppose the application shall within 14 days notify the applicant and the appropriate officer of the Crown Court, in writing, of his opposition, giving the reasons therefor.

(6) An application under paragraph (1) shall be determined by a judge of the Crown Court without a hearing, unless the judge otherwise directs, and the appropriate officer of the Crown Court shall notify the parties of the time and place of any such hearing.

(7) The appropriate officer of the Crown Court shall notify all the parties and any person who is to accompany the witness (if known) of the decision of the Crown Court in relation to an application under paragraph (1). Where leave is granted, the notification shall state—

(a) where the witness is to give evidence on behalf of the prosecutor, the name of the witness, and, if known, the name, occupation and relationship (if any) to the witness of the person who is to accompany the witness and,

(b) the location of the Crown Court at which the trial should take place.

(8) The period specified in paragraph (3) may be extended, either before or after it expires, on an application made in writing, specifying the grounds of the application and sent to the appropriate officer of the Crown Court, and a copy of the application shall be sent by the applicant to every other party to the proceedings. The appropriate officer of the Crown Court shall notify all the parties of the decision of the Crown Court.

(9) An application for extension of time under paragraph (8) shall be determined by a judge of the Crown Court without a hearing unless the judge otherwise directs.

(10) A witness giving evidence through a television link pursuant to leave granted under paragraph (7) shall be accompanied by a person acceptable to a judge of the Crown Court and, unless the judge otherwise directs, by no other person.

Evidence through television link where witness is outside United Kingdom

23B.—(1) Any party may apply for leave under section 32(1) of the Criminal Justice Act 1988 for evidence to be given through a live television link by a witness who is outside the United Kingdom.

(2) An application under paragraph (1), and any matter relating thereto which, by virtue of the following provisions of this rule, falls to be determined by the Crown Court, may be dealt with in chambers by any Judge of the Crown Court.

(3) An application under paragraph (1) shall be made by giving notice in writing, which shall be in the form prescribed in Schedule 6 or a form to the like effect.

(4) An application under paragraph (1) shall be made within 28 days after the date of the committal of the defendant or, as the case may be, of the giving of a notice of transfer under section 4(1)(c) of the Criminal Justice Act 1987, or of the preferral of a bill of indictment in relation to the case.

(5) The period of 28 days in paragraph (4) may be extended by the Crown Court either before or after it expires, on an application made in writing, specifying the grounds of the application. The appropriate officer of the Crown Court shall notify all the parties of the decision of the Crown Court.

(6) The notice under paragraph (3) or any application under paragraph (5) shall be sent to the appropriate officer of the Crown Court and at the same time a copy thereof shall be sent by the applicant to every other party to the proceedings.

(7) A party who receives a copy of a notice under paragraph (3) shall, within 28 days of the notice, notify the applicant and the appropriate officer of the Crown Court, in writing—
   (a) whether or not he opposes the application, giving his reasons for any such opposition, and
   (b) whether or not he wishes to be represented at any hearing of the application.

(8) After the expiry of the period referred to in paragraph (7), the Crown Court shall determine whether an application under paragraph (1) is to be dealt with—
   (a) without a hearing, or
   (b) at a hearing at which the applicant and such other party or parties as the court may direct may be represented,
and the appropriate officer of the Crown Court shall notify the applicant and, where necessary, the other party or parties, of the time and place of any such hearing.

(9) The appropriate officer of the Crown Court shall notify all the parties of the decision of the Crown Court in relation to an application under paragraph (1) and, where leave is granted, the notification shall state—
   (a) the country in which the witness will give evidence,
   (b) if known, the place where the witness will give evidence,
   (c) where the witness is to give evidence on behalf of the prosecutor, or where disclosure is required by section 11 of the Criminal Justice Act 1967 (alibi) or by rules under section 81 of the Police and Criminal Evidence Act 1984 (expert evidence), the name of the witness,
   (d) the location of the Crown Court at which the trial should take place, and
   (e) any conditions specified by the Crown Court in accordance with paragraph (10).

(10) The Crown Court dealing with an application under paragraph (1) may specify that as a condition of the grant of leave the witness should give the evidence in the presence of a specified person who is able and willing to answer under oath or affirmation any questions the trial judge may put as to the circumstances in which the evidence is given, including questions about any persons who are present when the evidence is given and any matters which may affect the giving of the evidence.

Video recordings of testimony from child witnesses

23C.—(1) Any party may apply for leave under section 32A of the Criminal Justice Act 1988 to tender in evidence a video recording of testimony from a witness where—
   (a) the offence charged is one to which section 32(2) of that Act applies;
   (b) in the case of an offence falling within section 32(2)(a) or (b), the proposed witness is under the age of 14 or, if he was under 14 when the video recording was made, is under the age of 15;
   (c) in the case of an offence falling within section 32(2)(c), the proposed witness is under the age of 17 or, if he was under 17 when the video recording was made, is under the age of 18; and

(d) the video recording is of an interview conducted between an adult and a person coming within sub-paragraph (b) or (c) above (not being the accused or one of the accused) which relates to any matter in issue in the proceedings;

and references in this rule to an offence include references to attempting or conspiring to commit, or aiding, abetting, counselling, procuring or inciting the commission of, that offence.

(2) An application under paragraph (1) shall be made by giving notice in writing, which shall be in the form prescribed in Schedule 7 or a form to the like effect. The application shall be accompanied by the video recording which it is proposed to tender in evidence and shall include the following, namely—

(a) the name of the defendant and the offence or offences charged;

(b) the name and date of birth of the witness in respect of whom the application is made;

(c) the date on which the video recording was made;

(d) a statement that in the opinion of the applicant the witness is willing and able to attend the trial for cross-examination;

(e) a statement of the circumstances in which the video recording was made which complies with paragraph (4) below;

(f) the date on which the video recording was disclosed to the other party or parties.

(3) Where it is proposed to tender part only of a video recording of an interview with the witness, an application under paragraph (1) must specify that part and be accompanied by a video recording of the entire interview, including those parts which it is not proposed to tender in evidence, and by a statement of the circumstances in which the video recording of the entire interview was made which complies with paragraph (4) below.

(4) The statement of the circumstances in which the video recording was made referred to in paragraph (2)(e) and (3) above shall include the following information, except in so far as it is contained in the recording itself, namely—

(a) the times at which the recording commenced and finished, including details of any interruptions;

(b) the location at which the recording was made and the usual function of the premises;

(c) the name, age and occupation of any person present at any point during the recording; the time for which he was present; his relationship (if any) to the witness and to the defendant;

(d) a description of the equipment used including the number of cameras used and whether they were fixed or mobile; the number and location of microphones; the video format used and whether there were single or multiple recording facilities;

(e) the location of the mastertape if the video recording is a copy and details of when and by whom the copy was made.

(5) An application under paragraph (1) shall be made within 28 days after the date of the committal for trial of the defendant, or of the giving of a notice of transfer under section 53 of the Criminal Justice Act 1991, or of consent to the preferment of a bill of indictment in relation to the case, or of the service of Notice of Appeal from a decision of a youth court or magistrates' court, as the case may be.

(6) The period of 28 days in paragraph (5) may be extended by a judge of the Crown Court, either before or after it expires, on an application made in writing, specifying the grounds of the application. The appropriate officer of the Crown Court shall notify all the parties of the decision of the Crown Court.

(7) The notice under paragraph (2) or (6) shall be sent to the appropriate officer of the Crown Court and at the same time, copies thereof shall be sent by the applicant to every other party to the proceedings. Copies of any video recording required by paragraph (2) or (3) to accompany the notice shall at the same time be sent to the court and to any other party who

has not already been served with a copy or in the case of a defendant acting in person, shall be made available for viewing by him.

(8) A party who receives a copy of a notice under paragraph (2) shall, within 14 days of service of the notice, notify the applicant and the appropriate officer of the Crown Court, in writing—

(a) whether he objects to the admission of any part of the video recording or recordings disclosed, giving his reasons why it would not be in the interests of justice for it to be admitted; and

(b) whether he would agree to the admission of part of the video recording or recordings disclosed and if so, which part or parts; and

(c) whether he wishes to be represented at any hearing of the application.

(9) After the expiry of the period referred to in paragraph (8), a judge of the Crown Court shall determine whether an application under paragraph (1) is to be dealt with—

(a) without a hearing; or

(b) where any party notifies the appropriate officer of the Crown Court pursuant to paragraph (8) that he objects to the admission of any part of the video recording and that he wishes to be represented at any hearing, or in any other case where the judge so directs, at a hearing at which the applicant and such other party or parties as the judge may direct may be represented,

and the appropriate officer of the Crown Court shall notify the applicant and, where necessary, the other party or parties, of the time and place of any such hearing.

(10) The appropriate officer of the Crown Court shall within 3 days of the decision of the Crown Court in relation to an application under paragraph (1) being made, notify all the parties of it in the Form prescribed in Schedule 8 or a form to the like effect, and, where leave is granted, the notification shall state whether the whole or specified parts only of the video recording or recordings disclosed are to be admitted in evidence.

Procedure for applications in proceedings for sexual offences

23D.—(1) An application for leave under section 41(2) of the 1999 Act must be made in writing to the appropriate officer of the Crown Court and must either—

(a) be received by that officer within 28 days of—

(i)   the committal of the defendant, or

(ii) the consent to the preferment of a bill of indictment in relation to the case, or

(iii) the service of notice of transfer under section 53 of the Criminal Justice Act 1991, or

(iv) where a person is sent for trial under section 51 of the Crime and Disorder Act 1998, the service of copies of the documents containing the evidence on which the charge or charges are based under paragraph 1 of Schedule 3 to that Act, or within such period as the Court may in any particular case determine, or

(b) be accompanied by a full written explanation specifying the reasons why the application could not have been made within the 28 days mentioned above.

(2) Such an application must contain the following—

(a) a summary of the evidence it is proposed to adduce and of the questions it is proposed to put to any witness;

(b) a full explanation of the reasons why it is considered that the evidence and questions fall within section 41(3) or (5) of the 1999 Act;

(c) a summary of any document or other evidence to be submitted in support of such evidence and questions;

(d) where it is proposed that a witness at the trial give evidence as to the complainant's sexual behaviour, the name and date of birth of any such witness.

(3) A copy of the application must be sent to all the parties to the proceedings at the same time as it is sent to the appropriate officer of the Crown Court.

(4) Where a copy of the application is received by the prosecutor more than 14 days before the date set for the trial to begin, the prosecutor must, within 14 days of the receipt of the application, notify the other parties to the proceedings and the appropriate officer of the Crown Court in writing whether or not—

(a) he opposes the application, giving reasons for any such opposition, and

(b) he wishes to be represented at any hearing of the application.

(5) Where a copy of the application is received by a party to the proceedings other than the prosecutor more than 14 days before the date set for the trial to begin, that party may make observations in writing on the application to the appropriate officer of the Court, but any such observations must be made within 14 days of the receipt of the application and be copied to the other parties to the proceedings.

(6) In considering any application under this rule, the Court may request a party to the proceedings to provide the Court with such information as it may specify and which the Court considers would assist it in determining the application.

(7) Where the Court makes such a request, the person required to provide the information must do so within 14 days of the Court making the request or by such time as the Court considers appropriate in the circumstances of the case.

(8) An application under paragraph (1) must be determined by a judge of the Crown Court following a hearing if—

(a) the prosecutor has notified the approprite officer that he opposes the application; or

(b) the copy of the application was received by any of the parties to the proceedings less than 14 days before the date set for the trial to begin.

(9) An application under paragraph (1) must be determined by a judge of the Crown Court following a hearing in any case where he considers such a hearing is appropriate in the circumstances of the particular case.

(10) The date and time of the hearing must be—

(a) determined by the Crown Court or the appropriate officer of the Court after taking into consideration—

(i)   any time which a party to the proceedings has been given to respond to a request for information; and

(ii) the date fixed for any other hearing relevant to the proceedings; and

(b) notified by the appropriate officer of the Crown Court to all the parties to the proceedings.

(11) Except where paragraph (8) or (9) applies, an application under paragraph (1) must be determined by a judge of the Crown Court without a hearing.

(12) The appropriate officer of the Crown Court must, as soon as possible after the determination of an application made in accordance with paragraph (1), give notice of the decision and the reasons for it to all the parties to the proceedings.

(13) An application under section 41(2) of the 1999 Act may be made orally where the application is made after the trial has begun.

(14) The person making the application under paragraph (13) must—

(a) give reasons why the applicant failed to make the application in writing in accordance with paragraph (1); and

(b) provide the Court with the information set out in paragraph (2)(a) to (d).

(15) In this rule, 'the 1999 Act' means the Youth Justice and Criminal Evidence Act 1999.

Restrictions on cross-examination of witness

24B.—(1) This rule and rules 24C and 24D apply where an accused is prevented from cross-examining a witness in person by virtue of section 34 or 35 of the 1999 Act.

(2) The Court shall explain to the accused as early in the proceedings as is reasonably practicable that he—

(a) is prevented from cross-examining a witness in person; and

(b) should arrange for a legal representative to act for him for the purpose of cross-examining the witness.

(3) The accused shall notify the appropriate officer of the Court within 7 days of the Court giving its explanation, or within such other period as the Court may in any particular case allow, of the action, if any, he has taken.

(4) Where he has arranged for a legal representative to act for him, the notification shall include details of the name and address of the representative.

(5) The notification shall be in writing.

(6) The appropriate officer of the Court shall notify all other parties to the proceedings of the name and address of the person, if any, appointed to act for the accused.

(7) Where the Court gives its explanation under paragraph (2) to the accused either within 7 days of the day set for the commencement of any hearing at which a witness in respect of whom a prohibition under section 34 or 35 of the 1999 Act applies may be cross-examined or after such a hearing has commenced, the period of 7 days shall be reduced in accordance with any directions issued by the Court.

(8) Where at the end of the period of 7 days or such other period as the Court has allowed, the Court has received no notification from the accused it may grant the accused an extension of time, whether on its own motion or on the application of the accused.

(9) Before granting an extension of time, the Court may hold a hearing at which all parties to the proceedings may attend and be heard.

(10) Any extension of time shall be of such period as the Court considers appropriate in the circumstances of the case.

(11) The decision of the Court as to whether to grant the accused an extension of time shall be notified to all parties to the proceedings by the appropriate officer of the Court.

Appointment by the Court

24C.—(1) Where the Court decides, in accordance with section 38(4) of the 1999 Act, to appoint a qualified legal representative, the appropriate officer of the Court shall notify all parties to the proceedings of the name and address of the representative.

(2) An appointment made by the Court under section 38(4) of the 1999 Act shall, except to such extent as the Court may in any particular case determine, terminate at the conclusion of the cross-examination of the witness or witnesses in respect of whom a prohibition under section 34 or 35 of the 1999 Act applies.

Appointment arranged by the accused

24D.—(1) The accused may arrange for the qualified legal representative, appointed by the Court under section 38(4) of the 1999 Act, to be appointed to act for him for the purpose of cross-examining any witness in respect of whom a prohibition under section 34 or 35 of the 1999 Act applies.

(2) Where such an appointment is made—

(a) both the accused and the qualified legal representative appointed shall notify the Court of the appointment; and

(b) the qualified legal representative shall, from the time of his appointment, act for the accused as though the arrangement had been made under section 38(2)(a) of the 1999 Act and shall cease to be the representative of the Court under section 38(4) of that Act.

(3) Where the Court receives notification of the appointment either from the qualified legal representative or from the accused but not from both, the Court shall investigate

whether the appointment has been made, and if it concludes that the appointment has not been made, paragraph (2)(b) shall not apply.

(4) An accused may, notwithstanding an appointment by the Court under section 38(4) of the 1999 Act, arrange for a legal representative to act for him for the purpose of cross-examining any witness in respect of whom a prohibition under section 34 or 35 applies.

(5) Where the accused arranges for, or informs the Court of his intention to arrange for, a legal representative to act for him, he shall notify the Court, within such period as the Court may allow, of the name and address of any person appointed to act for him.

(6) Where the Court is notified within the time allowed that such an appointment has been made, any qualified legal representative appointed by the Court in accordance with section 38(4) of the 1999 Act shall be discharged.

(7) The appropriate officer of the Court shall, as soon as reasonably practicable after the Court receives notification of an appointment under this rule or, where paragraph (3) applies, after the Court is satisfied that the appointment has been made, notify all the parties to the proceedings—

(a) that the appointment has been made;
(b) where paragraph (4) applies, of the name and address of the person appointed; and
(c) that the person appointed by the Crown Court under section 38(4) of the 1999 Act has been discharged or has ceased to act for the Court.

(8) In rule 24B, 24C and this rule, 'the 1999 Act' means the Youth Justice and Criminal Evidence Act 1999.

Crown Court (Special Measures Directions and Directions Prohibiting Cross-Examination) Rules 2002
2002 No. 1688 (L. 5)

PART I   GENERAL

Citation, commencement and interpretation

1.—(1) These Rules may be cited as the Crown Court (Special Measures Directions and Directions Prohibiting Cross-examination) Rules 2002 and shall come into force on 24th July 2002.

(2) In these Rules—

'the Act' means the Youth Justice and Criminal Evidence Act 1999;

'the Rules' means the Crown Court Rules 1982.

PART II   SPECIAL MEASURES DIRECTIONS

Application for special measures direction

2.—(1) An application by a party in any criminal proceedings for the court to give a special measures direction under section 19 of the Act must be made in writing in the form prescribed in the Schedule to these Rules or a form to the like effect.

(2) If the application is for a special measures direction—

(a) enabling a witness to give evidence by means of a live link, the information sought in Part B of the form prescribed in the Schedule to these Rules must be provided;
(b) enabling a video recording of an interview of a witness to be admitted as evidence in chief of the witness, the information sought in Part C of that form must be provided.

(3) The application under paragraph (1) above must be sent to the appropriate officer of the Crown Court and at the same time a copy thereof must be sent by the applicant to every other party to the proceedings.

(4) The application must be received by the appropriate officer within 28 days of—

    (a) the committal of the defendant; or

    (b) the consent to the preferment of a bill of indictment in relation to the case; or

    (c) the service of a notice of transfer under section 53 of the Criminal Justice Act 1991; or

    (d) where a person is sent for trial under section 51 of the Crime and Disorder Act 1998, the service of copies of the documents containing the evidence on which the charge or charges are based under paragraph 1 of Schedule 3 to that Act; or

    (e) the service of a Notice of Appeal from a decision of a youth court or a magistrates' court.

(5) A party to whom an application is sent in accordance with paragraph (3) above may oppose the application for a special measures direction in respect of any, or any particular, measure available in relation to the witness, whether or not the question whether the witness is eligible for assistance by virtue of section 16 or 17 of the Act is in issue.

(6) A party who wishes to oppose the application must, within 14 days of the date the application was served on him, notify the applicant and the appropriate officer of the Crown Court in writing of his opposition and give reasons for it.

(7) In order to comply with paragraph (6) above—

    (a) a party must in the written notification state whether he—

        (i) disputes that the witness is eligible for assistance by virtue of section 16 or 17 of the Act;

        (ii) disputes that any of the special measures available would be likely to improve the quality of evidence given by the witness or that such measures (or a combination of them) would be likely to maximise the quality of that evidence; and

        (iii) opposes the granting of a special measures direction; and

    (b) where the application relates to the admission of a video recording, a party who receives a recording must provide the information required by rule 8(5) below.

(8) Except where notice is received in accordance with paragraph (6) above, the court may—

    (a) determine the application in favour of the applicant without a hearing; or

    (b) direct a hearing.

(9) Where a party to the proceedings notifies the appropriate officer of the Crown Court in accordance with paragraph (6) above of his opposition to the application, the court must direct a hearing of the application.

(10) Where a hearing of the application is to take place in accordance with paragraph (8) or (9) above, the appropriate officer of the Crown Court shall notify each party to the proceedings of the time and place of the hearing.

(11) A party notified in accordance with paragraph (10) above may be present at the hearing and be heard.

(12) The appropriate officer of the Crown Court must, within 3 days of the decision of the Crown Court in relation to an application under paragraph (1) above being made, notify all the parties of the decision, and if the application was made for a direction enabling a video recording of an interview of a witness to be admitted as evidence in chief of that witness, the notification must state whether the whole or specified parts only of the video recording or recordings disclosed are to be admitted in evidence.

Application for an extension of time

3.—(1) An application may be made in writing for the period of 28 days specified in rule 2(4) above to be extended.

(2) The application may be made either before or after that period has expired.

(3) The application must be accompanied by a statement setting out the reasons why the applicant is or was unable to make the application within that period and a copy of the application and the statement must be sent to every other party to the proceedings.

(4) An application for an extension of time under this rule shall be determined by a judge of the Crown Court without a hearing unless the judge otherwise directs.

(5) The appropriate officer of the Crown Court shall notify all the parties of the judge's decision.

Late applications

4.—(1) Notwithstanding the requirements of rule 2 above—

  (a) an application may be made for a special measures direction orally at the trial; or
  (b) the court may of its own motion raise the issue whether a special measures direction should be given.

(2) Where an application is made in accordance with rule 4(1)(a) above—

  (a) the applicant must state the reasons for the late application; and
  (b) the court must be satisfied that the applicant was unable to make the application in accordance with rule 2 above.

(3) The court shall determine before making a special measures direction—

  (a) whether to allow other parties to the proceedings to make representations on the question;
  (b) the time allowed for making such representations (if any); and
  (c) whether the question should be determined following a hearing at which the parties to the proceedings may be heard.

Discharge or variation of a special measures direction

5.—(1) An application to the court to discharge or vary a special measures direction under section 20(2) of the Act must be in writing and each material change of circumstances which the applicant alleges has occurred since the direction was made must be set out.

(2) An application under paragraph (1) above must be sent to the appropriate officer of the Crown Court as soon as reasonably practicable after the change of circumstances occurs.

(3) The applicant must also send copies of the application to each party to the proceedings at the same time as the application is sent to the appropriate officer.

(4) A party to whom an application is sent in accordance with paragraph (3) above may oppose the application on the ground that it discloses no material change of circumstances.

(5) Rule 2(6) to (12) above shall apply to an application to discharge or vary a special measures direction as it applies to an application for a direction.

Renewal application following a material change of circumstances

6.—(1) Where an application for a special measures direction has been refused by the court, the application may only be renewed ("renewal application") where there has been a material change of circumstances since the court refused the application.

(2) The applicant must—

  (a) identify in the renewal application each material change of circumstances which is alleged to have occurred; and
  (b) send the renewal application to the appropriate officer of the Crown Court as soon as reasonably practicable after the change occurs.

(3) The applicant must also send copies of the renewal application to each of the parties to the proceedings at the same time as the application is sent to the appropriate officer.

(4) A party to whom the renewal application is sent in accordance with paragraph (3) above may oppose the application on the ground that it discloses no material change of circumstances.

(5) Rule 2(6) to (12) above and rules 7 and 8 below apply to a renewal application as they apply to the application which was refused.

Application for special measures direction for witness to give evidence by means of a live television link

7.—(1) Where the application for a special measures direction is made, in accordance with rule 2(2)(a) above, for a witness to give evidence by means of a live link, the following provisions of this rule shall also apply.

(2) A party who seeks to oppose an application for a child witness to give evidence by means of a live link must, in order to comply with rule 2(5) above, state why in his view the giving of a special measures direction would not be likely to maximise the quality of the witness's evidence.

(3) However, paragraph (2) above does not apply in relation to a child witness in need of special protection within the meaning of section 21(1)(b) of the Act.

(4) Where a special measures direction is made enabling a witness to give evidence by means of a live link, the witness shall be accompanied at the live link only by persons acceptable to a judge of the Crown Court.

Video recording of testimony from witnesses

8.—(1) Where an application is made for a special measures direction enabling a video recording of an interview of a witness to be admitted as evidence in chief of the witness, the following provisions of this rule shall also apply.

(2) The application made in accordance with rule 2(1) above must be accompanied by the video recording which it is proposed to tender in evidence and must include—

(a) the name of the defendant and the offence to be charged;

(b) the name and date of birth of the witness in respect of whom the application is made;

(c) the date on which the video recording was made;

(d) a statement as to whether, and if so at what point in the video recording, an oath was administered to, or a solemn declaration made by, the witness;

(e) a statement that, in the opinion of the applicant, either—
   (i) the witness is available for cross-examination; or
   (ii) the witness is not available for cross-examination and the parties have agreed that there is no need for the witness to be so available;

(f) a statement of the circumstances in which the video recording was made which complies with paragraph (4) below; and

(g) the date on which the video recording was disclosed to the other party or parties.

(3) Where it is proposed to tender part only of a video recording of an interview with the witness, the application must specify that part and be accompanied by a video recording of the entire interview, including those parts which it is not proposed to tender in evidence, and by a statement of the circumstances in which the video recording of the entire interview was made which complies with paragraph (4) below.

(4) The statement of the circumstances in which the video recording was made referred to in paragraphs (2)(f) and (3) above shall include the following information, except in so far as it is contained in the recording itself,—

(a) the times at which the recording commenced and finished, including details of interruptions;

(b) the location at which the recording was made and the usual function of the premises;

(c) in relation to each person present at any point during, or immediately before, the recording—
    (i)   their name, age and occupation;
    (ii) the time for which each person was present; and
    (iii) the relationship, if any, of each person to the witness and to the defendant;
(d) in relation to the equipment used for the recording—
    (i)   a description of the equipment;
    (ii) the number of cameras used;
    (iii) whether the cameras were fixed or mobile;
    (iv) the number and location of the microphones;
    (v)   the video format used; and
    (vi) whether it offered single or multiple recording facilities and, if so, which were used; and
(e) the location of the mastertape if the video recording is a copy and details of when and by whom the copy was made.

(5) A party who receives a recording under paragraph (2) above must within 14 days of its receipt, notify the applicant and the appropriate officer of the Crown Court, in writing—

(a) whether he objects to the admission under section 27 of the Act of any part of the video recording or recordings disclosed, giving his reasons why it would not be in the interests of justice for the recording or any part of it to be admitted;
(b) whether he would agree to the admission of part of the video recording or recordings and if so, which part or parts; and
(c) whether he wishes to be represented at any hearing of the application.

(6) Notwithstanding the provisions of rule 2 and this rule, any video recording which the accused proposes to tender in evidence need not be sent to the prosecution until the close of the prosecution case at the trial.

(7) The court may determine an application by the accused to tender in evidence a video recording even though the recording has not, in accordance with paragraph (6) above, been served upon the prosecution.

(8) Where a video recording which is the subject of a special measures direction is sent to the prosecution after the direction has been made, the prosecutor may apply to the court for the direction to be varied or discharged.

(9) An application under paragraph (8) above may be made orally to the court.

(10) A prosecutor who makes an application under paragraph (8) above must state—

(a) why he objects to the admission under section 27 of the Act of any part of the video recording or recordings disclosed, giving his reasons why it would not be in the interests of justice for the recording or any part of it to be admitted; and
(b) whether he would agree to the admission of part of the video recording or recordings and if so, which part or parts.

(11) The court must, before determining the application,—

(a) direct a hearing of the application; and
(b) allow all the parties to the proceedings to be present and be heard on the application.

(12) The appropriate officer of the Crown Court must notify all parties to the proceedings of the decision of the court as soon as may be reasonable after the decision is given.

(13) Any decision varying a special measures direction must state whether the whole or specified parts of the video recording or recordings subject to the application are to be admitted in evidence.

Expert evidence

9. Any party to the proceedings who proposes to adduce expert evidence (whether of fact or opinion) in connection with an application or renewal application for, or for varying

or discharging, a special measures direction must, not less than 14 days before the date set for the trial to begin—

> (a) furnish the other party or parties to those proceedings with a statement in writing of any finding or opinion which he proposes to adduce by way of such evidence; and
>
> (b) where a request is made to him in that behalf by any other party to those proceedings, provide that party also with a copy of (or if it appears to the party proposing to adduce the evidence to be more practicable, a reasonable opportunity to examine) the record of any observation, test, calculation or other procedure on which such finding or opinion is based and any document or other thing or substance in respect of which any such procedure has been carried out.

PART III   DIRECTIONS PROHIBITING CROSS-EXAMINATION

Amendment of the Crown Court Rules

10.—(1) After rule 24D of the Rules[6], there shall be inserted the following rule—

'Prohibition on cross-examination of particular witness

24E.—(1) An application by the prosecutor for the court to give a direction under section 36 of the 1999 Act in relation to any witness must be sent to the appropriate officer of the Crown Court and at the same time a copy thereof must be sent by the applicant to every other party to the proceedings.

(2) In his application the prosecutor must state why, in his opinion—

> (a) the evidence given by the witness is likely to be diminished if cross-examination is undertaken by the accused in person;
>
> (b) the evidence would be improved if a direction were given under section 36(2) of the 1999 Act; and
>
> (c) it would not be contrary to the interests of justice to give such a direction.

(3) On receipt of the application the appropriate officer of the Crown Court must refer it—

> (a) if the trial has started, to the trial judge;
>
> (b) if the trial has not started when the application is received—
>
>> (i) to the judge who has been designated to conduct the trial; or
>>
>> (ii) if no judge has been designated for that purpose, to such judge who may be designated for the purposes of hearing that application.

(4) Where a copy of the application is received by a party to the proceedings more than 14 days before the date set for the trial to begin, that party may make observations in writing on the application to the appropriate officer of the Crown Court, but any such observations must be made within 14 days of the receipt of the application and be copied to the other parties to the proceedings.

(5) A party to whom an application is sent in accordance with paragraph (1) above who wishes to oppose the application must give his reasons for doing so to the appropriate officer of the Crown Court and the other parties to the proceedings.

(6) Those reasons must be notified—

> (a) within 14 days of the date the application was served on him, if that date is more than 14 days before the date set for the trial to begin;
>
> (b) if the trial has begun, in accordance with any directions issued by the trial judge; or
>
> (c) if neither sub-paragraph (a) nor sub-paragraph (b) apply, before the date set for the trial to begin.

(7) Where the application made in accordance with (1) above is made before the date set for the trial to begin and—

    (a) is not contested by any party to the proceedings, the court may determine the application without a hearing;

    (b) is contested by a party to the proceedings, the court must direct a hearing of the application.

(8) Where the application is made after the trial has begun—

    (a) the application may be made orally; and

    (b) the trial judge may give such directions as he considers appropriate to deal with the application.

(9) Where a hearing of the application is to take place, the appropriate officer of the Crown Court shall notify each party to the proceedings of the time and place of the hearing.

(10) A party notified in accordance with paragraph (9) above may be present at the hearing and be heard.

(11) The appropriate officer of the Crown Court must, as soon as possible after the determination of an application made in accordance with paragraph (1) above, give notice of the decision and the reasons for it to all the parties to the proceedings.

(12) A person making an oral application under paragraph (8)(a) above must—

    (a) give reasons why the application was not made before the trial commenced; and

    (b) provide the court with the information set out in paragraph (2) above.'

(2) In each of the provisions set out in paragraph (3) below, for 'section 34 or 35' substitute 'section 34, 35 or 36'.

(3) Those provisions are—

    (a) rule 24B(1);

    (b) rule 24B(7);

    (c) rule 24C(2);

    (d) rule 24D(1);and

    (e) rule 24D(4).

(4) In rule 24D(8) after '24C' insert ',24E'.

PART C

European Convention on Human Rights

Convention for the Protection of Human Rights and Fundamental Freedoms
(Rome, 4.11.1950)[1]

The governments signatory hereto, being members of the Council of Europe,

Considering the Universal Declaration of Human Rights proclaimed by the General Assembly of the United Nations on 10th December 1948;

Considering that this declaration aims at securing the universal and effective recognition and observance of the rights therein declared;

Considering that the aim of the Council of Europe is the achievement of greater unity between its members and that one of the methods by which that aim is to be pursued is the maintenance and further realisation of human rights and fundamental freedoms;

Reaffirming their profound belief in those fundamental freedoms which are the foundation of justice and peace in the world and are best maintained on the one hand by an effective political democracy and on the other by a common understanding and observance of the human rights upon which they depend;

Being resolved, as the governments of European countries which are like-minded and have a common heritage of political traditions, ideals, freedom and the rule of law, to take the first steps for the collective enforcement of certain of the rights stated in the Universal Declaration,

Have agreed as follows:

Article 1
The High Contracting Parties shall secure to everyone within their jurisdiction the rights and freedoms defined in Section 1 of this Convention.

SECTION I

Article 2
1. Everyone's right to life shall be protected by law. No one shall be deprived of his life intentionally save in the execution of a sentence of a court following his conviction of a crime for which this penalty is provided by law.

2. Deprivation of life shall not be regarded as inflicted in contravention of this article when it results from the use of force which is no more than absolutely necessary:

---

[1] European Treaty Series, No. 5. Text amended according to the provisions of Protocol No. 3 (ETS No. 45), which entered into force on 21 September 1970, of Protocol No. 5 (ETS No. 55), which entered into force on 20 December 1971, and of Protocol No. 8 (ETS No. 118), which entered into force on 1 January 1990, and comprising also the text of Protocol No. 2 (ETS No. 44) which, in accordance with Article 5, paragraph 3, therefor, has been an integral part of the Convention since its entry into force on 21 September 1970.

(a) in defence of any person from unlawful violence;
(b) in order to effect a lawful arrest or to prevent the escape of a person lawfully detained;
(c) in action lawfully taken for the purpose of quelling a riot or insurrection.

Article 3
No one shall be subjected to torture or to inhuman or degrading treatment or punishment.

Article 4
1. No one shall be held in slavery or servitude.
2. No one shall be required to perform forced or compulsory labour.
3. For the purpose of this article the term 'forced or compulsory labour' shall not include:
   (a) any work required to be done in the ordinary course of detention imposed according to the provisions of Article 5 of this Convention or during conditional release from such detention;
   (b) any service of a military character or, in case of conscientious objectors in countries where they are recognised, service exacted instead of compulsory military service;
   (c) any service exacted in case of an emergency or calamity threatening the life or well-being of the community;
   (d) any work or service which forms part of normal civic obligations.

Article 5
1. Everyone has the right to liberty and security of person. No one shall be deprived of his liberty save in the following cases and in accordance with a procedure prescribed by law:
   (a) the lawful detention of a person after conviction by a competent court;
   (b) the lawful arrest or detention of a person for non-compliance with the lawful order of a court or in order to secure the fulfilment of any obligation prescribed by law;
   (c) the lawful arrest or detention of a person effected for the purpose of bringing him before the competent legal authority on reasonable suspicion of having committed an offence or when it is reasonably considered necessary to prevent his committing an offence or fleeing after having done so;
   (d) the detention of a minor by lawful order for the purpose of educational supervision or his lawful detention for the purpose of bringing him before the competent legal authority;
   (e) the lawful detention of persons for the prevention of the spreading of infectious diseases, of persons of unsound mind, alcoholics or drug addicts or vagrants;
   (f) the lawful arrest or detention of a person to prevent his effecting an unauthorised entry into the country or of a person against whom action is being taken with a view to deportation or extradition.
2. Everyone who is arrested shall be informed promptly, in a language which he understands, of the reasons for his arrest and of any charge against him.
3. Everyone arrested or detained in accordance with the provisions of paragraph 1(c) of this article shall be brought promptly before a judge or other officer authorised by law to exercise judicial power and shall be entitled to trial within a reasonable time or to release pending trial. Release may be conditioned by guarantees to appear for trial.
4. Everyone who is deprived of his liberty by arrest or detention shall be entitled to take proceedings by which the lawfulness of his detention shall be decided speedily by a court and his release ordered if the detention is not lawful.
5. Everyone who has been the victim of arrest or detention in contravention of the provisions of this article shall have an enforceable right to compensation.

Article 6

1.   In the determination of his civil rights and obligations or of any criminal charge against him, everyone is entitled to a fair and public hearing within a reasonable time by an independent and impartial tribunal established by law. Judgment shall be pronounced publicly but the press and public may be excluded from all or part of the trial in the interests of morals, public order or national security in a democratic society, where the interests of juveniles or the protection of the private life of the parties so require, or to the extent strictly necessary in the opinion of the court in special circumstances where publicity would prejudice the interests of justice.

2.   Everyone charged with a criminal offence shall be presumed innocent until proved guilty according to law.

3.   Everyone charged with a criminal offence has the following minimum rights;

(a) to be informed promptly, in a language which he understands and in detail, of the nature and cause of the accusation against him;

(b) to have adequate time and facilities for the preparation of his defence;

(c) to defend himself in person or through legal assistance of his own choosing or, if he has not sufficient means to pay for legal assistance, to be given it free when the interests of justice so require;

(d) to examine or have examined witnesses against him and to obtain the attendance and examination of witnesses on his behalf under the same conditions as witnesses against him;

(e) to have the free assistance of an interpreter if he cannot understand or speak the language used in court.

Article 7

1.   No one shall be held guilty of any criminal offence on account of any act or omission which did not constitute a criminal offence under national or international law at the time when it was committed. Nor shall a heavier penalty be imposed than the one that was applicable at the time the criminal offence was committed.

2.   This article shall not prejudice the trial and punishment of any person for any act or omission which, at the time when it was committed, was criminal according to the general principles of law recognised by civilised nations.

Article 8

1.   Everyone has the right to respect for his private and family life, his home and his correspondence.

2.   There shall be no interference by a public authority with the exercise of this right except such as is in accordance with the law and is necessary in a democratic society in the interests of national security, public safety or the economic well-being of the country, for the prevention of disorder or crime, for the protection of health or morals, or for the protection of the rights and freedoms of others.

Article 9

1.   Everyone has the right to freedom of thought, conscience and religion; this right includes freedom to change his religion or belief and freedom, either alone or in community with others and in public or private, to manifest his religion or belief, in worship, teaching, practice and observance.

2.   Freedom to manifest one's religion or beliefs shall be subject only to such limitations as are prescribed by law and are necessary in a democratic society in the interests of public safety, for the protection of public order, health or morals, or for the protection of the rights and freedoms of others.

Article 10

1.   Everyone has the right to freedom of expression. This right shall include freedom to hold opinions and to receive and impart information and ideas without interference by public authority and regardless of frontiers. This article shall not prevent States from requiring the licensing of broadcasting, television or cinema enterprises.

2.   The exercise of these freedoms, since it carries with it duties and responsibilities, may be subject to such formalities, conditions, restrictions or penalties as are prescribed by law and are necessary in a democratic society, in the interests of national security, territorial integrity or public safety, for the prevention of disorder or crime, for the protection of health or morals, for the protection of the reputation of rights of others, for preventing the disclosure of information received in confidence, or for maintaining the authority and impartiality of the judiciary.

Article 11

1.   Everyone has the right to freedom of peaceful assembly and to freedom of association with others, including the right to form and to join trade unions for the protection of his interests.

2.   No restrictions shall be placed on the exercise of these rights other than such as are prescribed by law and are necessary in a democratic society in the interests of national security or public safety, for the prevention of disorder or crime, for the protection of health or morals or for the protection of the rights and freedoms of others. This article shall not prevent the imposition of lawful restrictions on the exercise of these rights by members of the armed forces, of the police or of the administration of the state.

Article 12

Men and women of marriageable age have the right to marry and to found a family, according to the national laws governing the exercise of this right.

Article 13

Everyone whose rights and freedoms as set forth in this Convention are violated shall have an effective remedy before a national authority notwithstanding that the violation has been committed by persons acting in an official capacity.

Article 14

The employment of the rights and freedoms set forth in this Convention shall be secured without discrimination on any ground such as sex, race, colour, language, religion, political or other opinion, national or social origin, association with a national minority, property, birth or other status.

Article 15

1.   In time of war or other public emergency threatening the life of the nation any High Contracting Party may take measures derogating from its obligations under this Convention to the extent strictly required by the exigencies of the situation, provided that such measures are not inconsistent with its other obligations under international law.

2.   No derogation from Article 2, except in respect of deaths resulting from lawful acts of war, or from Articles 3, 4 (paragraph 1) and 7 shall be made under this provision.

3.   Any High Contracting Party availing itself of this right of derogation shall keep the Secretary General of the Council of Europe fully informed of the measures which it has taken and the reasons therefor. It shall also inform the Secretary General of the Council of Europe when such measures have ceased to operate and the provisions of the Convention are again being fully executed.

Article 16
Nothing in Articles 10, 11 and 14 shall be regarded as preventing the High Contracting Parties from imposing restrictions on the political activity of aliens.

Article 17
Nothing in this Convention may be interpreted as implying for any State, group or person any right to engage in any activity or perform any act aimed at the destruction of any of the rights and freedoms set forth herein or at their limitation to a greater extent than is provided for in the Convention.

Article 18
The restrictions permitted under this Convention to the said rights and freedoms shall not be applied for any purpose other than those for which they have been prescribed.

PART D

Civil Statutes

Police (Property) Act 1897
(1897, c.30)

1. (1) Where any property has come into the possession of the police in connexion with their investigation of a suspected offence a court of summary jurisdiction may, on application, either by an officer of police or by a claimant of the property, make an order for the delivery of the property to the person appearing to the magistrate or court to be the owner thereof, or, if the owner cannot be ascertained, make such order with respect to the property as to the magistrate or court may seem meet.

(2) An order under this section shall not affect the right of any person to take within six months from the date of the order legal proceedings against any person in possession of property delivered by virtue of the order for the recovery of the property, but on the expiration of those six months the right shall cease.

2. (1) A Secretary of State may make regulations (limited by subsection (2)) for the disposal of property which has come into the possession of the police under the circumstances mentioned in this Act in cases where the owner of the property has not been ascertained and no order of a competent court has been made with respect thereto.

(2)—(2B) Regulations.

(3) Where property is a perishable article or its custody involves unreasonable expense or inconvenience, it may be sold at any time, but the proceeds of sale shall not be disposed of until they have remained in the possession of the police for a year. In any other case the property shall not be sold until it has remained in the possession of the police for a year.

(4) Regulations may be made by the Secretary of State as to the investment of money and audit of accounts.

Civil Evidence Act 1968
(1968, c. 64)

PART II   MISCELLANEOUS AND GENERAL

Convictions, etc. as evidence in civil proceedings

11   Convictions as evidence in civil proceedings

(1) In any civil proceedings the fact that a person has been convicted of an offence by or before any court in the United Kingdom or by a court-martial there or elsewhere shall (subject to subsection (3) below) be admissible in evidence for the purpose of proving, where to do so is relevant to any issue in those proceedings, that he committed that offence, whether he was so convicted upon a plea of guilry or otherwise and whether or not he is a party to the civil

proceedings; but no conviction other than a subsisting one shall be admissible in evidence by virtue of this section.

(2) In any civil proceedings in which by virtue of this section a person is proved to have been convicted of an offence by or before any court in the United Kingdom or by a court-martial there or elsewhere—

(a) he shall be taken to have committed that offence unless the contrary is proved; and

(b) without prejudice to the reception of any other admissible evidence for the purpose of identifying the facts on which the conviction was based, the contents of any document which is admissible as evidence of the conviction, and the contents of the information, complaint, indictment or charge-sheet on which the person in question was convicted, shall be admissible in evidence for that purpose.

(3) Nothing in this section shall prejudice the operation of section 13 of this Act or any other enactment whereby a conviction or a finding of fact in any criminal proceedings is for the purposes of any other proceedings made conclusive evidence of any fact.

(4) Where in any civil proceedings the contents of any document are admissible in evidence by virtue of subsection (2) above, a copy of that document, or of the material part thereof, purporting to be certified or otherwise authenticated by or on behalf of the court or authority having custody of that document shall be admissible in evidence and shall be taken to be a true copy of that document or part unless the contrary is shown.

(5) Nothing in any of the following enactments, that is to say—

(a) [Section 14 of the Powers of Criminal Courts (Sentencing) Act 2000] (under which a conviction leading to discharge is to be disregarded except as therein mentioned);

(b) section 9 of the Criminal Justice (Scotland) Act 1949 (which makes similar provision in respect of convictions on indictment in Scotland); and

(c) section 8 of the Probation Act (Northern Ireland) 1950 (which corresponds to the said section 12) or any corresponding enactment of the Parliament of Northern Ireland for the time being in force,

shall affect the operation of this section; and for the purposes of this section any order made by a court of summary jurisdiction in Scotland under section 1 or section 2 of the said Act of 1949 shall be treated as a conviction.

(6) In this section 'court-martial' means a court-martial constituted under the Army Act 1955, the Air Force Act 1955 or the Naval Discipline Act 1957 or a disciplinary court constituted under section [52G] of the said Act of 1957, and in relation to a court-martial 'conviction', means a finding of guilty which is, or falls to be treated as, the finding of the court, and 'convicted' shall be construed accordingly.

12 Findings of adultery and paternity as evidence in civil proceedings

(1) In any civil proceedings—

(a) the fact that a person has been found guilty of adultery in any matrimonial proceedings; and

(b) the fact that a person has been found to be the father of a child in relevant proceedings before any court in England and Wales [or Northern Ireland] or has been adjudged to be the father of a child in affiliation proceedings before any court in the United Kingdom

shall (subject to subsection (3) below) be admissible in evidence for the purpose of proving, where to do so is relevant to any issue in those civil proceedings, that he committed the adultery to which the finding relates or, as the case may be, is (or was) the father of that child, whether or not he offered any defence to the allegation of adultery or paternity and whether or not he is a party to the civil proceedings; but no finding or adjudication other than a subsisting one shall be admissible in evidence by virtue of this section.

(2) In any civil proceedings in which by virtue of this section a person is proved to have been found guilty of adultery as mentioned in subsection (1)(a) above or to have been found or adjudged to be the father of a child as mentioned in subsection (1)(b) above—

(a) he shall be taken to have committed the adultery to which the finding relates or, as the case may be, to be (or have been) the father of that child, unless the contrary is proved; and

(b) without prejudice to the reception of any other admissible evidence for the purpose of identifying the facts on which the finding or adjudication was based, the contents of any document which was before the court, or which contains any pronouncement of the court, in the other proceedings in question shall be admissible in evidence for that purpose.

(3) Nothing in this section shall prejudice the operation of any enactment whereby a finding of fact in any matrimonial or affiliation proceedings is for the purposes of any other proceedings made conclusive evidence of any fact.

(4) Subsection (4) of section 11 of this Act shall apply for the purposes of this section as if the reference to subsection (2) were a reference to subsection (2) of this section.

(5) In this section—

'matrimonial proceedings' means any matrimonial cause in the High Court or a county court in England and Wales or in the High Court in Northern Ireland, any consistorial action in Scotland, or any appeal arising out of any such cause or action;

'relevant proceedings' means—

(a) proceedings on a complaint under section 42 of the National Assistance Act 1948 or section 26 of the Social Security Act 1986;

(b) proceedings under the Children Act 1989;

(c) proceedings which would have been relevant proceedings for the purposes of this section in the form in which it was in force before the passing of the Children Act 1989;

(e) proceedings which are relevant proceedings as defined in Section 8(5) of the Civil Evidence Act (Northern Ireland) 1971.

13   Conclusiveness of convictions for purposes of defamation actions

(1) In an action for libel or slander in which the question whether a person did or did not commit a criminal offence is relevant to an issue arising in the action, proof that at the time when that issue falls to be determined, that person stands convicted of that offence shall be conclusive evidence that he committed that offence; and his conviction thereof shall be admissible in evidence accordingly.

(2) In any such action as aforesaid in which by virtue of this section a person is proved to have been convicted of an offence, the contents of any document which is admissible as evidence of the conviction, and the contents of the information, complaint, indictment or charge-sheet on which that person was convicted, shall, without prejudice to the reception of any other admissible evidence for the purpose of identifying the facts on which the conviction was based, be admissible in evidence for the purpose of identifying those facts.

(2A) In the case of an action for libel or slander in which there is more than one plaintiff—

(a) the references in subsections (1) and (2) above to the plaintiff shall be construed as references to any of the plaintiffs, and

(b) proof that any of the plaintiffs stands convicted of an offence shall be conclusive evidence that he committed that offence so far as that fact is relevant to any issue arising in relation to his cause of action or that of any other plaintiff.

(3) For the purposes of this section a person shall be taken to stand convicted of an offence if but only if there subsists against him a conviction of that offence by or before a court in the United Kingdom or by a court-martial there or elsewhere.

(4) Subsection (4) to (6) of section 11 of this Act shall apply for the purposes of this section as they apply for the purposes of that section, but as if in the said subsection (4) the reference to subsection (2) were a reference to subsection (2) of this section.

(5) The foregoing provisions of this section shall apply for the purposes of any action begun after the passing of this Act, whenever the cause of action arose, but shall not apply for the purposes of any action begun before the passing of this Act or any appeal or other proceedings arising out of any such action.

Privilege

14   Privilege against incrimination of self or spouse

(1) The right of a person in any legal proceedings other than criminal proceedings to refuse to answer any question or produce any document or thing if to do so would tend to expose that person to proceedings for an offence or for the recovery of a penalty—

    (a) shall apply only as regards criminal offences under the law of any part of the United Kingdom and penalties provided for by such law; and

    (b) shall include a like right to refuse to answer any question or produce any document or thing if to do so would tend to expose the husband or wife of that person to proceedings for any such criminal offence or for the recovery of any such penalty.

(2) In so far as any existing enactment conferring (in whatever words) powers of inspection or investigation confers on a person (in whatever words) any right otherwise than in criminal proceedings to refuse to answer any question or give any evidence tending to incriminate that person, subsection (1) above shall apply to that right as it applies to the right described in that subsection; and every such existing enactment shall be construed accordingly.

(3) In so far as any existing enactment provides (in whatever words) that in any proceedings other than criminal proceedings a person shall not be excused from answering any question or giving any evidence on the grounds that to do so may incriminate that person, that enactment shall be construed as providing also that in such proceedings a person shall not be excused from answering any question or giving any evidence on the ground that to do so may incriminate the husband or wife of that person.

(4) Where any existing enactment (however worded) that—

    (a) confers powers of inspection or investigation; or

    (b) provides as mentioned in subsection (3) above,

further provides (in whatever words) that any answer or evidence given by a person shall not be admissible in evidence against that person in any proceedings or class of proceedings (however described, and whether criminal or not), that enactment shall be construed as providing also that any answer or evidence given by that person shall not be admissible in evidence against the husband or wife of that person in the proceedings or class of proceedings in question.

(5) In this section 'existing enactment' means any enactment passed before this Act; and the references to giving evidence are references to giving evidence in any manner, whether by furnishing information, making discovery, producing documents or otherwise.

15   *(Repealed by the Patents Act 1977, s. 132, Sch. 6.)*

16   Abolition of certain privileges

(1) The following rules of law are hereby abrogated except in relation to criminal proceedings, that is to say—

    (a) the rule whereby, in any legal proceedings, a person cannot be compelled to answer any question or produce any document or thing if to do so would tend to expose him to a forfeiture; and

(b) the rule whereby, in any legal proceedings, a person other than a party to the proceedings cannot be compelled to produce any deed or other document relating to his title to any land.

(2) The rule of law whereby, in any civil proceedings, a party to the proceedings cannot be compelled to produce any document relating solely to his own case and in no way tending to impeach that case or support the case of any opposing party is hereby abrogated.

(4) In section 43(1) of the Matrimonial Causes Act 1965 (under which the evidence of a husband or wife is admissible in any proceedings to prove that marital intercourse did or did not take place between them during any period, but a husband or wife is not compellable in any proceedings to give evidence of the matters aforesaid), the words from 'but a husband or wife' to the end of the subsection shall cease to have effect except in relation to criminal proceedings.

(5) A witness in any proceedings instituted in consequence of adultery, whether a party to the proceedings or not, shall not be excused from answering any question by reason that it tends to show that he or she has been guilty of adultery; . . .

17 Consequential amendments relating to privilege

(1) In relation to England and Wales—

(a) section 1(3) of the Tribunals of Inquiry (Evidence) Act 1921 (under which a witness before a tribunal to which that Act has been applied is entitled to the same privileges as if he were a witness before the High Court) shall have effect as if after the word 'witness', in the second place where it occurs, there were inserted the words 'in civil proceedings'; and

(b) section 8(5) of the Parliamentary Commissioner Act 1967 (which provides that, subject as there mentioned, no person shall be compelled for the purposes of an investigation under that Act to give any evidence or produce any document which he could not be compelled to give or produce in proceedings before the High Court) shall have effect as if before the word 'proceedings' there were inserted the word 'civil';

and, so far as it applies to England and Wales, any other existing enactment, however framed or worded, which in relation to any tribunal, investigation or inquiry (however described) confers on persons required to answer questions or give evidence any privilege described by reference to the privileges of witnesses in proceedings before any court shall, unless the contrary intention appears, be construed as referring to the privileges of witnesses in civil proceedings before that court.

(2) . . .

(3) Without prejudice to the generality of subsection (2) to (4) of section 14 of this Act, the enactments mentioned in the Schedule to this Act shall have effect subject to the amendments provided for by that Schedule (being verbal amendments to bring those enactments into conformity with the provisions of that section).

(4) Subsection (5) of section 14 of this Act shall apply for the purposes of this section as it applies for the purposes of that section.

General

18 General interpretation and savings

(1) In this Act 'civil proceedings' includes, in addition to civil proceedings in any of the ordinary courts of law—

(a) civil proceedings before any other tribunal, being proceedings in relation to which the strict rules of evidence apply; and

(b) an arbitration or reference, whether under an enactment or not,

but does not include civil proceedings in relation to which the strict rules of evidence do not apply.

(2) In this Act—

'court' does not include a court-martial, and, in relation to an arbitration or reference, means the arbitrator or umpire and, in relation to proceedings before a tribunal (not being one of the ordinary courts of law), means the tribunal;

'legal proceedings' includes an arbitration or reference, whether under an enactment or not;

and for the avoidance of doubt it is hereby declared that in this Act, and in any amendment made by this Act in any other enactment, references to a person's husband or wife do not include references to a person who is no longer married to that person.

(3) Any reference in this Act to any other enactment is a reference thereto as amended, and includes a reference thereto as applied, by or under any other enactment.

(4) Nothing in this Act shall prejudice the operation of any enactment which provides (in whatever words) that any answer or evidence given by a person in specified circumstances shall not be admissible in evidence against him or some other person in any proceedings or class of proceedings (however described).

In this subsection the reference to giving evidence is a reference to giving evidence in any manner, whether by furnishing information, making discovery, producing documents or otherwise.

(5) Nothing in this Act shall prejudice—

(a) any power of a court, in any legal proceedings, to exclude evidence (whether by preventing questions from being put or otherwise) at its discretion; or

(b) the operation of any agreement (whenever made) between the parties to any legal proceedings as to the evidence which is to be admissible (whether generally or for any particular purpose) in those proceedings.

(6) It is hereby declared that where, by reason of any defect of speech or hearing from which he is suffering, a person called as a witness in any legal proceedings gives his evidence in writing or by signs, that evidence is to be treated for the purposes of this Act as being given orally.

19 (*Repealed by the Northern Ireland Constitution Act 1973, s. 41, Sch. 6, Pt. I.*)

20   Short title, repeals, extent and commencement

This Act may be cited as the Civil Evidence Act 1968.

(2) . . .

(3) This Act shall not extend to Scotland or, . . . to Northern Ireland.

Family Law Reform Act 1969
(1969, c. 46)

PART III   PROVISIONS FOR USE O F SCIENTIFIC TESTS IN DETERMINING PARENTAGE

20   Power of court to require use of scientific tests

(1) In any civil proceedings in which the parentage of any person falls to be determined, the court may, either of its own motion or on an application by any party to the proceedings, give a direction—

(a) for the use of scientific tests to ascertain whether such tests show that a party to the proceedings is or is not the father or mother of that person; and

(b) for the taking, within a period specified in the direction, of bodily samples from all or any of the following, namely, that person, any party who is alleged to be the father or mother of that person and any other party to the proceedings;

and the court may at any time revoke or vary a direction previously given by it under this subsection.

(1A) Tests required by a direction under this section may only be carried out by a body which has been accredited for the purposes of this section by—

(a) the Lord Chancellor, or

(b) a body appointed by him for the purpose.

(2) The individual carrying out scientific tests in pursuance of a direction under subsection (1) above shall make to the court a report in which he shall state—

(a) the results of the tests;

(b) whether any party to whom the report relates is or is not excluded by the results from being the father or mother of the person whose parentage is to be determined; and

(c) in relation to any party who is not so excluded, the value, if any, of the results in determining whether that party is the father or mother of that person;

and the report shall be received by the court as evidence in the proceedings of the matters stated in it.

(2A) Where the proceedings in which the parentage of any person falls to be determined are proceedings on an application under section 55A or 56 of the Family Law Act 1986, any reference in subsection (1) or (2) of this section to any party to the proceedings shall include a reference to any person named in the application.

(3) A report under subsection (2) of this section shall be in the form prescribed by regulations made under section 22 of this Act.

(4) Where a report has been made to a court under subsection (2) of this section, any party may, with the leave of the court, or shall, if the court so directs, obtain from the person who made the report a written statement explaining or amplifying any statement made in the report, and that statement shall be deemed for the purposes of this section (except subsection (3) thereof) to form part of the report made to the court.

(5) Where a direction is given under this section in any proceedings, a party to the proceedings, unless the court otherwise directs, shall not be entitled to call as a witness the tester, or any other person to whom anything necessary for the purpose of enabling those tests to be carried out was done, unless within fourteen days after receiving a copy of the report he serves notice on the other parties to the proceedings, or on such of them as the court may direct, of his intention to call the tester or that other person; and where (the tester or) any such person is called as a witness the party who called him shall be entitled to cross examine him.

(6) Where a direction is given under this section the party on whose application the direction is given shall pay the cost of taking and testing bodily samples for the purpose of giving effect to the direction (including any expenses reasonably incurred by any person in taking any steps required of him for that purpose) and of making report to the court under this section, but the amount paid shall be treated as costs incurred by him in the proceedings.

21   Consents, etc., required for taking of bodily samples

(1) Subject to the provisions of subsection (3) and (4) of this section, a bodily sample which is required to be taken from any person for the purpose of giving effect to a direction under section 20 of this Act shall not be taken from that person except with his consent.

(2) The consent of a minor who has attained the age of sixteen years to the taking from himself of a bodily sample shall be as effective as it would be if he were of full age; and where a minor has by virtue of this subsection given an effective consent to the taking of a bodily sample it shall not be necessary to obtain any consent for it from any other person.

(3) A bodily sample may be taken from a person under the age of sixteen years, not being such a person as is referred to in subsection (4) of this section, (a) if the person who has the

care and control of him consents; or (b) if that person does not consent, if the court considers that it would be in his best interests for the sample to be taken.

(4) A bodily sample may be taken from a person who is suffering from mental disorder within the meaning of [the Mental Health Act 1983] and is incapable of understanding the nature and purpose of scientific rests if the person who has the care and control of him consents and the medical practitioner in whose care he is has certified that the taking of a bodily sample from him will not be prejudicial to his proper care and treatment.

(5) The foregoing provisions of this section are without prejudice to the provisions of section 23 of this Act.

23   Failure to comply with direction for taking bodily tests

(1) Where a court gives a direction under section 20 of this Act and any person fails to take any step required of him for the purpose of giving effect to the direction, the court may draw such inferences, if any, for that fact as appear proper in the circumstances.

(2) Where in any proceedings in which the parentage of any person falls to be determined by the court hearing the proceedings there is a presumption of law that that person is legitimate, then if—

(a) a direction is given under section 20 of this Act in those proceedings, and
(b) any party who is claiming any relief in the proceedings and who for the purpose of obtaining that relief is entitled to rely on the presumption fails to take any step required of him for the purpose of giving effect to the direction,

the court may adjourn the hearing for such period as it thinks fit to enable that party to take that step, and if at the end of that period he has failed without reasonable cause to take it the court may, without prejudice to subsection (1) of this section, dismiss his claim for relief notwithstanding the absence of evidence to rebut the presumption.

(3) Where any person named in a direction under section 20 of this Act fails to consent to the taking of a bodily sample from himself or from any person named in the direction of whom he has the care and control, he shall be deemed for the purposes of this section to have failed to take a step required of him for the purpose of giving effect to the direction.

24   Penalty for personating another, etc., for purpose of providing bodily sample

If for the purpose of providing a bodily sample for a test required to give effect to a direction under section 20 of this Act any person personates another, or proffers a child knowing that it is not the child named in the direction, he shall be liable—

(a) on conviction on indictment, to imprisonment for a term not exceeding two years, or
(b) on summary conviction, to a fine not exceeding the statutory maximum.

25   Interpretation of Part III

In this Part of this Act the following expressions have the meanings hereby respectively assigned to them, that is to say—

'bodily sample' means a sample of bodily fluid or bodily tissue taken for the purpose of scientific tests;

'excluded' means excluded subject to the occurrence of mutation . . .

'scientific tests' means scientific tests carried out under this Part of the Act and made with the object of ascertaining the inheritable characteristics of bodily fluids or bodily tissue.

PART IV   MISCELLANEOUS AND GENERAL

26   Rebuttal of presumption as to legitimacy and illegitimacy

Any presumption of law as to the legitimacy or illegitimacy of any person may in any civil proceedings be rebutted by evidence which shows that it is more probable than not that that person is illegitimate or legitimate, as the case may be, and it shall not be necessary to prove that fact beyond reasonable doubt in order to rebut the presumption.

Civil Evidence Act 1972
(1972, c. 30)

2 Rules of court with respect to expert reports and oral expert evidence

(3) Notwithstanding any enactment or rule of law by virtue of which documents prepared for the purpose of pending or contemplated civil procedings or in connection with the obtaining or giving of legal advice or in certain circumstances privileged from disclosure, provision may be made by rules of court—

(a) for enabling the court in any civil proceedings to direct, with respect to medical matters or matters of any other class which may be specified in the direction, that the parties or some of them shall each by such date as may be so specified (or such later date as may be permitted or agreed in accordance with the rules) disclose to the other or others in the form of one or more expert reports the expert evidence on matters of that class which he proposes to adduce as part of his case at the trial; and

(b) for prohibiting a party who fails to comply with a direction given in any such proceedings under rules of court made by virtue of paragraph (a) above from adducing in evidence, except with the leave of the court, any statement (whether of fact or opinion) contained in any expert report whatsoever in so far as the statement deals with matters of any class specified in the direction.

(4) Provision may be made by rules of court as to the conditions subject to which oral expert evidence may be given in civil proceedings.

(5) Without prejudice to the generality of subsection (4) above, rules of court made in pursuance of that subsection may make provision for prohibiting a party who fails to comply with a direction given as mentioned in subsection (3)(b) above from adducing, except with the leave of the court, any oral expert evidence whatsoever with respect to matters of any class specified in the direction.

(6) Any rules of court made in pursuance of this section may make different provision for different classes of cases, for expert reports dealing with matters of different classes, and for other different circumstances.

(7) References in this section to an expert report are references to a written report by a person dealing wholly or mainly with matters on which he is (or would if living be) qualified to give expert evidence.

3 Admissibility of expert opinion and certain expressions of non-expert opinion

(1) Subject to any rules of court made in pursuance of this Act, where a person is called as a witness in any civil proceedings, his opinion on any relevant matter on which he is qualified to give expert evidence shall be admissible in evidence.

(2) It is hereby declared that where a person is called as a witness in any civil proceedings, a statement or opinion by him on any relevant matter on which he is not qualified to give expert evidence, if made as a way of conveying relevant facts personally perceived by him, is admissible as evidence of what he perceived.

(3) In this section 'relevant matter' includes an issue in the proceedings in question.

4 Evidence of foreign law

(1) It is hereby declared that in civil proceedings a person who is suitably qualified to do so on account of his knowledge or experience is competent to give expert evidence as to the

law of any country or territory outside the United Kingdom, or of any part of the United Kingdom other than England and Wales, irrespective of whether he has acted or is entitled to act as a legal practitioner there.

(2) Where any question as to the law of any country or territory outside the United Kingdom, or of any part of the United Kingdom other than England and Wales, with respect to any matter has been determined (whether before or after the passing of this Act) in any such proceedings as are mentioned in subsection (4) below, then in any civil proceedings (not being proceedings before a court which can take judicial notice of the law of that country, territory or part with respect to that matter)—

    (a) any finding made or decision given on that question in the first-mentioned proceedings shall, if reported or recorded in citable form, be admissible in evidence for the purpose of proving the law of that country, territory or part with respect to that matter; and

    (b) if that finding or decision, as so reported or recorded, is adduced for that purpose, the law of that country, territory or part with respect to that matter shall be taken to be in accordance with that finding or decision unless the contrary is proved:

Provided that paragraph (b) above shall not apply in the case of a finding or decision which conflicts with another finding or decision on the same question adduced by virtue of this subsection in the same proceedings.

(3) Except with the leave of the court, a party to any civil proceedings shall not be permitted to adduce any such finding or decision as is mentioned in subsection (2) above by virtue of that subsection unless he has in accordance with rules of court given to every other party to the proceedings notice that he intends to do so.

(4) The proceedings referred to in subsection (2) above are the following, whether civil or criminal, namely—

    (a) proceedings at first instance in any of the following courts, namely the High Court, the Crown Court, a court of quarter sessions, the Court of Chancery of the county palatine of Lancaster and the Court of Chancery of the county palatine of Durham;

    (b) appeals arising out of any such proceedings as are mentioned in paragraph (a) above;

    (c) proceedings before the Judicial Committee of the Privy Council on appeal (whether to Her Majesty in Council or to the Judicial Committee as such) from any decision of any court outside the United Kingdom.

(5) For the purposes of this section a finding or decision on any such question as is mentioned in subsection (2) above shall be taken to be reported or recorded in citable form, if, but only if, it is reported or recorded in writing in a report, transcript or other document which, if that question had been a question as to the law of England and Wales, could be cited as an authority in legal proceedings in England and Wales.

5   Interpretation, application to arbitrations etc. and savings

    (3) Nothing in this Act shall prejudice—

        (a) any power of a court, in any civil proceedings, to exclude evidence (whether by preventing questions from being put or otherwise) at its discretion; or

        (b) the operation of any agreement (whenever made) between the parties to any civil proceedings as to the evidence which is to be admissible (whether generally or for any particular purpose) in those proceedings.

6   Short title, extent and commencement

    (1) This Act may be cited as the Civil Evidence Act 1972.

    (2) This Act shall not extend to Scotland or Northern Ireland.

Matrimonial Causes Act 1973
(1973, c. 18)

19.   (1) Any married person who alleges that reasonable grounds exist for supposing that the other party to the marriage is dead may present a petition to the court to have it presumed that the other party is dead and to have the marriage dissolved, and the court may, if satisfied that such reasonable grounds exist, grant a decree of presumption of death and dissolution of the marriage.

(3) In any proceedings under this section the fact that for a period of seven years or more the other party to the marriage has been continually absent from the petitioner and the petitioner has no reason to believe that the other party has been living within that time shall be evidence that the other party is dead until the contrary is proved.

48.   (1) The evidence of a husband or wife shall be admissible in any proceedings to prove that marital intercourse did or did not take place between them during any period.

(2) In any proceedings for nullity of marriage, evidence on the question of sexual capacity shall be heard in camera unless in any case the judge is satisfied that in the interests of justice any such evidence ought to be heard in open court.

Solicitors Act 1974
(1974, c. 47)

18.   (1) Any list purporting to be published by authority of the Society and to contain the names of solicitors who have obtained practising certificates for the current year before 2nd January in that year shall, until the contrary is proved, be evidence that the persons so named as solicitors holding practising certificates for the current year are solicitors holding such certificates.

(2) The absence from any such list of the name of any person shall, until the contrary is proved, be evidence that that person is not qualified to practise as a solicitor under a certificate for the current year, but in the case of any such person an extract from the roll certified as correct by the Society shall be evidence of the facts appearing in the extract.

Patents Act 1977
(1977, c. 37)

100.   (1) If the invention for which a patent is granted is a process for obtaining a new product, the same product produced by a person other than the proprietor of the patent or a licensee of his shall, unless the contrary is proved, be taken in any proceedings to have been obtained by that process.

(2) In considering whether a party has discharged the burden imposed upon him by this section, the court shall not require him to disclose any manufacturing or commercial secrets if it appears to the court that it would be unreasonable to do so.

Supreme Court Act 1981
(1981, c. 54)

69.   (5) Where for the purpose of disposing of any action or other matter which is being tried in the High Court by a judge with a jury it is necessary to ascertain the law of any other country which is applicable to the facts of the case, any question as to the effect of the evidence given with respect to that law shall, instead of being submitted to the jury, be decided by the judge alone.

72.   (1) In any proceedings to which this subsection applies a person shall not be excused, by reason that to do so would tend to expose that person, or his or her spouse, to proceedings for a related offence or for the recovery of a related penalty—
>   (a) from answering any question put to that person in the first mentioned proceedings; or
>   (b) from complying with any order made in those proceedings.

(2) Subsection (1) applies to the following civil proceedings in the High Court, namely—
>   (a) proceedings for infringement of rights pertaining to any intellectual property or for passing off;
>   (b) proceedings brought to obtain disclosure of information relating to any infringement of such rights or to any passing off; and
>   (c) proceedings brought to prevent any apprehended infringement of such rights or any apprehended passing off.

(3) Subject to subsection (4), no statement or admission made by a person—
>   (a) in answering a question put to him in any proceedings to which subsection (2) applies; or
>   (b) in complying with any order made in any such proceedings, shall, in proceedings for any related offence or for the recovery of any related penalty, be admissible in evidence against that person or (unless they married after the making of the statement or admission) against the spouse of that person.

(4) Nothing in subsection (3) shall render any statement or admission made by a person as there mentioned inadmissible in evidence against that person in proceedings for perjury or contempt of court.

(5) In this section—

'intellectual property' means any patent, trade mark, copyright, registered design, technical or commercial information or other intellectual property;

'related offence,' in relation to any proceedings to which subsection (1) applies, means—
>   (a) in the case of proceedings within subsection (2)(a) or (b)—
>>   (i) any offence committed by or in the course of the infringement or passing off to which those proceedings relate; or
>>   (ii) any offence not within sub-paragraph (i) committed in connection with that infringement or passing off, being an offence involving fraud or dishonesty;
>   (b) in the case of proceedings within subsection (2)(c), any offence revealed by the facts on which the plaintiff relies in those proceedings;

'related penalty,' in relation to any proceedings to which subsection (1) applies means—
>   (a) in the case of proceedings within subsection (2)(a) or (b), any penalty incurred in respect of anything done or omitted in connection with the infringement or passing of to which those proceedings relate;
>   (b) in the case of proceedings within subsection (2)(c), any penalty incurred in respect of any act or omission revealed by the facts on which the plaintiff relies in those proceedings.

(6) Any reference in this section to civil proceedings in the High Court of any description includes a reference to proceedings on appeal arising out of civil proceedings in the High Court of that description.

Civil Jurisdiction and Judgments Act 1982
(1982, c. 27)

32   Overseas judgments given in proceedings brought in breach of agreement for settlement of dispute

(1) Subject to the following provisions of this section, a judgment given by a court of an overseas country in any proceedings shall not be recognised or enforced in the United Kingdom if—

(a) the bringing of those proceedings in that court was contrary to an agreement under which the dispute in question was to be settled otherwise than by proceedings in the courts of that country; and

(b) those proceedings were not brought in that court by, or with the agreement of, the person against whom the judgment was given; and

(c) that person did not counterclaim in the proceedings or otherwise submit to the jurisdiction of that court.

(2) Subsection (1) does not apply where the agreement referred to in paragraph (a) of that subsection was illegal, void or unenforceable or was incapable of being performed for reasons not attributable to the fault of the party bringing the proceedings in which the judgment was given.

(3) In determining whether a judgment given by a court of an overseas country should be recognised or enforced in the United Kingdom, a court in the United Kingdom shall not be bound by any decision of the overseas court relating to any of the matters mentioned in subsection (1) or (2).

(4) Nothing in subsection (1) shall affect the recognition or enforcement in the United Kingdom of—

(a) a judgment which is required to be recognised or enforced there under the 1968 Convention or the Lugano Convention

(b) a judgment to which Part I of the Foreign Judgments (Reciprocal Enforcement) Act 1933 applies by virtue of section 4 of the Carriage of Goods by Road Act 1965, section 17(4) of the Nuclear Installations Act 1965, section 6 of the International Transport Conventions Act 1983, section 5 of the Carriage of Passengers by Road Act 1974 or section 6(4) of the Merchant Shipping Act 1995.

Civil Evidence Act 1995
(1995, c. 38)

Admissibility of hearsay evidence

1   Admissibility of hearsay evidence

(1) In civil proceedings evidence shall not be excluded on the ground that it is hearsay.

(2) In this Act—

(a) 'hearsay' means a statement made otherwise than by a person while giving oral evidence in the proceedings which is tendered as evidence of the matters stated; and

(b) references to hearsay include hearsay of whatever degree.

(3) Nothing in this Act affects the admissibility of evidence admissible apart from this section.

(4) The provisions of sections 2 to 6 (safeguards and supplementary provisions relating to hearsay evidence) do not apply in relation to hearsay evidence admissible apart from this section, notwithstanding that it may also be admissible by virtue of this section.

Safeguards in relation to hearsay evidence

2   Notice of proposal to adduce hearsay evidence

(1) A party proposing to adduce hearsay evidence in civil proceedings shall, subject to the following provisions of this section, give to the other party or parties to the proceedings—

    (a) such notice (if any) of that fact, and

    (b) on request, such particulars of or relating to the evidence,

as is reasonable and practicable in the circumstances for the purpose of enabling him or them to deal with any matters arising from its being hearsay.

(2) Provision may be made by rules of court—

    (a) specifying classes of proceedings or evidence in relation to which subsection (1) does not apply, and

    (b) as to the manner in which (including the time within which) the duties imposed by that subsection are to be complied with in the cases where it does apply.

(3) Subsection (1) may also be excluded by agreement of the parties; and compliance with the duty to give notice may in any case be waived by the person to whom notice is required to be given.

(4) A failure to comply with subsection (1), or with rules under subsection (2)(b), does not affect the admissibility of the evidence but may be taken into account by the court—

    (a) in considering the exercise of its powers with respect to the course of proceedings and costs, and

    (b) as a matter adversely affecting the weight to be given to the evidence in accordance with section 4.

3   Power to call witness for cross-examination on hearsay statement

Rules of court may provide that where a party to civil proceedings adduces hearsay evidence of a statement made by a person and does not call that person as a witness, any other party to the proceedings may, with the leave of the court, call that person as a witness and cross-examine him on the statement as if he had been called by the first-mentioned party and as if the hearsay statement were his evidence in chief.

4   Considerations relevant to weighing of hearsay evidence

(1) In estimating the weight (if any) to be given to hearsay evidence in civil proceedings the court shall have regard to any circumstances from which any inference can reasonably be drawn as to the reliability or otherwise of the evidence.

(2) Regard may be had, in particular, to the following—

    (a) whether it would have been reasonable and practicable for the party by whom the evidence was adduced to have produced the maker of the original statement as a witness;

    (b) whether the original statement was made contemporaneously with the occurrence or existence of the matters stated;

    (c) whether the evidence involves multiple hearsay;

    (d) whether any person involved had any motive to conceal or misrepresent matters;

    (e) whether the original statement was an edited account, or was made in collaboration with another or for a particular purpose;

(f) whether the circumstances in which the evidence is adduced as hearsay are such as to suggest an attempt to prevent proper evaluation of its weight.

Supplementary provisions as to hearsay evidence

5   Competence and credibility

(1) Hearsay evidence shall not be admitted in civil proceedings if or to the extent that it is shown to consist of, or to be proved by means of, a statement made by a person who at the time he made the statement was not competent as a witness.

For this purpose 'not competent as a witness' means suffering from such mental or physical infirmity, or lack of understanding, as would render a person incompetent as a witness in civil proceedings; but a child shall be treated as competent as a witness if he satisfies the requirements of section 96(2)(a) and (b) of the Children Act 1989 (conditions for reception of unsworn evidence of child).

(2) Where in civil proceedings hearsay evidence is adduced and the maker of the original statement, or of any statement relied upon to prove another statement, is not called as a witness—

(a) evidence which if he had been so called would be admissible for the purpose of attacking or supporting his credibility as a witness is admissible for that purpose in the proceedings; and

(b) evidence tending to prove that, whether before or after he made the statement, he made any other statement inconsistent with it is admissible for the purpose of showing that he had contradicted himself.

Provided that evidence may not be given of any matter of which, if he had been called as a witness and had denied that matter in cross-examination, evidence could not have been adduced by the cross-examining party.

6   Previous statements of witnesses

(1) Subject as follows, the provisions of this Act as to hearsay evidence in civil proceedings apply equally (but with any necessary modifications) in relation to a previous statement made by a person called as a witness in the proceedings.

(2) A party who has called or intends to call a person as a witness in civil proceedings may not in those proceedings adduce evidence of a previous statement made by that person, except—

(a) with the leave of the court, or

(b) for the purpose of rebutting a suggestion that his evidence has been fabricated.

This shall not be construed as preventing a witness statement (that is, a written statement of oral evidence which a party to the proceedings intends to lead) from being adopted by a witness in giving evidence or treated as his evidence.

(3) Where in the case of civil proceedings section 3, 4 or 5 of the Criminal Procedure Act 1865 applies, which make provision as to—

(a) how far a witness may be discredited by the party producing him,

(b) the proof of contradictory statements made by a witness, and

(c) cross-examination as to previous statements in writing,

this Act does not authorise the adducing of evidence of a previous inconsistent or contradictory statement otherwise than in accordance with those sections.

This is without prejudice to any provision made by rules of court under section 3 above (power to call witness for cross-examination on hearsay statement).

(4) Nothing in this Act affects any of the rules of law as to the circumstances in which, where a person called as a witness in civil proceedings is cross-examined on a document used by him to refresh his memory, that document may be made evidence in the proceedings.

(5) Nothing in this section shall be construed as preventing a statement of any

description referred to above from being admissible by virtue of section 1 as evidence of the matters stated.

7   Evidence formerly admissible at common law

(1) The common law rule effectively preserved by section 9(1) and (2)(a) of the Civil Evidence Act 1968 (admissibility of admissions adverse to a party) is superseded by the provisions of this Act.

(2) The common law rules effectively preserved by section 9(1) and (2)(b) to (d) of the Civil Evidence Act 1968, that is, any rule of law whereby in civil proceedings—

- (a) published works dealing with matters of a public nature (for example, histories, scientific works, dictionaries and maps) are admissible as evidence of facts of a public nature stated in them,
- (b) public documents (for example, public registers, and returns made under public authority with respect to matters of public interest) are admissible as evidence of facts stated in them, or
- (c) records (for example, the records of certain courts, treaties, Crown grants, pardons and commissions) are admissible as evidence of facts stated in them,

shall continue to have effect.

(3) The common law rules effectively preserved by section 9(3) and (4) of the Civil Evidence Act 1968, that is, any rule of law whereby in civil proceedings—

- (a) evidence of a person's reputation is admissible for the purpose of proving his good or bad character, or
- (b) evidence of reputation or family tradition is admissible—
  - (i) for the purpose of proving or disproving pedigree or the existence of a marriage, or
  - (ii) for the purpose of proving or disproving the existence of any public or general right or of identifying any person or thing,

shall continue to have effect in so far as they authorise the court to treat such evidence as proving or disproving that matter.

Where any such rule applies, reputation or family tradition shall be treated for the purposes of this Act as a fact and not as a statement or multiplicity of statements about the matter in question.

(4) The words in which a rule of law mentioned in this section is described are intended only to identify the rule and shall not be construed as altering it in any way.

Other matters

8   Proof of statements contained in documents

(1) Where a statement contained in a document is admissible as evidence in civil proceedings, it may be proved—

- (a) by the production of that document, or
- (b) whether or not that document is still in existence, by the production of a copy of that document or of the material part of it,

authenticated in such manner as the court may approve.

(2) It is immaterial for this purpose how many removes there are between a copy and the original.

9   Proof of records of business or public authority

(1) A document which is shown to form part of the records of a business or public authority may be received in evidence in civil proceedings without further proof.

(2) A document shall be taken to form part of the records of a business or public authority if there is produced to the court a certificate to that effect signed by an officer of the business or authority to which the records belong.

For this purpose—
- (a) a document purporting to be a certificate signed by an officer of a business or public authority shall be deemed to have been duly given by such an officer and signed by him; and
- (b) a certificate shall be treated as signed by a person if it purports to bear a facsimile of his signature.

(3) The absence of an entry in the records of a business or public authority may be proved in civil proceedings by affidavit of an officer of the business or authority to which the records belong.

(4) In this section—

'records' means records in whatever form;

'business' includes any activity regularly carried on over a period of time, whether for profit or not, by any body (whether corporate or not) or by an individual;

'officer' includes any person occupying a responsible position in relation to the relevant activities of the business or public authority or in relation to its records; and

'public authority' includes any public or statutory undertaking, any government department and any person holding office under Her Majesty.

(5) The court may, having regard to the circumstances of the case, direct that all or any of the above provisions of this section do not apply in relation to a particular document or record, or description of documents or records.

10   Admissibility and proof of Ogden Tables

(1) The actuarial tables (together with explanatory notes) for use in personal injury and fatal accident cases issued from time to time by the Government Actuary's Department are admissible in evidence for the purpose of assessing, in an action for personal injury, the sum to be awarded as general damages for future pecuniary loss.

(2) They may be proved by the production of a copy published by Her Majesty's Stationery Office.

(3) For the purposes of this section—
- (a) 'personal injury' includes any disease and any impairment of a person's physical or mental condition; and
- (b) 'action for personal injury' includes an action brought by virtue of the Law Reform (Miscellaneous Provisions) Act 1934 or the Fatal Accidents Act 1976.

General

11   Meaning of 'civil proceedings'

In this Act 'civil proceedings' means civil proceedings, before any tribunal, in relation to which the strict rules of evidence apply, whether as a matter of law or by agreement of the parties.

References to 'the court' and 'rules of court' shall be construed accordingly.

12   Provisions as to rules of court

(1) Any power to make rules of court regulating the practice or procedure of the court in relation to civil proceedings includes power to make such provision as may be necessary or expedient for carrying into effect the provisions of this Act.

(2) Any rules of court made for the purposes of this Act as it applies in relation to proceedings in the High Court apply, except in so far as their operation is excluded by agreement, to arbitration proceedings to which this Act applies, subject to such modifications as may be appropriate.

Any question arising as to what modifications are appropriate shall be determined, in default of agreement, by the arbitrator or umpire, as the case may be.

13 Interpretation

In this Act—

'civil proceedings' has the meaning given by section 11 and 'court' and 'rules of court' shall be construed in accordance with that section;

'document' means anything in which information of any description is recorded, and 'copy', in relation to a document, means anything onto which information recorded in the document has been copied, by whatever means and whether directly or indirectly;

'hearsay' shall be construed in accordance with section 1(2);

'oral evidence' includes evidence which, by reason of a defect of speech or hearing, a person called as a witness gives in writing or by signs;

'the original statement', in relation to hearsay evidence, means the underlying statement (if any) by—

(a) in the case of evidence of fact, a person having personal knowledge of the fact, or

(b) in the case of evidence of opinion, the person whose opinion it is; and

'statement' means any representation of fact or opinion, however made.

14 Savings

(1) Nothing in this Act affects the exclusion of evidence on grounds other than that it is hearsay.

This applies whether the evidence falls to be excluded in pursuance of any enactment or rule of law, for failure to comply with rules of court or an order of the court, or otherwise.

(2) Nothing in this Act affects the proof of documents by means other than those specified in section 8 or 9.

(3) Nothing in this Act affects the operation of the following enactments—

(a) section 2 of the Documentary Evidence Act 1868 (mode of proving certain official documents);

(b) section 2 of the Documentary Evidence Act 1882 (documents printed under the superintendence of Stationery Office);

(c) section 1 of the Evidence (Colonial Statutes) Act 1907 (proof of statutes of certain legislatures);

(d) section 1 of the Evidence (Foreign, Dominion and Colonial Documents) Act 1933 (proof and effect of registers and official certificates of certain countries);

(e) section 5 of the Oaths and Evidence (Overseas Authorities and Countries) Act 1963 (provision in respect of public registers of other countries).

16 Short title, commencement and extent

(1) This Act may be cited as the Civil Evidence Act 1995.

(2) The provisions of this Act come into force on such day as the Lord Chancellor may appoint by order made by statutory instrument, and different days may be appointed for different provisions and for different purposes.

(3) An order under subsection (2) may contain such transitional provisions as appear to the Lord Chancellor to be appropriate; and subject to any such provision, the provisions of this Act shall not apply in relation to proceedings begun before commencement.

(4) This Act extends to England and Wales.

(5) Section 10 (admissibility and proof of Ogden Tables) also extends to Northern Ireland.

As it extends to Northern Ireland, the following shall be substituted for subsection (3)(b)—

(b) 'action for personal injury' includes an action brought by virtue of the Law Reform (Miscellaneous Provisions) (Northern Ireland) Act 1937 or the Fatal Accidents (Northern Ireland) Order 1977.

(6) The provisions of Schedule 1 and 2 (consequential amendments and repeals) have the same extent as the enactments respectively amended or repealed.

Civil Procedure Rules 1998

CPR Part 32 Evidence

CONTENTS OF THIS PART

32.1   Power of court to control evidence

(1) The court may control the evidence by giving directions as to—

    (a) the issues on which it requires evidence;

    (b) the nature of the evidence which it requires to decide those issues; and

    (c) the way in which the evidence is to be placed before the court.

(2) The court may use its power under this rule to exclude evidence that would otherwise be admissible.

(3) The court may limit cross-examination.

32.2   Evidence of witnesses—general rule

(1) The general rule is that any fact which needs to be proved by the evidence of witnesses is to be proved—

    (a) at trial, by their oral evidence given in public; and

    (b) at any other hearing, by their evidence in writing.

(2) This is subject—

    (a) to any provision to the contrary contained in these Rules or elsewhere; or

    (b) to any order of the court.

32.3   Evidence by video link or other means
The court may allow a witness to give evidence through a video link or by other means.

32.4   Requirement to serve witness statements for use at trial
(1) A witness statement is a written statement signed by a person which contains the evidence which that person would be allowed to give orally.

(2) The court will order a party to serve on the other parties any witness statement of the oral evidence which the party serving the statement intends to rely on in relation to any issues of fact to be decided at the trial.

(3) The court may give directions as to—
    (a) the order in which witness statements are to be served; and
    (b) whether or not the witness statements are to be filed.

32.5   Use at trial of witness statements which have been served
(1) If—
    (a) a party has served a witness statement; and
    (b) he wishes to rely at trial on the evidence of the witness who made the statement,
he must call the witness to give oral evidence unless the court orders otherwise or he puts the statement in as hearsay evidence. (Part 33 contains provisions about hearsay evidence)

(2) Where a witness is called to give oral evidence under paragraph (1), his witness statement shall stand as his evidence in chief unless the court orders otherwise.

(3) A witness giving oral evidence at trial may with the permission of the court—
    (a) amplify his witness statement; and
    (b) give evidence in relation to new matters which have arisen since the witness statement was served on the other parties.

(4) The court will give permission under paragraph (3) only if it considers that there is good reason not to confine the evidence of the witness to the contents of his witness statement.

(5) If a party who has served a witness statement does not—
    (a) call the witness to give evidence at trial; or
    (b) put the witness statement in as hearsay evidence,
any other party may put the witness statement in as hearsay evidence.

32.6   Evidence in proceedings other than at trial
(1) Subject to paragraph (2), the general rule is that evidence at hearings other than the trial is to be by witness statement unless the court, a practice direction or any other enactment requires otherwise.

(2) At hearings other than the trial, a party may rely on the matters set out in—
    (a) his statement of case; or
    (b) his application notice,
if the statement of case or application notice is verified by a statement of truth.

32.7   Order for cross-examination
(1) Where, at a hearing other than the trial, evidence is given in writing, any party may apply to the court for permission to cross-examine the person giving the evidence.

(2) If the court gives permission under paragraph (1) but the person in question does not attend as required by the order, his evidence may not be used unless the court gives permission.

32.8   Form of witness statement
A witness statement must comply with the requirements set out in the relevant practice direction.

(Part 22 requires a witness statement to be verified by a statement of truth)

32.9   Witness summaries

(1) A party who—

(a) is required to serve a witness statement for use at trial; but

(b) is unable to obtain one,

may apply, without notice, for permission to serve a witness summary instead.

(2) A witness summary is a summary of—

(a) the evidence, if known, which would otherwise be included in a witness statement; or

(b) if the evidence is not known, the matters about which the party serving the witness summary proposes to question the witness.

(3) Unless the court orders otherwise, a witness summary must include the name and address of the intended witness.

(4) Unless the court orders otherwise, a witness summary must be served within the period in which a witness statement would have had to be served.

(5) Where a party serves a witness summary, so far as practicable rules 32.4 (requirement to serve witness statements for use at trial), 32.5(3) (amplifying witness statements), and 32.8 (form of witness statement) shall apply to the summary.

32.10   Consequence of failure to serve witness statement or summary

If a witness statement or a witness summary for use at trial is not served in respect of an intended witness within the time specified by the court, then the witness may not be called to give oral evidence unless the court gives permission.

32.11   Cross-examination on a witness statement

Where a witness is called to give evidence at trial, he may be cross-examined on his witness statement whether or not the statement or any part of it was referred to during the witness's evidence in chief.

32.12   Use of witness statements for other purposes

(1) Except as provided by this rule, a witness statement may be used only for the purpose of the proceedings in which it is served.

(2) Paragraph (1) does not apply if and to the extent that—

(a) the witness gives consent in writing to some other use of it;

(b) the court gives permission for some other use; or

(c) the witness statement has been put in evidence at a hearing held in public.

32.13   Availability of witness statements for inspection

(1) A witness statement which stands as evidence in chief is open to inspection unless the court otherwise directs during the course of the trial.

(2) Any person may ask for a direction that a witness statement is not open to inspection.

(3) The court will not make a direction under paragraph (2) unless it is satisfied that a witness statement should not be open to inspection because of—

(a) the interests of justice;

(b) the public interest;

(c) the nature of any expert medical evidence in the statement;

(d) the nature of any confidential information (including information relating to personal financial matters) in the statement; or

(e) the need to protect the interests of any child or patient.

(4) The court may exclude from inspection words or passages in the statement.

32.14   False statements

(1) Proceedings for contempt of court may be brought against a person if he makes, or causes to be made, a false statement in a document verified by a statement of truth without an honest belief in its truth. (Part 22 makes provision for a statement of truth)

(2) Proceedings under this rule may be brought only—
  (a) by the Attorney General; or
  (b) with the permission of the court.

32.15   Affidavit evidence

(1) Evidence must be given by affidavit instead of or in addition to a witness statement if this is required by the court, a provision contained in any other rule, a practice direction or any other enactment.

(2) Nothing in these Rules prevents a witness giving evidence by affidavit at a hearing other than the trial if he chooses to do so in a case where paragraph (1) does not apply, but the party putting forward the affidavit may not recover the additional cost of making it from any other party unless the court orders otherwise.

32.16   Form of affidavit

An affidavit must comply with the requirements set out in the relevant practice direction.

32.17   Affidavit made outside the jurisdiction

A person may make an affidavit outside the jurisdiction in accordance with—
  (a) this Part; or
  (b) the law of the place where he makes the affidavit.

32.18   Notice to admit facts

(1) A party may serve notice on another party requiring him to admit the facts, or the part of the case of the serving party, specified in the notice.

(2) A notice to admit facts must be served no later than 21 days before the trial.

(3) Where the other party makes any admission in response to the notice, the admission may be used against him only—
  (a) in the proceedings in which the notice to admit is served; and
  (b) by the party who served the notice.

(4) The court may allow a party to amend or withdraw any admission made by him on such terms as it thinks just.

32.19   Notice to admit or produce documents

(1) A party shall be deemed to admit the authenticity of a document disclosed to him under Part 31 (disclosure and inspection of documents) unless he serves notice that he wishes the document to be proved at trial.

(2) A notice to prove a document must be served—
  (a) by the latest date for serving witness statements; or
  (b) within 7 days of disclosure of the document,
whichever is later.

PD 32 Practice Direction—Written Evidence

(This Practice Direction Supplements CPR Part 32)

Evidence in general

1.1   Rule 32.2 sets out how evidence is to be given and facts are to be proved.

1.2   Evidence at a hearing other than the trial should normally be given by witness statement (see paragraph 17 onwards). However a witness may give evidence by affidavit if he wishes to do so (and see paragraph 1.4 below).

1.3   Statements of case (see paragraph 26 onwards) and application notices may also be used as evidence provided that their contents have been verified by a statement of truth.

(For information regarding evidence by deposition see Part 34 and PD 34)

1.4   Affidavits must be used as evidence in the following instances:

(1) where sworn evidence is required by an enactment, statutory instrument, rule, order or practice direction,

(2) in any application for a search order, a freezing injunction, or an order requiring an occupier to permit another to enter his land, and

(3) in any application for an order against anyone for alleged contempt of court.

1.5   If a party believes that sworn evidence is required by a court in another jurisdiction for any purpose connected with the proceedings, he may apply to the court for a direction that evidence shall be given only by affidavit on any pre-trial applications.

1.6   The court may give a direction under rule 32.15 that evidence shall be given by affidavit instead of or in addition to a witness statement or statement of case:

(1) on its own initiative, or

(2) after any party has applied to the court for such a direction.

1.7   An affidavit, where referred to in the Civil Procedure Rules or a practice direction, also means an affirmation unless the context requires otherwise.

Affidavits

Deponent

2   A deponent is a person who gives evidence by affidavit or affirmation.

Heading

3.1   The affidavit should be headed with the title of the proceedings (see paragraph 4 of the practice direction supplementing Part 7 and paragraph 7 of the practice direction supplementing Part 20); where the proceedings are between several parties with the same status it is sufficient to identify the parties as follows:

	Number:
A.B. (and others)	Claimants/Applicants
C.D. (and others)	Defendants/Respondents
	(as appropriate)

3.2   At the top right hand corner of the first page (and on the backsheet) there should be clearly written:

(1) the party on whose behalf it is made,

(2) the initials and surname of the deponent,

(3) the number of the affidavit in relation to that deponent,

(4) the identifying initials and number of each exhibit referred to, and

(5) the date sworn.

Body of affidavit

4.1   The affidavit must, if practicable, be in the deponent's own words, the affidavit should be expressed in the first person and the deponent should:

(1) commence 'I (*full name*) of (*address*) state on oath . . .',

(2) if giving evidence in his professional, business or other occupational capacity, give the address at which he works in (1) above, the position he holds and the name of his firm or employer,

(3) give his occupation or, if he has none, his description, and

(4) state if he is a party to the proceedings or employed by a party to the proceedings, if it be the case.

4.2   An affidavit must indicate:

(1) which of the statements in it are made from the deponent's own knowledge and which are matters of information or belief, and

(2) the source for any matters of information or belief.

4.3 Where a deponent:

(1) refers to an exhibit or exhibits, he should state 'there is now shown to me marked ". . ." the (*description of exhibit*)', and

(2) makes more than one affidavit (to which there are exhibits) in the same proceedings, the numbering of the exhibits should run consecutively throughout and not start again with each affidavit.

Jurat

5.1 The jurat of an affidavit is a statement set out at the end of the document which authenticates the affidavit.

5.2 It must:

(1) be signed by all deponents,

(2) be completed and signed by the person before whom the affidavit was sworn whose name and qualification must be printed beneath his signature,

(3) contain the full address of the person before whom the affidavit was sworn, and

(4) follow immediately on from the text and not be put on a separate page.

Format of affidavits

6.1 An affidavit should:

(1) be produced on durable quality A4 paper with a 3.5 cm margin,

(2) be fully legible and should normally be typed on one side of the paper only,

(3) where possible, be bound securely in a manner which would not hamper filing, or otherwise each page should be endorsed with the case number and should bear the initials of the deponent and of the person before whom it was sworn,

(4) have the pages numbered consecutively as a separate document (or as one of several documents contained in a file),

(5) be divided into numbered paragraphs,

(6) have all numbers, including dates, expressed in figures, and

(7) give the reference to any document or documents mentioned either in the margin or in bold text in the body of the affidavit.

6.2 It is usually convenient for an affidavit to follow the chronological sequence of events or matters dealt with; each paragraph of an affidavit should as far as possible be confined to a distinct portion of the subject.

Inability of deponent to read or sign affidavit

7.1 Where an affidavit is sworn by a person who is unable to read or sign it, the person before whom the affidavit is sworn must certify in the jurat that:

(1) he read the affidavit to the deponent,

(2) the deponent appeared to understand it, and

(3) the deponent signed or made his mark, in his presence.

7.2 If that certificate is not included in the jurat, the affidavit may not be used in evidence unless the court is satisfied that it was read to the deponent and that he appeared to understand it. Two versions of the form of jurat with the certificate are set out at Annex 1 to this practice direction.

Alterations to affidavits

8.1 Any alteration to an affidavit must be initialled by both the deponent and the person before whom the affidavit was sworn.

8.2 An affidavit which contains an alteration that has not been initialled may be filed or used in evidence only with the permission of the court.

Who may administer oaths and take affidavits

9.1 Only the following may administer oaths and take affidavits:

(1) Commissioners for oaths,

(2) Practising solicitors,

(3) other persons specified by statute,

(4) certain officials of the Supreme Court,

(5) a circuit judge or district judge,

(6) any justice of the peace, and

(7) certain officials of any county court appointed by the judge of that court for the purpose.

9.2   An affidavit must be sworn before a person independent of the parties or their representatives.

Filing of affidavits

10.1   If the court directs that an affidavit is to be filed, it must be filed in the court or Division, or Office or Registry of the court or Division where the action in which it was or is to be used, is proceeding or will proceed.

10.2   Where an affidavit is in a foreign language:

(1) the party wishing to rely on it—

    (a) must have it translated, and

    (b) must file the foreign language affidavit with the court, and

(2) the translator must make and file with the court an affidavit verifying the translation and exhibiting both the translation and a copy of the foreign language affidavit.

Exhibits

Manner of exhibiting documents

11.1   A document used in conjunction with an affidavit should be:

(1) produced to and verified by the deponent, and remain separate from the affidavit, and

(2) identified by a declaration of the person before whom the affidavit was sworn.

11.2   The declaration should be headed with the name of the proceedings in the same way as the affidavit.

11.3   The first page of each exhibit should be marked:

(1) as in paragraph 3.2 above, and

(2) with the exhibit mark referred to in the affidavit.

Letters

12.1   Copies of individual letters should be collected together and exhibited in a bundle or bundles. They should be arranged in chronological order with the earliest at the top, and firmly secured.

12.2   When a bundle of correspondence is exhibited, the exhibit should have a front page attached stating that the bundle consists of original letters and copies. They should be arranged and secured as above and numbered consecutively.

Other documents

13.1   Photocopies instead of original documents may be exhibited provided the originals are made available for inspection by the other parties before the hearing and by the judge at the hearing.

13.2   Court documents must not be exhibited (official copies of such documents prove themselves).

13.3   Where an exhibit contains more than one document, a front page should be attached setting out a list of the documents contained in the exhibit; the list should contain the dates of the documents.

Exhibits other than documents

14.1   Items other than documents should be clearly marked with an exhibit number or letter in such a manner that the mark cannot become detached from the exhibit.

14.2   Small items may be placed in a container and the container appropriately marked.

General provisions
15.1   Where an exhibit contains more than one document:
(1) the bundle should not be stapled but should be securely fastened in a way that does not hinder the reading of the documents, and
(2) the pages should be numbered consecutively at bottom centre.

15.2   Every page of an exhibit should be clearly legible; typed copies of illegible documents should be included, paginated with 'a' numbers.

15.3   Where affidavits and exhibits have become numerous, they should be put into separate bundles and the pages numbered consecutively throughout.

15.4   Where on account of their bulk the service of exhibits or copies of exhibits on the other parties would be difficult or impracticable, the directions of the court should be sought as to arrangements for bringing the exhibits to the attention of the other parties and as to their custody pending trial.

Affirmations
16   All provisions in this or any other practice direction relating to affidavits apply to affirmations with the following exceptions:
(1) the deponent should commence 'I (*name*) of (*address*) do solemnly and sincerely affirm . . .', and
(2) in the jurat the word 'sworn' is replaced by the word 'affirmed'.

Witness statements

Heading
17.1   The witness statement should be headed with the title of the proceedings (see paragraph 4 of the practice direction supplementing Part 7 and paragraph 7 of the practice direction supplementing Part 20); where the proceedings are between several parties with the same status it is sufficient to identify the parties as follows:

	Number:
A.B. (and others)	Claimants/Applicants
C.D. (and others)	Defendants/Respondents
	(as appropriate)

17.2   At the top right hand corner of the first page there should be clearly written:
(1) the party on whose behalf it is made,
(2) the initials and surname of the witness,
(3) the number of the statement in relation to that witness,
(4) the identifying initials and number of each exhibit referred to, and
(5) the date the statement was made.

Body of witness statement
18.1   The witness statement must, if practicable, be in the intended witness's own words, the statement should be expressed in the first person and should also state:
(1) the full name of the witness,
(2) his place of residence or, if he is making the statement in his professional, business or other occupational capacity, the address at which he works, the position he holds and the name of his firm or employer,
(3) his occupation, or if he has none, his description, and
(4) the fact that he is a party to the proceedings or is the employee of such a party if it be the case.

18.2   A witness statement must indicate:
(1) which of the statements in it are made from the witness's own knowledge and which are matters of information or belief, and
(2) the source for any matters of information or belief.

18.3   An exhibit used in conjunction with a witness statement should be verified and identified by the witness and remain separate from the witness statement.

18.4   Where a witness refers to an exhibit or exhibits, he should state 'I refer to the (*description of exhibit*) marked "..." '.

18.5   The provisions of paragraphs 11.3 to 15.4 (exhibits) apply similarly to witness statements as they do to affidavits.

18.6   Where a witness makes more than one witness statement to which there are exhibits, in the same proceedings, the numbering of the exhibits should run consecutively throughout and not start again with each witness statement.

Format of witness statement

19.1   A witness statement should:

(1) be produced on durable quality A4 paper with a 3.5 cm margin,
(2) be fully legible and should normally be typed on one side of the paper only,
(3) where possible, be bound securely in a manner which would not hamper filing, or otherwise each page should be endorsed with the case number and should bear the initials of the witness,
(4) have the pages numbered consecutively as a separate statement (or as one of several statements contained in a file),
(5) be divided into numbered paragraphs,
(6) have all numbers, including dates, expressed in figures, and
(7) give the reference to any document or documents mentioned either in the margin or in bold text in the body of the statement.

19.2   It is usually convenient for a witness statement to follow the chronological sequence of the events or matters dealt with, each paragraph of a witness statement should as far as possible be confined to a distinct portion of the subject.

Statement of truth

20.1   A witness statement is the equivalent of the oral evidence which that witness would, if called, give in evidence; it must include a statement by the intended witness that he believes the facts in it are true.

20.2   To verify a witness statement the statement of truth is as follows:

'I believe that the facts stated in this witness statement are true'

20.3   Attention is drawn to rule 32.14 which sets out the consequences of verifying a witness statement containing a false statement without an honest belief in its truth.

Inability of witness to read or sign statement

21.1   Where a witness statement is made by a person who is unable to read or sign the witness statement, it must contain a certificate made by an authorised person.

21.2   An authorised person is a person able to administer oaths and take affidavits but need not be independent of the parties or their representatives.

21.3   The authorised person must certify:

(1) that the witness statement has been read to the witness,
(2) that the witness appeared to understand it and approved its content as accurate,
(3) that the declaration of truth has been read to the witness,
(4) that the witness appeared to understand the declaration and the consequences of making a false witness statement, and
(5) that the witness signed or made his mark in the presence of the authorised person.

21.4   The form of the certificate is set out at Annex 2 to this practice direction.

Alterations to witness statements

22.1   Any alteration to a witness statement must be initialled by the person making the statement or by the authorised person where appropriate (see paragraph 21).

22.2   A witness statement which contains an alteration that has not been initialled may be used in evidence only with the permission of the court.

Filing of witness statements

23.1   If the court directs that a witness statement is to be filed, it must be filed in the court or Division, or Office or Registry of the court or Division where the action in which it was or is to be used, is proceeding or will proceed.

23.2.   Where the court has directed that a witness statement in a foreign language is to be filed:

(1) the party wishing to rely on it must—
    (a) have it translated, and
    (b) file the foreign language witness statement with the court, and
(2) the translator must make and file with the court an affidavit verifying the translation and exhibiting both the translation and a copy of the foreign language witness statement.

Certificate of court officer

24.1   Where the court has ordered that a witness statement is not to be open to inspection by the public or that words or passages in the statement are not to be open to inspection the court officer will so certify on the statement and make any deletions directed by the court under rule 32.13(4).

Defects in affidavits, witness statements and exhibits

25.1   Where:

(1) an affidavit,
(2) a witness statement, or
(3) an exhibit to either an affidavit or a witness statement,

does not comply with Part 32 or this practice direction in relation to its form, the court may refuse to admit it as evidence and may refuse to allow the costs arising from its preparation.

25.2   Permission to file a defective affidavit or witness statement or to use a defective exhibit may be obtained from a judge in the court where the case is proceeding.

Statements of case

26.1   A statement of case may be used as evidence in an interim application provided it is verified by a statement of truth.

26.2   To verify a statement of case the statement of truth should be set out as follows:

'[I believe] [the (*party on whose behalf the statement of case is being signed*) believes] that the facts stated in the statement of case are true'.

26.3   Attention is drawn to rule 32.14 which sets out the consequences of verifying a witness statement containing a false statement without an honest belief in its truth. (For information regarding statements of truth see Part 22 and the practice direction which supplements it.)

(Practice directions supplementing Parts 7, 9 and 17 provide further information concerning statements of case.)

ANNEX 1

Certificate to be used where a deponent to an affidavit is unable to read or sign it

Sworn at . . . this . . . day of . . . Before me, I having first read over the contents of this affidavit to the deponent [*if there are exhibits, add* 'and explained the nature and effect of the exhibits referred to in it'] who appeared to understand it and approved its content as accurate, and made his mark on the affidavit in my presence.

Or, (after, *Before me*) the witness to the mark of the deponent having been first sworn that he had read over etc. (*as above*) and that he saw him make his mark on the affidavit. (*Witness must sign*).

Certificate to be used where a deponent to an affirmation is unable to read or sign it

Affirmed at ... this ... day of ... Before me, I having first read over the contents of this affirmation to the deponent [*if there are exhibits, add* 'and explained the nature and effect of the exhibits referred to in it'] who appeared to understand it and approved its content as accurate, and made his mark on the affirmation in my presence.

Or, (after, *Before me*) the witness to the mark of the deponent having been first sworn that he had read over etc. (*as above*) and that he saw him make his mark on the affirmation. (*Witness must sign*).

ANNEX 2

Certificate to be used where a witness is unable to read or sign a witness statement

I certify that I [*name and address of authorised person*] have read over the contents of this witness statement and the declaration of truth to the witness [*if there are exhibits, add* 'and explained the nature and effect of the exhibits referred to in it'] who appeared to understand (a) the statement and approved its content as accurate and (b) the declaration of truth and the consequences of making a false witness statement, and made his mark in my presence.

CPR Part 33 Miscellaneous Rules About Evidence

CONTENTS OF THIS PART

33.1   Introductory
In this Part—
    (a) 'hearsay' means a statement made, otherwise than by a person while giving oral evidence in proceedings, which is tendered as evidence of the matters stated; and
    (b) references to hearsay include hearsay of whatever degree.

33.2   Notice of intention to rely on hearsay evidence
  (1) Where a party intends to rely on hearsay evidence at trial and either—
    (a) that evidence is to be given by a witness giving oral evidence; or
    (b) that evidence is contained in a witness statement of a person who is not being called to give oral evidence; that party complies with section 2(1)(a) of the Civil Evidence Act 1995 by serving a witness statement on the other parties in accordance with the court's order.

(2) Where paragraph (1)(b) applies, the party intending to rely on the hearsay evidence must, when he serves the witness statement—

(a) inform the other parties that the witness is not being called to give oral evidence; and

(b) give the reason why the witness will not be called.

(3) In all other cases where a party intends to rely on hearsay evidence at trial, that party complies with section 2(1)(a) of the Civil Evidence Act 1995 by serving a notice on the other parties which—

(a) identifies the hearsay evidence;

(b) states that the party serving the notice proposes to rely on the hearsay evidence at trial; and

(c) gives the reason why the witness will not be called.

(4) The party proposing to rely on the hearsay evidence must—

(a) serve the notice no later than the latest date for serving witness statements; and

(b) if the hearsay evidence is to be in a document, supply a copy to any party who requests him to do so.

33.3   Circumstances in which notice of intention to rely on hearsay evidence is not required

Section 2(1) of the Civil Evidence Act 1995 (duty to give notice of intention to rely on hearsay evidence) does not apply—

(a) to evidence at hearings other than trials;

(aa) to an affidavit or witness statement which is to be used at trial but which does not contain hearsay evidence;

(b) to a statement which a party to a probate action wishes to put in evidence and which is alleged to have been made by the person whose estate is the subject of the proceedings; or

(c) where the requirement is excluded by a practice direction.

33.4   Power to call witness for cross-examination on hearsay evidence

(1) Where a party—

(a) proposes to rely on hearsay evidence; and

(b) does not propose to call the person who made the original statement to give oral evidence, the court may, on the application of any other party, permit that party to call the maker of the statement to be cross-examined on the contents of the statement.

(2) An application for permission to cross-examine under this rule must be made not more than 14 days after the day on which a notice of intention to rely on the hearsay evidence was served on the applicant.

33.5   Credibility

(1) Where a party—

(a) proposes to rely on hearsay evidence; but

(b) does not propose to call the person who made the original statement to give oral evidence; and

(c) another party wishes to call evidence to attack the credibility of the person who made the statement,

the party who so wishes must give notice of his intention to the party who proposes to give the hearsay statement in evidence.

(2) A party must give notice under paragraph (1) not more than 14 days after the day on which a hearsay notice relating to the hearsay evidence was served on him.

33.6 Use of plans, photographs and models as evidence

(1) This rule applies to evidence (such as a plan, photograph or model) which is not—

    (a) contained in a witness statement, affidavit or expert's report;

    (b) to be given orally at trial; or

    (c) evidence of which prior notice must be given under rule 33.2.

(2) This rule includes documents which may be received in evidence without further proof under section 9 of the Civil Evidence Act 1995.

(3) Unless the court orders otherwise the evidence shall not be receivable at a trial unless the party intending to put it in evidence has given notice to the other parties in accordance with this rule.

(4) Where the party intends to use the evidence as evidence of any fact then, except where paragraph (6) applies, he must give notice not later than the latest date for serving witness statements.

(5) He must give notice at least 21 days before the hearing at which he proposes to put in the evidence, if—

    (a) there are not to be witness statements; or

    (b) he intends to put in the evidence solely in order to disprove an allegation made in a witness statement.

(6) Where the evidence forms part of expert evidence, he must give notice when the expert's report is served on the other party.

(7) Where the evidence is being produced to the court for any reason other than as part of factual or expert evidence, he must give notice at least 21 days before the hearing at which he proposes to put in the evidence.

(8) Where a party has given notice that he intends to put in the evidence, he must give every other party an opportunity to inspect it and to agree to its admission without further proof.

33.7 Evidence of finding on question of foreign law

(1) This rule sets out the procedure which must be followed by a party who intends to put in evidence a finding on a question of foreign law by virtue of section 4(2) of the Civil Evidence Act 1972.

(2) He must give any other party notice of his intention.

(3) He must give the notice—

    (a) if there are to be witness statements, not later than the latest date for serving them; or

    (b) otherwise, not less than 21 days before the hearing at which he proposes to put the finding in evidence.

(4) The notice must—

    (a) specify the question on which the finding was made; and

    (b) enclose a copy of a document where it is reported or recorded.

33.8 Evidence of consent of trustee to act

A document purporting to contain the written consent of a person to act as trustee and to bear his signature verified by some other person is evidence of such consent.

CPR Part 34 Depositions and Court Attendance by Witnesses

CONTENTS OF THIS PART

34.1 Scope of this part

(1) This Part provides—

    (a) for the circumstances in which a person may be required to attend court to give evidence or to produce a document; and

    (b) for a party to obtain evidence before a hearing to be used at the hearing.

(2) In this Part, reference to a hearing includes a reference to the trial.

34.2 Witness summonses

(1) A witness summons is a document issued by the court requiring a witness to—

    (a) attend court to give evidence; or

    (b) produce documents to the court.

(2) A witness summons must be in the relevant practice form.

(3) There must be a separate witness summons for each witness.

(4) A witness summons may require a witness to produce documents to the court either—

    (a) on the date fixed for a hearing; or

    (b) on such date as the court may direct.

(5) The only documents that a summons under this rule can require a person to produce before a hearing are documents which that person could be required to produce at the hearing.

34.3 Issue of a witness summons

(1) A witness summons is issued on the date entered on the summons by the court.

(2) A party must obtain permission from the court where he wishes to—

    (a) have a summons issued less than 7 days before the date of the trial;

    (b) have a summons issued for a witness to attend court to give evidence or to produce documents on any date except the date fixed for the trial; or

    (c) have a summons issued for a witness to attend court to give evidence or to produce documents at any hearing except the trial.

(3) A witness summons must be issued by—

    (a) the court where the case is proceeding; or

    (b) the court where the hearing in question will be held.

(4) The court may set aside(GL) or vary a witness summons issued under this rule.

34.4 Witness summons in aid of inferior court or of tribunal

(1) The court may issue a witness summons in aid of an inferior court or of a tribunal.

(2) The court which issued the witness summons under this rule may set it aside.

(3) In this rule, 'inferior court or tribunal' means any court or tribunal that does not have power to issue a witness summons in relation to proceedings before it.

34.5   Time for serving a witness summons

(1) The general rule is that a witness summons is binding if it is served at least 7 days before the date on which the witness is required to attend before the court or tribunal.

(2) The court may direct that a witness summons shall be binding although it will be served less than 7 days before the date on which the witness is required to attend before the court or tribunal.

(3) A witness summons which is—

    (a)   served in accordance with this rule; and

    (b)   requires the witness to attend court to give evidence, is binding until the conclusion of the hearing at which the attendance of the witness is required.

34.6   Who is to serve a witness summons

(1) A witness summons is to be served by the court unless the party on whose behalf it is issued indicates in writing, when he asks the court to issue the summons, that he wishes to serve it himself.

(2) Where the court is to serve the witness summons, the party on whose behalf it is issued must deposit, in the court office, the money to be paid or offered to the witness under rule 34.7.

34.7   Right of witness to travelling expenses and compensation forloss of time

At the time of service of a witness summons the witness must be offered or paid—

    (a)   a sum reasonably sufficient to cover his expenses in travelling to and from the court; and

    (b)   such sum by way of compensation for loss of time as may be specified in the relevant practice direction.

34.8   Evidence by deposition

(1) A party may apply for an order for a person to be examined before the hearing takes place.

(2) A person from whom evidence is to be obtained following an order under this rule is referred to as a 'deponent' and the evidence is referred to as a 'deposition'.

(3) An order under this rule shall be for a deponent to be examined on oath before—

    (a)   a judge;

    (b)   an examiner of the court; or

    (c)   such other person as the court appoints.

(Rule 34.15 makes provision for the appointment of examiners of the court)

(4) The order may require the production of any document which the court considers is necessary for the purposes of the examination.

(5) The order must state the date, time and place of the examination.

(6) At the time of service of the order the deponent must be offered or paid—

    (a)   a sum reasonably sufficient to cover his expenses in travelling to and from the place of examination; and

    (b)   such sum by way of compensation for loss of time as may be specified in the relevant practice direction.

(7) Where the court makes an order for a deposition to be taken, it may also order the party who obtained the order to serve a witness statement or witness summary in relation to the evidence to be given by the person to be examined.

(Part 32 contains the general rules about witness statements and witness summaries)

34.9   Conduct of examination

(1) Subject to any directions contained in the order for examination, the examination must be conducted in the same way as if the witness were giving evidence at a trial.

(2) If all the parties are present, the examiner may conduct the examination of a person not named in the order for examination if all the parties and the person to be examined consent.

(3) The examiner may conduct the examination in private if he considers it appropriate to do so.

(4) The examiner must ensure that the evidence given by the witness is recorded in full.

(5) The examiner must send a copy of the deposition—

    (a) to the person who obtained the order for the examination of the witness; and

    (b) to the court where the case is proceeding.

(6) The party who obtained the order must send each of the other parties a copy of the deposition which he receives from the examiner.

34.10   Enforcing attendance of witness

(1) If a person served with an order to attend before an examiner—

    (a) fails to attend; or

    (b) refuses to be sworn for the purpose of the examination or to answer any lawful question or produce any document at the examination,

a certificate of his failure or refusal, signed by the examiner, must be filed by the party requiring the deposition.

(2) On the certificate being filed, the party requiring the deposition may apply to the court for an order requiring that person to attend or to be sworn or to answer any question or produce any document, as the case may be.

(3) An application for an order under this rule may be made without notice.

(4) The court may order the person against whom an order is made under this rule to pay any costs resulting from his failure or refusal.

34.11   Use of deposition at a hearing

(1) A deposition ordered under rule 34.8 may be given in evidence at a hearing unless the court orders otherwise.

(2) A party intending to put in evidence a deposition at a hearing must serve notice of his intention to do so on every other party.

(3) He must serve the notice at least 21 days before the day fixed for the hearing.

(4) The court may require a deponent to attend the hearing and give evidence orally.

(5) Where a deposition is given in evidence at trial, it shall be treated as if it were a witness statement for the purposes of rule 32.13 (availability of witness statements for inspection).

34.12   Restrictions on subsequent use of deposition taken for the purpose of any hearing except the trial

(1) Where the court orders a party to be examined about his or any other assets for the purpose of any hearing except the trial, the deposition may be used only for the the purpose of the proceedings in which the order was made.

(2) However, it may be used for some other purpose—

    (a) by the party who was examined;

    (b) if the party who was examined agrees; or

    (c) if the court gives permission.

34.13   Where a person to be examined is out of the jurisdiction—letter of request

(1) Where a party wishes to take a deposition from a person outside the jurisdiction, the High Court may order the issue of a letter of request to the judicial authorities of the country in which the proposed deponent is.

(2) A letter of request is a request to a judicial authority to take the evidence of that person, or arrange for it to be taken.

(3) The High Court may make an order under this rule in relation to county court proceedings.

(4) If the government of a country allows a person appointed by the High Court to examine a person in that country, the High Court may make an order appointing a special examiner for that purpose.

(5) A person may be examined under this rule on oath or affirmation or in accordance with any procedure permitted in the country in which the examination is to take place.

(6) If the High Court makes an order for the issue of a letter of request, the party who sought the order must file—

    (a) the following documents and, except where paragraph (7) applies, a translation of them—

        (i) a draft letter of request;

        (ii) a statement of the issues relevant to the proceedings;

        (iii) a list of questions or the subject matter of questions to be put to the person to be examined; and

    (b) an undertaking to be responsible for the Secretary of State's expenses.

(7) There is no need to file a translation if—

    (a) English is one of the official languages of the country where the examination is to take place; or

    (b) a practice direction has specified that country as a country where no translation is necessary.

34.14   Fees and expenses of examiner of the court

(1) An examiner of the court may charge a fee for the examination.

(2) He need not send the deposition to the court unless the fee is paid.

(3) The examiner's fees and expenses must be paid by the party who obtained the order for examination.

(4) If the fees and expenses due to an examiner are not paid within a reasonable time, he may report that fact to the court.

(5) The court may order the party who obtained the order for examination to deposit in the court office a specified sum in respect of the examiner's fees and, where it does so, the examiner will not be asked to act until the sum has been deposited.

(6) An order under this rule does not affect any decision as to the party who is ultimately to bear the costs of the examination.

34.15   Examiners of the court

(1) The Lord Chancellor shall appoint persons to be examiners of the court.

(2) The persons appointed shall be barristers or solicitor-advocates who have been practising for a period of not less than three years.

(3) The Lord Chancellor may revoke an appointment at any time.

PD 34 Practice Direction—Depositions and Court Attendance by Witnesses

This Practice Direction Supplements CPR Part 34

Witness summonses

Issue of witness summons

    1.1   A witness summons may require a witness to:

(1) attend court to give evidence,

(2) produce documents to the court, or

(3) both,

on either a date fixed for the hearing or such date as the court may direct.

1.2   Two copies of the witness summons should be filed with the court for sealing, one of which will be retained on the court file.

1.3   A mistake in the name or address of a person named in a witness summons may be corrected if the summons has not been served.

1.4   The corrected summons must be re-sealed by the court and marked 'Amended and Re-Sealed'.

Witness summons issued in aid of an inferior court or tribunal

2.1   A witness summons may be issued in the High Court or a county court in aid of a court or tribunal which does not have the power to issue a witness summons in relation to the proceedings before it.

2.2   A witness summons referred to in paragraph 2.1 may be set aside by the court which issued it.

2.3   An application to set aside a witness summons referred to in paragraph 2.1 will be heard:

(1) in the High Court by a Master at the Royal Courts of Justice or by a district judge in a District Registry, and

(2) in a county court by a district judge.

2.4   Unless the court otherwise directs, the applicant must give at least 2 days' notice to the party who issued the witness summons of the application, which will normally be dealt with at a hearing.

Travelling expenses and compensation for loss of time

3.1   When a witness is served with a witness summons he must be offered a sum to cover his travelling expenses to and from the court and compensation for his loss of time.

3.2   If the witness summons is to be served by the court, the party issuing the summons must deposit with the court:

(1) a sum sufficient to pay for the witness's expenses in travelling to the court and in returning to his home or place of work, and

(2) a sum in respect of the period during which earnings or benefit are lost, or such lesser sum as it may be proved that the witness will lose as a result of his attendance at court in answer to the witness summons.

3.3   The sum referred to in 3.2(2) is to be based on the sums payable to witnesses attending the Crown Court.

3.4   Where the party issuing the witness summons wishes to serve it himself, he must:

(1) notify the court in writing that he wishes to do so, and

(2) at the time of service offer the witness the sums mentioned in paragraph 3.2 above.

Depositions

To be taken in England and wales for use as evidence in proceedings in courts in England and Wales

4.1   A party may apply for an order for a person to be examined on oath before:

(1) a judge,

(2) an examiner of the court, or

(3) such other person as the court may appoint.

4.2   The party who obtains an order for the examination of a deponent before an examiner of the court must:

(1) apply to the Foreign Process Section of the Masters' Secretary's Department at the Royal Courts of Justice for the allocation of an examiner,

(2) when allocated, provide the examiner with copies of all documents in the proceedings necessary to inform the examiner of the issues, and

(3) pay the deponent a sum to cover his travelling expenses to and from the examination and compensation for his loss of time.

4.3   In ensuring that the deponent's evidence is recorded in full, the court or the examiner may permit it to be recorded on audiotape or videotape, but the deposition must always be recorded in writing by him or by a competent shorthand writer or stenographer.

4.4   If the deposition is not recorded word for word, it must contain, as nearly as may be, the statement of the deponent; the examiner may record word for word any particular questions and answers which appear to him to have special importance.

4.5   If a deponent objects to answering any question or where any objection is taken to any question, the examiner must:

(1) record in the deposition or a document attached to it—

   (a) the question,

   (b) the nature of and grounds for the objection, and

   (c) any answer given, and

(2) give his opinion as to the validity of the objection and must record it in the deposition or a document attached to it.

The court will decide as to the validity of the objection and any question of costs arising from it.

4.6   Documents and exhibits must:

(1) have an identifying number or letter marked on them by the examiner, and

(2) be preserved by the party or his legal representative who obtained the order for the examination, or as the court or the examiner may direct.

4.7   The examiner may put any question to the deponent as to:

(1) the meaning of any of his answers, or

(2) any matter arising in the course of the examination.

4.8   Where a deponent:

(1) fails to attend the examination, or

(2) refuses to:

   (a) be sworn, or

   (b) answer any lawful question, or

   (c) produce any document,

the examiner will sign a certificate of such failure or refusal and may include in his certificate any comment as to the conduct of the deponent or of any person attending the examination.

4.9   The party who obtained the order for the examination must file the certificate with the court and may apply for an order that the deponent attend for examination or as may be. The application may be made without notice.

4.10   The court will make such order on the application as it thinks fit including an order for the deponent to pay any costs resulting from his failure or refusal.

4.11   A deponent who wilfully refuses to obey an order made against him under Part 34 may be proceeded against for contempt of court.

4.12   A deposition must:

(1) be signed by the examiner,

(2) have any amendments to it initialled by the examiner and the deponent,

(3) be endorsed by the examiner with—

   (a) a statement of the time occupied by the examination, and

   (b) a record of any refusal by the deponent to sign the deposition and of his reasons for not doing so, and

(4) be sent by the examiner to the court where the proceedings are taking place for filing on the court file.

4.13   Rule 34.14 deals with the fees and expenses of an examiner.

Depositions to be taken abroad for use as evidence in proceedings before courts in England and Wales

5.1   Where a party wishes to take a deposition from a person outside the jurisdiction, the High Court may order the issue of a letter of request to the judicial authorities of the country in which the proposed deponent is.

5.2   An application for an order referred to in paragraph 5.1 should be made by application notice in accordance with Part 23.

5.3   The documents which a party applying for an order for the issue of a letter of request must file with his application notice are set out in rule 34.13(6). They are as follows:

(1) a draft letter of request is set out in Annex A to this practice direction,

(2) a statement of the issues relevant to the proceedings,

(3) a list of questions or the subject matter of questions to be put to the proposed deponent,

(4) a translation of the documents in (1), (2) and (3) above unless the proposed deponent is in a country—

  (a) of which English is one of the official languages, or

  (b) listed at Annex B to this practice direction, unless the particular circumstances of the case require a translation,

(5) an undertaking to be responsible for the expenses of the Secretary of State, and

(6) a draft order.

5.4   The above documents should be filed with the Masters' Secretary in Room E214, Royal Courts of Justice, Strand, London WC2A 2LL.

5.5   The application will be dealt with by the Senior Master of the Queen's Bench Division of the High Court who will, if appropriate, sign the letter of request.

5.6   Attention is drawn to the provisions of rule 23.10 (application to vary or discharge an order made without notice).

5.7   If parties are in doubt as to whether a translation under paragraph 5.3(4) above is required, they should seek guidance from the Foreign Process Section of the Masters' Secretary's Department.

5.8   A special examiner appointed under rule 34.13(4) may be the British Consul or the Consul-General or his deputy in the country where the evidence is to be taken if:

(1) there is in respect of that country a Civil Procedure Convention providing for the taking of evidence in that country for the assistance of proceedings in the High Court or other court in this country, or

(2) with the consent of the Secretary of State.

5.9   The provisions of paragraphs 4.1 to 4.12 above apply to the depositions referred to in this paragraph.

Depositions to be taken in England and Wales for use as evidence in proceedings before courts abroad pursuant to letters of request

6.1   RSC, ord. 70 in CPR, sch. 1, relates to obtaining evidence for foreign courts and should be read in conjunction with this part of the practice direction.

6.2   The Evidence (Proceedings in Other Jurisdictions) Act 1975 applies to these depositions.

6.3   Where a foreign court sends a letter of request under which it is proposed that an application to give effect to the request be made by an agent in England or Wales of a party to the foreign proceedings, the application should be made by an application notice (see CPR, Part 23) and should be supported by a witness statement or affidavit exhibiting:

(1) the letter of request;

(2) a statement of the issues relevant to the proceedings;

(3) a list of questions or the subject matter of questions to be put to the proposed deponent;

(4) a translation of the documents in (1), (2) and (3) above if necessary; and

(5) a draft order.

6.4   Where the application to give effect to the request is made by the Treasury Solicitor (see RSC, ord. 70, r. 3 in CPR, sch. 1), he must provide to the court:

(1) a statement of the issues relevant to the proceedings;

(2) a list of questions or the subject matter of questions to be put to the proposed deponent;

(3) a translation of:

(a) the documents in (1) and (2) above and

(b) the letter of request, if necessary; and

(4) a draft order.

6.5   The order for the deponent to attend and be examined together with the evidence upon which the order was made must be served on the deponent.

6.6   Attention is drawn to the provisions of r. 23.10 (application to vary or discharge an order made without notice).

6.7   Arrangements for the examination to take place at a specified time and place before an examiner of the court or such other person as the court may appoint shall be made by the applicant for the order (i.e. the agent referred to in para. 6.3 or the Treasury Solicitor) and approved by the Senior Master.

6.8   The provisions of paragraphs 4.2 to 4.12 apply to the depositions referred to in this paragraph, except that the examiner must send the deposition to the Senior Master. (For further information about evidence see Part 32 and the practice direction which supplements it)

ANNEX A

DRAFT LETTER OF REQUEST

To the Competent Judicial Authority of

in the   of

I [name] Senior Master of the Queen's Bench Division of the Supreme Court of England and Wales respectfully request the assistance of your court with regard to the following matters.

1.   A claim is now pending in the   Division of the High Court of Justice in England and Wales entitled as follows

[set out full title and claim number]

in which [name] of [address] is the claimant and [name] of [address] is the defendant.

2.   The names and addresses of the representatives or agents of [set out names and addresses of representatives of the parties].

3.   The claim by the claimants is for:—

(a) [set out the nature of the claim]

(b) [the relief sought, and]

(c) [a summary of the facts.]

4.   It is necessary for the purposes of justice and for the due determination of the matters in dispute between the parties that you cause the following witnesses, who are resident within your jurisdiction, to be examined. The names and addresses of the witnesses are as follows:—

5.   The witnesses should be examined on oath or if that is not possible within your laws or is impossible of performance by reason of the internal practice and procedure of your court or by reason of practical difficulties, they should be examined in accordance with whatever procedure your laws provide for in these matters.

6.   Either/

The witnesses should be examined in accordance with the list of questions annexed hereto.
Or/

The witnesses should be examined regarding [*set out full details of evidence sought*]

N.B. Where the witness is required to produce documents, these should be clearly identified.

7.   I would ask that you cause me, or the agents of the parties (if appointed), to be informed of the date and place where the examination is to take place.

8.   Finally, I request that you will cause the evidence of the said witnesses to be reduced into writing and all documents produced on such examinations to be duly marked for identification and that you will further be pleased to authenticate such examinations by the seal of your court or in such other way as is in accordance with your procedure and return the written evidence and documents produced to me addressed as follows:—

Senior Master of the Queen's Bench Division
Royal Courts of Justice
Strand
London WC2A 2LL
England

ANNEX B

Countries where the translation referred to in paragraph 5.3(4) above should not be required:
Australia
Canada (other than Quebec)
Holland
New Zealand
The United States of America

INDEX